9/94 Ingram

GENERALS IN BLUE

GENERALS

IN BLUE

Lives of the Union Commanders

BY EZRA J. WARNER

Louisiana State University Press

BATON ROUGE AND LONDON

To him whose "bones are dust
and his good sword rust."

ISBN 0-8071-0882-7
LIBRARY OF CONGRESS CATALOG CARD NUMBER 64-21593
COPYRIGHT © 1964, 1992 BY DOROTHY J. WARNER
ALL RIGHTS RESERVED
MANUFACTURED IN THE UNITED STATES OF AMERICA
DESIGNED BY THEO JUNG
1993 printing

The paper in this book meets the guidelines for permanence and durability
of the Committee on Production Guidelines for Book Longevity of the
Council on Library Resources. ∞

PREFACE

GENERALS IN BLUE appears as the inescapable companion to
Generals in Gray, published in 1959. The author's purpose remains fixed: to tell the complete story of the men who led the
brigades, divisions, corps, and armies which won the war for the
Union. Many of the generals will not emerge in the pages which
follow as examples of nineteenth-century recitude—stiff and
chilly as so many figures in a waxwork museum. In point of fact,
quite a number will not even vaguely resemble the models of
Christian virtue extemporized by a generation of editors whose
cardinal motto was *De mortuis nil nisi bonum.* Even if a man
was a drunkard, thief, coward, or malcontent, contemporary
obituary notices (almost universally employed and relied upon
by editors of latter-day compendiums) are laudatory. Derelictions
of character or execution are glossed over and positive knowledge
of absolute guilt or chicanery is ignored entirely. That there
were 110 resignations and only 3 men cashiered of 583 men appointed to the grade of general officer demonstrates that many
men were allowed to honorably leave the service under dubious
circumstances.

No matter, the author has enjoyed, over a period of six
years, tracking down the heroes and rogues of the Union Army,
to say nothing of the inexhaustible supply of mediocrity which
lay in between. That there were heroes by the dozen is incon-
trovertible: what American, North or South, can fail to be thrilled
by the words of the dying General James Clay Rice at Spotsylvania, who, with a leg shot off, when asked by his brigade surgeon
on which side he would be most comfortable, replied, "Turn my
face to the enemy." That the "enemy" have not been so for a
century takes nothing from the naked courage of such a man,
dying at the age of thirty-five. At the bottom of the totem pole,
as far as the question of personal courage is concerned, might be
General James H. Ledlie, nominally in command of the leading
division of the IX Corps in the attack on the Petersburg Crater,

but actually comfortably seated in a bombproof some hundreds of yards to the rear "plying himself with rum borrowed from a brigade surgeon." (Catton, *A Stillness at Appomattox*, 246.) Six months later General Ledlie was permitted to resign.

The rest of the spectrum embraced nearly six hundred professional soldiers, farmers, lawyers, politicians, engineers, teachers, and men who were marshaled from all walks of life to meet the national emergency. That they did preserve the Union (and at the same time extinguish slavery) is self-evident; *how* they did so and *who* they were is another matter. All of this should be, in the author's estimate, informative and in some cases unthought of. Be that as it may, whether tall and handsome or squat and unprepossessing, models of courage or arrant cowards, honest and upright or paltry and knavish, popularity-seeking, raffish, debauched, and profane or modest, quiet, and moral, they are set down here as their contemporaries saw them behind the scenes and as the lens of history's microscope brings them into focus a hundred years later.

E. J. W.

La Jolla, California
June, 1964

ACKNOWLEDGMENTS

No WORK of this scope can be written without extensive research. By the same token, the results of the research place the author under great obligation to literally hundreds of people who filled in postcards, examined records, looked at grave markers, and supplied invaluable information. For especial favors I am indebted to: William G. Smith, Washington, D. C.; Mrs. Faye B. Reeder, Columbus, Ohio; the late Charles R. Barker, Lansdowne, Pa.; that eminent historian and friend Thomas R. Hay, Locust Valley, N. Y.; Mrs. Ralph H. Conant, Augusta, Me.; Miss Margaret A. Flint, Springfield, Ill.; my friend John R. Peacock, High Point, N. C.; and the inimitable Stanley F. Horn of Nashville, Tenn., whose writings are history. To Ralph Newman of Chicago, possessor of an encyclopedic knowledge touching every phase of Lincoln and the Civil War, my thanks are due for getting the project off the ground in the first place. Hirst D. Milhollen of the Library of Congress and Miss Josephine Cobb of the National Archives have been unfailingly helpful in searching out obscure photographs in their respective official files, and Mr. Milhollen generously loaned the author many negatives from his private collection. I also wish to offer my grateful appreciation to the following, who, in their private or official capacities as representatives of libraries and historical societies or as individuals, rendered priceless help—in many instances above and beyond the call of duty:

Mrs. James B. Adams, Worcester, Mass.; Miss Olive Adams, Nelsonville, N. Y.; Miss Elsie Anderson, Washington, D. C.; Mrs. Kathryn P. Arnold, Chattanooga Public Library, Chattanooga, Tenn.; the late James W. Arrott, Sapello, N. M.; Robert Athearn, University of Colorado, Boulder, Colo.; James M. Babcock, Detroit Public Library, Detroit, Mich.; F. Clever Bald, University of Michigan, Ann Arbor, Mich.; Miss Dorothy Barck, New York State Historical Association, Cooperstown, N. Y.; T. C. Barnwell,

Roslyn, N. Y.; Edward E. Barthell, Ludington, Mich.; John E. Becker, Waterloo, N. Y.; Amos Bedell, Ossining, N. Y.; Mrs. Marion Hatch Bowman, Chicago, Ill.; Palmer Bradley, Houston, Tex.; Charles N. Branham, U. S. Military Academy Foundation, West Point, N. Y.; Colonel Campbell H. Brown, Nashville, Tenn.; Miss Josephine B. Brown, Warren Public Library, Warren, Ohio; Kenneth W. Brown, Old Town, Me.; Lieutenant Colonel Earl K. Buchanan, U. S. Military Academy, West Point, N. Y.; Mrs. Randolph Buck, St. Augustine, Fla.; John R. Buckingham, Parkland, Pa.; T. T. Burchell, Manchester, Ky.; Mrs. Frances H. Buxton, Oakland Public Library, Oakland, Calif.; Reverend Charles I. Carpenter, Milford, Del.; Kent Castor, Chillicothe, Ohio; Harry Chase, Pomfret Center, Conn.; Mrs. Lois R. Clark, Westport, Conn.; G. Glenn Clift, Kentucky Historical Society, Frankfort, Ky.; Thomas A. Cloutier, Oswego, N. Y.; Frank E. Cofran, Superintendent of Cemeteries, Portland, Me.; Mrs. Robert Colby, Mason, Mich.; Mrs. Myrtle Comes, Jersey City, N. J.; Mrs. Mary C. Connor, Concord, N. H.; Mrs. Roy O. Cook, Algiers, Algeria; Kenneth C. Cramer, Hanover, N. H.; Miss Pollyanna Creekmore, Lawson-McGhee Library, Knoxville, Tenn.; Bernarr Cresap, Florence State College, Florence, Ala.; Mrs. Gardiner Criswell, Columbia Public Library, Columbia, Pa.; Mrs. Dorothy Thomas Cullen, The Filson Club, Louisville, Ky.

Mrs. Stuart H. Danovitch, Chicago Historical Society, Chicago, Ill.; Miss Frances Davenport, Connecticut State Library, Hartford, Conn.; James R. Davidson, Wellsville, Ohio; Bertrand O. DeForest, Sr., Baldwin, N. Y.; Miss Rose Demorest, Carnegie Library, Pittsburg, Pa.; Mrs. Dorothy Dennis, East St. Louis, Ill.; Miss Ruth E. Dickey, Indiana State Library, Indianapolis, Ind.; Miss Dorothy Dodd, State Librarian, Tallahassee, Fla.; J. T. Dorris, Eastern Kentucky State College, Richmond, Ky.; Mrs. Constance K. Draper, Atlanta, Ga.; Deane DuComb, Carlyle, Ill.; Miss Sharon DuMolin, Chicago Historical Society, Chicago, Ill.; Miss Rena Durkan, Amherst College, Amherst, Mass.; Mrs. Byron H. Eaton, Salem, N. Y.; Ralph B. Eckley, Monmouth, Ill.; Mrs. Janet M. Edwards, Berkshire Athenaeum, Pittsfield, Mass.; Joseph L. Eisendrath, Chicago, Ill.; Miss Helen Eldridge, Newburgh Free Library, Newburgh, N. Y.; Kimball C. Elkins, Harvard College Library, Cambridge, Mass.; J. G. Engle, Clarkboro, N. J.; Miss Carol Evans, Georgetown University Libraries, Washington, D. C.; Miss Lois M. Fawcett, Minnesota Historical Society, St. Paul, Minn.; Miss A. Feeley, Jersey City, N. J.; William Dale Fisher, American Consul, Florence, Italy; William Fitzgerald, Florence, Ky.; Mrs. Sarah W. Flannery, Boston Public Library, Boston, Mass.; Paris Fletcher, Worcester, Mass.; Miss Barbara P. Fluck, Franklin Library, Franklin, Mass.; Miss Doris A. Foley, Keokuk Public Library, Keokuk, Iowa; Miss Clara E. Follette, Vermont Historical Society, Montpelier, Vt.;

John D. Forbes, Woodlawn Cemetery, New York, N. Y.; Mrs. Grant Foreman, Oklahoma Historical Society, Oklahoma City, Okla.; Sidney Forman, U. S. Military Academy, West Point, N. Y.; Mrs. Mayme Kelley Foster, Harrodsburg, Ky.; Miss Llerena Friend, University of Texas Library, Austin, Tex.; Lewis B. Furr, Tallulah, La.

Herbert L. Ganter, College of William and Mary Library, Williamsburg, Va.; Kenneth Gardner, San Diego, Calif.; Dr. James W. Gibbon, Charlotte, N. C.; Mrs. Aloys Gilman, State Department of History and Archives, Des Moines, Iowa; Miss Margaret Gleason, State Historical Society of Wisconsin, Madison, Wis.; Miss Alice B. Good, State Department of Archives and History, Phoenix, Ariz.; Miss Eleanora Gralow, Fisk Public Library, Natchez, Miss.; Francis C. Haber, Maryland Historical Society, Baltimore, Md.; Leonard Hale, Pikeville, Tenn.; Mrs. Leona M. Hall, San Diego Public Library, San Diego, Calif.; A. J. Hanna, Rollins College, Winter Park, Fla.; Harry B. Harvey, Hastings on Hudson, N. Y.; Robert J. Head, San Francisco, Calif.; Miss Ruby Hemphill, Portsmouth, Ohio; James J. Heslin, The New-York Historical Society, New York, N. Y.; Mrs. C. D. Hetz, San Diego, Calif.; Max L. Heyman, Los Angeles Valley College, Van Nuys, Calif.; Miss Ann C. Hibler, Portland, Ore.; Bradford M. Hill, Boston Public Library, Boston, Mass.; Horace E. Hillery, Patterson, N. Y.; Kenneth B. Holmes, Columbia, Mo.; Mrs. Hazel W. Hopper, Indiana State Library, Indianapolis, Ind.; L. A. Hopkins, San Francisco, Calif.; Stanley F. Horn, Nashville, Tenn.; Donald W. Howe, Ware, Mass.; Mrs. Katherine A. Howell, Camden, N. J.; Miss Anne Hubley, New Jersey Historical Society, Newark, N. J.; Miss Aurora Hunt, Whittier, Calif.; Mrs. J. Warren Hutchens, Bridgeport, Conn.; Miss Ethel L. Hutchins, Public Library of Cincinnati and Hamilton County, Cincinnati, Ohio; Miss Lucile L. Hutson, Erie County Historical Society, Sandusky, Ohio; A. J. White Hutton, Chambersburg, Pa.; Mrs. Brewer Jean, Louisville, Ky.; John R. Jewkes, Jersey City, N. J.; Al Johnson, Congressional Cemetery, Washington, D. C.; Alfred H. Johnson, Carrollton, Ill.; Miss E. Frances Jones, Carnegie Public Library, East Liverpool, Ohio; T. K. Jones, Lubbock, Tex.; Floyd S. Judah, San Francisco, Calif.

W. A. Keleher, Albuquerque, N. M.; Miss Barbara Kell, Missouri Historical Society, St. Louis, Mo.; Campbell Dirck Keyser, Arlington, Va.; H. Irvine Keyser II, Baltimore, Md.; R. Campbell Keyser, Morristown, N. J.; Roy E. Kimball, Metropolitan District Commission, Belchertown, Mass.; Mrs. Leland W. Knight, Westbrook, Me.; Mrs. McCook Knox, Washington, D. C.; Rabbi Bertram W. Korn, Philadelphia, Pa.; Wilbur G. Kurtz, Atlanta, Ga.; Miss Gladys Ladu, New York State Library, Albany, N. Y.; Van Buren Lamb, Jr., Summit, N. Y.; Buxton L. Layton, New Orleans, La.; Miss Constance E. Lee, California State Library,

Sacramento, Calif.; Miss Elizabeth C. Litsinger, Enoch Pratt Free Library, Baltimore, Md.; Frederick Loescher, Spring Valley, N. Y.; George King Logan, New Orleans Public Library, New Orleans, La.; Mrs. E. B. Loughin, Michigan State Library, Lansing, Mich.; Joseph A. McCarthy, Swan Point Cemetery, Providence, R. I.; Miss Mary E. McCoy, Monmouth, Ill.; Raymond McCoy, Santa Fe, N. M.; Mrs. Irene McCreery, Toledo Public Library, Toledo, Ohio; Mrs. H. K. McJunkin, Swissvale, Pa.; Mrs. Loring McMillen, Staten Island Historical Society, Richmondtown, N. Y.: R. Gerald McMurtry, Lincoln National Life Foundation, Ft. Wayne, Ind.: Rex E. Magee, Washington, D. C.; Miss Clare Malone, Yonkers Public Library, Yonkers, N. Y.; Miss Leah Simpson Marshall, Grand Army of the Republic, Lansing, Mich.; Mrs. Laura Maxon, Brownville, N. Y.; Miss Pauline Maxton, Reading Public Library, Reading, Pa.; Mrs. Elma A. Medearis, Museum of New Mexico Library, Santa Fe, N. M.; J. Metzler, Arlington National Cemetery, Washington, D. C.; Nyle H. Miller, Kansas Historical Society, Topeka, Kan.; Miss Helen E. Mook, Buffalo and Erie County Public Library, Buffalo, N. Y.; Mrs. Maurice Moore, Lynchburg, Va.; Colonel W. J. Morton, U. S. Military Academy, West Point, N. Y.; Mrs. Jane S. Moyer, Easton Public Library, Easton, Pa.; John Mullane, Public Library of Cincinnati and Hamilton County, Cincinnati, Ohio; John A. Munroe, University of Delaware, Newark, Del.; Jack W. Musgrove, State Department of History and Archives, Des Moines, Iowa.

Mrs. Harvey F. Nagle, Pottsville, Pa.; Frank W. Nash, Cherryfield, Me.; Clarence Nelson, Yonkers, N. Y.; Miss Dawn P. Nye, South Kingstown, R. I.; Joseph M. O'Donnell, U. S. Military Academy, West Point, N. Y.; Reverend Gerald B. O'Grady, Geneva, Switzerland; B. Joseph O'Neil, Boston Public Library, Boston, Mass.; Miss Beth Oyler, Salt Lake City Public Library, Salt Lake City, Utah; Dr. Caroline L. Paine, Glendale, Calif.; R. E. Pairan, Chillicothe, Ohio; Miss Alberta Pantle, Kansas State Historical Society, Topeka, Kan.; Major John W. Parker, Ohio Soldiers and Sailors Home, Sandusky, Ohio; Reverend DeWolf Perry, Charleston, S. C.; William J. Petersen, State Historical Society of Iowa, Iowa City, Iowa; Miss Alice J. Pickup, Buffalo Historical Society, Buffalo, N. Y.; Miss Margaret Pierson, Indiana State Library, Indianapolis, Ind.; Russell H. Porter, Paris, France; R. H. Potter, Jr., Connecticut State Library, Hartford, Conn.; Mrs. Marie C. Preston, Denter Street Museum, Geneseo, N. Y.; Jack H. Putnam, Pikeville, Tenn.; Robert Quarles, Jr., Tennessee Historical Society, Nashville, Tenn.

Frank H. Ramsey, Beaufort, S. C.; Alfred C. Raphelson, University of Michigan, Flint, Mich.; Kenneth W. Rapp, U. S. Military Academy, West Point, N. Y.; Mrs. Helen S. Ray, New London, N. H.; M. B. Reed, Tacoma Cemetery Association, Tacoma,

Wash.; Miss Ruth Richardson, Cedar Rapids Public Library, Cedar Rapids, Iowa; Miss Helen Richter, Des Moines Park Board, Des Moines, Iowa; Chester L. Roadhouse, Davis, Calif.; Charles Roberts, British Cemetery Corporation, Buenos Aires, Argentina; Will E. Robinson, South Dakota State Historical Society, Pierre, S. D.; James H. Rodabaugh, Ohio Historical Society, Columbus, Ohio; Rutherford D. Rogers, New York Public Library, New York, N. Y.; William C. Rogers, Community Cemetery, Monroe, N. Y.; Paul B. Rowen, Los Angeles, Calif.; Christopher A. Russell, Baltimore, Md.; Mrs. Virginia B. Sampson, Island Cemetery, Newport, R. I.; Miss Emily Sanders, New York, N. Y.; Mrs. LeRoy Sanders, Historical Society of Berks County, Reading, Pa.; Miss Mari Sandoz, New York, N. Y.; Miss Mahala Saville, University of Mississippi Library, University, Miss.; Mrs. Lewis Sawyer, Chicago Historical Society, Chicago, Ill.; W. M. Schnure, Selinsgrove, Pa.; Charles B. Scott, Oxford, Neb.; Maxine Serre, Toulon, France; Fred Shelley, New Jersey Historical Society, Newark, N. J.; Mrs. J. K. Shishkin, Museum of New Mexico, Santa Fe, N. M.; Floyd C. Shoemaker, State Historical Society of Missouri, Columbia, Mo.; Mrs. Walter A. Simpson, Sewell, N. J.; Theodore Sizer, Yale University, New Haven, Conn.; Miss Elizabeth Sloan, Free Public Library, Burlington, Iowa; Martin A. Slough, Amarillo, Tex.; Mrs. Elsie Hawes Smith, Barre, Mass.; Hugh W. Smith, Times-Picayune Publishing Company, New Orleans, La.; Mrs. S. H. Smith, La Jolla, Calif.; Mrs. Nina W. Smithers, De Peyster, N. Y.; Paul G. Sotirin, Milwaukee Public Library, Milwaukee, Wis.; Lawrence N. Spears, Chattanooga, Tenn.; H. E. Stahl, Claymont, Del.; Mrs. Ernest J. Stiefel, St. Paul Park, Minn.; Miss Lois Stombaugh, Indiana State Library, Indianapolis, Ind.; Kenneth Stone, Beverly Hills, Calif.; Mrs. Elleine H. Stones, Detroit Public Library, Detroit, Mich.; Winston J. Stratton, Brooklyn, N. Y.; W. H. Struss, Brooklyn, N. Y.; Boyd B. Stutler, Charleston, W. Va.; Earl G. Terko, Albany Cemetery Association, Albany, N. Y.; Dr. Frederick Tilberg, Gettysburg National Military Park, Gettysburg, Pa.; Ronald V. T. Tilyard, Walpole, N. H.; John Barr Tompkins, University of California Library, Berkeley, Calif.; Franklin A. Towne, Norway, Me.; Robert J. Trenchard, Dundee, N. Y.; Miss Prudence B. Trimble, Historical Society of Western Pennsylvania, Pittsburgh, Pa.; Justin G. Turner, Beverly Hills, Calif.; W. W. Turner, Jasper, Tenn.; Miss Louise W. Turpin, Brooklyn Public Library, Brooklyn, N. Y.

Leon de Valenger, Jr., State Archivist, Dover, Del.; James L. Van Alen, Newport, R. I.; Peter N. Vanden Berge, New Brunswick Theological Society, New Brunswick, N. J.; William W. Vanderhoof, Elizabeth, N. J.; Dorothy M. Vaughan, Public Library, Portsmouth, N. H.; Mrs. Kay Wade, State Historical Society of Missouri, Columbia, Mo.; Edward S. Wallace, East Haddam, Conn.; William S. Wallace, Las Vegas, N. M.; Joseph A. Walsh, Jersey City, N. J.; Clyde C. Walton, Illinois State Historian, Springfield, Ill.; Afton Wardle, Salt Lake City Public Library, Salt Lake City, Utah; Neil B. Watson, Sr., The Green-Wood Cemetery, Brooklyn, N. Y.; Miss Elizabeth H. Webster, Tryon, N. C.; Whitman B. Welles, Greenfield, Mass.; Mrs. M. C. Wheelwright, Des Moines, Iowa; Mrs. James T. White, Cumberland, Md.; Mrs. Walter C. White, Gates Mills, Ohio; Dr. Minna C. Wilkins, Staten Island, N. Y.; John R. Williams, Jersey City, N. J.; Miss Louise Wood, Indiana State Library, Indianapolis, Ind.; William N. Woodbury, Birmingham, Ala.; Mrs. C. S. Woodward, Little Rock, Ark.; Miss Muriel H. Wright, Oklahoma Historical Society, Oklahoma City, Okla.; B. C. Yates, Kennesaw Mountain National Battlefield Park, Marietta, Ga.; Robert J. Younger, Dayton, Ohio; William G. Smith, Washington, D. C.

E. J. W.

CONTENTS

INTRODUCTION

THE UNITED STATES was no more unprepared for the Civil War than it was for any of the wars in which it has fought before or since. Public sentiment, nourishing the delusion that swarms of patriots would answer a call to arms and successfully repel enemies without or within, disapproved of the large, standing armies maintained by European monarchies. That we had been bailed out of the Revolution by the French; that England was preoccupied by a vastly more important theater during the War of 1812; and that the Mexicans, like our own troops, were little more than an armed mob, escaped the notice of all but a handful of professional officers (few of whom had commanded as large a detachment as a battalion in action) in the minimal Regular Army of the United States. Accordingly, as the year 1861 dawned, with South Carolina already out of the Union and a dozen more states teetering on the brink of secession, the United States possessed an army of 1,108 officers and 15,259 enlisted men, divided into nineteen line regiments and eleven staff corps. In the absence of a retirement system many of the officers were either superannuated or "awaiting orders" since they were of no use on active duty. The table of organization, as provided for in the act of March 3, 1855, exhibits 724 line officers—only 76 were field grade, 4 were general officers, and 312 were officers of the staff (95 attached to the medical department). Eleven of the 19 colonels of the line had fought in the War of 1812 as commissioned officers; the commissary general had held his post since 1818, the chief engineer and chief topographical engineer since 1838, and 2 of the 4 generals since 1841. From this roster and from the ranks of those who had resigned from the service because of stultified promotion plus the state militia officers and Mexican War veterans came the experienced officer corps for an army which would number two and one-half million.

As a consequence of the desperate need for officers and as a logical concomitant to the American political system, politically inspired appointments and promotions were made without end, many to the prejudice of the lives of the men in the ranks. Not only were incompetents shielded from the rightful consequences of their mistakes, but scores of gallant officers failed to receive the acknowledgment on the part of the government to which they were entitled. On April 29, 1864, General Henry W. Halleck, then acting as chief of staff of the army, wrote General William T. Sherman, who was poised to launch the campaign against Atlanta, "It seems little better than murder to give important commands to such men as Banks, Butler, McClernand, Sigel, and Lew Wallace, and yet it seems impossible to prevent it." (*Official Records*, XXXIV, Pt. 3, pp. 332-33.) Ludwell H. Johnson in his *Red River Campaign* has well summarized this unfortunate situation: "A sincere conviction that the only salvation of the country lay in the continued ascendancy of the Republican party [led] easily to acts which, while they strengthened that party, seriously impeded the progress of the war. . . . Political overtones of this nature were implicit in the removal from command of McClellan, Buell, and Porter, and the appointment and retention of Butler, Pope, Hooker, Frémont, Banks, *et al.*"

On the other hand, of all the officers to whom the Union should have been grateful, Benjamin F. Davis (West Point, 1854), colonel of the 8th New York Volunteer Cavalry, was the man. Born in Alabama and appointed to the Military Academy from Mississippi, he was the only officer from the Deep South who remained loyal to the Union, forsaking his family and friends to do so. He was commanding a brigade of cavalry at Beverly Ford, Virginia, on June 9, 1863, when he was killed in action. He was not even awarded the brevet of brigadier general, although brevet promotions had become almost as common as Good Conduct medals did later.

Years after the war Brigadier General Anson Mills, U. S. Army, who had himself won the brevet of lieutenant colonel in 1864, wrote in his *My Story*: "Prior to the Civil War the Government established a satisfactory system of brevets, conferred on officers who distinguished themselves in action, so regulated that rights to promotion of those commissioned in special corps might not be infringed, while allowing the beneficiary to exercise rank and command by authority of his brevet whenever placed on duty with a mixed command. . . . During the Civil War, however, the conferring of brevets was so overdone by political and other influences that in one or two instances a captain in a noncombative corps acquired the rank of major general. The situation was so absurd and confusing that Congress passed a law declaring that under no circumstances should a brevet be exercised for rank or command. This rendered brevets practically worthless." (p. 209). This is about as clear an exposition of the situation as can be found, and it overlooks only one factor: since brevets constituted an acknowledgment by the government of the recipient's services, they *were* as prized, especially among volunteer officers, as the Distinguished Field Cross and the Distinguished Service Medal are today. That many deserving officers failed to receive them and that they were overdone cannot be denied.

It was possible to hold four separate and distinct ranks at one and the same time. Many officers of the Regular Army, who held substantive and brevet rank, obtained leaves in order to accept commissions in the volunteer service, where substantive and brevet rank also existed. Ranald S. Mackenzie at the end of the war was a full-rank brigadier general of volunteers, a major general of volunteers by brevet, and a brigadier general by brevet in the Regular Army, although his substantive rank in the Regulars was captain of engineers.

The absurd situations in which this often resulted may be illustrated by one instance. William H. Emory was colonel of the 5th U. S. Cavalry, a regiment in which George Custer was one of the junior captains. Yet Custer's commission as major general of volunteers dated from April 15, 1865, Emory's from September 25, 1865. Although young men—many of them volunteers— fought the war and gained the largest popular reputations, the regular establishment in 1866 looked like the Army register of a past generation. At this time there were thirty lineal rank colonels, who it might be supposed were the division and corps commanders of the Armies of the Potomac, Ohio, Tennessee, Cumberland, etc., and the other Federal forces which had swept to victory after four years of war. Such a supposition would have been naïve. In point of fact, twenty of these colonels are virtually unknown today (as they were a century ago); of the remainder only E. R. S. Canby remains a prominent figure. Who were the other nine? T. W. Sherman, Daniel Butterfield, T. J. Wood, W. H. Emory, Silas Casey, W. B. Franklin, S. P. Heintzelman, E. C. Carrington, and David Hunter. (For a measure of their relative importance the reader is referred to their sketches herein.) It is fair to say—as did Colonel W. A. Graham, leading expert on the battle of the Little Big Horn, in his book *The Custer Myth* —that "but for the blaze of glory that formed the setting for [Custer's] dramatically tragic [death] at the hands of yelling savages, he would probably be just another name of a long list of names in our histories of the Civil War, in which as 'The Boy General' he made an outstanding record as a leader of Cavalry, as did also numerous others who have been long since all but forgotten."

Unlike the Confederate service, that of the United States provided for only two grades of general officers: brigadier and major general. This arrangement was not modified until 1864 when the grade of lieutenant general was revived in order to make Ulysses S. Grant general-in-chief, who up until that time was ranked not only by Halleck but also by George B. McClellan and John C. Frémont. In the course of the Civil War, 583 individuals (including Grant) served in the Union armies as general officers of full rank, and 1,367 others were brevetted as such.

Since we have only recently been subjected to the humbug attendant upon the demise of the alleged "last survivor" of the Civil War, it may be appropriate to note the actual last survivors of the 583 full-rank generals. Only eight outlived World War I, two major generals and four brigadiers; all but one of these were gone by the end of 1926. Brigadier General Adelbert Ames lived to witness the Great Depression, the inauguration of Franklin D. Roosevelt, and to walk about the golf course with another nonagenarian John D. Rockefeller. General Ames died on April 13, 1933, aged ninety-eight. Apparently the last survivor of the brevet-rank generals (later a brigadier general in the Regular Army) was Brevet Brigadier General Aaron S. Daggett, U. S. Volunteers, who died on May 14, 1938, a month before his one hundred-first birthday.

As was emphasized in *Generals in Gray,* the Civil War was a young man's war. The average age of the 132 major generals in 1861 was thirty-nine; that of the 450 brigadiers was thirty-seven. Grant had not reached his thirty-ninth birthday when Fort Sumter was fired upon; Sherman was only forty-one; Philip Sheridan thirty or thirty-one; and George H. Thomas a venerable forty-four. Brigadier General (and Brevet Major General) Galusha Pennypacker, U. S. Volunteers, was not old enough to cast his vote in 1864; only sixteen years old at the outbreak of war, he was twenty when appointed a full-rank brigadier on April 28, 1865, to rank from February 18. At the other end of the spectrum was that highly efficient relic of a bygone age, the septuagenarian John Ellis Wool, who was born three years after Yorktown, was a general officer since 1841, and who served with distinction until his retirement in 1863. Generally speaking, as the war got older, the generals—through retirement, resignation, and consequent promotion—got younger; and the average age of those on active duty in 1865, particularly those discharging field duty, was substantially younger than it was in 1861.

To a much greater extent than in the Confederate Army, high command was entrusted to individuals whose claims to preferment rested exclusively upon political considerations. President Lincoln, master politician that he was, walked on the blade of a knife during the entire war. It was his task to reconcile the conflicting interests of a number of diametrically opposed groups and to enlist them in a war to save the Union. No abolitionist himself, he nevertheless had to satisfy the radical wing of the Republican party as well as the pro-Union Democrats in the border states, many of whom were slaveowners. The emotional and pragmatic concepts of the two factions could not have been more divergent. Unfortunately, many innocents were led to the slaughter by generals whose claims the administration could not ignore and still remain in power. In any event, the appointments to lead troops had to be made from at least four distinct factions other than that of professional soldiers: hard-core abolitionists, high-tariff protectionists, foreign language immigrant groups (particularly the Irish and German), and War Democrats. If based upon the performance in the field of battle the results of these selections reflect most unfavorably in retrospect when compared to the choices of Jefferson Davis. Yet who is to say that had Benjamin F. Butler been snubbed, or N. P. Banks, or Lew Wallace, or T. F. Meagher, or Franz Sigel, or Jeremiah Boyle, that the war could have been won at all? The question not infrequently resolved itself into a choice between a competent West Point graduate in subordinate command at the front, and a New England (or New York or Ohio) politician, the mention of whose name swayed thousands of votes. It was thus that simple—and that complex.

At all events, an analysis of the antebellum occupations of the Union general officers is illuminating to the extent that it illustrates the difference in background between the generals of the North and those of the South:

	U. S. A.	C. S. A.
Lawyers, jurists	126	129
Professional soldiers	194	125
Businessmen	116	55
Farmers	23	42
Politicians	47	24
Educators	16	15
Civil engineers	26	13
Students	8	6
Doctors	11	4
Ministers	1	3
Frontiersmen, peace officers	2	3
Indian agents	0	2
Naval officers	3	2
Editors	6	1
Unclassified	4	1
Totals	583	425

In the foregoing classification the emphasis of each general's antebellum career was used in determining his occupation or profession. Quite naturally, many politicians were also lawyers, and some West Point graduates had resigned to become civil engineers, businessmen, and educators. Newspaper editors who, as much as any other profession, were responsible for bringing on the war joined the Union standard six to one vis-à-vis their Southern counterparts. By another standard of comparison Northern businessmen who sprang to the colors outnumbered Southerners more than two to one—perhaps illustrating the far greater preoccupation with mercantile pursuits in the North. By the same token, only half as many Northern farmers achieved general's rank as did those on the Southern side, a region principally devoted to agriculture. Most of the civil engineers on both sides were West Point graduates who saw no immediate promotion in the army and who had resigned to survey and construct the rapidly growing United States railway system.

Lincoln's choices were limited: they were decided by appointing the best-placed instead of the best-qualified. Even so, the bulk of generals were professionals or had, at least, experienced some professional training, as is demonstrated by the following table:

West Point graduates	217
Nongraduates of West Point	11
Graduates of other military schools	9
Regular Army (and Navy) officers	36
State militia officers	40
European emigré officers	20
Others with Mexican War background, etc.	62
Inexperienced civilians	188
Total	583

In this connection it is interesting to note that, aside from the U. S. Military Academy, Norwich University at Northfield, Vermont, furnished more officers to the war than did any other military school. Originally founded in Norwich, Vermont, by Captain Alden Partridge (the fifteenth graduate of West Point and for twelve years a faculty member), it was subsequently located in Middletown, Connecticut, before its final location in Northfield. The school contributed 523 of her men to the Union and 34 to the Confederacy. Among the former were six major generals, nine brigadiers, eighteen brevet brigadiers, more than a hundred field grade officers, and a host of company officers who received their primary military education there.

According to the definitive *Memorandum Relative to the General Officers in the Armies of the United States during the Civil War, 1861-1865* (published by the War Department in 1906 but in reality a compilation by former Confederate General Marcus J. Wright), there were 583 individuals appointed to the substantive grade of general officer (or who already held such rank) for services rendered during the Civil War. At the time of the surrender of Joseph E. Johnston's army to Sherman, which for all practical purposes marks the end of the war, 374 were in grade, an attrition of 209 or nearly 40 per cent. The causes for this decrease are set forth in comparison with those in the Confederate Army during the same period in the following table:

	U. S. A.	C. S. A.
Killed in action or died of wounds	47	77
Resigned	110	19
Died by accident or disease	18	15
Appointments cancelled	22	5
Declined appointment	1	3
Killed in "personal encounters"	1	2
Committed suicide	1	1
Retired	6	1
Cashiered or dismissed	3	1
Other	0	2
Totals	209	126

When it is considered that 425 men were appointed as general officers in the army of the Confederate States, the figures above are suggestive, particularly in the first two categories. Of all Federal generals appointed, 8 per cent were killed in action or died of wounds; the figure for Confederate generals was 18 per cent. The relative percentage of resignations was 19 per cent and 4.5 per cent respectively. Obviously the North was far better supplied not only with the tools of war but with the men to use them. General John Beatty, a distinguished division commander under Sherman, resigned from the army in January, 1864, so that his younger brother William, who was conducting their joint banking business in Cardington, Ohio, could get a taste of soldiering. At the other end of the spectrum, any number of Federal generals with charges hanging over their heads were permitted to resign; only three were cashiered or dismissed. (The sketches herein document this occurrence.)

The question of allegiance to the "Old Flag" and its effect upon Southern-born officers of the Old Army is interesting. Broadly speaking, loyalty to the Union manifested itself in inverse ratio to how far south lay the general's place of birth and upbringing. With the single exception of B. F. Davis, no individual born and raised south of the thirty-fifth parallel of latitude failed to resign and go with his state. (With one or two exceptions the same is true of civilians.) Progressing northward some division of sentiment was evident in East Tennessee, which was overwhelmingly Union, but much less than in her sister state to the east, North Carolina. Kentucky, Maryland, and Missouri, however, were bitterly divided, with Virginia (including the area which is now West Virginia) favoring the Confederacy by probably 80 per cent. Despite the adherence of a number of men from the border states and upper South to the Union, it must be admitted that those officers who later became distinguished in most cases were found fighting under the Stars and Bars. If the names of Winfield Scott (whose service extended only until his retirement in November, 1861) and George Thomas, both Virginians, are omitted, one casts about in vain for Federal general officers from Southern states whose contribution to the war was particularly significant. As a matter of fact, almost 70 per cent of the North's generals were born in New England, New York, New Jersey, Pennsylvania, and Ohio, although many subsequently moved to the West during the tide of emigration which marked the twenties, thirties, and forties. Another 8 per cent were of foreign birth (in contrast to the Confederacy's 2 per cent), illustrating the relatively larger influx of Europeans to Northern ports in the decades preceding 1861. So sparse was settlement in the states of Michigan, Illinois, and Wisconsin that only 16 of the 583 were born there, although many others were, of course, resident in those states when the war broke out. (Appendix II gives a complete breakdown of the Union generals' birthplaces.)

It is perhaps not surprising that the best fighters of the war, with few exceptions, were born in the areas which they later defended. As Lincoln said about the Pennsylvania-born George Gordon Meade immediately before the battle of Gettysburg: "Meade will fight well on his own dunghill." (Cleaves, *Meade of Gettysburg*, 123.) Most of the Northern-born officers who attached themselves to the Confederate cause were relatively undistinguished; by the same token, the Southern-born who clung to the old Union contributed little, with the particular exceptions already noted.

No major war could be more truly called a "civil" war. General Philip St. George Cooke was both the father-in-law of the famous Jeb Stuart and the father of General John R. Cooke, a distinguished Confederate infantry brigadier. President Zachary Taylor's brother was commissary general of the U. S. Army, his daughter had been Jefferson Davis' first wife, and his only son was a Confederate lieutenant general. Robert E. Lee's nephew was Federal General John Pope's aide-de-camp. Lincoln himself had a host of in-laws either in sympathy with, or actively fighting for, the Southern cause. Further instances of divided families can be cited virtually without end: there were the Terrill brothers and the McIntosh brothers arrayed on opposite sides, brother against brother, with both Terrills and one McIntosh killed in action. And these were only the names in the headlines; endless rows of headstones from the Atlantic to the Mississippi and beyond attest to the savage partisan nature of the struggle.

For better understanding of the photographs of the generals and as a matter of general interest, a brief survey of uniform and dress of the army is in order. On March 3, 1861, Adjutant General Lorenzo Thomas (whose predecessor in office Samuel Cooper had resigned only six days before and was the ranking general of the Confederacy), set forth in detail the regulations thereto. These regulations were modified in only a few minor details during the war, and, for that matter, for a generation. Essentially, the full-dress uniform of the army today—"dress blues"—derives from that day.

Quoting from General Thomas' General Orders No. 6, all officers were to wear "a frock coat of dark blue cloth, the skirt to extend from two-thirds to three-fourths of the distance from the top of the hip to the bend of the knee; single-breasted for Captains and Lieutenants; double-breasted for all other grades." Button arrangement was to be "For a Major General—two rows of buttons on the breast, nine in each row, placed by threes. . . . For a Brigadier General—the same as for a Major General, except that there will be only eight buttons in each row . . . placed in pairs." This portion of the directive makes it relatively easy to determine an officer's rank from a photograph and accordingly helps to date the photograph. Thus, if a full-rank brigadier and major general by brevet is shown wearing nine buttons in groups of threes, it is safe to assume that the photograph was taken after the close of hostilities when he had donned the uniform of his brevet rank. He could wear this uniform on ceremonial occasions and, curiously enough, on court-martial duty. To continue with the regulations, "seven buttons in each row . . . placed in equal distances" was prescribed for colonels, lieutenant colonels, and majors. For company grade officers there was to be "one row of nine buttons . . . placed at equal distances." The collar and cuffs of general officers' uniforms were to be of "dark blue velvet"; those of field grade officers "of the same color and material as the coat." Unlike the Confederate service, trousers of general officers were unadorned by a stripe although staff officers (excepting ordnance officers) wore a narrow gold stripe and regimental officers that of their branch—cavalry, yellow; artillery, scarlet; infantry, blue. A distinction again appears between the United States and Confederate services as to insignia of rank. Shoulder straps and epaulettes remained in favor in the Union, whereas the Confederates went to the European custom of designating rank by collar insignia. Both governments originally prescribed stand-up collars; however, these frequently went by the board, by general consent, in the field. Confederate officers habitually sewed their stars on the lapels of their uniform coats. The familiar bars, oak leaves, eagles, and stars were prescribed for the U. S. Army then as now with two exceptions: the shoulder straps of second lieutenants were void of insignia, and the bars of first lieutenants and captains were gold instead of silver, as they are today.

From reviewing photographs of the period, one is forced to the conclusion that a deliberately careless or offhand style of dress must have been *de rigueur* on both sides. The author possesses a photograph of his great-uncle and West Point graduate General James M. Warner, taken by Brady in Washington immediately after the grand review of the armies in May, 1865. The spit-and-polish tradition of West Point is nowhere apparent in this photograph; the youthful brigadier gazes serenely from a velvet and much-tasselled armchair, collar of his uniform turned down in the style of today's double-breasted suit, wearing a white shirt with turn-down collar and a bow tie all askew with ends uneven. (He also appears to be somewhat in need of a shave.)

The custom was prevalent in the Union as well as in the Confederacy, for general officers to take great liberties with regulations governing dress. Grant, while campaigning with the Army of the Potomac, habitually wore an enlisted man's tunic with the shoulder straps of a lieutenant general sewn on to it; Butler, on the other hand, added all manner of gold braid to the sleeves and collar of his uniform coat; and the flamboyant Custer appeared at Appomattox "dressed in a blue sack with the largest shoulder straps of a Major General I ever saw . . . with a gorgeous red scarf and in it a gold pin near two inches in length and breadth and in big letters 'George A. Custer, Major General.'" (Haskell, "Memoirs.")

Since the United States government was intact at the war's end whereas the Confederacy was in flight with many of its records destroyed forever, the determination of who was and who was not entitled to be called "general" was a far less difficult task in this volume than it was in *Generals in Gray*. A number of authoritative sources are available, all of which closely agree. The previously mentioned General Wright's *Memorandum Relative to the General Officers* carries the names of 583 men who were accorded the full rank of brigadier or major general in the Federal service during the course of the Civil War, a figure which includes General Grant, who was the Union's only lieutenant general. The lives of these men are treated *in extenso* herein. Additionally, 1,367 other officers (some of whom served regularly in no higher grade than that of major) received brevet promotions to brigadier general and, in a few instances, to major general as the triumphant Union forces were mustered out. The names of these 1,367 will be found listed alphabetically in Appendix I.

In all there were 1,950 generals, which would seem a very large number. However, in addition to these, a number of men were appointed by their state governors to command state troops at various times during emergencies but at no time were mustered into United States service. Their names will not be found in the present work which deals—as did *Generals in Gray*—with appointees of the central government. Another class, perhaps worthy of mention, were those officers appointed "acting brigadier general" by field commanders but whose appointments did not subsequently receive presidential sanction.

It is the author's fond, and perhaps misguided, expectation that the lives of these patriots—and patriots they were from whatever motive—may point up the ideal of freedom for which our world fights today. Here then is the full complement of the GENERALS IN BLUE!

GENERALS IN BLUE

John Joseph Abercrombie was born in Baltimore, Maryland. Upon the authority of a daughter, the date was March 4, 1798; however, his gravestone reports "March 28, 1798." (1) He was a son-in-law of General Robert Patterson of Mexican War fame and a brother-in-law of Brigadier General Francis E. Patterson, U. S. Volunteers. Considerable mystery surrounds his early life, and some sources record his birthplace as Tennessee. In any event, he was graduated from the Military Academy in 1822, standing thirty-seventh in a class of forty. Abercrombie established a long and gallant army record during his service at many posts in the South and Northwest. He was promoted to first lieutenant of infantry in 1828, to captain in 1836, to major in 1847, to lieutenant colonel in 1852, and to full colonel at the outbreak of the Civil War. Meanwhile, he received the brevet promotions of major for gallant and meritorious services in Florida, and of lieutenant colonel in the Mexican War. He was appointed brigadier general of volunteers on August 31, 1861. In the early part of the war he was in field command: at Falling Waters, Virginia; at Seven Pines, where he was wounded; and at Malvern Hill during the withdrawal of George B. McClellan's army to Harrison's Landing. With the use of younger officers in the field, Abercrombie's activities were confined mainly to garrison and administrative duties, including command of depots around Fredericksburg and White House, Virginia, during U. S. Grant's Overland campaign. Brevetted brigadier general in the Regular Army on March 13, 1865, and retired from active service the following June 12, he continued on court-martial duty until 1869. He then made his home in Roslyn, Long Island, where he died on January 3, 1877. He is buried in Woodlands Cemetery, Philadelphia.

Robert Allen was born in West Point, a hamlet of Morrow County, Ohio, on March 15, 1811. (2) Lit-

Valley. In this latter post he supplied U. S. Grant's army at Vicksburg, W. T. Sherman's army through the Georgia campaign, the great Federal base at Nashville, and the various secondary expeditions in that theater, and the troops in New Mexico, on the Plains, and in the Northwest. In his forty-six years in the army—from 1832 until his retirement in 1878 as assistant quartermaster general—he reputedly disbursed some $111 million (equivalent today to almost $3 billion) without a penny being disallowed by the Treasury. After retirement, General Allen traveled abroad. He died on August 5, 1886, in Geneva, Switzerland, where he is buried in the cemetery of Chêne-Bougeries.

tle is known of his life before he was admitted to the Military Academy at the age of twenty-one. He was graduated in the lower third of the class of 1836 and was commissioned into the 2nd Artillery. He performed routine garrison duties at various points until the outbreak of the Mexican War in 1846, when he transferred from the line to the Quartermaster's Department. Chief quartermaster of the Pacific Division of the army in the 1850's, he was brevetted major for gallant and meritorious conduct at Cerro Gordo and achieved the rank of major in 1861. In the course of his distinguished Civil War career— during which he was successively promoted to colonel, to brigadier general of volunteers, and to brevet major general in both the volunteers and the regular establishment —he acted as chief quartermaster of the turbulent Department of Missouri, and his authority soon extended to the entire Mississippi

Benjamin Alvord was born August 18, 1813, in Rutland, Vermont. He was the lineal descendant of one Alexander Alvord who had settled in Connecticut about 1645. Young Alvord entered the Military Aca-

4

demy at the age of sixteen and was graduated in the class of 1833. For the next twenty-one years he was an officer of the 4th Infantry, serving with it continuously except for a two-year tour of duty as an instructor at West Point. During the Florida War against the Seminoles he was with his regiment, and in the Mexican War he fought at Palo Alto and Resaca de la Palma under Zachary Taylor and in the advance on Mexico City under Winfield Scott. He was brevetted major for his services during the latter operation and, after some garrison duty in the early 1850's, changed from line to staff by accepting an appointment as paymaster with rank of major. From 1854 until 1862 Alvord was chief paymaster of the Department of Oregon—an area which included the present states of Oregon and Washington as well as much of Idaho. On April 15, 1862, he was appointed a brigadier general of volunteers and placed in command of the recently created District of Oregon, serving there until the spring of 1865. His principal problem during the war years was that of mediating between the Nez Percés, whose treaty rights had been repeatedly ignored and violated, and the whites who swarmed into the region in search of gold. General Alvord was relieved from command of the district in late March, 1865, and was ordered East. He resigned his volunteer commission in August and the following month became paymaster at New York City. From that time until his retirement in 1880, General Alvord was, successively, chief paymaster at Omaha, chief paymaster of the Department of the Platte, and paymaster general of the U. S. Army after 1872. He was made brigadier general, U. S. Army, in 1876. Meantime, he had become well known for his research and writings in a variety of technical fields, especially mathematics and agriculture in the West. Alvord died in Washington, D. C., on October 16, 1884, and was buried near his birthplace in Rutland.

Adelbert Ames was born in Rockland, Maine, on October 31, 1835. In his youth he became a sailor and was mate on a clipper ship. He left the sea in 1856 to enter the U. S. Military Academy where he was graduated fifth in the

class of May 6, 1861. He went almost immediately to the front as a lieutenant of artillery and was badly wounded at First Manassas. This gallantry won him the rank of brevet major in the Regular Army and later the Congressional Medal. Returning to duty, Ames remained in the Washington defenses until the spring of 1862 when he took part in the Peninsular campaign and was brevetted lieutenant colonel for services at Malvern Hill. As colonel of the 20th Maine Volunteers, he led his troops in the Maryland campaign, at Fredericksburg, and at Chancellorsville. On May 20, 1863, he was appointed brigadier general of volunteers. While commanding a brigade in the XI (Howard's) Corps at Gettysburg, he received the brevet of colonel in the regular service. During the siege of Petersburg, Ames was in divisional command; he later participated in the capture of Fort Fisher, North Carolina. For gallantry in this last operation and for meritorious services throughout the war, he was brevetted major general of volunteers and brigadier and major general, U. S. Army. His contribution to the Federal war effort was second to none of his age and experience, but General Ames later embarked upon a political career in Mississippi which ultimately tarnished his Civil War fame. In 1868 he was appointed provisional governor under the Reconstruction acts, and resigned from the army in 1870 to accept election to the United States Senate by the "carpetbag legislature." Four years later he became governor, but after the state was reclaimed by the whites in 1875, Ames offered his resignation to the Democratic legislature in return for the withdrawal of articles of impeachment. He left the state in 1876 to reside in Tewksbury, Massachusetts, and later in Florida. His remaining fifty-seven years of life contrasted sharply with those of fame and turbulence in his earlier career. Dur-

ing the Spanish-American War he served briefly as a brigadier general of volunteers. This was his last public service before his death at Ormond, Florida, on April 13, 1933. This last survivor of the full-rank general officers on either side of the conflict was buried in Hildreth Cemetery, Lowell, Massachusetts. General Ames's wife was a daughter of General Benjamin F. Butler.

Jacob Ammen was born on January 7, 1806, in Botetourt County, Virginia, but his parents moved north and he grew up in Ohio and was then appointed to the U. S. Military Academy. After being graduated from there in the class of 1831, he remained in the army only until his resignation in 1837. He served two tours of duty at the Academy as an instructor, was present in Charleston Harbor in 1832-33 during the nullification proceedings, and taught mathematics at

various colleges in Kentucky, Indiana, and Mississippi. He reentered Federal service as captain of a company of the 12th Ohio six days after the bombardment of Fort Sumter. During the early part of the war he participated, as colonel of the 24th Ohio, in the western Virginia campaign and later in the battle of Shiloh and in the subsequent siege of Corinth. He was promoted to brigadier general of volunteers on July 16, 1862, having mainly administrative duties in garrison commands and courts-martial. He resigned on January 14, 1865, to become a surveyor and civil engineer before settling on a farm near Beltsville, Maryland, in 1872. He was a member of the board of visitors to the Military Academy and was also deputed by the Secretary of the Navy to accompany the Isthmus of Panama commission to examine canal routes. In 1891 General Ammen removed to Lockland, Ohio, where he died on February 6, 1894. He is buried in Spring Grove Cemetery, Cincinnati.

Robert Anderson was born at "Soldier's Retreat" near Louisville, Kentucky, on June 14, 1805. His father, a lieutenant colonel of the Continental line, had moved from Virginia to Kentucky after the American Revolution. Commissioned into the 3rd Artillery after being graduated from West Point in 1825, Anderson was assigned to artillery and ordnance duty at various places. He participated in the Black Hawk, Florida, and Mexican Wars, and was brevetted twice for gallantry. He also served on various artillery boards while translating a number of French artillery texts. He received the rank of major in 1857 and, in November, 1860, was ordered to Charleston Harbor to command the three United States forts there—Castle Pinckney, Moultrie, and the unfinished Sumter—in the face of South Carolina's imminent secession. This assignment was dictated by both military and political considerations: Anderson was a Kentucky-born proslavery officer whose wife was a Georgian, but he was also highly competent and respected in his profession and his loyalty was unquestioned. Anderson, who had established his headquarters at Moultrie, realized his untenable position and moved his command to Sumter. The South Carolina authorities immediately declared this act a violation of the status quo previously agreed upon in Washington. When the steamer *Star of the West* appeared to reinforce him, Anderson—not wishing to provoke war and having only vague instructions from Washington—permitted it to be driven off. A formal demand for surrender was finally presented. Anderson refused and beginning in the early morning of April 12, 1861, sustained a thirty-four hour bombardment which made further resistance suicidal. Accepting the terms offered by the Confederates, he marched out with colors flying and saluted his flag with fifty guns. His conduct served to unify the North. Arriving in New York as a hero, he was appointed brigadier general in the Regular Army by President Abraham Lincoln on May 15, 1861. After commanding for a short time in Kentucky, where he helped maintain the state's nominal allegiance to the Union, he fell ill, was relieved in October, and retired in 1863. He raised the United States flag over Sumter on April 14, 1865, exactly four years after he had hauled it down. He was brevetted major general the same year. He died in Nice, France, on October 26, 1871, but his remains were returned to the United States for burial at West Point.

Christopher Columbus Andrews was born at Hillsboro, New Hampshire, on October 27, 1829. A precocious young man, he was admitted to the Massachusetts bar at the age of twenty-one after three terms at Francestown Academy in New Hampshire and a stint at Harvard Law School. He began practice in Newton, Massachusetts, but in 1854 went to Kansas. Andrews soon r e c e i v e d a political appointment as clerk in the Treasury Department in Washington. His writing talent led him to contribute accounts of his travels East and West to various newspapers.

In 1857 he established residence in St. Cloud, Minnesota, and in 1859 became a member of the Minnesota state senate. He enlisted as a private in 1861, but was soon commissioned c a p t a i n of the 3rd Minnesota. Taken prisoner near Murfreesboro, Tennessee, in July 1862, he was exchanged in October of that year and appointed lieutenant colonel. He was colonel in command of the regiment in the Arkansas campaign of 1863; on January 5, 1864, he was appointed brigadier general of volunteers. For his part in the assault and capture of Fort Blakely, Alabama, during the Mobile campaign, Andrews was brevetted major general of volunteers on March 9, 1865. Mustered out in January, 1866, he returned to St. Cloud and became prominent in state politics. President Grant appointed him minister to Sweden and Norway in 1869, a post he occupied until 1877. He was then successively a newspaper editor, a district supervisor of the

1880 census in Minnesota, a consul general to Brazil, and chief warden and forest commissioner of Minnesota. From 1911 until his death in St. Paul on September 21, 1922, he was secretary of the state forestry board. General Andrews' writings extended over many fields, among them law, history, and military tactics, and included his impressions of the foreign countries in which he had served as a government representative. He is buried in Oakland Cemetery, St. Paul.

George Leonard Andrews was born at Bridgewater, Massachusetts, on August 31, 1828. After finishing the state normal school in Bridgewater, he attended West Point and

was graduated at the head of the class of 1851. He worked in the Engineer Corps on the construction of Fort Warren in Boston Harbor and, after a brief tour at the Academy as an assistant professor, Andrews resigned in 1855 to pursue the

profession of civil engineer. He rèturned to the army as lieutenant colonel of the 2nd Massachusetts Infantry, of which he became colonel in June, 1862. On November 10, 1862, he was appointed brigadier general of volunteers and was involved in some of the early battles in the Eastern theater of war, including Cedar Mountain and Sharpsburg. He served with General N. P. Banks's expedition to Louisiana as chief of staff, taking part in the siege and capture of Port Hudson. Until joining the attack on Mobile, Andrews was placed in command of a district near Baton Rouge and charged with the organization and training of Negro troops raised from the vicinity of the Mississippi. He was mustered out in August, 1865, having been brevetted a major general of volunteers. His civil occupations included being a planter in Mississippi from 1865 until 1867, a United States marshal of Massachusetts until 1871, and a professor of Frènch at West Point. Retiring in 1892, he made his residence in Brookline. Massachusetts, where he died April 4, 1899. He is buried in Mt. Auburn Cemetery, Cambridge.

Lewis Golding Arnold was born in Perth Amboy, New Jersey, (3) on January 15, 1817. At sixteen he was appointed to the Military Academy from that state and in 1837 was graduated tenth in a class of fifty. Arnold had a distinguished record in the army before the Civil War; he served in the Florida War during 1837-38; assisted in transferring the Cherokees to the West; was on the Canadian frontier a year later; and after several years of garrison duty won the brevets of captain and major for gallant and meritorious conduct in the Mexican War. He was commissioned captain in the Regular Army in 1847 and major at the outbreak of the Civil War. Arnold

participated in the defense of Fort Pickens, Florida, in August, 1861, and was subsequently in command of the work until May 9, 1862. On January 24, 1862, he was appointed brigadier general of volunteers and assigned for some months to command the Department of Florida. In the fall he was transferred to the command of New Orleans but, on November 10, while reviewing his troops, suffered a stroke from which he never recovered. On sick leave until 1864, he was retired on February 8 of that year when it became apparent that he was permanently paralyzed. (4) He died in South Boston, Massachusetts (now a part of Boston), on September 22, 1871, and was buried in St. Mary's Cemetery, Newton Lower Falls, Massachusetts.

Richard Arnold, descending from an old New England family which included the notorious Benedict, was the son of a Rhode Island governor and United States Congressman. He was born in Providence on April 12, 1828, and was graduated from West Point in 1850. Commissioned into the artillery, Arnold at first performed routine duties—at Key West and San Francisco, on the Northern Pacific Railroad exploration, in Washington Territory, and as aide-de-camp to General John E. Wool. As a captain of the 5th Artillery, he commanded a battery at First Manassas and lost all of his guns while covering the retreat of the panic-stricken Federal volunteers. The following spring he entered the Peninsular campaign as chief of artillery of Franklin's division, but was soon appointed acting inspector general of the VI Corps. With the withdrawal of George B. McClellan's army to Harrison's Landing, Arnold

won the brevet of major for services at the battle of Savage's Station. In November, 1862, Arnold was promoted to brigadier general of volunteers and assigned to duty as chief of artillery, Department of the Gulf. He engaged in the siege of Port Hudson, in the ill-fated Red River campaign under N. P. Banks (at one time as a cavalry commander), and in the capture of Fort Morgan in Mobile Bay. Thereafter, his war service was confined to membership on a retirement board for disabled officers. At the end of the war he received the brevets through major general, in both the r e g u l a r and volunteer service. However, his regular rank was only that of a captain of the 5th Artillery, for his promotion to major did not occur until 1875. He was made lieutenant colonel only five days before his death, which occurred at Governors Island, New York, on November 8, 1882, while he was acting assistant inspector general, Department of the East. He was buried in Swan Point Cemetery, Providence.

Alexander Sandor Asboth was born in Keszthely in the county of Zala, Hungary, on December 18, 1811. He was graduated from the academy at Selmecbanya and, after receiving a government appointment as an engineer, worked in various parts of Hungary. During the Hungarian revolt of 1848 against the temporal power of Austria, he associated himself with Lajos Kossuth and followed him to exile in America in 1851. By 1861 Asboth had become a citizen and offered his services to the Federal government. General John C. Frémont, who had known him in New

York, applied for his services and appointed him brigadier general of volunteers and chief of staff. But the appointment was not recognized in Washington and lapsed until Asboth was duly appointed on March 21, 1862. During the same month he was wounded while in command of a division at Pea Ridge (Elkhorn Tavern). The following year he was in command at Columbus, Kentucky, and later of the District of West Florida. In 1864, at the battle of Marianna, he was badly wounded in the left cheek bone and the left arm. In 1866 General Asboth was appointed United States minister to the Argentine Republic and Uruguay. By this time he had been accorded the brevet rank of major general of volunteers for gallant and faithful service during the war. The wound in his cheek failed to heal, and on January 21, 1868, he died at Buenos Aires, probably of a malignancy. He was first buried in the British Cemetery in the Victoria District. In 1923 the Victoria District became a public park and the cemetery was moved to the Chacarita District. (5)

Christopher Columbus Augur was born on July 10, 1821, in Kendall, New York, but was taken the same year by his widowed mother to Michigan, from where he was appointed to the Military Academy in 1839. The class of 1843, in which Augur stood sixteenth of thirty-

nine graduates, furnished ten general officers to the North and three to the South, excluding brevet promotions. Augur performed routine garrison duty for some years, fought creditably in the Mexican War, and during the 1850's saw frontier service. He was promoted through grades and, on May 14, 1861, attained the rank of major in the Regular Army. After spending the first months of the war as commandant of cadets at West Point,

he was posted to the Washington defenses. He was appointed brigadier general of volunteers on November 12, 1861, and saw his first active field service on the line of the Rappahannock during the Peninsular campaign. Placed in command of Sigel's old division of the V Corps, Augur was one of several professional soldiers victimized by N. P. Banks's poor showing at Cedar Mountain and was severely wounded in the Federal rout. For his conduct here he was brevetted c o l o n e l in the regular establishment and commissioned as major general of volunteers on August 9, 1862. Banks asked for him as second in command of the New Orleans expedition that fall, and Augur commanded the left wing of the army during the siege of Port Hudson. From October, 1863, until the end of the war he commanded the XXII Corps and the Department of Washington. He was brevetted brigadier and major general, U. S. Army for gallant services; appointed colonel of the 12th Infantry in March, 1866; and brigadier general, U. S. Army, in 1869. General Augur commanded various military departments in the West and South during the postbellum years, and was retired in 1885. He died in Georgetown, D. C., on January 16, 1898, and was buried in Arlington National Cemetery.

William Woods Averell was born on November 5, 1832, in the village of Cameron, New York. In his youth he worked as a drug clerk in the nearby county seat of Bath. He was appointed to West Point in 1851 and was graduated in four years, ranking in the lower third of his class. Averell's antebellum army

career included garrison duty at Jefferson Barracks, Missouri; a tour at the Cavalry School in Carlisle, Pennsylvania; and two years of rugged service against the southwestern Indians, during which he was severely wounded and invalided from 1859 until the outbreak of the Civil War. As acting assistant adjutant general to General Andrew Porter, Averell took part in the battle of First Manassas and was then commissioned colonel of the 3rd Pennsylvania Cavalry. He participated in the Peninsular campaign as commander of a brigade; in the campaign which culminated at Sharpsburg; at Fredericksburg, in December, 1862; and in various skirmishes of the mounted branch of the Army of the Potomac. His 2nd Cavalry Division won the first claimed victory of the Federal horse over the Confederates at Kelly's Ford, Virginia, in March, 1863—an action said to have been the turning point of cavalry fighting in the Eastern theater. Meanwhile he was appointed brigadier general of volunteers on September 26, 1862. After taking part in George Stoneman's famous but ill-starred raid on Richmond during the campaign of Chancellorsville, (6) Averell was employed in minor operations in western Virginia until Philip Sheridan's Shenandoah campaign. At the end of the war he was brevetted brigadier and major general, U. S. Army, and resigned on May 18, 1865. He served as United States consul general to British North America (French Canada) from 1866 until 1869, and then invented a number of devices which rendered him financially independent. He died at Bath, New York, February 3, 1900, and was buried there.

Romeyn Beck Ayres was born at the crossroads of East Creek in Montgomery County, New York, on December 20, 1825. His father, a country physician, trained him so

13

thoroughly in Latin that Ayres was regarded as an authority in it among the cadets at the Military Academy from 1843 until his graduation in 1847. He served in garrison in Puebla and Mexico City after active hostilities in the Mexican War had ceased, and then had routine duty in many sections of the United States. He was advanced to captain of the 5th Artillery on May 14, 1861. He commanded a battery at First Manassas and continued with the Army of the Potomac until the surrender of Robert E. Lee at Appomattox. His leadership was conspicuous as an artillery commander at Sharpsburg and Fredericksburg, and as a brigade and division commander of infantry from Chancellorsville to Five Forks and Appomattox. At the end of the war Ayres was awarded the brevets of brigadier and major general, U. S. Army, and in 1866 was appointed lieutenant colonel of the newly created 28th Infantry. With the contraction of the Regular Army in the 1870's, General Ayres performed garrison duty at a number of posts, including Little Rock, Arkansas; Jackson Barracks, Louisiana; Key West, Florida; and other places in the South. On July 15, 1879, he was promoted to colonel of the 2nd Artillery, and supervised various army posts in Florida. He died at Fort Hamilton in New York Harbor on December 4, 1888; his remains were taken to Arlington National Cemetery for burial.

Joseph Bailey was born on May 6, 1825, probably at Pennsville, Ohio, (7) but was taken by his parents to Illinois at an early age. He studied civil engineering there and, in 1847, moved to Wisconsin to be-

come a lumberman. On July 2, 1861, he was mustered into Federal service as captain of a company of the 4th Wisconsin Infantry. Most of Bailey's war service was under General Benjamin F. Butler and then General N. P. Banks in the Department of the Gulf, during which time he was promoted to colonel of his regiment. His flair for engineering had distinguished him at Port Hudson and New Orleans, but Banks's Red River expedition afforded him the opportunity of a lifetime. The success of this joint army-navy venture depended upon high water in the Red River. However, on the retreat to Alexandria, after the repulse at Mansfield and Pleasant Hill, it was found that the thirty-three naval vessels could not be gotten over the shoals. Despite the opposition of most of the professional engineers of both services, Bailey obtained permission from Banks to construct a pair of wing dams from the sides of the

14

river, in order to raise the water level enough to bring the fleet through to safety. The Herculean efforts of 3,000 men, including several hundred lumbermen from Maine regiments, finally pushed the fleet through a sixty-six foot spillway on May 12, 1864. In reward, Bailey received the thanks of Congress, the brevet of brigadier general, and a sword from Admiral David D. Porter. He later participated in the reduction of Mobile, and was promoted to full brigadier general of volunteers and brevet major general. After the war he settled in Vernon County, Missouri, and was elected sheriff in the fall of 1866. On March 21, 1867, near Nevada, Missouri, he was shot and killed by a pair of bushwackers whom he had arrested. General Bailey is buried in Evergreen Cemetery, Fort Scott, Kansas.

Absalom Baird, grandson of a surgeon in the Revolutionary Army, and great-grandson of a lieutenant in the French and Indian Wars, was born at Washington, Pennsylvania, on August 20, 1824. He was graduated from Washington College and in 1849 from West Point, ranking ninth in a class of forty-three. Commissioned in the artillery, he campaigned against the Seminoles in Florida, instructed for six years at the Academy, and did a tour of duty on the Texas frontier. Baird transferred from line to staff at the outbreak of the Civil War and was present at First Manassas as adjutant of Tyler's division. In the spring of 1862 he took part in the Peninsular campaign as inspector general and chief of staff of the IV (Keyes's) Corps. Appointed brigadier general of volunteers on

April 28, Baird's subsequent Civil War career was in the Western theater. As a division commander under William S. Rosecrans, and later under George H. Thomas and W. T. Sherman, he played a prominent part in all the operations of the forces which swept Braxton Bragg out of Tennessee, held the famous Horseshoe Ridge at Chickamauga, maneuvered Joseph E. Johnston from Dalton to Atlanta, and moved through Georgia to Savannah and up the Atlantic coast until the final capitulation by General Johnston in North Carolina. However, Baird was never advanced beyond divisional command, nor were the several recommendations for his promotion to major general of volunteers acted upon. At the end of the war he was brevetted major general in both the volunteers and the Regular Army, mustered out of volunteer service in 1866, and reverted to his regular rank of major and assistant inspector general. He served at various times as inspector general of many military departments and, in 1885, was appointed inspector general of the army, first with the rank of colonel and, in the same year, with that of brigadier. Retired in 1888, he died near Relay, Maryland, on June 14, 1905, and was buried in Arlington National Cemetery.

Edward Dickinson Baker was born in London on February 24, 1811. At the age of four he was brought to Philadelphia where he was apprenticed to a weaver. His family later lived in New Harmony, Indiana, and in Belleville, Illinois. Having little formal education,

Baker read law and was admitted to the bar at the age of nineteen. A private soldier in the Black Hawk War, he subsequently moved to Springfield where he became a member of the so-called Lincoln "coterie." (Abraham Lincoln later named his second son after Baker.) He attained stature as an orator and was soon immersed in politics. He was a representative in the Illinois general assembly; defeated Lincoln to become a representative to Congress; served in the Mexican War as colonel of the 4th Illinois Infantry; was again elected to Congress from a district in which he had lived only three weeks; was a presidential elector in 1848; and four years later moved to California where he became a prominent lawyer and public speaker. In 1860 Baker moved to Oregon at the request of the Republican party of the newly admitted state and, in October of that year, was elected to the United States Senate. Having already done much to hold the Pacific Coast to the Union, he did even more by several remarkable speeches, in and out of the Senate. Soon after Lincoln's inauguration Baker assisted in raising a "California" regiment, recruited in New York and Pennsylvania and named the 71st Pennsylvania. (8) He declined the appointment of brigadier general of volunteers in May, 1861, accepted that of colonel in June, and on September 21, 1861, was appointed major general of volunteers. Under the law, acceptance of the latter commission would have required his resignation from the Senate, but he had neither accepted nor declined the appointment at the time he was killed in action while commanding a brigade at the mishandled affair of Ball's Bluff (Leesburg) on October 21, 1861. (9) He was buried at the Presidio, San Francisco.

La Fayette Curry Baker was born at Stafford, New York, on October 13, 1826, supposedly a great-grand-

son of Remember Baker of "Green Mountain Boys" fame. Baker's reputation for untruthfulness and the fact that much of the information about him stems from his own writing, (10) make it difficult to pinpoint his antebellum career. He probably grew up in Michigan and during 1848-60 lived in New York, Philadelphia, and San Francisco while working as a jack-of-all-trades. He is rumored to have been a vigilante and claim-jumper while in San Francisco. He returned East in the early Civil War days and became a spy for General Winfield Scott. He later ingratiated himself with Secretary of State William H. Seward and with Secretary of War Edwin M. Stanton. As a special provost marshal of the War Department, operating in the lavish corruption of wartime Washington, he performed valuable services by ferreting out all sorts of abuses against the government, meanwhile lining his own pockets.

At the end of the war part of the reward for the capture of the Abraham Lincoln conspirators was taken from him because "he was building a big hotel in Lansing." He was appointed colonel of the 1st District of Columbia Cavalry on May 5, 1863, and was promoted to brigadier general of volunteers on April 26, 1865, presumably for his part in tracking down John Wilkes Booth and his conspirators. He came to grief as a star witness against President Andrew Johnson during the latter's impeachment trial, when he could not produce damaging letters he had alleged to exist. He died in Philadelphia on July 3, 1868, and was buried there in the Mutual Family Cemetery. (11)

Nathaniel Prentiss Banks was born in Waltham, Massachusetts, on January 30, 1816. Nicknamed "the Bobbin Boy of Massachusetts" because he had gone to work at an early age in a cotton mill which his

father superintended, Banks had little formal education. At the age of twenty-three he was admitted to the bar, but failed seven times to become a member of the Massachusetts legislature before winning a seat. He was speaker of the Massachusetts house, presided over the Constitutional Convention of 1853, and the same year was elected to Congress—the first of ten terms under five different party affiliations. Elected Speaker of the House of Representatives after 133 ballots in 1856, Banks showed moderation in deciding among factions during the bitter slavery debates. In 1858 he was elected governor of Massachusetts, serving until January, 1861, when Lincoln appointed him a major general of volunteers after Banks proffered his services. Many West Point officers could not be made to understand that, however substandard Banks's qualifications were for the job of a field commander, he contributed immeasurably in recruits, morale, money, and propaganda to the Federal cause. He was expelled from the Shenandoah with the loss of 30 per cent of his force during Stonewall Jackson's celebrated Valley campaign and, in August, 1862, was again defeated by Jackson at Cedar Mountain. Banks was responsible for costly assaults at Port Hudson, which was compelled to surrender anyway after the capitulation of Vicksburg, and was the commander, if not the author, (12) of the ill-fated Red River campaign of 1864. After the evacuation of Alexandria during the retreat of the expedition, Banks was superseded by General E. R. S. Canby. Having received the thanks of Congress for "the skill, courage, and endurance

which compelled the surrender of Port Hudson," General Banks was mustered out of military service in August, 1865, and was almost immediately elected to Congress—his first of six terms, five as a Republican and one as a Democrat, in the postwar years. During the same period he was elected once to the Massachusetts senate and served nine years as United States marshal for the state. Before the end of his last term in the House of Representatives he retired to his home in Waltham where he died on September 1, 1894, and was buried in Grove Hill Cemetery.

Francis Channing Barlow, the son of a minister, was born in Brooklyn, New York, on October 19, 1834, but was raised in his mother's hometown, Brookline, Massachusetts. Graduated from Harvard in 1855, he went to New York, studied law, was admitted to the bar in 1858, and practiced until the out-

break of the war. Barlow enlisted as a private in the 12th New York, a three-month regiment from which he was mustered out in August. He reentered the army as lieutenant colonel of the 61st New York to commence a meritorious military career. As colonel of the 61st and later as brigadier general of volunteers (September 19, 1862), he served throughout the Peninsular campaign and at Sharpsburg under George B. McClellan, where he was severely wounded. At Chancellorsville, Barlow's brigade was a part of Howard's XI Corps which was driven off the field in confusion by S t o n e w a l l Jackson's celebrated flank attack. In the retirement of the XI Corps to Cemetery Ridge on the first day of Gettysburg, Barlow was wounded by a ball which temporarily paralyzed his arms and legs. Left for dead on the field, he was succored by Confederate General John B. Gordon. He did not rejoin the army until the inception of Grant's Overland campaign, in which he commanded a division of Hancock's II Corps. The high point of his career occurred in the dawn hours at Spotsylvania where, on May 12, 1864, his and David Birney's divisions captured some three thousand Confederates, including two generals, thirty stands of colors, and twenty guns. Soon after the investment of Petersburg he went on sick leave, but returned to active duty in time to be present at Sayler's Creek and the closing scenes of the war. He was promoted to major general of volunteers on May 25, 1865. General Barlow then entered politics and was twice elected secretary of the state of New York; served as United States marshal; was elected state attorney general,

in 1871, and initiated the prosecution of the "Tweed Ring." After the expiration of his term he practiced law until his death in New York City on January 11, 1896; he was buried in Brookline.

John Gross Barnard was born at Sheffield, Massachusetts, on May 19, 1815. A relative, General Peter Buel Porter, Secretary of War under John Quincy Adams, secured him an appointment to the Military Academy, from which he was

graduated second in the class of 1833. During forty-eight years in the Corps of Engineers, despite an inherited deafness, Barnard achieved high rank in a body of men whose duties included the construction of coast defenses, the improvement of rivers and harbors, and the supervision of West Point. Before the Civil War he served in the construction of fortifications along the Atlantic Coast, the Pacific

19

Coast, and the Delaware breakwater. He assisted in the improvement of New York Harbor, in work in the Gulf of Mexico at Tampico, and in the survey of the Mexican War battlefields. Upon the outbreak of the Civil War he was charged with constructing the defenses of Washington. He had been promoted to major in the Regular Army in 1858 and, on September 23, 1861, was appointed brigadier general of volunteers. Barnard was chief engineer of the Army of the Potomac under George B. McClellan, then in charge of the Washington defenses until U. S. Grant's assumption of command, when Barnard became chief engineer of the armies in the field on the staff of the lieutenant general. For his distinguished services he received the brevets of major general in both the Regular Army and the volunteers. On December 28, 1865, he was commissioned colonel, Corps of Engineers. General Barnard's postbellum contributions were also valuable to his country. Ordered to recast the whole approach to coastal defenses occasioned by the obsolescence of wooden vessels and muzzle loading guns, he did so with success. He advocated the use of parallel jetties in improving the mouth of the Mississippi (a system in use today). He also wrote many scientific treatises and made several valuable contributions to the history of the Civil War. Retired in 1881, he died at Detroit, Michigan, on May 14, 1882, and was buried in Sheffield, Massachusetts.

James Barnes was born in Boston, Massachusetts, on December 28, 1801. Upon graduation from the

Boston Latin School, he went into business for some years, but later secured an appointment to the Military Academy, from which he was graduated in the class of 1829. He worked at West Point as an instructor until his resignation from the army in 1836. Until the outbreak of the Civil War, Barnes was a civil engineer for railroads in New York, Massachusetts, Virginia, North Carolina, and the Midwest. Appointed colonel of the 18th Massachusetts in July 1861, he served commendably with the Army of the Potomac in the Washington defenses and in the Peninsular campaign, and was appointed a brigadier general of volunteers on November 29, 1862. At Sharpsburg, Fredericksburg, and Chancellorsville he commanded a brigade in Morell's division of the V Corps. Temporarily placed in command of the 1st (Griffin's) Division of the corps after Chancellorsville, he seems to have lost control of his troops at Gettysburg (though Vincent's brigade of his division seized and held Little Round Top at the instance of General Gouverneur K. Warren and probably saved the battle for the Union). He was wounded here, and upon his return to service was posted to garrison and prison duty for the balance of the war. On March 13, 1865, he was brevetted major general of volunteers "for Meritorious Services during the Rebellion" and was mustered out of service early the following year. In 1868 he was appointed to a United States commission to investigate the building of the Union Pacific Railroad and telegraph line. He died in Springfield, Massachusetts, on February 12, 1869, and was buried in Springfield Cemetery.

Joseph K. Barnes (13) was born in Philadelphia on July 21, 1817. After attending school in Northampton, Massachusetts, and Har-

vard University, he studied medicine and was graduated from the University of Pennsylvania in 1838. Barnes was appointed to the medical corps of the army in 1840. He saw three years of service against the Florida Seminoles, was with the "Army of Occupation" which crossed the Rio Grande during the Mexican War, and was later with General Winfield Scott's forces in the capture of the city of Mexico. When the Civil War opened, Barnes was ordered east from Vancouver barracks. In 1862, while on duty in Washington as a surgeon with the rank of major, he was noticed by Secretary of War Edwin M. Stanton, who was looking for a replacement for Surgeon General William Alexander Hammond. Barnes supplanted Hammond, first as "acting surgeon general" and subsequently as brigadier general and surgeon general on August 22, 1864. Barnes conducted himself admirably, and attracted a group of brilliant men to the army medical service. (14) Brevetted major general, U. S. Army, on March 13, 1865, he officiated at the deathbeds of two presidents of the United States: he closed the eyes of Abraham Lincoln, and sixteen years later attended the mortally wounded James A. Garfield. General Barnes was retired on June 30, 1882, and died in Washington on April 5, 1883. He was buried in Oak Hill Cemetery.

Henry Alanson Barnum (15) was born at Jamesville, Onondaga County, New York, on September 24, 1833. Securing his early education at Syracuse (New York) Institute, he was successively a teacher,

law student, and member of the bar and of the local militia company. He enlisted at the beginning of the Civil War and was at once elected captain of a company of the 12th New York. This regiment fought at First Manassas and was swept from the field in utter confusion, although one account reported that Barnum's company "remained firm." (16) At the battle of Malvern Hill during the withdrawal of George B. McClellan's army from the White House to Harrison's Landing, Barnum was wounded and, presumed dead, was left on the field after leading a charge at the head of his regiment. The remains of another officer were buried under a headboard bearing Barnum's name. Actually, Barnum was taken to the Malvern house by his own men, where he was captured by the Confederates and imprisoned in Richmond; he was later exchanged. His wound bothered him until the end of the war, and necessitated

several leaves of absence from the 149th New York, a regiment he had organized. He fought with this regiment at Gettysburg in Geary's division of the XII (Slocum's) Corps, and was transferred with it when the XI and XII Corps were consolidated after Chickamauga and sent west. At Lookout Mountain he sustained another wound, but took part in the Atlanta campaign, where he was again wounded. He later commanded a brigade in the "March to the Sea." At Savannah he led the Federal advance over the already evacuated defenses. Barnum received postbellum the brevets of brigadier and major general of volunteers and was also appointed full brigadier on May 31, 1865. After the war he served in various public sinecures and was active in the Grand Army of the Republic. He died in New York City on January 29, 1892, and was buried in Oakwood Cemetery, Syracuse.

William Farquhar Barry was born in New York City on August 18, 1818. Prior to his admission to West Point, he had received private tutoring in the classics. Graduated from the Military Academy in 1838, he served on the Canadian border for some years and then in Mexico, ultimately as aide-de-camp to General W. J. Worth. Barry was promoted to captain, 2nd Artillery, in 1852, fought the Seminoles in Florida, and helped pacify the warring factions in Kansas. Serving first in the defense of Fort Pickens, Florida, Barry acted as chief of artillery to Irvin McDowell at First Manassas, and subsequently to George B. McClellan in organizing and implementing the ordnance of the Army of the Potomac. He was ap-

Henry in Baltimore on July 18, 1879, General Barry served in command of the northern frontier during the Fenian disturbances, and then at various artillery posts. He was buried in Forest Lawn Cemetery, Buffalo, New York, his wife's hometown. Jointly with General J. G. Barnard, Barry wrote a history of the engineer and artillery operations of the Army of the Potomac through the Peninsular campaign.

Joseph Jackson Bartlett was born in Binghamton, New York, on November 21, 1834. (17) Admitted to the state bar in 1858, he was practicing law at the outbreak of the Civil War. Bartlett enlisted upon the first call for troops and at El-

pointed brigadier general of volunteers on August 20, 1861, and took an active part in the Peninsular campaign the following spring. Transferred to Washington as chief of artillery of the huge defense system which encircled the city, he concurrently served on a number of important boards of ordnance. In 1864 he was assigned as chief of artillery on the staff of General W. T. Sherman, commanding the Military Division of the Mississippi. He participated in all the actions of the Atlanta campaign, in the subsequent North Georgia campaign, and in the campaign of the Carolinas which terminated with the surrender of the Confederate forces under General Joseph E. Johnston. Barry received all the brevet promotions in both the volunteers and the Regular Army up to and including the grade of major general. He was promoted to colonel, 2nd Artillery, on December 11, 1865. Until his death at Fort Mc-

mira on May 21, 1861, was elected captain of one of the companies organized into the 27th New York Volunteers (infantry). When the regiment chose its field officers,

Henry W. Slocum (later corps and army commander) was elected colonel and Bartlett, major. Following the promotion of Slocum and the resignation of the lieutenant colonel, Bartlett became colonel on September 21, 1861, and was made a brigadier general of volunteers on October 4, 1862. Under a statute which required Senate confirmation during the current Congressional session, his first appointment as brigadier general expired on March 4, 1863; however, he was reappointed on March 30 and duly confirmed. Bartlett is believed to have participated in every battle fought by the Army of the Potomac from Manassas to Appomattox, except for the campaign of Second Manassas where the VI Corps was not engaged. Repeatedly commended by his superiors in reports, from the Union debacle at Bull Run to the surrender of Robert E. Lee's army, Bartlett progressed from the command of a regiment to that of a division, first in the VI Corps and subsequently in the V Corps. General Bartlett's characteristic aplomb was shaken during the Mine Run campaign in the autumn of 1863: Confederate horseman Jeb Stuart records that he sent a detail to capture Bartlett in his "exposed" camp at New Baltimore, Virginia, and that the latter "saved himself by precipitate flight in his nether garments." (18) On the morning of April 12, 1865, Bartlett received the stacked arms of the Army of Northern Virginia at Appomattox Court House. He won the brevet of major general toward the close of the war, and in postbellum years served as United States minister to Sweden and deputy commissioner of pensions un-

der President Grover Cleveland. He died in Baltimore on January 14, 1893, and was buried in Arlington.

William Francis Bartlett was born in Haverhill, Massachusetts, on June 6, 1840, (19) and was a member of the class of 1862 at Harvard when the Civil War broke out. He enlisted as a private the day Fort Sumter was surrendered and in August, 1861, became a captain of the

20th Massachusetts Infantry. He lost a leg at Yorktown in the spring of 1862 during the Peninsular campaign, but recovered sufficiently to be present with his class and receive his degree in June of that year and to become colonel of the 49th Massachusetts in November. The regiment was ordered to Louisiana with N. P. Banks, and took part in the siege and capture of Port Hudson in July, 1863, where Bartlett was twice wounded and thereafter compelled to be on horseback at all times. He was a prime target for marksmen, though

24

Confederate officers reputedly told their men not to shoot at the one-legged Yankee. At the outset of U. S. Grant's Overland campaign Bartlett organized the 57th Massachusetts, which he led at the battle of the Wilderness, sustaining still another wound. He was appointed brigadier general of volunteers on June 20, 1864 and at the battle of The Crater was taken prisoner, his cork leg shattered by bullets. After several weeks in Libby Prison, General Bartlett was exchanged and put in command of the 1st Division of the IX Corps, which he led with distinction until the end of hostilities. He received the brevet of major general on March 13, 1865, for gallant and meritorious services. Mustered out in July, 1866, he engaged for some time in business with the government-owned Tredegar Iron Works in Richmond, Virginia. Then he moved to Pittsfield, Massachusetts, the home of his wife. He died there on December 17, 1876, and was buried in Pittsfield Cemetery.

Henry Baxter was born in Sidney Plains, Delaware County, New York, on September 8, 1821. At the age of ten he moved with his father to the village of Jonesville in Michigan. In 1849 Baxter crossed the plains to California, remaining until 1852, when he returned to Jonesville to engage in the milling business. Soon after the beginning of the Civil War he was elected captain of a local company which was mustered in as Company C of the 7th Michigan Infantry. He became its lieutenant colonel on July 1, 1862, and was appointed brigadier general of volunteers on March 12, 1863. In the course of the Peninsu-

lar campaign, Baxter was severely wounded in the abdomen. After recovering, he fought at Fredericksburg in command of the regiment in Howard's division of the II. Corps and led the assaulting boat party which drove out Confederate skirmishers from the riverfront buildings to secure the crossing. Here his left shoulder was shattered by a bullet, and he was again invalided for some months. At Gettysburg, commanding a brigade in the I Corps, he lost his entire staff and half his men. During U. S. Grant's Overland campaign against Richmond in the spring of 1864, General Baxter commanded a brigade of the V Corps. At the Wilderness a rifle ball passed through his leg and killed his horse. On April 1, 1865, he was brevetted major general for gallantry at the Wilderness and the battle of Five Forks. Mustered out in August, 1865, he returned to Jonesville and served two years as register of deeds. In 1869 President Grant appointed him minister resident to the Republic of Honduras, a post he occupied until the vagaries of Central American politics forced his retirement in 1872. Returning to Jonesville, he engaged in the lumber business for a year until his death of pneumonia on December 30, 1873. He was buried in Jonesville Cemetery. (20)

George Dashiell Bayard was born in Seneca Falls, New York, on December 18, 1835, but grew up in Iowa, where he learned fencing from an exiled Hungarian colonel. He was appointed to West Point in

1852 and graduated four years later as a second lieutenant of cavalry. Bayard's antebellum career was spent on frontier duty in Kansas and Colorado, where he is reputed to have provoked a Kiowa-Comanche uprising by killing Kiowa Chief Big Pawnee in September, 1859. (21) Soon after the beginning of the Civil War, Bayard was ap-

pointed colonel of the 1st Pennsylvania Cavalry, with which he served in the defenses of Washington, on the line of the Rappahannock, and in the Shenandoah during the Valley campaign of Stonewall Jackson. In this last operation he took part in the battle of Port Republic and in a number of skirmishes. Appointed chief of cavalry of the III Corps and brigadier general of volunteers on April 28, 1862, he engaged in hostilities on the Rapidan River, in the battle of Cedar Mountain in August, 1862, and in the defenses of the capital after the Union defeat at Second Manassas. Under General Ambrose E. Burnside, Bayard took part in the campaign and battle of Fredericksburg in command of a brigade of six regiments. While at the headquarters of General W. B. Franklin, commanding the "Left Grand Division" in this battle, he was struck and mortally wounded by a piece of shell on December 13, 1862, and died the following day. He was buried at Princeton, New Jersey.

George Lafayette Beal was born in Norway, Maine, on May 21, 1825. When George was a small boy, his family moved to Portland where he attended the city schools and later Westbrook Seminary. In 1840 he was apprenticed to a Boston bookbinder, returning to Norway ten years later to practice his trade. He became an agent of the Canadian Express Company in 1853, enlisted as a private in the Norway Light Infantry (a militia company) in 1855, and rose to captain by the outbreak of war. Beal was probably the first man, and the Norway Light Infantry the first

unit, to enlist for active duty in the state of Maine. Mustered in as Company G of the 1st Maine, a three-month regiment, the unit did guard duty in Washington until it was mustered out in August, and then reorganized as the 10th Maine with Beal appointed its colonel. The 10th Maine fought at Cedar Mountain, where it suffered 173 casualties in thirty minutes, and at Sharpsburg, where Beal was wounded and his horse killed. When the regiment was mustered out in May, 1863, Beal recruited the 29th Maine, which took part in Banks's Red River campaign in the XIX Corps. Beal was in brigade command part of the time, and led the rear guard of the army during the retreat. Subsequently, the XIX Corps was transferred to the Shenandoah Valley and placed under Philip Sheridan. Beal fought at Winchester and Fisher's Hill in command of a brigade, but does not appear to have been present at Ce-

dar Creek. He was appointed a brigadier general of volunteers on November 30, 1864, and brevet major general on March 13, 1865, for gallant service. Serving briefly thereafter in western North Carolina, he was mustered out in January, 1866. After the war General Beal was adjutant general of Maine from 1880 to 1885, and state treasurer from 1888 to 1894. He died in Norway on December 11, 1896, and was buried in South Paris, Maine. (22)

John Beatty was born near Sandusky, Ohio, on December 16, 1828. Educated in the local schools, he established with his brother the Beatty Brothers Bank (later the First National Bank) in Cardington, Ohio, about 1854. He was a Republican presidential elector in 1860. In April of 1861 he raised one of the companies of the 3rd Ohio, a regiment of which he soon became lieutenant colonel and with

which he served in George B. Mc-
Clellan's western Virginia campaign. Promoted to colonel and
transferred to Kentucky, he took
part in Ormsby Mitchel's raid into
Tennessee and North Alabama and
then fought at Perryville. He was
appointed brigadier general of volunteers on November 29, 1862, and
was in command of a brigade at
Murfreesboro, where two horses
were killed under him. He took a
distinguished part in the Tullahoma, Chickamauga, and Chattanooga campaigns and accompanied
W. T. Sherman's column to the relief of Ambrose E. Burnside's beleaguered command at Knoxville.
In January, 1864, he resigned his
commission and returned to his
banking business so that his brother could enter the army. In 1868
General Beatty was elected to Congress and was twice reelected. Moving to Columbus, Ohio, in 1873, he
opened a bank and served as president until 1903. He held many offices in the Republican party, was
a candidate for governor of Ohio
in 1884, and served as president of
the Ohio Chickamauga and Chattanooga Military Park Commission
from 1891 to 1895. Beatty published his Civil War diary in 1879,
and later wrote several historical
novels, financial treatises, and mis-
cellaneous articles. He died in Columbus on December 21, 1914, and
was buried in Oakland Cemetery,
Sandusky.

Samuel Beatty was born in Mifflin
County, Pennsylvania, on December 16, 1820. His family moved to
Stark County, Ohio, in 1829, settling on the farm in Jackson
Township where Beatty spent his
entire life, except for his service in

two wars. Having little formal education, Beatty enlisted in 1846 and
served a year as first lieutenant of
the 3rd Ohio Infantry in the Mexican War. In 1857 he was elected
sheriff of Stark County and was reelected in 1859. On April 27, 1861,
he was elected captain of Company
A, 19th Ohio Infantry, and colonel of the regiment on May 29. He
fought competently at Shiloh and
in the "siege" of Corinth, was in
command of the brigade at Perryville and Murfreesboro, and was
promoted to brigadier general of
volunteers on November 29, 1862.
At Chickamauga his brigade was in
H. P. Van Cleve's division of the
XXI Corps and, in the Chattanooga campaign, in Thomas J.
Wood's division of Granger's IV
Corps, which took part in the
famous storming of Missionary
Ridge. Beatty participated in the
Atlanta campaign and in the battles of Franklin and Nashville.
During this last operation he was in

divisional command, Wood having been advanced to direction of the IV Corps. On March 13, 1865, General Beatty was brevetted major general of volunteers for "long and gallant service in the field" and, on January 15, 1866, was honorably mustered out. The records do not reveal why he did not receive a full major generalcy. (23) He returned to his farm in Ohio to live uneventfully: four years before his death on May 26, 1885, he was listed unpretentiously in a county history as "Farmer; P. O. Massillon." General Beatty was buried in the Massillon City Cemetery.

William Worth Belknap was born in Newburgh, New York, on September 22, 1829. He attended Princeton College, studied law, was

admitted to the bar in 1851, and commenced practice in Keokuk, Iowa. A member of the Iowa legislature in 1857-58, he was commissioned major of the 15th Iowa in

December 1861. Belknap rendered gallant service with the western armies on every field from Shiloh to Bentonville. Meantime he was promoted to lieutenant colonel in August, 1862, to colonel in June, 1863, and to brigadier general of volunteers on July 30, 1864—upon the recommendation of W. T. Sherman —and was brevetted major general on March 13, 1865. He was repeatedly commended for bravery and personal disregard of danger, and commanded the 4th Division of the XVII Corps in the Atlanta campaign, the "March to the Sea," and the Carolina campaign. Returning to civilian life, Belknap received the appointment of collector of internal revenue in Iowa. In 1869 he became President U. S. Grant's Secretary of War. In this capacity he became mired in the corruption which characterized the postwar period. On March 2, 1876, the "unquestioned evidence of the malfeasance in office by General William W. Belknap" was reported to the House of Representatives, and Belknap was impeached by unanimous vote. The specific charge was that the post trader at Fort Sill had paid Belknap some $24,000 over a period of years for immunity from removal. In the subsequent trial before the Senate thirty-five Senators voted guilty and twenty-five not guilty, short of the two-thirds necessary for conviction. However, all but three of the Senators voting not guilty stated they did so because they felt that Belknap's resignation, which Grant had accepted prior to the trial, removed him from the Senate's jurisdiction. Thereafter, General Belknap lived in Philadelphia and Washington, D. C., practicing law in the latter city. He died on October 13, 1890, and was buried in Arlington National Cemetery.

Henry Washington Benham was born in Connecticut (24) on April 17, 1813. The place was probably Meriden, where his father and step-father resided. Benham entered Yale in 1832, but later secured an appointment to the Military Academy, from which he was graduated

first in the class of 1837. He was commissioned into the Corps of Engineers, engaged mainly in the construction of coast defenses, and was promoted to captain. He took part in the Mexican War, was wounded slightly at Buena Vista, declined a majority in the 9th Infantry in 1855, and continued his engineering duties. Appointed chief engineer of the Department of the Ohio, he took part in George B. McClellan's western Virginia campaign and led the advance guard of General T. A. Morris' column in

pursuing Confederate General Robert S. Garnett from Laurel Hill to Corrick's Ford, where Garnett was killed. (25) This action won Benham the brevet of colonel in the Regular Army, a commission as brigadier general of volunteers, and assignment to a line command, but his talents were entirely unsuited to his new duties. He was criticized by General William S. Rosecrans, McClellan's successor, and was relieved by General David Hunter after his unsuccessful attack on Secessionville, South Carolina, in June, 1862. In August of that year his brigadier's commission was revoked (the revocation was later canceled by President Lincoln) and Benham returned to his proper sphere. From the spring of 1863 until the end of the war he commanded the engineer brigade of the Army of the Potomac, rendering service which was rewarded by the brevets of major general in both the regular and volunteer establishments. On March 7, 1867, he was commissioned colonel, Corps of Engineers and, until his retirement from active service in 1882, he was in charge of constructing the defenses of the harbors of Boston and New York. He died in New York City on June 1, 1884, and was removed for burial to Congressional Cemetery in Washington, D.C.

William Plummer Benton was born in New Market, Frederick County, Maryland, on December 25, 1828. When he was four months old his father died; his mother moved to Richmond, Indiana, in 1836, where he received his early education. At the age of eighteen he enlisted for Mexican War service and as a private in the Regiment of Mounted

Riflemen participated in the battles of Contreras, Churubusco, Chapultepec, and the capture of Mexico City. He returned to Indiana to finish his legal studies and was ad-

mitted to the bar in 1851. During 1852-54 he served as district attorney of Wayne County and from 1856 to 1858 was judge of the common pleas court. Reportedly the first man in the county to respond to Lincoln's call for seventy-five thousand volunteers, he was unanimously elected captain of the 8th Indiana Infantry (three-month regiment) on April 27, 1861, and colonel of the same regiment on September 5 of that year upon its reenlistment for three years or the duration of the war. After service in the western Virginia campaign in the summer of 1861, Benton's regiment was ordered to Missouri in September. He is said to have commanded a brigade at Elkhorn Tavern (Pea Ridge), although the *Official Records* show another

officer, not later promoted to brigadier, in command of the brigade of which Benton and his regiment were a part. (26) On April 28, 1862, Benton was appointed brigadier general of volunteers and fought at the battles of Port Gibson, Jackson (where he was slightly wounded), Champion Hills, Big Black River, in the siege of Vicksburg, and in the campaign against Mobile. For his services in this last campaign he was brevetted major general on March 26, 1865. At Vicksburg he commanded a brigade of the XIII Corps, first under the politician John A. McClernand and subsequently under the professional Edward O. C. Ord. Mustered out in July, 1865, Benton resumed his law practice in Richmond. The following year he went to New Orleans as an agent of the government, but died of yellow fever on March 14, 1867. He was buried there in Greenwood Cemetery. (27)

Hiram Gregory Berry was born in Rockland, Maine, in a district then known as Thomaston, on August 27, 1824. He was the son of a veteran of the War of 1812 and grandson of a soldier of the Revolution. In his early years he was a carpenter, contractor, bank president, Democratic member of the state legislature, mayor of Rockland, and captain of the local militia company. On June 15, 1861, he became colonel of the 4th Maine Volunteer Infantry, a regiment organized at Rockland for three-year service, and a month later accompanied it to First Manassas. His whole military service was with the Army of the Potomac, during which time he was advanced from colonel to ma-

jor general of volunteers and extolled by his superiors. As a brigadier he commanded in the Peninsular campaign, where Philip Kearny, Joseph Hooker, S. P. Heintzelman, and George B. McClellan mentioned him in their official reports. He did not take part in the campaigns of Second Manassas and Sharpsburg because of illness, but returned to the army in time for the battle of Fredericksburg, where he commanded a brigade in the III Corps. Promoted to major general on November 29, 1862, Berry took Hooker's old division of the III Corps into the battle of Chancellorsville, under the command of General Daniel E. Sickles. In the confused fighting which occurred on the early morning of May 3, 1863, in the course of which the Federals attempted to regroup after Stonewall Jackson's celebrated flank march of the previous afternoon, Berry was killed at the head of his command. According to General Joseph B. Carr, his successor in

command, Berry was mortally wounded at 7 A.M. and died within a half-hour. (28) He was buried in Achorn Cemetery, Rockland.

Daniel Davidson Bidwell was born in Black Rock (now a part of Buffalo), New York, on August 12, 1819. An influential citizen of Buffalo for more than twenty years before the war, he was prominently identified with the various military organizations of the city and held the office of police justice. Bidwell resigned this position to enlist as a private in the 65th New York Infantry, was appointed brigade inspector, and later transferred to the 74th New York. On October 21, 1861, he was appointed colonel of

the 49th New York and served with this regiment throughout the Peninsular campaign. From the Seven Days until South Mountain he is said to have commanded a brigade, although the records do not substantiate this nor do the army returns indicate his presence in the Maryland campaign which culminated at Sharpsburg (Antietam). At the bloody fiasco on the Rappahannock River, when Ambrose E. Burnside attempted to drive Robert E. Lee from his unassailable position in the rear of Fredericksburg, Bidwell, who was again in command of the 49th New York, took an honorable part. He fought at Chancellorsville and on May 31 was in command of the 3rd Brigade, 2nd Division, VI Corps, as senior colonel, in the absence of General Thomas H. Neill. Bidwell continued with the VI Corps at Gettysburg, again in regimental command, and participated in the Overland campaign of 1864 and in the battles around Petersburg. On June 9, 1864, (29) General George G. Meade recommended him for promotion to brigadier general; on August 11 the appointment was made. He accompanied the VI Corps, now under General Horatio G. Wright, to the Shenandoah and fought at Winchester, Fisher's Hill, and Cedar Creek in permanent command of his brigade. At Cedar Creek, during the Union reverse on the early morning of October 19, 1864, Bidwell was mortally wounded by a shell, "while behaving with conspicuous gallantry." He was buried in Forest Lawn Cemetery, Buffalo.

Henry Warner Birge, descendant of an old colonial family, was born in Hartford, Connecticut, on August 25, 1825. At the outbreak of the Civil War he was a merchant in Norwich, Connecticut, and a member of the governor's staff. Birge was appointed major of the 4th Connecticut Infantry (later named

the 1st Heavy Artillery), the first regiment in the state to enlist for three years. He resigned in order to recruit the 13th Connecticut and was mustered in as its colonel in February, 1862. Birge took part with General Benjamin F. Butler's forces in the capture of New Orleans. In 1863 he commanded the 3rd Brigade, 4th Division, of the XIX Corps, in the campaign to reduce Port Hudson. After abortive attempts against the position, Birge was selected to lead an "elite storming party" in a third assault when the garrison capitulated upon learning of the surrender of Vicksburg. Birge was appointed brigadier general of volunteers on September 19, 1863, and commanded a brigade, and at times a division, in the Red River campaign of 1864, where he was warmly commended by General N. P. Banks. His brigade went to Virginia, then to Savannah, where it served as garrison for the town.

The brigade became a division of the X Corps, and took part in the campaign of the Carolinas with Birge as its commander. After General Joseph E. Johnston's surrender at Greensboro, North Carolina, Birge was assigned to the command of the district of Savannah; in the meantime he was brevetted major general on February 25, 1865. He resigned on October 18 and returned to civil life. After the war he engaged in cotton planting and in the lumber business in Georgia and later invested in a number of enterprises in Texas and the West. He finally established residence in New York City, where he died on June 1, 1888. He was buried in· Yantic Cemetery, Norwich.

David Bell Birney, son of antislavery leader James G. Birney, was born at Huntsville, Alabama, on May 29, 1825. The family moved to Cincinnati when the boy was thirteen. After graduation from Andover

young Birney entered business, studied law, and was admitted to the bar. He moved to Philadelphia, was active in business, and practiced law from 1856 until the outbreak of the Civil War, meanwhile studying military subjects which equipped him better professionally than most volunteer officers mustered into service. Birney began as lieutenant colonel of the 23rd Pennsylvania, a three-month militia regiment. When his unit became a three-year regiment he was commissioned its colonel and on February 17, 1862, became brigadier general of volunteers. His first important field command was a brigade· of General Philip Kearny's division of the III Corps, which he led through the Peninsular campaign. He was tried and acquitted of disobedience of an order allegedly issued by General S. P. Heintzelman at the battle of Fair Oaks (Seven Pines), was restored to command, and fought at Chantilly in support of John Pope's Army of Virginia. Succeeding Kearny in command of the division, Birney served with distinction with the Army of the Potomac until July, 1864. He was again charged with dereliction of duty at Fredericksburg, but the charge was not substantiated and Birney was, in fact, highly praised by General George Stoneman. Birney was promoted to major general to rank from May 20, 1863, for his able leadership at Chancellorsville and commanded the III Corps at Gettysburg after the wounding of General Daniel Sickles. He took part in the Overland campaign and on July 23, 1864, was selected by U. S. Grant to command the X Corps. However, he fell ill with a virulent species of malaria, was ordered home, and died in Philadelphia on October 18, 1864. He was buried in Woodlands Cemetery there.

William Birney, elder brother of General David Bell Birney and son of antislavery leader James G. Birney, was born on his father's plantation in Madison County, Alabama, on May 28, 1819. The family moved first to Huntsville, Alabama, and subsequently to Cincinnati, where William began the practice of law. For a period of five years, including the revolutionary year of 1848, he resided on the Continent and in England, contributing numerous articles to Eng-

lish and American newspapers. Returning to the United States, he established the daily *Register* at Philadelphia in 1853, and on May 22, 1861, entered Federal service as a captain of the 1st New Jersey Infantry. In September, 1861, he be-

came major of the 4th New Jersey and its colonel on January 13, 1863. With these two regiments Birney took part in all the battles and campaigns of the Army of the Potomac up through Chancellorsville, during which the 4th New Jersey acted as guard to the Federal trains. On May 22, 1863, Birney was simultaneously appointed colonel of the 22nd U. S. Colored Infantry and brigadier general of volunteers. In this dual capacity he enlisted seven Negro regiments, freed the inmates of the Baltimore slave prisons, expedited emancipation in Maryland, and served in Florida after the battle of Olustee (Ocean Pond). During the latter part of the war he commanded a division of Negro troops in the X Corps, and during the Appomattox campaign, a division of the XXV Corps under General Godfrey Weitzel, with which he was present at the surrender of the Army of Northern Virginia. Brevetted major general on March 13, 1865, General Birney was mustered out in August and resided in Florida for several years. He then moved to Washington where he practiced law, served for a time as United States attorney for the District of Columbia, and wrote prolifically on a variety of subjects including history and religion. His best-known work was a biography of his father, published in 1890. The general died at his home in Forest Glen, Maryland, on August 14, 1907, and was buried in Oak Hill Cemetery, Georgetown, D. C.

Francis Preston Blair, Jr., the son of an advisor to Andrew Jackson and brother of Montgomery Blair, Lincoln's first postmaster-general, was born at Lexington, Kentucky, on February 19, 1821. Blair attended school in Washington, where he contributed to his father's paper,

the *Globe*. He was graduated from Princeton, studied law at Transylvania, and began practicing with his brother Montgomery, in St. Louis in 1842. In the Southwest at the outbreak of the Mexican War, he served briefly as attorney general of New Mexico Territory, then returned to St. Louis to fight the extension of slavery into the territories (even though he owned slaves). He was elected to Congress in 1856 on the Free-Soil ticket, was defeated for reelection two years later, but won again in 1860. Blair's formation of the Union party in Missouri, his capacity as an orator, his efforts for Lincoln during and after the Chicago convention of 1860, his organization of the "Wide Awakes" and "Home Guards" to combat the secession activities of Governor Claiborne Jackson, and

the influence of other members of his family, were instrumental in saving Missouri for the Union. He declined a brigadier generalcy in 1861 to avoid political complications at home. In the Thirty-seventh Congress he distinguished himself as chairman of the Committee on Military Defense, where he persistently advocated an all-out war effort. In 1862 Blair enlisted seven regiments for the war, and was appointed a brigadier general of volunteers on August 7 and a major general on November 29. His military career began as a brigade commander in the Yazoo expedition during the campaign against Vicksburg and terminated with his successive direction of the XV Corps and XVII Corps in the march through Georgia and into the Carolinas. He was an intimate friend of W. T. Sherman who, together with U. S. Grant, repeatedly praised his leadership. Blair resigned from service in November, 1865, virtually a pauper, having expended his fortune for the Union cause. After an unsuccessful venture in a Mississippi cotton plantation he reentered Missouri politics on a moderate platform and was twice nominated for lucrative positions by President Johnson, only to have the Radical-controlled Senate refuse confirmation. He ran as vice-presidential candidate in 1868 on Horatio Seymaus's ticket, but became increasingly unpopular with the Radical Republicans because of his desire to restore the ex-Confederate States to the Union on easy terms. Chosen United States Senator from Missouri in 1871 to fill an unexpired term, he served until 1873, when he retired because of ill health. He died in St. Louis on July 8, 1875, and was buried in Bellefontaine Cemetery.

Louis (Ludwig) Blenker was born in Worms, Germany (then in the principality of Hesse Darmstadt), on May 12, 1812. He served as apprentice to a jeweler, belonged to the Bavarian Legion, was Prince Otto's escort after his election as king of Greece in 1837, studied

medicine, and engaged in the wine business. In 1848 he participated in the revolution against the monarchy and had to seek asylum in Switzerland, but was expelled the following year and came to the United States, where he settled in Rockland County, New York, cultivated a farm, and later engaged in business in New York City. His reputation as a revolutionary patriot enabled him to recruit a regiment which was mustered into Federal service as the 8th New York Infantry with Blenker as colonel. He was appointed brigadier general of volunteers on August 9, 1861. At

First Manassas, Blenker had commanded a brigade, part of Colonel Dixon Miles's division which was in reserve at Centreville during the battle. Despite Colonel Miles's alleged drunkenness, it appears that the reserve division performed capably in covering the rear of the Union forces retiring in confusion toward Washington. Blenker later commanded a division which was originally destined for George B. McClellan on the Peninsula; however, Abraham Lincoln's solicitude for the safety of Washington resulted in its being sent to aid John C. Frémont against Stonewall Jackson in the Shenandoah. Although there was no overt criticism of Blenker's conduct or dispositions at the battle of Cross Keys, he was ordered to Washington, D. C., following General Franz Sigel's arrival in the Shenandoah and on March 31, 1863, was honorably discharged. He died on his farm in Rockland County on October 31 of that year and was buried in Rockland Cemetery, Sparkill, New York.

James Gillpatrick Blunt was born in Trenton, a village of Hancock County, Maine, on July 21, 1826. At fifteen he went to sea for five years. He later was graduated from a medical college in Columbus, Ohio, commenced practice in New Madison, Ohio, and in 1856 settled in Greeley, Kansas. Opposed to slavery, he soon allied himself with John Brown. Blunt was a member of the Wyandotte constitutional convention in 1859 and served as chairman of the committee on militia. Contrary to some accounts, Blunt's entrance into the Civil War was actually an extension of

his Jayhawker career, like that of his superior, Senator James H. Lane. Lane recruited the "Kansas Brigade," a force that was not at first admitted into Federal service. Blunt, acting as a regimental commander under Lane, participated in some minor affairs in Kansas and the Indian Territory. However, on April 8, 1862, he was duly appointed a brigadier general of volunteers and distinguished himself in a number of skirmishes and battles. He chastised Confederate General Douglas H. Cooper and his Cherokees and Choctaws at Old Fort Wayne that autumn and in November became commander of the Army of the Frontier, with which he defeated General J. S. Marmaduke at Cane Hill. Acting in concert with General F. J. Herron he repulsed T. C. Hindman at Prairie Grove; captured Van Buren, Arkansas; again defeated Cooper at Honey Springs, Indian Territory, in July 1863; and in 1864 successfully opposed the "Missouri Raid" of General Sterling Price. Meantime he was promoted to major general of volunteers on March 16, 1863 (to rank from November 29, 1862). For four years after the war Blunt practiced medicine in Leavenworth, Kansas, after which he moved to Washington, where he was for many years a claims agent. Blunt spent his last years in a government hospital for the insane in Washington, D. C. He died there on July 27, 1881, and was buried in Leavenworth.

Henry Bohlen was born in Bremen, Germany, on October 22, 1810. He emigrated to the United States as a youth and amassed a considerable fortune as a liquor dealer. Said to have served in the Mexican War, when the Civil War came, Bohlen was instrumental in recruiting the 75th Pennsylvania Volunteer Infantry, a Philadelphia regiment whose rolls were studded with such names as Matzdorff, Gerke, Ehrlich, Koerper, and Sauer. He became its

colonel on September 30, 1861. The regiment wintered near Washington, attached to Louis Blenker's division which in March, 1862, was ordered to report to General John C. Frémont in the Mountain Department. Bohlen went with it and was promoted to brigadier general of volunteers on April 28, 1862. In the course of Stonewall Jackson's celebrated Valley campaign, Bohlen was under the command first of the dubious Blenker and then of the scholarly but inept Carl Schurz in the corps of the even more hapless Franz Sigel. Bohlen performed capably at Cross Keys and helped cover the retreat of the units of the Army of Virginia which had fought at Cedar Mountain under the command of N. P. Banks. On August 22, 1862, Bohlen's brigade was pushed back across Freeman's Ford on the Rappahannock while conducting a seemingly purposeless reconnaissance in the face of Jackson's whole force. At this ford, four miles above the present village of Remington, Virginia, Bohlen was killed while attempting to recross the river with his command. His remains now lie in Laurel Hill Cemetery, Philadelphia.

James Bowen was born in New York City on February 25, 1808. Independently wealthy by inheritance, Bowen was the first president of the Erie Railroad and was in the forefront of New York's civic leaders. He served as a member of the legislature during 1848-49 and was president of the first board of New York City police commissioners in 1855. He was also an intimate friend of such public figures as Daniel Webster, Thurlow Weed, and William H. Seward. In the first year of the Civil War he was instrumental in recruiting a number of regiments and on October 11, 1862, accepted a commission as brigadier general of volunteers. At the age of fifty-four, Bowen was considered too old for field service and was assigned to New Orleans as provost marshal general of the Department of the Gulf. Bowen was a trained executive and ran his office in much the same way as he had the Erie Railroad. Nevertheless, in company with a number of officers who had accompanied N. P. Banks on the Red River expedition, Bowen was relieved from duty with the Department of the Gulf and resigned his commission on July 27, 1864. The following March he received the brevet of major general "for meritorious service." Surviving the war by more than twenty years, General Bowen served a long period as commissioner of charities

39

of New York, was a prominent clubman, and was said to have been a literary critic. He died in his summer home at Dobbs Ferry, New York, September 29, 1886, and was buried in the Presbyterian Cemetery there.

Jeremiah Tilford Boyle was born May 22, 1818, in Mercer County (now Boyle County), Kentucky. (30) He received his education at Centre College, Princeton, and at Transylvania University, where he studied law. After graduation he

commenced practice in Danville, Kentucky. Boyle owned slaves and was a Whig; nevertheless, he became one of the most fervent Unionists in the state. On November 9, 1861, he was appointed a brigadier general of volunteers and the following spring participated "with conspicuous gallantry" in the battle of Shiloh, where he commanded a brigade in T. L. Crittenden's division of Don Carlos Buell's

forces. On May 27, 1862, Secretary of War Edward M. Stanton directed him "to take command of the forces in Kentucky . . . on account of his intimate knowledge of the requirements of the service in his State. . . ." Boyle's administration of what was later denominated the District of Kentucky, as well as his military capabilities, has been the subject of considerable disagreement. He was certainly no strategist nor tactician. Regularly organized Confederate cavalry as well as guerrillas raided throughout the state while Boyle did little more than telegraph for reinforcements. Louisville, Boyle's own headquarters, lay in the palm of Braxton Bragg's hand during the Kentucky invasion of 1862 and was saved only by Bragg's ineptness. Boyle's civilian policy alienated all but the most zealous Union sympathizers, embracing as it did his ruthless punishment of persons suspected of "disloyalty," use of troops to control elections, and assessment of damages caused by guerrillas upon the citizens living nearby. In January, 1864, he was summarily relieved and ordered to report with his division to Knoxville, whereupon he resigned. General Boyle then interested himself in the railroad business and in land speculation. He died a wealthy man in Louisville on July 28, 1871, and was buried in Danville.

Luther Prentice Bradley was born in New Haven, Connecticut, on December 8, 1822. Before moving to Chicago in 1855, he held various commands in the Connecticut militia, where he acquired a basic military education. In Chicago he worked as a bookkeeper and sales-

man and served as a captain of the 1st Illinois Militia and as lieutenant colonel of the "Chicago Legion." On November 6, 1861, Bradley was mustered into Federal service as lieutenant colonel of the 51st Illinois Infantry. He subsequently fought with his regiment at the capture of Island No. 10, at New Madrid, Missouri, and at the occupation of Nashville under D. C. Buell. He was promoted to colonel on October 15, 1862, and participated in the campaign and battle of Murfreesboro. At the battle of Chickamauga he commanded a brigade in McCook's XX Corps and was severely wounded. He was advanced to brigadier general of volunteers, to rank from July 30, 1864. Bradley participated in the Atlanta campaign, during which he commanded a brigade in Newton's division of the IV Corps, Army of the Cumberland. For his services at Resaca he was subsequently brevetted brigadier general in the Regular Army; he received the brevet

of colonel for gallantry at Chickamauga. Bradley was detached along with the IV Corps to oppose John B. Hood's invasion of Tennessee. At the battle of Franklin he was wounded again and is not shown present at the battle of Nashville, where his brigade was under the command of its senior colonel. On July 28, 1866, General Bradley was appointed lieutenant colonel of the newly organized 27th U. S. Infantry. He became colonel in 1879 and was retired on December 8, 1886, having reached the statutory age of sixty-four. He died in retirement in Tacoma, Washington, on March 13, 1910, and was buried in Arlington National Cemetery. (31)

Edward Stuyvesant Bragg was born on February 20, 1827, at the crossroads hamlet of Unadilla, New York. He was educated in the local academies and at what is now Hobart College. He read law and was admitted to the bar in 1848. Two

years later he moved to Fond du Lac, Wisconsin. A Douglas Democrat in politics, Bragg served as district attorney of Fond du Lac County and was a delegate to the Charleston presidential convention of 1860. Staunchly espousing the cause of the Union, he raised a company which became part of the 6th Wisconsin Infantry and was elected its captain. The regiment was mainly employed in garrisoning the defenses of Washington, D. C., until August, 1862, when it took part in the campaign of Second Manassas. By this time Bragg had been advanced to the grade of lieutenant colonel and, until the end of the war, participated in all but one fight in which the Army of the Potomac was engaged—he was absent from the field of Gettysburg because of illness. The unit of which the 6th Wisconsin was a part, and which Bragg commanded for many months, was the celebrated "Iron Brigade." He was promoted to colonel in March, 1863, and brigadier general of volunteers to rank from June 25, 1864. During the war he was once nominated as a Democrat to Congress from his district but was defeated. After the war he reentered politics as a delegate to the Union national convention of 1866, was elected state senator in 1867, and was a delegate to the Democratic national convention of 1872. He served four terms in Congress and was twice the chairman of the Wisconsin delegation to Democratic conventions. In seconding the nomination of Grover Cleveland for the presidency in 1884, Bragg eyed the Tammany-controlled New York delegation and coined the celebrated political slogan, "We love

him for the enemies he has made!" Cleveland subsequently rewarded him with an appointment as minister to Mexico. In 1896 Bragg's lifelong loyalty to the Democratic party wavered on the "free silver" issue, and he refused to support William Jennings Bryan. Thereafter he supported the Republican ticket nationally and was appointed United States consul general at Hong Kong by Theodore Roosevelt in 1902, a post which he held for four years. He died in Fond du Lac on June 20, 1912, and was buried there.

John Milton Brannan (32) was born in Washington, D. C., on July 1, 1819. While serving as a messenger in the House of Representatives in 1837, he was appointed to the Military A c a d e m y by Representative Ratliff Boon of Indiana with the signed approval of 114 other Congressmen. (33) After graduation he was posted to the artillery as a brevet second lieuten-

ant. He served in routine garrison duty at various posts and was regimental adjutant of the 1st Artillery in the war with Mexico, winning the brevet of captain for gallantry at Contreras and Churubusco. He was appointed brigadier general of volunteers on September 28, 1861. After serving creditably on the South Atlantic coast, Brannan commanded an infantry division under W. S. Rosecrans in the Tullahoma campaign and under General G. H. Thomas at Chickamauga. In the latter battle he lost 38 per cent of his command in the effort to hold Horseshoe Ridge, the last Union position on that bloody field. Following the relief of Rosecrans by U. S. Grant, Brannan was himself relieved from infantry command and was made chief of artillery of the Army of the Cumberland; nonetheless, he was at the same time brevetted colonel in the Regular Army for gallant services during the battle. He supervised the defenses of Chattanooga and took part in the Atlanta campaign; after the occupation of Atlanta in September, he was in charge of construction of the Union defenses and after October, 1864, conducted an inspection tour of the Department of the Cumberland. At the end of the war he was brevetted major general in both the regular and volunteer services. Reverting to his regular rank of major, 1st Artillery, Brannan's postbellum service included tours of duty at such artillery installations as Fort Trumbull, Connecticut; Fort Wadsworth, New York; and Ogdensburg, New York; he also briefly commanded troops in Tallahassee, Florida, during the weeks when Samuel J. Tilden was deprived of

the presidency by the supporters of Rutherford B. Hayes. (34) Retired as colonel of the 4th Artillery in 1882, he thereafter made his home in New York, where he died on December 16, 1892, and was buried in Woodlawn Cemetery.

Mason Brayman was born in Buffalo, New York, on May 23, 1813. At the age of twenty-two he was editor of the Buffalo *Bulletin* and in later years edited newspapers in Illinois and Kentucky.

After admission to the New York bar, he settled in Monroe, Michigan, where he was city attorney for a time. Moving to Illinois in 1842, he practiced law. Among other activities he wrote an introduction to the *Revised Statutes;* attempted to settle the disputes between the Mormons and their hostile neighbors at Nauvoo; served as a regent of the University of Illinois; reported the proceedings of the state constitutional convention of 1847 for the St. Louis *Union;* and acted as general solicitor for the new Illinois Central Railroad, whose right-of-way he helped secure. Soon after the outbreak of the Civil War, Brayman volunteered for service and in August, 1861, was commissioned major of the 19th Illinois Infantry. He was advanced to colonel in April, 1862, and was appointed brigadier general of volunteers to rank from September 24, 1862. Brayman fought at Belmont, Fort Donelson, and Shiloh and commanded the post at Bolivar, Tennessee, u n t i l J u n e, 1863. Thereafter he commanded Camp Dennison, Ohio, and, during the last year of the war, the post of Natchez, Mississippi. Brevetted major general for gallant and meritorious services, General Brayman retired to private life. He lived in Missouri and Arkansas for a time in connection with some railroad interests. He then became editor of the *Illinois State Journal.* In 1873 he moved to Wisconsin, but three years later was appointed governor of Idaho Territory. Returning to Wisconsin upon the expiration of his term of office, he moved some years later to Kansas City, where he resided until his death on February 27, 1895. He is buried at Ripon, Wisconsin. (35)

Henry Shaw Briggs was born in Lanesboro, Massachusetts, on August 1, 1824. He was the son of George Nixon Briggs, six-term representative in Congress and governor of Massachusetts from 1843 to 1851. Young Briggs was graduated from Williams College in 1844, was admitted to the Massachusetts bar in 1848, and in 1856 represented Pittsfield in the state legislature.

At the outbreak of the Civil War he was captain of the "Allen Guard," a local militia company which, as part of the 8th Massachusetts Mili-

tia, arrived in Annapolis several days after the capitulation of Fort Sumter. The 8th Massachusetts, a three-month regiment, was soon disbanded and on June 21, 1861, Briggs was mustered into Federal service as colonel of the 10th Massachusetts Infantry. After training and duty in the defenses of Washington, the regiment was engaged in George B. McClellan's Peninsular campaign in the spring of 1862. At the battle of Seven Pines (Fair Oaks), Briggs received bullet wounds through both thighs. During his convalescence he was appointed a brigadier general of volunteers to rank from July 17, 1862. Briggs's health was undermined by his wounds, and he did little active field campaigning after his return to the army. Toward the end of the war he commanded the draft rendezvous at Alexandria which dispatched draftees to the various commands of the Army of the Potomac. Honorably mustered out of service in December, 1865, General Briggs was state auditor of Massachusetts until 1869; he then became judge of the district court of Central Berkshire and for the last fourteen years of his life was appraiser at the Boston Custom House. He died in Pittsfield on September 23, 1887, and was buried there. (36)

James Sanks Brisbin was born in the village of Boalsburg, Pennsylvania, on May 23, 1837. After obtaining a good classical education, he taught school and won prominence as an antislavery ora-

tor. At the beginning of the Civil War, Brisbin enlisted as a private in a Pennsylvania regiment; however, on April 26, 1861, he was appointed a second lieutenant in the 1st U. S. Cavalry (a regular unit then called the 1st Dragoons). While in charge of a detachment of recruits from Carlisle barracks destined for service with the 2nd Artillery, Brisbin was twice wounded at the battle of First Manassas and was praised for his conduct there. He was promoted through grades in the volunteer service and became a brigadier on May 1, 1865; he also won the brevets of major general of volunteers and colonel in the Regular Army. He served in the Peninsular campaign as a captain of the 6th Cavalry, took part in the Blue Ridge expedition, and won the brevet of major at the battle of Beverly Ford. In the Gettysburg campaign, he commanded the Pennsylvania state cavalry and acted as chief of cavalry on the staff of General Albert L. Lee during the Red River campaign, where at Sabine Crossroads, he was again wounded. Toward the close of hostilities he was chief of staff to General Stephen G. Burbridge, who was in command of the District of Kentucky and, subsequently, in Tennessee. Mustered out of the volunteers on January 15, 1866, Brisbin served with distinction in the post-Civil War army. He was promoted to major, 2nd Cavalry, in 1868; to lieutenant colonel, 9th Cavalry, in 1885; and to colonel, 1st Cavalry, in 1889. In 1876 he commanded the battalion of cavalry which formed part of John Gibbon's column in the Little Big Horn campaign. An aspiring author, Brisbin was the author of *The Beef Bonanza, or, How to Get Rich on the Plains*. He died in Philadelphia on January 14, 1892, and his remains were taken to Red Wing, Minnesota, for burial.

John Rutter Brooke was born on July 21, 1838, in Montgomery County, Pennsylvania, and secured his early education at what is now Collegeville and in West Chester, Pennsylvania. On April 20, 1861, he entered Federal service as a captain of the 4th Pennsylvania Infan-

try. At First Manassas, this three-month regiment marched away on the eve of the battle while the rest of the Union Army was moving in to fight. Becoming colonel of the 53rd Pennsylvania in November, Brooke took part in the Peninsular campaign and was in temporary command of a brigade of Sumner's II Corps at Sharpsburg. He reverted to command of his regiment at Fredericksburg, and was given permanent command of the 4th Brigade of the 2nd Division of the II Corps, which he directed at Chancellorsville and Gettysburg. On the second day at Gettysburg the 2nd Division was ordered to support Daniel E. Sic-

kles' poorly deployed III Corps, and in the desperate fighting around the wheatfield Brooke was wounded. He received the praise of his division commander, John C. Caldwell, for his conduct. The following winter, Brooke commanded a convalescent camp at Harrisburg. He returned to the army and participated in Grant's Overland campaign of 1864. For distinguished services at the Wilderness and Spotsylvania, his long delayed appointment as brigadier general of volunteers was conferred, to rank from May 12, 1864. Critically wounded at Cold Harbor in June, Brooke returned to duty in September, although temporarily incapacitated for field service. He served on court-martial duty until the spring of 1865, when he was given command of a division of recruits in the Army of the Shenandoah under General Winfield S. Hancock. Brooke was brevetted major general of volunteers and was appointed to the Regular Army on July 28, 1866, as lieutenant colonel, 37th Infantry; he was promoted to colonel in 1879; to brigadier in 1888, and to major general in 1897. During the Spanish War he commanded the pestiferous camp at Chickamauga Park, Georgia, where the I and III Corps were trained. Shortly thereafter he took part in the Puerto Rican campaign under Nelson A. Miles and was military governor first of Puerto Rico and then of Cuba after the evacuation of the islands by Spain. His last command was that of the Department of the East. He retired on July 21, 1902, having reached the statutory age of sixty-four. His remaining years were spent quietly, mainly in Philadelphia, where he died on September 5, 1926. He was buried in Arlington National Cemetery. General Booke was the next to the last survivor of the 583 Union generals of full rank.

William Thomas Harbaugh Brooks was born in Lisbon (then New Lisbon), Ohio, on January 28, 1821. He obtained an appointment to West Point at sixteen and was graduated forty-sixth of fifty-two members in the class of 1841—a class which contributed twenty general

officers to the Union and Confederate armies. Posted to the 3rd Infantry, Brooks took part in the Florida War of 1842-43, performed garrison duty at various points, and won the brevets of captain and major for gallant and meritorious conduct in the war with Mexico. Until the beginning of the Civil War, he served as aide to General David E. Twiggs and on frontier Indian duty; he was made a captain in 1851. Appointed a brigadier general of volunteers on

September 28, 1861, Brooks took part the following spring in the Peninsular campaign. He commanded a brigade of W. F. Smith's division in the IV Corps at Williamsburg, and in the VI Corps during the Seven Days battles, when he was wounded at Savage's Station. He later fought at Crampton's Gap and at Sharpsburg, where he was again wounded. Brooks was advanced to the command of a VI Corps division, which he directed at the battle of Fredericksburg and in the campaign of Chancellorsville. From May, 1863, until April, 1864, he commanded the Department of Monongahela, with headquarters at Pittsburgh, after which he directed the 1st Division of the XVIII Corps and then a division of the X Corps in the operations at Cold Harbor and around Petersburg. He was promoted to major general on June 10, 1863, but the promotion was revoked on April 6, 1864. (37) Brooks's poor health, which had necessitated numerous sick leaves during his army career, became worse. He resigned as volunteer brigadier general and as major of the 18th Infantry on July 14, 1864, to take up residence on a farm near Huntsville, Alabama. There, Brooks was treated with esteem and affection by his Southern neighbors. He died on July 19, 1870, and was buried in Maple Hill Cemetery, Huntsville, in a grave marked with a Confederate emblem secured in concrete. (38)

Egbert Benson Brown was born in Brownsville, New York, on October 4, 1816. (39) As a young man he sailed half-way around the world on a whaler. (40) He settled in

Toledo in the early 1840's, where he became a respected grain dealer and erected the first steam elevator in the town. After serving successively as city clerk, councilman, and briefly as mayor of Toledo (41) he removed to St. Louis in 1852, where he engaged in the railroad business. Brown was active in the movement that held Missouri to the Union and in August, 1861, was commissioned lieutenant colonel of the 7th M i s s o u r i Infantry, a regiment mustered i n t o Federal service. However, he resigned his commission the following May to accept appointment as a brigadier general of the Missouri state militia and was appointed a brigadier general of U.S. Volunteers to rank from November 29, 1862. Brown participated creditably in numerous skirmishes and in January, 1863, was praised for his defense of Springfield, where he was severely wounded in the shoulder and lost the use of one arm. He commanded the District of Central Mis-

souri later that year and through 1864, resisting innumerable guerrilla raids and skirmishing with raiding parties of Confederates from Arkansas and the Indian Territory. During Sterling Price's raid into Missouri in the autumn of 1864, Brown commanded a brigade of cavalry. At the battle of Westport he was relieved of command and arrested by General Alfred Pleasonton for alleged failure to obey an order to attack. Apparently no charges were preferred, since Brown assumed command in January, 1865, of the District of Rolla, where he served until the end of the war. (42) Appointed United States pension agent at St. Louis in 1866, he resigned two years later to operate a farm in Illinois. (43) From 1881 to 1884 he was a member of the state board of equalization. Brown's later life is almost totally obscure. (44) He died in the home of a granddaughter at West Plains, Missouri, on February 11, 1902, and was buried in Cuba, Missouri, next to his wife, who had died four years earlier. (45)

Robert Christie Buchanan, a nephew by marriage of President John Quincy Adams, was born in Baltimore, Maryland, on March 1, 1811. During Adams' administration Buchanan obtained an appointment to the Military Academy and was graduated in 1830. He took part in the Black Hawk War of 1831-32 and in the campaign against the Florida Seminoles during 1837-38 and was promoted to captain of the 4th Infantry. In the Mexican War, Buchanan distinguished himself at Palo Alto, Resaca de la Palma, and at Molino del Rey. He won successively the

expired at the opening of the next session of Congress (March 4, 1863), at which time he assumed command of the defenses of Fort Delaware. (46) In 1864 he became colonel of the 1st Infantry through seniority and at the close of the war was brevetted brigadier and major general, U. S. Army. His chief postbellum work was as commander of the Department of Louisiana; at the instructions of the Republican Radicals he enforced upon the prostrate state a Negro governor and a carpetbag legislature. Buchanan was retired in 1870 and died in Washington, D. C., on November 29, 1878. He was buried in Rock Creek Cemetery.

brevets of major and lieutenant colonel. He served on garrison and recruiting duty for some years and, at the outbreak of the Civil War, his regiment defended Washington until the spring of 1862, when Buchanan was given command of the "Regulars," a brigade of old army troops in Sykes's division of the V Corps. With these men he participated with distinction in the battles of the Seven Days and was twice brevetted. He was present at Second Manassas under General Fitz John Porter. Although Porter was here made the goat of John Pope's ineptitude and subsequently cashiered, Buchanan was praised in Pope's report. Promoted to brigadier of volunteers to rank from November 29, 1862, he commanded the Regulars at Sharpsburg and at F r e d e r i c k s b u r g, where his deportment was highly commended, although his casualties were heavy. The Senate failed to act upon Buchanan's nomination to brigadier, and his appointment

Catharinus Putnam Buckingham was born in what is now Zanesville, Ohio, on March 14, 1808. At the age of seventeen he secured an appointment to West Point; he was graduated sixth in the class of 1829, whose number two man was Robert E. Lee, with whom Buckingham is

said to have been on intimate terms. (47) After brief service on topographical duty, Buckingham was an instructor at the Academy until his resignation in 1831. He taught at Kenyon College, Ohio, for a time, and from 1849 until 1861 was proprietor of an ironworks in Knox County. When the war came, Buckingham served successively as assistant adjutant general, commissary general, and adjutant general of Ohio; on July 16, 1862, he was appointed brigadier general of U.S. Volunteers. He was attached to the War Department on special duty and was the officer who bore the dispatch relieving General George B. McClellan from the command of the Army of the Potomac on November 7, 1862. Resigning his commission on February 11, 1863, to return to private business, Buckingham and his brothers erected a grain elevator in New York, which proved unprofitable. He then moved to Chicago, his home for the rest of his life, where he built the Illinois Central grain elevators—a project with which he was connected until 1873—and was president of the Chicago Steel Works. He also found time to write two mathematical treatises. He died in Chicago on August 30, 1888, and was buried in Woodlawn Cemetery, Zanesville.

Ralph Pomeroy Buckland was born on January 20, 1812, either in Leyden, Massachusetts, or in Ravenna, Ohio: his parents moved in the year of his birth. At the age of eighteen he sailed down the Ohio and Mississippi rivers with a flatboat of produce and subsequently remained in New Orleans for three years. Returning to Ohio,

he studied law, was admitted to the bar, and began practice at Fremont in 1837. Affiliated with the Whig party, he held a number of local offices, including that of mayor, and was a delegate to the Whig convention of 1848; however, he was carried by the free-soil controversy into the Republican fold. Having served two terms in the state senate, he entered Federal service in January, 1862, as colonel of the 72nd Ohio Volunteer Infantry. At Shiloh he commanded a brigade in the division of W. T. Sherman, who commended Buckland for resisting the Confederate assault on the first day of the battle. Buckland accompanied Sherman to Memphis and after being appointed brigadier general on November 29, 1862, commanded a brigade of the XV Corps in the Vicksburg campaign. In January, 1864, he assumed command of the District of Memphis, where he served until January 6, 1865; at this time he resigned his commission in order to accept the seat in Congress to which he had been elected *in absentia*. He was brevetted major general of volunteers for faithful and meritorious service on March 13, 1865. After two consecutive terms, Buckland resumed his law practice in Fremont, but his interest in public affairs did not abate. In 1870 he became president of the Ohio Soldiers' and Sailors' Orphans Home; in 1876 he was a delegate to the Republican convention which nominated Rutherford B. Hayes, who had been his law partner; and from 1878 to 1881 he was government director of the Union Pacific Railroad. General Buckland died in Fremont on May 27, 1892, and was buried in Oakwood Cemetery there.

Don Carlos Buell, a descendant of a Welshman who came to Connecticut in the 1630's, was born in what is now Lowell, Ohio, on March 23, 1818. Having passed most of his boyhood in the home of an uncle in Lawrenceburg, Indiana, he was appointed to West Point in 1837 and was graduated in the celebrated class of 1841, which contributed twenty general officers to the Civil War. Buell's class standing, thirty-second out of fifty-two, caused him to be posted to the 3rd Infantry, with which he served against the Florida Indians, on garrison and frontier duty, and in the Mexican War. He was severely wounded at the battle of Churubusco and won the brevets of captain and major. Buell then transferred from line to staff and for the next thirteen years performed the duties of the adjutant general's department, serving at the headquarters of a number of military departments on the fron-

tier, as well as in the East, including Washington. At the outbreak of war he was in San Francisco as adjutant of the Department of the Pacific with rank of lieutenant colonel. Prior to his departure from the coast he was commissioned a brigadier general of volunteers on May 17, 1861. After his arrival in Washington in September, he assisted in organizing and training the embryonic Army of the Potomac. George B. McClellan selected Buell to lead a force from Kentucky (the Army of the Ohio) into East Tennessee by way of Louisville and Knoxville. Because of the lack of roads and rail facilities, Buell urged an alternative: an advance via the Cumberland and Tennessee rivers toward Nashville. Despite the opposition of both Abraham Lincoln and McClellan, Buell's idea was carried out with only minor changes. Buell's plan may have been a contributing factor to the success of U. S. Grant, whose victories at Forts Henry and Donelson enabled Buell with his fifty thousand men to march into Nashville virtually unopposed. He later arrived at Shiloh in time to stem the Confederate assault of the first day and turn almost certain defeat into victory. Buell then served under Henry W. Halleck in the Corinth campaign, and was promoted to major general of volunteers on March 22, 1862. In June he was detached with four divisions under orders to advance on Chattanooga and to repair the Memphis & Charleston Railroad as he went. Buell's forces were continuously harassed by Confederate cavalry, and John H. Morgan arrested the advance in July by destroying Buell's line of supply to Louisville. In September, Buell moved into Kentucky to resist the invasion of the state by the Confederates Braxton Bragg and Edmund Kirby Smith. He occupied Louisville unopposed and on October 8 fought the bloody but indecisive battle of Perryville. Bragg yielded the field to the Federals, but Buell followed too slowly. As a result, he was relieved from command on the twenty-fourth of the month, and on the thirtieth was succeeded by W. S. Rosecrans. Accused of dilatory tactics, he was investigated by a military commission in November, but no recommendations were made. After more than a year of awaiting orders, he was mustered out of volunteer service in May, 1864, and on June 1 resigned his regular commission. Although subsequently recommended by U. S. Grant for restoration to duty, he was not recommissioned and consequently retired to a civilian career, operating an ironworks and a coal mine in Kentucky, where he set-

tled. He was also for a time (1885-89) a government pension agent. During the war Buell ignored political considerations; he had a Southern-born wife and he was a friend of McClellan. He was also reserved in manner and was thought to be unfriendly to the administration. These deficiencies were not compensated for by his abilities as organizer, disciplinarian, and logistician. He died at his home in the now abandoned village of Airdrie, a mile from the hamlet of Paradise, Kentucky, on November 19, 1898, and was buried in Bellefontaine Cemetery, St. Louis.

John Buford, half-brother of General Napoleon B. Buford and cousin of Confederate General Abraham Buford, was born in Woodford County, Kentucky, on March 4, 1826. In the early 1840's his parents moved to Rock Island, Illinois, from where he was appointed to West Point. Upon his graduation in 1848, he posted to the 2nd

Dragoons and saw much frontier service in Texas, New Mexico, Kansas, and in the Utah Expedition of 1857-58. In 1861 the regiment was marched overland to Fort Leavenworth, Kansas, thence to Washington in October. It was redesignated as the 2nd Cavalry, and Buford was one of its captains. During the following winter he acted as a staff major and assistant inspector general in the Washington defenses. At this time General John Pope, fresh from his western successes, procured Buford a brigadier's commission to rank from July 27, 1862, and command of the reserve cavalry brigade of the newly constituted Army of Virginia. In the campaign of Second Manassas, Buford performed yeoman's service before he was so badly wounded in the withdrawal of the Federal army across Bull Run that he was reported dead. In the Maryland campaign he acted as chief of cavalry of the Army of the Potomac under George B. McClellan and at Fredericksburg, under Ambrose E. Burnside. Upon the reorganization of the c a v a l r y under Joseph Hooker, Buford again took command of the reserve brigade. He participated with great credit in the attempt by George Stoneman to capture Richmond and free the Union prisoners there, although this action reflected poor judgment on the part of Hooker since it deprived him of his whole cavalry corps immediately before he plunged into the tangled wilderness around Chancellorsville. In the subsequent campaign of Gettysburg Buford, now c o m m a n d i n g a division, reached the apogee of his career, on July 1, 1863. With one man to about a yard of front, he

ordered one of his brigades, under Colonel (later General) William Gamble, to dismount in order to oppose the advance of A. P. Hill's Confederate corps on the road from Cashtown. This permitted the deployment of the leading units of Reynolds' I Corps and the establishment of some order in the crumbling Federal defenses. After engaging in numerous cavalry combats, General Buford was stricken with typhoid fever during the Rappahannock campaign in the autumn of 1863. He died in Washington on December 16, 1863, and was buried in West Point. His commission as major general of volunteers was presented to him on his deathbed.

Napoleon Bonaparte Buford, half-brother of John Buford, was born in Woodford County, Kentucky, on January 13, 1807. After receiving an education in the plantation schools, he was appointed to the West Point class of 1827. His most

distinguished classmate was the future Confederate General Leonidas Polk, who thirty-five years later wrote to his wife: "[Buford] is as good a fellow as ever lived, and most devotedly my friend; a true Christian, a true soldier, and a gentleman, every inch of him." Following his graduation, Buford served as a lieutenant of artillery for eight years, but resigned in 1835 to engage in private business as a civil engineer. In 1843 he removed to Rock Island, Illinois, where he was successful as a merchant, banker, and railroad president. In 1861 he was bankrupted by the repudiated Southern state bond holdings of his bank. Assigning his property to his creditors, Buford accepted the colonelcy of the 27th Illinois Regiment, which he had recruited himself. He was promoted to brigadier general of volunteers on April 15, 1862, and was awarded the brevet of major general "for gallant and meritorious services" in 1865. Meanwhile, he took part in the battle of Belmont; the campaign against Island No. 10; the battle of Corinth; and the early stages of the Vicksburg campaign. During the latter part of the war he was in command of the District of Arkansas at Helena, where he dealt capably with the droves of cotton speculators, smugglers, and carpetbaggers. After being mustered out of service in August, 1865, General Buford briefly held several successive Federal appointments. He later took up residence in Chicago and died there on March 28, 1883. He was buried at Rock Island.

Stephen Gano Burbridge, grandson of a Revolutionary War veteran, was born in Scott County, Kentucky,

on August 19, 1831. He attended Georgetown College and Kentucky Military Institute, practiced law, and engaged in farming. He was commissioned colonel of the 26th Kentucky (Union) Infantry on Au-

gust 27, 1861, and brigadier general of volunteers to rank from June 9, 1862. Burbridge took part in the battle of Shiloh and commanded a brigade of the XIII Corps in the expedition which reduced the Post of Arkansas and also in the Vicksburg campaign. Early in 1864 he succeeded General Jeremiah T. Boyle in the command of the District of Kentucky. Boyle had been execrated, but Burbridge was actively loathed by a majority of the population over whom he had extensive civil and military powers. He was moderately successful in the field—he was, for example, awarded the brevet of major general on July 4, 1864, for repulsing John H. Morgan's abortive invasion of the state

—but his administration of Kentucky earned him the enmity of the duly constituted civil authorities as well as of the populace. Among his arbitrary measures were the arrest of persons suspected of opposing the reelection of Lincoln; the regulation of commodity prices to force farmers to sell to the Federal government at figures below the Cincinnati market; and the establishing of a system of reprisals against civilians to suppress guerrilla depredations—a system originated by Boyle but expanded by Burbridge. Relieved from his command in January, 1865, he resigned his commission in December. After the Civil War he and his family were socially and financially ostracized. In 1867 he confessed that he was not "able to live in safety or do business in Kentucky" and complained that "my services to my country have caused me to be exiled from my home." He was a frequent but unsuccessful supplicant for Federal office. General Burbridge died in Brooklyn, New York, on December 2, 1894, and was buried in Arlington National Cemetery.

Hiram Burnham was born in Narraguagus (now Cherryfield), Maine. According to the modest stone in Pine Grove Cemetery there, he was "killed in battle . . . September 9, 1864, ae. 50 years," the only discoverable clue to the date of his birth. Prior to the outbreak of the Civil War, he is described by a collateral descendant as having been "a very active man in Cherryfield . . . County Commissioner and also coroner. He was a lumberman and a leader of men." Burnham was mustered into service on July 15, 1861, as colonel of the

6th Maine, a regiment he had helped recruit and which lost thirteen commissioned officers in action in less than twelve months. The 6th Maine took part in the Peninsular campaign as a part of Winfield S. Hancock's brigade of W. F. Smith's division of the IV Corps. Here Burnham began to gain the notice of his commanding officers, eventually winning the

commission of brigadier general of volunteers to rank from April 26, 1864. At Antietam (Sharpsburg) the division was part of the VI Corps. At the battle of Fredericksburg in December, 1862, where the corps was not heavily engaged, Burnham was in brigade command for a time. In the celebrated campaign of Chancellorsville, the VI Corps, under John Sedgwick, was ordered to take the heights at Fredericksburg which had cost Ambrose E. Burnside heavy casualties five months previously. Here the 6th Maine had its major and four of its ten captains shot dead on a field which did not greatly distinguish either Sedgwick or his Confederate opposite, Jubal Early. Again mainly in reserve at Gettysburg, Burnham fought gallantly in the Overland campaign of the spring of 1864. He was promoted to brigadier general of volunteers to rank from April 26, 1864, and in the subsequent operations against Petersburg commanded a brigade of the XVIII Corps. While engaged in a probing operation to determine the degree of Confederate resistance at a position then known to the Confederates as Fort Harrison (on the outer line of the Richmond defenses, below Chaffin's Bluff) Burnham was killed on September 29, 1864. (48)

William Wallace Burns was born in Coshocton, Ohio, on September 3, 1825. At seventeen he was appointed to the Military Academy, from which he was graduated in 1847, ranking twenty-eighth in a class of thirty-eight. This class numbered future Confederate division commander Henry Heth as its bottom man. Posted to the infantry, Burns served during the Mexican War on recruiting duty, then spent several years at various Indian posts in the West and Southwest. In 1858 he accepted a staff commission as commissary of subsistence with rank of captain. In the first months of the Civil War, he acted as George B. McClellan's chief commissary in the West Virginia campaign. He was appointed a brigadier general of volunteers on September 28, 1861, and in the Peninsular campaign the following spring commanded a brigade of John Sedgwick's division of the II Corps,

during which he was wounded and favorably mentioned by McClellan. On sick leave for some months, he commanded the 1st Division of the IX Corps at the bat-

tle of Fredericksburg. Burns evidently preferred administration to field command, for on March 20, 1863, he resigned his volunteer commission and reverted to his staff rank of major and commissary. He served as chief commissary in the Department of the Northwest until the close of the war and later discharged with distinction the same duties in various Southern departments. General Burns was promoted to lieutenant colonel in the commissary service in 1874 and to colonel in 1884. Meantime he had been brevetted brigadier general for gallant and meritorious services. He was retired on September 3, 1889, and died at Beaufort, South Carolina, April 19, 1892. He was buried in Arlington National Cemetery.

Ambrose Everett Burnside, the most unwilling and, perhaps, most unsuitable commander of the Army of the Potomac, was born on May 23, 1824, at Liberty, Union County, Indiana. His father, born in South Carolina, had been a slave owner but freed his slaves when he moved to Indiana. After receiving a primary school education, Burnside was apprenticed to a tailor and subsequently was a partner in a shop in Liberty. At nineteen, however, his father's political connections procured for him an appointment to West Point, from which he was graduated in 1847 as a brevet second lieutenant, 2nd Artillery. In the Mexican War he was confined mainly to garrison duty in Mexico City. He afterward served in garrison duty and on the southwestern frontier, where he was slightly wounded in a skirmish with Apaches in 1849. He resigned his commission in 1853 and in Bristol, Rhode Island, engaged in the manufacture of a breech-loading rifle which he had invented while in the army—a venture which failed. Burnside's genial personality won for him, during the antebellum years, appointment as major general of the state militia, nomination to Congress as a Democrat, and a job with the Illinois Central Railroad under his friend, George B. McClellan. At the outbreak of war Burnside organized the 1st Rhode Island Infantry, a three-month regiment which was one of the first to reach Washington. He was in command of a brigade at First Manassas and was appointed a brigadier general of volunteers on August 6, 1861. Having become something of a favorite of President Lincoln, he was given command of the

expedition against the coast of North Carolina, an eminently successful venture which gave the Federals a base of operations. One of the few early Union successes, Burnside's feat was rewarded by promotion to major general of volunteers to rank from March 18, 1862. In July some of Burnside's troops were withdrawn to be sent to the Army of the Potomac and, some sources say, in the next few weeks he twice declined the command of that army. At Sharpsburg in September, McClellan assigned him direction of his own IX Corps and Joseph Hooker's I Corps. Burnside's overly precise construction of his orders on this field caused delay and loss of an opportunity to crush the weak Confederate position opposite "Burnside's Bridge." On November 10, 1862, after McClellan had incessantly appealed for more men and materiel in order to assume the offensive, Burnside was made commander, accepting the responsibility as an order to be obeyed. The following month the tragedy of Fredericksburg was acted out—nearly thirteen thousand casualties were sustained by the Army of the Potomac in a series of assaults against the impregnable Confederate position. Although Burnside's subordinate commanders opposed the abortive "Mud March," by which he proposed again to cross the Rappahannock above Fredericksburg, he persisted in the plan. He afterward offered the President the choice of relieving him or of dismissing some and relieving others of his subordinates, including five major generals and two brigadiers. Lincoln thereupon gave the army command to Hooker, whose dismissal Burnside had urged. In March, 1863, Burnside was assigned to command the Department of the Ohio. Here he arrested and tried by military commission Copperhead ex-Congressman Clement L. Vallandigham for uttering seditious sentiments. In the autumn of 1863 Burnside ably defended Knoxville against the forces of Confederate General James Longstreet. The following spring Burnside's old IX Corps was recruited to full strength and was for a time an independent unit supporting the Army of the Potomac, an awkward arrangement dictated by Burnside's being senior in rank to George G. Meade, the nominal army commander. The IX Corps took part with U. S. Grant in the Overland campaign and in the operations culminating in the siege of Petersburg. In the celebrated battle of the Crater (July, 1864), Burnside's troops failed to exploit a fifty-yard gap in the Confederate line caused by the explosion of a Federal mine. This circumstance ultimately resulted in

his resignation from the service on April 15, 1865. General Burnside continued to enjoy the confidence of his civilian friends, occupying numerous railroad and industrial directorships after the close of hostilities. In the course of his business career he was elected three times governor of Rhode Island (1866, 1867, 1868). In 1874 he was elected a United States Senator from Rhode Island and served until his death at Bristol, Rhode Island, on September 13, 1881. General Burnside was buried in Swan Point Cemetery, Providence, Rhode Island.

Cyrus Bussey was born at Hubbard, Ohio, on October 5, 1833. Four years later his family moved to Indiana. There, at the age of sixteen, Bussey started a business at Dupont, a hamlet in Jefferson County. In 1855 he established himself in Bloomfield, Iowa. He was elected to the Iowa senate in

1858 and to the Democratic National Convention of 1860, which nominated Stephen A. Douglas for the presidency. At the outbreak of the Civil War, Bussey was appointed by the governor to command the militia in southeastern Iowa, with rank of lieutenant colonel, and on August 10, 1861, he was mustered into Federal service as colonel of the 3rd Iowa Cavalry. He commanded a small force in addition to his own regiment at Elkhorn Tavern (Pea Ridge) and was in command of a full brigade of cavalry during Frederick Steele's successful expedition against Arkansas Post. After a few months in charge of the District of Eastern Arkansas, Bussey commanded a cavalry division of the Army of the Tennessee during the campaign which resulted in the capitulation of Vicksburg. He was appointed brigadier general of volunteers on January 5, 1864. During the remainder of the war he was in brigade and divisional command in western Arkansas, where he restored discipline and fought the corrupt practices of contractors and cotton speculators. Brevetted major general to rank from March 13, 1865, Bussey returned to civilian pursuits as a merchant in St. Louis and then New Orleans. He was president of the New Orleans Chamber of Commerce for six years and a prime mover in the adoption of the jetty system which protects the mouth of the Mississippi. Having become a Republican, General Bussey served as a delegate to the conventions of 1868 and 1884 and as Assistant Secretary of the Interior in 1889, in which capacity he liberally awarded pensions to "deserving" Union veterans. He later

established a law office in Washington, where he died on March 2, 1915. He was buried in Arlington National Cemetery.

Richard Busteed, born in Cavan, Ireland, on February 16, 1822, was the son of a Dublin barrister who once held a colonel's commission in the British army. The family moved to the island of St. Lucia for a time; returned to Ireland; moved again to London, Ontario; and

thence successively to Cincinnati, Hartford, and New York City, where the father and son engaged in newspaper work. Young Busteed studied law and was admitted to the bar in 1846. Soon attaining distinction in several extradition cases, he was elected corporation counsel of New York City in 1856 and served until 1859. Meantime he was active in politics as a Democrat and supported Stephen A. Douglas in 1860, earning a reputation as a bitter opponent of Abraham Lincoln but as a strong Union man. In October, 1861, he organized an independent battery of field artillery known variously as Captain Busteed's Battery, the Chicago Light Artillery, and Battery C, Chicago Light Artillery. On November 7, 1861, two days before the battery's transfer to the 1st Regiment, New York Light Artillery, Busteed resigned his captain's commission. He makes no further appearance in the records until August 7, 1862, when he was appointed a brigadier general of volunteers, an appointment which expired by law on March 4 since his name was not sent to the Senate for confirmation. Meantime, he served in the occupation forces under the immediate command of General Erasmus D. Keyes, protecting the Federal stronghold of Fort Monroe on the Virginia Peninsula. In September, 1863, Lincoln appointed Busteed judge of the U. S. District Court for Alabama, anomalously, since Alabama was almost entirely under Confederate control. Busteed opened his court in the autumn of 1865 and inaugurated a flood of trials resulting in few convictions but high costs. Allegedly, Busteed conspired with other court officials to swindle the businessmen they prosecuted. In the course of a nine-year tenure he handed down several important opinions, one of which decreed the unconstitutionality of the Congressionally prescribed test oath so far as it applied to attorneys practicing before United States courts. This decision was upheld by the Supreme Court. Although Busteed strengthened his affiliation with the Democratic party through association with some of its New York officials who visited Washington, he supported Republican candidates in the 1872 campaign. He resigned from office in 1874 to avoid impeachment and returned to New York to resume his law practice. He died there on September 14, 1898, and was buried in Woodlawn Cemetery.

Benjamin Franklin Butler was born in Deerfield, New Hampshire, on November 5, 1818. Although diminutive in stature and having a cast in one eye, he was aggressive, dynamic, and resourceful. After the death of his father, his mother operated a boarding house in Lowell, Massachusetts. Young Butler went to Colby College in Maine, graduating in 1838. He returned to Lowell, taught school, was admitted to the bar in 1840, and soon built a large criminal practice with offices in Boston and Lowell. He was elected as a Democrat to the Massachusetts house of repre-

sentatives in 1853 and to the state senate in 1859. The following year Butler was a delegate to the Democratic convention which met in Charleston, where he voted fifty-seven consecutive times to nominate Jefferson Davis for President of the United States. Butler later joined with other seceders from the Baltimore convention in backing the extreme States' Rights candidate, John C. Breckinridge. Before the decade was out, however, Butler was one of the foremost Republican Radicals to howl for the head of Andrew Johnson, whose fall from favor was occasioned by his soft policy toward such men as Davis and Breckinridge. As a brigadier general of the Massachusetts militia, Butler entered the war in dramatic fashion: five days after the bombardment of Sumter he lifted the blockade of Washington with the 8th Massachusetts. He was the first volunteer major general appointed by Lincoln (to rank from May 16, 1861), and although his military exploits were not such as to earn him a place beside Napoleon and Marlborough, in other respects his contributions to the Union cause were little short of monumental. Badly defeated in the action at Big Bethel while in command of Fort Monroe, Butler was the first to apply the term "contraband-of-war" to slaves of Southern masters who fled into the Union lines. In August, Butler commanded the successful amphibious attack on Hatteras Inlet and the following May entered New Orleans with his troops—the city had already surrendered to the fleet under Admiral David G. Farragut. Appointed military governor, Butler's subsequent conduct of office was controversial. He was vilified in the South and declared an outlaw by President Davis and was even accused of stealing the silverware from the house in which he made his headquarters. That he governed effectively and performed useful service is impossible to deny, but that he lined his own pockets and those of his family and friends seems equally evident. He was removed in December, 1862, but was given command of the Army of the James in 1863. This army consisted of two corps which U. S. Grant intended to employ as a part of the over-all strategy of the 1864 campaign. Butler's ineptness resulted in his entire force being bottled up at Bermuda Hundred by a greatly inferior force under the Confederate General P. G. T. Beauregard. After some service in New York City in November, 1864, Butler was ordered by Grant to return home and await orders in January, 1865. He resigned his commission on November 30. Elected to Congress as a Republican in 1866, Butler served until 1875, meantime, as noted above, taking a prominent part in the impeachment of Andrew Johnson in 1868. Loathed by conservative Democrats and Republicans alike in Massachusetts, Butler repeatedly ran for governor of the state from 1871 until 1882, when he was finally elected. In 1878 he was elected once again to Congress, this time as a Greenbacker—the third of his political affiliations. He was presidential candidate of this party in 1884. General Butler died in Washington, D. C., on January 11, 1893, and was buried in his wife's family cemetery in Lowell. His daughter married General Adelbert Ames.

Daniel Butterfield was born on October 31, 1831, in Utica, New York, the son of John Butterfield of the Overland Mail Company. After graduation from Union College at the age of eighteen, he studied law, traveled extensively in the South, and entered business as superin-

tendent of the eastern division of the American Express Company of which his father was part owner. Apparently he was in Washington at the time of the bombardment of Sumter, for on April 16, 1861, F. B. Heitman's *Historical Register* mentions his enrollment as first sergeant of the "Clay Guards" of that city. He was mustered into Federal service as colonel of the 12th New York Militia on May 2, 1861, the first Union regiment to set foot on Virginia soil (May 24). After service with General Robert Patterson at Martinsburg, Butterfield was appointed brigadier general of volun-

teers to rank from September 7, 1861, and assigned to command a brigade in George W. Morell's division of Fitz John Porter's V Corps. He was wounded at Gaines's Mill in the Peninsular campaign and thirty years later was awarded the Medal of Honor for his conduct on that day. Present at Second Manassas, his brigade was under the command of its senior colonel during the Maryland campaign, which culminated in the battle of Sharpsburg. Butterfield succeeded Morell as division commander on October 30, and after the removal of Porter, commanded the V Corps at Fredericksburg; he was appointed major general to rank from November 29, 1862. Upon Joseph Hooker's accession to command of the Army of the Potomac, Butterfield became his chief of staff and helped design the celebrated corps badges of the army. Continuing as chief of staff under General George G. Meade, Butterfield was severely wounded at Gettysburg. He subsequently engaged in an acrimonious debate with his chief over the meaning of Meade's famous order of July 1st (49) and in October accompanied Hooker to the western army. In the Atlanta campaign he commanded a division of the XX Corps before becoming ill; he saw no further field service after this. Meantime, he had been appointed a lieutenant colonel in the Regular Army in 1861 and colonel of the 5th Infantry on July 1, 1863. In 1865 he was brevetted brigadier and major general, U. S. Army. The general's postbellum career was notable for its multifarious business, military, and civic connections. Both before and after his resignation from the army in 1870, General Butterfield's name appeared countless times in the public eye—as a friend to General U. S. Grant, as a director of numerous corporations, and as an unofficial ambassador to several foreign countries. One of his most enduring claims to fame was the bugle call "Taps," which he composed at Harrison's Landing in 1862. He died in his summer home at Cold Spring, New York, on July 17, 1901. By special dispensation of the War Department, he was buried at West Point.

George Cadwalader was born in Philadelphia on May 16, 1806, to a noted family. He studied law and was admitted to the bar; meanwhile he interested himself in the local

militia organizations. In 1844, as brigadier general, he was instrumental in suppressing in Philadelphia the "anti-foreign" riots which erupted from the activities of the American or Know-Nothing party.

At a critical moment, General Cadwalader was hung in effigy by anti-Catholics, who had already erected a gallows to hang him *in corpore*. Three years later he was commissioned a brigadier general of volunteers and distinguished himself in the Mexican War, receiving the brevet of major general for gallantry at Chapultepec. Cadwalader left the management of his large private interests in 1861. He was a major general of Pennsylvania troops in the early months of the war and on April 25, 1862, was commissioned a major general of United States Volunteers. In this capacity he served on boards of inquiry, in garrison commands, as advisor to the President and the Secretary of War, and on various military commissions. From August, 1863, until the end of the war General Cadwalader commanded the post at Philadelphia. With the end of hostilities, he resigned on July 5, 1865, and returned to private life. After the war he devoted himself to his private interests. General Cadwalader died at his home in Philadelphia on February 3, 1879, and was buried in the cemetery of Christ Church. As was the case with many of the contenders in the great struggle of the 1860's, Cadwalader had close family connections in the South; his wife Frances (Mease) was a granddaughter of United States Senator Pierce Butler of South Carolina.

John Curtis Caldwell was born in Lowell, Vermont, on April 17, 1833. After graduation from Amherst College in Massachusetts, he took up teaching and in 1861 was the principal of Washington Academy at East Machias, Maine.

Mustered into Federal service as colonel of the 11th Maine on November 12, 1861, and promoted to brigadier general of volunteers to

rank from April 28, 1862, he compiled a war record that was adequate though not spectacular. He commanded a brigade of the II Corps in the Peninsular campaign. Although he was not present at Sharpsburg, he suffered two superficial wounds at Fredericksburg (where one of his regiments broke to the rear) and was again with his brigade at Chancellorsville. At Gettysburg he was temporarily in command of the II Corps after the wounding of Winfield S. Hancock, and in the autumn of 1863 during the Mine Run campaign, he again led the II Corps. Relieved from duty in the Army of the Potomac on March 25, 1864, Caldwell was one of eight general officers assigned as a guard of honor to the body of President Abraham Lincoln during the procession from

Washington to Springfield. General Caldwell was mustered out of service in January, 1866, and in the same year was admitted to the Maine bar. Thereafter, he received many state and Federal appointments, including those of adjutant general of Maine (1867-69), U. S. consul at Valparaiso, Chile (1869-74), and U. S. minister to Uruguay (1874-82). From 1885 to 1897 he was chairman or secretary of the Kansas state board of pardons. With the election of William McKinley to President in 1896, Caldwell went the following year to Costa Rica as U. S. consul, where he served at San José until 1909. Returning to Topeka that year, he made his home with one or another of his children until his death at the home of a daughter in Calais, Maine, on August 31, 1912. The general was buried next to his wife in East Machias. (50)

Robert Alexander Cameron was born in Brooklyn, New York, on February 22, 1828. His parents moved to Valparaiso, Indiana, in the early 1840's. Here young Cameron attended the public schools and Indiana Medical College. After his graduation in 1849, he studied at Rush Medical College in Chicago. Cameron seemingly lost his desire to be a doctor and in 1857 purchased the Valparaiso *Republican,* which he published for some years, in the meantime serving as a Lincoln delegate at the 1860 Republican convention in Chicago and a member of the Indiana house of representatives. Upon the outbreak of the Civil War, Cameron entered the Union army as captain of the 9th Indiana (a three-month regiment), which saw service under

George B. McClellan in western Virginia. Reenlisting for the war, Cameron was successively lieutenant colonel of the 19th Indiana, lieutenant colonel and colonel of the 34th Indiana, and brigadier general of volunteers from August 11, 1863. Meantime he had taken part in the operations against Island No. 10 and New Madrid, the capture of Memphis, and the siege of Vicksburg. He commanded a division of the XIII Corps in the Red River campaign of 1864 and briefly the corps itself. From then until the war's end he was in district command at Thibodaux, Louisiana, in the Department of the Gulf and was brevetted major general as of March 13, 1865. General Cameron soon resigned his commission and became interested in establishing farm colonies in the new state of Colorado. In 1870 he was instrumental in founding the city of Greeley and the following year was elected president of its

board of trustees. However, he soon resigned in order to assume the superintendency of the colony which established Colorado Springs; later he took part in a luckless venture to establish Fort Collins, Colorado. After this he resided in San Francisco for a few years, then returned to Colorado and served as a postal clerk in Denver and warden of the state penitentiary at Canon City. He died on March 15, 1894, on a farm he had established near Canon City, and was buried there.

Charles Thomas Campbell was born in Franklin County, Pennsylvania, on August 10, 1823. At the age of twenty-three he took part in the Mexican War as a lieutenant, and later as captain, of the 11th U. S. Infantry; he was honorably discharged on August 14, 1848. Four years later he won election to the lower house of the Pennsylvania legislature. On May 29, 1861, Campbell was again mustered into

service as captain of Battery A, Pennsylvania Light Artillery. When the various batteries were regimented, Campbell became successively lieutenant colonel and colonel of the 1st Pennsylvania Artillery, meantime taking part in the action at Dranesville. In February, 1862, he resigned to accept the colonelcy of the 57th Pennsylvania Infantry, which he took into the battle of Seven Pines in the Peninsular campaign as a part of Philip Kearny's division of the III Corps. Here he was wounded three times and had his horse shot out from under him. Seven months later, with one arm still in a sling, he commanded the 57th Pennsylvania Infantry at Fredericksburg, where he was shot through the liver and given up for dead. Partially fit for duty by the following May, he was ordered to report for assignment in the Department of the Northwest and until the end of the war exercised district command in Wisconsin. He had been appointed brigadier general to rank from November 29, 1862, and when the appointment expired by statute on March 4, 1863, he was reappointed to rank from March 13. After the war he went to Dakota Territory as inspector of Indian agencies and operated the pioneer stage line into the Black Hills, making his home in Yankton, South Dakota. Subsequently he was one of the founders of the town of Scotland, South Dakota, where he served as mayor, owned a substantial part of the townsite, and operated for many years the Campbell House. General Campbell died on April 15, 1895, from the effects of a fall on the steps of his own hotel in Scotland. He was buried in Yankton. (51) He car-

ried the scars of seven different wounds acquired in the Mexican and Civil wars.

William Bowen Campbell was born on a farm in Sumner County, Tennessee, on February 1, 1807. Educated as a lawyer, he commenced practice in Carthage, Tennessee, and in 1836 took a gallant part in the war with the Seminoles as cap-

tain of the 2nd Tennessee Mounted Volunteers, whose colonel was William Trousdale. The following year Campbell defeated Trousdale for Congress in a campaign which pitted the Whigs against the Democratic followers of ex-President Andrew Jackson. Retiring after three terms, Campbell reentered military service as colonel of the 1st Tennessee Infantry in the war with Mexico. This regiment, known as the "Bloody First," fought at Monterey, Vera Cruz, and Cerro Gordo. In 1851 Campbell was elected governor of Tennessee over his old opponent Trousdale. His campaign slogan was "Boys, Follow Me," a cry he had immortalized at the battle of Monterey. He was the last Whig governor of Tennessee. A decade later, he was forced to preside at the dissolution of his party when, after supporting John Bell and strongly opposing secession, he found Bell swearing allegiance to the Confederacy. As the most distinguished Middle-Tennessee loyalist, he was wooed by both the Confederate and Washington governments. From the latter he accepted a brigadier general's commission on June 30, 1862, which he resigned on January 26, 1863. Thereafter, he labored unceasingly for the restoration of Tennessee to the Union on a conservative basis; he was a champion of Andrew Johnson and his policies in the early Reconstruction years. This failed to arouse the enthusiasm of the Republican Radicals, who opposed the seating of Campbell upon his election to the House of Representatives in 1865. He died in Lebanon, Tennessee, on August 19, 1867, and was buried there.

Edward Richard Sprigg Canby was born at Piatt's Landing, Boone County, Kentucky, on November 9, 1817. (52) After attending the local school at nearby East Bend and Wabash College in Crawfordsville, Indiana, where his father had bought property, Canby received an appointment to the Military Academy. He was graduated, ranking next to last in the class of 1839. Until the outbreak of the Mexican War, Canby fought Seminoles in Florida; assisted in removing the Creeks, Cherokees, and Choctaws to Arkansas; and served in garrison

and on recruiting duty. As chief of staff of a brigade in the Mexican War, he won the brevets of major and lieutenant colonel; in subsequent staff duty on the Pacific Coast and in Washington, he was promoted to major of the 10th Infantry in the army reorganization of 1855. In the five years preceding the Civil War, Canby did considerable frontier duty, and the bombardment of Fort Sumter found him operating from Fort Defiance, New Mexico Territory, which then included all of present-day Arizona. On May 14, 1861, he was appointed colonel of the newly authorized 19th Infantry and put in command of the Department of New Mexico. There, the following January, he opposed the invasion of Confederate General Henry H. Sibley, whose ultimate object was the conquest of California. Although defeated at Valverde, Canby drew Sibley away from his supplies and saw the demoralized

67

and half-starved Confederates retreat to Texas. In the course of this
campaign Canby's Fabian tactics
gave rise to the widely circulated
untruth that Sibley and Canby
were brothers-in-law. (53) On May
31, 1862, Canby was appointed a
brigadier general of volunteers and
ordered to the East. For the next
eighteen months he performed staff
duties, except for a period following the draft riots of 1863 when he
commanded at New York City. He
was promoted to major general of
volunteers to rank from May 7,
1864, and was placed in command
of the Military Division of West
Mississippi, an area embracing the
states from Missouri to the Gulf
Coast and from Texas to Florida.
After reorganizing the forces of
N. P. Banks who were retreating
from the abortive Red River campaign, Canby set about the capture
of Mobile and its forts—an enterprise which was at length undertaken in August in conjunction
with the navy. Admiral David G.
Farragut's passage of the forts protecting Mobile Bay was followed by
the reduction of the forts themselves by General Gordon Granger
in September, 1864. For planning
the expedition, Canby received official thanks from President Lincoln.
When the town of Mobile surrendered on April 12, 1865, Canby received acknowledgment from the
President and the War Department. In May, at the end of the
war, Canby accepted the surrender of the forces commanded by
Generals Richard Taylor and Edmund Kirby Smith. Having been
brevetted through all the grades in
both the volunteer and regular
services, Canby was promoted to
brigadier general, U. S. Army, in

the reorganization of 1866. For five
years he served at various points in
the occupied Southern states and in
Washington. In 1870 he accepted
the command of the Department of
Columbia and in 1873 that of the
Division of the Pacific. On April
11, 1873, while negotiating with the
Modoc Indians for removal from
their stronghold in the Lava Beds
of Siskiyou County, California,
General Canby was attacked without warning by Captain Jack and
mortally wounded. He was shot
through the head and killed by another Indian and stabbed by yet
another. His remains were taken
to Indianapolis for burial in Crown
Hill Cemetery.

James Henry Carleton was born
on December 27, 1814, in Lubec,
Maine, five months after his parents
had fled nearby Eastport on Moose
Island after the British occupation.
(54) As a young man he had literary aspirations and corresponded
from Boston with Charles Dickens.

After participating as a lieutenant of militia in the 1839 Aroostook War (a bloodless encounter occasioned by the conflict over the Maine-New Brunswick boundary, which nearly involved the United States in a third war with Great Britain), Carleton was appointed a second lieutenant of the 1st U. S. Dragoons on October 18, 1839. In 1846 he accompanied Stephen W. Kearny's Rocky Mountain expedition and the following year served on General John E. Wool's staff in Mexico, where he was brevetted major for gallantry at Buena Vista. From the close of the Mexican War until the beginning of the Civil War, Carleton was chiefly employed in scouting and exploring expeditions. In the spring of 1862 he recruited and organized the "California column," which he led from the Colorado River to the Rio Grande. He was commissioned brigadier general of volunteers to rank from April 28, 1862. At this time Carleton relieved General Edward R. S. Canby as commander of the Department of New Mexico, where he remained until the end of the war and was frequently a center of controversy in a sparsely settled and highly partisan area. He was eventually relieved from command on September 19, 1866. Meantime he had been brevetted through all grades to that of major general in both the Regular Army and the volunteer service, and on July 31, 1866, he was appointed lieutenant colonel of the 4th Cavalry. Seven years later he died of pneumonia at San Antonio, Texas, January 7, 1873, and was buried in Mount Auburn Cemetery, Cambridge, Massachusetts. General Carleton's son, Henry Guy Carleton (1852-1910)

became a distinguished New York playwright.

William Passmore Carlin was born in the Richwoods neighborhood, near Carrollton, Illinois, November 24, 1829. His appointment to West Point in 1846 was obtained through a competitive examination in his Congressional district. After his graduation in 1850, he was posted

to the 6th Infantry as a brevet second lieutenant. In the decade preceding the Civil War, Carlin did garrison duty, participated in William S. Harney's expedition against the Sioux in 1855, in Edwin V. Sumner's campaign against the Cheyenne in 1857, and in Albert Sidney Johnston's celebrated Mormon expedition of 1858. At the outbreak of hostilities Carlin was a captain in the regular service. On August 15, 1861, he was commissioned colonel of the 38th Illinois Infantry. Stationed in the then

Southwest (Missouri and Arkansas), Carlin performed creditably in a number of minor operations and distinguished himself in the battle of Perryville, Kentucky, in October, 1862. The following month he was promoted to brigadier general of volunteers. He fought at Stone's River, in the Tullahoma campaign (which forced the Confederate Army under Braxton Bragg from Tennessee) and at Chickamauga and Chattanooga. Taking a gallant part in the Atlanta campaign, he commanded a division at the battle of Jonesboro. During the campaign of the Carolinas he directed the 1st Division of the XIV Corps. He was brevetted major general in both the volunteers and regular services and reverted to his regular rank of major of infantry after the war. In 1867 and 1868 he acted as assistant commissioner of the Freedmen's Bureau in Tennessee and for the following four years was in garrison command at various points in the South. He returned to frontier duty in the West, commanding at various posts, and was promoted to lieutenant colonel in 1872 and to colonel in 1882. On May 17, 1893, he was appointed brigadier general and in the same year was retired. He then established residence in Spokane, Washington, meantime traveling widely in the United States and abroad. General Carlin died near Whitehall, Montana, on board a Northern Pacific train on October 4, 1903. He was buried in Carrollton. (55)

Eugene Asa Carr was born in Erie County, New York, on March 20, 1830. At sixteen he secured an appointment to West Point and

was graduated in the class of 1850, ranking just ahead of William P. Carlin. Originally commissioned into the Regiment of Mounted Riflemen (3rd Cavalry), Carr commenced a distinguished career of forty-three years, most of it on the frontier, in the mounted arm of the service. He was severely wounded by Indians in Texas in 1854 and was promoted to captain in 1858 in the old 1st Cavalry, a regiment which numbered among its field officers, R. E. Lee, J. E. Johnston, and W. J. Hardee. Carr's first Civil War service was at the battle of Wilson's Creek, Missouri, August 10, 1861. Six days later he was commissioned colonel of the 3rd Illinois Cavalry and on March 7, 1862, brigadier general of volunteers. While still a colonel, Carr commanded a brigade of cavalry and directed the 4th (infantry) Division, at the battle of Elkhorn Tavern where he was three times wounded and won the Congressional Medal of Honor for distinguished gallantry. In the campaign that culminated in the surrender of Vicksburg, Carr commanded a division of the XIII Corps. Thereafter, he served in Arkansas where, in command of a cavalry division, he took part in Frederick Steele's Camden campaign until 1865. In February of that year, Carr commanded a division of the XVI Corps and participated in the campaign against Mobile. Brevetted major general in both the regular and volunteer forces, Carr soon returned to the western frontier, reverting to his regular rank of major, 5th Cavalry. A long series of campaigns took him over much Indian country in Kansas, Colorado, Nebraska, Arizona, New Mexico, the Dakotas, and Montana. He was promoted to lieutenant colonel (1873), colonel (1879), and brigadier general (1892). His exploits were legion as a famous and experienced Indian fighter of the post-Civil War period. Retired in 1893, he lived in Washington, where he was much interested in the National Geographic Society. He died on December 2, 1910, and was buried at West Point.

Joseph Bradford Carr was born August 16, 1828, in Albany, New York, the child of Irish immigrants. At an early age he was apprenticed to a tobacconist and continued in this business until the outbreak of the Civil War. Meantime, he became interested in military affairs while living in Troy, New York, and by 1861 was a colonel of militia. Carr was a prime mover in the organization of the 2nd New York Infantry, a two-year regiment. He was mustered into United States service

as a colonel on May 14, 1861. Sent to Fort Monroe, the 2nd New York Infantry took part in the famed action at Big Bethel. Carr commanded a brigade in Joseph Hooker's division of the III Corps during the Peninsular campaign and at Second Manassas and on September 7, 1862, was promoted to brigadier general of volunteers. He fought creditably at Fredericksburg, Chancellorsville (where he briefly commanded the division of mortally wounded Hiram G. Berry), and at Gettysburg, where he was commended by his immediate commander A. A. Humphreys. In the fall of 1863 he was given command of a division in Winfield S. Hancock's II Corps. By the following May, Carr's original commission as brigadier had not been acted upon by the Senate in the session in which he was nominated and had expired on March 4, 1863. Reappointed on March 30, 1863, the Senate, for reasons not apparent in the records, refused as late as May, 1864, to confirm Carr as of the date of his first commission. Accordingly, he stood junior to his own brigade commanders and on May 2, U. S. Grant ordered Carr to report to General Benjamin F. Butler for assignment in the Army of the James. (56) Carr commanded a division of Negro troops in that army and, for a time, the Union defenses on the York and James rivers. At the end of the war he was brevetted major general of volunteers and mustered out. He engaged in the manufacturing business in Troy, served as secretary of state for New York from 1879 to 1885, and in the latter year was an unsuccessful Republican candidate for lieutenant governor. General Carr died in Troy, on February 24, 1895, and was buried there.

Henry Beebee Carrington was born on March 2, 1824, in Wallingford, Connecticut. He was graduated in the Yale class of 1845. In early manhood he became a profound classical scholar and historian and also a dedicated Abolitionist. Removing to Columbus, Ohio, in 1848, Carrington obtained a law degree at Yale and practiced his profession in partnership with William Dennison, later Ohio's Civil War governor. Carrington was prominent in the Abolitionist movement and was an intimate of Salmon P. Chase. Having reorganized the state militia in 1857 at the behest of Chase, then governor, Carrington became state adjutant general and in 1861 was commissioned a colonel in the Regular Army of the United States as a reward for his efforts in organizing, equipping, and dispatching nine

regiments of Ohio militia to aid General George B. McClellan in the western Virginia campaign. His logistic effort did much to hold the area to the Union in a time of general panic. In 1862, as a brigadier

general of volunteers, he superintended in Indiana the recruitment of tens of thousands of men for the Union cause. At the same time—in Indiana and Ohio—he ruthlessly suppressed the disloyal Sons of Liberty, the Supreme Court later holding Carrington's military tribunals illegal since neither Indiana nor Ohio was technically "in rebellion." Mustered out of volunteer service in 1865, Carrington joined his regiment in 1866 and became a notoriety as a result of the Fetterman Massacre near Fort Phil Kearny, Dakota Territory. Immediately prior to this debacle, the unfortunate Fetterman, as untrained in Indian warfare as his superior, wrote to a friend: "We are afflicted with an incompetent commanding officer. . . ." Carrington survived this stricture to live for half a century, during which he occupied a prominent position in Indian negotiations, was a prolific contributor to historical publications, and wrote a number of history books. He died in Boston on October 26, 1912, and was buried in Fairview Cemetery, Hyde Park, Massachusetts.

Samuel Sprigg Carroll was born on September 21, 1832, in Takoma Park near Washington, D. C., where his father was clerk of the Supreme Court. Carroll was graduated from West Point in 1856, ranking forty-fourth in a class of

forty-nine—number forty-five was the later famous Confederate cavalry commander Fitzhugh Lee. Routine frontier service was followed by a year of quartermaster duty at Carroll's alma mater. He was ap-

pointed colonel of the 8th Ohio Infantry in December, 1861, and the following spring commanded a brigade in James Shields's division during the celebrated Shenandoah Valley campaign and in James B. Ricketts' division of the III Corps in the battle of Cedar Mountain. Five days later Carroll was wounded while inspecting his pickets on the Rapidan but returned to duty for the battle of Fredericksburg. In the spring of 1863 he was transferred at his own request to the II Corps, a brigade of which he led at Chancellorsville and Gettysburg and in the Bristoe Station and Mine Run operations of that fall. Carroll was wounded again at the Wilderness on May 5, 1864, and temporarily disabled by yet another wound at Spotsylvania on the thirteenth, while temporarily in command of John Gibbon's division. (57) Meanwhile, he was appointed brigadier general of volunteers to rank from May 12. Carroll was unable to return to duty until December, when he was assigned command of the Department of West Virginia. At the end of the war he commanded a provisional division of the embryo Army of the Shenandoah at Winchester. In 1868 and 1869 General Carroll served as acting assistant inspector general of the division of the Atlantic and on June 9, 1869, he was retired as a major general, U. S. Army, for disability resulting from wounds received in battle. Thereafter, he made his home in Washington, and died in Montgomery County, Maryland, on January 28, 1893. He was buried in Oak Hill Cemetery, Georgetown. His sister was the wife of General Charles Griffin.

Samuel Powhatan Carter, the only American officer to achieve the ranks of major general in the army and rear admiral in the navy, was born in Elizabethton, East Tennessee, on August 6, 1819. He entered Princeton in 1837 but early in 1840 was appointed midshipman in the navy. After three years' duty with

the Pacific squadron, one year on the Great Lakes, and another on the frigate *Potomac* with his home squadron, Carter was ordered to the Naval Academy at Annapolis, from which he was graduated in the class of 1846. Until the outbreak of the Civil War he performed varied duties, afloat and ashore, and in the meantime was promoted to lieutenant, a grade then subordinate only to commander and captain. When he proclaimed his fidelity to the Union in a widely publicized letter, Andrew Johnson and other East Tennessee opponents of secession requested his services to whip up

Union sentiment in that area, with the result that in July, 1861, Carter was detailed from the navy to the War Department. From that time on he was referred to as General Carter, though he usually signed himself "Lieutenant, U. S. Navy (on special duty)." Subsequently, he adopted "Acting Brigadier-General" until his formal commissioning at that grade in the volunteer service on May 1, 1862. Most of Carter's war service was in Kentucky and Tennessee, where he took part in the battle of Fishing Creek, the operations culminating in the surrender of Cumberland Gap in June, 1862, Ambrose E. Burnside's occupation of East Tennessee, and the siege of Knoxville, where he commanded the cavalry division of the XXIII Corps. During the Carolina campaign of 1865, Carter commanded an infantry division of the XXIII Corps under John M. Schofield and was brevetted major general of volunteers to rank from March 13, 1865. Mustered out the following January, Carter resumed the naval rank of commander he had received during the war. He became a captain in 1870, a commodore in 1878, and was retired in 1881; the next year he was advanced to the rank of rear admiral on the retired list. He died in Washington on May 26, 1891, and was buried in Oak Hill Cemetery, Georgetown.

Silas Casey was born at East Greenwich, Rhode Island, July 12, 1807. After receiving an education in neighborhood schools, he was appointed to the Military Academy in 1822 and was graduated four years later. During the next thirty-five years he performed many duties for

the Regular Army. He was promoted to first lieutenant ten years after graduation and to captain in 1839. In the course of the Mexican War, Casey distinguished himself with General Winfield Scott's army in the battles of Contreras, Churubusco, Molino del Rey, and Chapultepec where, as captain of the 2nd Infantry, he was brevetted major and lieutenant colonel for gallant and meritorious conduct. Until the outbreak of the Civil War, Casey served mainly on the Pacific Coast and was commissioned lieutenant colonel of the reconstituted 9th Infantry in 1855. Appointed a brigadier general of volunteers on August 31, 1861, Casey's principal Civil War field service was at the battle of Seven Pines (Fair Oaks) in the Peninsular campaign, where his division of Erasmus D. Keyes's IV Corps bore the brunt of the first Confederate attack by A. P. Hill's troops. (Casey's Redoubt at Seven Pines was named for him.) (58)

Even though his position was overrun here, Casey was brevetted brigadier general in the Regular Army and commissioned major general of volunteers from May 31, 1862. Until the end of the war he commanded a provisional brigade in the Washington defenses and served as president of a board to examine candidates for officers of Negro troops. He was mustered out of volunteer service in July, 1865, and reverted to his permanent rank of colonel of the 4th Infantry, to which he had been promoted in October, 1861. Three years later he was retired on his own application after forty-six consecutive years of service. General Casey compiled and edited *Infantry Tactics,* which was adopted by the government in 1862, and a similar volume "for Colored Troops," adopted in 1863. He died in Brooklyn, New York, January 22, 1882, and was buried on the Casey family farm at North Kingstown, Rhode Island. One of his daughters married General Lewis C. Hunt.

Robert Francis Catterson (59) was born on March 22, 1835, on a farm near Beech Grove, Marion County, Indiana. He was the son of an Irish immigrant who died when Robert was five. Catterson was educated at Adrian College, Michigan, and at Cincinnati Medical College; he had just commenced practice at Rockville, Indiana, when the Civil War broke out. (60) Volunteering almost at once, he was mustered into Company A of the 14th Indiana Infantry on April 23, 1861. He was promoted to first sergeant in June, to second lieutenant the same month, to first lieutenant the following March, and to captain in

May, 1862. In October he was appointed lieutenant colonel of the 97th Indiana and in November became its colonel. He fought his first pitched battle at Kernstown in the Shenandoah Valley campaign of 1862 and his last at Bentonville in the campaign of the Carolinas in 1865. Meanwhile, he engaged (with repeated commendations by his superior officers) in the occupation of Memphis by W. T. Sherman, the siege of Vicksburg, the Tullahoma campaign, the battle of Chattanooga, the Atlanta campaign, and the "March to the Sea." During the march northward from Savannah, which culminated in the surrender of Joseph E. Johnston in North Carolina, Catterson commanded a brigade of C. R. Woods's division of Logan's XV Army Corps. Catterson was finally promoted to brigadier general of volunteers to rank from May 31, 1865. He never returned to medicine, but went to Arkansas after being mustered out and engaged unsuccessfully in cotton speculation. He then became commander of the Arkansas Negro militia used by Governor Powell Clayton to fight the Ku Klux Klan. But he later fell out with Clayton during the latter's successful campaign for the U. S. Senate, and as a result lost his position of United States marshal. From 1872 to 1874 Catterson was mayor of Little Rock. In the latter year he played a prominent part in the so-called Brooks-Baxter War on the side of Brooks. With the end of Reconstruction, General Catterson moved to Minneapolis, where he sold farm implements for a time and tried farming; he was not successful in either occupation. Incapacitated by a stroke, he died in the Veterans' Hospital in San Antonio, Texas, March 30, 1914, and was buried in the National Cemetery there. (61)

Joshua Lawrence Chamberlain, born September 8, 1828, in Brewer, Maine, was descended on his father's side from a long line of volunteer soldiers dating back to colonial days. He was educated at a military academy in Ellsworth, Maine, and was graduated from Bowdoin College in 1852 and from the Bangor Theological Seminary in 1855. Chamberlain returned to Bowdoin the same year as a professor. On August 8, 1962, Chamberlain was commissioned lieutenant colonel of the 20th Maine. He participated in twenty-four engagements, ranging from skirmishes to pitched battles, including Sharpsburg, Fredericksburg, Chancellorsville, Gettysburg (for gallantry here he was later awarded the Medal of Honor), Spotsylvania, Cold Har-

bor, and Five Forks. He was wounded six times and was given a field promotion to brigadier general by General U. S. Grant after one of the initial assaults against Petersburg in which he was thought to have been mortally wounded. At Appomattox, Chamberlain was detailed to receive the formal surrender of the Army of Northern Virginia. Brevetted major general for his conduct at Five Forks, he declined a commission in the regular service and was mustered out in January, 1866. The same autumn he was elected governor of Maine and was reelected three times, serving until 1870. For the next thirteen years he occupied the presidency of Bowdoin and until 1885 continued there as a lecturer in political science and public law. Meantime, as major general of the state militia, he ameliorated a tense situation which threatened anarchy in the state legislature as the result of an alliance between

the Democratic and Greenback parties against the Republicans. Subsequently, General Chamberlain occupied himself with various business enterprises in Florida; served as surveyor of the port of Portland, Maine; and wrote a number of historically valuable treatises on his native state and on the various Civil War campaigns in which he had served. He died in Portland on February 24, 1914, and was buried in Pine Grove Cemetery, Brunswick, Maine.

Alexander Chambers was born in Great Valley, Cattaraugus County, New York, on August 23, 1832. When he was an infant, his family moved to nearby Ellicottville, the county seat. Here he attended the common school, and was appointed to West Point in 1849. He was graduated forty-third of fifty-two in the class of 1853 (John Bell Hood was forty-fourth) and was commissioned into the 5th Infantry. With

this regiment he performed routine frontier and garrison duties until the outbreak of the Civil War when, as a newly commissioned captain of the 18th Infantry, he was detailed to recruiting duty in Iowa. Chambers was appointed colonel of the 16th Iowa Infantry on March 24, 1862, and with it took part in the battle of Shiloh, where he was twice wounded and was brevetted major in the Regular Army for gallant services. He was again severely wounded at Iuka and brevetted lieutenant colonel, and he was brevetted colonel for his services during the Vicksburg campaign. Shortly thereafter he was appointed a brigadier general of volunteers (to rank from August 11, 1863) and served as such until April 6, 1864, when his appointment was negated by the Senate—this action was taken, according to a descendant, (62) because Chambers was not a legal resident of Iowa. From August, 1863, until the close of the war, General Chambers was in garrison and on furlough with his brigade, served as mustering officer in Iowa, and commanded a battalion of his Regular Army regiment near Chattanooga. He was brevetted brigadier general, U. S. Army, on March 13, 1865, in the omnibus promotions of that date. From that time until his death twenty-three years later, Chambers' career was uneventful—garrison duty, frontier service, and "unassigned" while awaiting orders. By the process of seniority, he was ultimately advanced to colonel of the 17th Infantry on March 1, 1886. During the brief remainder of his life General Chambers often was on sick leave. He died in San Antonio, Texas, on January 2, 1888, and was buried in

Owatonna, Minnesota, the town to which his parents had moved in 1859.

Stephen Gardner Champlin was born in Kingston, New York, July 1, 1827. After an early education in the common schools of the neighborhood, he attended Rhinebeck Academy, studied law, and in 1850 began a practice in Albany. Three years later he removed to Grand

Rapids, Michigan. Here he was successively judge of the recorder's court and prosecuting attorney of Kent County. On June 10, 1861, he was mustered into Federal service as major of the 3rd Michigan Infantry (one of two regiments so designated), which was organized at Grand Rapids to serve three years. Champlin was commissioned colonel of the unit on October 22, 1861. Meanwhile, he was commended by General George B. McClellan for his dispositions in a minor affair at Bailey's Corners, Virginia. During the Peninsular campaign in the spring of 1862, Champlin received a wound in the hip, "considered not dangerous, though severe," (63) at the battle of Seven Pines. He was highly commended here by his superior Philip Kearny and by his brigade commander General Hiram G. Berry. During the campaign of Second Manassas Champlin returned to duty too soon: according to General O. M. Poe, "his wounds from Fair Oaks (Seven Pines) broke out afresh and he is now completely prostrated." Kearny's report of the battle, prepared but unsigned when he died the following day at Chantilly, again commended Champlin, whom he described as "disabled." (64) Thereafter Champlin was placed in charge of the recruiting office in Grand Rapids and was promoted to brigadier general of volunteers to rank from November 29, 1862. He died from the effects of his wounds on January 24, 1864, in Grand Rapids, and was buried there in Fulton Street Cemetery.

Edward Payson Chapin was born August 16, 1831, in Waterloo, Seneca County, New York, the youngest of six children of a Presbyterian minister. Securing his early education in the village school, at seventeen he began to read law in Waterloo. He completed his legal education in Buffalo and Ballston Spa, was admitted to the bar soon after his twenty-first year, and commenced practice in Buffalo. Prior to 1861 Chapin had taken an interest in the local militia and in September of that year he was mustered into serv-

ice as captain of a company (which became part of the 44th New York) recruited in Erie County and named "Ellsworth's Avengers," after Colonel Elmer Ellsworth of the New York Fire Z o u a v e s. Chapin was promoted to major and to lieutenant colonel and meantime distinguished himself at Yorktown during the Peninsular campaign, in which he commanded the regiment as a major and was seriously wounded. On July 4 he was commissioned colonel of the 116th New York (part of the troops guarding Baltimore) until he was sent in November to Ship Island, Mississippi, as a part of N. P. Banks's expedition. In March, 1863, the regiment took part in the operations against Port Hudson which enabled David G. Farragut's fleet to run the batteries. On April 30 Chapin commanded a brigade consisting of the 21st Maine, the 48th and 49th Massachusetts, and the 116th New York, in Christopher

C. Augur's division of the XIX Corps. On May 27 Banks ordered an assault on the Confederate works, which in his own words resulted in "severe losses" with no corresponding gain. Among the casualties was Chapin, killed in the ditch below the parapet. Four months later he was posthumously promoted to brigadier general of volunteers to rank from the day of his death. General Chapin's remains were sent north for burial in Maple Grove Cemetery, Waterloo. (65)

George Henry Chapman was born in the village of Holland, Massachusetts, November 22, 1832. At the age of six he was taken to Indiana, where his father and uncle

published newspapers, successively at Terre Haute and Indianapolis. Young Chapman attended the Marion County Seminary and in 1847 was appointed a midshipman in the navy. After three years' service he resigned and subsequently published a newspaper of his own, the *Indiana Republican*. Meanwhile he studied law and was admitted to the bar in 1857. He was appointed an assistant clerk to the House of Representatives in 1860, but resigned this post in October, 1861, to accept the majority of the 3rd Indiana Cavalry. Chapman was regularly promoted through grades: lieutenant colonel in 1862, colonel in 1863, brigadier general in 1864, and brevet major general in 1865. In the meantime he was uniformly lauded by all his superiors. He participated in the campaigns of Second Manassas, Sharpsburg, Fredericksburg, Chancellorsville, and Gettysburg (where his regiment in William Gamble's brigade of John Buford's division was the first to face the Confederates advancing along the road from Cashtown). In U. S. Grant's sledgehammer movement to Petersburg and in the Shenandoah Valley against the forces of the Confederate General Jubal Early, Chapman commanded first a brigade and then a division in the autumn and winter of 1864-65. Following the dispersal of the remnants of Early's little army at Waynesboro, March 2, 1865, the divisions of George A. Custer and Thomas C. Devin were selected by Philip Sheridan to accompany him to the Petersburg front. Chapman was left in the valley with a brigade of three small regiments and some artillery. His military career is obscure after this time. He resigned on January 7, 1866, to accept the judgeship of the Marion County (Indiana) Criminal Court, where he served five years. In the 1870's he was receiver for two different financially embarrassed railroads and in 1880 was elected to the Indiana state senate. He died near Indianapolis, June 16, 1882, and was buried in Crown Hill Cemetery. (66)

Augustus Louis Chetlain, the son of Swiss parents who came to the United States by way of Canada, was born in St. Louis, Missouri, December 26, 1824. He was taken to Galena, Illinois, as an infant. After attending local schools, he became a clerk. In 1852 he went into busi-

ness for himself; by 1859 he was wealthy. Selling his business, he traveled in Europe and participated actively in the 1860 presidential campaign. When the Civil War came Chetlain was elected, at the suggestion of U. S. Grant, captain of a volunteer company recruited in Galena, and when the company was made part of the 12th Illinois Infantry, he became first lieutenant colonel and then colonel in April,

1862. In the absence of its regular colonel (John McArthur) in brigade command, Chetlain led the regiment at the capture of Forts Henry and Donelson and at the battles of Shiloh, Iuka, and Corinth. On December 18, 1863, he was commissioned brigadier general of volunteers, and organized and recruited Negro troops in Tennessee and Kentucky, with headquarters at Memphis. On January 26, 1865, he was assigned to the command of the Post and Defenses of Memphis, a subdistrict of the District of West Tennessee under the command of the Department of Mississippi. He was brevetted major general of volunteers on June 18, 1865, and mustered out the following January. Chetlain was collector of internal revenue at Salt Lake City from 1867 to 1869, and United States consul at Brussels for the next three years. In 1872 he established himself in the banking business in Chicago, where he was president of the Home National Bank, organizer of the Industrial Bank of Chicago, director of the Chicago Stock Exchange, member of the Board of Education, an active philanthropist, and was prominent for many years in the Military Order of the Loyal Legion and the Grand Army of the Republic. He wrote his *Recollections of Seventy Years* in 1893. General Chetlain died in Chicago on March 15, 1914, and was buried in Greenwood Cemetery, Galena.

Morgan Henry Chrysler was born in Ghent, Columbia County, New York, September 30, 1822. After a common school education, he was a farmer for most of his life, residing at various points in Columbia and

81

Peninsular campaign; in Irvin Mc-Dowell's III Corps in the campaign of Second Manassas; and in the subsequent Maryland campaign and the battle of Chancellorsville. After Chancellorsville the regiment and Chrysler were honorably mustered out due to expiration of term of service. Chrysler was immediately authorized to reorganize the discharged men into a cavalry regiment, which was duly mustered in as the 2nd New York Veteran Cavalry. After being stationed at Washington during the winter of 1863-64, Chrysler and his regiment were sent to New Orleans and there joined the Department of the Gulf. Taking part in N. P. Banks's Red River expedition in Gooding's 5th Brigade of A. L. Lee's cavalry division, Chrysler's veterans performed their remaining duty in the lower South, taking part in the final campaign against Mobile with Chrysler in command of a brigade in the division of T. J. Lucas. Mustered out in 1866 after being briefly employed as military governor of the District of Northern Alabama, General Chrysler retired to private life. He died in Kinderhook, New York, August 24, 1890, and was buried in the nearby village of Valatie.

William Thomas Clark was born June 29, 1831, in Norwalk, Connecticut. He reportedly struck out on his own at the age of thirteen. Admitted to the New York bar in 1854, he moved two years later to Davenport, Iowa, where he commenced practice. In 1861 he recruited the 13th Iowa Infantry. He was first lieutenant and adjutant of this regiment until March 6, 1862, when he was appointed captain and assistant adjutant general of volun-

Saratoga counties and at New Haven, Connecticut. At the outbreak of the Civil War, Chrysler enlisted as a private in a company which became a part of the 30th New York Infantry. According to Edward M. Collier's *A History of Old Kinderhook,* Chrysler was one of only four men in Federal service during the war who rose from private to major general, (67) a rank to which he was promoted by brevet on March 13, 1865. Meantime, he became captain of the 30th New York on June 1, 1861, major in March, 1862, lieutenant colonel in August, 1863, and colonel of a regiment of cavalry in December, 1863. On November 11, 1865, he was appointed a full brigadier general of volunteers—next to the last such appointment made for wartime service. (68) Chrysler served with the 30th New York in winter quarters near Washington until the spring of 1862; on the line of the Rappahannock during the

feated for reelection in 1871 by a conservative Democrat, but certified by the corrupt Republican governor who threw out more than three thousand adverse votes, Clark was subsequently expelled from the House of Representatives by unanimous vote of both parties. He soon obtained a place in the Bureau of Internal Revenue, which he occupied until his death in New York City on October 12, 1905. He was buried in Arlington National Cemetery.

Cassius Marcellus Clay was born on his father's estate, White Hall, in Madison County, Kentucky, October 19, 1810. Rebellious against authority from an early age and turbulent in his relations with everyone, he was graduated from Yale in 1832 after spending a year there. Although his father was a slaveholder, Clay hated slavery and was embittered by defeat in his 1836 campaign for the Kentucky legislature. In 1845 he established

teers. Until the end of the war, he had staff rank and eventually was promoted to lieutenant colonel and assistant adjutant general, and to brigadier general of volunteers on May 31, 1865. He was brevetted brigadier general for gallant and distinguished services at the battle of Atlanta, where he had served as James B. McPherson's adjutant, and also major general in November, 1865, for gallant and meritorious service during the war. Next, still holding his volunteer commission in the army, he arrived in Texas a full-blown carpetbagger. After helping to organize a bank in Galveston, he was soon closely allied with the leader of the town's Negroes, who succeeded in 1869 in electing Clark to the United States House of Representatives as an exponent of "reconstructed" Texas. Clark advocated the sale of west Texas lands for the benefit of railroads in which he was reputed to have an interest. De-

an antislavery newspaper in Lexington, which his fellow-townsmen got rid of by shipping its physical properties to Cincinnati in Clay's absence. In 1846 Clay volunteered for the Mexican War—in contradistinction to his stand against annexation of Texas, a natural result of his opposition to slavery. He performed capably as a captain of the 1st Kentucky Cavalry, was captured by the Mexicans, and ultimately freed. In the years prior to 1860, Clay became an outstanding figure in the Republican party in Kentucky and thus claimed the gratitude of Abraham Lincoln after the latter's election. Reportedly, Lincoln offered Clay the ministry at Madrid to pacify him for the loss of the vice-presidency Clay had anticipated. He declined this appointment, but later accepted the Russian ministry, at the same time rejecting a commission as major general of volunteers because of the government's failure to abolish slavery. From April 11, 1862, until he resigned on March 11, 1863, he was a duly commissioned major general of United States volunteers. Clay was in Russia from 1863 until 1869. He soon fell out with the new President, U. S. Grant and from then until his death at ninety-two was in constant disagreement with every recognized form of authority, changing from one political party to another. After marrying a young girl and fortifying his home against attack, he was adjudged a lunatic. He died at White Hall, on July 22, 1903, and was buried in nearby Richmond Cemetery.

Powell Clayton was born in Delaware County, Pennsylvania, on August 7, 1833. After attending a mil-

itary academy in nearby Bristol and an engineering school in Wilmington, Delaware, he moved to Kansas in 1855 to engage in civil engineering at Leavenworth. As early as

April 29, 1861, Clayton had a company of militia at Fort Leavenworth. A month later he was formally mustered into Federal service as a captain of the 1st Kansas Infantry. In December he became lieutenant colonel of the 5th Kansas Cavalry and in March, 1862, its colonel. He was made a brigadier general of volunteers on August 1, 1864. In the interval, and thereafter until he was mustered out, Clayton served primarily in Missouri and Arkansas. He fought at Wilson's Creek and after the capture of Little Rock in September, 1863, was assigned to command the post at Pine Bluff, where in October he repulsed an attack by Confederate General J. S. Marmaduke. Soon after the war, he bought a plantation and engaged in cotton farming. In 1868 Clayton was elected the first carpetbag governor of Arkansas, "neither the worst nor the best" (69) of this gentry, according to one of his biographers; he remained Republican boss of Arkansas from then until his death. One of Clayton's acts as governor was the expenditure of $300,000 for Negro militia, under the command of General Robert F. Catterson, to put down the Ku Klux Klan. He also sponsored a $10 million increase in the bonded debt of the state. After Clayton had been elected U. S. Senator, he paid R. J. T. White, the Arkansas secretary of state, $30,000 to resign in order that Lieutenant Governor J. M. Johnson could be appointed to the post. (Clayton did not wish Johnson to succeed him as governor.) Opponents freely aired charges of venality, corruption, and election fraud against him. Defeated for reelection in 1876 by the re-enfranchised conservatives, General Clayton returned to Arkansas and in 1882 established his residence in Eureka Springs, where he managed hotels and railroads. From 1897 until 1905 he was ambassador to Mexico in the administrations of William McKinley and Theodore Roosevelt. About 1912, he moved to Washington, where he died on August 25, 1914. He was buried in Arlington National Cemetery.

Gustave Paul Cluseret was born in Suresnes, France, on June 13, 1823. In 1841 he was admitted to St. Cyr, then the West Point of France. Seven years later he was made a chevalier of the Legion of Honor for helping suppress the insurrection of June, 1848, against the

Orleanist régime. With the return to power of the Bonapartists, he was temporarily retired but soon reinstated. He served in Algeria and in the Crimea and was promoted to captain in 1855. Resigning his commission in 1858, he commanded the French Legion in Giu-

seppe Garibaldi's forces and was wounded at the siege of Capua. Among many military adventurers who flocked to the United States at the outbreak of the Civil War, Cluseret arrived in January, 1862, and was commissioned colonel and aide-de-camp on the staff of General George B. McClellan. Soon afterward he joined John C. Frémont's entourage, was given a brigade, and fought tenaciously at the battle of Cross Keys. For his services here he was promoted to brigadier general of volunteers to rank from October 14, 1862. After service in the Shenandoah, he was reported in arrest (charges unstated) in January, 1863, when General-in-Chief Henry W. Halleck (in responding to William S. Rosecrans' request that Cluseret be detailed to him) telegraphed: "If you knew him better, you would not ask for him. You will regret the application as long as you live. . . ." (70) Cluseret resigned on March 2, 1863; the following year he edited a weekly in New York which advocated Frémont for the presidency while vehemently opposing the renomination of Abraham Lincoln. Returning to Europe in 1867, Cluseret soon had a price placed upon his head by the British government for his alleged complicity in the Fenian uprisings, was jailed by the French government for inflammatory magazine articles, and was ultimately allowed to leave France by claiming he was a naturalized American. Returning after the fall of Napoleon III, he schemed against the provisional government and was condemned to death—although the sentence was not executed—during the period of the Commune. In later years he was four times elected to the Chamber of Deputies from Toulon. General Cluseret died near Hyères, Department of the Var, August 22, 1900. He was buried in the Old Cemetery of the Commune in Suresnes. (71)

John Cochrane, grandson of Surgeon General John Cochran of the Revolutionary Army (the final "e" was added by Cochrane's father), was born in Palatine, New York, August 27, 1813. After graduation from Hamilton College, he was admitted to the bar in 1834 and twelve years later moved to New York City. For thirty years

before the Civil War he was a staunch Democrat and upheld the Southern viewpoint on most issues. As a states' righter, he served in Congress from 1857 until 1861. A delegate to the Democratic convention of 1860, he firmly believed and stated that the North was responsible for Southern discontent. Nevertheless, when secession came, he supported the Union, recruited the 65th New York Infantry, and on June 11, 1861, was mustered into Federal service as its colonel. He was promoted to brigadier general of volunteers on July 17, 1862, but resigned "because of his health" the following February. (72) In the interim he commanded his regiment at Fair Oaks (Seven Pines) during the Peninsular campaign, was in command of a brigade that reached the field of Sharpsburg the day after the battle, and was also in Newton's division of the VI Corps at Fredericksburg.

Soon after his retirement from the army, he was elected attorney general of New York on the ticket of the Republican-Union party which endorsed the Abraham Lincoln administration. The following year, however, dissatisfied with many of the President's policies, he allowed himself to be nominated for vice-president (running with John C. Frémont) by the Cleveland convention. The ticket was withdrawn in September, and Cochrane actively campaigned for Lincoln against the Democratic candidate General George B. McClellan. In 1872 he supported Horace Greeley and was largely responsible for his nomination in the so-called Liberal Republican—in reality the Democratic—convention of that year. A member of Tammany Hall, and its Sachem in 1889, General Cochrane also belonged to various patriotic societies and was president of the Society of the Cincinnati at the time of his death in New York on February 7, 1898. He was buried in the Rural Cemetery at Albany, New York.

Patrick Edward Connor was born in County Kerry, Ireland, March 17, 1820, and was brought to New York City as a child by his parents. He had little education and at the age of nineteen enlisted in the army. After service against the Seminoles and at various garrisons, he was discharged upon the expiration of his enlistment; in 1846 he went to Texas, where he enlisted in an independent company of Texas volunteers and was subsequently promoted to first lieutenant and later to captain. He participated in the battles of Palo Alto, Resaca de la Palma, and Buena Vista; re-

signed his commission May 24, 1847; and in 1849 went to Redwood City, California, where he engaged in mining. On September 4, 1861, Connor was appointed colonel of the 3rd California Infantry and assigned to command the District of Utah (which included what is now Nevada), with headquarters at Salt Lake City. Three miles east of Salt Lake City he established Fort Douglas, which earned him the enmity of the Mormons, whose antipathy for Connor was cordially reciprocated. The purpose of Connor's assignment was to keep the central mail road open to California, where it had been shifted after the southern route through Texas had been taken over by the Confederates. The major hazard, roaming bands of Bannocks, Shoshones, Sioux, Cheyenne, and Arapaho, was successfully overcome by Connor and his small forces. His defeat of the Bannocks and Shoshones on Bear River, Idaho, won him the commission of brigadier general of volunteers to rank from March 30, 1863. At the end of the war he was brevetted major general. In August, 1865, he established Fort Connor (later Fort Reno) on the Powder River in Wyoming and won a substantial victory over the Arapaho on the Tongue River. During the latter expedition, an alleged failure to concert his forces with those of two other columns marching from the Missouri resulted in their demoralization from defeat and privation and Connor's removal from command. Mustered out in 1866, he spent the remainder of his life in Salt Lake City, where he established the first daily newspaper in the state and industriously promoted the mining industry. He died in Salt Lake, December 17, 1891, and was buried in Fort Douglas Cemetery.

Selden Connor (73) was born in Fairfield, Maine, on January 25, 1839. He was graduated from Tufts College in the class of 1859

and then studied law at Woodstock, Vermont. On May 2, 1861, he was mustered into service as a private in the 1st Vermont Infantry, a three-month regiment which participated in the battle of Big Bethel on the Virginia Peninsula on June 10. Mustered out on August 15, Connor was appointed lieutenant colonel of the 7th Maine on August 22. With this regiment he fought through the Peninsular campaign of 1862, at Sharpsburg, Fredericksburg (where he was slightly wounded), and Gettysburg—at times in regimental command. On January 11, 1864, Connor was appointed colonel of the 19th Maine. At the battle of the Wilderness on May 6, the regiment's gallant conduct materially assisted in restoring the morale of Winfield S. Hancock's II Corps which had been shattered by James Longstreet's initial attack on that day. In the melee Connor's thigh bone was shattered by a bullet, a wound which incapacitated him for further service. He was promoted to brigadier general of volunteers to rank from June 11, 1864, and was mustered out of the service on April 7, 1866. The same month a fall in his home fractured his injured leg and he was confined to his house for two years. In 1868 he was appointed assessor of internal revenue; in 1874, collector for the Augusta district; and the year following, was nominated for governor on the Republican ticket. General Connor was elected by a sizeable majority and twice reelected, serving from January, 1876, until January, 1879. From 1882 until 1886, during the administration of President Arthur, Connor was United States pension agent and was reappointed to the position by President William McKinley in 1897. A full brigadier general at the age of twenty-five, General Connor was among the nine survivors of this rank at the time of his death in Augusta, Maine, on July 9, 1917. He was buried in Forest Grove Cemetery, Augusta.

John Cook was born in Belleville, Illinois, on June 12, 1825. His mother was related by marriage to Mrs. Abraham Lincoln; his father, Daniel P. Cook, was an early Illinois member of Congress for whom

Cook County (C h i c a g o) was named. Left an orphan at an early age, Cook was educated by his grandfather, Governor (and U. S. Senator) Ninian Edwards, and attended college in Jacksonville, Illinois. After learning the mercantile business in St. Louis, he entered into a partnership with his uncle in Springfield, Illinois, and later dealt

in real estate. In 1855 he was elected mayor of Springfield; the following year, sheriff of Sangamon County; and then state quartermaster general. On April 25, 1861, Cook was commissioned colonel of the 7th Illinois Infantry, the first infantry regiment mustered into service in Illinois. For gallantry at the capture of Fort Donelson, where he commanded a brigade in C. F. Smith's division, Cook was promoted to brigadier general on March 21, 1862. After some Indian duty against the Sioux in the Department of the Northwest under General John Pope, Cook was assigned to the command of the District of Illinois, with headquarters at Springfield. He remained there until the end of the war. On August 24, 1865, he was brevetted major general of volunteers and mustered out the same day. In 1868, General Cook was elected to the lower house of the Illinois legislature from Sangamon County and in 1879 was awarded the Sioux agency in South Dakota known as the Rosebud. The later years of his life were spent in and near Ransom, Michigan, where he died on October 13, 1910. He was buried in Oak Ridge Cemetery, Springfield.

Philip St. George Cooke was born, June 13, 1809, in Leesburg, Virginia. Although he compiled a long and meritorious record in his country's service prior to the Civil War, his principal distinctions thereafter were that his son John Rogers Cooke was one of the outstanding infantry brigadiers of Robert E. Lee's Army of Northern Virginia and his son-in-law was the renowned leader of Confederate cavalry, Jeb Stuart. Cooke's adult

life, including his writings in retirement, was concerned with the U. S. Army, which he entered in 1823 as a plebe at West Point. Graduating in 1827, he spent six years at various western stations, served in the Black Hawk War, became first lieutenant of the new 1st Dragoons; went on numerous trips of exploration into the Far West; led the celebrated Mormon battalion from Sante Fe to California during the Mexican War; took part in the Utah expedition of 1857-58; wrote a treatise on cavalry tactics for the army; and was an observer of the Italian War of 1859-60. In 1861, Cooke's family divided over the issue of secession: two daughters and their husbands and one son defected to the Confederacy, Cooke and his other daughter and her husband adhered to the Union. Since 1858 he had been colonel of the 2nd Dragoons, and on November 12, 1861, was commissioned brigadier general in the Regular

Army. During the early part of the war he commanded the brigade of regular cavalry in the Washington defenses and had the direction of a division in the Peninsular campaign of 1862. He saw no further field service, but was employed on courts-martial, in district command, and as general superintendent of the recruiting service. Following the war he exercised various departmental commands and served on boards for promotion, retirement, and tactics. Having been brevetted a major general, U. S. Army, in 1865, General Cooke was retired in 1873 after more than fifty years' service. He wrote a number of books of an autobiographical nature dealing mainly with army life on the frontier. He died in Detroit, Michigan, March 20, 1895, and was buried in Elmwood Cemetery.

James Cooper, a native of Frederick County, Maryland, was born on May 8, 1810. He received his education at St. Mary's College, Emmitsburg, Pennsylvania, and at Washington College (now Washington and Jefferson) in Washington, Pennsylvania, from which he was graduated in 1832. He then studied law in the office of Thaddeus Stevens in Gettysburg. Admitted to the bar in 1834, he was elected to Congress as a Whig in 1838 and served until 1843. In the next five years Cooper was four times a member of the Pennsylvania legislature, serving one term as speaker, and was attorney general of the state in 1848. The following year he was elected to the United States Senate. During his single term as Senator, he was a member of the celebrated "committee of thirteen," which wrote the compromise measures of 1850. In 1861 his Whig principles, outspoken opposition to the Kansas-Nebraska Bill, firm adherence to the

administration, and the accident of his Maryland birth, impelled Abraham Lincoln to appoint him a brigadier general of volunteers and to authorize him to recruit a "brigade of Loyal Marylanders," with rank from May 17, 1861. During Stonewall Jackson's Valley campaign in the spring of 1862, General Cooper briefly commanded a brigade in Franz Sigel's division of N. P. Banks's army. Early in September he was ordered to take charge of a paroled prisoner-of-war camp near Columbus, Ohio; soon after, he was appointed commandant of Camp Chase (also near Columbus), a Union camp of instruction which was converted into a military prison after the Union capture of Forts Henry and Donelson. Here he died on March

28, 1863. His remains were taken to Frederick, Maryland, for interment in Mount Olivet Cemetery.

Joseph Alexander Cooper was born November 25, 1823, on a farm near Cumberland Falls in Whitley County, Kentucky, but was taken by his parents to the adjoining Tennessee county of Campbell. In the fall of 1847 Cooper served briefly in the Mexican War as a member of the 4th Tennessee Infantry. He returned to Campbell County to engage in farming near Jacksboro. Like many East Tennesseeans, Cooper was an antisecession Whig; he was elected a delegate to the 1861 Union convention at Knoxville. After some months spent in recruiting men from his county, he was mus-

tered into service at Whitesburg, Kentucky, as a captain of the 1st Tennessee (Union) Infantry. He fought at Wild Cat Mountain and

91

Fishing Creek (Mill Springs) under General George H. Thomas and in March, 1862, was made colonel of the 6th Tennessee. This regiment was in George W. Morgan's command at Cumberland Gap and retreated with it to the Ohio. After being refitted, Cooper and his men saw hard service at Murfreesboro defending ordnance trains; Cooper fought also at Chickamauga and in the Chattanooga campaign. In the course of the Atlanta campaign Cooper was promoted to brigadier general of volunteers to rank from July 30, 1864; in this capacity he commanded a brigade of the 2nd Division of the XXIII Corps from June 4 until he was temporarily advanced to divisional command after the battle of Jonesboro. He was again in command of his brigade—and intermittently commanded the 2nd Division —at Franklin and Nashville and in the closing operations of the war in North Carolina under General John M. Schofield. Brevetted major general for gallant and meritorious services at Nashville, Cooper was mustered out in 1866. In 1868 he was an unsuccessful candidate for U. S. Senator from Tennessee. The following year President U. S. Grant rewarded him with the sinecure of collector of internal revenue for the Knoxville District, an office he held for ten years. In 1880, he moved to Stafford County, Kansas, where he again engaged in farming. For more than thirty-five years a deacon of the Baptist Church, General Cooper was a longtime moderator of the South Central Baptist Association of Kansas. He died in Stafford on May 20, 1910. He was buried in the National Cemetery at Knoxville, Tennessee.

Joseph Tarr Copeland was born at Newcastle, Maine, on May 6, 1813. After graduation from Harvard College, he studied law in the office of Daniel Webster and in the early 1840's moved to Michigan. There he settled in St. Clair; was judge of the county court from 1846 to 1849; and was elected circuit judge in

1851, an office which made him automatically a justice of the supreme court of Michigan. (He is reputed to have built the first sawmill in Bay City, Michigan.) In 1859, Judge Copeland, now retired from the bench, bought an estate near Pontiac, Michigan, where he was living when the war came. In August 1861, he was commissioned lieutenant colonel of the 1st Michigan Cavalry, which formed a portion of the forces of General N. P. Banks in the Shenandoah Valley the following spring. In August, 1862, Copeland was commissioned colonel of the 5th Michigan Cavalry and was appointed brigadier general of volunteers to rank from November 29, 1862, and assigned to the command of the Michigan cavalry brigade, with duty in Washington. On the eve of the battle of Gettysburg, Copeland's regiments were taken from him and assigned to General George Á. Custer; a week after the battle Copeland was assigned to command the depot for drafted men at Annapolis Junction, Maryland. From then until the end of the war, General Copeland was in charge at Annapolis, at another draft rendezvous at Pittsburgh, and lastly of the post and military prison at Alton, Illinois. He resigned on November 8, 1865. There seems to have been no reflection on Copeland's integrity or patriotism in his relief from active field service: he was overage for a cavalry commander and with the change of army commanders from Joseph Hooker to George G. Meade, the entire Cavalry Corps was overhauled. After his retirement General Copeland lived on his Pontiac estate, which he operated as a resort hotel until 1878, when he moved to Orange Park, Florida. There he died on May 6, 1893, and was buried in Magnolia Cemetery. Senator Royal S. Copeland (1868-1938) of New York was his nephew. (74)

Michael Corcoran was born in Carrowkeel, County Donegal, Ireland, September 21, 1827. The son of an officer in the British army, he received a good education, and at the age of eighteen was appointed in the Irish constabulary. The repressive measures taken by the organization against his countrymen impelled him to resign his commission in 1849 and to emigrate to the

United States. He settled in New York and obtained a clerkship, first in the post office and later in the city register's office. Entering the 69th New York Militia as a private, he rose to colonel. Upon the occasion of the visit of the Prince of Wales (later Edward VII) in 1860, Corcoran refused to parade his regiment in the Prince's honor. For this insubordination he was court-martialed, and his trial was still pending at the outbreak of the Civil War, when the charges were dismissed to permit him to bring his command to the defense of Washington. The 69th Militia, which was not mustered into Federal service, fought at the battle of Manassas (Bull Run) in W. T. Sherman's brigade and here Colonel Corcoran was wounded and captured. Corcoran became a pawn in a game played by the Union and Confederate authorities: he was reserved for reprisal in the event of the execution of the crews of captured privateers by United States authorities. After being shuttled back and forth between a number of Confederate prison camps, Corcoran was exchanged in August, 1862, and was promoted to brigadier general of volunteers to rank from the date of the battle of Manassas the previous year. In the spring of 1863, while commanding a division of three brigades in the army of North Carolina, he took part in the Suffolk campaign in southeastern Virginia. Shortly after the battle of Gettysburg, General Corcoran and his brigade, "The Irish Legion," were transferred to the Department of Washington and assigned to Rufus King's division; Corcoran succeeded to command of the division in October. On December 22, 1863, while riding in the company of General Thomas Meagher near Fairfax Court House, Virginia, where his division was in winter quarters, Corcoran's horse fell, killing him. He was buried in Calvary Cemetery, Long Island City, New York.

John Murray Corse was born April 27, 1835, in Pittsburgh, Pennsylvania; at the age of seven he was taken by his parents to Burlington, Iowa, where his father operated a book and stationery business and served six times as mayor. Young Corse studied law, was admitted to the bar, and in 1860 was the Democratic candidate for secretary of state. (From 1853 to 1855 he was a student at the U. S. Military Academy, where his middle name was spelled Murry.) (75) He became major of the 6th Iowa in July, 1861, and served on the staff of General John Pope during the early operations on the Mississippi. Pro-moted to lieutenant colonel and to colonel, Corse demonstrated conspicuous ability at Corinth and in the Vicksburg campaign, after which he was promoted to brigadier general of volunteers from August 11, 1863. Corse was badly wounded—bruised by a spent ball—at the battle of Chattanooga, but returned to the army in time to serve as General W. T. Sherman's inspector general during the Atlanta campaign. On July 26, 1864, he was assigned to the command of the 2nd Division of the XVI Corps. In the course of Confederate General John B. Hood's move northward to sever Sherman's communications, Corse was the hero of the "battle of Allatoona Pass" in which S. G. French's Confederate division attempted to dislodge Corse's men from blockhouses designed to protect the Western and Atlantic Railroad. According to many accounts, no more severe fighting was ever experienced by men in Sherman's army; (76) there were more than 1,500 dead and wounded out of 5,200 engaged on both sides. The following day Corse telegraphed Sherman: "I am short of a cheekbone, and one ear, but am able to whip all hell yet." (77) He took part in the "March to the Sea" and in the campaign of the Carolinas as commander of the 4th Division of the XV Corps. Refusing a proffered appointment of lieutenant colonel in the Regular Army, General Corse was mustered out in 1866 with the brevet of major general and appointed collector of internal revenue at Chicago. Some years later he moved to Boston, where he became chairman of the state Democratic committee and received the postmastership of Boston from President Cleveland. He died at Winchester, Massachusetts, April 27, 1893, and was taken to Burlington for burial in Aspen Grove Cemetery.

Darius Nash Couch was born on a farm in Putnam County, New York, on July 23, 1822. After a common school education, he entered West Point and was graduated in the class of 1846 along with George B. McClellan and Stonewall Jackson. Forty-four graduates survived to fight in the Civil War and nineteen of these became general officers of full rank in either the United States or Confederate armies. Couch was brevetted for gallant and meritorious conduct in the Mexican War and after eight years' service as a lieutenant of artillery, mainly at eastern stations, resigned his commission in 1855 in order to enter the copper fabricating business of his wife's family at Taunton, Massachusetts. Couch

was colonel of the 7th Massachusetts volunteers in Washington on the eve of the battle of First Manassas, an engagement in which this regiment did not participate. With the accession of his classmate McClellan

to chief command of the Union armies, Couch was promoted to brigadier general of volunteers on August 9, 1861, with rank from May 17. After a winter spent in training the raw recruits of the Army of the Potomac, he compiled a distinguished record in the Peninsular campaign of the following spring, commanding a division of Keyes's IV Corps. Illness plagued Couch, and in July, 1862, he tendered his resignation, which McClellan refused to forward to the War Department. Instead Couch was immediately appointed major general to rank from July 4. He commanded his division at Sharpsburg (Antietam) and the II Corps at Fredericksburg under Ambrose E. Burnside and at Chancellorsville under Joseph Hooker. His distrust of

Hooker's capacity for high command was profound and unconcealed. After the debacle in the tangled Wilderness, Couch applied for relief from duty with the Army of the Potomac. This move, coupled with his close relationship with McClellan, ended his career. He commanded the Pennsylvania militia during the Gettysburg campaign and in 1864 was assigned a division of the XXIII Corps, which he led with distinction at the battle of Nashville (where he had a horse killed under him) and in the campaign of the Carolinas. General Couch resigned on May 26, 1865. After the war, because he was a Democrat and a McClellan supporter, he failed to gain the governorship of Massachusetts and could not hold the collectorship of the port of Boston, a post to which he had been appointed by President Andrew Johnson. After 1870, he lived in Norwalk, Connecticut, and in the ensuing years was at various times state quartermaster general and adjutant general. He died in Norwalk, February 12, 1897, and was buried in Taunton.

Robert Cowdin (occasionally misspelled "Coudin") was born in Jamaica, Vermont, on September 18, 1805. After receiving an education in his hometown, he moved to Boston at the age of twenty to engage in the lumber business. He was a member of the 2nd Massachusetts militia regiment and was its colonel at the outbreak of the Civil War. On May 25, 1861, Cowdin was mustered into Federal service as colonel of the 1st Massachusetts Infantry, the first volunteer regiment to be enlisted in the state for three-year service. The regiment took part with I. B. Richardson's brigade of Tyler's 1st Division in the battle of First Manassas (Bull Run), where Cowdin's horse was killed. In the spring of 1862, Cowdin participated in the Peninsular campaign, fighting at Williamsburg, Fair Oaks (Seven Pines), Glendale, and Malvern Hill. For bravery at Williamsburg, he was recommended for promotion by his brigade commander General Joseph Hooker. He was appointed brigadier general of volunteers to rank from September 26, 1862. During the fall and winter of 1862, General Cowdin commanded a brigade of John J. Abercrombie's division in the defenses of Washington. Perhaps because of his age, the Senate failed to confirm Cowdin to the grade of brigadier during the session in which he was nominated; accordingly, on March 4, 1863, the appointment expired. On March 30 he was relieved from duty and returned home. At the close of the war he became captain of the "Ancient and Honorable Artillery Company" of Boston. Both before and after his war service he directed various public institutions, serving ten terms on the council and board of aldermen. General Cowdin died in Boston, July 9, 1874, and was buried in Mount Auburn Cemetery, Cambridge. (78)

Jacob Dolson Cox descended from a Dutch colonial family which had settled in New York in 1705. He was born on October 27, 1828, in Montreal, Canada, where his father was engaged in a construction

project. Cox became a legal clerk, worked in a bank, and then attended Oberlin College, from which he was graduated in 1851. He resumed the study of law and in 1853 commenced practice in Warren, Ohio, the home of his wife's family. A strong abolitionist, he was a delegate to the 1855 Columbus convention which organized the Ohio Republican party and was elected to the state senate in 1858. There he came to know intimately state Senator James A. Garfield, Governor-elect William Dennison, and Governor Salmon P. Chase. Cox entered the army on April 23, 1861, as a brigadier general of Ohio state troops and was subsequently appointed a brigadier general of United States volunteers to rank from May 17, 1861. He took part in the campaign in western Virginia under General George B. McClellan and remained in command there until August, 1862, when he was assigned to John Pope's Army of Virginia. At South Mountain and Sharpsburg he commanded a division and for a short time led the IX Corps. He was appointed a major general of volunteers to rank from October 6, 1862, which expired the following March due to an excess of major generals over those provided for by law, but he was reappointed and confirmed on December 7, 1864. During most of the year 1863, Cox commanded the District of Ohio; the following year he directed a division of the XXIII Corps in the Atlanta campaign and at F r a n k l i n and Nashville. In 1865 he was in North Carolina with John M. Schofield, participating in the affair at Kinston, March 14, 1865, which connected Schofield's troops with W. T. Sherman's northbound columns. Before being mustered out, General Cox was elected governor of Ohio, an office which he occupied in 1866-67. However, his moderate views on Negro suffrage and his endorsement of President Andrew Johnson's Reconstruction policy resulted in his failure to win renomination. Having finally abandoned Johnson, Cox became Secretary of the Interior upon the accession of U. S. Grant. As a proponent of civil service reform, he soon became disenchanted with "the plans of our active political managers" and in the fall of 1870 submitted his resignation. Grant's characteristic rejoinder to what he felt to be insubordination by a junior officer was: "The trouble was that General Cox thought the Interior Department was the whole government, and that Cox was the Interior Department." Returning to Ohio, Cox resumed law practice in Cincinnati. In 1873 he became president of the Wabash Railway and in 1876 was elected to Congress, where he served one term. From 1881 until 1897 General Cox was dean of the Cincinnati Law School and for four years of that time also served as president of the University of Cincinnati. He declined President William McKinley's offer of the Spanish Ministry in 1897. During the last quarter-century of his life, General Cox was a prolific writer on military topics connected with the Civil War. One of these, a commentary on the battle and campaign of Second Manassas, reflected little credit on Cox, since it was a barefaced fraud which attempted to prevent the exoneration of Fitz John Porter and to sustain the reputations of those who had condemned Porter. (79) On August 4, 1900, Cox died near Gloucester, Massachusetts, while on a summer vacation with a son. He was buried in Spring Grove Cemetery, Cincinnati.

James Craig was born on February 28, 1817, in Washington County, Pennsylvania. His parents moved first to Mansfield, Ohio, and then

to New Philadelphia, Ohio, where Craig was admitted to the bar in 1839. In 1844 he went to St. Joseph, Missouri, his home for the rest of his life. As a captain of the Missouri Mounted Volunteers, he took part in the Mexican War and was honorably mustered out on November 8, 1848. Thereafter he served as state attorney for his district from 1852 until 1856, as a state senator, and as a Democratic Congressman from 1857 until March 3, 1861. Having been defeated for renomination in 1860, he resumed his law practice until Abraham Lincoln appointed him a brigadier general of United States volunteers to rank from March 21, 1862. The appointment was openly political, designed to retain Craig's Missouri Democratic admirers within the Union fold. In April, Craig was sent west with a detachment to protect the route of the Overland Mail and in November was assigned to the command of the District of

Nebraska. In May, 1863, he resigned his Federal commission, but in May, 1864, was appointed a brigadier in the Missouri State Militia, a post he resigned in January, 1865. General Craig had been instrumental while in the state senate in securing a charter for the Hannibal and St. Joseph Railroad, the first constructed west of the Mississippi, and he was its president from 1861 to 1872, except for two brief intervals. He built the Kansas City, St. Joseph & Council Bluffs Railroad and was its first president; he was also president of the St. Joseph & Denver Railroad, now the Grand Island branch of the Union Pacific. Toward the end of his life he served for two years as comptroller of the city of St. Joseph. He died there, October 21, 1888, and was buried in Mount Mora Cemetery. (80)

Samuel Wylie Crawford was born in Franklin County, Pennsylvania, November 8, 1829. After graduation from the University of Pennsylvania in 1846, he attended the university's medical school from which he was graduated in 1850. The following year he accepted an appointment as assistant surgeon in the army and served at various points on the western frontier until 1860. He was then stationed at Fort Moultrie in Charleston Harbor and later at Fort Sumter, where he had command of a battery during the bombardment which signaled the beginning of the Civil War. Soon after, he vacated his staff commission by becoming major of the newly authorized 13th Infantry. During the Shenandoah Valley campaign of 1862, Crawford, who had been promoted to brigadier general of volunteers to rank

from April 25, was highly praised by N. P. Banks, although "yet unassigned to [a] separate command." At Cedar Mountain his brigade suffered 50 per cent casualties; at Sharpsburg he commanded a division and was severely wounded. In May, 1863, Crawford was assigned to command the Pennsylvania Reserve Corps then in the defenses of Washington. He led them with great distinction at Gettysburg—where they made up the 3rd Division of Sykes's V Corps —and in all the operations of the Army of the Potomac until the close of the war. Crawford was brevetted for gallantry in the battles of the Wilderness, Spotsylvania, Five Forks, and the siege of Petersburg. In the meantime, he was brevetted through all grades to that of major general in both the regular and volunteer services and had also been commissioned lieutenant colonel of the 2nd Infantry on February 17, 1864. Mustered out of volunteer service in 1866, General Crawford served with his regiment at various points in the South and was promoted to colonel in 1869. On February 19, 1873, he was retired and in 1875 was promoted to brigadier on the retired list under a newly enacted statute. General Crawford subsequently made his home in Philadelphia where he died on November 3, 1892. He was buried in Laurel Hill Cemetery.

Thomas Leonidas Crittenden—son of United States Senator John J. Crittenden, younger brother of Major General George B. Crittenden of the Confederate Army, and first

cousin of General Thomas T. Crittenden—was born in Russellville, Kentucky, May 15, 1819. He was admitted to the bar in 1840 and two years later was elected commonwealth attorney for his district. At the outbreak of the Mexican War, Crittenden enlisted and served successively as aide to General Zachary Taylor (81) and as colonel of the 3rd Kentucky Infantry, whose major was John Cabell Breckinridge, later Vice-President of the United States and Confederate major general and Secretary of War. In 1849, President Taylor appointed Crittenden consul at Liverpool. In 1853 he returned to Kentucky and resided in Frankfort and Louisville. Adhering to the Union, as did his father, Crittenden became commander of those state forces which remained loyal after General Simon B. Buckner had led the others south for service in the Confederacy. Crittenden was commissioned a brigadier general of volunteers in September, 1861, and at the battle of Shiloh the following spring commanded the 5th Division of Don Carlos Buell's Army of the Ohio, which arrived in time to reinforce U. S. Grant's troops. Crittenden was commissioned major general on July 17, 1862. During the campaigns of Tullahoma and Chickamauga he was one of General William S. Rosecrans' principal lieutenants, commanding the XXI Corps in the latter campaign. Subsequently, Rosecrans attempted to transfer some of the responsibility for the disaster at Chickamauga by preferring charges against Crittenden, as well as against Generals Alex. McD. McCook and James S. Negley. All were formally acquitted following an exhaustive inquiry conducted at Nashville, but none of their military careers was thereafter embellished. Crittenden resigned his volunteer commission in December, 1864, and in January, 1866, was appointed state treasurer of Kentucky. Subsequently, President Andrew Johnson offered him a colonelcy in the Regular

Army, which he accepted, serving until retirement in 1881. General Crittenden died at Annandale, Staten Island, New York, October 23, 1893, and was buried in Frankfort, Kentucky.

Thomas Turpin Crittenden was born in Huntsville, Alabama, October 16, 1825. His father was a younger brother of Senator John J. Crittenden of Kentucky and he was, accordingly, a first cousin of both Major Generals George B. Critten-

den, C. S. Army, and Thomas L. Crittenden, U. S. Army. (He is also sometimes confused with another first cousin, Governor Thomas Theodore Crittenden of Missouri.) Crittenden's parents remained briefly in Alabama and then settled in Texas, where his father died and his mother took up a homestead near Galveston. He was graduated from Transylvania College at Lexington, Kentucky,

where he studied law; he commenced practice at Hannibal, Missouri. During the Mexican War, Crittenden served as a second lieutenant of a Missouri volunteer battalion for more than a year, after which he made his residence at Madison, Indiana. On April 19, 1861, he entered the service of the United States as captain of the 6th Indiana and was appointed its colonel on April 27. This was a three-month regiment which reenlisted for three years in September. It fought at Philippi and Corrick's Ford in the western Virginia campaign and after reorganization was stationed in Kentucky until the battle of Shiloh, where it was engaged on the second day. Crittenden was promoted to brigadier general on April 28, 1862. On July 13, 1862, while in command of the post at Murfreesboro, Tennessee, Crittenden and all the troops in the vicinity were surprised and captured by Confederate General Nathan B. Forrest, an action characterized by General Don Carlos Buell as follows: "Few more disgraceful examples of neglect of duty and lack of good conduct can be found in the history of wars." In justice to Crittenden, it must be said that he had assumed command only the day before and was not familiar with the arrangements in force for the protection of the town. Nevertheless, the incident virtually ended his career, and after his release in October he saw no further important service. He resigned on May 5, 1863. In 1868, General Crittenden moved to Washington and in 1885 retired and moved to San Diego, where he engaged in real estate development. He died while on a vacation trip at East Gloucester, Massachusetts, September 5, 1905, and is buried in Arlington National Cemetery. (82)

Marcellus Monroe Crocker was born February 6, 1830, in Franklin, Indiana. He entered West Point with the class of 1851, but left in

February, 1849, to study law; he began practice in Des Moines, Iowa. On May 27, 1861, he was mustered into the volunteer army as a captain of the 2nd Iowa Infantry and on May 31 became its major. In September he was made lieutenant colonel and in December, colonel of the 13th Iowa. During Crocker's association with the 2nd Iowa it performed mainly railroad guard duty in Missouri. The 13th Iowa's first important service was at Shiloh, where Crocker led it in the 1st Brigade of John McClernand's division and where it sustained 172 casualties. Shortly thereafter Crocker was given command of the "Iowa Brigade," 6th

Division, Army of the Tennessee. He took part in the battle of Corinth in October, 1862, and was promoted to brigadier general to rank from November 29 of that year. In the Vicksburg campaign he directed a division of James B. McPherson's XVII Corps. In September, 1863, his division conducted a minor raid into Louisiana; then it was in garrison at Natchez during the fall and winter. Crocker had long suffered from tuberculosis and in May, 1864, while the XVII Corps was en route to Georgia to join W. T. Sherman's army, he was relieved because of illness and the following month submitted his resignation, which was not accepted. Instead, he was ordered to duty in New Mexico, where it was thought his health might improve. In December, 1864, he felt so much better that he was ordered to report to General G. H. Thomas at Nashville. U. S. Grant remarked of Crocker at the time: "I have never seen but three or four division commanders his equal." (83) However, the order assigning him to Thomas (84) either miscarried or was countermanded, since in March he was ordered to Washington instead. (85) Here his condition gradually worsened, and he died on August 26, 1865. General Crocker's remains were returned to Des Moines for burial in Woodland Cemetery.

George Crook was born near Dayton, Ohio, September 8, 1828. Securing his early education in the common schools, he was graduated from West Point in 1852, ranking thirty-eighth in a class of forty-three, and was commissioned in the 4th Infantry. Until the outbreak of the Civil War, Crook was stationed

102

mainly in northern California and in Washington. On September 12, 1861, he was appointed colonel of the 36th Ohio and with his regiment served in western Virginia. In August, 1862, he was commissioned brigadier general and took part in the Maryland campaign, engaging in the battles of South Mountain and Sharpsburg in command of a brigade of three Ohio regiments, including his own. In 1863, Crook commanded a cavalry division of George H. Thomas' Army of the Cumberland and took part in the Chickamauga campaign. The following year he was again assigned to the Kanawha District in western Virginia where he defeated and routed the forces of Confederate General A. G. Jenkins at the battle of Cloyd's Mountain. That August he was given command of the Department of Western Virginia and, subsequently, of one of the three corps of Sheridan's army in the Shenandoah. He was promoted to major general of volunteers to rank from October 21, 1864. The following February he returned to the command of his department and made his headquarters at Cumberland, Maryland, at that time a town of some eight thousand inhabitants. Here, one of the most daring feats of the war was performed at Crook's expense. Crook's private rooms were in the Revere House, a hotel operated by one Daily (or Dailey), whose daughter Mary later became Crook's wife. Daily's son was a member of Captain Jesse McNeill's band of Confederate "Partisan Rangers." Early in the morning of February 21 these sixty young men overpowered or deceived the Union pickets and, in the face of some ten thousand Union troops, captured and made off with Generals Crook and Benjamin F. Kelley who was also engaged to a Cumberland belle. They were taken to Richmond, where they were paroled and subsequently exchanged—Crook, as of March 20, 1865. (86) During the final operations culminating in the surrender at Appomattox, General Crook commanded a division of cavalry in the Army of the Potomac and was brevetted major general in the regular service. In the army reorganization of 1866, Crook became lieutenant colonel of the 23rd Infantry. For the next twenty years he enjoyed unusually rapid promotion to the grade of major general and was constantly on the western frontier, pacifying the various tribes of hostile Indians. One of his few failures was against Geronimo's Southern Chiricahua Apaches; their surrender was engineered by General Nelson A. Miles a few months after Crook's relief.

From 1888 his headquarters was in Chicago, where he commanded the Division of the Missouri until his death on March 21, 1890. He was buried in Arlington National Cemetery.

John Thomas Croxton was born in Bourbon County, Kentucky, November 20, 1836. (87) He was graduated from Yale in 1857; studied law in Georgetown, Kentucky; and began practice in Paris, Kentucky,

in August, 1859. On October 9, 1861, Croxton was mustered into United States service as lieutenant colonel of the 4th Kentucky Mounted Infantry; he became its colonel the following May. He was made brigadier general of volunteers in July, 1864, and brevetted major general at the close of the war. In the interval he compiled a most creditable military record. His first battle was that of Mill Springs under George H. Thomas.

In command of his regiment, Croxton was present at Perryville, although not engaged, and in the campaign of Tullahoma, which maneuvered Braxton Bragg out of Tennessee. In the battle of Chickamauga, Croxton commanded a brigade of John M. Brannan's division of Thomas' XIV Corps. Here he was "s e v e r e l y and painfully wounded" on September 20 and eulogized by Brannan as the "gallant and dashing Croxton." During the Atlanta campaign, Croxton commanded a cavalry brigade which, after the capture of Atlanta, was sent with Thomas to Nashville. In Thomas' efforts to concentrate his forces before he could be struck by the hard-marching forces of John B. Hood, Croxton's command displayed considerable *esprit* in the face of Nathan B. Forrest's troopers. During the battle of Nashville, Croxton's brigade was prominent in the rout and dispersal of Hood's army. At the close of hostilities he was placed in command of the military District of Southwest Georgia, with headquarters at Macon. In December, 1865, General Croxton resigned his commission and returned to Kentucky, where he resumed his law practice and lived on his farm near Paris. A few years later he was a prime mover in establishing the Louisville *Commercial,* a Republican paper. In 1873, he accepted the office of United States minister to Bolivia. He died there, on April 16, 1874, and his body was returned to Paris for burial.

Charles Cruft was born in Terre Haute, Indiana, on January 12, 1826. After graduation from Wabash College in 1842, he taught

school, worked as a bank clerk, studied law, and was admitted to the bar in 1848. From 1855 until 1858 he served as president of the St. Louis, Alton, and Terre Haute Railroad. At the outbreak of the Civil War he was in Washington and witnessed the battle of First Manassas (Bull Run) as a spectator. On September 20, 1861, he was mustered into the volunteer army as colonel of the 31st Indiana Infantry. With this regiment he took part in the capture of Fort Donelson, where he commanded a brigade in Lew Wallace's division; the battle of Shiloh, where he was severely wounded in the leg and shoulder; and in the siege of Corinth. He was promoted to brigadier general of volunteers to rank from July 16, 1862. Cruft distinguished himself at the disastrous battle of Richmond, Kentucky; was present, but not engaged, at Perryville; and commanded a brigade of J. M.

Palmer's division at Murfreesboro and Chickamauga. Thereafter he was given command of a division in Granger's IV Corps, which he led in the battle of Chattanooga. Cruft and his division were sent to the relief of Knoxville; had a minor role in the Atlanta campaign; accompanied W. T. Sherman to Alabama; and then proceeded into Tennessee to oppose John B. Hood's invasion. At the battle of Nashville, Cruft commanded the "provisional division," Army of the Cumberland—an outfit composed primarily of detachments of Negro troops from the XIV, XV, XVII, and XX Corps "which had been unable to rejoin their proper commands in Georgia." At the end of the war Cruft was stationed at Huntsville, Alabama. He had been brevetted a major general to rank from March 5, 1865, and was honorably mustered out on August 24. Afterward he resumed residence in Terre Haute and revived his law practice. General Cruft rose high in the Masonic order, becoming a member of the Supreme Commandery, Knights Templar of the United States. He died in Terre Haute, March 23, 1883, and was buried there in Woodlawn Cemetery. (88)

George Washington Cullum was born in New York City, February 25, 1809. When he was a child, his parents moved to Meadville, Pennsylvania, from which state he was appointed to the Military Academy at the age of twenty. He was graduated third in the class of 1833 and was commissioned into the Engineer Corps. As an officer in this elite organization, Cullum had a prominent part in harbor

bequeathed to the Military Academy and the American Geographical Society. Cullum is best known for his monumental compilation, *Biographical Register of the Officers and Graduates of the United States Military Academy,* published in three volumes in 1890 and supplemented at ten-year intervals by a provision of his will. This work gives a minute record of the military service of every graduate of West Point. Although the work is open to criticism in some respects because of Cullum's intense anti-Confederate bias, its value transcends all such considerations. General Cullum died in New York City, February 29, 1892, and was buried in Green-Wood Cemetery, Brooklyn.

defɛnse work in most of the principal Atlantic Coast ports, performed instruction duty at West Point and at New York, but by 1861 was still only a captain. During the first months of the Civil War, Cullum served as aide to Winfield Scott, then commander in chief. His principal war service, however, was performed as chief of staff to General Henry W. Halleck, with rank of brigadier general of volunteers from November 1, 1861. After leaving Halleck's staff in September, 1864 General Cullum was superintendent of the Military Academy for two years. He then discharged various engineering duties until his retirement in 1874, with rank of colonel. The following year he married Halleck's widow, a granddaughter of Alexander Hamilton; he thus became a brother-in-law to General Schuyler Hamilton. He inherited a substantial fortune from his wife, much of which he

Newton Martin Curtis was born on May 21, 1835, in De Peyster, New York, the son of a veteran of the War of 1812. As a young man he had a varied career as a teacher in Illinois, law student, postmas-

ter of his native village, and manager of his father's farm. Upon the fall of Sumter, Curtis entered the army as captain of Company G of the 16th New York. While leading his unit at West Point on the Virginia Peninsula in May, 1862, he was "severely wounded." From that time until his participation in the two attacks on Fort Fisher, North Carolina, Curtis' war service was confined mainly to departmental duty, enlivened principally by his engagement in the battle of Cold Harbor and the subsequent investment of Petersburg as a part of Benjamin F. Butler's Army of the James. When Butler was dispatched to reduce Fort Fisher, the last seacoast stronghold of the Confederacy, Curtis commanded a brigade in the division of Adelbert Ames, who later became Butler's son-in-law. The affair became a fiasco when Butler called off the attack at the very moment of victory. Subsequently, in January, 1865, a new expedition under Quincy A. Gillmore successfully stormed the fort and Curtis was later awarded the Congressional medal for being the first Federal soldier inside the works. For many months he had been colonel of the 142nd New York; he was now speedily made brigadier general and brevetted major general of volunteers for his fearless conduct on that occasion. Mustered out in 1866, he made his home in Ogdensburg, New York. Thereafter, for almost half a century, General Curtis was a distinguished representative of his state. He was successively a collector of customs, special agent for the Treasury Department, member of the New York State Assembly, and

from 1891 to 1897 a representative in Congress. An avowed opponent of the death penalty for criminals, he wrote prolifically on the subject. He also made a contribution to Civil War history with his book, *From Bull Run to Chancellorsville.* He died in New York City, January 8, 1910, and was buried in Ogdensburg.

Samuel Ryan Curtis was born February 3, 1805, in Clinton County, New York. His father, a veteran of the Revolutionary War, and his mother were both originally from Connecticut. Soon after Cur-

tis' birth, the family moved to Licking County, Ohio, from which state he was appointed to West Point. After graduation in 1831, he served a year in garrison at Fort Gibson, Indian Territory, resigning on June 30, 1832. For the next seven years Curtis was a civil engineer in Ohio; in his free time he studied law and interested himself in the activities of the state militia. Upon the outbreak of the Mexican War he was appointed adjutant general of Ohio but soon accepted the colonelcy of the 2nd Ohio Volunteers, which he led with distinction in General Zachary Taylor's army. He moved to Keokuk, Iowa, and later lived in St. Louis. While in Keokuk he engaged in engineering and in the practice of law, was elected mayor in 1856, and the same year was elected to Congress, where he served three successive terms. Mustered into the Union army as colonel of the 2nd Iowa, he was appointed brigadier general of volunteers to rank from May 17, 1861, and resigned his Congressional seat on August 6 in order to accept the commission. The following spring he was in command of the Federal army which defeated the Confederates at the celebrated battle of Pea Ridge, Arkansas. For this achievement he was appointed major general on March 21, 1862. That autumn he was given command of the Department of the Missouri; however, his falling out with Governor William Gamble resulted in the removal of Curtis in May, 1863, by President Abraham Lincoln, who remarked that he had no authority to remove Gamble. General Curtis then commanded the Department of Kansas and later that of the Northwest until the close of the war. In August, 1865, he was commissioned to negotiate treaties with the Sioux, Cheyenne, and other Plains tribes and in November of that year was appointed to a commission to examine and

report upon the construction of the fledgling Union Pacific Railroad, then building west from Omaha. While on this work, he died at Council Bluffs, Iowa, December 26, 1866, and was buried in Oakland Cemetery, Keokuk.

George Armstrong Custer was born on December 5, 1839, in the hamlet of New Rumley, three miles east of Scio, Harrison County, Ohio. Destined to become one of the most celebrated and controversial figures to emerge

from the Civil War, he was called "Armstrong," "Autie" (his own childhood pronunciation of the former), "Fanny" (applied to him in his plebe year at West Point), or "Curly" (derived from the shoulder-length reddish locks he wore at times). During much of his boyhood he lived with his half-sister and his brother-in-law in Monroe, Michigan. Prior to entering West

Point in 1857, he taught school in Ohio. According to one story, Custer owed his appointment to the Military Academy to the father of a young lady who wished to get him out of the neighborhood. (89) His career at West Point was not particularly impressive: he graduated last in the class of June, 1861; had been close to expulsion in each of his four years because of excessive demerits; and was under detention at the time of his graduation. He was immediately ordered to duty with the Army of the Potomac and on the eve of the battle of First Manassas, the young lieutenant was detailed by Lieutenant General Winfield Scott to carry dispatches to General Irwin McDowell at Centerville. Perhaps the best appraisal of Custer's career in the Civil War was written by his fellow commander, Major General James Harrison Wilson: "The modest man is not always the best soldier. . . . Some of the best, while shamelessly sounding their own praises, were brave, dashing, and enterprising to an unusual degree." Custer was all these things. He served on the staffs of Generals George B. McClellan and Alfred Pleasonton, with the temporary rank of captain, until the spring of 1863, distinguishing himself on a dozen occasions. On June 29, 1863, he was jumped from first lieutenant to brigadier general of volunteers and was assigned to command a brigade in Judson Kilpatrick's division, which he led a few days later at Gettysburg. Until the end of the war Custer fought with the utmost distinction in all the cavalry battles of the Army of the Potomac; he was in command of a division in the Shenandoah and cut off the last avenue of escape for Robert E. Lee's army at Appomattox. (Here Philip Sheridan purchased the table on which U. S. Grant wrote the terms of surrender, for presentation to Mrs. Custer.) A week later he was made a full major general of volunteers, having been previously brevetted to the same rank in both the regular and volunteer services. In 1866, Custer was appointed lieutenant colonel of the newly authorized 7th Cavalry, remaining its active commander until his death. He took part in Winfield S. Hancock's expedition of 1867 against the Sioux and Cheyenne, but was court-martialed and suspended from duty for paying an unauthorized visit to his wife, although he was restored to duty the following year by Sheridan. He bears the blame for destroying an unoffending Cheyenne village on the Washita in November, 1868. He also took part in Stanley's Yellowstone expedition in 1873 and the next year he led an exploring expedition into the Black Hills, which precipitated the great Sioux (and Cheyenne) outbreak of 1876 and culminated in the battle of Little Big Horn on June 25, 1876. The campaign envisioned two supporting columns, one under Custer, the other under General John Gibbon, with General Alfred H. Terry in over-all command. Upon discovering the huge Indian village, Custer divided his own command into three battalions and without waiting for his supports led an attack which resulted in the extermination of his immediate command and a total loss of some 266 officers and men. On June 28 the bodies were given hasty burial on the field. In the following year, what may have been Custer's remains were disinterred and given a military funeral at West Point. Custer had been a prolific writer and Mrs. Custer, who survived him by fifty-seven years, helped to create what might be called the Custer myth. When all is said on both sides, Custer's military philosophy, eminently successful on scores of fields, was to pitch in against any odds and then extricate himself and his command later if the going got too rough. (90)

Lysander Cutler was born on February 16, 1807, in Worcester County, Massachusetts, the son of a farmer. Over his father's objections, he worked to improve the rudimentary education he had received in the local school; he studied surveying and then embarked upon a career as a schoolmaster.

At the age of twenty-one he moved to Dexter, Maine, where the pupils of the local school had "flogged and ejected" the last several teachers who had attempted discipline. Cutler spent his first day in authority in "the thorough flogging of every bully in the school." Soon after, he undertook various business enterprises, including woolen mills, a foundry, a flour mill, and a saw mill. He was also prominent in civic affairs as selectman, railroad director, college trustee (Tufts), militia colonel, and state senator. Ruined financially by the depression of 1857, he moved to Milwaukee, where he attempted to perfect title to certain iron ore deposits and subsequently operated as a grain broker. At the outbreak of the Civil War, Cutler was appointed colonel of the 6th Wisconsin, a regiment which ultimately became a unit of the famous "Iron Brigade." Cutler's first important service was in the campaign of Second Manassas, where he was severely wounded in the leg. At the Battle of Fredericksburg, he commanded, temporarily, a brigade of Abner Doubleday's division, I Corps, and he was commissioned a brigadier general, his rank to date from November 29, 1862. At the battles of Chancellorsville and Gettysburg he commanded the 4th brigade of Wadsworth's division. Fighting gallantly, his men suffered heavy losses. After the reorganization of the army in the spring of 1864, Cutler was assigned a brigade in the V Corps, and after James S. Wadsworth was killed at the Wilderness, Cutler assumed command of the 4th Division. By August 13, 1864, this organization's original regiments were reduced from 3,742 to 1,324 by attrition suffered in front of Petersburg, and its commander's health was wrecked by wounds and e x p o s u r e. Relieved from field duty at his own request in September, Cutler spent the balance of the war directing the Jackson, Michigan, draft rendezvous and was brevetted major general as of August 19, 1864. General Cutler resigned on June 30, 1865, and returned to Milwaukee, where he died July 30, 1866. He was buried in Forest Home Cemetery.

Napoleon J a c k s o n Tecumseh Dana was born on April 15, 1822, at Fort Sullivan, Eastport, Maine, where his father, an officer of the 1st Artillery, was stationed.

His paternal grandfather had been a Revolutionary naval o f f i c e r. Young Dana entered the Military Academy at the age of sixteen; he was graduated in 1842 and posted to the 7th Infantry. He fought in the M e x i c a n War—at Cerro Gordo he was so severely wounded that he was left for dead until picked up by a burial detail thirty-six hours later. In 1855 he resigned his commission to engage in the banking business in St. Paul, Minnesota, but maintained his interest in military affairs by serving as a brigadier of Minnesota militia. On October 2, 1861, he was appointed colonel of the 1st Minnesota, a regiment which he commanded at the disastrous battle of Ball's Bluff. The following spring, having been commissioned a brigadier general of volunteers, Dana commanded a brigade of John Sedgwick's division of the II Corps. In September he was badly wounded at Sharpsburg and incapacitated for months; he was promoted to major general, however, to rank from November 29, 1862. After his return to duty in July, 1863, General Dana saw no further important field service, but successively commanded the defenses of Philadelphia, the operations at Brazos Santiago Pass on the Texas Gulf Coast, the XIII Corps, and various districts along the Mississippi River which by the autumn of 1864 had ceased to be a theater of active operations. In December, 1864, he was placed in charge of the Department of Mississippi, a post he occupied until he submitted his resignation on May 27, 1865. Until 1871, General Dana was general agent of the American-Russian Commercial Company of San Francisco in Alaska and at Washington, D. C. He later was an excutive of several railroads; commissioner in charge of railroad pools at St. Louis; and deputy commissioner of pensions for the United States government from 1895 until 1897. In 1894 he had been placed on the army retired list as a captain. General Dana spent his last years in Portsmouth, New Hampshire, where he died on July 15, 1905, and was buried.

John Wynn Davidson was born in Fairfax County, Virginia, on August 18, 1824. His grandfather had been a general officer in the Revolution and his father, who was graduated from West Point in

1815, died in the service twenty-five years after his graduation. Young Davidson was graduated from the Academy in 1845 and, after frontier duty in Kansas and Wisconsin, took part in the Mexican War, mainly in California with the so-called Army of the West. He was promoted to captain of the 1st Dragoons in 1855,

fought Indians throughout New Mexico and California, and was wounded in an engagement with the Jicarilla Apaches. At the beginning of the Civil War he was stationed at Fort Tejon near Los Angeles, and it is alleged that he declined a commission in the Confederate Army. After duty in the Washington defenses, Davidson, appointed a brigadier general of volunteers to rank from February 3, 1862, perhaps in reward for his adherence to the Union, commanded creditably a brigade of W. F. Smith's division of Keyes's IV Corps in the Peninsular campaign. Late in the summer of 1862 he was assigned to the command of the District of St. Louis, his wife's hometown. The rest of his Civil War career was spent in Missouri and Arkansas, where he was commander of the Army of Southeast Missouri in 1863 and the Army of Arkansas in 1864 and chief of cavalry of the Department of West Mississippi in 1865. Meantime, he was b r e v e t t e d through all the grades to that of major general in both the Regular Army and volunteer service. After the war he was in the inspector general's department for a time and from 1868 until 1871 was professor of military science and tactics at Kansas Agricultural College. After holding various commands in Texas and the Indian Territory, he was promoted to colonel of the 2nd Cavalry in 1879. Two years later, while on duty at Fort Custer, Montana, he was injured when his horse fell with him. He died while on sick leave at St. Paul, Minnesota, June 26, 1881, and was buried in Arlington National Cemetery.

Henry Eugene Davies, (91) nephew of General Thomas A. Davies, was born in New York City on July 2, 1836. He was educated at Harvard, Williams, and Columbia colleges, finally graduating in 1857 from the latter. He then studied law, gained admission to the state

bar, and began practice. At the beginning of the Civil War, Davies became a captain in the 5th New York Infantry and fought at the battle of Big Bethel on June 10, 1861. In August he was appointed major of the 2nd New York Cavalry, called the "Harris Light Cavalry" in honor of United States Senator Ira Harris. The regiment was attached to Irvin McDowell's corps on the Rappahannock during the Peninsular campaign and saw its first hard service during the campaign of Second Manassas. Davies was promoted to lieutenant colonel in December, 1862, to colonel in June,

1863, to brigadier in September, 1863, and to major general at the end of the war. In June, 1863, the regiment suffered heavy casualties at Beverly Ford and Aldie, Virginia, while the army was en route to Pennsylvania. It was not engaged at Gettysburg, since it was stationed at Westminster, Maryland. From then until the close of the war General Davies was in brigade and divisional command in the Cavalry Corps of the Army of the Potomac: he took a gallant part in the raids on Richmond and in all the actions in the Shenandoah in 1864 and rendered outstanding service in the cavalry operations which culminated in the surrender of the Army of Northern Virginia at Appomattox—he was wounded on February 6, 1865, at Hatcher's Run. He resigned in January, 1866, while commanding the Middle District of Alabama, to return to his law practice in New York. He was city public administrator from 1866 until 1869 and assistant district attorney for the southern district of New York until 1872. During the later years of his life, while making his home in what is now Beacon, New York, General Davies wrote several books, including a biography of General Philip Sheridan. He died in Middleboro, Massachusetts, September 7, 1894, and was buried in the yard of St. Luke's Church at Beacon.

Thomas Alfred Davies, an uncle of General Henry E. Davies, was born December 3, 1809, on a farm in St. Lawrence C o u n t y, New York, when the area was virtually w i l d e r n e s s. After a common school education, he entered West

gaged in the siege of Corinth in April and May, 1862, and in the battle of Corinth on October 3 and 4. Until the close of the war, he commanded the Districts of Columbus, Kentucky (1862-63), Rolla, Missouri (1863-64), and North Kansas (1864-65). While in command of the District of Wisconsin, he was mustered out with the brevet of major general on August 24, 1865, and returned to New York. General Davies devoted many of his remaining years to writing on topics ranging from the esoteric (*Cosmogony: or Mysteries of Creation* and *Genesis Disclosed*) to the eminently practical (*How to Make Money, and How to Keep It*). He died near Ogdensburg, in St. Lawrence County, August 19, 1899, and was buried in the family cemetery at Oswegatchie, a hamlet near the southern boundary of the county.

Point at the age of sixteen and was graduated twenty-fifth in the class of 1829 in which Generals Robert E. Lee and Joseph E. Johnston of the Confederate Army stood respectively second and thirteenth in rank. Another future high-ranking Confederate in the same class was Lieutenant General T. H. Holmes. After serving on the frontier of Wisconsin, Davies resigned in 1831 to accept a position as a civil engineer on the Croton aqueduct which was to supply water to the city of New York. From 1841 until the outbreak of the Civil War, Davies was a merchant in New York. He went back into the army as colonel of the 16th New York, with which he took part in the Union disaster of First Manassas (Bull Run). He was subsequently on duty in the defenses of Washington, stationed at Alexandria until March 7, 1862, when he was made a brigadier general of volunteers. He was en-

Edmund Jackson Davis was born in St. Augustine, Florida, October 2, 1827; but as a child he was taken to Galveston, Texas, by his widowed mother. He studied law in Corpus Christi, was admitted to the bar, and practiced successfully in Brownsville, Laredo, and Corpus Christi. He served as district attorney for the Rio Grande Valley district and judge thereof from 1854 until 1861. It is stated that his defection from the Confederate cause arose from his defeat as a candidate to the Texas Secession Convention. At this juncture he crossed into Mexico and recruited the 1st Texas Cavalry, reportedly raised from large numbers of "disaffected Texas Unionists." As its commander, Davis held the rank of colonel of United States volun-

teers from October 26, 1862, and established "political beachheads" in Matamoras, across the Rio Grande from Brownsville. On November 10, 1864, he was made a brigadier general of United States volunteers. At the end of the war Davis was a delegate to the constitutional convention of 1866 and president of the convention of 1869. He advocated unrestricted Negro suffrage, the disfranchisement of all ex-Confederates, and the division of Texas into three states, among other proposals. With the help of the military he was elected governor in 1869 over General Andrew Jackson Hamilton by less than a thousand majority. It is alleged that as governor Davis was personally incorruptible; however, for his four-year term he was virtual dictator of the state, having absolute power of appointment over eight thousand state and local employees. Ousted by a majority of forty thousand Democratic

votes in 1873, Davis appealed unsuccessfully to General U. S. Grant in the White House to be sustained in office. He thereupon resumed his law business in Austin and died there on February 7, 1883. He was buried in the State Cemetery.

Jefferson Columbus Davis, the son of Kentucky parents, was born on March 2, 1828, in Clark County, Indiana. At the age of eighteen he served in the Mexican War as a volunteer in the 3rd Indiana and took part in the battle of Buena Vista. Two years later, June 17, 1848, he was commissioned directly into the Regular Army as a second lieutenant of the 1st Artillery. He was promoted to first lieutenant in 1852 and to captain in 1861. He was present at the bombardment of Fort Sumter. That August his good friend Governor Oliver P. Morton appointed him colonel of the 22nd Indiana

and in December he was made brigadier general of volunteers. He commanded a division at the battle of Elkhorn (Pea Ridge) in March, 1862, and at the siege of Corinth. On September 29 of that year he provoked a quarrel with his ex-commanding officer, General William Nelson, and shot him down in the lobby of the Galt House in Louisville. At least one impartial witness who was a friend of both men (92) felt that the act was cold-blooded murder, but no effective legal steps were taken against Davis. A few days later he was restored to duty, with the helping hand of the politically powerful Morton. Davis went on to distinguish himself as a division commander at Murfreesboro, at Chickamauga, and in the Atlanta campaign and as commander of the XIV Corps in the "March to the Sea" and in the Carolina campaign. He was not promoted in spite of his increased responsibilities and ended the war a major general by brevet only. One of his biographers set forth that "perhaps the administration felt about him as Dr. Johnson did about the American colonists, that he 'ought to be thankful for anything . . . short of hanging.'" After the war Davis became colonel of the 23rd Infantry, served in Alaska, and later took part in the chastisement of the Modocs who had murdered General Edward R. S. Canby. He died in Chicago on November 30, 1879, and now lies buried in Crown Hill Cemetery, Indianapolis, near his wife's home. (93)

George Washington Deitzler was born November 30, 1826, in Pine Grove, Pennsylvania, where he ob-

tained a rudimentary education in the common schools of the neighborhood. After a short residence in Illinois and California, Deitzler went to Lawrence, Kansas,

in March, 1855. Here he became prominent as a farmer, real estate dealer, and antislavery politician. Before the admission of Kansas to the Union (January 29, 1861), Deitzler was an incessant worker for the free-state cause, serving on committees, attending meetings, and writing for newspapers and periodicals. He was sent to Boston to see Amos Lawrence and the representatives of the Emigrant Aid Society, soon returning with a shipment of B e e c h e r ' s Bibles (Sharps rifles boxed up and labelled "books") to promote free-state migration. In the so-called Wakarusa War he was aide-de-camp to the commander of the free-state forces and was himself in command part of the time.

He served in the territorial legislature as speaker of the house of representatives, was later a member of the senate, and was mayor of Lawrence in 1860. At the outbreak of the Civil War he helped organize and was appointed colonel of the 1st Kansas Volunteer Infantry. He was severely wounded at the battle of Wilson's Creek that August and after partial recovery was promoted to brigadier general on April 4, 1863, to rank from November 29, 1862. He does not seem to have been on duty after February, 1863, when he was in command of a brigade of John McArthur's division of the XVII Corps at Lake Providence, Louisiana, during the Vicksburg campaign. He was on sick leave at Lawrence when he resigned on August 27, 1863. The following year, as major general in command of the Kansas militia, he opposed C o n f e d e r a t e General Sterling Price's abortive "Missouri Expedition." After the war General Deitzler was active in promoting the townsite of Emporia and in expanding railroads in the state. In 1872 he moved to San Francisco with his family, where he resided until 1884. In the latter year he visited Tucson, Arizona (where he proposed to move). On the morning of April 11 while driving a buggy back to town from a trip to examine some water rights, his team bolted from fright after a singletree came loose, the rig overturned, and Deitzler was killed instantly. (94). He is buried in Oak Hill Cemetery, Lawrence.

Richard Delafield, son of a New York merchant who had emigrated from England at the close of the

Revolution, was born in New York City, September 1, 1798. Entering the Military Academy at the age of sixteen, he graduated first in the class of 1818 and was reportedly the first cadet assigned a standing according to merit. Counting his four years at West Point, Delafield's army career spanned fifty-two years: promotions from second lieutenant to brevet major general; twelve years as superintendent of the Academy; and Chief of Engineers, U. S. Army, for the last two years of his active service. As a young officer he performed engineer duty at Hampton Roads during the administration of President James Monroe, on the Mississippi River from 1824 to 1832, and on the Atlantic Coast defenses from 1845 to 1855. Delafield was sixty-three when the Civil War came; he immediately joined the effort to equip and forward to the field the New York volunteers. At the same time he superintended the defenses of the Narrows, Governors Island, and Sandy Hook, in and near New York Harbor. On May 19, 1864, he was promoted to brigadier general and chief of engineers in the regular establishment, with rank from April 22; and at the close of the war he was made major general by brevet. The following year, "having been borne on the Army Register over forty-five years," General Delafield was retired from active service. During his remaining seven years he served on a commission for the improvement of Boston Harbor, on another relating to ocean encroachments at Sandy Hook, on the lighthouse board, and as a regent of the Smithsonian Institution. He died in Washington, D. C., November 5, 1873, and was buried in the family plot in Green-Wood Cemetery, Brooklyn, New York.

Elias Smith Dennis was born December 4, 1812, in Newburgh, New York. After spending his boyhood on Long Island, he migrated to Illinois and in 1838, in Carlyle, married the widow of Congressman Charles Slade. By this marriage he acquired title not only to a rather unsuccessful gristmill, but also to a stepson who later became a celebrated Western desperado, the notorious "Jack" or "Cap" Slade and who, in his early years, assisted in the mill. Despite his age, Dennis served in both houses of the Illinois legislature between 1842 and 1846 and in the 1850's was a U. S. marshal in Kansas Territory. On August 28, 1861, he was mustered into service as lieutenant colonel of the 30th Illinois Infantry. Dennis compiled a most creditable record in the war and

was commended at Fort Donelson and at a subsequent engagement in Tennessee by his superiors. He became colonel of the 30th Illinois on May 1, 1862, and brigadier general of volunteers to rank from November 29. During the Vicksburg campaign, commanding elements of Logan's division of McPherson's XVII Corps, he was sent to the "leased plantations in Louisiana," in and near Young's Point and Milliken's Bend. At the end of the war he was brevetted major general for gallant and meritorious services at the capture of Mobile. After a brief interval as military governor of Shreveport, General Dennis was mustered out in August. The widowed Dennis now took up residence in Madison Parish, Louisiana, an area well known to him through prior station in the vicinity. Here he was elected sheriff in 1880, after having for five years been the husband of a widow who owned a nearby plantation. In 1886 he moved

118

back to Carlyle and made his home with a son there. He died on December 17, 1894, in Carlyle, and was buried in the City Cemetery. Probably, no other officer of his rank, accomplishments, and distinction has had his career so completely overlooked by the contemporary n e w s p a p e r s upon the occasion of his death. No obituary appeared in the Chicago *Tribune,* nor any other Illinois paper; two days later the New York *Tribune* carried sixteen lines, having been apparently alerted by its southern Illinois correspondent. (95)

Frederick Tracy Dent was born on his father's farm near St. Louis, Missouri, on December 17, 1820. (96) He entered West Point at the

age of nineteen and was graduated thirty-third in the class of 1843. Of this class's thirty-nine members, twenty-seven were living in 1861, fifteen of whom became general officers of full rank in the Union or Confederate armies. One of these was Ulysses S. Grant, whom Dent introduced to his sister who in due course became Mrs. Grant. Dent's army career at various frontier posts was creditable, and in the course of the Mexican War he received two brevets for gallant and meritorious conduct, being badly wounded at Molino del Rey. At the outbreak of the Civil War, Dent was a captain of the 9th Infantry stationed in San Francisco, where he remained until March, 1863, when he was promoted to major of the 4th Infantry and ordered to duty in the East. He was stationed in New York City and served on a military commission to try prisoners of state until the spring of 1864, when Grant, who was now lieutenant general, appointed Dent "Aide-de-Camp to the General-in-Chief" with rank of lieutenant colonel. At the close of the war he served briefly as military governor of Richmond and was made a brigadier general of volunteers to rank from April 5, 1865, as well as a brigadier by brevet in the Regular Army. As a colonel of staff, U. S. Army, he served as President Grant's military secretary until 1873, when he was assigned to the command of Fort Trumbull, Connecticut (at New London), with rank of lieutenant colonel. General Dent was retired from active service as colonel of the 3rd Artillery on December 1, 1883, "upon his own application . . . having served over forty years." He then established residence in Washington, but five years later moved to Denver, Colorado, where one of his sons was practicing law. He died there on December 23, 1892. He is buried in Arlington National Cemetery, the simple inscription on his grave marker reciting his Regular Army rank of "Colonel, U. S. Army," and ignoring the volunteer rank which he also held. (97)

James William Denver was born October 23, 1817, on his father's farm, near Winchester, Virginia. At thirteen he moved with his parents to Wilmington, Ohio, where he studied civil engineering. He was

successively a surveyor, schoolteacher, lawyer, and newspaper editor in the years before the Mexican War, eventually settling in Platte City, Missouri. In 1847, he raised a company of volunteers which participated in General Winfield Scott's campaign against the city of Mexico. He was drawn to California in 1850 by the gold rush, and in 1852 he was elected to the state senate. The same year he killed the editor of California's leading newspaper in a duel over a criticism of Denver's management of the supply trains authorized by the legislature for the succor of overland emigrants. In 1853 he was secretary of the state of California and from 1855 to 1857 served as a Democrat in Congress. In the latter year, President Buchanan appointed him successively commissioner of Indian Affairs and secretary of Kansas Territory and in 1858, governor of the territory which included the present state of Colorado. He established Arapahoe County while governor and the city of Denver was named in his honor. Subsequently, he returned to C a l i f o r n i a and sought unsuccessfully to be elected United States Senator. He then returned to Ohio. On August 14, 1861, Abraham Lincoln, recalling Denver's services during the earlier Kansas troubles, appointed him a brigadier general of volunteers and assigned him to command the troops in that state as a sort of inspector general. In the course of the siege and capture of Corinth, subsequent to the battle of Shiloh, Denver commanded a brigade in W. T. Sherman's division. Thereafter, he was employed mainly in garrison duty in protecting the Federal supply lines until he resigned his commission on March 5, 1863. When the war ended, General Denver commenced the practice of law in Washington. The next year he was a delegate to the Soldiers' Convention at Cleveland and in 1870 was an unsuccessful candidate for Congress from his old home in Ohio. He remained active politically until his death in Washington on August 9, 1892. He was buried in Wilmington.

120

Gustavus Adolphus De Russy, scion of a military family of long tradition, was born in Brooklyn, New York, November 3, 1818. (His father, Brevet Brigadier General René E. De Russy, U. S. Army, and his uncle, Colonel Lewis G. De Russy of the Confederate Army, were both graduates of West Point and veterans of the War of 1812 and the Mexican War; his grandfather had been a midshipman in the Revolutionary Navy.) Young De Russy attended West Point for three years, but in 1838 was permitted to resign after being arrested for drinking. (98) Nine years later he was commissioned directly into the army as second lieutenant of the 4th Artillery and in the Mexican War won the brevets of first lieutenant and captain for gallantry at Contreras, Churubusco, and Chapultepec. At the outbreak of the Civil War, De Russy was a full-rank captain in the regular establishment and was highly commended by

George B. McClellan during the Peninsular campaign for bringing "two guns . . . into action under very difficult circumstances." (99) During the same campaign he commanded the Artillery Reserve of Heintzelman's III Corps and was again praised in orders for his conduct at Malvern Hill, winning the brevets of major and lieutenant colonel. He commanded the guns on Ambrose E. Burnside's left at Fredericksburg and in March, 1863, entered volunteer service as colonel of the 4th New York Artillery. Henry W. Halleck applied for his services soon after and De Russy was commissioned brigadier general of volunteers to rank from May 23, 1863, and assigned to the command of the "Defenses of Washington South of the Potomac." He remained there until the end of the war, when he was assigned to duty for a short interval in the Department of Alabama. With the brevets of major general of volunteers and brigadier general, U. S. Army, General De Russy returned to the regular service in 1866 as major of the 3rd Artillery. He was promoted to lieutenant colonel in 1879, to colonel in 1882, and retired the same year after an uneventful sixteen years in garrison. Subsequent to his retirement he made his home in Detroit, Michigan, where he became an esteemed member of the community by the time of his death on May 29, 1891. He was buried in Elmwood Cemetery there. (100)

Philippe Régis Dénis de Keredern de Trobriand was born near Tours, France, June 4, 1816, son of a baron who supported the

121

Bourbons until 1830, when he resigned his general's commission and retired from the army. Young De Trobriand in a lifetime spanning eighty years pursued, on several continents, the varied occupations of l a w y e r, p o e t, author, soldier, and bon vivant. Splendidly at home in all these metiers, he was excelled by few civilians as a regiment, brigade, and division commander of the Army of the Potomac. When Civil War began, De Trobriand, who had married a New York heiress, took out American citizenship and on August 28, 1861, was mustered into Federal service as colonel of the 55th New York, which had been recruited as the "Lafayette Guard." He saw his first hard action on the Peninsula in a brigade of Couch's division of Keyes's IV Corps and his last at Appomattox Court House where he commanded the 3rd Division of the II Corps. In the interval he directed a brigade of the III Corps

at Fredericksburg, Chancellorsville, and Gettysburg where he defended the center of Daniel Sickles' line in the celebrated peach orchard. Upon the consolidation of the III Corps he was assigned a brigade of the II Corps, which he led until his promotion to divisional command. He was commissioned brigadier general of volunteers to rank from January 5, 1864, and major general by brevet from April 9, 1865, the date of the surrender of the Army of Northern Virginia. The following year General De Trobriand accepted a colonel's commission in the regular service, although he was in France at the time, writing his *Quatre Ans de Campagnes a l'Armée du Potomac,* which was translated into English. From 1867 until his retirement he served intermittently with his regiment on the frontier between trips to Europe and in 1875 was a tactful representative of the Federal government in New Orleans during Reconstruction troubles. He remained in the Crescent City after his retirement, spending his summers with his daughter on Long Island. He died at Bayport, New York, on July 15, 1897, and was buried in St. Anne's Cemetery in nearby Sayville.

Charles Devens, Jr., was born April 4, 1820, in Charlestown, Massachusetts. His education was begun at the Boston Latin School and completed at Harvard University (1838) and Harvard Law School (1840), when he was admitted to the Massachusetts bar. Devens had a notable antebellum career as lawyer, state senator, United States marshal, orator, and militia officer. Forced to participate in the return of an escaped slave to his owner while serving as marshal, he attempted to purchase, unsuccessfully, the bondman's liberty with his own funds. Immediately upon receipt of the news of President Lincoln's call for seventy-five thousand volun-

teers, Devens, a militia brigadier, offered his services and was mustered into Federal service as major of the 3rd Battalion of Massachusetts Rifles, a ninety-day unit which was stationed at Baltimore until its discharge on the eve of First Manassas. Four days later, Devens was commissioned colonel of the 15th Massachusetts and fought at the debacle of Ball's Bluff that October, where a uniform button saved his life when he was struck by a rifle ball. Promoted to brigadier general of volunteers on April 15, 1862, he commanded a brigade of the IV Corps

at the battle of Seven Pines (Fair Oaks) during the Peninsular campaign and was again wounded. At Fredericksburg, Devens commanded a brigade of the VI Corps and at Chancellorsville, where he was wounded a third time, directed the 1st Division of Howard's XI Corps on the right of the Federal line. The 1st was virtually destroyed as a fighting unit by Stonewall Jackson's flank attack. Historians cannot explain the rewards of this celebrated piece of military ineptitude in which the corps commander was promoted to commander of the Army of the Tennessee under W. T. Sherman and Devens was advanced to brevet major general "for highly meritorious service." (101) Upon his return to active service, Devens commanded a division of the Army of the James during 1864 and 1865 and after the Confederate surrender c o m m a n d e d the District of Charleston, S o u t h Carolina. In 1867, General Devens was appointed a judge of the superior court and, in 1873, a justice of the Massachusetts supreme court. Four years later President Rutherford B. Hayes appointed him Attorney General of the United States, after he had declined the war portfolio. Devens was the recipient of numerous degrees and a participant in many commemoratory occasions in his state, where he was the object of universal affection. He died in Boston, January 7, 1891, and was buried in Mount Auburn Cemetery, Cambridge.

Thomas Casimer Devin, whose parents were natives of Ireland, was born in New York City on December 10, 1822. He received a

limited education in the common schools of the city, became a house painter, and joined the New York State militia, rising to lieutenant colonel of a regiment. When the C i v i l W a r c a m e, Devin was mustered into Federal service as a captain of the 1st New York Cavalry two days before First Manassas and on November 18, 1861, became colonel of the 6th New York Cavalry, which was also called the "2nd Ira Harris Guards," after the popular New York Senator. This regiment's first important service was in the Maryland campaign of 1862, with the battle of Antietam supposedly opened by one of its squadrons. After the battle of Fredericksburg, Devin was given the direction of a brigade under Alfred Pleasonton, who consistently urged Devin's appointment as brigadier. Devin fought well at Chancellorsville and Beverly Ford, and his brigade, in the command of John Buford, aided in holding back the

advance of Henry Heth's men on the first day at Gettysburg, enabling the Federal I Corps to reach the field before the position was lost. Early in 1864, the brigade took part in Judson Kilpatrick's raid on Richmond and in August of that year was sent to the Shenandoah Valley for service in Philip Sheridan's campaign against Jubal Early. Slightly wounded in the action at Crooked Run, Devin returned to his command to participate in the battles of Winchester, Fisher's Hill, and Cedar Creek, his commission of brigadier general (not issued until March 13, 1865) giving him rank as of the last-named battle. In the final operations of the cavalry during the Appomattox campaign, Devin commanded the 1st Division of the Cavalry Corps. At the close of the war he was brevetted major general of volunteers for gallant and meritorious service, in 1866 was appointed lieutenant colonel of the 8th U. S. Cavalry, and in 1877 became colonel of the 3rd Cavalry. General Devin's health was precarious after 1873 and in 1878 he returned to his home in New York City, where he died on April 4, 1878. He was buried in Calvary Cemetery, Long Island City, New York. Years older than most of his contemporaries at war's end, his finest accolade was: "Colonel Devin knew how to take his men into action and also how to bring them out." (102)

Joel Allen Dewey was born in Georgia, Vermont, September 20, 1840. In 1859 he enrolled in Oberlin College, at which time his home address was Austinburgh, Ohio. (103) He left college in the autumn of 1861 to become a second lieutenant of the 58th Ohio, with which he served until promoted to captain of the 43rd Ohio the following January. With the 43rd Ohio, Dewey was under fire at New Madrid, Missouri, under John

Pope, and at the battles of Iuka and Corinth. Until the opening of W. T. Sherman's campaign against Atlanta, his regiment performed garrison duty in West Tennessee. At this juncture, Dewey was commissioned lieutenant colonel of the 111th Colored Infantry, becoming its colonel on April 29, 1865. Until the end of the war, his regiment was employed mainly in guarding the line of the Nashville and Northwestern Railroad. In February, 1865, Dewey commanded the 111th Infantry, in a brigade of five Negro regiments commanded by another colonel. Hence, it is difficult to account for his promotion to full

brigadier general except as a reward to a volunteer officer who could be induced to command Negroes—not a desirable assignment at that time and one disdained by regular officers. On November 20, 1865, he was appointed brigadier general of volunteers, the last such appointment made during the Civil War. Dewey refused an appointment in the Regular Army following the close of the war; instead, he studied law in Albany, New York. Graduating in 1867, he was admitted to the Tennessee bar the same year and established himself at Dandridge, Tennessee. He married the daughter of a pioneer Jefferson County family in 1871. Under the administration of "Parson" Brownlow, Dewey was elected attorney general of the second judicial district of Tennessee in 1869 and reelected the following year to an eight-year term. He died suddenly in the Knoxville Courthouse of heart disease on June 17, 1873, and was buried in Dandridge. (104)

John Adams Dix was born in Boscawen, New Hampshire on July 24, 1798, son of Lieutenant Colonel Timothy Dix, Jr., a prominent merchant who died in the War of 1812. Young Dix was educated in the classics and in Spanish and French. At the age of fourteen, he fought at Lundy's Lane as an ensign, a commission which his father aided him in obtaining. Dix remained in the army until 1828, meanwhile studying law and obtaining admission to the District of Columbia bar. He settled in Cooperstown, New York, to manage his father-in-law's properties and soon became distinguished as county leader of the Jacksonian Democ-

125

racy, adjutant general of the state, secretary of state, state school superintendent, and a leading member of the powerful Albany Regency which controlled the state by means of the "spoils system." After a trip abroad in 1843, Dix was elected to the U. S. Senate in 1845 to fill an unexpired term and served until 1849. While in the Senate he advocated the free-soil policies which a decade later carried him out of the Democratic party. After ten uneventful years, during which he acted as president of two different railroads and practiced law in New York, Dix was appointed city postmaster by President James Buchanan, to clean up a defalcation scandal; soon after, in the last months of the administration, he was made Secretary of the Treasury. In this office, with the Civil War impending, Dix fired off a telegram to a harried Treasury official in New Orleans: "If anyone attempts to haul down the American flag, shoot him on the spot." With Abraham Lincoln as President, Dix was commissioned a major general of volunteers to rank from May 16, 1861, first on the list—as such he outranked all other volunteer officers until the end of the war. At sixty-three General Dix was considered too old for field service and performed department and garrison duties during the war, his most important and distinguished contribution being the suppression of the New York draft riots in 1863. Resigning in November, 1865, he served as minister to France during 1866-69 and in 1872 was elected governor of New York. Defeated for reelection in 1874 by Samuel J. Tilden, he spent his last years·in retirement and died in New York City on April 21, 1879. He was buried in Trinity Cemetery there.

Charles Cleveland Dodge, a son of the William E. Dodge and Melissa Phelps whose marriage cemented the present copper firm of Phelps Dodge Corp., was born on September 16, 1841, in Plainfield, New Jersey. On December 10, 1861, three months after his twentieth birthday, he was mustered into the army as captain of the 7th New York Cavalry, a regiment originally called the 1st Battalion New York Mounted Rifles, and was its colonel by August 13, 1862. His entire war service was spent in and near Suffolk, Virginia, under the immediate command of General John J. Peck and the department command of Major General John A. Dix, a New Yorker. In the months between May, 1862, and the siege of Suffolk by James Longstreet in April, 1863, Dodge performed commendably but seems to have incurred criticism from both Peck and Dix by the time he was nominated for brigadier general by President Abraham Lincoln (a grade to which he was confirmed to rank from November 29, 1862).

On March 17, 1863, Dix wrote Peck: "I do not intend that General Dodge shall command the cavalry . . . at Suffolk." (105) Peck had already expressed a preference for another officer, (106) who was junior to Dodge by date of commission as colonel and who would not be appointed brigadier general even by brevet until the omnibus promotions of March 13, 1865. Dodge, perhaps unwilling to be subordinated to the orders of a man junior in rank, although old enough to be his father, (107) resigned his commission as of June 12, 1863. During the draft riots in New York the following month, he volunteered his services which were used and officially appreciated by General John E. Wool. After the war, he was connected with innumerable business enterprises, including a partnership in Phelps Dodge Corp. At the time of his death he had been for some years the president of the New York and Boston Cape Cod Canal Co.; the canal, completed in 1914 by private capital, is now operated by the Federal government. Dodge died in New York on November 4, 1910, and was buried in Woodlawn Cemetery. (108)

Grenville Mellen Dodge was born on April 12, 1831, at Danvers, Massachusetts. He was educated at Durham Academy, New Hamp-

shire; and Captain Partridge's school in Norwich, Vermont, where he received a diploma in 1851 as a military and civil engineer. For the next decade, Dodge engaged mainly in railroad engineering and surveying in Illinois, Iowa, and Nebraska, making his home at Council Bluffs. He had organized a militia company, the Council Bluffs Guards, in

1856; on July 6, 1861, he was mustered into the U. S. Army as colonel of the 4th Iowa Infantry. He served in Missouri under John C. Frémont; commanded a brigade in the Army of the Southwest; and took part in the battle of Elkhorn (Pea Ridge), where he had three horses shot from under him and was severely wounded. Promoted to brigadier general to rank from March 21, 1862, and major general from June 7, 1864, Dodge was given steadily increasing responsibilities, first as commander of the District of the Mississippi and later as leader of the XVI Corps during the Atlanta campaign, where he was again wounded. In December, 1864, U. S. Grant put him in command of the Department of Missouri and in February, 1865, of the Department of Kansas as well. In these areas he operated against bands of guerrillas and hostile Indians with signal success until the end of the war. In January, 1866, Dodge was appointed chief engineer of the Union Pacific Railroad, which at the time had but forty miles of poorly laid track west of Omaha. Resigning his army commission in May, 1866, Dodge had located, laid, and equipped one thousand and eighty-six miles of rail by May, 1869. (By 1933, modernization had eliminated only thirty miles of curves from the track built by him sixty-four years before.) (109) In 1873, Dodge joined the Jay Gould organization and in the next decade was associated with the construction of more than nine thousand miles of road. After the war with Spain he constructed a line in Cuba. Meantime, he found time to serve a term in Congress (1867-69); survey

and map some sixty thousand miles of railroad; and act as one of the foremost railway lobbyists of his day. He was prominent in patriotic organizations in his later years. He died in Council Bluffs, January 3, 1916, and was buried there.

Charles Camp Doolittle was born March 16, 1832, in Burlington, Vermont, but at the age of four was taken by his parents to Montreal, and later to New York City. Doolittle attended school until age fifteen, when his father's insolvency

compelled him to go to work in a glassware emporium. In the late 1850's he moved to Hillsdale, Michigan, and on June 30, 1861, was commissioned first lieutenant of the 4th Michigan Infantry and captain in August. The regiment was heavily engaged on the Peninsula in 1862 and during the Seven Days battle sustained 249 casualties. On August 13, 1862, Doolittle was promoted to colonel of the 18th Michigan, which was involved in minor operations in Kentucky in 1862 and 1863 and served as provost guard at Nashville until June, 1864. He was ordered to Decatur, Alabama, with his command and participated in the defense operations under General Gordon Granger against the Confederate Army of Tennessee under General John B. Hood on October 30, 1864, an action which forced Hood to divert his army forty miles to a crossing of the Tennessee River at Tuscumbia and postponed the proposed invasion of Tennessee by many days. During the battle of Nashville, Colonel Doolittle commanded the 1st Brigade of Jacob D. Cox's 3rd Division of the XXIII (Schofield's) Corps. Promoted to brigadier general to rank from January 27, 1865, Doolittle was in command of the post of Nashville for a time and then of the northeastern district of Louisiana. With the brevet of major general of volunteers "for meritorious service during the war," General Doolittle was honorably mustered out of volunteer service on November 30, 1865. After the war he made his residence in Toledo, Ohio, where he became an employee of the First National Bank. When the Merchants National Bank was organized, Doolittle became its cashier and remained in this occupation until his death on February 20, 1903. He was for many years a leading elder of Westminster (Presbyterian) Church. He was buried in Woodlawn Cemetery. (110)

Abner Doubleday, more famous for the canard that he originated the game of baseball than for his military career, was born at Ballston

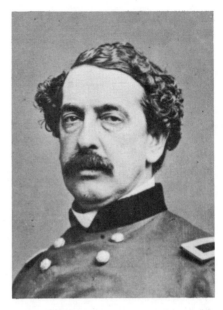

Spa, New York, June 26, 1819. His grandfather was a soldier of the American Revolution; his father was a two-term Congressman from New York; both of his brothers became volunteer colonels in the Civil War. Young Doubleday was graduated from West Point in 1842, ranking in the middle of a class which included such future Confederate celebrities as Gustavus W. Smith, A. P. Stewart, D. H. Hill, R. H. Anderson, Lafayette McLaws, Earl Van Dorn, and James Longstreet. Promotion was slow in the artillery branch to which he had been appointed and he was awarded no brevets in Mexico, where he served faithfully; in the spring of 1861 he was in garrison in the harbor of Charleston, where he is said to have aimed the first gun to reply to the Confederate batteries. After some service in the Shenandoah, following the surrender of Fort Sumter, Doubleday was made a brigadier of volunteers and as-

signed to a brigade of Irvin Mc-
Dowell's corps during the campaign of Second Manassas. At
Sharpsburg and Fredericksburg he
commanded a division of the I
Corps. In reserve at Chancellorsville, his command's greatest performance seemed to come at Gettysburg upon the collision of the
leading elements of the Army of
Northern Virginia with those of the
Union I Corps. After the fall of
General John F. Reynolds,
Doubleday assumed command of
the corps and was driven, along
with Howard's XI Corps, through
town and to the low hills beyond,
where the ultimate Federal line was
located on the order of Winfield S.
Hancock. Distrusting Doubleday's
ability to assume the initiative with
celerity (he was nicknamed "Forty-
eight Hours"), George G. Meade
assigned the temporary corps command to John Newton, (111)
Doubleday's old classmate.
Doubleday held no further active
command in the field and for the
rest of the war was on duty in
Washington. Brevetted major general for his service in 1865, he became colonel of the 35th Infantry
in 1867 and was retired in 1873.
In 1876, Doubleday published his
*Reminiscences of Forts Sumter and
Moultrie in 1860-61*. He made his
residence in Mendham, New Jersey,
where he died on January 26, 1893.
He was buried in Arlington National Cemetery.

Neal Dow, born in Portland,
Maine, March 20, 1804, is remembered better as an advocate of temperance and father of the Maine
anti-liquor law than as a Civil
War brigadier general of
volunteers. Of Quaker parentage,

he was educated in **Portland** and
New Bedford, Massachusetts. He
then entered his father's tanning
business and in this and other later
business ventures was markedly
successful. His preoccupation with
prohibition is explained by one of
his biographers as stemming from
"the intolerable amount of intem-
perance prevailing in Maine during
[Dow's] youth." (112) Dow served
as the militant head of a succession
of organizations which, in 1884,
caused the voters to overwhelmingly
approve a "bone-dry" law for the
state. In the meantime, Dow served
as mayor of Portland and lectured
widely on prohibition in this country and abroad. He was appointed
colonel of the 13th Maine Infantry
on November 23, 1861. The following February the command was
assigned to Benjamin F. Butler's
expedition for the capture of New
Orleans. Dow's vessel with twenty-
five hundred troops aboard ran
aground off the North Carolina

coast; however, he arrived safely at Ship Island, Butler's rendezvous. He was promoted to brigadier general to rank from April 28, 1862, and was assigned command of the former rebel forts of Jackson and St. Philip below the city. After serving for a time as commander of the District of Florida, Dow took part in the siege of Port Hudson; in the Union attack of May 27, 1863, he was wounded and, while recuperating, taken prisoner. Eight months in prison at Richmond and Mobile followed before his exchange for Confederate General "Rooney" Lee in March, 1864. His health undermined by prison life, General Dow resigned from the service in November. After the war he continued his activity in the cause of temperance, and in 1880 received 10,305 votes for President on the Prohibition ticket. General Dow died in Portland on October 2, 1897, and was buried in Evergreen Cemetery.

Alfred Napoleon Alexander Duffié, whose nickname "Nattie" went into the records as his middle name, was born in Paris on May 1, 1835, the son of a French count. He was graduated from the military college of St. Cyr in 1854, served in Algiers and Senegal as a lieutenant of cavalry, and won four decorations in the Crimea. Wounded in the battle of Solferino against the Austrians, he took leave of absence to come to the United States in 1859, where he met and married the daughter of a prominent Staten Island family. When the Civil War broke out Duffié resigned his commission in the French army and offered his services to the United States. On August 9, 1861, he was commis-

sioned captain of the 2nd New York Cavalry (Harris Light Cavalry) and was promoted to major in October. The following July he was appointed colonel of the 1st Rhode

Island Cavalry, with which he took part in the campaign of Second Manassas. In March, 1863, his distinguished services at the engagement of Kelly's Ford on the Rappahannock impelled General Joseph Hooker to request his promotion to brigadier and he was so commissioned to rank from June 23, 1863. He commanded a division of the Cavalry Corps under Alfred Pleasonton during the campaign of Chancellorsville and in the early phases of the Pennsylvania campaign; after this he was ordered to duty in the Department of West Virginia. His subsequent war service was in that department, operating under Benjamin F. Kelley, Franz Sigel, David Hunter, and George Crook. In October, 1864,

131

complaints were made of his command, then encamped around Cumberland, Maryland, and he was relieved. (113) A few days later he was captured by Confederate partisans near Bunker Hill, Virginia, and was not paroled until the end of February, 1865. In April, having been properly exchanged, he was assigned to duty in the Division of the Missouri, but received no further command and was mustered out in August. General Philip Sheridan had been unsparing in his condemnation of Duffié for allowing himself to be captured and had requested his dismissal. (114) After the war General Duffié served as United States consul at Cádiz, Spain, until his death there from tuberculosis on November 8, 1880. His remains were interred in Fountain Cemetery, West New Brighton, Staten Island, New York.

Ebenezer Dumont was born in the Ohio River hamlet of Vevay, Switzerland County, Indiana, on November 23, 1814. He was graduated from the University of Indiana, studied law, was admitted to the bar, and began practice in Vevay. In 1838 he served in the legislature and for the following six years was treasurer of his town. Dumont was captain and lieutenant colonel of the 4th Indiana volunteers during the war with Mexico, was again a member of the Indiana house in 1850 and 1853, and was a presidential elector for Franklin Pierce in 1852. He had meantime changed his residence to Indianapolis and here, on April 27, 1861, was again mustered into the service of the United States as colonel of the 7th Indiana V o l u n t e e r Infantry, a ninety-day regiment reorganized as

a t h r e e - y e a r regiment in September. The 7th Infantry fought well at Laurel Hill, Rich Mountain, and Corrick's Ford, in George B. McClellan's West Virginia campaign at the start of the war; Dumont was promoted to brigadier general of volunteers on September 3, 1861, almost immediately after assuming command of his newly mustered regiment. He was in action at Cheat Mountain and on the Greenbrier River against R. E. Lee that fall and the following January commanded the 17th Brigade of the Army of the Ohio. His command repulsed John H. Morgan's cavalry at Lebanon, Kentucky, in May and after September he commanded the 12th Division of D. C. Buell's army during Braxton Bragg's Kentucky invasion. Soon after the battle of Perryville, in which Dumont's division did not participate but remained at Frankfort, a portion of his command was captured at Hartsville,

Tennessee by a force under John H. Morgan. He went on sick leave in December and resigned his commission on February 28, 1863, to take his seat in Congress. He served until 1867, not running for a third term. U. S. Grant appointed him governor of the Idaho Territory but Dumont died in Indianapolis on April 16, 1871, before taking the oath of office. He was buried in Crown Hill Cemetery there.

Abram Duryée was born in New York City on April 29, 1815, shortly after the close of the second war with England in which his father and two uncles took part. His paternal grandfather was a veteran of

the Revolution. After attending the grammar school of Columbia College, Duryée became a mahogany importer and made a fortune. He became interested in the militia as early as 1833 and by 1849, in the course of zealous service, had been

promoted to colonel. He was twice wounded during the Astor Place riots of 1849 and in 1859 resigned his commission against the protests of his comrades. Two years later, however, with civil war in prospect, Duryée recruited a regiment of volunteers known as Duryée's Zouaves, which were mustered in as the 5th New York Infantry. With them he saw action at the first battle of the war at Big Bethel, Virginia. Abraham Lincoln appointed him a brigadier general of volunteers to rank from August 31, 1861, and he was assigned to instruct recruits until his plea for active duty resulted in his assignment to the command of a brigade of James B. Rickett's division in McDowell's III Corps during the campaign of Second Manassas. Duryée was twice wounded in this campaign and at South Mountain and Sharpsburg, he was again wounded on three occasions. But as senior brigadier, Duryée commanded the division for a time after the wounding of Ricketts. Upon returning to the army after a thirty-day leave, Duryée found the regiments of his division reassigned by orders from army headquarters; a new corps commander; and John Gibbon, junior by date of commission as brigadier general, assigned to the command of Rickett's old division. Duryée felt that he had been overslaughed and, failing to obtain satisfaction through official channels, tendered his resignation, which was accepted January 5, 1863. At the close of the war he was made a major general of volunteers by brevet for gallant and meritorious service in almost every engagement in which he had smelled powder. General Duryée served as police commissioner of

New York in 1873 and as dockmaster in 1884. He died on September 27, 1890, and was buried in Green-Wood Cemetery, Brooklyn. (115)

Isaac Hardin Duval (116) was born September 1, 1824, near the Ohio River at Wellsburg, in the strip of (West) Virgina between Ohio and Pennsylvania. After attendance at the c o m m o n schools of the neighborhood, he joined an elder brother in conducting a trading

post at Fort Smith, Arkansas. He became a hunter and trapper on the western plains and voyaged to Mexico and Central and South America. In 1849 Duval is said to have led the first emigrant train from Texas to California and two years after that took part in the Cuban insurrection of Narciso Lopez. In 1853 Duval returned to Wellsburg and entered the mercantile business. His section was attached more to the North than the South both geographically and by settlement (117); consequently he supported the Union and on June 1, 1861, was mustered into service as major of the 1st (West) Virginia Infantry—a three-month regiment mustered out in August and replaced in October by a three-year regiment. On September 19, 1862, he was appointed colonel of the 9th West Virginia. Duval spent most of his time in the West Virginia mountains chasing bushwhackers but also engaged in more than thirty battles and skirmishes, was wounded three times, and had eleven horses shot from under him. At the battle of Cloyd's Mountain in May, 1864, he led his regiment in a desperate, uphill charge against the Confederate breastworks—breaking the line, but suffering 30 per cent casualties in the process. He was made a brigadier general to rank from September 24, 1864, meantime participating in Philip Sheridan's Shenandoah Valley campaign in the Army of West Virginia under George Crook. With the brevet of major general for gallantry, Duval embarked upon a postwar career of persistent office-holding. He was successively state senator in West Virginia, state adjutant general, Congressman (1869-71), U. S. assessor of internal revenue, collector of internal revenue for twelve years, and member of the lower house of the state legislature. He died at Wellsburg on July 10, 1902, and was buried there.

William Dwight was born July 14, 1831, in Springfield, Massachusetts, a descendant of John Dwight who settled in Dedham in 1635. After attendance at a private military school, Dwight entered West Point in 1849. That he "resigned in 1853 before graduation" is generally reported in accounts of his life; however, he "was discharged . . . 31 January 1853 for deficiency in

studies." (118) He then engaged in manufacturing in Boston and Philadelphia until the beginning of the Civil War. In June, 1861, Dwight was commissioned lieutenant colonel of the 70th New York, a regiment whose colonel was Daniel Sickles. At the battle of Williamsburg on the Virginia Peninsula, Dwight's regiment suffered 50 per cent casualties and he was wounded, left for dead on the field, and taken prisoner by the Confederates. Soon exchanged and promoted to brigadier general to rank from November 29, 1862, Dwight commanded a brigade in Cuvier Grover's division of N. P. Banks's forces in Louisiana and was a leading participant in the reduction and surrender of Port Hudson. He acted as chief of staff to Banks during the celebrated Red River campaign and in this connection it was rumored that Dwight's principal interest was flushing out stores of Confederate cotton for shipment to Massachusetts mills. (119) In July, 1864, he was transferred to command a division of Emory's XIX Corps and in the Shenandoah Valley campaign fought at Winchester, Fisher's Hill, and Cedar Creek. For alleged defamatory statements relating to other commands at Winchester and because of the allegation that Dwight had retired to a place out of gunfire to take his lunch during the battle, he was subsequently put in arrest. (120) The charges seem to have died of inertia, and no action was taken; however, it is worth noting that Dwight's name was not included in the omnibus brevet promotions at the end of the war. Honorably mustered out on January 15, 1866, he had already moved to Cincinnati, where he became associated with his brothers in railroad management. He died in Boston on April 21, 1888, and was buried in Forest Hills Cemetery.

Alexander Brydie Dyer was born in Richmond, Virginia, on January 10, 1815. Appointed to West Point from the state of Missouri in 1833, he was graduated sixth in the class of 1837—Braxton Bragg stood fifth. Dyer served in the Florida War as a lieutenant of artillery and in 1838 transferred to the Ordnance Department. As chief of ordnance of the army invading New Mexico under S. W. Kearny, Dyer took part in some little publicized actions of the Mexican War, including the suppression of insurrection at Taos and the affair at

Santa Cruz de Rosales near Chihuahua City under Sterling Price who, like Braxton Bragg, became a prominent Confederate general. With the brevet (and later full) rank of captain, Dyer performed routine ordnance service until the outbreak of the Civil War when, although a native Virginian, he chose loyalty to the Union. He was put in charge of the Springfield armory in August, 1861, and soon quadrupled its production to manufacture a thousand rifles a day. He once declined the post of chief of ordnance proffered by Abraham Lincoln in January, 1862, (121) out of regard for the incumbent General James W. Ripley, but after Ripley's retirement, Dyer was promoted to the office, with rank of brigadier general, U. S. Army, on September 12, 1864. His contributions to the Union cause were great and ranged from the donation of his patented "Dyer shell" to resistance to the threats of "political demagogues, charlatan inventors, and knavish contractors" by whom he was surrounded. A court of inquiry requested by him resoundingly endorsed his stewardship of the ordnance bureau, after grievances of the same pressure groups were aired in Congress. At the termination of hostilities he was brevetted major general in the Regular Army "for Faithful, Meritorious, and Distinguished Services in the Ordnance Department." He continued in charge of this bureau, but his health began to give way in 1869. Five years later, on May 20, 1874, he died in Washington and was buried in Arlington National Cemetery. With the possible exception of Generals Winfield Scott (who went into retirement in November, 1861) and George H. Thomas, no native-born Southerner had so distinguished a Civil War career in the Union Army.

Amos Beebe Eaton was born on May 12, 1806, in the Hudson River town of Catskill, New York, where his father, a well-known botanist, was acting as agent and surveyor of the Livingston estates. Young Eaton was graduated from West Point in 1826 in the class which included Albert Sidney Johnston. As a lieutenant of infantry Eaton performed duty at various garrisons; and during the Florida War of 1837-41 discharged commissary and other staff details, having in the meantime been promoted to captain, commissary of subsistence, to rank from July 7, 1838. During the Mexican War, Eaton was chief commissary of subsistence of the army commanded by General Zachary Taylor and won the brevet of major for gallant and meritorious conduct at

Buena Vista. From the close of that war until 1855, Eaton operated as chief of commissariat of the Department of the Pacific at San Francisco and from then until 1861 as depot commissary at New York

City. At the outbreak of the Civil War he was accorded larger responsibilities, with attendant increase in rank. It is recorded that "millions . . . passed through his hands in the discharge of the important position committed to him, and in the selection of General Eaton the government was peculiarly fortunate." (122) Upon the retirement in 1864 of General Joseph P. Taylor (brother of his old commander and uncle of Confederate General Richard Taylor), Eaton was appointed commissary general of the U. S. Army to rank from June 29, 1864. In this capacity he served for a decade with rank of brigadier general. On March 13, 1865, he was brevetted major general, U. S.

Army, for "Faithful, Meritorious, and Distinguished Services in the Subsistence Department during the Rebellion." General Eaton was retired in 1874 by operation of the law of July 17, 1862, having served more than forty-five years. He and his wife then traveled extensively in Europe, returning in the autumn of 1876 to make their residence in New Haven, Connecticut, where their son was a professor at Yale. General Eaton died suddenly there, presumably of heart disease, on February 21, 1877, and was buried in Grove Street Cemetery.

John Edwards was born in Louisville, Kentucky, on October 24, 1815. (123) After a common-school education and admission to the state bar, he moved successively to Indiana, California, back to Indiana, and then to Iowa. Meantime he served in both houses of the Indiana legislature, as justice of the peace during the California

137

gold rush, and as member of both the Iowa constitutional convention and the lower house of the legislature where he was speaker from 1858 to 1860. He also founded a newspaper, the *Patriot*. In the early months of the Civil War, Edwards was appointed lieutenant colonel on the staff of Governor Samuel J. Kirkwood and in August, 1862, colonel of the 18th Iowa Infantry. This last command served in the Army of the Southwest under John M. Schofield; was garrisoned at Springfield during most of 1863; and in the fall of that year composed part of the garrison of Fort Smith, Arkansas, with Edwards as post commander. In the spring of 1864 the regiment took part in Frederick Steele's ill-fated Camden campaign, fighting at Prairie d'-Ane, Moscow, and Jenkins' Ferry. On September 24, 1864, Edwards was promoted to brigadier general of volunteers, and commanded first a brigade and then a division in the District of the Frontier with headquarters at Fort Smith; he remained at this post until the close of the war. Although not a recipient of the brevet of major general, Edwards was in 1866 rewarded by President Andrew Johnson with the post of assessor of internal revenue at Fort Smith, where he had settled. In 1870, General Edwards ran for Congress as a Liberal Republican, against the incumbent Thomas Boles, a former Confederate officer and native Arkansan who ran on a moderate ticket. Edwards presented credentials of election to the Forty-Second Congress and served from March 4, 1871, until February 9, 1872, when he was succeeded by Boles, who had successfully contested the election. With the day of

the carpetbagger rapidly coming to a close, Edwards was not a candidate for renomination and thereafter made his home in Washington, D. C., where his legal talents and his army service procured him a living. He died in Washington on April 8, 1894 and was buried in Arlington National Cemetery.

Oliver Edwards was born in Springfield Massachusetts, on January 30, 1835, and was graduated from high school there in 1852. Four years later he moved to Warsaw, Illinois, where he became a partner in a foundry. With the

outbreak of the Civil War, Edwards returned to Massachusetts, where he was mustered into the army as first lieutenant and adjutant of the 10th Massachusetts Infantry. General Darius N. Couch selected him as his aide-de-camp and in this capacity Edwards rendered gallant service during the Peninsular campaign. On September 4, 1862, he was commissioned colonel of the 37th Massachusetts and with it took part in the campaigns of Fredericksburg, Chancellorsville, and Gettysburg, in John Newton's division of the VI Corps. After duty in New York City quelling the draft riots, Edwards and his unit were returned to the Army of the Potomac. In the course of U. S. Grant's Overland campaign of 1864, Edwards was advanced to command of a brigade and at the battle of Spotsylvania Court House is said to have held the "Bloody Angle" for twenty-four continuous hours of fighting while in command of twenty-one Union regiments. He was with Philip Sheridan in the Shenandoah and was brevetted brigadier general of volunteers for gallantry at Spotsylvania and at the battle of Winchester. At this juncture Sheridan offered him the post of provost marshal general of the Middle Military Division, which he declined, preferring field command. In the final assault on the Petersburg lines in April, 1865, Edwards' brigade was in the forefront and he personally received the city's surrender. At Sayler's creek, on the road to Appomattox, Edwards captured Lieutenant General Richard S. Ewell, Major General Custis Lee, and an entire brigade of Confederates, for which was brevetted major general to rank from April 5, 1865. On May 19, 1865, he received the full rank of brigadier general of volunteers. After the war, he served as postmaster of Warsaw for a time and then became superintendent of a manufacturing company in Northampton, Massachusetts, where he patented several inventions. About 1875 he returned to Warsaw which was his home for the rest of his life, except for two or three years spent in England. Three times mayor of Warsaw, he died there on April 28, 1904, and was buried in Oakland Cemetery.

Thomas Wilberforce Egan, the son of Irish immigrants, was born in Watervliet, New York, on June 14, 1834. He received a solid schooling; but what his occupations were prior to 1861 is unknown. During this time he married an actress and fathered a son who died in childhood. Enlisting in the 40th New York, also known as the Constitution Guard and the Mozart Regiment, in April, 1861, he was commissioned its lieutenant colonel on July 1. The following year, at the battle of Seven Pines (Fair Oaks) in the Peninsular campaign, Egan put his colonel in arrest for misconduct, displayed conspicuous gallantry, and was commissioned colonel as of the date of his supe-

rior's discharge from the service. Egan was conspicuous on every field in which the Army of the Potomac took part. The losses of the 40th regiment were heavy and were compensated for only by the addition of recruits for the 87th New York in September, 1862, and the consolidation of veterans of the 37th, 38th, 55th, and 101st New York into the c o m m a n d after Chancellorsville. While commanding a brigade in the II Corps during the initial attacks on the defenses of Petersburg, Egan sustained a wound near the spine which resulted in a slight paralysis of his legs. Two months later he returned to duty and was promoted to brigadier general of volunteers on September 3, 1864. On November 14, 1864, during the course of a minor operation in command of John Gibbon's division of the II Corps, Egan was severely wounded in the right arm and disabled. Nevertheless, he returned to active duty in time to be assigned to one of the divisions of Hancock's Provisional Corps, with the brevet of major general to rank from October 27, 1864, "for gallant and distinguished service at the battle of Boydton Plank Road. . . ." After his separation from the army in 1866, General Egan was appointed a deputy collector in the New York Customs House, a position he held until about six years before his death. Alone and in obscurity, he died in a charity hospital on February 24, 1887. He was buried in Cypress Hills National Cemetery, Brooklyn, New York. (124)

Alfred Washington Ellet, one of fourteen children, was born October 11, 1820, at Penn's Manor,

Pennsylvania. He worked on his father's farm and studied civil engineering at Bristol Academy. In the years before the war he practiced his profession at various locations and on August 20, 1861, as a resident of Bunker Hill, Illinois, was commissioned a captain of the 59th Illinois Infantry. The following spring, when his brother, the celebrated engineer Charles Ellet, was ordered by the War Department to purchase vessels and convert them into rams, Alfred Ellet was commissioned an additional aide-de-camp with rank of lieutenant colonel and accompanied his brother who had been made colonel. They completed their fleet at Cincinnati and steamed down the river to Memphis, defeating the Confederate fleet there on June 6, 1862, and sinking or disabling eight of the nine enemy ironclads. Charles here received a wound which proved fatal fifteen days later, and the command devolved upon Alfred. With the *Monarch* and the *Lancaster* he steamed up the Yazoo and discovered and reported the presence of the Confederate ram *Arkansas*. Promoted to brigadier general of volunteers to rank from November 1, 1862, he was assigned to the Department of the Mississippi and placed in command of the Marine Brigade in 1863. After running the Vicksburg batteries in March, 1863, Ellet was engaged for some time in moving U. S. Grant's troops to the east bank of the Mississippi. In retaliation for information furnished the troops of Confederate J. R. Chalmers' command, Ellet burned Austin, Mississippi, which nearly resulted in the capture of one of his boats. He was on duty in New Orleans when he resigned his commission on December 31, 1864, to return to civil engineering. About 1868 he removed to El Dorado, Kansas, where he immediately became a prominent businessman and civic leader. With his son, Ellet organized one of the pioneer banks of the community and was instrumental in persuading an early railroad company (which is now part of the main line of the Santa Fe) to build through El Dorado. When he died there on January 9, 1895, his funeral "brought together the largest and most notable . . . concourse in the history of [El Dorado]." (125) He was buried in the local cemetery.

Washington Lafayette Elliott, son of Commodore Jesse Duncan Elliott, U. S. Navy, was born in Carlisle, Pennsylvania, March 31, 1825. During his boyhood he accompanied his father on cruises to the West Indies and abroad. He left

the sophomore class of Dickinson College to enter West Point, where he was a cadet from July 1, 1841, to June 30, 1844, leaving to study medicine. (126) However, on May 27, 1846, he was commissioned directly into the army as a second

lieutenant of Mounted Rifles. Participation in the siege of Vera Cruz was followed by illness and assignment to recruiting duty. He later served on the frontier and was made captain in 1854. After some service as a regular officer at Springfield and Wilson's Creek at the beginning of the Civil War, Elliott was commissioned into the volunteers as colonel of the 2nd Iowa Cavalry on September 14, 1861, and assigned to the command of General John Pope, with whom he took part in the operations against new Madrid and Island No. 10. Commanding a cavalry brigade during the siege of Corinth, he was in charge of the first cavalry raid of the war, against the Mobile & Ohio Railroad; on June 11, 1862, he was made a brigadier general of volunteers. He went east with Pope and at Second Manassas, where he was wounded, was chief of cavalry of the Army of Virginia. General Elliott was successively in command of the Department of the Northwest, of the 3rd Division of Sickles' III Corps at Chancellorsville and Gettysburg, and of the 1st Cavalry Division of the Army of the Cumberland during the relief of Ambrose E. Burnside in East Tennessee. In the Atlanta campaign he was chief of cavalry under General George H. Thomas and took part in the pursuit of John B. Hood. At the battle of Nashville he commanded a division of the IV Corps. After having been in command of the District of Kansas, he was mustered out of volunteer service on March 1, 1866, with the brevets of major general in both the Regular Army and volunteers, his regular rank being that of major, 1st Cavalry. This was shortly augmented by promotion to lieutenant colonel; in 1878 he became colonel, 3rd Cavalry, and was retired the following year. He then engaged in the banking business in San Francisco, where he died on June 29, 1888. He was buried in the Presidio there.

William Hemsley Emory was born on his father's estate (Poplar Grove) in Queen Annes County, Maryland, September 7, 1811. His grandfather, who came to the colonies from England, served in the American Revolution, and his father was a veteran of the War of 1812. Emory was graduated from West Point in 1831 but resigned

his commission in 1836 after five years with the 4th Artillery; in 1838 he was recommissioned as a first lieutenant in the Topographical Engineers. After serving as second in command of the northeastern boundary survey between the United States and Canada, he distinguished himself in the Mexican War, winning two brevets for gallantry. From then until the Civil War, he was active in making surveys, including one of the boundary between California and Mexico; in compiling maps of the country west of the Mississippi; and in writing valuable scientific works, such as his celebrated *Notes of a Military Reconnaissance from Fort Leavenworth in Missouri, to San Diego in California.* (127) At the outbreak of war in 1861, Emory was stationed in Indian Territory and is said to have been the only officer in Confederate territory who brought out all his troops without the loss of a man. Commissioned a brigadier general of volunteers on March 17, 1862, he took part in the Peninsular campaign under George B. McClellan; commanded a division under N. P. Banks in 1863; was raised to the command of the XIX Corps, with which he took part in the Red River campaign of 1864; and was afterward transferred to Virginia, where the XIX Corps served under Philip Sheridan in the Shenandoah. In 1865, Emory commanded the Department of West Virginia. Although he held the rank of colonel in the regular service as early as 1863, had been a brigadier of volunteers since March, 1862, and had won every brevet to and including that of major general in both the regular and volunteer organizations, he was not given the full rank of major general of volunteers until September 25, 1865, 126 in order of seniority of 131 appointees. (128) After the war he commanded various departments until his retirement with rank of brigadier general, U. S. Army, in 1876. He died in Washington on December 1, 1887, and was buried in the Congressional Cemetery. His wife was the great-granddaughter of Benjamin Franklin.

George Peabody Estey (also Este) was born in Nashua, New Hampshire, April 24, 1829. He was born and was buried under the name Estey; however, at the time he entered the army he adopted an older spelling and the name Este is rendered in all army records. He attended Dartmouth but did not graduate, visited California, and then studied law, practicing first in Galena, Illinois, and later in Toledo, Ohio, where he became a partner of Morrison R. Waite, later Chief Justice of the U. S. Supreme Court. Estey was appointed lieutenant colonel of the 14th Ohio on April 24, 1861, and became its colonel on November 20, 1862. The unit was engaged at Philippi, Laurel Hill, and Corrick's Ford in (West) Virginia and after its reenlistment for three years was stationed in Kentucky and fought at Mill Springs (Fishing Creek). Estey took part in the Tullahoma campaign but was apparently not present at Chickamauga or Chattanooga, where the regiment was commanded by its lieutenant colonel. He directed a brigade of the XIV Corps through the Atlanta campaign, the "March to the Sea," and the Carolina campaign. At Jonesboro, where his horse was shot from under him and he was wounded, he received the special commendation of his division commander, General Absalom Baird, for having "made as gallant a charge as ever was made." The brigade loss was 346 out of about 1,100 men engaged. Estey was made a brigadier general by brevet on December 9, 1864, and was commissioned to the full rank on June 26, 1865. He resigned from the army on December 4, 1865, and took up residence in Washington, D. C. Here he practiced law until his death in New York City on February 6, 1881. General Estey was buried in the Nashua Cemetery under a marker which spells his name Estey. (129) *History of Nashua, New Hampshire,* published in 1897, records the same spelling; however, Appleton's *Cyclopedia of American Biography* lists him under Este, as do most other published sources.

Henry Lawrence Eustis was born on February 1, 1819, in Fort Independence, Boston, Massachusetts,

where his father Major (later Colonel and Brevet Brigadier General) Abraham Eustis was stationed. Young Eustis was graduated from

Harvard in 1838 and accepted an appointment to West Point, where he was graduated first in the class of 1842, leading such luminaries as John Newton, William S. Rosecrans, G. W. Smith, A. P. Stewart, John Pope, Abner Doubleday, D. H. Hill, George Sykes, R. H. Anderson, Lafayette McLaws, Earl Van Dorn, and James Longstreet. Posted to the Corps of Engineers as a second lieutenant, he was in charge of the construction of Fort Warren in Boston Harbor and spent two years at West Point as assistant professor of engineering. Eustis resigned from the army in 1849 in order to become professor of engineering at Harvard, a post he occupied until his death, except for two years' service in the Civil War. On August 21, 1862, despite waning health, he was again mustered into the service of the United States as colonel of the 10th Massachusetts Volunteers. With this regiment, and later in command of a brigade in the division of his old classmate Newton in the VI Corps, he fought at Fredericksburg, in the Chancellorsville campaign, at Gettysburg, and in U. S. Grant's Overland campaign, which culminated in the battle of Cold Harbor in June, 1864. On June 27 his resignation was accepted, two stories having been advanced as a reason therefor. The first was "impaired health"; the other is to be found in a telegram sent by Assistant Secretary C. A. Dana to Secretary of War Edwin M. Stanton on June 12: "General Eustis is relieved . . . and ordered to Washington. He is to be informed that if he does not resign, charges of neglect of duty and general inefficiency will be preferred against him. He is said to eat opium." (130) Perhaps the two versions are not incompatible. Eustis, who had been promoted to brigadier general to rank from September 12, 1863, returned to Cambridge and resumed his academic pursuits until his death on January 11, 1885. He was buried in Mount Auburn Cemetery. He is the author of a number of articles on technical and scientific subjects.

Charles Ewing, youngest of three brothers who became Union generals and brother-in-law of General William T. Sherman, was born on March 6, 1835, in Lancaster, Ohio. He was the son of Thomas Ewing,

Senator from Ohio, Secretary of the Treasury, and Secretary of the Interior. Young Ewing's education was obtained at local schools, at a Dominican college, and at the University of Virginia. He studied law and was practicing in St. Louis at the outbreak of war. On May 14,

1861, he received a commission as captain of the newly authorized 13th U. S. Infantry. This regiment was stationed at Alton, Illinois, until ordered to Memphis in October, 1862, during the furore occasioned by Braxton Bragg's invasion of Kentucky. At the siege of Vicksburg, Ewing's regiment—or a battalion thereof—was a part of Francis P. Blair's division of Sherman's XV Corps, and Ewing won praise from Blair for his conduct during an assault on the Confederate works. Shortly afterward he was appointed assistant inspector general with rank of lieutenant colonel and assigned to Sherman's staff. Although there may have been nepotism in this, Ewing discharged his duties gallantly and was brevetted three times for services performed during the balance of the war, as he accompanied Sherman in many campaigns. After distinguished service at Chattanooga, in the Atlanta campaign, on the famous "March to the Sea," and in the campaign of the Carolinas which resulted in the surrender of the Confederacy's second most important army under Joseph E. Johnston, Ewing was brevetted colonel in the regular service to rank from March 13, 1865, five days after being commissioned a full rank brigadier general of volunteers. Although Sherman's influence had something to do with all this, Ewing's own record was unassailable. After brief service as a captain of the 22nd Infantry, to which he had transferred, he resigned in 1867, and began the practice of law in Washington. He died there on June 20, 1883, and was buried in Arlington National Cemetery.

Hugh Boyle Ewing, brother of Generals Charles and Thomas Ewing, was born in Lancaster, Ohio, October 31, 1826. His early education was received from private tutors and on July 1, 1844, he entered the Military Academy, from which he resigned on the eve of graduation

in 1848 because of deficiency in engineering. The following year he went to California during the gold rush. In 1852, Ewing returned east and commenced the practice of law, first in St. Louis and later in Leavenworth, Kansas, where he was associated with his brother Thomas and his foster brother William Tecumseh Sherman. (Sherman was taken into the Ewing household in 1829, after his own father died, and was reared there. Although he was never legally adopted, his relationship with the Ewing boys was one of foster brother. Subsequently, he married one of the Ewing girls.) Having returned to Ohio

in 1858, he was appointed to a staff position by Governor William Dennison in May, 1861; served under Generals George B. McClellan and William S. Rosecrans in western Virginia that summer; and in August became colonel of the 30th Ohio Volunteers. In the battles of South Mountain and Sharpsburg in September, 1862, Ewing distinguished himself in command of his regiment and then a brigade of the IX Corps, following which his command was assigned to Sherman's XV Corps in U. S. Grant's operations against Vicksburg; Ewing was promoted to brigadier general of volunteers on November 29, 1862. After the surrender of the city he succeeded to the command of William Sooy Smith's division of the XVI Corps, which had been transferred to Sherman's XV Corps. At the battle of Chattanooga, Ewing's division was the spearhead of Sherman's assault on the Confederate right wing, commanded by Patrick R. Cleburne, on Missionary Ridge and sustained heavy losses. The following February he was assigned to command of the post of Louisville, Kentucky. In February, 1865, he was ordered to join Sherman in North Carolina and was planning an expedition up Roanoke River when the end of the war came. Mustered out in 1866, General Ewing received the brevet of major general "for meritorious services," and soon after was appointed minister to Holland by President Andrew Johnson. He served in this capacity until 1870, when he returned to Washington and resumed the practice of law. In 1874 he purchased a farm near his birthplace, where he resided until his death on June 30, 1905. General Ewing is buried in Lancaster, Ohio. He is the author of two novels and numerous magazine articles.

Thomas Ewing, Jr., brother of Generals Charles and Hugh Ewing, was born in Lancaster, Ohio, August 7, 1829. At the age of nineteen, while his father was Secretary of the Interior, he became one of the private secretaries of President Zachary Taylor. Subsequently, he studied law in Cincinnati, gained admission to the bar,

and in 1856 moved to Leavenworth, Kansas, where he associated himself with the firm of Ewing, Sherman & McCook. Ewing was a staunch antislavery advocate and had much to do with preventing the admission of Kansas to the Union as a slave state. Elected the first chief justice of the state supreme court in 1861, he resigned in the autumn of 1862 to recruit the 11th Kansas Cavalry of which he became colonel. The regiment served as infantry at Cane Hill and Prairie Grove, Arkansas, in James G. Blunt's division of the Army of the Frontier. On March 13, 1863, Ewing was promoted to brigadier general and soon after was assigned to the command of the District of the Border, comprising Kansas and the western tier of Missouri counties. In an effort to suppress the bushwhackers who roamed the area, Ewing issued his notorious Order No. 11, which decreed expulsion of the inhabitants, loyal or disloyal, from the Missouri counties of Jackson, Cass, Vernon, and Bates. During Sterling Price's famous Missouri Raid in 1864, Ewing's command embraced the District of St. Louis, and he distinguished himself at the battle of Pilot Knob and in the subsequent retreat of the Federal forces. He resigned on February 23, 1865, with the brevet of major general and for the next few years practiced law in Washington, declining the posts of Secretary of War and Attorney General tendered him by President Andrew Johnson. In 1870, General Ewing returned to Lancaster and soon became identified with the Greenback wing of the Democratic party. He represented his district in Congress for two terms (1877-81) and was an unsuccessful candidate for governor of Ohio in 1879. From 1881 until his death on January 21, 1896, he practiced law in New York City. He was buried in Oakland Cemetery, Yonkers, New York.

Lucius Fairchild was born December 27, 1831, in Portage County, Ohio, while his parents were en route to the new capital of Wisconsin. His father became the first

treasurer of the state and the first mayor of Madison. Young Fairchild attended Carroll College at Waukesha for a time but soon went to California, where he remained for six years. In 1858, on his return to Wisconsin, he offered for public office and was elected clerk of the Dane County circuit court as a Democrat, a party allegiance which he forsook at the beginning of the Civil War to become a Republican. Fairchild enlisted five days after the bombardment of Fort Sumter as a private in the 1st Wisconsin, a ninety-day regiment; was elected captain in May; and took part in the skirmish at Falling Waters, Maryland, in July. The following month he became lieutenant colonel of the 2nd Wisconsin, which won fame as a unit of the celebrated "Iron Brigade." Meantime, he was mustered into service as a captain of the 16th U. S. Infantry, from which he obtained leave to act in his volunteer capacity. He greatly distinguished himself at Second Manassas, South Mountain, and Sharpsburg; was promoted to colonel on September 1, 1862; and was present at Fredericksburg and Chancellorsville. During the course of the first day's fighting in Reynolds' I Corps at Gettysburg, Fairchild's left arm was shattered, requiring amputation, and he fell into the hands of the Confederates. He saw no more service and resigned in November, having been promoted to brigadier general of volunteers to rank from October 19, 1863. While in the field he had been elected secretary of state of Wisconsin and in 1866 was elected governor, serving until 1872. For the next decade he held a succession of consular and diplomatic posts abroad, including the Spanish ministry. Upon his return to America in 1882, he found the political complexion of his state greatly changed, with a new faction of the Republican party in control. He was defeated for the nomination for U. S. Senator in 1885. Thereafter, he was chiefly known for the bitter partisanship of his views relative to the war and for his repeated "waving of the bloody shirt." He held a minor Federal appointment under Benjamin Harrison and at the time of his death in Madison on May 23, 1896, was commander in chief of the Military Order of the Loyal Legion. He was buried in Forest Hill Cemetery.

Elon John Farnsworth was born in the hamlet of Green Oak, Livingston County, Michigan, on July 30, 1837. At the age of seventeen he was taken by his parents to the village of Rockton, Illinois. The next year he entered the University of

Michigan but left in 1858 "with three or four of his associates after becoming involved in some unfortunate affair." (131) Farnsworth then joined Albert Sidney Johnston's Mormon expedition as a ci-

vilian foragemaster (132) and in 1861 enlisted in his uncle John F. Farnsworth's regiment, the 8th Illinois Cavalry of which he became first lieutenant and adjutant in September, 1861, and captain in December. Young Farnsworth seems to have served commendably in the 8th Illinois and on the staff of General Alfred Pleasonton; however, the annals of the war fail to account for his sudden promotion from captain to brigadier general, on the very eve of the battle of Gettysburg, to rank from June 29, 1863. (It is said that Pleasonton loaned him a blouse carrying the shoulder straps of a brigadier general upon receipt of the advice of Farnsworth's promotion at cavalry

headquarters; in after years Pleasonton wrote that "nature made him a general.") The newly appointed general led a night march in search of Confederate Jeb Stuart's forces and conducted a skirmish in the streets of Hanover, Pennsylvania, on July 1 and another near Hunterstown the following day, commanding a brigade of Judson Kilpatrick's division. Soon after the failure of George E. Pickett's charge on July 3, Kilpatrick thought he saw an opportunity to disrupt Robert E. Lee's lines as the broken fragments of the attack fell back toward Seminary Ridge. He accordingly ordered a charge of Farnsworth's regiments against the right flank of James Longstreet's position. The hopeless charge no doubt contributed to Kilpatrick's reputation as a "hell of a damned fool" (133) and resulted in the death of Farnsworth, who was shot to death near the Confederate battle line. His remains were buried in Rockton.

John Franklin Farnsworth, uncle of Elon J. Farnsworth and son of New England parents, was born in Eaton, a tiny village in Compton County, Quebec, Canada, on March 27, 1820. At an early age he became a resident of Ann Arbor, Michigan, where he studied law. He commenced practice in St. Charles, Illinois, but about 1852 moved to Chicago. In 1856, Farnsworth was elected to Congress, described at the time as "a full-blown Lovejoy abolitionist," although he had originally been a Democrat. He was reelected in 1858 but was defeated for renomination in 1860. In September of the following year he recruited the 8th Illinois Cavalry of which he was made colo-

nel. The regiment saw service on outpost duty in front of Washington and took part in the Peninsular campaign in the spring of 1862. During the Maryland campaign he was placed in command of a brigade in Alfred Pleasonton's division, which saw very limited service, its total casualties amounting to only thirty officers and men. Farnsworth was promoted to brigadier general of volunteers to rank from November 29 and was with his brigade at Fredericksburg where, according to Pleasonton's report, "the cavalry was massed . . . in rear of the ridge commanding the approaches to the upper bridges. This position was held . . . until the army had recrossed the Rappahannock." Meantime, Farnsworth was again elected to Congress, this time from St. Charles, and took his seat on March 4, 1863, resigning his commission the same day. He was reelected in 1864 and by virtue of successive elections held his seat until 1873. Allying himself closely with the Radical Republican element in Congress, Farnsworth voted for all the extreme Reconstruction measures, including the impeachment of President Andrew Johnson. With sentiment changing in favor of moderation, he failed to gain renomination in 1872 and in 1874 waged an unsuccessful campaign as a Democrat. General Farnsworth resumed his Chicago law practice when he left Congress and in 1880 moved to Washington, where he continued in practice until his death on July 14, 1897. He was buried in St. Charles.

Edward Ferrero, of Italian parentage, was born in Granada, Spain, on January 18, 1831. He was brought in infancy to New York, where his father became a dance teacher—a profession followed with marked success by young Ferrero, who taught dancing at West Point. At the outbreak of the Civil War, Ferrero was lieutenant colonel of a militia regiment and on October 14

was mustered into the service of the United States as colonel of the 51st New York Infantry, a regiment which he c o m m a n d e d in Ambrose E. Burnside's North Carolina expedition. At Second Manassas, Sharpsburg, and Fredericksburg, he was in charge of a brigade of the IX Corps and was promoted to brigadier general on September 10, 1862. However, this appointment lapsed the following March by failure of Senate confirmation, and his later reappointment, to rank from May 6, 1863, resulted in his being junior to General R. B. Potter, who had been Ferrero's major in the 51st Infantry but became his division commander in the Vicksburg campaign. At the siege of Knoxville by James Longstreet, Ferrero commanded a division and upon the return to the IX Corps to the Eastern theater, was given command of the newly organized colored division of the corps. At the celebrated battle of The Crater on July 30, 1864, Ferrero's men were supposed to follow Ledlie's forces in the assault on the Confederate line after the explosion. But Ledlie and Ferrero remained in a bombproof some yards in the rear, passing a bottle of rum back and forth, while the assaulting troops became a leaderless mass of humanity in the huge excavation. (134) The whole affair was a dismal failure; casualties amounted to almost thirty-eight hundred men; and a court of inquiry headed by Winfield S. Hancock found that Ferrero was culpable for "being in a bomb-proof habitually, where he could not see the operation of his troops [nor know] the position of two brigades of his division or whether they had taken Cemetery Hill or not." Nevertheless, he re-

ceived the brevet of major general in December for "meritorious service in the present campaign before Richmond and Petersburg." During the last months of the war he was stationed in the defenses of Bermuda Hundred. Returning to New York, he leased and managed a succession of large ballrooms. General Ferrero died on December 11, 1899, and was buried in Green-Wood Cemetery, Brooklyn.

Orris Sanford Ferry, son of a prosperous hat manufacturer, was born in Bethel, Connecticut, August 15, 1823. He was graduated from Yale in 1844, where he had distinguished

himself as an orator and as editor of the *Yale Literary Magazine*. In 1846 he was admitted to the bar and began practice in Norwalk. His public service included seven years as probate judge, two years as state attorney for Fairfield County, and two terms as a member of the Connecticut senate. After a defeat in 1856, he was elected as a Republican to Congress in 1858 but lost the election to a Democrat in 1860. When the Civil War began, Ferry was commissioned colonel of the 5th Connecticut immediately after the battle of First Manassas in July, 1861. He was promoted to brigadier general of volunteers on March 17, 1862, and was routinely brevetted major general on May 23, 1865. Meanwhile, he took part in the Shenandoah Valley campaign as commander of a brigade under the unfortunate James Shields and later commanded a brigade of Keyes's IV Corps on the Peninsula. His final war service was with the X Corps of Benjamin F. Butler's Army of the James. In 1866, General Ferry was elected by the Connecticut legislature to the U. S. Senate, the choice probably resulting from a d e a d l o c k between supporters of the two leading candidates. Ferry, who had been regarded as a staunch Radical upon the policies of amnesty, Reconstruction, and like issues, came out strongly for a policy of moderation and conciliation toward ex-Confederates. Nevertheless, he was whipped into line to vote for the impeachment of President Andrew Johnson. In 1872 he was reelected by a coalition of Democrats and Liberal Republicans but died in office from the results of a "progressive spinal disease" on November 21, 1875. He was buried in Norwalk Cemetery.

Francis Fessenden, younger brother of General James Deering Fessenden and son of Senator William Pitt Fessenden, Secretary of the Treasury under Abraham Lincoln, was born in Portland, Maine, March 18, 1839. After preliminary schooling in Portland he was graduated from Bowdoin College in

1858, studied law at Harvard, and gained admittance to the bar. Upon the outbreak of the war in 1861, Fessenden was at once commissioned a captain in the newly authorized 19th U. S. Infantry by Secretary of War Simon Cameron. Although his Civil War career was not undistinguished and he lost a leg in the Red River campaign, it is impossible to account for this appointment or for his subsequent advance to the full grade of major general on other grounds than his father's political prominence. Fessenden's first field service was at Shiloh, where he was wounded. After returning to duty, he became colonel of the 25th Maine Infantry in September, 1862, and served with this regiment in the defenses of Washington, until he was mustered out of volunteer service on July 10, 1863. From then until the following January, when he was remustered as colonel of the 30th Maine, he seems to have performed routine duty at his regular rank of captain. His regiment was ordered to New Orleans to take part in N. P. Bank's Red River campaign. At the battle of Pleasant Hill, Fessenden succeeded to the command of the 3rd Brigade of Emory's division of Franklin's XIX Corps upon the death of Colonel Lewis Benedict. At Monett's Ferry, Fessenden is credited with directing a charge which saved the retreating army. He was wounded, and his right leg was amputated a few days later. He was promoted to brigadier general of volunteers on May 10, 1864, and to major general on November 9, 1865; his duties after his recovery were mainly of an administrative nature in the neighborhood of Washington. During this period he was a member of the military commission which tried and c o n d e m n e d Henry Wirz, former Confederate commandant at Andersonville Prison. Upon the reorganization of the army in 1866, Fessenden was tendered a lieutenant colonelcy but declined it; he was retired with the rank of brigadier general. Resuming his law practice in Portland, he served a term as mayor of that city, was an overseer of Bowdoin for many years, and compiled his father's letters and papers. He died in Portland on January 2, 1906, and was buried there.

James Deering Fessenden, brother of General Francis Fessenden and son of William Pitt Fessenden, was

born at Westbrook, Maine, September 28, 1833. He was graduated from Bowdoin College in the class of 1852, pursued law studies, and was admitted to the bar in 1856, becoming a member of his father's

firm and showing great ability. Upon the outbreak of the war he recruited a company of riflemen who became part of the 2nd Regiment of U. S. Sharpshooters, an organization whose enlistment was not credited to any particular state or territory and which was commended repeatedly by the officers under whom it served. In March, 1862, Fessenden was assigned to the staff of General David Hunter, engaged in operations on the Carolina coast, and organized the first regiment of Negroes in the national service—an action subsequently disavowed by the government. As aide-de-camp with rank of colonel, he took part in Admiral Samuel F. DuPont's attack on Charleston in 1863. In the fall of that year he was ordered to duty with General Joseph Hooker (who was moving the XI and XII Corps to the western theater from the Army of the Potomac), on whose staff he served at the battles around Chattanooga and in the Atlanta campaign. Upon Hooker's relief from command Fessenden, at his own request, was ordered to report to General Philip Sheridan in the Shenandoah. He had meantime been made a brigadier general of volunteers to rank from August 8, 1864—a promotion difficult to justify except for the exalted political station of his father. At the battle of Cedar Creek he commanded a brigade of William Dwight's division of the XIX Corps. Thereafter he was in garrison at Winchester, Virginia, until the end of the war. After appearing in the grand review of the Union forces in Washington in May, 1865, he served in South Carolina and Georgia until he was mustered out in January, 1866. He had been brevetted major general of volunteers to rank from March 13, 1865. In the postwar years General Fessenden pursued his law practice; served three terms in the Maine legislature; and was a Federal register of bankruptcy for several years. He died in Portland on November 18, 1882, and was buried there.

Clinton Bowen Fisk was born at York, Livingston County, New York, on December 8, 1828. While an infant he was taken by his parents to Coldwater, Michigan. He obtained some education at the academy in nearby Albion and became successful as a merchant, miller, and banker in Coldwater,

only to be financially ruined by the panic of 1857. Fisk then moved to St. Louis and engaged in the insurance business. According to a cam-

paign biography published in 1888, he served in the Union home guards and took part in the capture of Camp Jackson in St. Louis in May, 1861. However, the records disclose no earlier service than his appointment as colonel of the 33rd Missouri Infantry on September 5, 1862. The same month he was ordered to organize a brigade and was commissioned brigadier general on November 24, 1862; he was brevetted major general in March, 1865. Meantime, his war service was almost entirely in Missouri and Arkansas, where he commanded the District of Southeast Missouri and later the Department of North Missouri. In both of these capacities he successfully opposed the recurrent raids and attacks of Generals Sterling Price, J. S. Marmaduke, and

Joseph O. Shelby on the state and its capital. At the close of the war Fisk, an avowed Abolitionist who neither drank nor swore, was appointed assistant commissioner of the Freedmen's Bureau for Kentucky and Tennessee. President Andrew Johnson remarked: "Fisk aint a fool, he wont hang everybody." He founded Fisk University, today a leading Negro institution, in an abandoned army barracks in Nashville and supported it with generous gifts for the remainder of his life. Fisk moved to New York where he once again began to prosper in the banking business; in 1874 President U. S. Grant appointed him to the board of Indian Commissioners, on which he served until his death. He had for years supported the Republican ticket, but in 1884, in keeping with his principles, supported the Prohibition candidate. In 1886 he ran for governor of New Jersey on the Prohibition ticket and two years later polled a quarter of a million ballots for President. He died in New York City on July 9, 1890, and was buried in Coldwater.

Manning Ferguson Force was born in Washington, D. C., on December 17, 1824. He was graduated from Harvard in 1845 and from its law school in 1848. The following year he moved to Cincinnati and was admitted to the Ohio bar in 1850. Eleven years later Force was mustered into the service of his country as major of the 20th Ohio Volunteer Infantry. He was promoted, successively, to lieutenant colonel, colonel, and brigadier general, meantime establishing a solid military repuation. His war service was entirely under U. S. Grant and W.

T. Sherman in the western armies. He took part in the reduction of Fort Donelson, the sanguinary battle of Shiloh, and the campaign of 1862-63 in Tennessee and Mississippi. During the siege of Vicksburg, Force commanded a brigade in McPherson's XVII Corps and was made brigadier general to rank from August 11, 1863. At the battle of Atlanta he earned a Congressional medal (awarded in 1892) and suffered a facial wound, first thought fatal, which disfigured him for life. Returning to duty in October, he commanded his old brigade in the "March to the Sea" and the 1st Division of the XVII Corps during the close of the Carolina campaign. He was brevetted major general "for especial gallantry before Atlanta." Rejecting proffered civil and military posts in the general government, Force retired to private life in 1866 and resumed his Cincinnati law practice. The same year he was elected judge of the common pleas court. He was reelected in 1871, ran unsuccessfully for Congress in 1876, was elected judge of the superior court in 1877, and was reelected in 1882. Declining nomination in 1887, he was named commandant of the Ohio Soldiers' and Sailors' Home at Sandusky, serving in this capacity until his death. In 1874, Force had married a sister of the wife of General John Pope and Pope died while visiting in Force's quarters at the home in 1892. General Force made a number of distinguished contributions to history and archaeology and also wrote several legal treatises, including the eighth edition of Walker's *Introduction to American Law* and the third edition of *Harris's Principles of Criminal Law*. He died at the home on May 8, 1899, and was buried in Spring Grove Cemetery, Cincinnati.

James William Forsyth was born in Maumee, Ohio, August 8, 1835. (135) He entered West Point in 1851; taking five years to graduate, he was commissioned a second lieutenant of the 9th Infantry on July 1, 1856. Prior to the outbreak of the Civil War his entire military service was performed in Washington Territory. Promoted to first lieutenant on March 15, 1861, he was for two months assistant instructor to a brigade of Ohio volunteers at Mansfield and on October 24 was promoted to captain. During George B. McClellan's Peninsular and Maryland campaigns Forsyth acted as inspector general to the provost marshal general of the Army of the Potomac. At Chickamauga, where he was acting assistant adjutant general on Philip Sheridan's staff, he won the brevet

of major. During 1864 and 1865 he was Sheridan's chief of staff; took part in the Richmond and Shenandoah campaigns; and was brevetted brigadier general of volunteers for gallantry at Winchester, Fisher's Hill, and Cedar Creek, colonel, U. S. Army for services at Five Forks, and brigadier general, U. S. Army for services during the war. On May 19, 1865, he was given the full rank of brigadier general of volunteers. In 1866 and 1867, after some duty in command of a brigade of cavalry, he was appointed assistant inspector general of the Department of the Gulf. From 1869 until 1873 he was assigned as Sheridan's aide-de-camp in the Division of the Missouri and was in Europe during the Franco-Prussian War; thereafter, until 1878, he was military secretary of the Division of the Missouri. Promoted to lieutenant colonel of the 1st Cavalry in 1878, Forsyth was on frontier duty with his regiment until his promotion to colonel of the 7th Cavalry in 1886 and assignment the following year to the command of Fort Riley, Kansas. In the next three years, while at Fort Riley, he originated and organized the cavalry and light artillery school for instruction which existed until World War II rendered horses obsolete in the army. Less to his credit was his command of the troops at the battle of Wounded Knee on the Pine Ridge Agency, South Dakota, December 29, 1890, where a pitiful remnant of the once-great Sioux nation was massacred in an action comparable to Lidice. Forsyth was made brigadier general, U. S. Army, in 1894 and commanded the Department of California until May 11, 1897, when he was promoted to major general. Two days later he was retired and went to live in Columbus, Ohio. He died there on October 24, 1906, and was buried in Greenlawn Cemetery.

John Gray Foster was born in Whitefield, New Hampshire, May 27, 1823. The family moved to Nashua when John was ten, and he received his early education there and at Hancock Academy. In 1842 he was appointed to the Military Academy and was graduated fourth in the class of 1846 in which George McClellan was second. Commissioned in the Corps of Engineers, he was at once attached to the company of sappers, miners, and pontoniers, just being organized to accompany General Winfield Scott's army for service in the war with Mexico. Foster won two brevets and was severely wounded at Molino del Rey. Thereafter he performed routine engineering duty until the outbreak of the Civil War. As chief engineer of the

fortifications of Charleston Harbor, he was a leading participant in the bombardment of Fort Sumter. In October, 1861, he was promoted from captain of engineers to brigadier general in the volunteer service, took a prominent part in

Ambrose E. Burnside's North Carolina expedition, and in July, 1862, was assigned to command of the Department of North Carolina. In the autumn of 1863 he took part in the operations designed to relieve Burnside at Knoxville and succeeded that officer in command of the Army and Department of the Ohio in December, but relinquished command in February due to injuries sustained when his horse fell with him. After returning to duty he commanded the Department of the South in the last year of the war and later the Department of Florida. He had been commissioned a major general of volunteers to rank from July 18,

1862, and was brevetted to the same rank in the regular service in March, 1865. The remainder of Foster's career was occupied by engineering duties of a routine nature. He became a lieutenant colonel, Corps of Engineers, in 1867 and thereafter engaged in survey and construction work on the coast of New England. In 1869 he published a treatise on underwater demolition which was for years considered to be the definitive authority on the subject. From 1871 until shortly before his death in 1874 he was assistant to the Chief of Engineers in Washington. His last active work was the superintendence of the Harbor of Refuge on Lake Erie. General Foster died in Nashua on September 2, 1874, and was buried in the Nashua Cemetery.

Robert Sanford Foster was born in Vernon, Indiana, on January 27, 1834. After a common school education he went to Indianapolis at the age of sixteen and learned the trade of tinner. With the outbreak of the Civil War he at once enlisted and on April 22, 1861, was mustered in as a captain of the 11th Indiana, a ninety-day regiment which saw limited service in western Virginia. In June, Foster transferred to the 13th Indiana as major and fought at Rich Mountain. He was promoted, successively, to lieutenant colonel and colonel and commanded the regiment in James Shields' division during the Shenandoah Valley campaign of 1862. He was ordered to the Peninsula and then to Suffolk, where his command was opposed to James Longstreet's in the spring of 1863. Foster was promoted to brigadier general of volunteers to rank from June 12, 1863. During Quincy A. Gillmore's siege operations against the city of Charleston in the fall and winter of 1863, Foster commanded a brigade stationed in the harbor at Folly Island. After a short period of duty in Florida in the spring of 1864, the brigade was returned to southeastern Virginia, where for a time Foster acted as chief of staff of Gillmore's X Corps in the Army of the James. From then until the end of the war Foster served gallantly on the Petersburg front, commanding first a brigade and then a division in the X Corps (merged into the XXIV Corps in December, 1864). On April 2, 1865, his division and that of General John W. Turner made repeated assaults on Fort Gregg, the hinge of the shattered Confederate line, at a cost of 714 casualties. (The Confederate position had to be held at all costs to enable Longstreet to organize an inner line to protect the withdrawal of Robert E. Lee's army). Having earned the brevet of major general, Foster resigned in September, 1865, after serving as a member of the military commission which tried the Abraham Lincoln conspirators. He declined a lieutenant colonelcy in the Regular Army in 1866 and until his death on March 3, 1903, resided in Indianapolis. He was city treasurer for five years, United States Marshal for Indiana from 1881 to 1885, and for many years president of the city board of trade. General Foster was buried in Crown Hill Cemetery.

William Buel Franklin was born on February 27, 1823, at York, Pennsylvania. He was graduated from West Point in 1843, ranking

first in the class in which U. S. Grant was twenty-first. Franklin's first commission was in the Corps of Topographical Engineers and he took part in the Great Lakes survey

of 1843-45 and in Philip Kearny's exploration of South Pass in the Rockies. During the Mexican War he was attached to John E. Wool's column and won a brevet for gallantry at Buena Vista. From the close of the Mexican War until 1861, Franklin was in Washington, where he was charged with the construction of the new Capitol dome and the monolithic Treasury addition. Upon the organization of the new Regular Army regiments at the outbreak of Civil War, Franklin was commissioned colonel of the 12th U. S. Infantry on May 14 and three days later, brigadier general in the volunteer service. At the debacle of First Manassas his brigade was in Samuel P. Heintzelman's division and consisted of two Massachusetts regiments, the 1st Minnesota and a battery of the 1st U. S. Artillery. The 4th Pennsylvania had already consigned its name to obloquy by claiming its discharge on the very morning of the battle, despite a personal appeal by General Irvin McDowell, the army commander. Franklin did as well with such material as could reasonably have been expected and in September was given the direction of a division in the Washington defenses. When the Army of the Potomac embarked upon the Peninsular campaign, Franklin led his division, and subsequently the VI Corps, with distinction. During the Maryland campaign he commanded the forces which penetrated Crampton's Gap in South Mountain and his corps at Sharpsburg. At Fredericksburg, Ambrose E. Burnside selected him to command the "Left Grand Division," consisting of his own corps and the I Corps of General John F. Reynolds. After all was over, Burnside complained bitterly that Franklin disobeyed orders, was partially responsible for the dismal failure of the Federal effort, and demanded his removal from the army. This set of circumstances effectively shattered Franklin's career. (136) Although Abraham Lincoln's refusal to cashier Franklin triggered Burnside's relief from the command of the Army of the Potomac, Franklin was never again restored to his previous status. Instead, after some months awaiting orders, he was relegated to the command of the XIX Corps in the expedition to Sabine Pass and in N. P. Banks's ill-fated Red River campaign, during which he was wounded. At the end of the war he served as president of the board for retiring disabled officers and, obviously out of favor, resigned both his regular and volunteer commissions. General Franklin was notably successful postbellum in many fields: for twenty-two years he was general manager of the Colt's Fire Arms Manufacturing Company in Hartford; he supervised the construction of the Connecticut capitol; he was a presidential elector for Samuel J. Tilden in 1876; and he was commissioner general of the United States for the Paris Exposition of 1888. He died in Hartford on March 8, 1903, and was buried in York, the town of his birth.

John Charles Frémont, the son of a French émigré dancing master and a Richmond, Virginia, housewife with whom he had eloped, was born in Savannah, Georgia, on January 21, 1813. He has been characterized by one of his biographers as "precocious, handsome, and daring"; he was also mercurial, headstrong, and unstable. All of these traits contributed to a career which soared in early life, stalled during the Civil War, and ended in utter frustration during the postbellum years. Frémont attended

Charleston College in South Carolina from 1829 until 1831 (when he was expelled) under the auspices of a prominent lawyer of the city; he was soon appointed a teacher of mathematics aboard the sloop of war *Natchez* at the instigation of J. R. Poinsett, Andrew Jackson's principal South Carolina lieutenant. In 1838, Frémont received an appointment in the army topographical engineers and transferred from sea to land, still under the guidance of Poinsett. Frémont's association with the distinguished scientist J. N. Nicollet, whom he accompanied on an expedition to western Minnesota, caused his meeting with Senator Thomas Hart

Benton, whose daughter Jessie married Frémont in 1841 despite her father's objections. From 1842 until the outbreak of the Mexican War, Frémont led several important expeditions through the American West. He played a leading part in the conquest of California; was loser in the Stockton-Kearny feud after the American occupation; and after a court-martial in Washington, in which he was found guilty of charges of mutiny and insubordination, resigned from the army on March 15, 1848. Soon after, gold was discovered in enormous quantities on his Mariposa estate in the Sierra foothills of California. In 1850 he was elected to a one-year term as U. S. Senator from the newly admitted state. In 1856, Frémont was selected as the presidential candidate of the newly formed Republican party, which gave him the nomination for largely negative reasons: his acquittal on charges brought against him in his court-martial and his silence on the slavery question. He polled 1,300,000 popular votes to James Buchanan's 1,800,000. Upon the outbreak of the Civil War, Abraham Lincoln appointed Frémont major general in the Regular Army to rank from May 14, 1861, and assigned him to the command of the ill-defined Department of the West, with headquarters at St. Louis. From then until his resignation from the service on June 4, 1864, Frémont was a controversial administrator and was shunted from command to command. A failure in the Valley campaign of the spring of 1862, he was relieved from command at his own request after being assigned to a command under General John Pope, whom

he detested. In 1864, Frémont was nominated for the presidency by a coalition of Radicals, Missouri Germans, and war Democrats. The supporters of Lincoln, embarrassed by Frémont's candidacy, effected a bargain by which Frémont withdrew in return for the ousting of the conservative Montgomery Blair from the Cabinet. By the autumn of 1864, Frémont had lost his California holdings and until the end of his life was to some extent dependent upon the literary endeavors of his wife. He served as territorial governor of Arizona from 1878 until 1887 and in the last year of his life was restored to the army roster as major general on the retired list. While temporarily residing in New York City he died on July 13, 1890, and was buried in Rockland Cemetery, Piermont-on-the-Hudson, New York.

William Henry French was born in Baltimore, Maryland, on January 13, 1815. He was appointed to the Military Academy from the District of Columbia and was graduated twenty-second of fifty students in the class of 1837, which included John Sedgwick, Joseph Hooker, and Confederates Braxton Bragg, Jubal Early, and John Pemberton. Posted to the 1st Artillery, he first served in one of the innumerable Creek-Seminole wars in Florida and in the Mexican War won the brevets of captain and major for gallantry and meritorious conduct. Upon the outbreak of the Civil War, French moved his garrison at Eagle Pass, Texas, to the mouth of the Rio Grande in sixteen days and embarked it for Key West. Having been promoted to brigadier general of volunteers to rank from Septem-

These were Major General David B. Birney, Brigadier General Henry Prince (who committed suicide in 1892), and Brigadier General Joseph B. Carr. Upon the consolidation of the various corps organizations in the spring of 1864, the III Corps disappeared and French was mustered out of volunteer service on May 6, 1864. Until the end of the war he served on various minor boards and through seniority attained the rank of colonel of the 4th Artillery. He died in Washington on May 20, 1881, and was buried in Rock Creek Cemetery.

James Barnet Fry was born on February 22, 1827, in the southwestern Illinois county seat of Carrollton. Entering West Point in 1843, he

ber 28, 1861, he was assigned to the Army of the Potomac and commanded a brigade of the II Corps in the Peninsular campaign and the 3rd division of the corps at Sharpsburg. He was promoted to major general to rank from November 29, 1862. After taking part in the battles of Fredericksburg and Chancellorsville, French was in charge of the District of Harpers Ferry during the Gettysburg campaign, but shortly after the wounding of General Daniel E. Sickles he succeeded to the command of the III Corps. At first enjoying the full confidence of George G. Meade, French lost his entire military reputation at Mine Run in the last days of November, 1863, when he was blamed, because of the slowness of his corps, for the Union failure to exploit a potential advantage over Robert E. Lee. (137) In an unpublished letter in the files of the War Department, French blamed his tardiness at Mine Run upon "one of his division commanders."

was graduated during the Mexican War in the class of 1847 and performed garrison duty in Mexico City the same year. Detailed as adjutant of the Military Academy from 1854 to 1859, at the outbreak

162

of the Civil War he was commanding a battery of light artillery in Washington. Beginning with March 16, 1861, Fry's entire army career was devoted to staff service. During his twenty years of service he attained the grades of brigadier general of volunteers, of brevet major general, U. S. Army, and during the last year of the war of provost marshal general of the United States. In the interim he served as Irvin McDowell's chief of staff during the campaign of First Manassas and for a year was D. C. Buell's chief of staff in the Army and the Department of the Ohio. For tenaciously clinging, during the remainder of his life, to the conviction that Buell's contribution to the Federal victory at Shiloh was substantial, Fry met with the disapproval of Grant and Sherman, who insisted upon the fiction that they had not been surprised at that battle. However, when the Bureau of the Provost Marshal General was created in the army hierarchy, Fry was recommended by Grant as "the officer best fitted" to direct it. The bureau was charged by law with the suppression of desertion, the reorganization of recruiting, and the enforcement of the conscription acts; Fry performed his duties outstandingly. Inevitably there were charges and counter-charges involving the fixing of state quotas and the notorious activities of bounty jumpers and their principals, the substitute brokers, all of which created dissension when Fry's later promotions occurred. But at the close of the war he had been confirmed through all grades to that of brevet major general, U. S. Army. In 1875 he was promoted to colonel in the adjutant general's department, his own bu-

reau ceasing to exist in 1866. Six years later he retired at his own request to continue his military writings, which were vastly informative and impressive in number. General Fry died in Newport, Rhode Island, on July 11, 1894, and was buried in the churchyard of St. James the Less, Philadelphia.

Speed Smith Fry was born in what is now Boyle County, Kentucky, on September 9, 1817. He attended Centre College at Danville, Kentucky, for a time but was graduated from Wabash College, Crawfordsville, Indiana, in 1840. He studied

law and in 1843 became a member of the Kentucky bar. When hostilities with Mexico began in 1846, Fry recruited a company of the 2nd Kentucky Infantry, which he commanded as captain until he was mustered out the following year. From 1857 until the outbreak of the Civil War he was county judge

163

of Boyle County. A staunch Unionist, he was appointed a colonel of the Union militia in July, 1861, and in October of that year was made colonel of the 4th Kentucky Infantry. In January, 1862, he took part in the battle of Fishing Creek. He was promoted to brigadier general of volunteers to rank from March 21, 1862, and served in George H. Thomas' division of Don Carlos Buell's army in the campaign of Shiloh, the division reaching the field after the fighting was over. (Buell went on record as condemning Fry as "inefficient.") Under Buell's successor William S. Rosecrans, Fry took part in the campaign of Stone's River (Murfreesboro), commanding a division, none of which was engaged save for one regiment and a battery, the balance being "detained" near Gallatin. From then until the end of the war he performed garrison duty, much of the time in command of Camp Nelson, the vast Union recruit and deployment depot south of Lexington. He was mustered out of the service on August 24, 1865, without being awarded the brevet of major general, usually automatic in the case of a brigadier with Fry's time in grade. For three years after 1869 General Fry was supervisor of internal revenue in Kentucky. At the time of his death on August 1, 1892, he was superintendent of the Soldiers' Home near Louisville. He was buried in Danville.

John Wallace Fuller was born at Harston, Cambridgeshire, England, on July 28, 1827. His father, a Baptist minister, brought the family to Oneida County, New York, in 1833, and much of young Fuller's education was obtained by reading in the

Utica bookstore in which he was employed at the age of fourteen. Between 1852 and 1861 he operated his own publishing business in Utica, served as city treasurer, was

an officer of militia, and moved to Toledo, Ohio, to establish a similar business there in 1858. At the outbreak of the Civil War, Fuller was detailed to drill troops at Grafton, (West) Virginia, and in August was appointed colonel of the 27th Ohio Volunteer Infantry. Serving under John Pope in the operations against New Madrid and Island No. 10, he commanded a brigade under William S. Rosecrans at the battles of Iuka and Corinth in the autumn of 1862, although garrison service in 1863 presumably prevented his promotion to brigadier until January 5, 1864. Thereafter, Fuller's command took a prominent part in the Atlanta campaign as a unit of the XVI Corps of McPherson's Army of the Tennessee, during which time he commanded his brigade and, at the battle of Atlanta, the 4th Division of the corps. Fuller's Brigade, although repeatedly reorganized and transferred from one unit to another, was a persistent designation in the Army of the Tennessee. During W. T. Sherman's "March to the Sea," the campaign from Atlanta to Savannah, Fuller reverted to the command of his brigade, now in Joseph A. Mower's division of Francis P. Blair's XVII Corps. He continued in command of the brigade through the campaign of the Carolinas and until the surrender of General Joseph E. Johnston at Durham Station, North Carolina. With the brevet of major general for meritorious service during the war, Fuller resigned on August 15, 1865, and returned to his home in Toledo. He engaged for the balance of his life in the wholesale boot and shoe business as senior partner of the firm of Fuller, Childs & Company. From 1874 until 1881 he also served as collector of customs for the city of Toledo. General Fuller died there on March 12, 1891, and was buried in Woodlawn Cemetery. He was one of a very small group of foreign-born officers who attained the grade of general in either the Federal or Confederate armies.

William Gamble was born at Duross, County Tyrone, Ireland, on January 1, 1818. He studied civil engineering and practiced this profession in northern Ireland before emigrating to the United States about 1838. The year following he enlisted in the Regular Army and was successively private, corporal, sergeant, and sergeant major of the 1st Dragoons (later re-

named the 1st Cavalry), until he received his honorable discharge in 1843. He then went to Chicago, where he worked as a civil engineer until the outbreak of the Civil War. In September, 1861, Gamble became lieutenant colonel of the 8th Illinois Cavalry and its colonel on December 5, 1862. The regiment's first war service was at Warrenton, Virginia, where it was stationed until the beginning of the Peninsular campaign. At Malvern Hill, Gamble was severely wounded in the chest and did not rejoin his command until the battle of Fredericksburg. By January 31, 1863, he was in command of a brigade, and on the first day of the battle of Gettysburg a vedette of his old regiment posted on the Cashtown Road fired the opening shot of that famous engagement. At the beginning of U. S. Grant's Overland campaign in May, 1864, Gamble was relieved from duty with the Army of the Potomac and assigned to the command of the cavalry division in the Department of Washington, where he served until the end of the war. Brevetted brigadier general of volunteers to rank from December 14, 1864, he was honorably mustered out of service on July 17, 1865. He was remustered shortly thereafter and on September 25, 1865, was appointed a full brigadier general of volunteers. Again mustered out in March, 1866, General Gamble was appointed major of the 8th Cavalry in July, 1866, when the postwar army reorganization was effected. That autumn his regiment was ordered to California. While accompanying it there via the Central American Transit route, he fell ill of cholera and died in Virgin Bay, Nicaragua, on December 20, 1866. (138) He was buried there in Virgin Grove Cemetery where, according to the Memorial Division of the Quartermaster General's Department, his remains still repose.

James Abram Garfield, twentieth President of the United States, was born on a pioneer farm in Cuyahoga County, Ohio, on November 19, 1831. Rendered fatherless as an infant, his early life was marked by deprivation, unceasing toil, and the ambition to obtain an education and better himself. He was graduated from Williams College in 1856, served as a schoolmaster, and in 1859 was elected to the Ohio senate as a Republican and ardent free-soiler. There he distinguished himself as a fluent and persuasive speaker and debater. With the advent of civil war, he aided in the recruitment of the 42nd Ohio, of which he was made lieutenant colonel in August, 1861, and colonel in

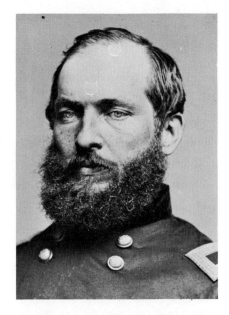

December. Garfield's principal distinction as a soldier was his zeal in mastering the profession and his willingness to study the manuals. Having impressed his superiors by his ability to turn recruits into soldiers, he was sent to D. C. Buell's army in Kentucky. Buell gave him command of a brigade and sent him to the Big Sandy Valley, where in January, 1862, he won an unimportant engagement over West Point Confederate Humphrey Marshall, an inept commander. Nevertheless, Garfield was promoted to brigadier general of volunteers to rank from January 11, 1862; he fought under Buell on the second day at Shiloh, when the latter rescued U. S. Grant and W. T. Sherman; and took part in the siege of Corinth in the division of T. J. Wood. From that time until autumn he was plagued by ill health but on November 17, 1862, was named to the military commission which drove Major General Fitz John Porter from the service. (139) The following spring Garfield became chief of staff to General William S. Rosecrans, who was commanding the Army of the Cumberland. At the disastrous battle of Chickamauga Rosecrans, the army commander, was completely discredited, but his chief of staff was awarded a promotion to major general. This appointment was made after Ohio elected Garfield to the U. S. House of Representatives. Garfield served nine terms in the House; he was elected to the Senate at the same time he was nominated for the presidency. (To describe his alleged complicity in the Crédit Mobilier and DeGolyer scandals and the complexities attending his election to the presidency and the choice of his Cabinet, is beyond the scope of this volume.) Four months after his inauguration on July 2, 1881, he was shot down in the Washington railroad depot, while en route to Williamstown for commencement exercises, by a mentally unbalanced office-seeker named Charles J. Guiteau. The ball, according to contemporary accounts, "entered by the back, fractured a rib, and lodged deep in the body." Amazingly enough, the President was kept alive for eleven weeks, surviving both the heat of midsummer Washington and removal to Elberon, New Jersey, on September 6. He succumbed there on September 19 and, after funeral obsequies reminiscent of Abraham Lincoln's, was buried in Lake View Cemetery, Cleveland, Ohio.

Kenner Garrard, a cousin of General Theophilus T. Garrard, was born at Fairfield, the home of his paternal grandfather in Bourbon County, Kentucky, while his mother was on a visit from the family home in Cincinnati. The best evidence is that the date was September 30, 1827, (140) although there are conflicting statements.

He attended Harvard for a time but left in his sophomore year to enter West Point, from which he was graduated eighth in the class of 1851. As a lieutenant of cavalry he saw service in the southwest and on the day of the bombardment of Sumter was captured at San Antonio by insurgent Texans not yet affiliated with the Confederacy. On parole until officially exchanged August 27, 1862, he was appointed colonel of the 146th New York the following month and took a gallant part in command of his regiment in the battles of Fredericksburg, Chancellorsville, and Gettysburg, where he succeeded to command of Stephen H. Weed's brigade of the V Corps after the death of the latter on Round Top. On July 23, 1863, Garrard was promoted to brigadier general of volunteers. In the fall of that year he commanded the brigade in the actions on the Rappahannock line; was briefly in command of the cavalry bureau at Washington; and in February, 1864, was given command of the 2nd Cavalry Division of the Army of the Cumberland, with which he operated during the campaign of Atlanta under General W. T. Sherman. In December, 1864, General Garrard was assigned once again to infantry, (141) and was given a division of the XVI Corps which, as a detachment from the Army of the Tennessee under the command of General A. J. Smith, distinguished itself at the battle of Nashville. Here Garrard received the brevet of major general of volunteers "for conspicuous gallantry." Toward the close of the war he took an important part in the capture of Mobile and on March 13, 1865, was brevetted brigadier and major general in the Regular Army. After serving for a time in command of the District of Mobile, he resigned his commission on November 9, 1866. Thereafter he devoted himself to his interests in Cincinnati and to the civic affairs of that city. He died on May 15, 1879, and was buried in Spring Grove Cemetery.

Theophilus Toulmin Garrard was born on June 7, 1812, at the Union Salt Works (then the Goose Creek Salt Works) near Manchester, Kentucky, in the same house in which he died almost ninety years later. He spent his childhood there, represented Clay County four different times from 1843 to 1860 in the state legislature, and was a captain of the 16th Infantry Kentucky Volunteers during the Mexican War. On September 22, 1861, he was appointed colonel of the 7th Kentucky (Union) Infantry and the following month was present at the battle of Wild

Cat Mountain (Rockcastle Hills) in Laurel County, the first engagement between Union and Confederate troops on Kentucky soil. In August, 1862, he was present at the battle of Richmond, directing a detachment of the 7th and 32nd Kentucky and 3rd (Union) Tennessee. During the East Tennessee raid of that winter he was attached to the staff of General Samuel P. Carter; he commanded a brigade in McClernand's XIII Corps at Grand Gulf, Port Gibson, and Baker's Creek. Immediately after this last battle and just before the investment of Vicksburg proper, Garrard, who had been promoted to brigadier general to rank from November 29, 1862, was ordered to report to

General Benjamin M. Prentiss at Helena, Arkansas. He was then in command successively of a detachment at Somerset, Kentucky; of the District of Somerset, which embraced four other nearby towns; and in January, 1864, at Cumberland Gap, of a mixed brigade of infantry and cavalry composing the District of the Clinch. General Garrard, for reasons not made apparent in the records was honorably mustered out of the service on April 4, 1864, although there is a reference to his being still on duty as late as the twelfth of that month. He spent his remaining forty years uneventfully in his old homestead in Clay County, farming and operating the salt works he owned. Death came to him on March 15, 1902, and he was buried in the cemetery at Garrard, Kentucky, a hamlet two miles south of Manchester. He was a first cousin of General Kenner Garrard's father. (142)

John White Geary was born December 30, 1819, at Mount Pleasant, Pennsylvania. He attended Jefferson College at Canonsburg, Pennsylvania, for a time, but was forced to leave upon the death of his father. For several years he pursued various activities: teaching school, clerking in a store, studying civil engineering and law, gaining entrance to the bar, and surveying in Kentucky. From the age of sixteen he had been a militia lieutenant and with the outbreak of the Mexican War was elected lieutenant colonel of the 2nd Pennsylvania Infantry and took part in Winfield Scott's advance from Vera Cruz to Mexico City. He was later advanced to colonel of his regiment. In the interval between the close of

the contest with Mexico and the bombardment of Sumter, Geary organized the postal service in California, served as first mayor of San Francisco, and for some months was

territorial governor of strife-torn Kansas. He threw his influence on the side of the antislavery faction in Kansas and his administration was not wholly satisfactory, resulting in his resignation in March, 1857, and his retirement to his farm in Westmoreland County, Pennsylvania. On June 28, 1861, he was made colonel of the 28th Pennsylvania Infantry and joined the command of General N. P. Banks at Harpers Ferry. Geary distinguished himself in several engagements, was wounded at Bolivar Heights, captured Leesburg in March, 1862, and was commissioned brigadier general of volunteers on April 25. Twice wounded at Cedar Mountain where he commanded the 2nd Brigade of Christopher C. Augur's

169

2nd Division of Banks's II Corps, he returned to duty in time to command the 2nd Division of the XII Corps at Chancellorsville and Gettysburg. Transferred to the west with the XI and XII Corps, he fought at Wauhatchie and Chattanooga and, after the XI and XII were consolidated into the XX Corps, commanded its 2nd Division in the "March to the Sea," and then served as military governor of Savannah. He was brevetted major general to rank from January 12, 1865, "for fitness to command and promptness to execute." Upon his return to Pennsylvania in 1866, he was elected governor on the Republican ticket (although he had been a lifelong Democrat) and served two terms, from January 1867 until January 1873. Eighteen days after the expiration of his second term he was suddenly stricken and died in Harrisburg. He was buried there in Harrisburg Cemetery.

George Washington Getty was born in Georgetown, D. C., October 2, 1819. He was appointed to the Military Academy at the age of sixteen and for the next forty-eight years made his career in the army. The class of 1840's forty-two graduates, in which Getty stood fifteenth, numbered such figures as W. T. Sherman and George H. Thomas of the Union and Richard S. Ewell, John P. McCown, Bushrod R. Johnson, J. G. Martin, William Steele, and Thomas Jordan of the Confederacy. Getty was brevetted for gallantry in the Mexican War, where he campaigned in Winfield Scott's army as an artillery lieutenant; he fought against the Florida Seminoles in 1849-50 and again in 1856-57. At the begin-

ning of the Civil War he was a captain of the 4th Artillery. In September, 1861, Getty was appointed lieutenant colonel and additional aide-de-camp in the volunteer service and commanded four batteries in the Peninsular campaign of 1862. He also fought at South Mountain and Sharpsburg during the Confederate invasion of Maryland, acting as chief of artillery of Ambrose E. Burnside's IX Corps. He was promoted to brigadier general of volunteers to rank from September 25, 1862, and at Fredericksburg commanded the 3rd Division of the IX Corps. In March, 1863, the division was sent to Suffolk, where the Federal army under John A. Dix successfully resisted James Longstreet's investment of the town, which guarded the southern approaches to Norfolk and Hampton Roads. After some subsequent engineering duty and command of a diversion to the South Anna River during the Get-

170

tysburg campaign, Getty served as acting inspector general of the Army of the Potomac in early 1864 and was then assigned a division of the VI Corps, which he lead at the Wilderness (where he was severely wounded), at the siege of Petersburg, and in Philip Sheridan's Shenandoah Valley campaign. His division made the initial breakthrough at Petersburg on April 2, 1865, and took part in the final campaign which terminated in the surrender of Robert E. Lee at Appomattox. He was brevetted a major general of volunteers in August, 1864, and in the regular service in March, 1865. Appointed colonel of the 38th Infantry in 1866, General Getty transferred to the 3rd Artillery in 1871, commanded the artillery school at Fort Monroe for six years, and was a member of the board which exonerated General Fitz John Porter in 1879. After retirement in 1883 he lived on a farm at Forest Glen, Maryland, where he died on October 1, 1901. He was buried in Arlington National Cemetery.

John Gibbon was born in Philadelphia, Pennsylvania, April 20, 1827. As a small boy, he was taken to Charlotte, North Carolina, from which state he was appointed to the Military Academy. He was graduated from there in 1847, ranking in the middle of the class; his most famous classmates were Ambrose P. Hill of the Confederacy and Ambrose E. Burnside of the Union. Prior to the outbreak of the Civil War, Gibbon saw service in Mexico, against the Florida Seminoles, and at the Academy where he was on duty for five years as an artillery instructor and quarter-

master. In 1861 he was a captain of the 4th Artillery, stationed at Fort Leavenworth. Although his wife was from Baltimore and three of his brothers entered the Confederate army, Gibbon adhered to the Union. After some months as chief of artillery in Irvin McDowell's divi-

sion, he was made a brigadier general of volunteers on May 2, 1862, and assigned to the command of the "Iron Brigade," which he led at Second Manassas and in the Maryland campaign. In November, 1862, Gibbon was advanced to command of the 2nd Division of John F. Reynolds' I Corps and was badly wounded at Fredericksburg the following month. Returning to duty after a three-month convalescence, he directed the 2nd Division of Winfield S. Hancock's II Corps—and on two occasions the corps itself—with conspicuous gallantry and distinction at Gettysburg, until he was again wounded and carried off the field. Upon his recovery he commanded the Cleveland and Philadelphia draft depots until the commencement of U. S. Grant's Overland campaign in 1864, when he assumed the direction of his old division. With it he fought in all the battles between the Wilderness and the investment of Petersburg, and was promoted to major general to rank from June 7, 1864. In January, 1865, he was given command of the newly organized XXIV Corps, Army of the James. At Appomattox he was one of the commissioners designated to receive the surrender of the Army of Northern Virginia. After the war General Gibbon received the usual brevets and was appointed colonel of the 36th U. S. Infantry and in 1869 of the 7th U. S. Infantry; his service was mainly against the Indians on the frontier, where the fallacy of pursuing the world's finest horsemen with foot soldiers was indelibly illustrated. Nevertheless, Gibbon's overall conduct of operations was highly commendable. He shared no blame in Custer's headstrong conduct at the Little Big Horn, arriving in time only to rescue the survivors of Custer's command and to bury the dead. The following year he conducted a successful campaign against the Nez Percés and on July 10, 1885, was made a brigadier general in the Regular Army. After retirement in 1891, he made his home in Baltimore where he died on February 6, 1896, serving at the time as commander in chief of the Military Order of the Loyal Legion. General Gibbon was buried in Arlington National Cemetery. He was the author of *The Artillerist's Manual*, published by the War Department in 1860, and of *Personal Recol-*

lections of the Civil War, written in 1885 but not published until 1928.

Alfred Gibbs was born on his father's estate of Sunswick, now within the confines of Astoria, Long Island, on April 22, 1823. He was a brother of chemist Oliver Wolcott Gibbs, son of mineralogist

George Gibbs, and grandson of Oliver Wolcott, Secretary of the Treasury in, the administrations of George Washington and John Adams. Young Gibbs attended school in White Plains, New York, and Dartmouth College before receiving an appointment to West Point, where he was graduated in 1846, ranking forty-second in the class. After receiving a wound and winning the brevets of first lieutenant and captain for gallantry in the Mexican War, he was attached to the headquarters of General Persifor F. Smith as aide-de-camp and

172

served as such until 1856. From then until the beginning of the Civil War, Gibbs was on frontier duty with his troop of Mounted Rifles and was again wounded in a skirmish with Apaches at Cook's Spring, New Mexico, in 1857. On July 27, 1861, Gibbs was captured at San Augustin Springs, New Mexico, by the Confederate forces under Lieutenant Colonel John R. Baylor, in the course of the Union retreat from Fort Fillmore. He was paroled but not exchanged for more than a year. In September, 1862, he became colonel of the 130th New York Volunteer Infantry and was on duty in the area of Suffolk, Virginia, under the command of General Erasmus D. Keyes. In August, 1863, his regiment was reorganized as cavalry under the name of 1st New York Dragoons, also known as the 19th New York Cavalry. With it he guarded the line of the Orange and Alexandria Railroad until November, when he assumed command of the Cavalry Reserve Brigade, Army of the Potomac, guarding trains until the spring of 1864. In Grant's offensive against Richmond, Gibbs's brigade became part of the 1st Cavalry Division, which saw much hard duty until transferred to the Shenandoah for service with Philip Sheridan. As of the date of the battle of Cedar Creek, October 19, 1864, Gibbs was promoted to brigadier general of volunteers. Until the surrender at Appomattox, his command played a large part in enveloping the renowned Army of Northern Virginia. Brevetted major general in both the regular and volunteer services, Gibbs became major of the 7th Cavalry in 1866. On December 26,

1868, he died suddenly at Fort Leavenworth, Kansas, of "congestion of the brain" and was buried in St. Mary's Cemetery, Portsmouth, Rhode Island.

Charles Champion Gilbert was born March 1, 1822, at Zanesville, Ohio. He was graduated from West Point in 1846, ranking twenty-first in the class in which George B. McClellan was second, and George E. Pickett was fifty-ninth and last. In the war with Mexico Gilbert

took part in the siege of Vera Cruz and later was in garrison there as a lieutenant of the 1st Infantry. During the five years after 1850, Gilbert served on the faculty of the Military Academy and did frontier duty in the Southwest. He was promoted to captain in December, 1855. On August 10, 1861, he was badly wounded at the battle of Wilson's Creek while commanding his company of regulars. After acting as inspector gen-

173

eral of the Department of the Cumberland, he served in the same capacity in the Army of the Ohio during the battle of Shiloh and the subsequent siege of Corinth. After the Union disaster at the battle of Richmond, Kentucky, General Horatio G. Wright, commanding the Department of the Ohio, appointed Gilbert "acting major general" to command the Army of Kentucky after the wounding of General William Nelson; on September 4, 1862, Gilbert was appointed brigadier general of volunteers by the President. Until this time his career had been auspicious, his conduct uniformly praised by his superiors, and he had won the brevet of major for gallantry at Shiloh. But now the Army of the Ohio under D. C. Buell absorbed Gilbert's forces and he was named commander of the III Provisional Corps of that army. He led the corps at the battle of Perryville in October; even though he was subsequently brevetted lieutenant colonel for gallant and meritorious services, it appears that his direction of the corps left much to be desired. The Buell Commission condemned him for failing to support Alex. McD. McCook's corps (on his left), which was driven back exposing Gilbert's own left flank; he was replaced and did not again hold field command. The Senate failed to act upon his nomination as brigadier and on March 4, 1863, his commission expired; he was not reappointed. In July of that year he became major of the 19th Infantry and performed desk duties until the end of the war. Thereafter, with regular promotion to lieutenant colonel (1868) and colonel (1881), he commanded various posts, mainly in the West, until his statutory retirement in 1886. He died in Baltimore on January 17, 1903, (143) and was buried in Cave Hill Cemetery, Louisville, Kentucky, his wife's hometown.

James Isham Gilbert was born July 16, 1823, in Louisville, Kentucky, but was taken by his parents in in-

fancy first to Illinois and then to Wisconsin, where he grew up and was educated in Prairie du Chien. In the years before the war Gilbert engaged in the rafting of lumber down the Mississippi, Indian trading, general merchandising, real estate, and operating livery stables in Illinois, Wisconsin, and Lansing, Iowa, a town which he laid out and resided in from 1851 until 1862. He entered the service as colonel of the 27th Iowa Infantry on October 3, 1862, and had no battle service until the spring of 1864, when the regiment was assigned to A. J.

174

Smith's detachment of the XVI Corps during the Red River campaign. Gilbert's gallant conduct throughout the campaign won him advancement to brigade command in June, 1864, and his distinguished services at the battle of Nashville in December resulted in his formal promotion to brigadier general on February 9, 1865. Here and in the subsequent campaign against Mobile, Gilbert commanded the 2nd Brigade of the 3rd Division of the Right Wing, XVI Corps. He was brevetted major general for "faithful and meritorious services" in the Mobile campaign and was mustered out on August 24, 1865. General Gilbert then established residence in Burlington, Iowa, where he resumed his 1851 partnership with his two brothers in the lumber business. Although this was a successful venture, in 1877 he embarked on a series of "extensive mining transactions" in Colorado which, according to his obituary, (144) "proved disastrous." In the last eighteen months of his life he resided in Topeka, Kansas, where on February 9, 1884, he died of a heart attack. General Gilbert was buried next to his wife in Aspen Grove Cemetery, Burlington.

Alvan Cullem Gillem was born in Gainesboro (145) in Middle Tennessee on July 29, 1830. After an early log-cabin schoolhouse education he was sent to Nashville and in 1847 entered the Military Academy, from which he was graduated, ranking eleventh in the class of 1851. Five of the graduates of this class who attained general officer's rank were Southerners: Gillem and Kenner Garrard of the Union and

Benjamin H. Helm, Junius Daniel, and Laurence S. Baker of the Confederacy. In the decade before the Civil War, Gillem discharged routine duties: against the Florida Seminoles, in various garrisons, and on the frontier of Texas. At the battle of Mill Springs (Fishing Creek) in 1862 he acted as General George H. Thomas' quartermaster and during the campaign of Shiloh his duties were extended to those of chief quartermaster of D. C. Buell's Army of the Ohio, as well as commander of its siege artillery. In May, 1862, he became colonel of the 10th Tennessee (Union) Infantry and served as provost marshal of Nashville for some time. At the instance of Andrew Johnson, then military governor of the state, Gillem was appointed adjutant general of Tennessee in June, 1863, and brigadier general of volunteers to rank from August 17. From then until the end of the war he was alternately occupied in the field and with the domestic problems arising from the reorganization of the state government under Union rule. A year later he took the field against the East Tennessee Confederates, a campaign with mixed results in which his forces killed the celebrated John H. Morgan. In January, 1865, Gillem was vice-president of the Tennessee convention and in April became a member of the legislature. Meantime, he served under George Stoneman in Western North Carolina, commanding a cavalry division. Brevetted major general, U. S. Army, for services on many fields, Gillem became colonel of the 28th Infantry in 1866. In January, 1868, he was appointed to command the Fourth Military District (Mississippi and Arkansas), under the Reconstruction plan. His policy of conciliation and moderation gained disfavor after Johnson's term came to an end, and Gillem was transferred to frontier duty in Texas. His last active service was against the Modocs who assassinated General Edward R. S. Canby in northern California. He arose from a sickbed to drive Captain Jack and his followers (the assassins) from their stronghold in the Lava Beds. On his return to Benecia Barracks, California, his condition worsened and he went on sick leave in January, 1875. On December 2 of that year, at his home at Soldier's Rest near Nashville, he died. He was buried in Mount Olivet Cemetery.

Quincy Adams Gillmore was born February 28, 1825, in what is now Lorain, Ohio. He was educated and taught school (for three years) in such nearby towns as Norwalk and Elyria before receiving an

appointment to West Point at the age of twenty. He was graduated at the head of the class of 1849, whose last-place man was James M. McIntosh of the Confederacy, and commissioned into the Corps of Engineers. Gillmore's pre-Civil War duties were mainly as an instructor at West Point and on active service at Hampton Roads and New York City. Gillmore was chief engineer of the Port Royal expedition in 1861-62, which effected a Union lodgement on the Carolina coast; however, his greatest claim to fame as a military engineer was his successful scheme to reduce Fort Pulaski, defending the water approach to Savannah, by establishing massed mortar batteries on nearby Tybee Island. He was promoted to brigadier general of volunteers to rank from April 28, 1862, and to major general from July 10, 1863. As commander of the Department of the South and of the X Corps, Gillmore rendered important service in the summer of 1863 in the Union effort to recapture Fort Sumter in Charleston Harbor. It was said that "his operations on Morris Island constitute a new era in the science of engineering and gunnery"; they included the capture of Batteries Wagner and Gregg and the long-range shelling of Charleston by the celebrated 8-inch Parrott rifle, the "Swamp Angel." In May, 1864, his corps was transferred to the Army of the James, where he came under the orders of General Benjamin F. Butler and, along with "Baldy" Smith's XVIII Corps, was bottled up at Bermuda Hundred by P. G. T. Beauregard. During Jubal Early's raid on Washington in July, Gillmore commanded two divisions of the XIX Corps and was severely injured when his horse fell with him. He was again placed in command of the department of the South in February, 1865, and commanded it to the end of the war, receiving brevets of brigadier and major general in the regular service on March 13, 1865. Emerging from the war as a major of engineers (after resignation of his volunteer commission), Gillmore became lieutenant colonel in 1874 and colonel in 1883. Meantime, he had a distinguished professional career, serving on a multitude of boards and commissions, both in and out of the army, and writing a number of learned books and treatises. He died in Brooklyn, New York, on April 7, 1888, and was buried at West Point.

George Henry Gordon was born in Charlestown, Massachusetts, on July 19, 1823. His widowed mother moved to Framingham, Massachusetts, when the boy was five. After

he was graduated from Framingham Academy, he entered West Point in the class of 1846, graduating forty-third of fifty-nine. As a young officer Gordon distinguished himself in Winfield Scott's army during the siege of Vera Cruz and the advance to Mexico City; he was twice wounded and was awarded a brevet promotion for gallantry at Cerro Gordo. After some routine duty he resigned his commission in the Mounted Rifles in 1854 to study law at Harvard and was admitted to the bar in 1857. Gordon recruited the 2nd Massachusetts early in 1861 and was made its colonel on May 24. During the first year of the war the regiment was on duty guarding the Upper Potomac and Frederick, Maryland. In the spring of 1862 Gordon served under the ill-fated N. P. Banks in the Shenandoah Valley campaign against Stonewall Jackson. On June 9, 1862, Gordon was promoted to brigadier general of volunteers. He fought at Cedar Mountain, Chantilly, South Mountain, and Sharpsburg and commanded for a time the 1st Division of the XII Corps. Left once again to guard the Upper Potomac during the campaign of Fredericksburg, he was sent to Suffolk, Virginia, during the siege of that place by James Longstreet, where Gordon commanded the reserve division of two brigades. Until the end of the war his duties were of a routine nature. In the autumn of 1863 he commanded a division of the forces laying siege to the harbor of Charleston and the following year served in Arkansas and in Florida. From November, 1864, until after the end of the war he was on duty in the Department of Virginia, commanding the Eastern district of the department from February, 1865, until he was mustered out with the brevet of major general. General Gordon was then a lawyer in Boston and authored numerous books dealing with his military experiences. He was also one of the founders of the Military Historical Society of Massachusetts. He died at Framingham on August 30, 1886, and was buried in Framingham Centre.

Willis Arnold Gorman was born near Flemingsburg, Kentucky, on January 12, 1816. He moved with his parents to Bloomington, Indiana, when he was nineteen. After studying law and gaining admission to the bar, he entered politics and was successively a functionary of the Indiana senate and a three-term member of the state house of representatives. In 1846 he became major of the 3rd Indiana Volunteers; fought at Buena Vista; and, upon the expiration of his regiment's enlistment, recruited the 4th Indi-

ana with which he fought at Puebla. In 1849, Gorman was elected to Congress from Indiana, serving until 1853 when he was appointed governor of the Minnesota Terri-

tory by President Franklin Pierce. At the end of his four-year term he took up the practice of law in St. Paul; was a member of the state constitutional convention and of the state legislature in 1859; and was a candidate for presidential elector for Stephen A. Douglas in 1860. On April 29, 1861, he was commissioned colonel of the 1st Minnesota Infantry, which acquitted itself well at First Manassas where it formed a part of W. B. Franklin's brigade of Samuel P. Heintzelman's division; Franklin praised the conduct of the regiment and its commander. The following month Gorman took part in the unfortunate affair at Ball's Bluff (Leesburg), in command of a brigade and was promoted to brigadier general to rank from September 7, 1861. At Seven Pines, in the Peninsular campaign, he directed the 1st Brigade of John Sedgwick's division of Edwin V. Sumner's II Corps and was commended by both Sumner and Sedgwick. He fought at Sharpsburg in the same capacity and on November 1, 1862, in the absence of the wounded Sedgwick, was in command of the division. Two weeks later he was assigned to command the District of Eastern Arkansas, with headquarters at Helena. Although supplanted as district commander by General Benjamin M. Prentiss, he remained in the district, participating in some minor operations during the Vicksburg campaign, until he was mustered out of service on May 4, 1864. He practiced law in St. Paul and was city attorney from 1869 until his death on May 20, 1876. General Gorman was buried in Oakland Cemetery, St. Paul.

Charles Kinnaird Graham was born in New York City on June 3, 1824. At the age of seventeen he entered the navy as a midshipman. During the Mexican War he saw service in the Gulf Squadron but resigned in 1848. He studied law and engineering and qualified to practice both professions. As an engineer he helped to lay out Central Park; in 1857 he constructed the dry docks at the Brooklyn Navy Yard. In 1861 he and four hundred other navy yard workmen enrolled in Daniel Sickles' "Excelsior Brigade"; Graham was successively appointed major, lieutenant colonel, and colonel of the regiment ultimately mustered in as the 74th New York. With it he took part in George B. McClellan's Peninsu-

lar campaign, fighting at Seven Pines (Fair Oaks) and in the Seven Days' battles which culminated at Malvern Hill. Bad health forced his retirement from the field for some time and he was employed on recruiting duty for almost a year but returned to lead a brigade in Birney's division of Sickles' III Corps at Chancellorsville. Meantime, he was promoted to brigadier general of volunteers in March to rank from November 29, 1862. On July 2, 1863, during the bloody combat in the Peach Orchard at Gettysburg, Graham was wounded and captured by the Confederates. Sent to Richmond, he was exchanged in September and in November, 1863, was assigned to command the army gunboats in Benjamin F. Butler's Army of the James. His principal exploit from this time until the end of the war was burning the home near Fredericksburg, of the brother of the Confederate Secretary of War, an act of retaliation ordered by General Butler because Montgomery Blair's house had been burned during General Jubal Early's invasion of Maryland. Graham was brevetted major general in 1865 and resumed civil engineering in New York. He was chief engineer of the department of docks from 1873 to 1875, surveyor of the port during 1878-83, and naval officer of the port until 1885. On April 15, 1889, General Graham died in Lakewood, New Jersey, and was buried in Woodlawn Cemetery, New York.

Lawrence Pike Graham was born at The Wigwam, the country home of his father in Amelia County, Virginia, on January 8, 1815. The elder Graham, a physician, was a veteran of both wars with England and Lawrence's three brothers, one of whom was George G. Meade's brother-in-law, were graduates of West Point. All four brothers ad-

hered to the Union cause. Having been educated by private tutors, young Graham was commissioned directly into the army in 1837 as a second lieutenant of dragoons and during the various Seminole disturbances in Florida was promoted to first lieutenant and to captain. In the Mexican War he won the brevet of major for gallant conduct at Palo Alto and Resaca de la Palma, was regularly promoted to major in 1858, and in August, 1861, was appointed a brigadier general of volunteers. The following October he was placed in charge of a brigade, composed of two New York and two Pennsylvania infantry regiments of the Army of the Potomac, which George B. McClellan was whipping into shape. This command in March, 1862, was assigned to Couch's division of Keyes's IV Corps, with Graham directing it in the siege of Yorktown. However, he soon fell ill and took no further part in the Peninsular campaign. In June he was assigned as chief of cavalry to the camp of instruction near Annapolis, where he rendered good service. He afterward acted as president of a general court-martial in St. Louis and of a board for the examination of invalid officers at Annapolis. Meantime, he became colonel of the 4th (U. S.) Cavalry in 1864 and on August 24, 1865, was mustered out of volunteer service with the brevet of brigadier general, U. S. Army, for gallant and meritorious service during the war. Five years later, during which his regiment's active duties were performed piecemeal at various frontier posts, General Graham was retired on December 15, 1870. He was then only fifty-five and in his remaining thirty-five years outlived his wife and both of his sons, one of whom was also a West Point graduate. He became one of the most accomplished Shakespearean scholars in Washington, where he lived from 1877. He died there on September 12, 1905, and was buried in Arlington National Cemetery. (146)

Gordon Granger was born on November 6, 1822, in Joy, New York, a hamlet in Wayne County. According to Cullum's *Register,* Granger received "at his home a good English education" before entering West Point in the class of 1845, fourteen of whose graduates became full-rank general officers. After graduation he served in the war with Mexico, winning the brevets of first lieutenant and captain for gallant and meritorious service. Until the outbreak of the Civil War, Granger's service was on the western frontier as an officer of the Mounted Rifles, which in 1861 became the 3rd U. S. Cavalry. At the

battle of Wilson's Creek, Missouri, in August, 1861, his conduct won him the colonelcy of the 2nd Michigan Cavalry and the following spring—in the campaigns against New Madrid and Island No. 10 and in the subsequent investment of Corinth—he commanded a brigade. He was commissioned brigadier general of volunteers on March 26, 1862, and major general to rank from September 17, 1862. On September 20, 1863, at the battle of Chickamauga, he marched his command, without orders, to the relief of the beleaguered George H. Thomas who was clinging precariously to Horseshoe Ridge with the remnant of his corps. Attacking with two brigades of his Reserve Corps and sustaining 44 per cent casualties in less than two hours, Granger contributed in great measure, by his heroic conduct, to saving William S. Rosecrans' army and the campaign in the western theater from total disaster. (147) At the battle of Chattanooga, Granger commanded the IV Corps and thereafter sometimes a corps and sometimes a division in the relief of Knoxville, the operations against Forts Gaines and Morgan, and the capture of Mobile in 1865. At the end of the war he received the brevet of major general in the Regular Army and in 1866 was appointed colonel of the 25th Infantry. He commanded the District of Memphis on two separate occasions during 1867-69 and the District of New Mexico intermittently from 1871 to 1876. During much of the time after the Civil War he was on sick leave; he died in Santa Fe on January 10, 1876, and was buried in Lexington, Kentucky, the home of his wife's family.

Robert Seaman Granger was born in Zanesville, Ohio, on May 24, 1816. His mother's brother, Henry Stanbery, was a law partner of Senator Thomas Ewing and later was President Andrew Johnson's Attor-

ney General. Granger was appointed to West Point in 1833 but did not graduate until 1838. Almost 50 per cent of his class attained the full rank of general officer in either the Union or Confederate armies; among them were P. G. T. Beauregard, Irvin McDowell, and W. J. Hardee. After his graduation from the Academy, Granger served in garrison at many points; in the Florida War (against the Seminoles); as an instructor at West Point; and in the War with Mexico, where he received regular promotion to captain, 1st Infantry. At the outbreak of the Civil War, while on duty in Texas, he was captured and paroled by the Confederates, but not exchanged for service in the field until August, 1862. He was promoted to major in the Regular Army in September, 1861, served on desk duty behind the lines for some months, was commissioned a brigadier of Kentucky volunteers soon after his release from parole, and in October, 1862, was appointed brigadier general of U. S. Volunteers. Granger's Civil War exploits were mainly confined to camp and garrison duty in Kentucky, Tennessee, and North Alabama, where he resisted the incursions of such Confederate worthies as John B. Hood, Joseph Wheeler, Nathan B. Forrest, and Philip D. Roddey—all of whom continuously plagued the Federal forces remaining in those areas after the principal theater of war had moved eastward to Chattanooga and Atlanta. During Hood's invasion of Tennessee, Granger was in command, successively, at Huntsville, Decatur, and Stevenson, Alabama. Brevetted major general in the regular service and promoted to lieutenant colonel of the 11th Infantry, General Granger discharged garrison duties at various points in Virginia and the South following the surrender of the Army of Northern Virginia until he was appointed superintendent of General Recruiting Service in 1871. Two years later he was retired on his own application, as colonel, 21st Infantry. He died on April 25, 1894, in Washington, and was buried in Zanesville.

Lewis Addison Grant was born in Winhall, Vermont, in Bennington County, on January 17, 1828. (148) He received his education in his native state, taught school for several years in New Jersey and

Massachusetts, studied law, and was admitted to the Windsor County (Vermont) bar in 1855. In the years before the war he practiced law in Bellows Falls with marked success. In August, 1861, Grant was commissioned major of the 5th Vermont, a regiment which became part of the illustrious "Vermont Brigade." At the battle of Savage's Station in the Peninsular campaign, during which Grant was lieutenant colonel, the regiment is claimed "to have suffered the heaviest loss in killed and wounded of any one regiment in a single action." (149) At the battle of Fredericksburg in December, 1862, Grant, now a colonel in command of the Vermont Brigade, was wounded. The following May, during the campaign of Chancellorsville, he led his command against the Confederate defenses on Salem Heights and captured three regimental flags. (Thirty years later he was awarded the Congressional

medal for this feat.) Having taken permanent command of the "Old Vermont Brigade" in February, 1863, he stayed with it until almost the close of the war. The command was actively engaged in most actions of the Army of the Potomac and in the Shenandoah Valley under Philip Sheridan. Grant distinguished himself at the battle of Cedar Creek, where Getty's division formed a line of battle upon which the routed Union forces were able to rally and from which position the victorious Federal assault of the afternoon was launched. He was promoted to brigadier general of volunteers to rank from April 27, 1864, and brevetted major general to rank from the date of the battle. He was again wounded during the breakthrough of Robert E. Lee's lines at Petersburg on April 2, 1865. Declining a commission in the regular service, he moved after the war from Vermont to Chicago, then to Des Moines, and finally to Minneapolis. From 1890 to 1893 he was assistant Secretary of War. When he died in Minneapolis on March 20, 1918, there were only seven men living of the 583 who had been appointed full-rank generals from 1861 to 1865. General Grant was buried in Lakewood Cemetery, Minneapolis.

Ulysses Simpson Grant, ranking general of the armies of the United States and eighteenth President, was born April 27, 1822, in the Ohio River hamlet of Point Pleasant, Ohio. He was baptized Hiram Ulysses; however, upon his admission to West Point in 1839 he was reported by the Congressman who had authored his appointment as Ulysses Simpson, Simpson being

his mother's maiden name. In his four years at the Academy he was outstanding only in equestrianism, a proficiency gained at his father's farm, where at the age of seven he had begun to haul wood with a team. "Sam" Grant was graduated twenty-first in a class of thirty-nine and on July 1, 1843, was brevetted a second lieutenant of infantry, there being no vacancy in any of the cavalry regiments for the best horseman at West Point. During the Mexican War he rendered distinguished service in the army of Zachary Taylor, whom Grant greatly admired. After the battle of Monterey, Grant's 4th Infantry was transferred to Winfield Scott's army of invasion at Vera Cruz, and as regimental quartermaster Grant discharged his staff duties with great ability and also took part in the fighting at Molino del Rey and Chapultepec, which won him the brevets of first lieutenant and captain. Assigned to the Pacific North-

west, he seems to have at times taken to the bottle, and after a warning from his commanding officer, resigned his army commission as of July 31, 1854. During the next six years he was successively (and unsuccessfully) a farmer, real estate salesman, candidate for county engineer (at St. Louis), and customhouse clerk. At length he was reduced to a clerkship in a leather store conducted by his two brothers in Galena, Illinois. At this point Grant's career started upward: within three years he commanded the armies of the United States, and within seven he was elected Chief Executive. Few army officers in American history have achieved such rapid advancement from relative obscurity. However, even at the outbreak of war Grant found no ready market for his talents and it was not until June 17, 1861, that he was appointed colonel of the 21st Illinois—despite his having offered his services to the adjutant general in Washington and to General George B. McClellan, then considering applications in Cincinnati. Grant's regiment was ordered to Missouri, where on August 7 he was appointed a brigadier general of volunteers to rank from May 17. The appointment stemmed from Grant's connection with Elihu B. Washburne, an important member of the Illinois Congressional delegation which parceled out the four Illinois brigadierships. After having been in command at Cairo for a time and having survived the ill-advised attack on Belmont, Missouri, Grant prepared to assault the center of the Confederate line protecting Nashville. The resulting surrender of Forts Henry and Donelson in February, 1862, won him vast stretches of Confederate-held territory, the acclaim of the nation, the sobriquet of "Unconditional Surrender," and a commission as major general of volunteers. Next followed the bloody battle of Shiloh, in which Grant and W. T. Sherman were surprised by Albert Sidney Johnston and nearly driven into the Tennessee River, before the arrival of D. C. Buell and the death of Johnston helped turn the tide. Until July, 1863, Grant occupied himself with plans to take the Confederate stronghold of Vicksburg, which would split the Confederacy in two and give the Union control of the last railroad leading east from the Mississippi. After one abortive attempt in the fall of 1862, Grant determined to march his troops down the west bank of the river to a rendezvous with David Porter's gunboats which were to run the batteries and then ferry Grant's men to the east bank. The plan was successful; after interposing between the forces of Joseph E. Johnston and John C. Pemberton, Grant defeated Johnston with his right, driving him out of Jackson, and with his left drove Pemberton into his fortifications at Vicksburg, after inflicting defeats on him at Baker's Creek (Champion's Hill) and Big Black River Bridge. The Confederate garrison capitulated July 4, 1863, and Grant was acclaimed and rewarded with the appointment to major general in the Regular Army. In November came the relief of William S. Rosecrans' beleaguered forces in Chattanooga, the replacement of Rosecrans by George H. Thomas in command of the Army of the Cumberland, and the routing of Braxton Bragg's army by

the combined forces of Thomas, Sherman, and Joseph Hooker. A gold medal, the revived grade of lieutenant general carrying with it command of all the armies, and the adulation of the Union were now bestowed upon Grant. At this juncture a coordinated plan was devised to bring about the downfall of the Confederacy: hurling George G. Meade's Army of the Potomac against Robert E. Lee's Army of Northern Virginia, Benjamin F. Butler's Army of the James against Lee's communications, and Sherman's forces (Armies of the Ohio, Tennessee, and Cumberland) against Johnston's Confederate Army of Tennessee—which was entrenched ninety miles northwest of Atlanta. Making his headquarters with the Army of the Potomac, Grant directed the sanguinary struggles of the Wilderness, Spotsylvania Court House, the North Anna, and Cold Harbor in May and June of 1864. Union losses were staggering and equaled the entire strength of Lee's army at the beginning of the campaign. Following the failure to take Petersburg by assault, the siege was on from June 18 until the breakthrough the following spring; the campaign was a gradual extension of the Federal lines to the left to gain possession of the rail lines which supplied Petersburg and Richmond, highlighted by numerous assaults which in the main were successfully resisted by Lee. Sheridan's victory at Five Forks on April 1, 1865, and the penetration of the main Confederate line the following morning compelled Lee to evacuate the two cities and march westward hoping to unite with Johnston. But he was brought to bay at Appomattox and on the morning of April 9 surrendered to Grant. On April 26 the war was virtually over when Johnston surrendered to Sherman in North Carolina. The following year Congress revived the grade of full general, unused since the days of Washington, and conferred it upon the general in chief. His siding with the Congressional Radicals and Secretary of War Edwin M. Stanton against President Andrew Johnson during the Tenure of Office Act imbroglio made Grant the inevitable Republican candidate for President in 1868. He was easily elected over his opponent Horatio Seymour. Grant doled out Cabinet positions with little regard for fitness; criticism was not brooked; and gifts were loosely accepted. However, Grant's abundance of simple honesty weathered the storms of the 1873 panic, the earlier factionalism which had impeached a President, the dispute with England, and the threat of crisis during the disputed election of 1876. Following his retirement from the presidency, Grant traveled abroad for two years and in 1880 was a leading contender for nomination to a third term—306 delegates remaining loyal until the end, when a coalition of Grant's opponents agreed upon James A. Garfield as the candidate. The last years of Grant's life were marked by want, misfortune, and agonizing illness. He lived in New York in a house and on a trust fund donated by admirers for a time, but the income failed and he entered a business in which his name could be exploited. The insolvency of the brokerage firm of Grant & Ward threw Grant into bankruptcy and his swords and souvenirs were lost

as security for a loan which he had been unable to repay. At length his friends succeeded in having his name restored to the retired list of the army, carrying with it a salary for life. In his last months he wrote his memoirs which were published by Mark Twain. The *Personal Memoirs of U. S. Grant* proved to be one of the greatest successes in the annals of publishing, earning nearly $450,000 for his family. Toward the end, speechless and racked by throat cancer, Grant wrote notes on slips of paper in order to finish the manuscript. He died on July 23, 1885, at Mount McGregor, New York, and his remains lie in a mausoleum on Riverside Drive in New York City.

George Sears Greene was born on May 6, 1801, in Apponaug, Rhode Island, the son of a shipowner ruined by the Embargo Act and the War of 1812. He intended to enter

Brown University, but a scarcity of money compelled him to seek work in New York. In 1819 he was appointed to West Point, graduated second in the class of 1823, and entered the 3rd Artillery. For the next thirteen years Greene acted as an engineering instructor, mainly at the Academy, and served in garrison at various New England points. He resigned in 1836 to become a civil engineer and was employed on various works in the East and South. He was engaged with construction of the Croton Reservoir in Central Park, New York, in January, 1862, when he reentered the army as colonel of the 60th New York Infantry. He served with his regiment in the vicinity of Washington until he was promoted to brigadier general of volunteers on April 28. One of the oldest field commanders in the service, General Greene had a distinguished career, in command of a brigade and at times of a division, commencing with the battle of Cedar Mountain in N. P. Banks's command and ending in the Carolina campaign, where he was in Absalom Baird's division of the XIV Corps. He fought at Sharpsburg and Chancellorsville and with great distinction at Gettysburg, where his lone brigade of the XII Corps, posted on Culp's Hill, repelled Confederate attacks on the Union line of communications on the Baltimore Pike. When the XI and XII Corps were transferred west, Greene accompanied them and at Wauhatchie, in October, 1863, was so severely wounded in the face that he did not return to field duty until 1865. After being mustered out of service in 1866, he resumed his profession in New York and else-

where, doing important work in Washington, Detroit, Troy, and Yonkers. He was president from 1875 to 1877 of the American Society of Civil Engineers; was president for a time of the New York Genealogical and Biographical Society; compiled a genealogy of the Greene family; and closely followed the affairs of the Academy of which he was the oldest living graduate for some years. General Greene died in Morristown, New Jersey, on January 28, 1899, and was buried at Warwick, Rhode Island. One of his sons was executive officer of the *Monitor* in her fight with the *Merrimack*.

David McMurtrie Gregg was born in Huntingdon, Pennsylvania, on April 10, 1833, a first cousin of Andrew Gregg Curtin, Civil War gov-

ernor of the state, and paternal grandson of Andrew Gregg, who served from 1791 to 1813 in the U. S. House and Senate. Gregg's early education was obtained at private schools and at what is now Bucknell University. In 1851, he was appointed to the Military Academy, from which he was graduated in 1855 and appointed a brevet second lieutenant of dragoons. After duty on the Indian frontier, he was in garrison at Fort Tejon, California, when the Civil War began. In January, 1862, he received the appointment of colonel of the 8th Pennsylvania Cavalry and, after capable service on the Peninsula and in the Maryland campaign under George B. McClellan, was appointed a volunteer brigadier general to rank from November 29, 1862. During George Stoneman's abortive raid against Richmond in the campaign of Chancellorsville, Gregg commanded a division. The following month he was covering the extreme right of the Union line at Gettysburg, when he fought a sharp cavalry battle against Jeb Stuart's troopers, which secured for the Federal army its last threatened artery. Although Alfred Pleasonton was in command of the cavalry, Gregg has been cited in some accounts as having "gained one of the most conspicuous cavalry victories of the war." In the course of Grant's Overland campaign against Richmond in 1864, General Gregg distinguished himself in command of the 2nd Division of the Cavalry Corps. It is difficult to explain his resignation from both regular and volunteer service on February 3, 1865. The records are silent and General Philip Sheridan notes in his autobiography: ". . . it is to be regretted he felt obliged a few months later to quit the service. . . ." (150) According to Cullum's *Register*, Gregg was a farmer near

Milford, Delaware, until Grant made him United States consul at Prague in 1874, where he served only briefly. Until his death on August 7, 1916, he resided in Reading, Pennsylvania, where he was buried in the Charles Evans Cemetery. In 1907 General Gregg published *The Second Cavalry Division of the Army of the Potomac in the Gettysburg Campaign.*

Walter Quintin Gresham, of English descent, was born near the hamlet of Lanesville, Indiana, on March 17, 1832. His early life included education in a log-cabin schoolhouse, teaching, clerking in

the office of a succession of county officials, attendance at a nearby seminary and at the state university, the study of law, admission to the bar in 1854, and the commencement of a successful practice. He was moderately opposed to slavery, despite the fact that Corydon, the county seat, was a station on the underground railroad. Gresham campaigned for office a number of times under several party labels, but was successful only once: in 1860 he was elected to the Indiana legislature as a Republican. In this capacity he fell out with Governor Oliver P. Morton, but recruited his own company and on March 10, 1862, was advanced to colonel of the 53rd Indiana. Gresham's regiment was not under fire at Shiloh, but acquitted itself well in the Vicksburg campaign, where it formed a part of Lauman's division of the XVI Corps. On August 11, 1863, Gresham was appointed brigadier general and assigned to command a brigade of the XVII Corps at Natchez. During the Atlanta campaign he led the 4th Division of the corps until on July 20 his knee was smashed by a sharpshooter's bullet —a wound which ended his military career. With the brevet of major general, he commenced the practice of law at New Albany, Indiana, as soon as he could maneuver on crutches. Despite his war record, Gresham was defeated in his bids for public office: twice for the House and once for the Senate. In 1883, President Chester A. Arthur appointed him Postmaster General; he served eighteen months, during which he curtailed the Louisiana state lottery by excluding it from the mails. The following year Gresham served briefly as Secretary of the Treasury until he accepted an appointment as United States circuit judge. A presidential hopeful in both the 1884 and 1888 Republican conventions, he flirted with the Populists in 1892 and the

following year, in reward for supporting Grover Cleveland, was named Secretary of State. He died in Washington during his term of office on May 28, 1895, and was buried in Arlington National Cemetery.

Benjamin Henry Grierson was born of Irish parentage in Pittsburgh, Pennsylvania, on July 8, 1826. He was educated at an academy in Y o u n g s t o w n, Ohio, and later

taught music there and at Jacksonville, Illinois. After 1856 he kept a store at Meredosia, a nearby hamlet on the Illinois River. When the Civil War came, Grierson entered the service as a volunteer aide-de-camp to General Benjamin M. Prentiss. He was commissioned major of the 6th Illinois Cavalry in October, 1861, and became its colonel the following April. During that spring and summer the regiment was engaged in a number

189

of skirmishes in Tennessee and Mississippi, its squadrons being posted at three different stations. In the latter part of December the regiment was reunited and took part in the pursuit of Earl Van Dorn after his Holly Springs raid. On April 17, 1863, under orders from U. S. Grant, Grierson left La Grange, Tennessee, in command of seventeen hundred men of the 6th and 7th Illinois and the 2nd Iowa in a raid southward through the heart of the C o n f e d e r a c y. In seventeen days the command marched eight hundred miles, repeatedly engaged the Confederates, ruined two railroads, and destroyed vast amounts of property, finally riding into Baton Rouge on May 2. For his feat Grierson was appointed brigadier general of volunteers to rank from June 3, 1863. He later commanded a cavalry division and at times the Cavalry Corps of the Army of the Mississippi during 1864 and 1865. In 1865 he took part in the campaign against Mobile. He was commissioned major general of volunteers on March 19, 1866, to rank from May 27, 1865, and was mustered out of volunteer service on April 30, 1866. Upon the reorganization of the Regular Army that July, Grierson was appointed colonel of the 10th Cavalry. The following year he was awarded the brevets of brigadier general and major general, U. S. Army. In the postwar years Grierson was stationed mainly in the Southwest, commanding at various times the Department of Arizona and the Districts of New Mexico and Indian Territory. He was promoted to brigadier general on April 5, 1890, and retired three months later. Residing in Jackson-

ville thereafter, he died at his summer home in Omena, Michigan, on September 1, 1911, and was buried in Jacksonville Cemetery.

Charles Griffin was born on December 18, 1825, in Granville, Ohio. He left Kenyon College to enter West Point in 1843; he was graduated four years later and was commissioned in the artillery. He

served under Winfield Scott in Mexico and then in the Southwest until his appointment to instruct in artillery tactics at the Military Academy in 1860. At the threat of war in January, 1861, Griffin was ordered to organize a field battery from the detachments of Regulars stationed at West Point; it was immediately ordered to the Capital and saw distinguished service at First Manassas, resulting in Griffin's receiving the brevet of major. In the course of the Peninsular campaign Griffin was promoted to brigadier general of volunteers to rank from June 9, 1862, and thereupon was assigned a brigade in Fitz John Porter's V Corps. This association at Second Manassas resulted in Porter's ruin by court-martial; however, Griffin was ultimately restored to command, even though he had staunchly defended Porter. (151) Griffin commanded a division of the corps at Fredericksburg under General Joseph Hooker, Porter's successor, and in the campaign of Chancellorsville under Daniel E. Sickles. He was absent because of illness during the Gettysburg campaign, although he arrived on the field July 3. In the course of the Richmond campaign General Griffin served continuously in command of his division of the V Corps at the Wilderness, Spotsylvania, Cold Harbor, and Petersburg, where his reputation as an idol of his men and a "hard case" as well was solidified. At one point during the Overland campaign, Grant thought George G. Meade should place Griffin under arrest for insubordinate remarks. Nonetheless, at Five Forks, Philip Sheridan relieved Gouverneur K. Warren with Griffin, a change of commanders which, despite Griffin's demonstrated ability, has found small favor among historians, mainly because of the alleged injustice to Warren. Griffin was commissioned major general of volunteers on April 2, 1865, and was one of the commissioners designated to carry out the surrender of the Army of Northern Virginia. Upon the reorganization of the Regular Army in 1866, Griffin was appointed colonel of the 35th Infantry and posted to duty in command of

the District of Texas. He refused to leave Galveston when an epidemic of yellow fever broke out there, and he died of the disease on September 15, 1867. He was buried in Oak Hill Cemetery, Georgetown, D. C. (152)

Simon Goodell Griffin was born in the New Hampshire hamlet of Nelson on August 9, 1824. Both of his grandfathers were veterans of the

American Revolution. After a rudimentary education interspersed with work on his uncle's farm, Griffin taught school, served in the legislature, studied law, and in 1860 gained admittance to the state bar. At the outbreak of war he was elected captain of a company of the 2nd New Hampshire and fought at First Manassas in Ambrose E. Burnside's brigade. The following October he resigned to become lieutenant colonel of the 6th New

Hampshire, with which he took part in Burnside's expedition on the Carolina coast. In April, 1862, Griffin became colonel of the regiment and that August led it at Second Manassas in Burnside's IX Corps, a command with which he was associated until the end of the war. The regiment suffered heavy losses in the attempt to carry "Burnside's Bridge" at Sharpsburg, and Griffin's men lost one third of their number at Fredericksburg. In May, 1863, he was assigned to command a brigade of the IX Corps and took part in the Vicksburg campaign. During the winter of 1863-64, Griffin commanded Camp Nelson, Kentucky, for a time, and then engaged in re-recruiting the New Hampshire regiments whose three-year enlistments were about to expire. During U. S. Grant's campaign against Petersburg and Richmond, Griffin commanded first his old brigade and then a division of the IX Corps. He was promoted to brigadier general to rank from May 12, 1864, and received the brevet of major general on April 2, 1865. Upon his muster out the following August it was recorded that he had not missed a day's duty during the war. General Griffin returned to New Hampshire and engaged in manufacturing in the town of Harrisville until 1873, meantime serving three terms in the state legislature and running twice, unsuccessfully, for a seat in Congress. He became interested in land and railroad speculation in Texas, where he spent a number of years. He returned to New Hampshire and settled in Keene, where he occupied himself with literary work and the interests of the Military Order of the Loyal Legion. General Griffin died in Keene on January 14, 1902, and was buried there.

William Grose, whose father and grandfathers fought the British in two wars, was born on December 16, 1812, near Dayton, Ohio. His father made two moves during his boyhood, first to Fayette County,

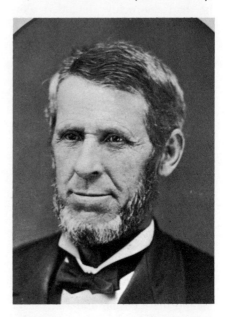

Indiana, and later to Henry County. Young Grose studied law while working as a farm laborer, was admitted to the bar, and began practice in New Castle, his home for the rest of a long life. Grose ran for Congress unsuccessfully as a Democrat in 1852 and four years later was a delegate to the first Republican National Convention. A few months after being elected common pleas judge, he was appointed on October 23, 1861, colonel of the 36th Indiana Infantry, the only regiment of Don Carlos Buell's army to participate in the first day's fighting at the bloody battle of Shiloh. (153) The month following his appointment Grose was assigned to command the brigade which had been Jacob Ammen's. He participated in all the operations of the Army of the Cumberland, in the Kentucky campaign, at Vicksburg, Chickamauga, and Chattanooga, and in the interminable series of skirmishes, fights, and maneuvers which made up the advance of W. T. Sherman's forces from Dalton to Atlanta. He was commissioned brigadier general to rank from July 30, 1864, while under fire in front of Atlanta. Subsequently, he accompanied General G. H. Thomas back to Tennessee and in the rout of John B. Hood's Confederate forces at Franklin and Nashville commanded a brigade in Nathan Kimball's division of Thomas J. Wood's IV Corps. Grose was brevetted major general to rank from August 13, 1865, while he was serving as president of a court-martial in Nashville. He resigned his commission on January 31, 1866, to return to civilian life, and later that year President Johnson named him collector of internal revenue for his area, a post he occupied until 1874. Thereafter, he served on a state commission to build mental hospitals. In 1887 he was elected to the Indiana senate. Four years later he published a regimental history of the 36th Indiana. On July 30, 1900, General Grose died at his home in New Castle and was buried in South Mound Cemetery.

Cuvier Grover was born in Bethel, Maine, July 29, 1828, a younger brother of Governor and Senator La Fayette Grover of Oregon. (154) Young Grover was prepared for college at the age of fifteen, but too young to enter West Point, he engaged in business in Boston for two years. In 1850 he was graduated fourth in his class from the Military Academy. His most important antebellum duty was in connection with the Northern Pacific Railroad exploration in 1853-54; he also served in the Mormon expedition and in frontier garrison duty. At the outbreak of the Civil War he was a captain of the 10th Infantry, stationed at Fort Union, New Mexico. (155) On leave of absence from November, 1861, until April, 1862, he was appointed a brigadier general of volunteers to rank from April 14, 1862. He won two brevets in the Regular Army for his conduct during the Peninsular campaign, where he led the 1st Brigade of Hooker's 2nd Division, Heintzelman's III Corps. Grover's brigade was then transferred to John Pope's Army of Virginia and with it engaged in the ill-fated campaign of Second Manassas, sustaining 486 casualties, mainly at Groveton in the assault on Stonewall Jackson's position behind the railroad embankment. Grover was then transferred to the Department of the Gulf, where he took charge of the 4th Division of N. P. Banks's XIX Corps. In this theater he commanded the right wing of Banks's forces at the siege of Port Hudson and was again moved, along with the corps, now under William H. Emory, to the seat of war in Virginia. For gallant services at Winchester and Fisher's Hill, Grover was brevetted major general of volunteers and for his conduct at Cedar Creek (where he was wounded) was awarded the brevet of brigadier general, U. S. Army. At the end of the war he was in command of the District of Savannah, Georgia, having won the brevet of major general, U. S. Army. He was appointed lieutenant colonel of the 38th Infantry, a Negro regiment, upon the reorganization of the army in 1866; was unassigned in 1869; and, subsequently, became colonel of the 1st Cavalry. In 1885 he went to Atlantic City in an effort to improve his health, but died there on June 6. He was buried at West Point.

Pleasant Adam Hackleman, son of an officer of the War of 1812, was born on November 15, 1814, in Franklin County, Indiana. He gained admittance to the state bar at the age of twenty-five and soon won distinction in the practice of his profession in Rushville, county seat of Rush County, Indiana. Hackleman was successively judge of the county probate court, clerk of the state house of representatives, county clerk, and in

1848 and 1858 an unsuccessful candidate for Congress. He was a delegate to the Republican National Convention which nominated Abraham Lincoln and was a delegate to the "Washington Peace Conference," which failed to arrest the coming Civil War. On May 20, 1861, he was commissioned colonel of the 16th Indiana Infantry, a regiment mustered into Federal service two days after the disaster at First Manassas and the first command to pass through Baltimore after the firing upon the 6th Massachusetts the preceding April. The regiment served under General N. P. Banks, attached to the brigade of General J. J. Abercrombie and took part in the Union misfortune at Ball's Bluff in October. On April 28, 1862, Hackleman was promoted to brigadier general of volunteers and in June was ordered to report to General U. S. Grant in Tennessee, where he was assigned to command a brigade of General Thomas A. Davies' division of the Army of

194

West Tennessee, consisting of the 52nd Illinois, the 2nd and 7th Iowa, and detachments from the 58th Illinois and the 8th, 12th, and 14th Iowa. At the battle of Corinth (following the earlier siege of Corinth after the battle of Shiloh), Hackleman was mortally wounded on October 3, 1862, while displaying conspicuous gallantry in rallying his own and other troops against the Confederate attack on the town by Generals Sterling Price and Earl Van Dorn. He died that night in a room at the Tishomingo Hotel in Corinth (156), and was buried in Rushville.

Henry Wager Halleck was born in Westernville, New York, on January 16, 1815. Early in life he ran away from home because of his dislike for farming and was adopted by his maternal grandfather, who sent him successively to the Hudson Academy, Union College (where he was elected to Phi

Beta Kappa), and West Point, from which he was graduated third in the class of 1839. An assistant professor while still an undergraduate at the Military Academy, Halleck first worked upon the fortifications of New York Harbor and in 1844 inspected those of France. Upon his return to the United States he wrote a *Report on the Means of National Defence,* which was published by Congress and won him an invitation from the Lowell Institute of Boston to deliver a series of lectures. These were published as *Elements of Military Art and Science,* a work which enjoyed wide circulation among soldiers for many years. En route to California by ship around the Horn at the outbreak of the Mexican War, Halleck translated Henri Jomini's monumental *Vie Politique et Militaire de Napoleon,* published in 1864. In California he discharged numerous important duties under the military government, including those of secretary of state, chief of staff in lower California, and lieutenant governor of the Mexican city of Mazatlán. At the conclusion of the war he was brevetted captain of engineers and in 1853 was regularly promoted. Meantime he served as aide to General Bennet Riley, as inspector and engineer of lighthouses, and as member of the board of engineers for Pacific Coast fortifications. He also played a prominent part in the formulation of the California constitution and studied law; upon his resignation from the army in 1854, he became head of the leading law firm in California, Halleck, Peachy & Billings. Refusing a state supreme court justiceship and a seat in the

U. S. Senate, Halleck turned his talents to business, writing, and the California militia; in all of these fields he was markedly successful, acquiring a fortune and publishing several authoritative books on mining law and international law. In 1855 he married a granddaughter of Alexander Hamilton and thus became the brother-in-law of Major General Schuyler Hamilton, U. S. Volunteers. At the beginning of the Civil War, General Winfield Scott recommended to Abraham Lincoln that Halleck be appointed major general in the regular service; this was accordingly done, with rank from August 19, 1861. (At the time he was ranked only by Scott himself, George B. McClellan, and John C. Frémont.) His brilliant accomplishments early in his career contrast strangely with the later estimates of his contemporaries. Lincoln came to regard him as "little more than a first rate clerk"; Edwin M. Stanton characterized him as "probably the greatest scoundrel and most bare-faced villain in America"; McClellan felt that he was "the most hopelessly stupid of all men in high position"; and Gideon Welles summed it all up by stating in his celebrated diary that "[Halleck] originates nothing, anticipates nothing . . . takes no responsibility, plans nothing, suggests nothing, is good for nothing." (157) In November, 1861, Halleck relieved Frémont at St. Louis and, in a demonstration of his undoubted talents as an administrator quickly brought order out of the chaos in which his predecessor had plunged the Department of the Missouri. A series of successes by his subordinates—U. S. Grant at Forts Henry and Donelson, Samuel R.

Curtis at Elkhorn Tavern (Pea Ridge), John Pope at Island No. 10, and Grant again at Shiloh—caused Halleck to shine in reflected glory, and his domain, enlarged to include Ohio and Kansas, was named the Department of the Mississippi. When he took the field himself, however, his shortcomings became immediately apparent. With twice the number of P. G. T. Beauregard's forces, he moved too slowly on the rail junction of Corinth, permitting the Confederates to evacuate the town at their leisure. Lincoln now called Halleck to Washington as general in chief. One of Grant's biographers acidly commented: "Unable to command successfully one army, he was ordered to Washington to command all the armies." (158) "Old Brains" now became known as "Old Wooden Head," as he plunged into a welter of minutiae, criticizing his subordinates for his own mistakes and frequently offering superfluous advice. (159) In general he allowed the main purpose of the war to be obscured by his preoccupation with the manner of raising men and material. Perhaps his worst fault was his continual effort to shift responsibility to the shoulders of others; his primary virtue was his unflinching insistence upon order and discipline —both sadly lacking in the early days of the war. With Grant's promotion to the chief command in March, 1864, Halleck was demoted to chief of staff but continued to discharge much the same duties as theretofore. After Appomattox he served briefly as commander of the Military Division of the James and in August, 1865, was transferred to the command of the Pacific with headquarters at San Francisco. In

1869 he was appointed to command the Division of the South, with headquarters at Louisville, where he died on January 9, 1872. He was buried in Green-Wood Cemetery, Brooklyn, New York.

Joseph Eldridge Hamblin was born on January 13, 1828, probably in Yarmouth, Massachusetts. He was educated in the Boston public schools; was employed by a firm of engine builders, first in Boston and then in New York; and in 1854 be-

came an insurance broker in the latter city. In 1851 he became a member of the 7th Regiment, New York National Guard. He resided in St. Louis from 1857 until 1861, returning to New York when the war began and accompanying the 7th Regiment to Washington a week after the fall of Sumter. On May 14 he was mustered into Federal service as first lieutenant and adjutant of the 5th New York Infantry, also known as "Duryée's Zouaves," with which he took part in the first battle of the war at Big Bethel on June 10. (160) After some engineering duty at Baltimore, Hamblin was promoted to captain and then transferred to the 65th New York as major. With successive promotions to lieutenant colonel (July, 1862) and colonel (May, 1863), he took part in the Peninsular campaign, the Maryland campaign, and the battles of Fredericksburg, Chancellorsville, and Gettysburg—the regiment was first a part of the 3rd Brigade of the 1st Division of the IV Corps and then, after Sharpsburg, of the 3rd Division of the VI Corps. Hamblin served under U. S. Grant from the Wilderness to Petersburg in the spring of 1864 and went to the Shenandoah with the VI Corps under Horatio G. Wright to participate in the battles of Winchester, Fisher's Hill, and Cedar Creek. At the latter battle he commanded a brigade, was severely wounded in the right leg, and received the brevet of brigadier general for "gallant and meritorious services." After his return to duty, he commanded the 3rd Brigade of Wheaton's 1st Division of the VI Corps at Hatcher's Run and in the other engagements leading up to Appomattox, winning the brevet of major general for conspicuous gallantry at Sayler's Creek. His commission as full brigadier general of volunteers dated from May 19, 1865. After the war General Hamblin reentered the insurance business in New York and in 1867 became adjutant general and chief of staff of the New York National Guard. At the time of his death in

New York on July 3, 1870, he was superintendent of agencies for the Commonwealth Fire Insurance Company. He was buried in Yarmouth.

Andrew Jackson Hamilton was born in Huntsville, Alabama, on January 28, 1815. He studied law and was admitted to the bar in 1841. Six years later he moved to

Fayette County, Texas, and in 1849 became state attorney general. He resided thereafter in Austin. In 1851-53 he served in the legislature and in 1859 was elected to Congress as an uncompromising Unionist, although speaking out for conciliation of the South. When other Texas representatives withdrew, Hamilton remained in his seat, returning to the state in March, 1861, to be again elected to the legislature as an opponent of secession. With the advent of war Hamilton came to be regarded as a traitor and in 1862 fled to Mexico and thence to Wash-

ington. Abraham Lincoln promptly appointed him a brigadier general of volunteers to rank from November 14, 1862, and military governor of Texas. Hamilton spent most of the balance of the war in New Orleans. A controversial figure in Washington, Hamilton was characterized by Gideon Welles as a "deceptive, vain, self-conceited partisan." His first appointment as brigadier general was not acted upon by the Senate and expired by law on March 4, 1863. However, Lincoln reappointed him to rank from September 18 and his appointment as governor was ratified by President Andrew Johnson in June, 1865, whereupon he resigned his military commission. The fourteen months of his provisional administration were characterized by tact, courage, efficiency, and moderation and in August, 1866, he was succeeded by a regularly elected set of officials. He then ascended the state supreme court bench, where his decisions reflected a conservative view; in 1868 he opposed the Reconstruction measure calling for disfranchisement of the Southern whites. This resulted in the conservatives' nominating him for governor in 1869, a race he lost. Hamilton's last appearance in the political arena came in 1873 when he sought to challenge the election of the Democrats, who had redeemed the state from the carpetbaggers, in the courts. Two years later, he died in Austin on April 11, 1875, and was buried in Oakwood Cemetery.

Charles Smith Hamilton was born in the hamlet of Westernville, New York, on November 16, 1822; early in his life his parents moved to Erie County and he was educated at the

Aurora Academy before receiving an appointment to West Point in 1839. Hamilton was graduated in the class of 1843, ranking five below U. S. Grant, and was brevetted a second lieutenant of infantry. In the course of the Mexican War he won promotion to the regular rank

of first lieutenant and the brevet of captain for gallantry and was badly wounded at Molino del Rey. In 1853, after five years of routine duty, he resigned to engage in farming and to manufacture flour at Fond du Lac, Wisconsin. At the outbreak of the Civil War, Hamilton promptly offered himself for service and on May 11, 1861, was commissioned colonel of the 3rd Wisconsin Infantry and six days later brigadier general of volunteers. He served in the Shenandoah during the winter of 1862 and commanded a division of Heintzelman's III Corps on the Peninsula until he was relieved by General George B.

McClellan after the siege of Yorktown on April 30, 1862, and superseded by General Philip Kearny. Powerful political pressure for his restoration to command failed to sway McClellan, who declared him "not fit to command a division." (161) Accordingly, he was dispatched to the western theater, where he performed most creditably at Iuka and Corinth in command of a division of William S. Rosecrans' Army of the Mississippi. During this period he was promoted to major general to rank from September 19, 1862, supposedly upon the interposition of Grant. At the same time that Hamilton was assuring Grant of his esteem and devotion, he privately assured Senator James R. Doolittle of Wisconsin that "Grant is a drunkard." After other criticisms of superiors, coupled with his efforts to obtain command of James B. McPherson's XVII Corps, Grant protested strongly to Washington, with the result that Hamilton offered his resignation. (162) It was promptly accepted on April 13, 1863. He returned to Fond du Lac and in 1869, paradoxically, was appointed United States marshal in Milwaukee by Grant. He was also a successful businessman in Milwaukee, member and president of the board of regents of the University of Wisconsin, and commander of the Wisconsin department of the Military Order of the Loyal Legion. General Hamilton died in Milwaukee on April 17, 1891, and was buried there in Forest Home Cemetery.

Schuyler Hamilton, a grandson of Alexander Hamilton, was born in New York City on July 25, 1822.

He entered the Military Academy at the age of fifteen and was graduated in 1841, ranking twenty-fourth in a class of fifty-two. He was commissioned second lieutenant, 1st Infantry, shortly before his nineteenth birthday. He served on the plains and as an assistant instructor in infantry tactics at West Point before the Mexican War. He won two brevets for gallantry in Mexico and was twice critically wounded, once by a ball in the abdomen and once by a lance which passed entirely through his chest, piercing his lung. He served as aide-de-camp to General Winfield Scott for seven years and resigned his commission in 1855. For a time Hamilton lived in California; however, at the outbreak of the war he was settled on a farm at Branford, Connecticut. He returned to Washington as a volunteer private in the 7th New York National Guard in April, 1861, and soon was again serving Scott as military secretary with the staff rank of colonel. Upon Scott's retirement Hamilton joined his brother-in-law Henry W. Halleck in St. Louis as assistant chief of staff of the Department of the Missouri. He was commissioned brigadier general of volunteers to rank from November 12, 1861. In the operations against New Madrid and Island No. 10 he commanded a division under John Pope and then participated in the slow advance upon and siege of Corinth under Halleck. Hamilton commanded the left wing of the Army of the Mississippi and William S. Rosecrans commanded the right wing. At this juncture Hamilton fell ill of malaria and went on sick leave. He was appointed major general of volunteers to rank from September 17, 1862, an appointment which would expire by law if not confirmed by the Senate by March 3, 1863. Understanding that the nomination of an officer unfit for service could not be submitted to the Senate for confirmation, Hamilton resigned on February 27, 1863. In later years he felt that he had been dealt an injustice and endeavored to be placed upon the retired list, without success. His remaining years were spent at his New York home, where he died on March 8, 1903. He was buried in Green-Wood Cemetery, Brooklyn.

Cyrus Hamlin, son of Senator and Vice-President Hannibal Hamlin, was born on April 26, 1839, at Hampden, Maine. He was educated at the Hampden Academy and at Colby College, Waterville, Maine, but left the latter school before graduation in order to study law. He was admitted to the bar in 1860 and began practice in York County, Maine. Hamlin did not enter military service until April, 1862, when he was mustered in as aide-de-camp with rank of captain and assigned to the staff of General John C. Frémont, for whom he discharged the duties of acting commissary of subsistence. He attracted Frémont's notice by his conduct at

the battle of Cross Keys and was among the first army officers to advocate the enlistment of Negroes. He was appointed colonel of the 80th U. S. Colored Infantry, February 12, 1863, although the regiment itself (originally called the 8th Corps d'Afrique) was not organized at Port Hudson, Louisiana, until September 1, 1863, and was not named until April 4, 1864. After the fall of Port Hudson in July, 1863, Hamlin's men were garrisoned there along with the balance of the Corps d'Afrique, consisting of eleven regiments divided into two divisions. The 1st Division contained two brigades (one

commanded by Hamlin); the 2nd Division, only its 2nd Brigade —the *Official Records* tersely remark, "The First Brigade disintegrated." (163) Hamlin commanded the district of Bonnet Carré, Louisiana, for some time and on December 13, 1864, was commissioned brigadier general of volunteers. In the omnibus promotions of 1865, Hamlin was brevetted major general. (164) He remained in New Orleans after the war as an active lawyer and carpetbagger and died of yellow fever on August 28, 1867, at the age of twenty-eight. General Hamlin was first buried in Girod Cemetery, New Orleans, but three months later was removed to the family ground in Mount Hope Cemetery, Bangor, Maine.

William Alexander Hammond was born on August 28, 1828, in Annapolis, Maryland. After obtaining his primary education in Harrisburg, Pennsylvania, he was graduated from New York University

201

Medical College in 1848. In 1849 he was appointed assistant surgeon in the Army Medical Corps and for ten years served at various posts, meantime publishing in 1857 a widely read treatise on nutrition. In 1860 he resigned to accept a professorship at the University of Maryland, which he gave up the following year together with a profitable practice in Baltimore, to go back into the army. A prime example of the evils of the seniority system, "the length of his previous service and the brilliance of his qualifications were . . . ignored [and] he was entered at the bottom of the list of assistant surgeons." (165) In the months that followed, Hammond's abilities were pressed upon the administration by a barrage of letters and physicians' delegations—in the main instigated by the pro-Hammond sanitary commission and General George B. McClellan—with the result that he was appointed surgeon general with rank of brigadier general, U. S. Army, on April 25, 1862. Hammond began at once to revitalize the moribund Medical Department: appropriations were increased tenfold; younger men were promoted to positions of responsibility; red tape was eliminated; and a much-needed ambulance corps was organized. Many of Hammond's edicts conflicted with other vested interests and soon his relations with the all-powerful Secretary of War Edwin M. Stanton began to deteriorate. (166) At length, after being ordered away from Washington and an acting successor named, Hammond demanded a court-martial. Having engaged in a game of power politics with Stanton, Hammond should not

have been surprised that, upon the flimsiest evidence, he was convicted of ungentlemanly conduct and dismissed from the service. He nevertheless enjoyed a most distinguished postbellum career: he became a pioneer in the treatment of nervous and mental diseases; a most successful practitioner; and wrote largely and authoritatively on a variety of subjects. He died in Washington on January 5, 1900, and was buried in Arlington National Cemetery. (167)

Winfield Scott Hancock, one of twin brothers, was born on February 14, 1824, in the Pennsylvania hamlet of Montgomery Square, eleven miles north of Norristown. Four years after his birth the family moved to Norristown, where his father studied law and his mother became a milliner. Young Winfield attended school in Norristown and in 1840 received an appointment to West Point, where he was grad-

uated eighteenth of twenty-five members four years later—probably the youngest graduate of that year. After two years' service in the Indian Territory, Hancock won a brevet for gallantry in Mexico, following which he took part in operations against the Seminoles in the Kansas War, in the Utah expedition against the Mormons as quartermaster under General William S. Harney with the forces sent to reenforce Albert Sidney Johnston, and as chief quartermaster at Los Angeles until the Civil War was well underway. (168) When he arrived in the East, General George B. McClellan at once secured Hancock's appointment as brigadier general of volunteers to rank from September 23, 1861. The following spring his brigade—containing one regiment each from Maine, New York, Pennsylvania, and Wisconsin—took a gallant part in the Peninsular and Maryland campaigns. In the course of the battle of Sharpsburg, Hancock succeeded to the command of the 1st Division of the II Corps after the mortal wounding of General Israel B. Richardson and was made major general to rank from November 29, 1862. He took a distinguished part in the battle of Fredericksburg; at Chancellorsville under Darius N. Couch, he employed parts of three regiments to cover his entire division front in the protection of the Union left flank and rear guard, while the balance of the Army of the Potomac retired across the Rappahannock. The employment of a skirmish line consisting of a man every three yards, which successfully resisted a series of heavy Confederate attacks, came to be regarded as a classic maneuver of defensive warfare. Two months later Hancock rode upon the field of Gettysburg on July 1, with broad discretionary powers from army commander George G. Meade, to find the I and XI Corps shattered and driven from their original positions; John F. Reynolds was dead and Oliver O. Howard was contentious about seniority. Brushing aside the objections of Howard, Hancock took command, ordered the Federal line anchored on Cemetery Ridge, advised Meade this was the place to fight, and threw up such a formidable front to the onrushing Confederates that General Robert E. Lee issued discretionary orders to General Richard S. Ewell relative to attacking. This cost the South the position of Culp's Hill and possibly the campaign. On the second day the left wing of the Federal army under Hancock successfully prevented James Longstreet's two divisions under John B. Hood and Lafayette McLaws from flanking the Union position on the Round Tops. The following day while his corps was repulsing George E. Pickett's celebrated charge against the Union left center, Hancock received a wound from which he never fully recovered (a bullet carried a nail and bits of wood from the pommel of his saddle into his thigh). (169) Disabled by his wound, he did not return to duty until the end of the year, when he reassumed command of the II Corps. Both he and the corps were conspicuous in the desperate fighting which marked U. S. Grant's advance on Petersburg, punctuated by the bloody battles of the Wilderness, Spotsylvania, Cold Harbor, Deep Bottom, Reams's Station, and the Boydton Plank

Road. On August 12, 1864, he was made brigadier general in the Regular Army. After his wound reopened in November, 1864, he went to Washington to attempt to recruit a "Veteran Reserve Corps." His efforts met with slight success, and in February, 1865, he assumed departmental command, which he exercised until the war's end. From 1866, Hancock, now a regular major general, saw varied service throughout the nation, ultimately assuming command of the Department of the East, with headquarters at Governors Island, New York, on November 8, 1877. In 1880, General Hancock, who had received the votes of a number of delegates at the 1868 Democratic National Convention, was nominated at Cincinnati for the presidency. He ran against James A. Garfield and lost by a narrow margin. On February 9, 1886, he died at Governors Island while still in command of the Department of the East, and was buried in Montgomery Cemetery, Norristown. Of all the accolades which came his way, including the thanks of Congress for his services at Gettysburg, perhaps the most revealing was that of one of his staff members: "One felt safe when near him." (170)

James Allen Hardie was born in New York City on May 5, 1823. Before receiving an appointment to West Point in 1839 by President Martin Van Buren, he attended Western Collegiate Institute at Pittsburgh and the Poughkeepsie Collegiate School in New York. Hardie was graduated from the Military Academy at the age of twenty, ranking eleventh in a class of thirty-nine cadets, and was pro-

moted to the 1st Artillery. He served in barracks, at his alma mater as an assistant professor, and in the Mexican War as major of the 1st New York Volunteers, a regiment sent to garrison San Francisco. After the Mexican War he was stationed at various points, was aide to General John E. Wool for a time, and was promoted to captain in 1857. At the outbreak of the Civil War he was adjutant general of the Department of Oregon. He was soon made lieutenant colonel and aide-de-camp to General George B. McClellan, and in the spring of 1862 accompanied the latter to the Virginia Peninsula as adjutant general of the Army of the Potomac. He acted in this capacity during the campaign in Maryland, which culminated in the battle of Sharpsburg. During the battle of Fredericksburg the new army commander Ambrose E. Burnside assigned Hardie to the headquarters of the "Left Grand Division" under W. B. Franklin, where he kept

Burnside informed of developments. Hardie was appointed brigadier general of volunteers to rank from November 29, 1862, but his name was not submitted to the Senate for confirmation and the records show that the appointment was revoked on January 22, 1863. (171) A month later he was appointed major and assistant adjutant general in the regular service (172) and in March, 1864, colonel and inspector general. He discharged the duties of this office with distinction until the end of the war, meantime carrying out a number of important special assignments for the War Department. In March, 1865, Hardie received the brevets of brigadier and major general, U. S. Army. After the war he continued as one of the four inspectors general holding the rank of colonel as authorized by the Act of 1866; he was stationed in various military departments and at army headquarters in Washington. He died on December 14, 1876, and was buried in Mount Olivet Cemetery. (173)

Martin Davis Hardin was born in Jacksonville, Illinois, June 26, 1837. (174) He was the grandson of U. S. Senator Martin Davis Hardin of Kentucky and the son of Major General John J. Hardin, Illinois Militia, who was killed at the battle of Buena Vista in the Mexican War while commanding the 1st Illinois Volunteer Infantry. Young Hardin was graduated from West Point in 1859 in a class which included the Confederate cavalry leader "Fightin'" Joe Wheeler. (175) After some routine service as a lieutenant of artillery in Oregon, Hardin embarked upon a combat career in the Civil War which has

few parallels in the annals of the army for gallantry, wounds sustained, and the obscurity into which he had lapsed a generation before his death. In the Peninsular campaign he acted as aide to Henry J. Hunt, chief of George B. McClellan's reserve artillery; was wounded twice at Second Manassas; commanded the 12th Pennsylvania Reserve Volunteers as colonel; was disabled by his wounds for various intervals from August, 1862, until June, 1863; commanded his regiment with distinction in the battle of Gettysburg and a brigade of the V Corps during the ensuing operations of Bristoe Station and Mine Run. That December, while inspecting his picket line near Catlett's Station on the Orange and Alexandria Railroad, he was bushwhacked by Rebel guerrillas and lost his left arm. He returned to duty and in the spring of 1864 sustained another wound at the crossing of the North Anna during U. S.

Grant's push toward Richmond. While convalescing he commanded the Washington defenses during Jubal Early's raid in July and continued in this command until the end of the war. Hardin received the regular rank of brigadier general of volunteers to rank from July 2, 1864, and at various stages all of the brevets through brigadier general in the Regular Army. In 1866 he was made major of the 43rd Infantry but four years later was retired as a brigadier general "for disability from wounds and loss of an arm in battle." Only thirty-three at this time, he studied law and practiced his profession in Chicago for a number of years. In later life he devoted much time to the affairs of the Military Order of the Loyal Legion and to writing, finally lapsing into total obscurity. He died in Saint Augustine, Florida, on December 12, 1923, one of the last survivors of the general officers on either side, and was buried in the National Cemetery there. (176)

Abner Clark Harding was born February 10, 1807, in East Hampton, Connecticut, but moved to Plainfield, New York, where he spent his boyhood years, tried to enlist in the navy, taught school, and engaged in business. He then moved to Bridgewater, New York, where he read law; to Lewisburg, Pennsylvania, where he was admitted to the bar and practiced for several years; and to Monmouth, Illinois, where he made his residence from 1838 until his death. He became interested in Illinois politics and was elected to a number of local and state offices and to the constitutional convention of 1848, being progressively a Jacksonian

Democrat, a regular Whig, an antislavery Whig, a Free-Soiler, and at the end a Republican. Around 1851 failing eyesight compelled him to turn from law to business. He was eminently successful, leaving at his death a fortune of $2 mil-

lion amassed from banking, railroad construction, and investments in farm lands. Harding's Civil War career was brief but highly creditable for a man of his age. He enlisted in the 83rd Illinois as a private but was soon commissioned its colonel. This regiment was recruited and mustered at Monmouth in August, 1862, and saw mainly bridge-guard duty until it became the Federal garrison of Fort Donelson a year after U. S. Grant had captured it from the Confederates. In February, 1863, two of the South's foremost cavalry leaders attempted to recapture the post in order to seize control of the Cumberland River: Generals Joe

Wheeler (in command) and N. B. Forrest surrounded the position and sent in a demand for surrender. Harding invited an attack which resulted in heavy Confederate casualties and the retirement of the Rebel forces and a breach between Wheeler and Forrest—the latter stating that he would never again fight under Wheeler. (177) For this exploit Harding was promoted to brigadier general to rank from March 13, 1863; however, in June he was compelled to resign from the service because of his failing eyesight. This handicap did not prevent his election to Congress in 1864 and his reelection in 1866. He died in Monmouth on July 19, 1874, and was buried there. (178)

Charles Garrison Harker was born on December 2, 1835, (179) at Swedesboro, New Jersey. He was left an orphan early in life and at the age of twelve or thirteen be-

came a clerk in a store in Mullica Hill, New Jersey, owned by N. T. Stratton, who served two terms in Congress from 1851 to 1855 and during this period procured for Harker an appointment to West Point. Harker entered the Academy in 1854 and was graduated in 1858 in the class which included the later Confederate brigadier Bryan M. Thomas. After service on the northwestern frontier, Harker was called east at the outbreak of the Civil War and was engaged in drilling Ohio troops, receiving the commission of colonel of the 65th Ohio Infantry on November 11, 1861. He joined Don Carlos Buell's Army of the Ohio and at Shiloh his regiment was attached to James A. Garfield's brigade of Thomas J. Wood's division. By the time of the battle of Perryville, Harker was commanding the 20th Brigade of Wood's division and assisted in "chasing [Braxton] Bragg out of Kentucky." At Murfreesboro in December, 1862, his conduct was so distinguished that Wood recommended him for promotion to brigadier general. At Chickamauga, Harker conducted the famous defense of the hill on which the Snodgrass house stood, which helped earn for G. H. Thomas the nickname "Rock of Chickamauga." On April 10, 1864, Harker was promoted to brigadier general to rank from the day of the battle. In the Atlanta campaign he commanded a brigade of nine regiments in Newton's division of Howard's IV Corps, Army of the Cumberland. On June 26, 1864, W. T. Sherman made the controversial decision to storm Joseph E. Johnston's intrenched line on Kennesaw Mountain, near Marietta, and the following day selected Newton's division to lead one of two columns of attack. Going into the battle mounted (he had already had four horses killed under him in previous fights but had escaped serious injury), Harker became a conspicuous target for Confederate sharpshooters and was mortally wounded in the abortive offensive, dying a few hours later. His remains were subsequently buried in the New Episcopal Cemetery in the village of his birth. (180)

Edward Harland was born in Norwich, Connecticut, on June 24, 1832, the grandson of an English watchmaker who came to America in 1773. After preparing for college in the local schools, he entered Yale and was graduated in 1853. He then studied law and was admitted to the bar in 1855. On May 11, 1861, he was mustered into Federal service as captain of Company D, 3rd Connecticut Volunteers, a

ninety-day regiment which distinguished itself on the field of First Manassas (Bull Run). (181) In September, Harland became colonel of the 8th Connecticut, which he led during Ambrose E. Burnside's expedition to North Carolina in the spring of 1862. At the battle of Sharpsburg that autumn Harland commanded a brigade of Isaac P. Rodman's division of Burnside's IX Corps, which was heavily engaged in the assault on the celebrated bridge over Antietam Creek. After the battle of Fredericksburg, where its losses were nominal, the brigade was transferred to southeast Virginia, and Harland was commissioned a brigadier general on April 4, 1863, to rank from the preceding November 29. From that time until the close of the war he commanded various districts and subdistricts in the Department of North Carolina. He resigned in June, 1865, to live in his native village of Norwich, practicing law and serving in both houses of the state legislature, as probate judge of the Norwich district, as adjutant general of Connecticut, and as a member of the state board of pardons. In 1890 he became president of the Chelsea Savings Bank, of which he had been elected a director in 1875. General Harland never married. He died in Norwich on March 9, 1915, and was buried in Yantic Cemetery. (182)

William Selby Harney was born on August 27, 1800, in Haysboro, Tennessee, a community on the Cumberland River (a few miles above Nashville) of which no trace remains today. (183) He attended the local academy and in 1818 was commissioned into the Regular

Army as a second lieutenant of infantry, with his birthplace and residence for some reason misrepresented in military records as Louisiana. (184) Harney distinguished himself in the Florida campaigns against the Creeks and Seminoles and rapidly attained promotion. By 1836 he was lieutenant colonel of the 2nd Dragoons (later the 2nd Cavalry) and in 1846, just prior to the war with Mexico, became its colonel. This promotion made him the senior cavalry officer under General Winfield Scott in the advance upon Mexico City. Scott distrusted Harney's judgment and relieved him of command. The ensuing imbroglio which resulted in Harney's restoration to command caused a great newspaper fanfare. In the end Scott was overruled by President James K. Polk, a neighbor of the Harney family in Tennessee, and Harney quickly vindicated his reputation by his gallant conduct at Cerro Gordo, for

which he received the brevet of brigadier to rank from April 18, 1847. From then until the outbreak of the Civil War, Harney enhanced his reputation by his feats against the warring Indians, but diminished it, after his promotion to brigadier general in the regular service, to rank from June 14, 1858, by his anti-British activities in the San Juan Island affair, while in command of the Department of Oregon. Recalled from the latter post, he was in command of the Department of the West, with headquarters at St. Louis, one of the four general officers of the line of the Regular Army when the Civil War began. (185) Harney had married into an old St. Louis family and by birthplace and other connections was allied with the pro-Southern element. (186) Accordingly, his agreement with Confederate General Sterling Price not to molest the Missouri State Guard so long as it committed no overt act against the Federal authority, was viewed with suspicion in Washington; he was relieved of command and saw no further service. Retired in 1863, at the close of the war he was brevetted major general. He lived in retirement on his estate at Pass Christian, Mississippi, and in St. Louis. He died in Orlando, Florida, on May 9, 1889, and was buried in Arlington National Cemetery.

Thomas Maley Harris was born on June 17, 1817, in Wood County (now Ritchie) on the Ohio River, in that part of Virginia which in 1862 became West Virginia. He studied medicine and in the years before the war practiced his profession at Harrisville and Glenville, Virginia. In the latter part of 1861, Harris aided in recruiting the 10th West Virginia and upon its muster was appointed first its lieutenant colonel and on May 20, 1862, its colonel. The regiment shared in the reverses sustained

during Stonewall Jackson's celebrated Shenandoah Valley campaign. In May, 1863, Harris and his regiment were ordered back to West Virginia and attached to William W. Averell's "Fourth Separate" brigade. After participation in some minor operations, it took part in the bloody fight at Cloyd's Mountain in May, 1864, where Confederate General A. G. Jenkins was mortally wounded. That summer Harris commanded a brigade under George Crook during Jubal Early's raid on Washington and subsequently in the Shenandoah Valley campaign, under the leadership of Philip Sheridan, distinguished himself in command of a

division of the Army of West Virginia at Winchester and at Cedar Creek. He was brevetted brigadier general of volunteers for his services at the latter battle and on March 29, 1865, was accorded full rank. Meantime, on December 19, 1864, Harris' division was ordered to the Petersburg front, where it was attached to the Army of the James and took part in the final operations against Robert E. Lee's army. After serving on the commission which tried the Abraham Lincoln conspirators, Harris was mustered out in 1866 with the brevet rank of major general for "gallant conduct in the assault on Petersburg." After the war General Harris served one term in the West Virginia legislature, was adjutant general of the state in 1869-70, and was pension agent at Wheeling from 1871 to 1877. In addition he practiced his profession and authored several medical essays and a religious tract entitled "Calvinism Vindicated." He also wrote a very prejudiced account of the Lincoln conspirators' trial, *Assassination of Lincoln*. He died in Harrisville on September 30, 1906, at the age of ninety, and was buried in the town cemetery. (187)

William Harrow was born in Winchester, Kentucky, on November 14, 1822. His family moved to Lawrenceville, Illinois, where he grew up, studied law, and was admitted to the bar. According to a biographical sketch compiled by his daughter, (188) he became friendly with Abraham Lincoln and traveled the Eighth Judicial Circuit with him. Harrow moved to Vincennes, Indiana, about 1859 and then to Mount Vernon, Indiana,

his wife's home, where he remained until the outbreak of the Civil War. After appointment in April, 1861, by the governor to captain of the "Knox County Invincibles," a militia company which became part of the 14th Indiana, Harrow was successively promoted to major, lieutenant colonel, and colonel. The regiment began its service in West Virginia; its first important battle, however, was that of Sharpsburg (Antietam) where, as a part of Nathan A. Kimball's 1st Brigade of William H. French's 3rd Division of the II Corps, it fought for four hours within sixty yards of the Confederate line with casualties of 181 killed and wounded, representing more than half its strength. On April 4, 1863, Harrow was appointed a brigadier general of volunteers to rank from the preceding November 29 and at Gettysburg commanded first a brigade and, after the wounding of John Gibbon, the 2nd Division of

the II Corps. After the Mine Run campaign of the fall of 1863, Harrow was transferred to the West and in the course of the Atlanta campaign commanded the 4th Division of the XV corps. In September, 1864, his division was broken up and its regiments transferred to other brigades and divisions. (189) He then seems to have been without assignment until January, 1865, when Oliver O. Howard, commanding the Army of the Tennessee, refused to assign him to duty and ordered him to report to W. T. Sherman (at Savannah), who in turn ordered him back to Washington. (190) On April 7, 1865, Harrow was ordered to report to Winfield S. Hancock at Winchester and on April 20, 1865, the records exhibit that his resignation was accepted. (191) General Harrow then returned to Mount Vernon to resume his law practice and to interest himself in politics, in which he had engaged in Illinois. Originally a Radical Republican, he became identified with the liberal movement in the presidential election of 1872 and was campaigning for Horace Greeley when he was killed in a train accident at New Albany, Indiana, on September 27, 1872. He was buried in Bellefóntaine Cemetery, Mount Vernon.

John Frederick Hartranft was born December 16, 1830, near Pottstown, Pennsylvania. After attendng Marshall College for a time, he was graduated from Union College in 1853 as a civil engineer. He transferred his interest to the field of law and in 1860 was admitted to the Montgomery County bar. At the beginning of the Civil War he was colonel of a militia regiment mustered into the service of the United States on April 20, 1861, as the 4th Pennsylvania Infantry, a three-

month regiment enlisted to suppress the rebellion. Ninety days later, on the eve of the battle of First Manassas, the entire regiment marched to the rear, turning their backs to the enemy and claiming expiration of service, despite personal pleas by Hartranft and by General Irvin McDowell, commander of the army. Hartranft volunteered for service with General W. B. Franklin during the ensuing battle, a decision which caused Congress to award him a Medal of Honor in 1886. He soon undertook the organization of the 51st Pennsylvania Regiment, was commissioned its colonel on November 16, 1861, and with it participated in Ambrose E. Burnside's occupation of the North Carolina coast in the spring of 1862. The defection of

his regiment at Bull Run probably retarded his promotion; he was not appointed a brigadier general until May 12, 1864, for services at the battle of Spotsylvania Court House. He was advanced to the command of a division at Petersburg and as of March 28, 1865, was brevetted major general for gallantry in successfully opposing the attack of the Confederate Second Corps on Fort Stedman, the last organized offensive by Robert E. Lee's Army of Northern Virginia. Soon after Hartranft found himself in a less congenial post—that of special provost marshal for the trial of those accused of the assassination of President Lincoln. General Hartranft showed unexpected consideration to the alleged conspirators, particularly Mrs. Surratt, who was hurried to the gallows on little evidence. Mustered out in 1866, he quickly became a power in Pennsylvania politics. From 1865 until 1885 he served as auditor general, governor for two terms, postmaster of Philadelphia, and collector of the port of Philadelphia from 1881 until 1885. He died in Norristown, Pennsylvania, on October 17, 1889, and was buried in Montgomery Cemetery.

George Lucas Hartsuff was born on May 28, 1830, in the tiny village of Tyre, (192) Seneca County, New York, but moved with his parents at the age of twelve to a farm in Livingston County, Michigan, where he obtained his early education and lived until his appointment to West Point in 1848. He was graduated four years later and assigned to the 4th Artillery. After some duty in Texas he served against the Florida Seminoles and in a skirmish near Fort Drane, Florida, suffering two severe wounds, one of which caused his death nineteen years later. In 1861, Hartsuff was brevetted captain in the adjutant general's department and went with the expedition which secretly

reenforced Fort Pickens. During the fall and winter of 1861-62 he was chief of staff to General William S. Rosecrans in West Virginia and on April 15, 1862, was appointed brigadier general of volunteers. He fought ably in Irvin McDowell's corps during the disastrous campaign which culminated at Second Manassas. (193) He was again severely wounded at Sharpsburg and disabled periodically for many months. Meantime, he was promoted to major general to rank from November 19, 1862. From April until November, 1863, General Hartsuff commanded the XXIII Corps but was again incapacitated by his wounds until March 13, 1865, when he took command of

the Bermuda front of the works for the siege of Petersburg between the James and Appomattox rivers. After the evacuation by the Confederates he commanded the District of Nottaway, with headquarters in Petersburg. After the war General Hartsuff, who had been brevetted brigadier and major general in the Regular Army, resumed his duties in the adjutant general's department, with rank of lieutenant colonel of staff. During the next five years he served in the Department of the Gulf, in the Fifth Military District composed of Louisiana and Texas, and in the Division of the Missouri. On June 29, 1871, he was retired at the grade of major general "for disability from wounds received in battle." Less than three years later he died of pneumonia at his home in New York City; a postmortem revealed that the infection stemmed from the scar on his lung caused by his old Florida wound. He was buried at West Point. (194)

Milo Smith Hascall was born on August 5, 1829, in the village of Le Roy, Genesee County, New York. (195) As a young man he joined three of his elder brothers at Goshen, Indiana, where he clerked in a store and taught school until his appointment to West Point in 1848. Graduating in 1852, he soon became dissatisfied with garrison duty in Newport Harbor, Rhode Island, and resigned the following year. From then until 1861 he had a successful career in Goshen and Elkhart County as a lawyer, railroad contractor, district attorney, and clerk of the county courts. Hascall immediately volunteered for service at the outbreak of the

Civil War and was appointed aide-de-camp to General T. A. Morris, brigadier of Indiana volunteers. On June 12, 1861, Hascall was appointed colonel of the 17th Indiana and with this regiment saw some minor action in West Virginia. In December he was sent to Louisville and given charge of a brigade of Thomas J. Wood's division of Don Carlos Buell's forces (Army of the Cumberland), which arrived at Shiloh the day after the battle and participated in the siege of Corinth under Henry W. Halleck. Hascall was promoted to brigadier general to rank from April 25, 1862. At the battle of Murfreesboro he had charge of his brigade and, after the wounding of Wood, of the division. Subsequent to this battle he was transferred to Ambrose E. Burnside's Army of the Ohio and spent several months collecting deserters while in command of the District of Indiana. In the autumn of 1863 he took part in the defense of Knoxville and the following spring commanded the 2nd Division, XXIII Corps, during the Atlanta campaign. On September 12, 1864, John M. Schofield, then commanding the Army of the Ohio, warmly commended Hascall and requested his promotion to major general of volunteers. (196) The fact that the recommendation was not acted upon may have influenced his decision to return to civilian life; in any event, he submitted his resignation, which was accepted on October 27, 1864. For a number of years thereafter General Hascall engaged in banking at Goshen and Galena, moving to Chicago in 1890 to enter the real estate business. He died at his residence in Oak Park, Illinois, on August 30, 1904, and was buried in Forest Home Cemetery, Forest Park, Illinois.

Joseph Abel Haskin was born in Troy, New York, on June 21, 1818. He was graduated tenth in the class of 1839 at West Point—the third man was Henry W. Halleck. Commissioned as a second lieutenant, 1st Artillery, Haskin served five years on the Maine frontier (during the "Disputed Territory" controversy with England. It was there, at Houlton, that he met and married his wife. In the Mexican War he served with Winfield Scott's army, lost his left arm at the storming of Chapultepec, and was brevetted captain and major for gallantry. Thereafter, he performed recruiting duty, was a quartermaster for three years, and was in garrison at various points throughout the South and Southwest. At the time of the secession of Louisiana he was a captain of the 1st Artillery and brevet major in command of the barracks and arsenal at Baton Rouge. On January 10, 1861, the governor, backed by a greatly superior force, summoned

him to surrender the U. S. government property under his command. Haskin, possessing no other alternative, was forced to comply. (197) Following garrison duty at various points, he was placed in charge of the northern defenses of Washington, where he served from 1862 until 1864. In the latter year he was appointed chief of artillery, Department of Washington, a post he occupied until the end of the war. He was instrumental in repelling the attack of the Confederate General Jubal Early on Fort Stevens in July, 1864, and for his services was promoted to brigadier general of volunteers with rank from August 5 and brevet brigadier general in the Regular Army the following March. As lieutenant colonel, 1st Artillery, he commanded first Fort

Independence in Boston Harbor and then, from 1866 until 1870, Forts Schuyler and Wood in New York Harbor. On December 15, 1870, General Haskin was retired from active service for disability from loss of an arm in battle. For the next two years he lived in Oswego, New York, where he contracted tuberculosis. His last two years were spent principally in Charleston in an attempt to regain his health. On August 3, 1874, he died in Oswego and was buried in Riverside Cemetery. His remains were moved to Arlington. (198)

Edward Hatch was born in Bangor, Maine, on December 22, 1832. After attending the local school, he spent two years at Norwich University, Vermont, went to sea for one voyage, and finally moved to Iowa to engage in the lumber business. On August 12, 1861, he was commissioned a captain of the 2nd Iowa Cavalry and ten months later,

215

its colonel. The regiment was present with John Pope at New Madrid and Island No. 10, at the siege of Corinth, and in October, 1862, took part in the battle of Corinth, where Hatch commanded a brigade. The following spring he participated in Benjamin H. Grierson's famous raid through central Mississippi—a diversionary effort ordered by General Grant during his advance on Vicksburg. During the winter of 1863-64 he engaged in raiding North Alabama and in December was wounded in a skirmish at Moscow, Tennessee. Hatch was commissioned brigadier general of volunteers to rank from April 27, 1864, upon the recommendation of Grierson. (199) While recovering from his wound he was placed in command of the cavalry depot at St. Louis (200) but in June was ordered to Memphis and after the fall of Atlanta was engaged in opposing John B. Hood's invasion of Tennessee, commanding a division of cavalry under J. H. Wilson. (Shortly before this campaign it was alleged that Hatch, while sparring with N. B. Forrest in North Mississippi, plundered the home of ex-Secretary of the Interior Jacob Thompson at Oxford while Mrs. Thompson looked on.) (201) The Federal cavalry during Hood's advance upon Nashville was clearly outclassed by the Confederates under Forrest; nevertheless, Hatch's division performed yeoman's service and its commander received the brevet of major general for gallantry during the campaign. Mustered out of volunteer service in January, 1866, Hatch was commissioned colonel of the 9th U. S. Cavalry upon the reorganization of the army on July 28 and was brevetted

brigadier and major general the following year. His postwar career embraced mainly frontier service: department command in the Southwest, chairman of a commission which in 1878 forced the Utes to yield a portion of their Colorado reservation, and an unsuccessful chase after the Apache chief Victorio in 1880. General Hatch died at Fort Robinson, Nebraska, April 11, 1889, and was buried in the National Cemetery at Fort Leavenworth, Kansas. (202)

John Porter Hatch was born in Oswego, New York, January 9, 1822. Receiving an appointment to West Point at the age of eighteen, he was graduated in the class of 1845, whose roster included William H. C. Whiting, "Baldy" Smith, T. J. Wood, Charles P. Stone, Fitz John Porter, Edmund Kirby Smith, John W. Davidson, and Gordon Granger. In the course of the Mexican War, as a second lieutenant of Mounted

Rifles, Hatch was twice brevetted for gallantry in the advance of General Winfield Scott's army on Mexico City. In the interval between the Mexican War and the Civil War Hatch performed garrison duty at dreary stations in Oregon, Texas, and New Mexico. He was acting as chief commissary in the Department of New Mexico when the war broke out. He was quickly brought east, commissioned brigadier general of volunteers to rank from September 28, 1861, and the following spring and summer was in command of N. P. Banks's cavalry in the Shenandoah Valley, which reflected little credit on either leader. Hatch commanded an infantry brigade until he was badly wounded at South Mountain, where he commanded the 1st Division of Joseph Hooker's corps. From that time until the end of the war he performed various duties of an administrative nature: on courts-martial, in command of cavalry rendezvous, and in garrison in the South. At the time of the surrender of General Joseph E. Johnston, Hatch was in charge of the District of Charleston. After muster out from the volunteers, he found himself major of the 4th U. S. Cavalry to which he had been promoted in 1863. He served again upon the western frontier and at various forts and encampments during the constantly recurring Indian troubles, with promotion to lieutenant colonel in 1873 and to colonel in 1881. For his wartime services he was accorded the brevets of brigadier general in the Regular Army and major general in the volunteers. Retired in 1886, he resided thereafter in New York City, where he died on April 12, 1901.

He was buried in Arlington National Cemetery.

Herman Haupt was born in Philadelphia, Pennsylvania, on March 26, 1817. (203) A child prodigy and mechanical genius, he was graduated from West Point at the age of eighteen, became principal assistant engineer of the state of

Pennsylvania at the age of nineteen, and published authoritative treatises on bridge construction while in his twenties. Haupt resigned from the Military Academy three months after graduation to enter the field of railroad engineering. In the next quarter-century he laid out, located, or constructed a half dozen of the more important railroad segments of New York, New England, and Pennsylvania, including a good part of the Juniata division of the Pennsylvania Railroad and the Allegheny and Hoosac tunnels. In the second year of the Civil War Haupt was sum-

217

moned to Washington as chief of construction and transportation on the U. S. Military Railroads (lines taken over by the government in the various war theaters) with rank of colonel and additional aide-de-camp from April 27, 1862. For a year and a half his engineering skill revived and maintained order in a vacuum which had reduced the operation of the Virginia roads to chaos. The complexity of this work was underscored in a telegram sent to Haupt by P. H. Watson, Assistant Secretary of War and an ex-railroad executive: "Be as patient as possible with the generals; some of them will trouble you more than they do the enemy." (204) On September 5, 1862, Haupt was appointed brigadier general of volunteers and for the next twelve months was addressed as a general officer and so signed himself in official dispatches. But, he did not accept this commission, which he did not want, preferring to serve without rank or pay, in order to devote time to his personal affairs, much involved by his advance of funds for the completion of a Massachusetts railroad. On September 14, 1863, he vacated the appointment by declining it and returning to private life. Haupt's postbellum career was also distinguished: besides publishing an impressive array of technical publications, he was chief engineer and general manager of many railroads, including the Northern Pacific, and was a pioneer in oil pipeline development and the use of compressed air for motors and mine machinery. General Haupt died of a heart attack on a train in Jersey City, New Jersey, on December 14, 1905, and was buried in West Laurel Hill Cemetery, Philadelphia.

John Parker Hawkins, brother-in-law of General Edward R. S. Canby, was born in Indianapolis on September 29, 1830. He was graduated from the Military Academy in the class of 1852, ranking 40th out of forty-three members, and was

brevetted second lieutenant of the 6th Infantry. So slow was promotion that two years elapsed before he received an appointment as a full-rank second lieutenant, this time in the 2nd Infantry. In the years before the Civil War, Hawkins served mainly on the northwestern frontier, being quartermaster of his regiment from 1858 until 1861. After the war broke out Hawkins shifted to the Commissary Department, serving as assistant commissary at St. Louis for a time, chief commissary of the District of Southwest Missouri, inspecting commissary of the Department of Missouri, chief commissary of the XIII Corps, and finally chief commissary of the Army of the Tennessee. Absent on sick leave for three months in 1863, he returned to command a brigade of Negroes and the District of Northeastern Louisiana until February, 1864. From then until the close of the war he was in garrison at Vicksburg commanding a Negro division, with which he took part in the campaign which resulted in the capture of Mobile. Hawkins had been made a brigadier general of volunteers in 1863 and in 1865 was given the brevets of major general in both the regular and volunteer services. Mustered out of volunteer service in February, 1866, he reverted to his regular rank of staff captain in the Subsistence Department and was not promoted to major until 1874. Meantime, and for many years thereafter, he served on commissary duty at various stations and was gradually promoted: to lieutenant colonel in 1889, to colonel in March, 1892, to commissary general of subsistence with rank of brigadier general on December 22, 1892. He headed the Subsistence Department until his retirement in September, 1894, at the statutory age of 64. General Hawkins lived twenty years after retirement, making his home in Indianapolis. He had married a daughter of Colonel Henry Knox Craig, chief of ordinance from 1851 until the outbreak of the Civil War, and interested himself in the genealogy of the Hawkins, Craig, and Canby families. He died in Indianapolis on February 7, 1914, and was buried in Crown Hill Cemetery there.

Joseph Roswell Hawley was born October 31, 1826, in the then-existing village of Stewartsville, North

Carolina, located in what is now Scotland County. His mother was from North Carolina, his father from Connecticut; when the boy was eleven the family returned to Connecticut and young Hawley was educated in the North, graduating from Hamilton College in 1847. During the 1850's he became a lawyer, was a delegate to the 1852 Free-Soil convention, was one of the organizers of the Connecticut Republican party, stumped the state for John C. Frémont in 1856, and became editor of the Hartford *Evening Press* the following year. At the inception of the Civil War, Hawley aided in recruiting the first company of the 1st Connecticut Volunteers, was commissioned its captain on April 22, 1861, and commanded it at First Manassas. He became lieutenant colonel of the 7th Connecticut in September, colonel in June, 1862, and on September 13, 1864, was made brigadier general of volunteers. With his regiment he took part in the Port Royal expedition, the investment of Fort Pulaski, the battles of James Island and Pocotaligo, the Florida expedition, and commanded the city of Fernandina, Florida, in January, 1863. He directed a brigade on Morris Island during the siege of Charleston and at the disastrous battle of Olustee (Ocean Pond), Florida, in February, 1864. He then went to Virginia as commander of a brigade in Alfred H. Terry's division, served throughout the operations against Petersburg, and, when Terry took command of the Fort Fisher expedition, succeeded to command of the division. At the end of the war he was in district command in the state of his birth. With the brevet of major general he was mustered out in 1866 and the same year was elected governor of Connecticut. In the next forty years General Hawley had a varied political career, including a celebrated controversy with his former commanding officer in the Army of the James, General Benjamin F. Butler. Hawley won and lost a number of congressional contests; he was elected three times to a seat in the lower house and defeated twice. He was elected U. S. Senator in 1881 and served by reelection until his death in Washington on March 18, 1905. He was buried in Cedar Hill Cemetery, Hartford, Connecticut.

Joseph Hayes was born September 14, 1835, at South Berwick, Maine. He was prepared for college at Andover and was a member of the class of 1855 at Harvard, although he was not awarded a B.A. until 1862 "as of the Class of 1855."

(205) After leaving college he was in the banking business in Wisconsin for a time, then pursued the profession of civil engineer in Iowa, returning to Boston in 1859 to become a real estate broker. Hayes was appointed major of the 18th

Massachusetts on July 26, 1861, although the regiment was not formally organized and mustered until August 24. With promotion to lieutenant colonel in August, 1862, and to colonel in March, 1863, he compiled a distinguished combat record on the Virginia Peninsula and at the battles of Sharpsburg, Fredericksburg (where his regiment charged Marye's Hill three separate times), Chancellorsville, and Gettysburg—all the time in the V Corps. On the morning of May 5, 1864, at the battle of the Wilderness, he was severely wounded by a bullet which made a deep furrow in his skull. Eleven days later both Gouverneur K.

Warren and George G. Meade recommended him for promotion to brigadier general and he was appointed to rank from May 12. On August 19 of that year Hayes was captured during Warren's attempt to seize the Weldon Railroad near Globe Tavern during the siege of Petersburg; he was not exchanged for almost six months. During his imprisonment he was paroled and selected to distribute supplies to Federal prisoners in the South. On April 3, 1865, General Hayes took command of the 1st Brigade of Ayres's 2nd Division of the V Corps and was present with it at Appomattox. Declining a proffered commission in the Regular Army, and with the brevet of major general for gallantry in action, he returned to private life. He became interested in mining in Colorado and in South America, was a broker in New York City, and was the head of a coal company. In later years General Hayes's old head wound is said to have made him a periodic dipsomaniac; (206) he became a virtual recluse in a small Pennsylvania village and cut himself off from his most intimate friends. A lifelong bachelor, he died in a private sanitarium in New York City on August 19, 1912, and was buried in South Berwick.

Rutherford Birchard Hayes, nineteenth President of the United States, was born in Delaware, Ohio, on October 4, 1822. He was educated at Norwalk, Ohio, at Middletown, Connecticut, and at Kenyon College, Gambier, Ohio. He then attended Harvard Law School, was admitted to the Ohio bar in 1845, and began practice in Lower Sandusky (now Fremont). In 1850 he

opened an office in Cincinnati and was successful in both law and local politics, as an active campaigner and speaker. First a Whig, he early became a Republican of the moderate school. With the coming of the Civil War, Hayes made patriotic speeches, aided in recruiting, and in June, 1861, entered the service as major of the 23rd Ohio. Although his military service has been de-

scribed as "varied and capable but not distinguished," (207) it appears that he exhibited considerable personal gallantry on a number of fields. He was wounded badly at South Mountain, where he led a charge; he aided in the capture of the Confederate General John H. Morgan during the latter's Ohio raid and headed his brigade in storming a strongly defended position at the battle of Cloyd's Mountain. He had been promoted to lieutenant colonel and to colonel and on October 19, 1864, was

221

appointed brigadier general. Meantime, he took a creditable part in Philip Sheridan's Shenandoah Valley campaign, commanding first a brigade and then a division of George Crook's Army of West Virginia. For "gallant and distinguished services" at Fisher's Hill and Cedar Creek he was awarded the brevet of major general in March, 1865. He had been elected to Congress the previous October and in June 1865, resigned his commission to take his seat. Reelected in 1866, he resigned in June, 1867, to run for governor of Ohio, was successful, and was reelected in 1869 but refused to run for a third term in 1871. The following year he was beaten for Congress because of the Republican party split and retired to his estate of Spiegel Grove near Fremont. In 1875, Hayes once again ran for governor in a campaign which attracted nationwide attention; his victory made him a national figure and an obvious candidate for the presidential nomination of his party in 1876. In the election of that year, early returns indicated that Hayes's Democratic opponent Samuel J. Tilden was a certain winner, and Hayes retired for the night in that belief. The Republican managers, however, caused the election boards in Louisiana and Florida, where carpetbag rule prevailed, to disqualify sufficient Tilden ballots to throw the electoral votes of those states to Hayes and make him the victor by a margin of one electoral vote: 185 to 184. The outraged Democrats screamed robbery, but an electoral commission was created which by strict party lines voted not to go behind the returns and to certify Hayes the winner—a decision announced only two days before the inaugural. Meantime, a deal was made between the two factions which provided for the withdrawal of the last remaining troops from the ex-Confederate states in return for the orderly inauguration of the Republican candidate. Hayes took the oath and within sixty days the troops were withdrawn; thereafter no Republican presidential candidate would carry a Southern state for forty-four years. Hayes's administration was marked by moderation and by efforts to promote civil service reform. The latter policy, coupled with termination of Federal occupation of the ex-Confederate states, lost Hayes much Republican support, leading one historian to remark that "within six weeks after his inauguration Hayes was without a party." (208) Prior to his election in 1876, Hayes had stated that he would serve but one term. Accordingly, in March, 1881, he returned to Spiegel Grove, where for the remainder of his life he pursued a variety of humanitarian causes and speaking engagements. He died at his home on January 13, 1893, and was first buried in Oakwood Cemetery, Fremont; his remains were removed in 1915 to the state park built on his former estate.

Isham Nicholas Haynie (209) was born on November 18, 1824, in the hamlet of Dover, Tennessee, which became famous a generation later as the site of Fort Donelson. He was taken to Illinois in childhood, received little education, worked as a farm laborer in order to accumulate the means to study law, and was admitted to the bar in 1846. During the Mexican War he served as a first lieutenant of the 6th Illinois Volunteers and in 1850 was a member of the Illinois legislature. To supplement his formal education, he entered the Kentucky law school and was graduated in 1852.

Four years later he was appointed judge of the court of common pleas at Cairo, Illinois. In 1860, Haynie canvassed the state as a presidential elector for Stephen A. Douglas. The following September, after the outbreak of the Civil War, Haynie recruited the 48th Illinois Infantry, which wintered at Cairo. The regiment participated in U. S. Grant's "reconnaissance" to Columbus, Kentucky; it was present at the capture of Forts Henry and Donelson, sustaining substantial casualties at the latter place, where Haynie temporarily commanded the 3rd Brigade of McClernand's 1st Division. (210) At Shiloh he was badly wounded, and the brigade suffered 585 casualties. On his return to duty, he was assigned to command the 1st Brigade of Logan's 3rd Division of McPherson's XVII Corps, whose headquarters was in Memphis in January, 1863, while Grant's whole army was preparing for the momentous operations against Vicksburg. Haynie was appointed brigadier general of volunteers to rank from November 29, 1862, but the Senate failed to act upon his nomination prior to the beginning of the new session of Congress and it expired by operation of law on March 4, 1863. Two days later Haynie was "relieved, on tender of his resignation. . . ." (211) He retired to the practice of law and later became adjutant general of Illinois. Haynie died in Springfield on May 22, 1868, and was buried there in Oak Ridge Cemetery.

Alexander Hays was born on July 8, 1819, in Franklin, Pennsylvania, and obtained his early education at Venango Academy, Mercer Academy, and Allegheny College. He left college in his senior year to enter West Point, from which he was graduated toward the bottom of the class of 1844. Among his classmates were Simon B. Buckner and Winfield S. Hancock; in the preceding class was U. S. Grant, with whom Hays formed a lasting friendship. In the Mexican War, Hays won a brevet for gallantry but resigned in 1848 to engage in the iron business near Franklin. Unsuccessful here, he went to California in quest of gold and thereafter became a construction engineer specializing in bridge building in western Pennsylvania. At the outbreak of the Civil War he was living in Pittsburgh. He reentered the

army as captain of the newly authorized 16th Infantry and as colonel of the 63rd Pennsylvania Volunteers. After a winter of training in the defenses of Washington, the 63rd Pennsylvania took part in the Peninsular campaign in the 1st Brigade of Kearny's division of Heintzelman's III Corps. Hays was brevetted major, lieutenant colonel, and colonel for gallantry on fields from Seven Pines to Gettysburg and was promoted to brigadier general of volunteers on September 29, 1862. He was severely wounded at Second Manassas and did not take part in the Maryland campaign. After his recovery he was posted to the Washington defenses, where he remained until June, 1863. At this time Hays was assigned to command the 3rd Division of the II Corps, which he led at Gettysburg with conspicuous gallantry. The following spring, prior to the commencement of Grant's Overland campaign, the III Corps was merged into the II

Corps. The three II Corps's divisions became two and because of seniority Hays was reduced to the command of a brigade of David B. Birney's division. On the morning of May 5, 1864, in the tangled Wilderness near the intersection of the Brock Road with the Orange Plank Road, Hays was killed by a Confederate bullet. Posthumously brevetted major general as of the day of his death, General Hays was buried in Allegheny Cemetery, Pittsburgh.

William Hays was born on May 9, 1819, in Richmond, Virginia, but at the time of his appointment to West Point in 1836 by Andrew Jackson, he was a resident of Nashville, Tennessee. (212) Hays was graduated in 1840, his classmates numbering W. T. Sherman, George H. Thomas, and Confederate Richard S. Ewell. In the years before the Mexican War, Hays served as a lieutenant of artillery at various

points in the northeast; then at the battles of Contreras, Churubusco, and Chapultepec, he won the brevets of captain and major. Except for some duty against the Seminoles, his career until the outbreak of the Civil War lapsed into routine garrison duty. After service in the Washington defenses during the winter of 1861, Hays commanded a brigade of horse artillery (213) in the Peninsular campaign and the reserve artillery of the army at Sharpsburg and Fredericksburg, with promotion to brigadier general of volunteers on December 27, 1862. He directed a brigade of William H. French's division of the II Corps at Chancellorsville, where early in the morning of May 3 he was captured, along with all but one member of his staff, by William D. Pender's brigade of the Confederate Second Corps. (214) However, by May 15 he was delivered at Fort Monroe. (215) There is no record of his subsequent service until the third day of the battle of Gettysburg, when George G. Meade, after the wounding of Winfield S. Hancock and John Gibbon, assigned Hays to command the II Corps, which he directed until September 13. From November, 1863, until February, 1865, Hays acted as provost marshal of the southern district of New York, after which he was assigned to command the 2nd Division of the II Corps, taking part in the siege of Petersburg and the pursuit of the Army of Northern Virginia. Three days before Appomattox, General A. A. Humphreys, who was commanding the corps, found everyone asleep at Hays's headquarters at 6:30 A.M. and relieved Hays with one of his brigade commanders. (216) This

unfortunate incident seemingly cost Hays the brevets of major general in the regular and volunteer services. Moreover, his regular rank of major, 5th Artillery, to which he had been advanced in 1863, was never further augmented and was his rank when he died at Fort Independence, Boston Harbor, February 7, 1875. First buried in Yonkers, New York, Hays's remains were moved to West Point in 1894.

William Babcock Hazen was born in West Hartford, Vermont, on September 27, 1830; however, at the age of three his parents took him to Hiram, Ohio, where he spent his boyhood and formed a close friendship with James A. Garfield. He was graduated from West Point at the age of twenty-five, with the brevet of second lieutenant of infantry. Hazen's pre-Civil War service was mainly in the Pacific Northwest and Texas, where he was severely wounded in a fight with

Comanches in 1859. From then until 1861 he was on sick leave, disabled by his wounds, but was promoted to captain of the 8th Infantry with the reorganization of the army following the fall of Fort Sumter. In October he became colonel of the 41st Ohio, and the following spring commanded a brigade of D. C. Buell's Army of the Ohio on the second day at Shiloh. With promotion to brigadier general in April, 1863, and major general in April, 1865, Hazen took a most commendable part in the successive campaigns and battles of Perryville, Stone's River, Tullahoma, Chickamauga, Chattanooga, Knoxville, Atlanta, the "March to the Sea," and the Carolinas. In August, 1864, he took command of the 2nd Division of the XV Corps and in May, 1865, led the corps in its grand review in Washington. By the end of the war he had received all the brevets through major general in the regular service and in July, 1866, was appointed colonel of the 38th Infantry, transferring to the 6th Infantry in 1869. Hazen put in years of duty on the western frontier, visited Europe as an observer with the German armies during the Franco-Prussian War, and became involved in the post-trader dispute, testifying to the extravagance and corruption which marked the system, which resulted in the resignation of U. S. Grant's Secretary of War, General William W. Belknap. In 1880, President Rutherford B. Hayes appointed Hazen chief signal officer with the staff rank of brigadier general, a post he held until his death. Because of the Signal Corps's management of the Weather Bureau. A. W. Greely's arctic expedition of 1881 came under Hazen's command and the general was bitterly critical of the supineness of Secretary of War Robert Lincoln in failing to authorize relief for the expedition. (217) When rescued in 1884, only seven of the party's twenty-five members were alive. Hazen died in Washington on January 16, 1887, and was buried in Arlington National Cemetery.

Charles Adam Heckman (218) was born on December 3, 1822, in Easton, Pennsylvania, and was educated there in the Minerva Seminary, graduating at the age of fifteen. At the outbreak of the

Mexican War he was clerking in a hardware store, a position he resigned to enlist in the Regiment of Voltigeurs and Foot Riflemen, a Regular Army unit organized for that war, whose lieutenant colonel was Joseph E. Johnston. Discharged as a sergeant in 1848,

(219) Heckman soon took up residence in Phillipsburg, New Jersey, and became a conductor on the Central Railroad of New Jersey, a vocation he pursued until the beginning of the Civil War in 1861. He was again mustered into the service of the United States on October 8, 1861, as lieutenant colonel of the 9th New Jersey, (220) and took part in Ambrose E. Burnside's expedition against the Carolina coast, with promotion to colonel from February 10, 1862, and to brigadier general to rank from November 29, 1862. His subsequent service was with the Army of the James. He commanded the defenses of Norfolk and Portsmouth during the winter of 1863-64. Early on the morning of May 16, 1864, at the battle of Drewry's Bluff, Heckman's brigade of the XVIII Corps was overwhelmed and its commander captured during a heavy fog, a disaster for which Heckman appears to have been partially responsible. (221) Prior to his exchange in September, he was one of the fifty-one Federal officers taken to Charleston and exposed to the fire of the Union batteries which were shelling the city at the time. (222) In September, 1864, Heckman commanded the 2nd Division of the XVIII Corps in the attempt to take Fort Harrison, apparently in a manner unsatisfactory to General Edward O. C. Ord, his corps commander, who criticized Heckman's direction of his division and omitted his name from a list of those "conspicuous for their gallantry." (223) In January and February, 1865, Heckman temporarily commanded the XXV Corps in the absence of Godfrey Weitzel but on March 23 was re-lieved from duty by U. S. Grant and ordered home. He resigned from the service on May 25 and despite his many months of division and corps command was not awarded the brevet of major general. After the war he was a public utility contractor and later a train dispatcher for the Jersey Central. He died on January 14, 1896, at his son's home in Germantown, Pennsylvania, and was buried in Easton.

Samuel Peter Heintzelman was born in Manheim, Pennsylvania, on September 30, 1805. At the age of seventeen he was appointed to

West Point and was graduated in 1826 in the same class with Albert Sidney Johnston. From his graduation until the Mexican War he engaged mainly in routine garrison duties and in recruiting and quartermaster service. In 1847-48 he won the brevet of major for gallantry at Huamantla and that of

lieutenant colonel in 1851 for his services in the Southwest—especially at Fort Yuma, California, on the Colorado River. He was commissioned colonel of the newly authorized 17th Infantry on May 14, 1861, and three days later, brigadier general of volunteers, with promotion to major general to rank from May 5, 1862. His star rose and fell during the campaign of First Manassas and that of George B. McClellan on the Virginia Peninsula, which occurred the following spring and summer. Heintzelman's performance was described by one authority as follows: "He somehow just missed being an effective corps commander." (224) At Bull Run, where Heintzelman was wounded, his division was driven from the field despite his heroic endeavors to rally it. At Yorktown on the Peninsula, where he commanded the III Corps, he advised McClellan that an assault on the comparatively weak forces of the Confederate General John B. Magruder would be impracticable. At Seven Pines on May 31, his personal gallantry in rallying the retiring Union troops accomplished little. His fortunes did not improve during the Seven Days and in the Second Manassas campaign under John Pope, where his attack on Stonewall Jackson at Groveton was repulsed. During the balance of the war Heintzelman was employed successively in command of portions of the Washington defenses, the Northern Department, and on court-martial duty. When peace came he commanded in Texas for a time and then served on various boards until his retirement with the rank of major general in 1869. After briefly engaging in business

in New York, General Heintzelman resided in Washington until his death on May 1, 1880. He was buried in Forest Lawn Cemetery, Buffalo, his wife's home.

Francis Jay Herron, who ranked as the youngest major general on either side in the Civil War at the time of his appointment, (225) was born in Pittsburgh on February 17, 1837. After attending what is now

Pitt University and clerking in a bank, he went to Dubuque, Iowa, in 1855 to join his brothers in establishing a bank. He tendered the services of his militia company, the "Governor's Grays," to President-elect Lincoln two months prior to the latter's inauguration. (226) His first muster-in was as captain of the 1st Iowa, with which he served in the disaster of Wilson's Creek under Nathaniel Lyon. In September, 1861, he became lieutenant colonel of the 9th Iowa and for his extraordinary heroism at Elkhorn Tavern

(Pea Ridge), where he was wounded and captured, was commissioned brigadier general of volunteers to rank from July 16, 1862. (Thirty years later he was awarded the Congressional medal for this exploit.) In December, 1862, Herron marched his two divisions a hundred and twenty-five miles in three days, without tents or equipment, from his encampment on Wilson's Creek to the battlefield of Prairie Grove, before the Confederate General T. J. Hindman could march half that distance and overwhelm the small Union force under General James G. Blunt. Although Hindman's timidity contributed to the Confederate reverse, Herron's feat was spectacular and turned defeat into victory. (227) For this deed, he was appointed major general of volunteers on March 10, 1863, to rank from November 29, 1862. In the last stages of the siege of Vicksburg, Herron's division of eight regiments plugged a gap on the extreme left of the Union line. Thereafter, he commanded the XIII Corps at Brownsville, Texas, the Northern District of Louisiana, and at the close of the war was appointed commissioner to negotiate treaties with the Indians. He resigned from the army on June 7, 1865. As a carpetbag lawyer in Louisiana, its United States marshal (1867-69) and acting secretary of state (1871-72), his stature and fortunes steadily diminished. In 1877, upon the withdrawal of Federal troops, General Herron moved to New York City, where he was reportedly connected with a manufacturing establishment until his death on January 8, 1902. However, his death certificate records

that he died in a "tenement" on West 99th Street, "Occupation: None." He was buried in Calvary Cemetery, Long Island City, New York. (228.)

Edward Winslow Hincks (229) was born on May 30, 1830, in Bucksport, Maine, where he received a common-school education. He moved to Bangor in 1845 and became a

printer for the *Whig & Courier*. In 1849 he removed to Boston and by 1855 was a member of the Massachusetts legislature. Probably at the instance of Benjamin F. Butler, under whom Hincks subsequently served, he was appointed a second lieutenant in the Regular Army at the same time he was serving as lieutenant colonel and colonel of a ninety-day regiment of Massachusetts militia. Resigning the former and mustered out of the latter, on August 3, 1861, he became colonel of the 19th Massachusetts Infantry, one of the regiments involved in the Ball's Bluff disaster in October. During George B. McClellan's Peninsular campaign, Hincks was wounded at the battle of Glendale and was warmly commended by both his brigade commander William W. Burns and division commander John Sedgwick. In the course of the Maryland campaign he was twice badly wounded at Sharpsburg. The following April he was promoted to brigadier general to rank from November 29, 1862, while convalescing from wounds; he then served on court-martial and recruiting duty until March, 1864, when he commanded the prison camp at Camp Lookout, Maryland, for two months. Thereafter, he commanded a Negro division of the XVIII Corps in the Petersburg offensive until July, 1864. From that time until the end of the war General Hincks again performed duties connected with draft and recruitment, resigning his volunteer commission on June 30, 1865. Upon the reorganization of the Regular Army in July, 1866, he was commissioned lieutenant colonel of the 40th Infantry. Three years later he transferred to the 25th Infantry and the following year, upon the contraction of the officer list, was retired with rank of colonel. Meantime, he had received the brevets of major general in the volunteer service and brigadier general in the Regular Army. After retirement General Hincks was governor of the National Home for Disabled Volunteers at Hampton, Virginia, until 1873, when he transferred to the same post at Milwaukee, Wisconsin, serving until 1880. He died in Cambridge, Massachusetts, on February 14, 1894,

and was buried in Mount Auburn Cemetery.

Ethan Allen Hitchcock, grandson of the leader of the "Green Mountain Boys" of Revolutionary War fame, was born at Vergennes, Vermont, on May 18, 1798. He was graduated from West Point in 1817

and after some routine duty in garrison and on recruiting service was commissioned a captain of the 1st Infantry in 1824. He compiled a most honorable, though stormy, record at the Military Academy, in the Florida War, on Indian duty in the Pacific Northwest, and in the war with Mexico, where he served as Winfield Scott's inspector general in the march on Mexico City. For his services Hitchcock was brevetted colonel and brigadier general and in 1851 was made colonel of the 2nd Infantry. Refused an extension of a four-month leave of absence for his health by Secretary of War Jefferson Davis, Hitchcock resigned in 1855 and went to St. Louis to live. He wrote many of his literary works here, devoting "himself to general literature and the peculiar philosophical investigations which had for years occupied his thoughts." (230) At the instance of General Scott and after having once before had the tender of his services rejected, Hitchcock was appointed major general of volunteers in February, 1862, only the sixth of this grade. He became successively an intimate of Edwin M. Stanton and Abraham Lincoln, commissioner for the exchange of prisoners, and in November, 1865, Commissary General of prisoners—a post which involved the adjustment of a vast number of complicated claims against the government. In 1867 he was mustered out of service and thereafter, because of his health, lived first in Charleston, South Carolina, and then in Sparta, Georgia, where he died on August 5, 1870. He was buried at West Point. Hitchcock was one of only a half-dozen West Point graduates born in the eighteenth century who became general officers during the Civil War.

Edward Henry Hobson was born on July 11, 1825, in Greensburg, Kentucky, a village on Green River in the central part of the state; his father was a steamboat operator and merchant. He attended school in Greensburg and in Danville, Kentucky, and at the age of eighteen went into business with his father. During the Mexican War he served with the 2nd Kentucky Infantry and was made first lieutenant for gallant conduct at the battle of Buena Vista. By 1861, Hobson had become prominent in commercial

circles and was president of the Greensburg Branch Bank of Kentucky. That autumn he recruited the 13th (Union) Kentucky Infantry (231) from the counties along Green River and was mustered in as its colonel on January 1, 1862. The regiment, assigned to Jeremiah T. Boyle's brigade of T. L. Crittenden's division, was present at Shiloh with Don Carlos Buell's forces. Thereafter, Hobson's service was almost entirely in Kentucky, first under the command of the dictatorial Boyle and later under that of Boyle's still more unpopular successor, Stephen G. Burbridge. Hobson's prime wartime accomplishment was probably at Buffington's Island, Ohio, where he helped compel the surrender of a part of the command of General John H. Morgan in July, 1863. The following June, Morgan, who had escaped from the Ohio penitentiary, turned the tables by capturing Hobson and his entire command near Cynthiana, Kentucky.

Hobson, who had been made a brigadier general in April, 1863 (to rank from November 29, 1862), entered into a quasi-parole arrangement with his captor to go to Cincinnati and attempt to effect his own exchange and those of his officers for some of Morgan's officers imprisoned in the North. (232) At the end of the war Hobson was stationed at Lexington in command of the "First Division, Department of Kentucky." (233). He was honorably mustered out in August, 1865. In the postbellum years Hobson joined the Radical Republicans, ran unsuccessfully for clerk of the state court of appeals, was made a district collector of internal revenue by U. S. Grant in 1869, and took a prominent part in business and the affairs of the Republican party and the Grand Army of the Republic. He died at an encampment of the latter in Cleveland on September 14, 1901, and was buried in the family graveyard at Greensburg.

Joseph Holt was born on the banks of the Ohio in Breckinridge County, Kentucky, on January 6, 1807. Educated at St. Joseph's and Centre colleges, he opened a law office in Elizabethtown at the age of twenty-one. He soon became noted as a magnetic speaker in behalf of the Democratic party, moved successively to Louisville and to Mississippi, was a newspaper editor and commonwealth's attorney, accumulated a substantial fortune, and in 1842 went into partial retirement to recuperate from tuberculosis. He emerged in 1856 to campaign for James Buchanan and was rewarded by receiving an appointment as commissioner of

patents, an office which took him to Washington, where he spent the rest of his life. In 1859 Holt became postmaster-general and during the last weeks of the Buchanan administration served as Secretary of War. Until the outbreak of the Civil War he was opposed to coercion of a state by the Federal government, denounced the personal liberty bills passed by some northern states in defiance of the Fugitive Slave Law, and interdicted abolitionist material from the mails within the borders of Virginia. However, his latent loyalty to the Union asserted itself and his decision hardened into an intense devotion to the Federal cause. Instrumental in holding a majority of Kentuckians to the North, Holt was appointed, by President Lincoln, judge advocate general of the army with rank of colonel on September 3, 1862 and that of brigadier general on June 22, 1864. In this office Holt implemented the administration's policy of keeping in jail without recourse to habeas corpus and trying by military commission individuals who would normally have been tried by civil courts. The most notable of these extralegal proceedings were the trials of ex-Congressman Clement L. Vallandingham of Ohio, the Lincoln conspirators, and Henry Wirz, commandant of Andersonville. None of these prosecutions was creditable to the government, the perjury of its witnesses in the trial of the President's assassins and the suppression of evidence and of the recommendation of mercy for Mrs. Surratt appearing particularly shocking. Holt retired in 1875 and died, blind and alone, in his Washington home on August 1, 1894. He was buried in the family cemetery at Holt, Kentucky. (234)

Joseph Hooker, grandson of a Revolutionary War captain, was born on November 13, 1814, in Hadley, Massachusetts. He obtained his early education at the Hopkins Academy in his native village; then he attended West Point from which he was graduated in 1837, ranking midway in the class. His army career prior to the outbreak of the Mexican War was highly commendable; he demonstrated qualities of leadership and executive ability. As a staff officer in Mexico under Generals P. F. Smith, Benjamin F. Butler, and Gideon J. Pillow, he took part in both Zachary Taylor's and Winfield Scott's campaigns and won the brevets of all the grades through lieutenant colonel for gallant and meritorious conduct, a record not surpassed by any first lieutenant in the service. Hooker was appointed captain of the 1st Artillery on October 29,

1848, but for some reason vacated the appointment the same day. From then until June 9, 1849, when he became assistant adjutant general of the Pacific Division, his service record does not disclose his activities. He was on leave of absence

during 1851-53 and resigned his commission on February 21, 1853, to engage in farming near Sonoma. During the next five years his career declined; one historian remarked that "the dashing army officer had descended almost to the level of beachcomber. . . ." (235) During this period Hooker apparently repented his decision to resign, for in a letter dated early in 1858 to Secretary of War John B. Floyd, Hooker dwelt upon his past services while requesting that his name "be presented to the President [Buchanan] as a candidate for a Lieut. Colonelcy. . . ." (236) Nothing came of this solicitation and until the beginning of the Civil War, Hooker eked out a living in

Oregon and California. On August 6, 1862, he was commissioned a brigadier general of volunteers to rank from May 17, his name standing two numbers above that of U. S. Grant. The following spring, at Williamsburg on the Virginia Peninsula, there was hard fighting as George B. McClellan advanced his force toward the capital of the Confederacy; Hooker's division of Samuel P. Heintzelman's III Corps was in the van. A press wire reading, "Fighting—Joe Hooker," appeared throughout the North as "Fighting Joe Hooker." (237) Hooker never lived the sobriquet down. In the ensuing actions of the Seven Days, Second Manassas, Sharpsburg, and Fredericksburg, Hooker exhibited solid qualifications as a combat officer in charge of his division and then of the I Corps. In the course of Ambrose E. Burnside's abortive effort to cross the Rappahannock and storm Robert E. Lee's position on the south side, Hooker, then in command of the "Center Grand Division," criticized his superior officer; as a consequence, his name headed the list of officers Burnside wished relieved as an alternative to his own relief. Nevertheless, Burnside was relieved and Hooker became commander of the Army of the Potomac. (Much of this elevation to command resulted from Hooker's association with Salmon P. Chase and the radical members of the Cabinet. Because of Chase's aspirations to the presidency in 1864, it has been widely stated that Hooker's principal recommendations for army command were that he looked like a great general and had no political ambitions.) In the campaign of Chancellors-

ville, Hooker moved 135,000 troops across the Rapidan and Rappahannock rivers with great adroitness and seemed about to crush Lee's Army of Northern Virginia. Suddenly obfuscated by Stonewall Jackson's counterstroke, which rolled up his right, Hooker later ordered a retreat upon the advice of a council of his corps commanders. He skillfully deployed his army so as to cover Washington and Baltimore while Lee advanced into Pennsylvania, a maneuver which won him the thanks of Congress. Refused the reenforcement of the Harpers Ferry garrison by Henry W. Halleck, he asked for relief and was supplanted by George G. Meade three days before the opening of the battle of Gettysburg. After the Chickamauga disaster in September, Hooker was sent west with the XI and XII Corps (under Oliver O. Howard and Henry W. Slocum), which were ultimately consolidated into the XX Corps. At Chattanooga in November, 1863, Hooker's troops drove a Confederate skirmish line off Lookout Mountain, an engagement which became celebrated in song and story as "The Battle Above the Clouds." Grant, who was present and in command of all the Union forces, trenchantly characterized it as "one of the romances of the war. There was no such battle and no action even worthy to be called a battle on Lookout Mountain." The New York *Tribune* remarked, "There were no clouds to fight above—only a heavy mist." (238) At this time Hooker was a brigadier general in the Regular Army and a major general of volunteers. After the death of James B. McPherson in front of Atlanta, W. T. Sherman promoted Hooker's subordinate Howard to command of the Army of Tennessee and Hooker asked to be relieved from command in "an army in which rank and service are ignored." Sherman promptly obliged him and Hooker's field service came to an end. A contemporary who saw Hooker late in 1864 "was much disappointed with his appearance: red-faced, very, with a lack-lustre eye and an uncertainty of gait and carriage that suggested a used-up man." (239) Thereafter, Hooker exercised departmental command until his retirement in 1868 as a major general. He died in Garden City, New York, on October 31, 1879, and was buried in Cincinnati, his wife's hometown. Appraisals of Hooker's accomplishments, morals, and military know-how have been the subject of discussion for more than a century. The term "hooker," denoting a woman of questionable virtue, is said to have derived from the class of females who frequented his headquarters—headquarters to which it was said "no gentleman cared to go and no lady could go."

Alvin Peterson Hovey, a remote cousin of General Charles E. Hovey, was born September 26, 1821, near Mount Vernon, Indiana. Orphaned at the age of fifteen, he was in succession bricklayer, schoolteacher, lawyer, officer of volunteers in the Mexican War (although he saw no service), member of the state constitutional convention, and circuit judge. In 1854 he was appointed to the state supreme court—the youngest man ever to serve on the Indiana bench up to that time. He served as U. S. District Attorney for a time, and in

1858 was an unsuccessful candidate for Congress on the Republican ticket. At the outbreak of the Civil War, Hovey was commissioned colonel of the 24th Indiana, and after some preliminary service in Missouri, took his regiment into the bloody battle of Shiloh in Morgan Smith's brigade of Lew Wallace's division. His gallantry in this battle was rewarded with a promotion to brigadier. That autumn (1862) he commanded a division in Arkansas under General Samuel R. Curtis and a division of General John McClernand's XIII Corps in the Vicksburg campaign. His division and two of McPherson's (Logan's and Crocker's) fought almost the entire battle of Champion's Hill. In December, 1863, he was sent to Indiana to organize and forward the troops being recruited there and to act as a go-between for General U. S. Grant and Governor Oliver Perry Morton. (240) During the preliminary stages of the

235

Atlanta campaign in May, 1864, Hovey commanded a division of the XXIII Corps, but early in June he was given a thirty-day leave and his division was broken up. (241) From then until the end of the war, with the brevet of major general (received July 4, 1864), he commanded the District of Indiana. During this period he was charged with the recruitment of ten thousand new troops, which he accomplished by asking for the enlistment of unmarried men only—these became known as "Hovey's Babies." After serving as U. S. minister to Peru from 1865 until 1870, Hovey returned to his law practice in Mount Vernon. He refused the Republican nomination for governor in 1872, was elected to Congress in 1886, and two years later finally accepted the governorship. He died in office at Indianapolis, November 23, 1891, and was buried in Bellefontaine Cemetery, Mount Vernon.

Charles Edward Hovey was born in Thetford, Vermont, April 26, 1827. He was graduated from Dartmouth in 1852, having for years taught school during vacation periods to augment his own slender means in order to finance his education. From then until the beginning of the Civil War, Hovey's career as an educator was enviable. He was successively principal of the F r a m i n g h a m (Massachusetts) High School, principal of the Peoria, Illinois, Boys' High School, superintendent of Peoria schools, president of the state teachers' association, member of the first state board of education, and founder of the original state teachers' university at Normal, Illinois. When the Civil War broke out in 1861, Hovey

organized the 33rd Illinois Infantry, a regiment largely comprised of teachers and students at Normal. He was commissioned colonel on August 15, 1861, and took the regiment to Missouri, where it saw service in a number of unimportant

actions during the winter. For reasons undisclosed by historical records Colonel Hovey was appointed a brigadier general of volunteers to rank from September 5, 1862; the Senate, however, declined to act upon the nomination within the statutory period and it expired by operation of law on March 4, 1863. In the interim he took a thoroughly commendable part in the capture of Arkansas Post in January, 1863, where General W. T. Sherman reported that he had been "wounded in his arm by a shell, but continued and still continues to command his brigade." (242) It is variously stated that he "was compelled to resign . . . owing to . . . a bullet which passed through both of his

236

arms . . ." (243), and that "he left the . . . service in May, 1863. . . ." (244) In any event he disappeared from the *Official Records,* but as of March 13, 1865, in the omnibus brevet promotions which accompanied the close of the war, he was promoted to major general. In the years following the war he lived in Washington. Having once briefly studied law in Framingham, he turned his undeniable talents as administrator and educator to the far more profitable business of pension lobbying, in which occupation he was eminently successful. General Hovey died in Washington, D. C., November 17, 1897, and was buried in Arlington National Cemetery.

Oliver Otis Howard was born November 8, 1830, in Leeds, Maine. He obtained his preliminary education at an academy in North Yarmouth, Maine, and by teaching school during vacations, he put himself through Bowdoin College

graduating from there in 1850. Four years later he was graduated from West Point, fourth in a class whose roster comprised such names as Custis Lee, Thomas H. Ruger, James Deshler, John Pegram, Jeb Stuart, Archibald Gracie, S. D. Lee, William D. Pender, John B. Villepigue, Shephen H. Weed, and others who would make their mark in the Civil War. (245) Howard's antebellum service was routine, more than half of it being at the Military Academy as an assistant professor of mathematics, where he was a first lieutenant of Ordnance at the outbreak of the war. His subsequent career must constitute one of the great paradoxes of American military history: no officer entrusted with the field direction of troops has ever equaled Howard's record for surviving so many tactical errors of judgment and disregard of orders, emerging later not only with increased rank, but on one occasion with the thanks of Congress. Howard was elected colonel of the 3rd Maine at the end of May, 1861, and resigned his regular commission on June 7. (246) At the battle of First Manassas (Bull Run), Howard commanded a brigade of three Maine and one Vermont regiments in Heintzelman's division. Although his command was driven from the field in disorder, along with a large part of the Union forces, he was rewarded with a commission as brigadier general of volunteers dating from September 3, 1861. During General George B. McClellan's campaign on the Peninsula, Howard commanded a brigade in the II Corps and lost his right arm at the battle of Seven Pines. Lack of courage was not a constituent of Howard's makeup, and in eighty days he was back in command, during the retreat to the Washington defenses after the disaster at Second Manassas (Bull Run), where Edwin V. Sumner assigned him to command of the rear guard of the army. At Sharpsburg Howard succeeded to command of the 2nd Division, II Corps, after the wounding of John Sedgwick and continued to lead the division at Fredericksburg. On March 31, 1863, Howard, who had been made a major general the preceding November 29, was assigned to command the XI Corps after the relief of its former commander, Franz Sigel (at his own request), an assignment galling to the many German officers and men in its ranks. (247) In the ensuing battle of Chancellorsville the XI Corps constituted the right of the Union army. Despite a positive order from General Joseph Hooker, Howard neglected to protect his exposed flank, was surprised by Stonewall Jackson's furious assault, and routed. At Gettysburg he was in command of the field on the first day after the death of John F. Reynolds and until the arrival of W. S. Hancock. Here he displayed a conspicuous lack of decision, but was voted the thanks of Congress for selecting Cemetery Hill and Ridge as a position for the I and XI Corps to fall back on. Although the evidence conclusively proves they were driven there, Howard's principal contribution was that he personally rallied the I Corps in the cemetery proper. That autumn (1863) the XI and XII Corps were ordered to Chattanooga under Hooker, and the following year Howard commanded the IV Corps in the Atlanta campaign. After the

death of James B. McPherson, General W. T. Sherman assigned him to command of the Army of Tennessee, which formed the right wing in the campaign of the Carolinas. He was appointed a brigadier general in the Regular Army at the close of the war, to rank from the date of the capture of Savannah. Howard had been deeply religious and an enthusiastic abolitionist even in his West Point days, but after the war his concern for the welfare of the Negro became almost a monomania. In May, 1865, Andrew Johnson appointed him first commissioner of the so-called "Freedmen's Bureau," but the organization soon became riddled by fraud, corruption, and inefficiency, which Howard's religious zeal, personal honesty, and lack of administrative ability were helpless to combat. In fact, he persistently and blindly refused to credit even the most readily demonstrated charges against his subordinates. He was exonerated by a court of inquiry in 1874 from accusations arising out of his conduct of the bureau; he then became the center of a conflict arising from his attempt to introduce colored members into a Congregational church which he helped to organize in Washington. He was instrumental in establishing Howard University and was director of a bank for Negroes in which they suffered heavy financial losses. During the 1870's and 1880's he served in Indian country, was superintendent of West Point, and after his promotion to major general in 1886, commanded the Division of the East until his retirement in 1894. Thereafter General Howard resided in Burlington, Vermont, writing, speaking, and engaging in all manner of religious and educational activities. Foremost among the latter was his aiding to establish Lincoln Memorial University at Harrogate, Tennessee, to offer a college education to the mountain people of the area. In 1893 he received the Congressional medal for bravery at Seven Pines where he had lost his arm. General Howard died in Burlington, October 26, 1909, and was buried in Lake View Cemetery.

Albion Parris Howe, a native of Maine, was born in Standish on March 13, 1818. Although first inclined to an academic career, at the instance of his state governor he re-

ceived an appointment to West Point at the age of nineteen and was graduated eighth in a class of fifty-two in 1841. Prior to the Mexican War, where he won a brevet promotion for gallantry during Winfield Scott's advance upon Mexico City, Howe served in the East and at his alma mater as an instructor. From then until the outbreak of the Civil War he saw much frontier duty intermingled with garrison stations in the eastern states, was promoted to captain in 1855, and was present with his battery at Harpers Ferry after the celebrated raid of John Brown. As an artillery officer by training, Howe's Civil War career was not as newsworthy as those of some of his colleagues; it was, however, creditable to a degree. After some service under George B. McClellan in western Virginia in 1861, he commanded an artillery brigade during the Peninsular campaign and was made a brigadier general of volunteers to rank from June 11, 1862. He then commanded an infantry brigade of the IV Corps in Maryland and the 2nd Division of the VI Corps at the battle of Fredericksburg. Directing the same command, he stormed Marye's Heights during the campaign of Chancellorsville, and at Gettysburg was lightly engaged, John Sedgwick's corps being held in reserve. After the Mine Run operations in the autumn of 1863, Howe was put in command of the Artillery Depot and in charge of the Office of the Inspector of Artillery at Washington—an obvious move by U. S. Grant and/or Sedgwick to remove him from infantry command. He remained in this capacity until 1866. Despite this seeming demotion, General Howe received all the brevets in both the regular and volunteer services through that of major general at the end of the war. He discharged a number of postbellum duties; the most distinguished of which was his assignment to the honor guard who stood watch upon the corpse of

Abraham Lincoln. Perhaps not so honorable was his membership on the commission which tried the Lincoln conspirators. He was retired as colonel of the 4th Artillery in 1882, and died in Cambridge, Massachusetts, on January 25, 1897. General Howe was buried in Mount Auburn Cemetery, Cambridge.

Joshua Blackwood Howell was born September 11, 1806, at the Howell homestead, Fancy Hill, near Woodbury, New Jersey. The family had owned this property on

the Delaware since 1688. His father was a colonel of New Jersey troops in the war of 1812, and his grandfather was a commissary with rank of colonel in the Revolution. (248) Howell obtained his early education in Woodbury and then studied law in Philadelphia, beginning his practice in Uniontown, Pennsylvania. He was a Democrat in politics and was a Stephen A. Douglas

elector in 1860. For some years prior to the Civil War he had been a brigadier general of Pennsylvania Militia; on November 12, 1861, he was mustered into Federal service as colonel of the 85th Pennsylvania. After spending the winter in the Washington defenses, the regiment was assigned to Keim's brigade of Casey's division of Keyes' IV Corps in the Peninsula by General George B. McClellan. Howell's regiment was ordered to New Bern, after which it took part in the expedition against Goldsboro, North Carolina. During the operations against Charleston in 1863, Howell commanded a brigade of Terry's division at the siege of Fort Wagner on Folly Island, and then on Morris Island. In April, 1864, the command was transferred to the Army of the James and posted at Bermuda Hundred and then designated the 1st Brigade, 1st (Terry's) Division, of Gillmore's X Corps. Howell at this juncture was way overage for a combat commander of that era; nevertheless, he distinguished himself on May 20, 1864, by retaking with his brigade a line of rifle pits previously captured by the Confederates. He continued to command his brigade until September 12, 1864, when his horse fell with him; he died from his injuries at X Corps headquarters near Petersburg, Virginia on the fourteenth. (249) Seven months later he was posthumously named a brigadier general to rank from the day of his fatal accident. (250) He lies buried in Eglington Memorial Gardens at Clarksboro, New Jersey.

Andrew Atkinson Humphreys, a native of Philadelphia, was born November 2, 1810. Both his father and grandfather were naval architects and constructors, the latter having drawn the plans for *Old Ironsides* and her five sister frigates. Young Humphreys was graduated from the Military Academy in 1831, and from that time until the beginning of the Civil War (with the ex-

ception of two years when he was employed by the government as a civil engineer on the Delaware River fortifications) was continuously on duty, much of the time in the Corps of Topographical Engineers which was engaged in hydrographical surveys of the Mississippi Delta. Humphreys became an aide to General George B. McClellan in 1861, was promoted brigadier general of volunteers in April, 1862, and during the Peninsular campaign served as chief topographical engineer of the Army of the Potomac. In September, 1862, he assumed command of a division of new troops in the V Corps, which

he led with distinction in the Maryland campaign, in the bloody assault on Marye's Heights at Fredericksburg, and at Chancellorsville. He was then transferred to a division of Daniel E. Sickles' III Corps; and for his services at Gettysburg, where he fought grimly in resisting the shattering assaults of John B. Hood and Layfayette Mc-Laws in an effort to redeem Sickles' ill-advised order pushing forward the line of the corps, was made a major general of volunteers and a brigadier by brevet in the Regular Army. Shortly thereafter, he acceded to General George G. Meade's request to become his chief of staff. He continued in this duty, greatly to the satisfaction of all concerned, until November, 1864. At this juncture Winfield S. Hancock was forced to quit field service because of his Gettysburg wound, and General Ulysses S. Grant selected Humphreys to succeed him in command of the II Corps, who were at this time much worn down and in need of reorganization. Under Humphreys' inspiriting leadership the corps took an honorable part in all of the operations leading up to the surrender of the Army of Northern Virginia at Appomattox. He received the brevet of major general, U. S. Army, for gallantry at Sayler's Creek. On August 8, 1866, he was made brigadier general, U. S. Army, and chief of engineers, where he served until his retirement in 1879. Much the oldest of the corps commanders of the Army of the Potomac at war's end, and by no means the least distinguished, General Humphreys took part in seventy engagements during a military career which spanned fifty-two years. He died in Washington,

D. C., December 27, 1883, and was buried in the Congressional Cemetery there.

Henry Jackson Hunt, a brother of Lewis Cass Hunt, was born on September 14, 1819, at Detroit, Michigan. Both his father and paternal grandfather were officers of the Reg-

ular Army. Orphaned at the age of ten, the young Hunt obtained his early education through the kindness of family friends and was graduated from West Point in 1839. He fought in Mexico in Winfield Scott's campaign as a lieutenant of artillery and won the brevets of captain and major for gallantry. From then until the beginning of the Civil War his most distinguished service was probably his membership on a board of three, the others being W. F. Barry and W. H. French, to revise the system of light artillery tactics. Their report was adopted by the War Department in 1860 and used throughout the Civil War by both sides. Hunt took a prominent part in the campaign of First Manassas (Bull Run), became chief of artillery of the Washington defenses, and during the winter of 1861-62 was in charge of training the artillery reserve of the Army of the Potomac. At Malvern Hill, the concluding battle of the Peninsular campaign, Hunt's hundred guns shattered the Confederate assaults, and at Fredericksburg he deployed the 147 pieces which inaugurated the battle. Meantime, he had served with distinction at Sharpsburg and had been made a brigadier general of volunteers on September 15, 1862. On the last day at Gettysburg, Hunt had seventy-seven guns in position along a narrow front on the left center of the Federal line, which a few minutes later blunted the celebrated charge of George E. Pickett and his supports. He remained as chief of artillery until June, 1864, when General Ulysses S. Grant put him in charge of all siege operations on the Petersburg front. Hunt was brevetted major general of volunteers for his services at Gettysburg and at the end of the war was given the same rank in the regular establishment, after which he reverted to his permanent rank of lieutenant colonel of the 3rd Artillery. In 1869 he became colonel of the 5th Artillery and until his death was regarded as the leading authority on that branch of the service. (251) During Reconstruction he was stationed for much of the time in the South, where he earned a reputation for fairness and moderation. (252) After his retirement in 1883 he became governor (1885) of the Soldier's Home in Washington, where he died on February 11, 1889, and was buried.

Lewis Cass Hunt, a brother of General Henry J. Hunt, was born at one of their father's duty stations, Fort Howard at Green Bay, Wisconsin, February 23, 1824. He was appointed to the Military Academy from Missouri and was graduated from there, ranked toward the bottom of the class of 1847. In the years before the Civil War he saw service in Mexico and the Pacific Northwest and commanded the U. S. detachment in the joint British American occupation of San Juan Island in 1859, having been promoted to captain, 4th Infantry, in 1855. He was ordered to Washington in 1861, took part in the Peninsular campaign of 1862 under General George B. McClellan, and was badly wounded at the battle of Seven Pines. A few days earlier (May 21, 1862) he had been made colonel of the 92nd New York. Following his recovery he was sent to

North Carolina, was promoted brigadier general of volunteers on November 29, 1862, and took part in John G. Foster's offensive movement against Kinston and Goldsboro, where he commanded one of the two brigades of Wessells' division and for which he received the brevet of lieutenant colonel in the Regular Army. From then until the end of the war he was successively in command of the draft rendezvous at New Haven, Connecticut, on special duty in Kansas and Missouri, and in command of the defenses of New York Harbor, with promotion to major, 14th Infantry, in 1863, and the brevet of brigadier general, U.S. Army, in 1865 for "Gallant and Meritorious Services during the Rebellion." In the postwar years he served at such widely scattered stations as Fort Wayne, Michigan; Greenville Barracks, Louisiana; Fort Totten, North Dakota; San Antonio, Texas; and Vancouver Barracks, Washington, being promoted lieutenant colonel in the regular army in 1868 and colonel of the 14th Infantry in 1881. He had suffered from chronic dysentery since his service in the Mexican War, and while stationed at San Diego on light duty in August, 1886, was ordered to Fort Union, New Mexico for his health. Six days after his arrival there on September 6, 1886, he died. After temporary interment in the post cemetery, his remains were conveyed to the National Cemetery at Fort Leavenworth, Kansas. General Hunt's wife was a daughter of General Silas Casey.

David Hunter, whose maternal grandfather, Richard Stockton, was a signer of the Declaration of Independence, was born in Washington on July 21, 1802. Cullum's *Register* states that "little is known of his early life before entering the Military Academy," from which he was graduated in 1822. Serving on frontier duty in what was then the Northwest—stationed at Fort Dear-

born (Chicago) from 1828 to 1831 —he met and married the daughter of the city's first permanent resident, John Kinzie. He resigned in 1836 in order to speculate in Chicago real estate, but six years later returned to the army as paymaster with the staff rank of major. In 1860 Hunter, then stationed at Fort. Leavenworth, Kansas, initiated a correspondence with the newly elected President Lincoln, which won for him an invitation to travel on the inaugural train to Washington in February, 1861. Almost immediately he became a prime example of Lincoln's inability—at that stage of the war— to select officers for high command, for he was

made the fourth ranking volunteer general. Hunter's Civil War record ranged from his order abolishing slavery in the Department of the South in March, 1862 (repudiated instantly by Lincoln) to his burning of the buildings of the Virginia Military Institute in 1864, following which he retired rapidly into the mountains of West Virginia. He had previously presided at the court-martial of Fitz John Porter—"organized to convict" as it was said—and would win the additional distinction of presiding at the trial of the Lincoln conspirators, Judge Advocate General Joseph Holt evidently feeling that he had a kindred spirit who could be depended upon to exclude all testimony favorable to the defense and unfavorable to summary execution. His confidence was not misplaced. Mrs. Surratt and three others were hurried to the gallows. Hunter accompanied the body of President Lincoln to Springfield. Hunter's field service embraced the First Manassas campaign, where he was wounded; the battle of Secessionville, during which he unsuccessfully attempted to take Charleston; and the battle of Piedmont, after which he yielded up the Shenandoah Valley to General Jubal Early, who promptly marched on Washington. In 1866 he was retired as colonel of cavalry with the brevets of brigadier and major general, U. S. Army. Thereafter he lived in Washington until his death on February 2, 1886; he was buried in Princeton, New Jersey.

Stephen Augustus Hurlbut was born November 29, 1815, in Charleston, South Carolina, the home of his mother. His father, a Unitarian

minister, was a native of Massachusetts. He resided in Charleston for thirty years, during which time he gained admission to the South Carolina bar and served as adjutant of a South Carolina regiment during one of the interminable Seminole uprisings in Florida. In 1845 he removed to Belvidere, Illinois, and soon became politically prominent; he was serving as a Republican member of the state legislature when the Civil War broke out. On June 14, 1861, Lincoln appointed him a brigadier general of volunteers, and he was advanced to major general on September 17, 1862. Hurlbut's military achievements were creditable; however, at the same time he seems to have exercised every opportunity to line his own pockets. He commanded the 4th Division of the Army of the Tennessee at Shiloh and in the ensuing campaign against Corinth, and during the next year was in garrison at Memphis in charge of the XVI Corps. In 1864 Hurlbut

was assigned to the command of the Department of the Gulf, where he used his official position to further his own ends, and in so doing harassed the carpetbag government of Louisiana, much to the discomfort of Lincoln. A special commission recommended his arrest and trial for corrupt practices; General Edward R. S. Canby so ordered, but the case was hushed up and allowed to die, and as of June 20, 1865, he was "honorably mustered out" of service. Hurlbut then returned to Belvidere, where he resumed his political prominence and was the first commander in chief of the Grand Army of the Republic. Well-founded charges of drunkenness and corruption leveled at him during this period of his life seem to have had little effect on his professional popularity. President Grant appointed him minister to Colombia as a reward for his having canvassed Illinois in 1868 as a presidential elector; and in 1872, after a failure two years previously, the general was elected to Congress, winning reelection in 1874. In 1881 President Garfield made him minister to Peru; and he was charged with unfortunate management of the post during the "War of the Pacific" and again seeking to provide financially for himself. He died at the ministry in Lima, March 27, 1882; his remains were returned to Belvidere for burial.

Rufus Ingalls, perhaps the only officer in a position of great responsibility who gave satisfaction to every commander of the Army of the Potomac from first to last, was born in Denmark, Maine, August 23, 1818. (253) He was graduated from West Point in the class of 1843 (254) and during the Mexican War won the brevet of first lieutenant for his services in northern New Mexico. Soon after, Ingalls accepted quartermaster duty, beginning a career of distinction in the U. S. Army. He was successively stationed at

Monterey, Los Angeles, Vancouver, Yuma, and Washington, D. C., joined Steptoe's expedition across the continent via Fort Leavenworth and Salt Lake, and at the outbreak of the Civil War was stationed at Fort Pickens, Florida. Almost immediately he was appointed chief quartermaster of the Army of the Potomac, and served successively under Generals George B. McClellan, Ambrose E. Burnside, Joseph Hooker, and George G. Meade. In June, 1864, his classmate and intimate, Ulysses S. Grant, with whom he had served in Mexico, made him chief quartermaster of all the armies operating against

Richmond, a post which he occupied until the end of the war. In the interval he had been promoted major in the quartermaster department in 1862, brigadier general of volunteers to rank from May 23, 1863, and had won all the brevets through that of major general in both the regular establishment and the volunteer forces. Upon the reorganization of the army in July, 1866, Ingalls became assistant quartermaster general with the staff rank of colonel. For the next sixteen years he was employed as chief quartermaster of the Division of the Pacific and the Division of the Missouri; and in 1881-82 was in charge of the quartermaster's depot in New York City. On February 23, 1882, he was promoted to quartermaster general of the army with the staff rank of brigadier general. Fifteen months later, at his own request, he was retired, having served forty years. It might be said of Ingalls, who arrived in Washington a week after First Manassas and was relieved from duty at City Point, the vast Union supply depot, on May 9, 1865, that corps and army commanders might come and go, but Ingalls went on forever. He died in New York City, January 15, 1893, and was buried in Arlington National Cemetery.

Conrad Feger Jackson, of an old Berks County, Pennsylvania family, was born in Alsace township, September 11, 1813, during the second war with England. He was in early life associated with the militia, as a lieutenant and adjutant of the "Reading Artillerists." At the outbreak of the Mexican War he had moved to Pottsville, Pennsylvania, and it is said that "he fought throughout the war as Captain," (255) although he is not so listed in F. B. Heitman's *Register*. Thereafter he is said to have secured a position in the United States Revenue Service. From then until the outbreak of the Civil War, he seems to have been employed by the Reading Railroad, residing in Pittsburgh, and associated with the "City Guard" militia company, which was mustered into the 9th Pennsylvania Reserves, a three-year regiment, on July 27, 1861, with Jackson as its colonel. The command, also known as the 38th

Pennsylvania Infantry, arrived in Washington a few days after the battle of First Manassas. While in winter quarters at Langley, Virginia, where the regiment had become a part of Ord's brigade of McCall's division, it took part in the little-publicized action at Dranesville, in December, 1861, virtually the first Northern victory of the war. Here the Federals inflicted a

loss of 194 men, horse and foot soldiers, on the celebrated Jeb Stuart and Powell Hill. In the course of General George B. McClellan's campaign on the Virginia Peninsula, the regiment, while attached to Porter's V Corps, was heavily engaged in the battles of Mechanicsville, Gaines's Mill, and Glendale, where Jackson directed the brigade for a time in the absence of General Truman Seymour. Subsequently, the command joined General John Pope's Army of Virginia and fought at Second Manassas under John F. Reynolds, with Jackson in command of the 3rd Brigade. He was promoted brigadier general of volunteers to rank from July 17, 1862. On August 30 Jackson was "taken sick on the field and obliged to retire" with, however, the encomiums of Reynolds. (256) Although it is generally stated that he "participated in the battles of South Mountain and Antietam" (257), the records exhibit that his brigade was commanded successively by its senior colonel and then by a lieutenant colonel. (258) At Fredericksburg, December 13, 1862, he was killed instantly by a bullet through the head, having "already shown distinguished gallantry on the day of his death." (259) He was buried in Allegheny Cemetery, Pittsburgh.

James Streshly Jackson was born on a farm in Fayette County, Kentucky, September 27, 1823. He received an excellent education at Centre College, Danville, Kentucky; Jefferson College, Canonsburg, Pennsylvania; and in the law department of Transylvania University, Lexington, Kentucky. He was admitted to the state bar

and commenced practice in Greenupsburg, Kentucky, in 1845. During the war with Mexico, Jackson served as a private in the 1st Kentucky Cavalry, a regiment which he aided in recruiting and of which he was later made third lieutenant, but he resigned, it is said, to escape court-martial after fighting a duel with his colonel. (260) In 1859 he removed to Hopkinsville, Kentucky, and the next year was elected to Congress as a Unionist. He served as a Congressman from March 4 until December 13, 1861, when he resigned to become colonel of the 3rd Kentucky (Union) Cavalry, which he had recruited and organized during the summer recess. Although "not actively engaged," he took part in the battle of Shiloh, where his regiment was attached to T. L. Crittenden's 5th Division of Buell's Army of the Ohio. (261) On July 19, 1862, he was appointed brigadier general of volunteers in accordance with the prevailing administration policy of reward-ing loyal border-state politicians with higher rank, whatever their military qualifications. In the case of Jackson advance in rank was merited; he seems to have been capable, and a few weeks later was assigned to the command of the cavalry of General William Nelson's Army of Kentucky. Although involved in the disaster at Richmond, he did not reach the vicinity of the battle until the following day, and his report to Nelson would tend to exculpate him from any blame. (262) In any event, upon the orders of General D. C. Buell, Jackson was assigned to the command of an infantry division of McCook's corps, Army of the Ohio, on September 29, 1862. At the battle of Perryville, October 8, 1862, Jackson and both of the brigade commanders of his division—singular to relate—were killed on the field. (263) General Jackson was buried in Riverside Cemetery, Hopkinsville.

Nathaniel James Jackson was born at Newburyport, Massachusetts, July 28, 1818. He learned the machinist's trade as a youth and at the outbreak of the Civil War was superintendent of the Hill mills at Lewiston, Maine. He became colonel of the 1st Maine, a ninety-day regiment, on May 3, 1861. Eight of the ten companies of this regiment had been units of the state militia in which Jackson had been prominent. During the campaign of First Manassas, the 1st Maine was not in action and was mustered out on August 3. A month later Jackson assumed command of the 5th Maine, which had also been recruited from the state militia. At the battle of Gaines's Mill on the Virginia Peninsula during George

B. McClellan's 1862 campaign, Jackson was wounded and carried from the field. He was present at South Mountain and Sharpsburg

and on September 24, 1862, was made a brigadier general. The XII Corps, of which Jackson's brigade of Geary's division was a part, was stationed at Harpers Ferry during the battle of Fredericksburg and at Chancellorsville where Jackson was not present, having suffered "a recent severe accident." (264) When able to perform light duty he was placed in command of the draft rendezvous on Riker's Island in New York Harbor and later of Hart's Island. On September 20, 1864, he was relieved from duty at the latter post and ordered to report to General W. T. Sherman at Atlanta, where he was assigned to the 1st Division of the XX Corps (former XI and XII Corps consolidated) under his old commander, A. S. Williams. With it he took

part in the celebrated "March to the Sea" and the campaign of the Carolinas. Soon after the battle of Averasboro, J. A. Mower having resumed permanent command of the XX Corps, Williams resumed permanent command of the 1st Division, and Jackson, its temporary commander, was relieved. With the brevet of major general he was honorably mustered out of service on August 24, 1865. His postwar career is obscure: by 1870 he was no longer a resident of Lewiston, and his obituary notice in the Newburyport paper records only that he "had a host of friends in this city, with whom he was wont to mingle during his summer vacations here." He died at the home of a son in Jamestown, New York, on April 21, 1892, and was buried in Newburyport—neither the Jamestown nor Buffalo papers noted his passing.

Richard Henry Jackson was a native of Ireland, born July 14, 1830, at Kinnegad, Westmeath County. (265) He emigrated to the United States as a young man, and on December 12, 1851, he enlisted in the 4th U. S. Artillery, serving successively as private, corporal, sergeant, and first sergeant of "L" company, in Florida and against the plains Indians. In 1859 he passed the promotional examinations and was commissioned a brevet second lieutenant of his regiment; when the Civil War broke out he was a first lieutenant. He engaged in the defense of Fort Pickens and in the capture of Pensacola, Florida, in 1861, and thereafter served with the X Corps in the Department of the South. During the operations against Fort

Sumter he was stationed on Folly Island in Charleston Harbor. His highest rank during hostilities was that of lieutenant colonel and assistant inspector general in the volunteer forces. For several months he was chief of artillery of the X Corps; when it was transported to the Army of the James to take part in the final operations against Petersburg, Jackson was assigned to direct the 2nd Division of Weitzel's XXV Corps, which he led until the close of the war. He was tardily rewarded with the grade of brigadier general of volunteers on May 19, 1865, together with the brevets of brigadier in the Regular Army and major general of volunteers. Following his muster-out in February, 1866, he reverted to his regular rank of captain, 4th Artillery, to which he had been appointed in 1862. This regular captaincy and his fine war record did not result in his promotion to major until 1880, and to lieutenant colonel until 1888—the grade which he occupied

at the time of his death at Fort McPherson, Atlanta, Georgia, on November 28, 1892. General Jackson was buried in the National Cemetery at West Point next to his son, who had died there during his cadetship four years before.

Charles Davis Jameson was born at Orono, Maine, on February 24, 1827, before Old Town was set off from Orono in 1840. After securing the rudiments of an education, he went into the lumber business, and it is said became one of the largest manufacturers and shippers on the Penobscot River. In the antebellum years he rose to the command of a militia regiment, and when the Civil War broke out, he was elected colonel of the 2nd Maine, which was originally enlisted for three months but subsequently mustered in for service of two years. Jameson affords a good illustration of a War Democrat, whose party principles changed sides after the Union was threatened. In 1860 he had been a

250

delegate to the Democratic convention at Charleston supporting Stephen A. Douglas for the presidency, and in both 1861 and 1862 was the party nominee for governor of the state. He led his regiment in the campaign of First Manassas, where it formed a part of Keyes's brigade of Tyler's division, and was commissioned brigadier general of volunteers to rank from September 3, 1861, for his part in protecting the Federal retreat to Centerville. During General George B. McClellan's Peninsular campaign in the spring and summer of 1862, Jameson commanded a brigade of Kearny's division of Heintzelman's III Corps. As "General of the Trenches" on May 4, 1862, he was the first to discover the Confederate evacuation of Yorktown. His brigade was in reserve at Williamsburg, but at Seven Pines it is reported that "his command went nigher to the city of Richmond than any other portion of McClellan's army—and he declared that he would have been in Richmond in less than two hours had [he] not been recalled." (266) When he might have made this statement is a matter of conjecture, since his official report of the battle indicates that the two regiments under his immediate command were flanked and forced to withdraw. (267) In any event General Samuel P. Heintzelman reported him "particularly distinguished . . . at the battle of Fair Oaks [Seven Pines], where his horse was shot under him. . . ." (268) Soon after this he contracted "camp fever" which forced him to take a leave of absence and to return to Maine. He died on a steamboat between Boston and Bangor on November 6, 1862,

and is buried in Riverside Cemetery, Stillwater, Maine. (269)

Andrew Johnson, seventeenth President of the United States, was born in Raleigh, North Carolina, on December 29, 1808. To say that his incidental commission as a brigadier general of volunteers while military governor of Tennessee during the Civil War was one of the least noteworthy events of his long and distinguished career would be a monumental understatement. In his youth he knew nothing but poverty, was apprenticed to a tailor, and was once advertised as a runaway. He moved to Tennessee at the age of eighteen, settled in Greeneville, and married the daughter of a shoemaker, who is popularly supposed to have taught her husband how to read and write while he sat cross-legged on his table stitching pantaloons. (270) His political career began with election to the village board of aldermen; he then became mayor and in 1835 was elected to the state legislature. He progressed subsequently to candidate for presidential elector in 1840, member of the state senate in 1841, Congressman in 1843, governor of Tennessee in 1853, and United States Senator in 1857. During all these years Johnson subscribed to the principles of Jacksonian democracy, although he quarreled with many of his own party. Resident in an area where slaves were few and violently opposed to pretensions by right of birth or fortune, he actively espoused the cause of "white representation," whereby slaves would count for nothing in state and national proration instead of the three-fifths of a white person which under the Constitution had been allotted them. This change would of course have given east Tennessee, where slaves were few, increased representation in both the legislature and Congress. Nevertheless, he claimed to be orthodox on the institution of slavery

per se, assailed the abolitionists on all occasions, and supported the doctrine which pronounced Congress powerless to bar slavery from the territories. In 1861, the period when Senators and representatives from the South were defecting to the newly formed Confederacy, Johnson was one of only two Senators from the thirteen states of the Confederacy who kept his seat and adhered to the Union. The other was L. W. Powell from the border state of Kentucky. In March, 1862, Johnson was appointed military governor of Tennessee, with commission of brigadier general of volunteers dating from March 4. He made his headquarters in Nash-

ville, which remained in the hands of Union troops from then until the war's end, and strove to reestablish the authority of the Federal government. Supported by the military and perforce compelled to exercise the arbitrary powers of a dictator, he at length brought about the restoration of civil government—an accomplishment which later served to exempt Tennessee from the worst features of Reconstruction. When in 1864 Lincoln was renominated by the Republicans under the Union party label, Johnson was a logical candidate for vice-president, relieving the party of the sectional character which previously had attached to it. Ill from typhoid during the previous winter, Johnson attended the inauguration only at Lincoln's earnest behest, arriving at the ceremonies intoxicated. After a rambling and pugnacious speech, he garbled the oath badly, embarrassing everyone present including Lincoln, who later absolved him by remarking, "He made a bad slip the other day, but . . . Andy ain't a drunkard." (271) Less than six weeks later he was sworn in as President and immediately confronted by the enormous complexities of the end of the war—demobilization, the newly liberated freedmen, and the problems arising from the thousands of ex-Confederates and the relationship of their former state governments to the Union. At first Johnson, caught up in the wave of hysteria which swept the North after Lincoln's assassination, thundered that "treason must be made infamous, and traitors . . . impoverished." Soon, however, the moderation which marked Lincoln's policies asserted itself and brought him into a power struggle with the Republican radicals in Congress. At the root of the struggle, as the latter clearly saw, was the increased representation of the white South in Congress occasioned by emancipation, which would be coupled with the return to power of the ex-Confederate leaders, unless the Negro vote could be controlled. Another factor in the conflict was the accident of fate which threw the executive power, with its vast patronage, into the hands of a Tennessee Democrat of the states' rights school. Such vindictive, bitter, and spoils-hungry men as Benjamin Wade, Benjamin F. Butler, Charles Sumner, and Thaddeus Stevens reasoned that this power must be nullified or, if necessary, its wielder removed from office. The President's naturally oppugnant nature did little to alleviate the situation, and his monotonous use of the veto power, even though most of the measures were passed over his veto, continuously worsened his already poor relations with the legislative branch. The climax of the battle was reached when, in defiance of the "Tenure of Office Bill," he suspended from office Secretary of War Edwin Stanton, who had been little more than an espionage agent for the Radicals. Soon afterwards, in February, 1868, Johnson was impeached for high crimes and misdemeanors. Chief Justice Salmon P. Chase presided over the Senate, organized for the occasion as a "Court of Impeachment." From a mass of irrelevant, and in many cases fraudulent, allegations, Johnson's counsel soon established that the only legal question of any importance involved was that of the Tenure of Office Act, a statute declared unconstitutional fifty-eight years later. The subsequent vote stood 35 to 19 for conviction, one less than the necessary two-thirds. "The single vote [cast for acquittal by Senator J. W. Grimes of Iowa, who was virtually driven from political life for his courage] marks the narrow margin by which the Presidential element in our system escaped destruction." (272) During the remainder of his term Johnson maintained his position vis-á-vis Congress, but with no more success than previously. His principal accomplishment in this period was the extension of his previous grants of amnesty until they embraced all classes of ex-Confederates without exception. In 1872 he was defeated in an attempt to be elected to the lower house of Congress, but two years later he was elected once again to the United States Senate, the only ex-President in history to achieve the distinction. He took his seat on March 5, 1875, and even then, the corruption of the Grant administration contrasted sharply with the courageous honesty of Johnson. He died on July 31, 1875, while visiting a daughter near Elizabethton, Carter County, Tennessee, and lies buried in the Andrew Johnson National Cemetery in Greeneville.

Richard W. Johnson (he had no middle name) was born February 27, 1827, near Smithland, Kentucky, a hamlet at the confluence of the Cumberland and Ohio rivers, of parents who had recently removed from Virginia. (273) His elder brother, who procured for him an appointment to West Point, was

later a surgeon in the Confederate Army. Johnson was graduated from the Military Academy in 1849 in a class which furnished five generals to the Union and eight to the Confederacy. All of his antebellum service was on the western frontier, first with infantry and after 1855 with the 2nd Cavalry. In keeping with the policy of giving responsible commands to loyal officers from the border states, Johnson was made a brigadier general of volunteers on October 11, 1861. (274) He was assigned a brigade of Alex. McD. McCook's division of the Army of the Ohio before the battle of Shiloh, but he missed the fighting itself because of illness. (275) That summer (1862), while pursuing the rebel General John Hunt Morgan, whom he had vowed to "capture . . . and bring . . . back in a band-box," (276) Johnson himself was defeated and forced to surrender by his numerically inferior adversary near Gallatin, Tennessee. Exchanged in December, he was given command of the 12th Division of the Army of the Cumberland and took part in the battles of Murfreesboro, Chickamauga, Chattanooga and the opening operations of the Atlanta campaign. On May 28, 1864, he was badly wounded at the battle of New Hope Church. Upon his recovery he was appointed chief of cavalry of the Military Division of the Mississippi, serving as such until October, after which he commanded a division under J. H. Wilson in the campaign against General John B. Hood which culminated in the battle of Nashville. For gallant and meritorious service he was awarded the brevet of major general in both the Regular and volunteer establishments. Retired as a major general in 1867 for disability from wounds received in battle, General Johnson had a distinguished postwar career as an educator and author. He was successively connected with the University of Missouri and the University of Minnesota as professor of military science; he was the Democratic candidate for governor of Minnesota in 1881; and wrote a number of military manuals and treatises. He died in St. Paul, Minnesota, on April 21, 1897, and was buried there in Oakland Cemetery.

Patrick Henry Jones was a native of Ireland, born in County Westmeath on November 20, 1830. He came to the United States as a boy of ten, worked on his father's farm in Cattaraugus County, New York, and then read law in Ellicottville, where he was admitted to the bar and practiced until the beginning of the Civil War. At this juncture he became a second lieutenant of

the 37th New York, known as the "Irish Rifles," a regiment which was in reserve at First Manassas. Jones was promoted first lieutenant in November, 1861, and major in January, 1862; he took part in the Peninsular campaign in Kearny's division of the III Corps and in the campaign of Second Bull Run. On October 8, 1862, Jones became colonel of the 154th New York, which was assigned to von Steinwehr's division of Howard's XI Corps. This command did not take part in the battle of Fredericksburg, (277) but at Chancellorsville in May, 1863, it was involved in the disaster which befell the corps as the result of Stonewall Jackson's famous flank march. Here Jones was wounded and taken prisoner—he was not exchanged until October. After the battle of Chickamauga the XI and XII Corps were ordered to Chattanooga although at the storming of Missionary Ridge the regiment was only nominally engaged. (278) In the spring of 1864, when the XX

Corps was formed from the consolidation of the XI and XII Corps, Jones's regiment was assigned to the 2nd Brigade of the 2nd Division ("Geary's White Stars"), with which it fought from Chattanooga to Atlanta, and then to the end of the Carolina campaign and the surrender of Johnston's army. On June 7 Jones was elevated to command of the brigade which he led thereafter. On April 18, 1865, he was appointed a brigadier general of volunteers to rank from the preceding December 6, and on June 17 he resigned his commission to return to his law practice in Ellicottville. He served as clerk of the New York State court of appeals from 1865 until he was appointed postmaster of New York City in 1869 by President Grant. Resigning in 1873, General Jones was elected register of New York the next year, serving until 1877, when he resumed his law practice. He died at Port Richmond, Staten Island, July 23, 1900, and was buried in St. Peter's Cemetery there.

Henry Moses Judah was born June 12, 1821, in Snow Hill on the eastern shore of Maryland, where his father, an Episcopal minister and native of Connecticut, was serving a parish. (279) He was graduated from West Point in 1843, thirty-fifth in a class of thirty-nine, Grant ranking twenty-first. His pre-Civil War military career was meritorious, and included the brevets of first lieutenant and captain for bravery in Mexico and extensive duty in the Pacific Northwest. At the outbreak of the Civil War, Judah, then a captain of the 4th Infantry, was stationed at Fort Yuma, California, across the Colorado

River from the present city of Yuma, Arizona. As a result of this geographical accident, he served nominally for a couple of months as colonel of the 4th California Infantry, a battalion organized in the gold rush area east of Sacramento. He resigned this command in November, 1861, returned to the East, and served in the Washington defenses until the following spring, when he was made a brigadier general of volunteers on March 21, 1862. As such he was acting inspector general of Ulysses S. Grant's army at Shiloh. After resigning this staff appointment, he commanded a division under Henry W. Halleck in the course of the approach on the rail junction of Corinth. During the winter of 1862-63, General Judah served as acting inspector general of the Army of the Ohio, and the following summer commanded a division of the XXIII Corps during the Confederate General John Hunt Morgan's incursion of Ohio. Although Morgan

was finally captured, Judah's direction of his troops seems to have left something to be desired in the minds of his superiors, (280) and he was relegated to routine administrative duties during the balance of the war. General Judah had been promoted major in the 4th Infantry on June 30, 1862, and after being mustered out of volunteer service, commanded the garrison at Plattsburg Barracks, New York. He died here, January 14, 1866, at the age of forty-five. His remains were taken to Westport, Connecticut, where they were placed in a tomb in Kings Highway Cemetery, known as the "Colonel Marvin Tomb," a sepulcher repeatedly desecrated by vandals. (281)

Thomas Leiper Kane, descended from a progenitor who had been a British loyalist during the Revolution, was born in Philadelphia on January 27, 1822. He was educated there and abroad, spending some years in Paris. Upon his return to the United States he studied law under the tutelage of his father, John K. Kane, who was a Federal judge for the eastern district of Pennsylvania, subsequently becoming a U. S. commissioner. In this capacity, the younger Kane, a confirmed abolitionist, fell afoul of the elder, who was strictly enforcing the Fugitive Slave Law, and was committed to jail for contempt. After serving as an active agent of the Underground Railroad, he associated himself with the Mormons, accompanied them in their wanderings, and in 1858 convinced Brigham Young that resistance to the U. S. Army would be unwise. Just before the Civil War he founded the village of Kane, Pennsylvania, in the northwestern part of the state, and here in 1861 he recruited the famous "Bucktails" from the local woodsmen and hunters. This regiment was named officially the 13th Pennsylvania Reserves but also was known as the First Pennsylvania

Rifles and as the 42nd Pennsylvania Volunteers. As its lieutenant colonel, Kane took part in the affair at Dranesville, Virginia, December 20, 1861, under the command of General Edward O. C. Ord, and was slightly wounded (282). On June 6, 1862, while in John C. Frémont's army opposing Stonewall Jackson in the Shenandoah, Kane was wounded and captured by the Confederates near Harrisonburg. (283) On September 7 he was appointed a brigadier general of volunteers, and a few days after Sharpsburg was ordered to duty in the XII Corps. He commanded a brigade of Williams' division at Chancellorsville, where he fell ill

of pneumonia. Supposedly rising from a hospital bed in Baltimore, he reached the battlefield of Gettysburg and resumed command of his brigade on the morning of July 2. Although the command was not heavily engaged in repelling the attack of Edward Johnson's Confederate division during the early morning hours of July 3, Kane was brevetted major general in 1865 for his services at the battle. (284) Kane was compelled by reasons of health to resign from the army in November, 1863, after which he lived in Kane and in Philadelphia. He was the first president of the state board of charities, a director of a number of business enterprises, and the author of three privately printed books. He died in Philadelphia, December 26, 1883, and was buried in Laurel Hill Cemetery.

August Valentine Kautz was born in the province of Baden, Germany, in or near Pforzheim, on January 5, 1828. (285) In the year of his birth, or soon thereafter, his parents emigrated to Brown County, Ohio, via Baltimore, Maryland. He attended school in Georgetown, Ohio, and during the first year of the Mexican War served as a private in the 1st Ohio Infantry. A year after his discharge he was appointed to West Point and was graduated in the class of 1852; he then served for a number of years in the Pacific Northwest, where he was twice wounded in operations against the Indians. With the reorganization of the Regular Army in May, 1861, Kautz was made a captain of the new 6th Cavalry, served in the Washington defenses and most creditably in General George B. Mc-

257

Clellan's Peninsular campaign. In September, 1862, he was appointed colonel of the 2nd Ohio Cavalry volunteer regiment and was sent to Fort Scott on the Kansas frontier. The following year, after some duty

in command of Camp Chase, Ohio, Kautz took part in the pursuit and capture of the rebel General John Hunt Morgan in the course of the latter's raid into Kentucky and Indiana. From April, 1864, until March, 1865, he commanded a division of cavalry in Benjamin F. Butler's Army of the James, having been made a brigadier general of volunteers on May 7, 1864. Kautz took part in a number of operations against the various Confederate lines of supply coming into Richmond and Petersburg, including the fight at Ream's Station on June 29, 1864, during James Harrison Wilson's raid. In none of these actions was he substantially successful, and in March, 1865, he was shifted to the command of a division of Negro troops in the XXV Corps at the head of which he entered the Confederate capital on April 3, 1865. In May and June Kautz had the dubious distinction of being one of the members of the military commission which acted out the farce of "trying" the conspirators in the assassination of President Lincoln. With the brevets of major general in both the Regulars and volunteers, Kautz became lieutenant colonel of the 34th Infantry in 1866, colonel of the 8th Infantry in 1874, and brigadier general, U. S. Army, in 1891. Meanwhile, he commanded effectively at various Indian posts on the frontier and wrote several military treatises. He died in Seattle, Washington, September 4, 1895, and was buried in Arlington National Cemetery.

Philip Kearny was born in New York City, June 2, 1815, the scion of great wealth and social position, and the nephew of General Stephen W. Kearny of Mexican War fame. In his early years he attended private schools, was graduated from Columbia University in 1833, studied law, and traveled widely. In 1836 he inherited a million dollars from his grandfather and at once embraced the military career which had been his goal since boyhood. A superb horseman, Kearny was commissioned second lieutenant in his uncle's regiment, the 1st Dragoons, in 1837. In 1839 he attended the French Cavalry School at Saumur, saw action with the Chasseurs d'Afrique in Algiers in 1840, and after his return to the United States acted as aide-de-camp successively to Generals Alexander Macomb and Winfield Scott, the generals-in-chief of the army. In 1846 his company served as escort for Scott during the advance on Mexico City, and at Churubusco his left arm was shattered, necessitating amputation. For his gallant conduct here he was brevetted major. After later service in California he resigned from the army in 1851 and went around the world. (286) Following several years spent on his

New Jersey estate, Kearny went abroad again in 1859 and served in Napoleon III's Imperial Guard during the Italian War. He is said to have taken part in every cavalry charge at Magenta and Solferino with the reins clenched in his teeth. When the Civil War broke out, Kearny hurried home and offered his services. He was among the first brigadier generals of volunteers appointed (August 7 to rank from May 17, 1861) and was assigned to command a brigade of New Jersey regiments in Franklin's division. During the course of the Peninsular campaign in the spring

of 1862, he rose to the command of a division of Samuel P. Heintzelman's III Corps and was made a major general as of July 4, 1862. At the close of the campaign of Second Manassas, during the indecisive engagement of Chantilly (Ox Hill) on September 1, 1862, Kearny inadvertently rode into the Confederate lines and was killed instantly by a rifle ball as he wheeled and spurred off. The originator of the "Kearny patch," the forerunner of the corps badges later developed by General Daniel Butterfield, Kearny was termed by General Scott "the bravest man I ever knew, and a perfect soldier." His remains, forwarded under a flag of truce by General Robert E. Lee, were first buried in Trinity Churchyard, New York City, but in 1912 were removed to Arlington National Cemetery.

William High Keim was born near Reading, Pennsylvania, on June 25, 1813. He attended Mt. Airy Military Academy in his native state, and accordingly took a great interest in the militia in subsequent years, rising through the various grades until he was commissioned major general on April 20, 1861. Meantime he was elected mayor of Reading in 1848 and a Democratic member of Congress, to fill a vacancy, in 1858. He was not a candidate for reelection, but in 1860 was made surveyor general of Pennsylvania, an office which he occupied until his death. Keim was second in command to Major General Robert Patterson of the Pennsylvania militia, (287) which was sent to the Shenandoah Valley to oppose and hold the forces of the Confederate Joseph E. Johnston at

259

Winchester, while Irvin McDowell's troops assailed P. G. T. Beauregard on the Manassas plains. Through the alleged supineness of Patterson, Johnston was able to transfer his entire force to Beauregard's front, with the result that the ensuing battle of First Bull Run became a Union disaster. Much contemporary obloquy was heaped on the venerable Patterson; to what extent blame should attach to Keim is moot. In any event, the Pennsylvania volunteers, together with Patterson and Keim, were mustered out on July 21, 1861. The latter, however, was appointed a brigadier general of United States volunteers on December 20, 1861. During the opening operation of General George B. McClellan's Peninsular campaign in the spring of 1862 Keim commanded the 2nd Brigade of Casey's division of Keyes' IV Corps. On May 8, 1862, following the battle of Williamsburg, Virginia, Keim wrote a report which he characterized as "owing to severe

indisposition . . . imperfect. . . ." (288) He had contracted what one of his biographers describes as "camp fever" (289) and ten days later died in Harrisburg, Pennsylvania. He was buried in Charles Evans Cemetery, Reading.

Benjamin Franklin Kelley was born April 10, 1807, in New Hampton, New Hampshire. At the age of nineteen he moved to Wheeling, in what is now West Virginia, and in 1851 became freight agent of the Baltimore and Ohio Railroad there. In May, 1861, Kelley raised the 1st (West) Virginia, a ninety-day regiment which he led at the battle of Philippi on June 3. (290) He was wounded severely during this engagement and upon recovery was commissioned brigadier general to rank from May 17. Virtually all of General Kelley's war service took place in West Virginia and Maryland, where his principal duty was to guard the line of the Baltimore and Ohio and to fend off

the constant incursions of Confederate raiders seeking to sever this vital line of communications. In consequence he took part in the pursuit of the Army of Northern Virginia after Gettysburg, the dispersal of Imboden's camp near Moorefield in November, 1863, and the engagements at Cumberland, Maryland, and Moorefield and New Creek, West Virginia in 1864. On February 21, 1865, a band of Confederate partisan rangers made a raid on Cumberland, Maryland, and carried off General Kelley along with General George Crook, his superior in command of the Department of West Virginia. Both Crook and Kelley were at the time engaged to belles of the town (whom they subsequently married), and the affair created a contemporary furore which has been studiously ignored by the biographers of both men. (291) After a brief sojourn in Richmond, Kelley was released by special exchange. He had been brevetted major general on August 5, 1864, and on June 1, 1865, resigned from the army. During the remainder of his life General Kelley held a succession of Federal positions as a reward for his wartime exploits: President Grant made him a collector of internal revenue for West Virginia in 1866 and superintendent of the Hot Springs, Arkansas, military reservation ten year later; in 1883 President Arthur appointed him an examiner of pensions. He died in Oakland, Maryland, on July 16, 1891, and is buried in Arlington National Cemetery.

John Reese Kenly was a lifetime resident of Baltimore, where he was born on January 11, 1818. He ob-

tained his education in the public schools of the city, studied law, was admitted to the Maryland bar in 1845, and was a member of the "Eagle Artillery" of Baltimore. During the Mexican War he served with distinction as captain and major of Maryland and Washington, D. C., volunteers; for his gallantry in the storming of Monterey he was awarded subsequently the thanks of the state legislature. On June 11, 1861, Kenly was commissioned by President Lincoln colonel of the 1st Maryland (Union) Infantry, a regiment with which he was posted to defend the upper Potomac. In the course of Stonewall Jackson's famous Shenandoah Valley campaign in the spring of 1862, Kenly was wounded and taken prisoner at the engagement of Front Royal, where at the cost of some six hundred casualties—most of whom were captured—the command "by its heroic resistance saved Banks' army." (292) Exchanged on August 15, Colonel Kenly became brigadier general on August 22, 1862, and was assigned to command the "Maryland Brigade," which joined the Army of the Potomac after the battle of Sharpsburg. It consisted of the 1st, 4th 6th, 7th, and 8th Maryland Infantry regiments, and during the autumn of 1862 and in 1863 was in western Maryland repelling—or attempting to repel—Confederate raids on the Baltimore and Ohio. This duty was punctuated by his command of the 3rd Division, I Corps, in the Bristoe (Virginia) campaign in the fall of 1863. Shortly after being relieved from duty with the Army of the Potomac at the beginning of General Ulysses S. Grant's Richmond campaign in 1864, General Kenly was assigned to command of the District of Delaware, with headquarters at Wilmington. (293) In the course of General Jubal Early's celebrated raid on Washington, Kenly pursued the retiring Confederates with a brigade of home guards and militia. Near Winchester part of a train which he was guarding was destroyed by the Confederates; an official inquiry seems ultimately to have resulted in his assignment to the command of the District of Eastern Shore, Maryland, with headquarters at Salisbury, Maryland, where he remained until the end of the war. He was brevetted major general in the omnibus promotions of 1865 and was mustered out in August of that year. Thereafter he resided in Baltimore, the recipient of a second vote of thanks from the Maryland legislature and a sword from the city itself. He died there on December 20, 1891, and was buried in Green Mount Cemetery.

John Henry Ketcham was born in Dutchess County, New York, December 21, 1832. (294) He procured an education at Suffield (Connecticut) Academy and then farmed near his home. He was a Dutchess County supervisor in 1854-55, member of the state assembly 1856-57, and state senator

1860-61. On October 11, 1862, he was mustered into service as colonel of the newly organized 150th New York—a regiment which did guard duty at Baltimore until the battle of Gettysburg where it was lightly engaged as a part of Lockwood's brigade, which after the battle became a part of Williams' division of the XII Corps. (295) In September, 1863, Ketcham and his men went west and until the beginning of the Atlanta campaign, with the rest of Williams' division, were stationed along the Nashville and Chattanooga Railroad between Murfreesboro and Bridgeport. The

XI and XII Corps became the XX Corps in April, 1864, and thereafter Ketcham led his regiment through the sanguinary battles of Resaca, Cassville, Dallas, Kennesaw, and the battles around Atlanta, where he was wounded and brevetted brigadier general of volunteers. Two days after he rejoined his regiment in front of Savannah, he was again severely wounded. (296) In January, 1865, he was assigned to duty according to his brevet rank; (297) however, the *Official Records* do not indicate that he was ever so employed subsequently. Although it appears that Ketcham never commanded more than a regiment in combat and although he had resigned his colonel's commission on March 2, 1865, in order to take the seat in Congress to which he had been elected the previous November, he was brevetted major general on March 13, 1865, and given the full rank of brigadier general on October 23, 1865! (298) During the next forty years General Ketcham was elected to the House of Representatives no less than seventeen times, was defeated once, and declined renomination once. He also served three years as a District of Columbia commissioner and was a delegate to numerous state and national Republican conventions. While a member of the Fifty-Ninth Congress, General Ketcham died, November 4, 1906, in New York City, and was buried in Valley View Cemetery, Dover Plains, in the county of his birth.

William Scott Ketcham was born in Norwalk, Connecticut, July 7, 1813, the son of an officer in the Regular Army who was also a native of Connecticut. Young Ketcham was graduated from West Point in 1834, standing thirty-two in a class of thirty-six. From then until the outbreak of the Civil War, he was on frontier duty in Florida and the West and did not take part in the war with Mexico, as he was stationed in Indian Territory (now Oklahoma) at the time. He was promoted to captain in the line in 1842, major in 1860, and lieutenant colonel the year following. During the war years Ketchum's career was soldierly but un-

spectacular. His services were confined entirely to matters of inspection, recruitment, boards of inquiry, the auditing of accounts and claims, and various other special assignments undertaken for the War and Treasury departments. He was made a brigadier of volunteers to rank from February 3, 1862, colonel of the 11th Infantry in 1864, and brevetted brigadier and major general, U. S. Army, at the close of the war. After being mustered out of volunteer service in 1866, he devoted the four remaining years of his army career to special duty in the adjutant general's office in Washington. Unassigned after March 15, 1869, he was retired at his own application on December 15, 1870. A few months later, while visiting a Baltimore boarding house, he died under mysterious circumstances on June 28, 1871. Subsequently the proprietress, a Mrs. Elizabeth G. Wharton, who owed Ketchum money, was formally indicted on a charge of having murdered him by poison. A change of venue was taken to Annapolis, where Mrs. Wharton was tried and found not guilty on January 24, 1872. Meanwhile General Ketchum's remains, which had been buried in Rock Creek Cemetery, Georgetown, D. C., were twice exhumed and examined by various medical authorities who testified for the state. Mrs. Wharton may have been beneficiary of the backward state of forensic medicine at the time, or of her own status as a female, since a review of the evidence presented at the trial hardly seems to warrant the verdict rendered. (299)

Erasmus Darwin Keyes was a native of Massachusetts, born in the village of Brimfield on May 29, 1810. His father, a well-known doctor, moved to Kennebec County, Maine, while Keyes was young; he was appointed to West Point from that state and was graduated in the class of 1832. Keyes compiled a glittering military record—even though he did not serve in the Mexican War—in the years before the Civil War, as an instructor at the Military Academy. A favorite

of General Winfield Scott, whose aide and military secretary he was on three different occasions, Keyes discharged duty in all three branches of the service, with promotion through grades to that of colonel, 11th Infantry in May, 1861. At the battle of First Manassas in July, he commanded a brigade of Tyler's division, whose conduct was no worse than that of other Federal troops, if no better. He was made a brigadier general of volunteers in August, third on the army list, to rank from May 17. When General George B. McClellan's big push against Richmond was organized in the spring of 1862, President Lincoln took it upon himself to name the corps commanders, and Keyes was assigned to the IV Corps, which he led in unexceptionable fashion during the Peninsular campaign. After the Army of the Potomac left the Peninsula, the IV Corps was left in the area as a part of General John Adams Dix's

Department of Virginia. During the Gettysburg campaign in 1863, Keyes, who had been made a major general for his services, fell afoul of General Dix's strategic plan to demonstrate heavily against Richmond in order to divert Confederate reenforcements from R. E. Lee's army which was in Pennsylvania. Keyes retired from a position near what is now Tallysville, Virginia, (300) in the face of what Dix deemed to be inferior forces. In the ensuing exchange, Dix seems to have had the last word. Keyes resigned in May, 1864, and moved to San Francisco, where he soon became financially successful and prominent. He interested himself in mining, in grape culture, and in the savings and loan business. While on a trip to Europe with his wife, he died in Nice, France, on October 14, 1895. He was ultimately buried at West Point.

James Lawlor Kiernan was born at Mount Bellew, County Galway, Ireland, October 26, 1837, the son of a retired British navy surgeon. (301) He appears to have been a most precocious young man, for after some preliminary studies at Trinity College, Dublin, he enrolled in 1854 at what is now the New York University Academy of Medicine and was graduated on March 4, 1857, some months before his twentieth birthday. He then practiced his profession on the lower East Side and, in conjunction with a brother-in-law who was also a physician, published the weekly New York *Medical Press* from 1859 until 1861. That spring he accompanied the famous 69th New York Militia to Washington and the battle of First Bull Run as an assistant

surgeon. He subsequently became surgeon of the 6th Missouri (Union) Cavalry, serving under John C. Frémont and at the battle of Pea Ridge (Elkhorn). At this juncture he is said to have become "tired of the medical department" and was appointed major of the 6th Missouri, an appointment which can not be substantiated by reference to any official source. (302) "Shortly afterward [he was] severely wounded through the left lung at Port Gibson, Mississippi, and left for dead in a swamp . . . was captured [but] succeeded in making his escape. . . ." He resigned, according to official account, as surgeon of the 6th Missouri on May 24, 1863, but was commissioned brigadier general of volunteers, it is said, by President Lincoln on August 1, 1863, and appointed to command of the post at Milliken's Bend on the Mississippi. (303) Because of failing health he resigned as of February 3, 1864. Soon after the war ended he received a consular post at Chinkiang, China, but remained there only a short time because of his health. Upon his return to New York City he returned to the practice of medicine and was appointed an examining physician in the pension bureau. He seems to have occupied this office until his death, November 26, 1869, at his residence on West 33rd Street, from "congestion of lungs." General Kiernan was buried in Green-Wood Cemetery, Brooklyn, New York, on November 29, 1869, the stone marking his grave reciting that he was "aged 32 years." (304)

Hugh Judson Kilpatrick (he dropped the "Hugh" upon admission to West Point) was born near Deckertown, New Jersey, January 14, 1836, the son of a farmer. He seems to have had little but a primary education in the local schools, but entered the Military Academy in 1856 and was graduated in the May class of 1861. Kilpatrick early recognized that the

path to promotion lay in the volunteer service, and on May 9, 1861, he became a captain of the 5th New York Infantry. At the skirmish of Big Bethel in June, billed as the first "battle" of the war, he became the first Regular officer to be wounded in action. In September, 1861, he became lieutenant colonel of the 2nd New York Cavalry, colonel in December, 1862, and on June 14, 1863, brigadier general of volunteers. In the meantime he successively commanded his regiment, a brigade, and later a division of cavalry in the Army of the Potomac, taking a creditable part in virtually every important cavalry action in the eastern theater, including Beverly Ford, Stoneman's raid, and Gettysburg. In February, 1864, while commanding the 3rd Cavalry Division, he undertook the celebrated raid on Richmond which was to free the Union prisoners there, but which resulted in a fiasco and the death of one-legged Colonel Ulric Dahlgren. (305) In April, General Ulysses S. Grant sent him south to take charge of a cavalry division in William T. Sherman's forces, and he was badly wounded at Resaca in the opening operations of the Atlanta campaign. He returned to duty in late July, guarded Sherman's communications, and raided and took part in several heavy skirmishes with his schoolmate, Joe Wheeler. Kilpatrick, nicknamed "Little Kil" and "Kil-Cavalry" (the latter because of the used-up condition of his horses), was a controversial and anomalous figure. He neither drank nor played cards but was a notorious Don Juan; it is recorded that he escaped from the embrace of an itinerant Southern belle in his underwear when

Confederate General Wade Hampton surprised his headquarters at dawn during the Carolina campaign. (306) He was much given to fictitious description of his own feats, vain, and careless of the truth. Nevertheless, Sherman in November, 1864, asserted, "I know that Kilpatrick is a hell of a damned fool, but I want just that sort of man to command my cavalry in this expedition." He accompanied the "March to the Sea" and the campaign which ended in North Carolina with the surrender of the army under General Joseph E. Johnston. Kilpatrick was brevetted major general, U. S. Army, in March and made major general of volunteers on June 19, 1865. At the end of the year he resigned both his regular and volunteer commissions to become minister to the Republic of Chile by appointment of President Johnson, serving until 1868. He switched his politics twice, was an unsuccessful candidate for Congress in 1880, and the following year was reappointed to the Chilean ministry by President Arthur. At this time Chile and Peru were engaged in a war, and Kilpatrick became embroiled in a diplomatic controversy with General Stephen Hurlbut who was his counterpart in Lima, presumably because he himself had a Chilean wife. In any event, by coincidence, the embattled diplomats both died at their posts, Kilpatrick in Santiago, December 4, 1881, and Hurlbut in Lima the following year; the former's remains ultimately came to rest at West Point.

Nathan Kimball was born in the southern Indiana hamlet of Fredericksburg on November 22, 1822

[1823]. (307) He attended what is now DePauw University from 1839 until 1841; then he taught school at Independence, Missouri. Shortly after, he took up the study of medicine under the tutelage of his wife's brother, practicing this profession until the beginning of the Mexican War in which he served as a captain of the 2nd Indiana Volunteers. This regiment behaved badly at Buena Vista, fleeing in disorder, but it is stated by Kimball's biographers that he "was able to rally his [own] company and continue fighting." After being mustered out, he continued to practice medicine at Loogootee, Indiana, where he was at the outbreak of the Civil War. Kimball became colonel of the 14th Indiana on June 7, 1861, and saw service at Cheat Mountain, western Virginia, in the fall of that year. The following March while commanding James Shields' division on the field at the battle of Kernstown (Shields having been wounded the previous evening), he inflicted upon Stonewall Jackson one of the few defeats suffered by the latter during his celebrated military career. Kimball was made a brigadier general on April 16, 1862, and led the 1st Brigade of French's division of the II Corps in the desperate fighting at Antietam Creek, where he lost over six hundred men either killed or wounded. At Fredericksburg he was himself badly wounded. The following summer he commanded a division of the XVI Corps at the siege of Vicksburg. After some detached duty he took part in the Atlanta campaign, first as a brigade—and after the battle of Peachtree Creek —as a division commander in the IV Corps. Before taking part in the battles of Franklin and Nashville, he was active in suppressing the activities of the disloyal Knights of the Golden Circle in southern Indiana. Kimball was brevetted major general in 1865 and soon after the end of the war became state commander of the newly organized Grand Army of the Republic, the American Legion of the day. He served two terms as state treasurer of Indiana and one term in the legislature. In 1873 President Grant appointed him surveyor general of the Utah Territory, where he thereafter made his home. President Hayes later appointed him postmaster of Ogden, Utah, an office which he held until his death there on January 21, 1898. He was buried in Weber, Utah.

John Haskell King was born, according to his grave marker in Arlington National Cemetery, in Sackets Harbor, New York, on February 19, 1820. His army dossier,

however, reflects that he was born in Michigan, where he was taken by his parents as a young boy. In any event he was appointed a second lieutenant of the 1st U. S. Infantry from Michigan, two months before his eighteenth birthday and pro- moted to first lieutenant in 1839 and captain in 1846. He served in Florida against the Seminoles, on the frontier at Vera Cruz during the Mexican War, and in Texas where, at the beginning of the Civil War, he defied the insurgent authorities and brought nine companies of Regulars safely to New York. King commanded detachments of Regular troops at Shiloh, Corinth, and in the battle of Murfreesboro, or Stone's River, where he was wounded. In April, 1863, he was appointed brigadier general of volunteers to rank from November 29, 1862, and on the first day at Chickamauga again commanded a brigade of Regulars in Baird's division of George Thomas' XIV

Corps, which along with Brannan's division of the same corps, "were thoroughly beaten up, fell back and were practically out of action for the rest of the day." (308) The following day, however, they fought magnificently on Horseshoe Ridge, doing much to save W. S. Rosecrans' army from destruction and sustaining the largest number of casualties in the battle. In the course of the Atlanta campaign he was in brigade and divisional command, and he was present at Resaca, New Hope Church, Kennesaw Mountain, and Peachtree Creek, commanding for a time the 1st Division of the IV Corps. From July, 1864, until the end of the war he commanded a brigade of five battalions of Regulars in the District of the Etowah under General James B. Steedman. General King was brevetted major general in the Regular Army on March 13, 1865, and in the volunteer service on May 31, 1865. At the end of the war, and a year before the reorganization of the army in 1866, he was promoted colonel of the 9th Infantry. He served at various stations on the western frontier until he was retired for age in 1882. Thereafter he made his home in Washington, where he died on April 7, 1888, and, as noted above, was buried in Arlington National Cemetery.

Rufus King was born in New York City on January 26, 1814, the scion of a family long distinguished in the annals of colonial and post-Revolutionary America. (309) After attending the preparatory department of Columbia College, where his father was president, he was graduated from West Point in 1833, but resigned his commission

three years later to become a civil engineer. From 1839 until the outbreak of the Civil War, King owned and edited a series of newspapers in Albany, New York, and Milwaukee, Wisconsin. At the same time he served as adjutant general of New York for four years, was prominent in framing the Wisconsin constitution of 1848, and served as superintendent of Mil-

waukee schools and as one of the first regents of the state university. Although he had been appointed minister to the Papal States by Lincoln, he resigned upon the bombardment of Sumter and was appointed one of the first volunteer brigadier generals, ranking from May 17, 1861. He organized the celebrated "Iron Brigade" of Wisconsin regiments, which went on to glory under other commanders, but his own war career left much to be desired. After duty in the Washington defenses during the winter

269

of 1861-62, he was assigned a division of General Irvin McDowell's III Corps and occupied the line of the Rappahannock until the campaign of Second Manassas. After the presence of Stonewall Jackson's Confederate corps in the Manassas area became known, McDowell posted James B. Ricketts' division in Thoroughfare Gap and King's division at Gainesville to prevent the junction of James Longstreet's corps with that of Jackson. King pulled back without orders, compelling Ricketts to do the same, thus opening the door to the Union debacle on August 30. Although King's troops fought well at Groveton on the twenty-ninth, it was rumored in army circles that their commander had been drunk. A subsequent court of inquiry, convened at the request of McDowell, determined that King had willfully disobeyed orders and, furthermore, had been guilty of a "grave error" by retiring. At this juncture he was appointed to Fitz John Porter's court-martial, thus affording the rather unusual military spectacle of an officer reprimanded for dereliction sitting in judgment upon another officer charged with the loss of the same battle. (310) He had no further important duty, and his failing health—he was an epileptic —is said to have compelled his resignation in 1863. Thereafter he went to Rome as minister until the mission was closed by the refusal of Congress to vote funds for its continuance. After a year's service as deputy collector of customs in New York City, he retired from public life in 1869. He died in New York on October 13, 1876, and was buried in Grace Churchyard, Jamaica, Long Island.

Edmund Kirby, born at Brownville, New York, March 11, 1840, grandson of Major General Jacob Brown, commander in chief of the U. S. Army from 1815 until his death in 1828, and a second cousin of General Edmund Kirby Smith of the Confederacy, had perhaps the

most singular career of any officer who took part in the Civil War. (311) His father was Brevet Colonel Edmund Kirby, a paymaster in the army, who died in 1849, and his mother was Eliza Brown. Young Kirby received an appointment to West Point in 1856; he was graduated in May, 1861, tenth in a class of forty-five members. Immediately posted to the 1st Artillery, he was promoted from second lieutenant to first lieutenant in a matter of eight days. This was to be his last promotion until he lay upon his deathbed. He commanded a section of a battery and later the battery itself throughout all the battles in the eastern theater of war, beginning with First Manassas and ending at Chancellorsville, and including Ball's Bluff, Seven Pines, and the Seven Days battles, the Maryland campaign, and the battle of Fredericksburg. On May 3, 1863, Lieutenant Kirby was in command of a II Corps battery near the Chancellor House, when his thigh was fractured by a piece of case shot. It was proposed to move him to the rear, but he instantly commanded, "No! take off that gun first." (312) Eventually he was taken to Washington, where he lingered for some weeks in a base hospital, condemned to death by a wound which in World War II would have been considered routine. Lincoln sent him a commission as brigadier general of volunteers "in recognition of his brilliant abilities, undaunted courage, and faithful service." (313) Oddly enough, although the appointment and confirmation is set forth by both F. B. Heitman's *Register* and the *Memorandum Relative to the General Officers . . . , USA*, General G. W. Cullum in his Register ignores it completely. Despite this, Kirby was subsequently referred to in the *Official Records* as "General Kirby." (314) One of the youngest full-rank general officer in the Federal army at the time of his appointment, he died on the day of his appointment, May 28, 1863. He lies buried in the village of his birth.

Edward Needles Kirk was born February 29, 1828, in Jefferson County, Ohio. He was educated at the Friends' Academy in Mount Pleasant, Ohio, taught school for a time, in 1853 was admitted to the bar, and after a year of practice

in Baltimore, Maryland, settled in Sterling, Illinois. Kirk was instrumental in recruiting the 34th Illinois Infantry in August, 1861, and on September 7 was commissioned its colonel. The regiment was stationed at various points in Kentucky until the battle of Shiloh where Kirk commanded a brigade of four regiments, including his own, in Alexander Mc.D. McCook's division of D. C. Buell's Army of the Ohio. The brigade was heavily engaged on the second day and sustained 346 casualties—Kirk himself was wounded. That fall his brigade was attached to Sill's division of McCook's Corps, but it did not fight at either Richmond or Perryville, although it took an active part in Braxton Bragg's invasion of Kentucky. At the same time McCook applied for Kirk's promotion, and as a result he was made a brigadier general of volunteers on November 29, 1862. The following month in the battle

271

of Murfreesboro the XIV Corps, or Army of the Cumberland, under W. S. Rosecrans, who had replaced Buell, was pitted against the Confederate Army of Tennessee under Bragg. The right wing was commanded by McCook, its 2nd Division by Brigadier General R. W. Johnson, and the 2nd Brigade of the latter by Kirk. At daybreak on December 31, 1862, three Confederate infantry brigades overwhelmed McCook's extreme right, consisting of the brigades of Kirk and August Willich; the latter being the flank brigade, while J. A. Wharton's cavalry came in on the right and rear. Kirk's outposts were ready for the assault, having seen the oncoming gray-clad masses, but Willich's men were caught with their arms stacked, cooking breakfast. Another Confederate attack under P. R. Cleburne succeeded the first, completing the rout. Willich's horse was shot and he was taken prisoner; Kirk "received a severe wound, which disabled him." (315) He was ultimately taken to his home in Sterling, where he lingered for nearly seven months, dying on July 21, 1863. (316) General Kirk was buried in Rosehill Cemetery, Chicago.

Joseph Farmer Knipe, whose ancestors came from Mannheim, Germany, to America before the Revolution, was born in Mount Joy, Pennsylvania, March 30, 1823. After a rudimentary education in the schools of Mannheim and Lebanon, Pennsylvania, he learned the trade of shoemaker in Philadelphia, and in 1842 enlisted as a private in the Regular Army. Soon after he took part in the Dorr Rebellion in Rhode Island, (317) a

minor episode of American history, and then fought in the Mexican War. From 1848 until the outbreak of the Civil War he was employed by the Pennsylvania Railroad in Harrisburg. During the first call of 75,000 volunteers "to suppress illegal combinations," Knipe served as a brigade inspector of Pennsylvania militia and was commissioned colonel of the 46th Pennsylvania Volunteer Infantry on August 1, 1861. With this regiment he fought under General N. P. Banks in the Shenandoah and at Cedar Mountain where he was wounded. In the Maryland campaign Knipe led a brigade of the XII Corps after the fatal wounding of General Joseph K. F. Mansfield. During the Gettysburg campaign, still not recovered from the wound received at Cedar Mountain, he served with the hapless Pennsylvania militia called out against veteran Confederates for the occasion. Ordered to Tennessee after the Chickamauga defeat, with the XI and XII Corps under Joseph Hooker (a command which, decimated at Gettysburg, was combined to become the XX Corps), Knipe took part in all the battles leading up to the fall of Atlanta, commanding for a time the 1st Division of the XX Corps. Long before this on April 15, 1863, he had been promoted brigadier general of volunteers to rank from November 29, 1862. He was later sent to Memphis to reorganize and recruit cavalry deserters and having accomplished this duty, reported to General G. H. Thomas in Nashville only to find the city besieged by J. B. Hood's Confederates. By assignment of Thomas, Knipe commanded a division of J. H. Wilson's Cavalry Corps which won a decisive victory during the retirement of Hood's ragged legions at the battle of Nashville, Knipe being credited with the capture of six thousand men and eight flags. He received no brevet promotions, but in 1866 was appointed postmaster of Harrisburg, Pennsylvania, by President Johnson, an office which he occupied until the election of Ulysses S. Grant, by whom he was immediately displaced. Thereafter he occupied a number of state and federal posts in Washington, Kansas, and Pennsylvania, where he died, in Harrisburg, August 18, 1901. General Knipe was buried in Old Harrisburg Cemetery.

Wladimir Krzyzanowski was born July 8, 1824, in the Prussian Polish city of Raznova. Like myriads who took part in the revolutions which swept Europe in the 1840's, he was forced to emigrate and came to the United States in 1846, becoming a civil engineer in New York. In 1861 he was instrumental in recruiting a regiment of Germans and Poles which was mustered into service as the 58th New York Volunteers. After duty at Washington the regiment fought under John C. Frémont at the battle of Cross Keys against Stonewall Jackson and in

the campaign of Second Manassas in Schurz's division of Sigel's I (later XI) Corps, where "Kriz," as he was known in the army, commanded a brigade. The command was not engaged at Sharpsburg or Fredericksburg, but in May, 1863, at Chancellorsville, shared in the disaster which befell Joseph Hooker's right when it was overwhelmed by Jackson's famous flank march. On November 29, 1862, Krzyzanowski had been appointed a brigadier general, but the Senate failed to act on the appointment and it expired by law on March 4, 1863. (318) The XI Corps was again badly mauled at Gettysburg, and in the fall of 1863 was sent west with the XII Corps under the command of Hooker. Krzyzanowski's brigade took part in the battle of Chattanooga and subsequently became part of the 4th Division of the XX Corps. Its commander, however, was detached during the Atlanta campaign to command the post of Bridgeport, Alabama, vital railroad crossing of the Tennessee River. He continued in the defense of the Nashville & Chattanooga Railroad and was in command of the post at Stevenson, Alabama at the end of hostilities. He was brevetted brigadier general of volunteers on March 2, 1865, and honorably mustered out of service on October 1. General Krzyzanowski was then given a succession of minor appointments in California, Alaska, and South America by the Federal government. He was appointed special agent of the Treasury Department in the New York custom house in 1883, an office which he held until his death, January 31, 1887. He was buried in Arlington National Cemetery.

Frederick West Lander, a native of Salem, Massachusetts, was born on December 17, 1821, of a distinguished American pioneer family. Privately educated, he studied for a career in engineering. After doing survey work on a number of eastern railroads, he was engaged on the survey of the Northern Pacific route in 1853; in the decade of the 1850's he participated in five transcontinental surveys, including that of the overland wagon road. At the outbreak of the Civil War, Lander went to Texas to ascertain the extent of Union sentiment there. He was later an aide to George B. McClellan at the engagements of Phi-

lippi and Rich Mountain; on August 6, 1861, he was commissioned brigadier general of volunteers to rank from May 17, and took command of a brigade of Stone's division. The day after the Federal disaster at Ball's Bluff, Lander was wounded in a skirmish at Edwards Ferry, which he was holding with a company of sharpshooters. He was soon promoted to divisional command and on January 5, 1862, successfully defended the town of Hancock, Maryland, against assault by an allegedly superior force of Confederates under Stonewall Jackson. (319) His division was then put into camp at Paw Paw, Virginia (now West Virginia), on the upper Potomac, and on February 14, 1862, he led in person an attack on a "rebel nest" in nearby Bloomery Gap. (320) In writing his report of this engagement, he applied for relief from command "my health [being] too much broken to do any severe work." (321) Immediate relief was not forthcoming, and two weeks later, while preparing to move his command to support N. P. Banks in the Shenandoah, he was mortally striken by a "congestive chill." After more than twenty hours under morphine, he died on March 2, 1862, at Camp Chase, Paw Paw, (322) and was buried in the Broad Street Burial Ground in Salem. Lander, besides pursuing his engineering and military careers, was an accomplished writer and the author of numerous patriotic poems of the Civil War. His wife, the English actress Jean Davenport (an early day Shirley Temple), delighted audiences in Europe and America for forty years.

Jacob Gartner Lauman was born January 20, 1813, in Taneytown, Maryland; but as a young boy moved with his parents across the state line to nearby York County, Pennsylvania, where he received his education in the local academy. In 1844 he moved to Burlington,

Iowa, and engaged in business until the outbreak of the Civil War. On July 11, 1861, Lauman was mustered into Federal service as colonel of the 7th Iowa Infantry. He served under U. S. Grant in Missouri and was severely wounded on November 7, 1861, in the battle of Belmont, while cutting a way through the Confederate lines. He distinguished himself at the capture of Fort Donelson, where, in command of a brigade of C. F. Smith's division, he was one of the first to enter the Confederate works. For this service he was commissioned brigadier general on March 22, 1862, to rank from the previous day. At the battle of Shiloh Lauman commanded a brigade of Hurlbut's division of the Army of the Tennessee, which sustained 458 casualties. During the Vicksburg campaign Lauman directed the 4th Division of the XVI Corps detachment under Washburn, which was first attached to Sherman's XV Corps and later to Ord's XIII Corps. Following the surrender of the Confederacy's last stronghold on the Mississippi, Lauman accompanied W. T. Sherman's forces, consisting of three army corps, in its mission to retake Jackson, Mississippi, the state capital. In the course of getting his division into its assigned position in front of the city on July 12, 1863, Lauman's men were badly mauled by the intrenched Confederates, one of his brigades losing 465 out of 880 present for duty. Edward O. C. Ord, claiming the whole affair was conducted by Lauman "without orders, and directly in violation of the instructions as to the position he was to take," (323) relieved him from command and ordered him to report to General Grant at Vicksburg. Ord was sustained by Sherman in this action, and on July 15 Grant ordered Lauman to return to Iowa and await orders. (324) Despite the fact that he seems never again to have been on duty, he was duly brevetted major general as of March 13, 1865, for the usual "gallant and meritorious services during the war." He died in Burlington on February 9, 1867, and was buried in Aspen Grove Cemetery.

Michael Kelly Lawler was born in County Kildare, Ireland, on November 16, 1814; his parents brought him to the United States in March 1816. (325) After residing in New York City and Frederick

County, Maryland, the family came to Gallatin County, Illinois, where they settled. Michael married the daughter of a large landowner in the vicinity and by 1840 was farming on a large scale for the day and time. For some years he commanded a company of militia and during the Mexican War distinguished himself as a captain of the 3rd Illinois in the engagements which marked Winfield Scott's advance from Vera Cruz to Mexico City. Until the beginning of the Civil War he farmed and kept a general store in Shawneetown, the county seat. Early in 1861 he and his regiment, the 18th Illinois, were mustered into service by U. S. Grant, then a captain on the staff of the adjutant general of Illinois. Lawler enforced discipline in his regiment by knocking down recalcitrants with his fists, by feeding emetics to drunks in the guardhouse, and by threats of violence to officers and men alike. Brought before a court-martial for these alleged "offenses," he was handsomely acquitted by Henry W. Halleck, then the department commander. In the assault on Fort Donelson, Lawler was wounded; in May, 1863, after being promoted to brigadier general (ranking from November 29, 1862), he commanded a brigade at Port Gibson, during the Vicksburg campaign. At the siege of Vicksburg proper he delivered one of the most audacious assaults made during the war, capturing more than eleven hundred Confederates. During the balance of the war he was employed in brigade and divisional command at various points in Louisiana and Texas and at the end of hostilities was in charge of the District of East Louisiana at Baton Rouge. He was brevetted major general as of March 13, 1865. After being mustered out of service General Lawler spent several years buying and selling horses in the area where he had been stationed. He lived uneventfully on his farm near Equality, Illinois, during his remaining years, where he died on July 26, 1882, and is buried in a nearby country churchyard. (326)

James Hewett Ledlie was born in Utica, New York, on April 14, 1832. He was educated at Union College in Schenectady and became a civil engineer engaged in railroad construction. Shortly after the outbreak of war he became major of

the 19th New York Infantry, subsequently named the 3rd New York Artillery. This regiment, at the expiration of its original term of service, mutinied and 23 of the original 206 offenders were sentenced to the Dry Tortugas. Ledlie was promoted lieutenant colonel, colonel, and then brigadier general on December 24, 1862; the latter rank expired on March 4, 1863, for lack of Senate confirmation.

(He was reappointed on October 27, 1863, and in due course confirmed.) Meantime, Ledlie had served unexceptionably on the Carolina coast, commanding an artillery brigade under John G. Foster, and in district and post command at various points in the Federal Department of Virginia and North Carolina. In the course of the fierce fighting around Spotsylvania Court House in May, 1864, Ledlie joined the Army of the Potomac and was assigned to the command of a brigade in Ambrose E. Burnside's IX Corps. The following month, after Petersburg was invested, he became commander of the 1st Division of the corps. At the end of July his division was selected to lead the Federal assault upon the Confederate works after the explosion of the celebrated Union mine. At 4:45 A.M. on the morning of July 30, 170 feet of Confederate entrenchment was disintegrated, creating a "crater" 60 feet across and 30 feet deep. While Ledlie's men struggled to get over their own parapet—no provision had been made for ladders or steps —and while the possession of Petersburg and the end of the war may have rested in the palms of their hands, Ledlie huddled "in a bombproof ten rods in rear of the main line. . . ." (327) In September he was criticized by a court of inquiry, and in December was virtually read out of the service by George G. Meade on U. S. Grant's orders. (328) He resigned on January 23, 1865. After the war he continued his career as a railroad engineer in the west and south. Ledlie died at New Brighton, Staten Island, on August 15, 1882, and was buried in Forest Hill Cemetery, Utica.

Albert Lindley Lee was born in Fulton, New York, on January 16, 1834. He was graduated from Union College at Schenectady in 1853 and then studied law. He moved to the Kansas Territory to practice his

profession and in 1861 became a justice of the state supreme court. Lee resigned from the bench to be mustered into military service as major of the 7th Kansas Cavalry on October 29, 1861. After some minor operations in Kansas and western Missouri, the regiment was brought to the east bank of the Mississippi and was active in the operations incident to U. S. Grant's movements against Vicksburg. Lee was appointed a brigadier in April, 1863 (to rank from November 29, 1862), and acted as chief of staff to John McClernand at Champion's Hill and the battle of the Big Black River. During the siege of Vicksburg he was wounded, and after rejoining the army, Lee was ordered to the command of General N. P. Banks in New Orleans, where he became chief of cavalry of the Department of the Gulf. He commanded the cavalry division in Banks's ill-fated Red River campaign, winning few laurels—the consensus being that the cavalry was no better handled than the infantry. In August, 1864, he was assigned to the command of the cavalry division of the department with headquarters at Baton Rouge. Soon afterwards General Edward R. S. Canby superseded Banks in command of a greatly expanded territory. Lee was continued at his post, but the records indicate that his relations with his superior rapidly deteriorated. Soon after the New Year he was ordered to report to the Adjutant General in Washington, who, however, returned him to "his proper command" in the Department of the Gulf a week later. On April 2, 1865, by orders of Canby, Lee was to "remain in this city [New Orleans] until further orders. This order to date from February 3, 1865." (329) On May 4, 1865, General Lee's resignation was accepted by the War Department, and he was duly mustered out. After the war he spent much of his time in Europe and New York City where he engaged in business. At the time of his death in New York, December 31, 1907, he was retired. He was buried in Mt. Adnah Cemetery in his birthplace.

Mortimer Dormer Leggett was born on a farm near Ithaca, New York, April 19, 1821. At the age of fifteen he was taken by his parents to Geauga County, Ohio, where he

278

helped his father to hew a farm from the wilderness. By his own unaided efforts he secured an excellent education, was admitted to the bar in 1844, and in 1846 moved to Akron. One of the founders of the graded-school system in Ohio, he lived successively in Akron, Warren, and Zanesville, serving as school superintendent in all three towns while practicing law. For a time he was professor of law in the Ohio Law College at Poland and a law partner of General Jacob D. Cox. (330) During the first months of the Civil War, Leggett served as a civilian aide on the staff of his friend, George B. McClellan, in western Virginia; he was commissioned colonel of the 78th Ohio in January, 1862. (331) This regiment was present but not seriously engaged at Donelson and Shiloh; one man was killed and nine were wounded at Shiloh, where it was a part of Lew Wallace's division. By the fall of 1862

Leggett had progressed to brigade command and was formally commissioned on April 15, 1863, to rank from the preceding November 29. During the campaign which culminated in the surrender of Vicksburg, Leggett was distinguished as commander of a brigade in Logan's division of McPherson's XVII Corps. In the Atlanta campaign he directed a division of the corps and on July 22 ably defended a key position on the left of the Federal line which came to be known as Leggett's Hill. For a time in the autumn of 1864 he commanded the corps and marched with Sherman to the sea and in the campaign of the Carolinas in the ensuing months, being brevetted major general of volunteers as of September 1, 1864. At the time of the surrender of Joseph E. Johnston in North Carolina, General Leggett was again directing the 3rd Division of the corps. On August 21, 1865, he was made a full major general but resigned on September 28 to return to private life. He practiced law in Zanesville until 1871 when President Grant appointed him commissioner of patents, a post in which he served three years. In 1884 he organized a company which became highly successful and ultimately a part of the General Electric Company. General Leggett died in Cleveland, January 6, 1896, where he was buried in Lakeview Cemetery.

Joseph Andrew Jackson Lightburn was born at Webster, Pennsylvania, south of Pittsburgh, on September 21, 1824, one of eleven children. (332) About 1838 the family moved to Lewis County (West) Virginia, where the father became a prosperous farmer and miller. In 1842 Lightburn unsuccessfully competed for a West Point cadetship against a neighbor youth who would one day become the celebrated Stonewall Jackson. From 1846 until 1851 he served in the Regular Army as private, corporal,

and sergeant, mainly on recruiting duty. In 1861, as a staunch Unionist, he was elected to the loyalist convention in Wheeling which led to the establishment of the state of West Virginia in 1863. (333) He was commissioned colonel of the 4th West Virginia Infantry in August, 1861, and took part in the unsuccessful engagements of Charleston and Gauley Bridge in 1862. In December of that year he was ordered to the theater of operations in the Vicksburg area where he commanded the 2nd Brigade of Francis P. Blair's division of the XV Corps. On March 16, 1863, he was made a brigadier general of

volunteers, and at Chattanooga in November, 1863, he served under W. T. Sherman in the attack on Missionary Ridge. The following spring he took part in the Atlanta campaign in Morgan Smith's division. His brigade was roughly handled at Kennesaw, where it sustained 171 killed and wounded, but distinguished itself under the leadership of Lightburn and Smith at the Augusta railroad cut in front of Atlanta on July 22. Here in the face of Confederate fire front and rear, it retrieved a lost situation and some previously captured Federal artillery. On August 24, 1864, while taking part in the operations which shifted Sherman's forces west and south around Atlanta, Lightburn was struck in the head by a rifle bullet; after his recovery he was assigned to duty in West Virginia and Maryland. At this time he made the acquaintance of a future President, Captain William McKinley, and figured in the kidnapping of Generals George Crook and Benjamin Kelley by the Confederates in Cumberland, Maryland. At the close of the war General Lightburn resumed his former occupations at Weston (West Virginia), and in 1867 was ordained as a minister in the Baptist Church, an avocation to which he was irresistibly drawn. He was an exemplary power in his church until his death at his old home on Broad Run in Lewis County, May 17, 1901. (334) He was buried in Broad Run Churchyard.

Henry Hayes Lockwood, probably the only army general to be buried in the Naval Academy Cemetery, was born in Kent County, Delaware, August 17, 1814, and was graduated from West Point in 1836.

(335) He served in the war against the Seminoles for a time, but resigned in 1837 to become a farmer. In 1841 Lockwood was appointed professor of mathematics at Annapolis; then during the Mexican War he served aboard the frigate *United States* and took part in the capture of Monterey, California. After the war he was again on duty at the Naval Academy, teaching such subjects as natural philosophy, astronomy, field artillery, gunnery, and infantry tactics. He became colonel of the 1st Delaware Infantry on May 25, 1861, and brigadier general of volunteers on August 8, 1861. During the first two years of the Civil War he had command of the eastern shore of Maryland and Virginia and the defenses of the Lower Potomac. In the Gettysburg campaign he was on active field duty, directing the 2nd Brigade of A. S. Williams' division of Slocum's XII Army Corps, two of the three regiments of his command having been recruited from the Potomac area. On July 17, 1863, Lockwood's troops were detached from the Army of the Potomac and ordered to reenforce the garrison on Maryland Heights across the Potomac from Harpers Ferry. Later that year he was placed in charge of the Middle Department, with headquarters at Baltimore, and in 1864 commanded some provisional troops called out to repel Jubal Early's raid on Washington. After Early's retirement into Virginia, Lockwood was assigned to the command of the "Third Separate Brigade" and a geographical area within the Middle Department which embraced the counties of Frederick, Carroll, Harford, the eastern shore of Maryland, and all of Baltimore with the exception of the coastal defenses; he continued this command until his muster out in 1865. He returned to the Naval Academy and served as professor of natural and experimental philosophy until 1870 when he was assigned to the Naval Observatory in Washington where he remained until his retirement in 1876. He then made his residence in Georgetown, D. C., where he died on December 7, 1899, and was buried at Annapolis.

John Alexander Logan, perhaps the Union's premier civilian combat general, was born February 9, 1826, paradoxically enough on a farm in Jackson County in the "Little Egypt" area of southern Illinois. Many of the inhabitants of this area came from the slave states, and it was a Democratic stronghold which largely supported disunion during the 1860's. Logan's early education was fragmentary, but included the study of

law; he served in the Mexican War as a second lieutenant of Illinois volunteers, was elected to the Illinois legislature, was a presidential elector for James Buchanan in 1856, and in 1858 went to Congress as a Free-Soil Democrat. In 1860 he attended the Democratic National Convention in Charleston as a Stephen A. Douglas supporter and was re-elected to Congress that fall. During the winter 1860-61 Logan repeatedly manifested his support for the Union, declaiming his sentiments far and wide. (336) He combined a talent for bombastic oratory, a large store of self-interest, a genuine love of the Union, and inherent abilities as a leader to produce a record hardly surpassed in the era for its versatility. After the special session of Congress in 1861, Logan, who had fought at Bull Run as a volunteer in a Michigan regiment, returned to southern Illinois and recruited the 31st Illinois, of which he was

commissioned colonel in September. "Black Jack," as he was known because of his black eyes and hair and swarthy complexion, became an instant success as a field commander in the western armies. He was present at Belmont, where his horse was killed, and at Fort Donelson, where he was wounded. Shortly after he was made a brigadier to rank from March 21, 1862. During Henry W. Halleck's "siege" of Corinth, following the battle of Shiloh, Logan commanded a brigade and division of U. S. Grant's Army of the .Tennessee. During the winter campaign in northern Mississippi which preceded the final operations against Vicksburg, Logan, who was made a major general on March 13, 1863, to rank from the preceding November 29, directed the 3rd Division of McPherson's XVII Corps; and for his services during the siege of the town, where his troops made the desperate assault on the Confederate works which followed the mine explosion, he was awarded the Congressional Medal. During the Atlanta campaign Logan commanded with great distinction the XV Corps and was wounded at Dallas, Georgia. When James B. McPherson was killed in front of Atlanta on July 22, 1864, the command of the Army of the Tennessee devolved temporarily upon Logan. It was subsequently determined between W. T. Sherman and G. H. Thomas, who was then commanding the Army of the Cumberland, that a West Pointer Oliver O. Howard should succeed to the permanent command of the XV Corps—this move caused Logan to hate West Point from the bottom of his heart. (337) Actually Sherman's distrust for political generals "off the field," even though he considered Logan "perfect in combat," determined the appointment. After aiding to carry Illinois for the Republican party in 1864 Logan returned to his corps, which he led from the Savannah campaign until the surrender of General Joseph E. Johnston in North Carolina. After the close of the war he served either as a Congressman or a Senator from Illinois almost uninterruptedly until his death. Meanwhile, he was instrumental in the organization of various veterans' societies, untiring in the movement to award pensions to Union veterans, and a dedicated disciple of the "bloody shirt" society at every election. (338) His usefulness on the national scene waned as he grew older, however, and in 1884 he was the unsuccessful Republican nominee for vice-president. He died in Washington while a member of the Senate on December 26, 1886, and is buried in Soldiers Home National Cemetery.

Eli Long was born in Woodford County, Kentucky, on June 16, 1837. He attended the Frankfort military school, was graduated in 1855, and the following year was appointed, directly from civilian life, a second lieutenant of the 1st U. S. Cavalry. After service on the frontier he became a first lieutenant on March 1, 1861, and captain on May 24 in the promotions incident to the withdrawals of those officers who had elected to "go South." He transferred to the 4th Cavalry in August in order to secure active duty, and at the bat-

tle of Murfreesboro was wounded in the arm while commanding Company K. Soon after he was appointed colonel of the 4th Ohio Cavalry, a regiment of volunteers whose morale had suffered greatly a few days before by being compelled to surrender to the Confederate raider, John Hunt Morgan. (339) Long revitalized the command and led it in the Tullahoma and Chickamauga campaigns; he directed a brigade in the latter. During the Atlanta campaign in June, 1864, his brigade joined the Cavalry Corps of the Army of the Cumberland, and Long was promoted brigadier general of volunteers on August 18, 1864. At the end of October he was sent to Nashville to take charge of Kenner Garrard's division, which he was to collect, equip, and remount, pending future operations. These were not long in coming; they included the Confederate General J. B. Hood's

283

thrust into Tennessee and culminated in the decisive battle of Nashville in December and General James Harrison Wilson's raid from west to east through what remained of the Confederacy in the spring of 1865. During this period Long commanded the 2nd Division of Wilson's Cavalry Corps, was badly wounded for the fifth time at Selma, and after the fighting was over was assigned to command of the military district of New Jersey. General Long was awarded every brevet in both the regular and volunteer services for gallant and meritorious service up to and including the grade of major general. He was retired from the army with the rank of major general in 1867 (reduced to brigadier in 1875), (340) and subsequently took up residence in Plainfield, New Jersey. Here, according to his obituary in the Plainfield *Courier-News* of January 8, 1903, he practiced law and was borough recorder. He died in a New York City hospital as the result of an operation on January 5, 1903, and was buried in Hillside Cemetery, Plainfield. (341)

Charles Russell Lowell, nephew of the poet, was born January 2, 1835, in Boston. He was graduated from Harvard at the head of the class of 1854 and then spent several years traveling abroad. At the beginning of the Civil War, he was managing an iron works in Maryland. On May 14, 1861, he accepted a commission as captain in the 3rd (later 6th) U. S. Cavalry. He served throughout the Peninsular campaign and at its close was assigned to the staff of General George B. McClellan. During the

battle of Sharpsburg (Antietam), Lowell displayed such gallantry while carrying orders under fire and rallying broken troops that he was chosen to carry the captured Confederate battle flags to Washington. In the autumn of 1862 he recruited and organized the 2nd Massachusetts Cavalry of which he was commissioned colonel on May 10, 1863. During the winter of 1863-64 he was in charge of the outer defenses of Washington, and the following July Lowell was engaged in repelling the raid of the Confederate Jubal Early—an operation which brought rebel troops within sight of the Capitol dome for the last time in the war and even placed President Lincoln under fire. (342) In the course of the ensuing Shenandoah Valley campaign between Early and Philip H. Sheridan, Lowell commanded a brigade of Merritt's division of the Cavalry Corps (then under the command of A. T. A. Torbert), comprised of his

284

own old regiment, the 6th Pennsylvania, and three regiments of Regulars. He distinguished himself in the battle at Winchester on September 19, and on October 9 took a leading part in the rout of Rosser's command at Tom's Brook, where Sheridan's orders to Torbert were "to whip the rebel cavalry or get whipped." (343) During his three years' service Lowell had twelve horses shot from under him without sustaining a scratch himself. At Cedar Creek on October 19, however, his luck ran out: he was wounded early in the day, and refusing to leave the field, he was at the head of his brigade when he sustained a mortal wound, during the successful Union counterattack which virtually dispersed Early's army. He died the following day at Middletown, Virginia, and was buried in Mount Auburn Cemetery, Cambridge, Massachusetts. Upon the personal intercession of Sheridan, Lowell's commission as brigadier general of volunteers was signed on the day of the battle.

Thomas John Lucas was born September 9, 1826, in the Ohio River town of Lawrenceburg, Indiana. He followed his father's trade of watchmaker until 1847 when he entered the Mexican War as a second lieutenant of the 4th Indiana Volunteers for a service of fourteen months. In 1861 he became lieutenant colonel of the 16th Indiana and with it took part in the Federal debacle at Ball's Bluff, Virginia. Upon the promotion of Colonel Pleasant A. Hackleman to brigadier, Lucas became commander of the regiment which was remustered for three

years or the duration of the war. The 16th Indiana met further misfortune at the battle of Richmond, Kentucky, during Braxton Bragg's invasion—two hundred were killed or wounded and six hundred were captured. The prisoners were paroled and exchanged; the command was reorganized and after furlough was

sent to U. S. Grant's army to take part in the Vicksburg campaign in John McClernand's (later Ord's) XIII Corps. In the course of these operations Lucas was wounded three times. Next he was assigned to direct a brigade of cavalry in the division commanded successively by Generals A. L. Lee and Richard Arnold during N. P. Banks's abortive Red River expedition. On November 10, 1864, Lucas was made a brigadier general of volunteers, and in the operations designed to take the city of Mobile, he commanded first a brigade and then a division, leading raids into west Florida, south Georgia, and Alabama. Brevetted major general to rank from March 26, 1865, "for faithful and meritorious service against the city of Mobile," he was commanding a brigade of cavalry at Vicksburg at the war's end. He returned to civilian life in Lawrenceburg early in 1866. From 1875 until 1881 General Lucas was employed in the U. S. Revenue Service, and from 1881 until 1885, during the administrations of Presidents Garfield and Arthur, was postmaster of his hometown. In 1886 he ran unsuccessfully for Congress on the Republican ticket. Lucas died on November 16, 1908, and was buried in Greendale Cemetery in Dearborn County, Indiana.

Nathaniel Lyon, who more than any other man saved Missouri for the Union in 1861, was born July 14, 1818, in that part of the Connecticut "town" of Ashford which is now a part of Eastford. (344) After a common-school education and a few months at the Brooklyn, Connecticut academy, Lyon matriculated at West Point and was graduated in 1841, ranking eleventh in a class of fifty-two. During the years before the war he fought against the Florida Seminoles and although denouncing the participation of the United States in the Mexican War, was nevertheless brevetted captain for gallantry in the conflict. For several years thereafter he was on duty in California. Lyon's political and military concepts became fixed in the period 1854-61, while he was stationed in "Bleeding Kansas." Even though he was far from being an abolitionist and was not even in favor of disturbing slavery where it existed, he developed an unconditional adherence to the Union. As commander of the St. Louis arsenal after February, 1861, he used this uncompromising attitude—which he would force if necessary upon those of secessionist proclivities—to provide the keynote for the removal of General William S. Harney as commander at St. Louis and for the subsequent meetings between the secessionist Governor Claiborne Jackson; his lieutenant, Sterling Price, later a Confederate major general; Francis P. Blair, a Union Congressman who would also become a Union major general; and Lyon. The upshot of these conferences was summarized by Lyon's remark, "This means war." In the meantime, Lyon rendered impotent the secessionist threat to Missouri's largest city, by seizing the encampment of the pro-Confederate Missouri militia under General D. M. Frost at

Camp Jackson in St. Louis. He was jumped from captain of the 2nd Infantry to brigadier general of volunteers on May 17, 1861, and in subsequent months attempted to drive the pro-Confederate elements from the state. After a series of minor operations he determined to attack the Confederate forces under Ben McCulloch on Wilson's Creek near Springfield, Missouri. This encounter on August 10, 1861, termed "the hardest four hours' fighting that up to that time had ever taken place on the American continent," (345) resulted in a Pyrrhic victory for McCulloch's Confederates and in the death of Lyon. (346) He was buried in a cemetery near his birthplace.

William Haines Lytle, born in Cincinnati, Ohio, November 2, 1826, was the descendant of a family which had figured prominently in the shaping of America since

the middle of the eighteenth century. His father Robert was for many years a dedicated disciple of Andrew Jackson in Congress and for a time surveyor general of the United States. Young Lytle, although predisposed to a military career, studied and practiced law until the beginning of the war with Mexico. He entered the service as a second lieutenant of the 2nd Ohio Volunteers and was mustered out as captain July 25, 1848. In the interval before the Civil War, Lytle practiced law in Cincinnati, was twice elected to the legislature, was an unsuccesssful candidate for lieutenant governor of Ohio, and in 1857 by appointment of Governor Salmon P. Chase became a major general of militia. This period of his life was further distinguished by his poetical writings upon which his principal claim to fame rests. (347) Lytle was commissioned colonel of the 10th Ohio on May 3, 1861. The regiment was initiated into battle on September 10, 1861, at Carnifex Ferry, (West) Virginia, where Lytle was badly wounded by a ball which passed through his leg and killed his horse. (348) After his recovery he commanded a recruit rendezvous at Bardstown, Kentucky, and subsequently a brigade in D. C. Buell's Army of the Ohio which served in Alabama and during Buell's march into Kentucky to oppose the invasion of the Confederate Braxton Bragg. At the battle of Perryville, which marked the retirement of Bragg southward, Lytle commanded a brigade of Alexander McD. McCook's corps and was wounded and left on the field for dead. Captured by the Confederates and restored to health, he was promoted brigadier general of volunteers on November 29, 1862, although not officially declared exchanged until February 4, 1863. At the battle of Chickamauga Lytle, while in command of the 1st Brigade of Sheridan's division of the XX Corps, was mortally wounded as he led a charge against the victorious Confederates on September 20, 1863, in an effort to protect the rear of his command. (349) He died the same day, and was ultimately buried in Spring Grove Cemetery, Cincinnati.

John McArthur was born November 17, 1826, in the parish of Erskine on the River Clyde in Renfrewshire, Scotland. He learned his

father's trade of blacksmithing, and at the age of twenty-three he emigrated to the United States and settled in Chicago where he soon became successful as proprietor of the Excelsior Iron Works. During the antebellum years he interested himself in a militia company called the "Chicago Highland Guards" of which he was captain in 1861. On May 3, 1861, he was appointed colonel of the 12th Illinois Infantry, a ninety-day regiment which was remustered in August to serve three years. It inaugurated its military service by garrisoning Cairo, and before the year was out McArthur was directing the 1st Brigade of C. F. Smith's 2nd Division, District of Cairo, as the army under Ulysses S. Grant was then known. From the capture of Forts Henry and Donelson in February, 1862, until the end of the war, the tall, brawny Scot compiled a combat record second to none in the capacity in which he served. Promoted brigadier general in March, 1862, he succeeded to command of W. H. L. Wallace's division after the latter was mortally wounded on the bloody field of Shiloh, and he led a division of the Army of the Tennessee under Edward Ord at Iuka and Corinth. He directed one of McPherson's XVII Corps's divisions during the Vicksburg campaign, and was commander of the city itself until August, 1864. On the fifth of that month he was ordered by W. T. Sherman to the Atlanta area to protect the latter's line of communications stretching north toward Chattanooga. In November he brought the 1st Division of the XVI Corps back to Nashville from Missouri where it had been occupied resisting Sterling Price's raid; the following month at the battle of Nashville, his four thousand men rolled up John B. Hood's left on the first day of the battle. For this exploit of "conspicuous gallantry and efficiency," he was brevetted major general. Thereafter he served under Edward Canby in the campaign which concluded the war and was stationed at Selma, Alabama, during the summer of 1865. His postbellum career was by no means so successful: he failed to revive his ironworks; the great Chicago Fire of 1871 occurred while he was commissioner of public works; and as postmaster of the city, he was further humiliated by the loss of Federal funds in a bank failure in which he was held personally liable by judicial decree. Prominent in Scottish and veterans organizations until his death, General McArthur died May 15, 1906, in Chicago and was buried in Rosehill Cemetery.

George Archibald McCall, one of the oldest West Point graduates to perform active field duty during the Civil War, was born in Philadelphia on March 16, 1802. Twenty years and three months later he became the 311th graduate of the Military Academy and was posted to the 1st Infantry. Much of his early military career was spent in Florida where he was employed almost continuously until 1842 against the warlike Seminoles, for five years serving as aide-de-camp to General Edmund P. Gaines. During the Mexican War, McCall, who was by then a captain of the 4th Infantry, was brevetted major and lieutenant colonel for gallantry at Palo Alto and Resaca de la Palma in Zachary Taylor's army. In 1850 after a leave of absence in Europe and promotion to major of the 3rd Infantry, he was named one of the two inspectors general with the staff rank of colonel of the army. Mc-

Call resigned his army commission in 1853 to retire to his country estate, Belair, near West Chester, Pennsylvania, but volunteered for duty again when the shooting started in 1861. Commissioned major general of Pennsylvania Volunteers by Governor Andrew G. Curtin on May 15, 1861, he was made brigadier general of U. S. Volunteers two days later by President Lincoln, and subsequently commanded "the Pennsylvania Reserves" as a division of the Army of the Potomac. He planned the operation against Dranesville, Virginia, in December, 1861. And at Mechanicsville, Virginia, during George B. McClellan's Peninsular campaign in the spring of 1862, perhaps McCall's most notable exploit of the war was his forming the advance of Porter's V Corps as they opposed the assault of A. P. Hill's Confederates across the Chickahominy in June, 1862. A few days later on June 30, he was taken prisoner at the battle of Glendale (Frayser's Farm) when he rode into the 47th Virginia while attempting to reconnoiter his position without staff officers. Confined in Libby Prison, Richmond, until August 18, 1862, he was paroled and exchanged for Confederate General Simon Bolivar Buckner, who had been taken prisoner at Fort Donelson. (350) After his release McCall was on sick leave until he resigned March 31, 1863. He retired to Belair where he died on February 26, 1868. He was buried in Christ Church Cemetery, Philadelphia.

George Brinton McClellan, one of the most controversial figures in American military history, was born in Philadelphia, Pennsylvania, on December 3, 1826, of distinguished Connecticut ancestry. His first cousin was Major Henry B. McClellan, chief of staff to Confederate General Jeb Stuart. George McClellan attended local preparatory schools and, for a time, the University of Pennsylvania, leaving the university in 1842 in order to enter West Point. He was graduated in 1846, ranking second in a class of fifty-nine—a class which contributed twenty full-rank general officers to the Union and Confederate armies. (351) McClellan was appointed a brevet second lieutenant in the Corps of Engineers. During the Mexican War, while attached to General Winfield Scott's forces, he excited much favorable mention in reports for his zeal, gallantry, and ability for constructing roads and bridges along the route over which the army made its way, and won the brevets of first lieutenant and captain. In the course of the next decade his duties were var-

ied and his accomplishments many. For three years he was an instructor at West Point, meanwhile translating into English and adapting to American usage a French treatise on bayonet exercises. He then served on engineering duty at Fort Delaware; in the expedition under Captain Randolph B. Marcy (his future father-in-law) to explore the sources of the Red River; in various surveys of possible transcontinental

railroad routes; and as a member of a board of officers sent abroad to study the armies of Europe and the Crimean War. The "McClellan saddle," adapted by McClellan from the Hungarian, was a direct result of this European trip and remained standard equipment in the army until mechanization eliminated horses. In 1857 he resigned his commission of captain in the 1st Cavalry, to which he had been appointed in 1855, to become chief engineer of the Illinois Central

Railroad. At the outbreak of the Civil War he was living in Cincinnati and was president of the Ohio & Mississippi Railroad. On April 23, 1861, he became major general of Ohio Volunteers, with command of all the forces of the state, by appointment of Governor William Dennison. Three weeks later, such was his élan, efficiency in organization, capability, and personal magnetism, that President Lincoln, who had never seen him, was impelled to appoint him major general in the Regular Army, where he was outranked only by the aged and infirm General-in-Chief Winfield Scott, whose commission dated from the time McClellan was a boy of fourteen. At the beginning of hostilities two of the main prizes contended for by the two governments were Kentucky and the western counties of Virginia. McClellan, whose authority embraced both areas, refused to acknowledge the so-called "neutrality" of Kentucky, thus doing much to hold the state to the Union; in what is now West Virginia he acted swiftly to insure the allegiance of its people by personally commanding the Rich Mountain campaign— a victory for the Federal arms which maintained control of the Baltimore & Ohio Railroad and most of transmontane Virginia for the balance of the war. This success, minor as it may seem in retrospect, coupled with Irvin McDowell's disaster at First Manassas (Bull Run), precipitated McClellan into command of the Army of the Potomac in August and into the office of General-in-Chief of the Armies of the United States on November 1, 1861, upon the retirement of General Scott. In two bounds a resigned subaltern, who was only thirty-five years old, took charge of the greatest military establishment ever assembled by the nation up to that time. Reaching Washington five days after the Bull Run debacle, he brought order out of chaos, reduced the several dissident commands to a state of discipline, and won for himself a regard by his men which would not soon be equaled. The description of McClellan's subsequent military operations amounts to lost opportunities and frustration. Greatly against his own judgment, but on orders of the administration, he moved against the Confederates via the Virginia Peninsula in the spring of 1862. Against his strenuous protests, a part of his army was retained for the defense of Washington. He vastly overestimated the forces opposing him led by Joseph E. Johnston, who was wounded at Seven Pines and replaced by Robert E. Lee for the subsequent battles of the Seven Days, and when McClellan retired to Harrison's Landing on the James River after a campaign magnificent in conception but undistinguished in execution, he laid himself open to the charge made by Confederate Colonel William Allan: "[He] was not conspicuous for his energy and skill in handling large bodies of troops. He directed . . . strategy . . . , but left . . . tactics . . . almost entirely to his subordinates." (352) Insisting that his failure lay in lack of support from Washington, and, as usual, greatly overestimating the enemy's forces, McClellan refused to reassume the offensive until given reinforcements which the administration and Henry W. Halleck, now general-in-chief, were unwilling to provide. As a result the Army of the Potomac was ordered north by water, and as its units arrived at Alexandria, they were assigned to General John Pope's Army of Virginia—a force organized to attempt the capture of Richmond via the line of the Orange & Alexandria Railroad. This expedition soon foundered on the rock of Pope's bombast and ineptness as a tactician, and McClellan was once again called upon to reorganize the weary and dispirited forces in the eastern theater. Some gauge of his popularity with the troops may be appreciated by the veritable tempest of cheers, echoing over the Manassas plains, which greeted the news that "Little Mac" had been restored to command. Again he was at his best —doing the job he knew best—and in short order hope revived in the ranks, in the halls of Congress, and at northern firesides. As Lee moved toward and crossed the upper fords of the Potomac, McClellan protected Washington on a line between Frederick and the river. A few days later on September 17, 1862, the battle of Antietam Creek (Sharpsburg) occurred—the bloodiest one day fight of the war— where McClellan fought Lee's numerically inferior Confederates in a drawn battle which elicited few laurels on either side. The great Lee had no business being where he was, having left a large portion of his footsore and ragged troops as stragglers in Virginia; and the great organizer McClellan permitted the battle to be fought in detail by subordinates. Subsequently McClellan could not be induced to move against Lee again until what

he deemed serious shortages of equipment and horses could be made good which exasperated the administration, although there is some evidence that certain items were deliberately withheld by Secretary of War Edwin Stanton. In any event on November 7, 1862, he was handed an order by the War Department messenger General C. P. Buckingham directing him to turn the army over to his good friend Ambrose E. Burnside and to proceed to his home in Trenton, New Jersey, to await orders which never came. Nominated for President by the Democratic party on a "peace at any price" platform in 1864, he attempted, without success, to reconcile the party line with his own oft-stated conviction that the war should be vigorously prosecuted and won the electoral votes of only three states. He resigned his army commission on election day. His postbellum career was marked chiefly by the three years, 1878-81, during which he served as governor of New Jersey. He died on October 29, 1885, at Orange, New Jersey, and was buried in Riverview Cemetery, Trenton. Although McClellan unquestionably possessed military talents of a high order and the unbounded confidence of his subordinates, there were deficiencies in his makeup which prevented him from becoming one of history's great commanders. However, it has been observed in perhaps his greatest testimonial that "the effect of this man's presence upon the Army of the Potomac—in sunshine or in rain, in darkness or in daylight, in victory or defeat—was electrical, and too wonderful to make it worthwhile attempting to give a reason for it."

John Alexander McClernand, as much underestimated for his role as a politician and sustainer of the Union as he has veen vilified for his ineptness and intriguing as a military commander, was born in the Kentucky backwoods near Har-

dinsburg on May 30, 1812, but the family moved to Shawneetown, Illinois, when he was quite young. His career in many respects resembled that of Lincoln: he was largely self-educated, was admitted to the bar in 1832, took part in the Black Hawk War, was an Illinois assemblyman, and served a number of terms in Congress. During his years in Congress, his bombastic oratory, adherence to Jacksonian principles, and dislike of abolitionists made him the favorite of his constituents, many of whom, like himself, were natives of slave-holding states. In 1860 he was defeated for the speakership of the House of Representatives by a coalition which opposed his moderate sen-

timents on slavery and disunion. At this juncture as Civil War became a reality, McClernand, whose only previous military service had been that of a private from June to August, 1832, against Chief Black Hawk, became a brigadier general of volunteers, ranking from May 17, 1861—a political selection by President Lincoln dictated by the need of holding southern Illinois Democrats to the Union cause. (353) McClernand's chief failing as a troop commander, aside from inexperience, was his fatal proclivity to display the fruits of victory, no matter how garnered, upon his own standards. A major general from March 21, 1862, he played a subversive role in the army, seeking to supplant George B. McClellan in the East and criticizing U. S. Grant's maneuvers in the West. After conducting an expedition which reduced the Post of Arkansas in January, 1863 (354), he commanded the XIII Corps in the operations against Vicksburg, and after a disastrous assault on the Confederate works there, he "furnished the press with a congratulatory order, extolling his men as the heroes of the campaign." (355) This effusion broke the camel's back, and he was sent home by Grant, to the relief of the other corps commanders, W. T. Sherman and James B. McPherson. The following year, however, McClernand again commanded the XIII Corps by then widely dispersed in Louisiana and Texas. He retained this command until his resignation from the army on November 30, 1864. He resided in Springfield after the war. He retained his allegiance to the Democratic party and in 1876 served as chairman of the

293

national convention which nominated Samuel J. Tilden. General McClernand died in Springfield, September 20, 1890, and was buried there.

Alexander McDowell McCook, the highest ranking of the fourteen "Fighting McCooks" who saw Civil War service, was born in Columbiana County, Ohio, on April 22, 1831. (356) He was the brother of Daniel McCook, Jr., and of Rob-

ert Latimer; Edward Moody McCook was his first cousin. He was graduated from West Point in 1852, requiring five years to complete the four-year course, and was posted to the 3rd Infantry. After garrison duty, he served on the frontier and later was an instructor in tactics at the Military Academy until the outbreak of the Civil War. Four days after the surrender of Fort Sumter he was commissioned colonel of the 1st Ohio Volunteers, which he led at First Ma-

nassas in July as part of Tyler's division. McCook was made a brigadier general of volunteers on September 3, 1861, and major general the following July. In the meantime he commanded a brigade in Kentucky and the 2nd Division of the Army of the Ohio, under D. C. Buell, at the capture of Nashville, the battle of Shiloh, and the subsequent "siege" of Corinth by Henry W. Halleck. During the battles and campaigns of Perryville, Murfreesboro, Tullahoma, and Chickamauga, he directed the XX Corps, and in the latter was charged with the blame, along with T. L. Crittenden of the XXI Corps, for the Union disaster. (357) Although subsequently officially exonerated by a court of inquiry, which he had himself requested, it is worthy of note that he was not again given command of troops in the field and awaited orders until November, 1864. Despite the seeming distrust in which he was held by his superiors, he was awarded the brevets of brigadier and major general in the Regular Army at the end of the war and was promoted to lieutenant colonel, 26th Infantry, in 1867. Significantly, during the Regular Army reorganization which followed the end of the war in July, 1866, McCook's rank of captain, 3rd Infantry, was not augmented, certainly a unique circumstance for one who was a major general of volunteers and by brevet in the Regulars. Nevertheless, McCook advanced in the service to colonel (1880), brigadier general (1890), and major general (1894); he retired in 1895. In the interval he had discharged much duty on the frontier, was aide to General W. T. Sherman, and in 1896 represented the United States at the coronation of Nicholas II of Russia. He died in Dayton, Ohio, June 12, 1903, and was buried in Cincinnati.

Daniel McCook, Jr., brother of Alexander McD. and Robert L. McCook and cousin of Edward M. McCook, was born at Carrollton, Ohio, July 22, 1834. He is said to have "graduated at Alabama university, Florence, Alabama, in 1858." (358) He then studied law in Steubenville, Ohio, and in 1860 moved to Leavenworth, Kansas, where he became a law partner of the future Union generals, W. T. Sherman and Thomas Ewing. With the outbreak of the Civil War, the office was closed and soon all three partners were in the army. During the summer of 1861 McCook served as a captain of the 1st Kansas Infantry and was present at the battle of Wilson's Creek. He was subsequently chief of staff of Thomas' 1st Division, Army of the

Ohio, during the Shiloh campaign, although these troops did not arrive in time to take part in the battle itself. On July 15, 1862, McCook was commissioned colonel of the 52nd Ohio and was at once assigned to command a brigade in the division of his old law partner, Sherman. At Perryville his brigade, composed of three Illinois regiments and his own 52nd Ohio, was in Sheridan's division; it was not engaged at Murfreesboro, as most of Fry's division of which it was then a part was employed as train guards during the battle. At Chickamauga McCook's regiments, augmented by the 69th Ohio, were attached to Granger's "Reserve Corps" and were only lightly engaged, sustaining only thirty-four casualties including eighteen missing. After the battle of Chattanooga he took part in the pursuit of the retreating Confederates toward Ringgold and then marched to the relief of Ambrose E. Burnside at Knoxville. In the course of the Atlanta campaign his brigade was attached to Jefferson C. Davis' division of the XIV Corps, Army of the Cumberland. For the disastrous assault on the heights of Kennesaw, June 27, 1864, Sherman selected McCook's brigade to lead the way. McCook, recognizing the adverse odds, had recited Horatius' speech to his men just before zero hour. (359) He reached the Confederate works where he fell mortally wounded. He was taken to the home of his brother George in Steubenville, Ohio, where he died on July 17, 1864, having been made a brigadier general of volunteers the previous day. He was buried in Spring Grove, Cemetery, Cincinnati. (360)

Edward Moody McCook, a first cousin of Union generals Alexander McD., Daniel, Jr., and Robert L. McCook was born on June 15, 1833, in Steubenville, Ohio. (361) At the age of sixteen after an education in the local public schools, he went to Colorado, then a part of

Kansas Territory, and was one of the first settlers of the Pike's Peak region—an area which he represented in the Kansas territorial legislature of 1859. Meanwhile he had become a lawyer with a flourishing practice. Upon the fall of Fort Sumter McCook made his way to Washington and on May 8, 1861, was appointed a lieutenant of cavalry in the Regular Army. He also served as major, lieutenant colonel, and colonel of the 2nd Indiana Cavalry. By the time of the battle of Shiloh (in which he was not actively engaged), he was commanding this regiment as lieutenant colonel. He commanded at Perryville a brigade of cavalry, consisting of his own and three Kentucky regiments, and at Chickamauga a division of cavalry of the Army of the Cumberland. As of April 27, 1864, he was made a brigadier general of volunteers. In the course of the Georgia campaign he was sent with his command to cut the Macon railroad south of Atlanta, which he succeeded in doing at Lovejoy's Station but at the cost of 950 men captured while attempting to rejoin the main army. The railroad was soon repaired, and the principal damage seems to have been done to the houses of civilians in the neighborhood, by virtue of which "McCook . . . made his name a horror." (362) He accompanied the forces of General G. H. Thomas back to Tennessee and in the closing weeks of the war took part in J. H. Wilson's raid through Alabama and Georgia, and was present at Selma on the occasion of N. B. Forrest's defeat there. He was brevetted repeatedly for gallant and meritorious conduct, ultimately being promoted to the brevet rank of brigadier in the Regular Army and major general in the volunteers. Resigning from the army in 1866, General McCook served for three years as United States minister to Hawaii; in 1869 he became territorial governor of Colorado, serving intermittently until 1875 when he retired from public life. Thereafter, he administered his financial interests, which included extensive real estate holdings, mining interests, and investments in European telephone companies and which made him at one time the largest taxpayer in Colorado. He died on September 9, 1909, in Chicago and was buried in Union Cemetery, Steubenville.

Robert Latimer McCook was a brother of Generals Alex. Mc.D. and Daniel McCook and a first cousin of General Edward McCook. (363) He was born in New Lisbon (then Lisbon), Ohio, December 28, 1827. After attending the local public schools, he studied law and practiced for more than a decade in Steubenville, Columbus, and Cincinnati. In 1861 McCook organized the 9th Ohio Infantry, becoming its colonel on May 8. He fought in the West Virginia campaign under George B. McClellan that summer and on September 10, 1861, took part in the action of Carnifix Ferry, where he commanded one of W. S. Rosecrans' three infantry brigades. The following January McCook greatly distinguished himself at the battle of Mill Springs, (364) where he directed one of Thomas' brigades and was wounded. On March 22 he was promoted brigadier general to rank from the previous day. After participating in Henry W. Hal-

leck's snail-like advance on Corinth, subsequent to the battle of Shiloh, McCook took part in the movements preliminary to Braxton Bragg's invasion of Kentucky. In the course of the march of D. C. Buell's forces from Stevenson, Alabama, eastward across Tennessee, McCook was ill and was riding on a bed in an open carriage on August 5, 1862. He and a small escort were well in advance of his brigade when he stopped at the house of a man named Petit, between Winchester and Decherd, Tennessee, to make inquiry about a campsite for the night. Here a band of Confederate partisan rangers and regular cavalry, under the command of Captain J. M. Hambrick (later lieutenant colonel of the 4th Alabama Cavalry), attacked the party and dispersed the escort. McCook's driver turned the carriage around and headed for the Union advance, some three miles distant, but was soon caught, surrounded by the Rebel troopers, and ordered to halt. In the ensuing melee McCook was shot through the abdomen, a wound invariably fatal in those days. He survived for twenty-four hours, dying at noon on August 6, 1862, in a nearby house where the Confederates had left him. He was buried in Spring Grove Cemetery, Cincinnati. His assailant, who had been an officer in a regularly mustered Confederate cavalry company and who on the day in question held an appointment from General E. Kirby Smith as captain of partisan rangers, was later tried for murder by a military court. (365)

Irvin McDowell was born, October 15, 1818, at Columbus, Ohio, and prior to his appointment to the

Military Academy in 1834, was educated in France. He was graduated in the class of 1838, ranking in the middle, and from 1841 to 1845 he taught tactics at the Academy to cadets who would later as Confederate generals haunt him on the

battlefield. As aide-de-camp to General J. E. Wool in the Mexican War, McDowell received the brevet of captain for gallant conduct at Buena Vista and thereafter, until the outbreak of the Civil War, was occupied in the office of the adjutant general of the army. On May 14, 1861, through the intervention of Secretary of the Treasury Salmon P. Chase, who had become his patron, McDowell was appointed a brigadier general in the Regular Army, although in the twenty-three years of his service he had never commanded so much as a squad in the field. By July political considerations demanded an advance by the half-trained Federals upon the half-trained Rebels under the command of General P. G. T. Beauregard at Manassas Junction, where the railroad from Richmond to Alexandria met the one from the Shenandoah Valley. The resulting Union disaster stemmed as much from misfortune as ineptitude, since both sides were equally "overmatched" at that stage of the war. Nevertheless, McDowell, who had conceived a good plan on paper, failed to inspire either his subordinate officers or his troops. He was then supplanted by George B. McClellan, but in March, 1862, he was made a major general of volunteers and assigned to command a corps of the Army of the Potomac. In keeping with President Lincoln's awkward efforts to handle strategy at this stage of the war, McClellan was not consulted about McDowell's appointment and McDowell was detached to "protect" Washington while McClellan undertook the Peninsular campaign. In the subsequent campaign of Second Manassas, McDowell commanded the III Corps of John Pope's Army of Virginia. His conduct, along with Pope's, was severely criticized in this, the second Union debacle with which he was connected; and he did little in the eyes of unbiased historians to redeem himself when he later appeared as a witness against General Fitz John Porter in the latter's court-martial when McDowell himself was under investigation at the same time for the same offenses. (366) Protected in his seniority by a politically influenced inquiry which had "exonerated" both him and Pope of blame for their management at Second Manassas, McDowell, at least, was exiled, and after two years of relative inactivity, was assigned on

July 1, 1864, to the command of the Department of the Pacific. By virtue of the relentless operation of the seniority system, he became a major general in the regular establishment on November 25, 1872, having commanded successively the Departments of the East and the South. He returned to San Francisco in 1876 to take command of the Division of the Pacific, a post which he occupied until his retirement in 1882. General McDowell died in San Francisco, May 4, 1885, and was buried at the Presidio, a military post whose grounds and buildings he had done much to improve during his service there.

George Francis McGinnis was born in Boston, Massachusetts, March 19, 1826. His mother died in his infancy and he lived with an aunt in Hampden, Maine, until he was eleven, when his father, a hatter by trade, took him to Chillocothe, Ohio. In 1846 he went to the Mexican War as a lieutenant of the 2nd

Ohio Volunteers and was mustered out as a captain on July 25, 1848. McGinnis moved to Indianapolis in 1850 and having learned his father's trade, began the manufacture of hats there. On April 15, 1861, almost as soon as the news of the fall of Fort Sumter was known, he enlisted as a private in Lew Wallace's 11th Indiana, a three-month regiment of which he became lieutenant colonel in a few days and colonel after its remuster for three years in August, 1861. During the campaign in western Virginia in the early summer of 1861, the regiment was not seriously engaged, but in succeeding months McGinnis won commendation by Wallace for his handling of his men at the capture of Fort Donelson, and later at Shiloh where he temporarily commanded the 1st Brigade of the division. The following February he took part in the Yazoo Pass expedition against Vicksburg and during the campaign against the city proper directed a brigade in McClernand's XIII Corps. His association with the latter (to say nothing of Wallace), against whom much hostility existed in Regular Army circles. did little for McGinnis' career. After the Vicksburg campaign he occupied a succession of unimportant posts, occasionally in divisional command, in N. P. Banks's Department of the Gulf, in the later Military Division of West Mississippi, and in the Department of Arkansas. He had been made a brigadier general on April 4, 1863, to rank from November 29, 1862, and at the end of active fighting he was in command of an infantry regiment, two cavalry companies, and a battery at the mouth of

White River in Arkansas. Mustered out without a brevet, he settled in Indianapolis, and from 1867 until 1871 was county auditor. He later operated a fiduciary business and served in various county and state offices. In 1900 President McKinley appointed him postmaster of Indianapolis. He died on May 29, 1910, in Indianapolis, and his ashes were buried in Crown Hill Cemetery there. (367)

John Baillie McIntosh was born on June 6, 1829, at Fort Brooke, Florida (the site of Tampa), where his father, a Regular Army officer later killed in the Mexican War, was

stationed. He was the brother of the Confederate brigadier, James M. McIntosh, and great-grand-nephew of the Revolutionary general who killed Button Gwinnett, causing his signature to become the highest priced of all autographs of a signer of the Declaration of Independence. (368) During the war

with Mexico John served aboard the *U.S.S. Saratoga* as midshipman, resigning from the navy soon after to reside in New Brunswick, New Jersey, where he engaged in business with his father-in-law. In 1861, feeling that his brother's defection to the Confederate cause constituted a blot on the family honor, he reentered the service of the United States as a second lieutenant of the 2nd (Regular) Cavalry. He compiled a most distinguished record from the beginning of the war until the last shot was fired. He was brevetted major in the Regular Army for services during the Peninsular campaign under George B. McClellan in 1862; and after taking part in the Maryland campaign against General Robert E. Lee, he was made colonel of the 3rd Pennsylvania Cavalry on November 15, 1862. Upon the reorganization of the cavalry of the Army of the Potomac in the spring of 1863, McIntosh was assigned a brigade under Alfred Pleasonton and fought at Kelly's Ford and during the Chancellorsville operations in May. Following Gettysburg, William W. Averell, his former division commander, pronounced him the inferior of no officer in command of a cavalry brigade in Federal service. In May, 1864, after recuperating from injuries received when his horse fell with him, he resumed command of his brigade. At the battle of Winchester in September, 1864, he received the wounds which necessitated the amputation of his right leg. For his gallantry in this battle he won the brevet of brigadier in the Regular Army. Commissioned major general by brevet in both the regular and volunteer services at the end of the war, he became lieutenant colonel of the 42nd Infantry in 1866 and was retired in 1870 as a brigadier general. Thereafter General McIntosh made his residence in New Brunswick, where he died on June 29, 1888, and was buried in Elmwood Cemetery.

Thomas Jefferson McKean was born on August 21, 1810, in the northern Pennsylvania hamlet of Burlington. He was graduated from West Point in 1831, but after

several tours of garrison duty resigned his commission in 1834 to become a civil engineer. This occupation was interrupted by his service as adjutant of the 1st Pennsylvania Volunteers in the so-called "Florida War" of 1837-38. He moved to Marion, Iowa, which was to be his home for the rest of his life, in 1840 and four years later was a member of the state constitutional convention. He had the curious distinction of serving

throughout the Mexican War as an enlisted man, failing to obtain a commission despite his age and experience. In 1861, however, his talents were recognized by appointment as paymaster of volunteers in June and brigadier general to rank from November 21. Since a man in his fifties was then deemed too old for field duty, most of McKean's service was performed in command of a succession of military districts, including several in Missouri; those of Nebraska and South Kansas; West Florida; Morganza, Louisiana; and the post of Corinth, Mississippi. During the battle of Corinth in October, 1862, he commanded the 6th Division of the Army of West Tennessee and for a month in the autumn of 1864 was chief of cavalry of the Department of the Gulf. He was brevetted major general of volunteers at the end of the war and was mustered out in August, 1865. General McKean then returned to Marion where he was elected mayor. From 1866 until 1869 he farmed near the town and in 1868 was a delegate to the Republican National Convention in Chicago which nominated U. S. Grant. For his efforts in the latter's behalf he was tended the post of pension agent for the eastern district of Iowa the following year but he declined the appointment. On April 19, 1870, General McKean died in Marion and was buried there in Oak Shade Cemetery.

Ranald Slidell Mackenzie was born in Westchester County, New York, July 27, 1840. (369) His family surname was not actually Mackenzie, for his father (a brother of the Confederate diplomat, John Slidell,

of the Mason and Slidell affair) had added Mackenzie to his own name out of admiration for a maternal uncle. By virtue of the Slidell relationship Mackenzie became connected by marriage with Confederate General P. G. T. Beauregard, whose second wife was the sister of John Slidell's wife. For a brief time just prior to the outbreak of the Civil War, Beauregard was superintendent of the Military Academy and thus Mackenzie's commanding officer. (370) Mackenzie, who had commenced his higher education at Williams in 1855, withdrew in order to accept an appointment to West Point, where he was graduated on June 17, 1862, ranking first in the class. (371) Posted to the Corps of Engineers, the young second lieutenant rendered notable service at Second Manassas, Fredericksburg, Chancellorsville, Gettysburg, and in U. S. Grant's Overland campaign of 1864 which resolved itself into the siege of Petersburg and Richmond.

During this period Mackenzie was brevetted repeatedly for gallantry and in July, 1864, became colonel of the 2nd Connecticut Heavy Artillery, a volunteer regiment which was hastily transported to Washington the same month to oppose Jubal Early's raid against the capital. Thereafter, while following the fortunes of Philip H. Sheridan in the Shenandoah Valley, he commanded a brigade in Wheaton's division of Wright's VI Corps until he was wounded at Cedar Creek on October 19. After his recovery and promotion to the rank of brigadier general, he was transferred with most of Sheridan's forces to the Petersburg front. Here Mackenzie commanded a division of cavalry in the Army of the James; his performance led Grant to remark, "I regarded Mackenzie as the most promising young officer in the army." (372) At the close of the war he was brevetted major general of volunteers and brigadier general in the Regular Army, and on March 6, 1867, he became colonel of the 41st Infantry. On December 15, 1870, he was transferred to the 4th Cavalry and commenced a series of campaigns against the Plains Indians which far outshone the exploits of General G. A. Custer. (373) In 1873 he led the celebrated raid into Coahuila which destroyed the villages of a renegade band of Lipans and Apaches who had been marauding at will in the United States; this gross violation of Mexican sovereignty was undertaken on the verbal orders of Sheridan. (374) After the Custer debacle Mackenzie so soundly thrashed the victorious and belligerent northern Cheyennes in the Powder River expedition that they soon

302

after surrendered. He subsequently was instrumental in pacifying the tribes over a vast territory in Colorado, Texas, New Mexico, and Arizona. Wounded six times during the Civil War, he received a seventh wound, which caused him agonizing pain for the rest of his life, in an Indian fight on the Staked Plain in 1871. In 1884 he was retired with the rank of brigadier general for disability in line of duty. His constitution wrecked by wounds and prolonged exposure during his arduous years of service, Mackenzie's mind ultimately gave way, and he died at New Brighton, Staten Island, New York on January 19, 1889. He was buried at West Point.

Justus McKinstry, chiefly celebrated for having been one of the most thoroughgoing rogues ever to wear a United States uniform, was born July 6, 1814, in New York State, probably in Columbia County. (375) He moved with his

parents to Michigan as a young boy and was appointed to the Military Academy from there. He was graduated in the class of 1838 which furnished an unusually large proportion of general officers to the Union and Confederate armies. McKinstry's early career was meritorious, and at the battles of Contreras and Churubusco in the war with Mexico, while a quartermaster with the staff rank of captain, he commanded a company of volunteers in such gallant fashion that he was awarded the brevet of major. He subsequently served on quartermaster duty on the United States-Mexico boundary and in California, and at the outbreak of the Civil War was in St. Louis as chief quartermaster of the Department of the West. On September 2, 1861, he was made a brigadier general of volunteers (376) and commanded a division under John C. Frémont in the latter's march to Springfield. While in charge of the quartermaster's department, he had found ample opportunity to line his own pockets at the expense of the government. Among the exactions levied upon the contractors who wished to do business with his office was a three-thousand dollar silver service for Mrs. McKinstry. The contractors' usual procedure for absorbing these obligations was for one contractor to bill another for goods at an enormous advance in price; these goods would then be sold to the quartermaster's department at "market." One St. Louis firm admitted profits of $280,000 on sales of $800,000 in a few months under the administration of McKinstry. (377) Upon the succession of General David Hunter to command of the department, McKinstry's peculations were investigated. And after a year in arrest he was cashiered, January 28, 1863, "for neglect and violation of duty, to the prejudice of good order and military discipline," the only such sentence handed a general officer in the war. His later record is obscure. For a time he was a stockbroker in New York; then he went to Rolla, Missouri, as a "land agent." He died in St. Louis on December 11, 1897, and was buried in Highland Cemetery, Ypsilanti, Michigan, the home of a son.

Nathaniel Collins McLean was born on February 2, 1815, (378) at Ridgeville, Warren County, Ohio. He was the son of Congressman, Postmaster-general and Supreme Court Justice, John McLean. Young McLean was graduated from Augusta College (Kentucky) in 1834 and in 1838 received a law degree at Harvard. This same year he was married, and moved to Cincinnati

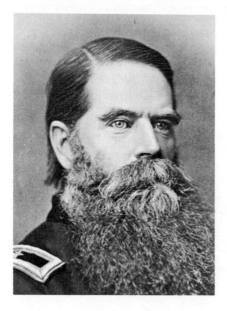

where he started his law practice. In the autumn of 1861 he was commissioned colonel of the 75th Ohio which he led the following May at the engagement of McDowell, (West) Virginia. Although promoted brigadier general to rank from November 29, 1862, he was not involved in any important affair until the battle of Chancellorsville where his and Von Gilsa's brigades of Devens' division of the XI Corps, constituting the right of the Army of the Potomac, were overwhelmed by the onrushing Confederates on the evening of May 2, 1863. Charles Devens was wounded and the command devolved upon McLean who was unable to reform the shattered units until he had retreated all the way to Joseph Hooker's headquarters at the Chancellor house. For this he incurred the displeasure of his corps commander, Oliver O. Howard. (379) In spite of this McLean was assigned on May 18 to duty with Ambrose E. Burnside in Cincinnati and was promptly made provost marshal general of the Department of the Ohio. During the early weeks of the Atlanta campaign, he commanded a brigade of Schofield's XXIII Corps, but at New Hope Church on May 27, 1864, he was again criticized severely by Howard (who was then commanding the IV Corps) for various sins of omission. (380) The following month he was assigned to a minor command in Kentucky. Another chance at field service yet remained to him: he accompanied the XXIII Corps to the Carolinas in command of a brigade under John M. Schofield. The Corps rendezvoused with W. T. Sherman at Goldsboro, North Carolina, on

March 28, 1865, after being transported from Tennessee to Virginia by rail, and from the Potomac to Fort Fisher by ship. For reasons not disclosed by the records, McLean elected to resign his commission on April 20, 1865. After resuming his law practice in Cincinnati for a time, he retired to a farm in Minnesota. Subsequently he lived for many years at Bellport, Long Island, where he died January 4, 1905, and was buried.

James Winning McMillan, a native of Clark County, Kentucky, was born on April 28, 1825. A wanderer, he was never in one place for

long. He fought in the Mexican War first as a sergeant of the 4th Illinois and later as a private in a battalion of Louisiana volunteers; honorably discharged in 1848, he went to Indiana and engaged in business at various and sundry places. In 1861 the 21st Indiana was organized at Indianapolis and he was appointed its colonel. (381) The following spring the regiment took part in Benjamin F. Butler's occupation of New Orleans and on August 5, 1862, sustained 126 casualties while aiding in the defense of Baton Rouge against the attack by John C. Breckinridge.. His command was next stationed at Berwick Bay until February, 1863; on April 4, 1863, McMillan was promoted brigadier general to rank from November 29, 1862. From March to May, 1864, he commanded a brigade, and at times the 1st Division, of Emory's XIX Corps, in N. P. Banks's ill-fated Red River expedition. During this expedition he fought gallantly at Mansfield, Pleasant Hill, and Monett's Ferry; at the battle of Mansfield (Sabine Cross-Roads) the 1st Division did much to stem the panicky Federal retreat from the battlefield. In July, 1864, the XIX Corps was ordered to the Shenandoah Valley of Virginia to serve under Philip Sheridan; McMillan, now in permanent command of the division, fought well at Winchester, and· at Cedar Creek, and had his greatest day when the savage assault of Jubal Early's Confederates threatened for a time to rout Sheridan's whole army. The lightly regarded XIX Corps was driven from its camp, but McMillan deployed his division so as to give troops in rear an opportunity to form a front. Following this campaign he commanded the 1st Division of the Department of West Virginia with headquarters at Grafton until the end of the war. In March, 1865, he was brevetted major general and resigned his commission in May. After the war he resided for a time in Kansas, but in 1875 was appointed a member of the board of review in the pension office in Washington. General McMillan held this position until his death on March 9, 1903. He was buried in Arlington National Cemetery.

John McNeil, a Canadian born in Halifax, Nova Scotia, February 14, 1813, moved while young to Boston where he learned the trade of hatter. Prior to 1840 he went to St.

Louis, then the hub of the fur industry upon which his livelihood depended. He was a member of the Missouri legislature in 1844-45, and from 1855 until the beginning of the Civil War he was president of the Pacific Insurance Company in St. Louis. McNeil's entire Civil War service was within the confines of the state of Missouri. A captain of a volunteer company early in 1861, McNeil became: colonel of the 3rd Missouri (Union) Infantry on May 8, from which he was mustered out in August; colonel of the 2nd

Missouri State Militia Cavalry in June 3, 1862; and brigadier general of U. S. Volunteers to rank from November 29, 1862. In the interim he had been sent to various points in the state and commanded a number of districts and subdistricts, mainly operating against the multitude of pro-Confederate partisans and guerrillas. In the course of Confederate General Sterling Price's famous "Missouri expedition" of 1864, McNeil and General Egbert B. Brown both ran afoul of Major General Alfred Pleasonton, who had been sent west to stamp out the rebels in Missouri. Both generals were relieved of their command at the battle of Westport; Brown mainly because he had only one operable arm, (382) and McNeil because, like Brown, he had not attacked when ordered. Nevertheless, General McNeil commanded the district of Central Missouri until April 12, 1865, when he resigned and was brevetted major general of volunteers. After the war he was twice clerk of the criminal court of St. Louis County, county sheriff, and commissioner to the Centennial Exhibition in Philadelphia in 1876. After 1878 he occupied a series of Federal offices, including those of inspector in the Indian service and superintendent of the St. Louis branch post office. He died in St. Louis on June 8, 1891, and was buried there in Bellefontaine Cemetery.

James Birdseye McPherson was born, November 14, 1828, on a farm near the present village of Clyde, Ohio. He was compelled at the age of thirteen (when his father, a mentally unstable and unsuccessful blacksmith, became in-

306

competent) to go to work in a nearby backwoods store in order to assist his mother in supporting the family. As a result of his employer's interest in aiding the young "store boy," McPherson spent two years at the Norwalk Academy (Ohio) and received an appointment to West Point at the rather advanced age of twenty. (383) He was graduated in 1853, ranked first in a class which included the celebrated Union and Confederate figures, Philip H. Sheridan and John Bell Hood. Eleven years after graduation, Hood's battle orders at Atlanta would result in the death of McPherson on an isolated woods road near the beleaguered city. Commissioned into the Corps of Engineers, in keeping with his class standing, McPherson served on both coasts in connection with harbor and seacoast defense and supervised the fortification of the celebrated Alcatraz Island in San Francisco Bay. After the outbreak of the Civil War no Union officer

had a more meteoric rise than McPherson. A first lieutenant of engineers as late as August of 1861, by October 8, 1862, he ranked as a major general of volunteers and commanded a division of the XIII Corps. In the interim he served as aide-de-camp to Henry W. Halleck; as chief engineer to U. S. Grant during the campaign of Forts Henry and Donelson, the battle of Shiloh, and the subsequent "advance" upon Corinth; and as superintendent of railways in West Tennessee. On August 19, 1862, he was appointed a brigadier general of volunteers, and soon after the battle of Corinth in October, 1862, in which his only part was the transporting of some troops who participated in the subsequent pursuit of the Confederate General Earl Van Dorn, he was promoted major general of volunteers. In January, 1863, McPherson obtained command of the XVII Corps which fought throughout the Vicksburg campaign in a manner which won the lively praise of both Grant and his chief lieutenant, W. T. Sherman, and won McPherson a promotion to brigadier in the Regular Army from August 1, 1863. On March 26, 1864, he assumed command of Sherman's old Army of the Tennessee, which he led in the subsequent campaign in north Georgia. During this campaign the affair at Snake Creek Gap, which might have dispersed Joseph E. Johnston's Confederates, came to nothing because of seemingly excessive caution by McPherson, and the handling of his troops thereafter was largely directed by Sherman himself. McPherson died while attempting with a single orderly to reach his command from

Sherman's headquarters after Hood's massive blow against the Federal left in front of Atlanta on July 22, 1864. Sherman's tears rolled through his beard and down on the floor when he viewed the body of his friend laid upon a door torn from its hinges and improvised as a bier. (384) A bachelor, McPherson had applied for a leave months previously to wed a Baltimore belle to whom he was engaged. The leave was refused by Sherman who felt that McPherson's presence was indispensable in the coming campaign. He was buried in the orchard where he played as a boy, and in 1881 a monument, erected over his grave through the efforts of the Society of the Army of the Tennessee, was dedicated by such luminaries as ex-President Hayes and Generals Sherman, Manning F. Force, and Mortimer D. Leggett. (385)

Jasper Adalmorn Maltby was born in Kingsville, Ohio, November 3, 1826. In the spring of 1847 he enlisted in the 15th U. S. Infantry for service in the Mexican War and later was severely wounded at Chapultepec. (386) After muster out on August 3, 1848, as a private, (387) he became a gunsmith in Galena, Illinois, and operated what today would be called a sporting goods store until the outbreak of the Civil War in 1861. He enlisted in the 45th Illinois Volunteers and was appointed its lieutenant colonel on December 26, 1861. The regiment, whose colonel was then John E. Smith, took part in U. S. Grant's offensive against Fort Henry and later Fort Donelson where Maltby was disabled for a time by a leg wound. After the promotion of

Smith, Maltby became colonel, and during the Vicksburg campaign he led the command with such ardor that it was chosen for the post of honor upon the occupation of the city after the Confederate capitulation. At this time the 45th Illinois was a part of Smith's brigade, Logan's division of McPherson's XVII Corps. On August 4, 1863, Maltby was promoted to brigadier general. Thereafter he and his brigade were stationed in and near Vicksburg, much of the time serving as garrison of the post. Then in June, 1865, General Maltby was given command of a subdistrict which embraced several counties in Mississippi and which he directed until he was honorably mustered out of the service on January 15, 1866. Although a fellow-townsman and friend of Grant's, he was not awarded a brevet promotion and in fact seems to have been shelved after Vicksburg —several who had been his juniors subsequently overslaughing him. After his muster-out General Maltby determined to try his fortunes in the city of which he had been commander for so long and engaged in "mercantile pursuits" there, although still maintaining a residence in Galena. In September, 1867, General Edward Ord, who at the time commanded the military department which embraced Vicksburg, appointed him mayor of the city. Three months later, on December 12, 1867, he died of yellow fever and was buried in Greenwood Cemetery, Galena. (388)

Joseph King Fenno Mansfield, the descendant of emigrants from England who arrived in America soon after the Pilgrims, was born December 22, 1803, in New Haven, Connecticut. Mansfield entered West Point two months before his fourteenth birthday, and was graduated five years later, ranking second in the class of 1822. As a young

engineer officer he was mainly engaged in the construction of the defenses of the Southern coast until the Mexican War, in which he served as chief engineer under General (later President) Zachary Taylor. He fought gallantly at Fort Brown, Monterey, and Buena Vista —sometimes in the command of troops—and won the brevets of major, lieutenant colonel, and colonel in the Regular Army. In 1853, upon the recommendation of the Secretary of War, Jefferson Davis, Mansfield was appointed to the staff rank of colonel in the inspector general's department, an office which demanded much travel on the frontier. On May 18, 1861 (to rank from the fourteenth), Mansfield was appointed a brigadier general in the regular service and assigned to command of Washington and its environs by Lincoln. He promptly seized and fortified the positions on the south side of the Potomac which later became a portion of the ring of forts surrounding Washington. After McClellan took chief command following First Bull Run, Mansfield was assigned to command of the XII Corps. At Sharpsburg, September 17, 1862, Mansfield led his command into action to support Joseph Hooker's I Corps on the Federal right, "which was visibly melting away." (389) "Seeing his raw recruits waver," Mansfield rode into the forefront of battle where the fire was hottest. Horse and rider were shot down and on the following day, September 18, 1862, General Mansfield died of his wounds. Six months after his death, on March 12, 1863, he was promoted major general of volunteers to rank from July 18, 1862. General

Mansfield's remains were buried in Indian Hill Cemetery, Middletown, Connecticut.

Mahlon Dickerson Manson was born in Piqua, Ohio, February 20, 1820. After obtaining his early education in the local schools, he moved to Montgomery County, Indiana, where he taught school for a year. He studied medicine in Cincinnati for a time and in 1847-48 served as captain of the 5th Indiana Volunteers. In the 1850's he was a member of the Indiana legislature meanwhile pursuing the occupation of druggist in Crawfordsville, Indiana. On April 17, 1861, three days after the surrender of Fort Sumter became known, Manson was mustered into Federal service as captain of the 10th Indiana, becoming its colonel in May. That July Manson commanded the regiment at the battle of Rich Mountain, (West) Virginia, and the following January directed a brigade under G. H. Thomas at

Fishing Creek (Kentucky). The latter was a complete victory over the Confederate forces under General F. K. Zollicoffer and reestablished Federal morale in the area. Manson was made a brigadier general of volunteers as of March 24, 1862. In the course of the Union disaster at Richmond, Kentucky, during General Braxton Bragg's invasion of the state, Manson was wounded and captured on October 30, 1862; he was exchanged the following December. During the raid of the celebrated Confederate John H. Morgan into Ohio and Indiana in July, 1863, Manson was occupied in resisting the draft of the Rebel General John Pegram upon the beef cattle in the neighborhood of Lebanon. Briefly after Chickamauga Manson commanded the XXIII Corps, but in the Atlanta campaign was reduced to command of a brigade of Cox's division of the corps which had become the Army of the Ohio. He was badly wounded by the explosion of a shell near Resaca, Georgia, on May 14, 1864, which is said to have compelled his resignation from service on December 21, 1864. Manson was a lifelong Democrat and in the years following the war stood for public office on a number of occasions: unsuccessful as candidate for lieutenant governor of Indiana in 1864, he served in Congress from 1871-73; then was state auditor; lieutenant governor; and district collector of internal revenue. He died in Crawfordsville on February 4, 1895, and was buried in Oak Hill Cemetery.

Randolph Barnes Marcy was born on April 9, 1812, at Greenwich, Massachusetts, a village in northeastern Hampshire County which was abandoned and then inundated by the Quabbin Reservoir in 1938. He was graduated from the Military Academy in the class of 1832, ranking twenty-ninth among forty-five students. During the next fourteen years he served almost entirely on the frontier in Michigan and Wisconsin. With promotion to captain

of infantry in 1846, Marcy was engaged in the Mexican War battles of Palo Alto and Resaca de la Palma, but was then detached on recruiting duty and received no brevet promotions at the close of the war. Thereafter, until 1859, he was on duty at various points in the Southwest, escorting emigrants, locating military posts, exploring the wilderness, and accompanying Albert Sidney Johnston on the expedition against the Mormons in Utah. After a few months as acting inspector general of the Department of Utah, he was ordered East to prepare from his voluminous notes a guidebook on western travel—this was published by the War Department in 1859 under the title, *The Prairie Traveler*. (390) Meanwhile he accepted a staff appointment as paymaster with the rank of major and served in the Pacific Northwest until May, 1861. At this juncture Marcy became chief of staff to General George B. McClellan, whose father-in-law he had become the previous year. On August 9, 1861, Marcy was appointed to be one of the four inspectors general of the Regular Army, with staff rank of colonel authorized by the acts of July 29 and August 3, 1861, (391) although his duties were entirely with McClellan until the latter's relief from command of the Army of the Potomac after the battle of Sharpsburg. He was appointed brigadier general of volunteers on September 28, 1861, but this appointment expired by operation of law on March 4, 1863, the Senate having failed to confirm him in the grade. (392) From July, 1863, until the end of the Civil War he performed inspection duties in a number of military departments and at army headquarters in Washington. On December 12, 1878, General Marcy was promoted to inspector general of the U. S. Army with the staff rank of brigadier general—at long last accorded the stature to which his duties and responsibilities had entitled him since 1861. He was retired at his own request in 1881. Surviving his son-in-law McClellan by two years, General Marcy died at West Orange, New Jersey, on November 2, 1887, and was buried in Riverview Cemetery in Trenton, New Jersey.

Gilman Marston was born August 20, 1811, at Orford, New Hampshire, on the Connecticut River. Brought up on his father's farm, he taught school in order to finance his college education at Dartmouth. After he was graduated in 1837, he served for a time as head of a preparatory school in Indianapolis; he was graduated from Harvard Law School in 1840, was admitted to the bar the following year, and began practice in Exeter, New Hampshire. In the years from 1845 to 1889 Marston was elected to the state legislature thirteen times; to the state constitutional conventions of 1850 and 1876; to Congress three times, serving from 1859 to 1863 and from 1865 to 1867; declined an appointment as governor of the Idaho Territory in 1870; and was appointed to the U. S. Senate for four months in 1889. In May and June, 1861, Marston recruited the 2nd New Hampshire which he led at First Bull Run (Manassas) in Burnside's brigade of Hunter's

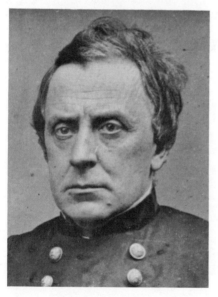

division. During the Peninsular campaign his regiment was a part of Grover's brigade of Hooker's division and at Fredericksburg was assigned to J. B. Carr's brigade of Sickles' division. In the interval he was on leave, commanded at Centreville on the line of the Orange & Alexandria Railroad, and was promoted brigadier general on November 29, 1862. Prior to the campaign of Chancellorsville he was relieved from duty with the Army of the Potomac and ordered to Washington for assignment by General Samuel P. Heintzelman who was commanding that department. After Gettysburg Marston was directed to establish a prison camp in Maryland; this camp became the well-known Point Lookout pen. The area was subsequently designated as the District of Saint Mary's under the general command of General Benjamin F. Butler. In the spring of 1864, just prior to Grant's Overland campaign against Richmond, Marston was assigned to a brigade of "Baldy" Smith's XVIII Corps with which he was involved in the disastrous attack on Robert E. Lee's intrenched lines at Cold Harbor in June, 1864—a movement which left seven thousand Federals dead and dying at small cost to the Confederates. Soon thereafter he was assigned to duty in eastern Virginia, and after having received the thanks of the New Hampshire Legislature, he discharged routine duty until his resignation, "to take effect April 20, 1865." He died July 3, 1890, and was buried in Exeter, New Hampshire.

John Henry Martindale, the son of a five-term Whig Congressman, was born, March 20, 1815, in Sandy Hill

(now Hudson Falls), New York. He was appointed to West Point in 1831 and was graduated in the class of 1835, ranking third. Disappointed at not being posted to the Corps of Engineers, he resigned his commission early in 1836 without ever having served with troops. He then studied law and, after admission to the bar in 1838, commenced practice in Batavia, New York, where he served two terms as district attorney; after 1851, he practiced in Rochester. A decade later he was one of the advocates of the use of Regular Army officers as drill instructors and the immediate graduation of the first and second classes at West Point—both recommendations were adopted by the War Department. On August 9, 1861, he was commissioned brigadier general of volunteers and the following spring served throughout the Peninsular campaign as commander of a brigade in Porter's division of Heintzelman's

III Corps. Martindale was investigated by a court of inquiry after Porter charged that he had declared that he would surrender rather than desert his wounded after Malvern Hill. After acquittal and restoration to duty, he acted as military governor of Washington, D. C., until the spring of 1864 when he led a division of "Baldy" Smith's XVIII Corps at Cold Harbor, Bermuda Hundred, and Petersburg. He subsequently commanded the XVIII Corps for a time, but was forced to resign because of his health as of September 13, 1864. At the end of the war Martindale was brevetted major general of volunteers to rank from March 13, 1865, paradoxically enough, "for gallant and distinguished service at the battle of Malvern Hill, Virginia." (393) Upon his retirement General Martindale returned to his law practice in Rochester, and for years thereafter he was prominent in handling personal injury cases against the New York Central Railroad. He was elected attorney general of New York, serving from 1867 until 1869, and was vice-president of the National Asylum for Disabled Volunteer Soldiers for eleven years. In the course of a trip abroad for his health, he died in Nice, France, December 13, 1881, and was buried in Batavia.

John Sanford Mason was born in Steubenville, Ohio, August 21, 1824, and after attending the local schools, was appointed to the Military Academy in 1843. From his graduation in 1847 until his retirement forty-one years later at the statutory age of sixty-four, Mason pursued an exclusively military career. His service began with garri-

son duty in Tampico during the Mexican War and ended with the colonelcy of the 9th U. S. Infantry at Fort Whipple, Arizona. In the interval he served in such widely separated posts as Fort Adams at Newport, Rhode Island, San Diego, California, and Fort Vancouver, Washington, where he was stationed when the Civil War broke out. In October, 1861, he was appointed colonel of the 4th Ohio Volunteer Infantry, a regiment with which he fought in western Virginia during that fall and winter under the command of General James Shields. In George B. McClellan's Peninsular campaign Mason served briefly at Harrison's Landing. He is not mentioned in the *Official Records* again until the battle of Fredericksburg, where he commanded a brigade of Sedgwick's II Corps of the "Right Grand Division." Mason had been promoted to brigadier general on November 29, 1862 (although listed at Fredericksburg as colonel), and

in April, 1863, was assigned to muster and recruit duty, first in Ohio, and for the last two years of the war in California and Nevada. In 1865 he was brevetted through grades to that of brigadier general, U. S. Army. Promoted to major of the 17th Infantry in 1864, General Mason stood duty in a number of posts on the western frontier in the 1870's and 1880's, receiving promotions to lieutenant colonel in 1873 and colonel in 1883. His stations included the states and territories of Texas, New Mexico, Wyoming, the District of Columbia, Ohio, and Arizona. After retirement in 1888 General Mason resided in Washington, D. C., where he died November 29, 1897, and was buried in Arlington National Cemetery.

Charles (Karl) Leopold Matthies was born May 31, 1824, in Bromberg, Prussia (now Bydgoszcz, Poland). He was educated in the

university at Halle, worked on his father's farm for a time, and served in the Prussian army. In 1849 he emigrated to the United States and settled in Burlington, Iowa, where he engaged in the liquor business. He is said to have been the first man in the United States to offer a military company to the government, making the tender through Governor Samuel J. Kirkwood of Iowa on January 9, 1861. (394) On May 14, 1861, he was mustered in as a captain of the 1st Iowa Volunteers; he was made lieutenant colonel of the 5th Iowa on July 23, 1861, colonel on May 23, 1862, and brigadier general of volunteers on April 4, 1863, to rank from the preceding November 29. His war record was not undistinguished; he led his regiment in Missouri in the early months of the war, at Island No. 10, and in the siege of Corinth. At the battle of Iuka, his regiment, part of Sanborn's brigade of C. S. Hamilton's division, sustained 217 casualties out of 482 men engaged. During the offensive against Vicksburg under U. S. Grant, Matthies, who had received his promotion to brigadier, commanded a brigade of the 3rd Division of Sherman's XV Corps from Grand Gulf to Jackson and thence to the envelopment of the city itself. After the battle of Chickamauga, Matthies' brigade, along with the rest of the XV Corps now under James B. McPherson, was hurried to Chattanooga, where, in the celebrated attack on Missionary Ridge, November 25, 1863, he "was struck by a bullet in the head, which felled [him] to the ground." (395) By February, 1864, he was temporarily commanding a division of the XV Corps at Cleveland, Tennessee, and in the

early stages of the Atlanta campaign was on field duty, but failing health compelled him to accept assignment to the post of Decatur, Alabama, in May, 1864. He resigned on May 16 and returned to his home in Burlington where he died on October 16, 1868. He was buried in Aspen Grove Cemetery. At the time of his death he was a member of the Iowa senate. (396)

George Gordon Meade was born December 31, 1815, in Cadiz, Spain. His father, a wealthy American merchant, was financially ruined by his adherence to the cause of Spain

during the Napoleonic wars. (397) While his sisters and brothers married into high stations both in the North and South, Meade was found an appointment to West Point. (398) After preparatory work at Mount Hope Institution in Baltimore, he entered the Military Academy in 1831 and was graduated four years later, ranking nineteenth in a class of fifty-six members. At this time he had no desire to remain in the army, and after some service in Florida and at the Watertown (Massachusetts) Arsenal, he resigned in 1836 to pursue a career in civil engineering. In 1842, however, he sought restoration to the army and on May 19 was appointed a second lieutenant in the Corps of Topographical Engineers. From then until 1861, with an interlude of Mexican War service, Meade was continuously employed as a military engineer in the construction of lighthouses and breakwaters and in coastal and geodetic survey work. During the war with Mexico he was present at Palo Alto, Resaca de la Palma, and Monterey and was awarded the brevet of first lieutenant. Soon after the beginning of the Civil War on August 31, 1861, Meade, by then a captain in his corps, was made a brigadier general of volunteers at the instance of Governor Andrew G. Curtin of Pennsylvania and was given command of one of the three Pennsylvania brigades then organized. After a winter spent in work on the Washington defenses, he joined George B. McClellan on the Peninsula in June and fought during the Seven Days battles at Mechanicsville, Gaines's Mill, and Glendale where he was severely wounded in two places almost simultaneously. Partially recovered, he led his brigade in Irvin McDowell's corps at Second Manassas; at South Mountain and Sharpsburg he commanded a division in Hooker's I Corps, succeeding John F. Reynolds who had been ordered to Harrisburg to enlist and train men for defense against the threatened invasion of the state. At Freder-

icksburg Reynolds commanded the I Corps and Meade its 3rd Division in Franklin's "Left Grand Division." (399) A few days later Meade was appointed to the command of the V Corps which he led at Chancellorsville. After this Federal debacle the administration decided not to risk another battle under Joseph Hooker, who had replaced Ambrose E. Burnside after Fredericksburg. Meade was given command of the Army of the Potomac on June 28, 1863, after Reynolds had taken himself out of competition for the position, Darius N. Couch had been transferred at his own request, and John Sedgwick and Henry W. Slocum had agreed that they would willingly serve under their junior. Meade was immediately confronted with Robert E. Lee's ragged and hungry legions who were fanned out over the Pennsylvania countryside. (400) In the ensuing Gettysburg campaign, the Army of the Potomac prevailed under his leadership even though on the first day Reynolds was killed and the I and XI Corps were badly mauled and driven through the town to the heights beyond. On July 2 and 3 successive Confederate assaults on the right, left, and center were repulsed with the infliction of frightful losses on attackers and attacked alike. Nevertheless, the decimated Southerners were compelled to retire toward the Potomac on July 5; they crossed the river on the night of July 13. That they were permitted to "escape" brought a torrent of criticism upon the head of Meade, including a message from Henry W. Halleck indicating President Lincoln's "dissatisfaction." Meade at once offered to resign, but the administration beat a hasty retreat, and he was appointed a brigadier general in the Regular Army on July 7, 1863, to rank from July 3. He was awarded the thanks of Congress by resolution the following January 28. In the next six months there occurred in the eastern theater of war only the rather indecisive campaigns of Bristoe Station and Mine Run—neither showered any particular glory on either Meade or Lee. The following spring U. S. Grant, newly appointed lieutenant general and general-in-chief, elected to make his headquarters with the Army of the Potomac. Since Burnside had been restored to the command of his old IX Corps, which was to operate with the Army of the Potomac, an awkward arrangement developed: Grant gave orders to Meade governing the movements of his army but separately to Burnside, who ranked Meade by seniority, although he was only a corps commander. From this time until Lee's surrender at Appomattox Court House, Meade was Grant's subordinate, although nominally in command of the Army of the Potomac until the end. He fought the army through the Wilderness, Spotsylvania, Cold Harbor, and the long months in front of Petersburg. He was finally rewarded with the grade of major general, U. S. Army, after both W. T. Sherman and Philip Sheridan, the latter his subordinate, had been appointed. (401) At the close of the war he was assigned, successively, to the command of departments and divisions in the East and South and was in charge of the military Division of the Atlantic, headquarters at Philadel-

phia when he died on November 6, 1872, from pneumonia. He was buried in Laurel Hill Cemetery.

Thomas Francis Meagher, son of a wealthy merchant and "the counterpart of some rash, impolitic, poetic, personage from Irish poetry or fiction," (402) was born in Waterford, Ireland, on August 3, 1823. As a disciple of "Irish liberty," he took part in the various independence movements—many of which were opposed to each other—and in 1849 was banished to Tasmania by a benevolent British government. Three years later he escaped to California and from there made his way to New York. He found in Manhattan a milieu which exactly suited his talents and his rabble-rousing oratory quickly made him the darling of the Young Ireland group. In 1861 he organized a Zouave company which became one of the units of the 69th New York Militia; this command, whose colonel was Michael Cor-

coran, fought at First Manassas with Meagher as its major, in Sherman's brigade. The following winter Meagher organized in New York City the "Irish Brigade" and was appointed by President Lincoln a brigadier general of volunteers on February 6, 1862, to rank from February 3. The Irish Brigade took part in all the battles of the Army of the Potomac from Bull Run to Chancellorsville—none of its exploits, however, exceeding the hopeless charge against the entrenched Confederate position on Marye's Hill behind the city of Fredericksburg in December, 1862. When he was refused permission to recruit his decimated ranks and it was proposed to extinguish the brigade organization by distributing its units among other commands, Meagher—who apparently regarded the brigade as a symbol of Irish glory rather than as a unit of the U. S. Army—submitted his resignation as of May 14, 1863, and went home. The resignation, however, was not accepted and was cancelled on December 23. In 1864 and 1865 he exercised command at various points in the rear of W. T. Sherman's armies, and on May 15, 1865, while stationed at Savannah, he again resigned from the service. Later that year he was appointed territorial secretary of Montana and, in the absence of the governor, served as acting governor for more than a year. On July 1, 1867, during a drunken spree at Fort Benton, Montana, he presumably fell from the deck of a steamboat into the Missouri River under mysterious circumstances and was drowned. His body was not recovered, and his last resting place is unknown. (403)

Montgomery Cunningham Meigs was born on May 3, 1816, in Augusta, Georgia, where his father, a noted obstetrician had his practice. His grandfather had served as a professor at Yale and president of the University of Georgia in a day before the slavery issue

had become a political factor. During Montgomery's childhood, the family moved to Philadelphia, his mother's home. He attended the University of Pennsylvania before entering West Point in the class of 1836. From his graduation until the opening of the Civil War, Meigs had a part in a wide range of engineering projects undertaken by the Army Engineers; the most outstanding were the construction of the Potomac Aqueduct and the additions to the Capitol which included the House and Senate wings and the dome. (404) On May 14, 1861, Meigs was promoted from captain of engineers to colonel of the 11th Infantry and the following day was made quartermaster general of the U. S. Army with rank of brigadier general. He served as quartermaster general with great distinction throughout the war and until his retirement in 1882. It has been estimated that from 1861 until 1866 he disbursed a billion and a half dollars upon his own order—the largest expenditure in military history up to that time. Every penny of the sum was accounted for, even though it must be confessed that large sums, by the very nature of the circumstances, found their way into the hands of speculators and dishonest contractors. He was brevetted major general, U. S. Army, July 5, 1864, for distinguished and meritorious services. In the postbellum years General Meigs traveled widely in this country and abroad, studying the organizations of foreign military establishments for comparison with that of the United States. After his retirement he acted as architect of the Pension Office Building in Washington, and among other scientific activities, he served as a regent of the Smithsonian Institution. (405) When he died in Washington, January 2, 1892, the simple tribute contained in General Orders dated January 4 was perhaps his highest accolade: "The Army has rarely possessed an officer . . . who was entrusted by the government with a greater variety of weighty responsibilities, or who proved himself more worthy of confidence." He was buried in Arlington National Cemetery.

Solomon Meredith was born in Guilford County, North Carolina, May 29, 1810. At the age of nineteen he moved to Wayne County,

Indiana, where by working as a farm laborer he was able to pay for a fair education for himself. A natural leader of men, Meredith became sheriff of the county at the age of twenty-four, serving two terms, and then was elected for four terms in the legislature. In 1849 he was appointed United States marshal for the district of Indiana. As a well-known peace officer and lawmaker, his selection by Governor Oliver P. Morton to be colonel of the 19th Indiana was not surprising. This brigade saw its first heavy action in the course of the Second Manassas campaign, during the attack of Stonewall Jackson's Confederates on Rufus King's Union division: the 19th Indiana suffered about 220 casualties and Meredith himself was severely wounded. (406) He was promoted brigadier general on October 6, 1862. At Chancellorsville his brigade of one Michigan, two Indiana, and three Wisconsin regiments, called during the war, the "Iron Brigade,"

was in Wadsworth's division of Reynolds' I Corps. Meredith's and Cutler's brigades opened the infantry action at Gettysburg, but Meredith was again wounded on the first day of fighting and incapacitated until November. Early in 1864 he was assigned to command of the post of Cairo, Illinois, and in September of that year to the post at Paducah, Kentucky, where he remained until the end of the war. On August 14, 1865, somewhat belatedly, he was brevetted major general of volunteers. His service record in the Civil War years was most distinguished, despite the fact that he was older by a decade, and in many cases by a generation, than most of his colleagues. (His three sons were all in the army during the war, two of them losing their lives.) From 1867 until his retirement in 1869 General Meredith served as surveyor general of the Montana Territory. After retiring to his farm, Oakland, near Cambridge City, Indiana, he devoted himself to raising prize livestock. He died there on October 2, 1875, and was buried in Riverside Cemetery.

Sullivan Amory Meredith, a native of Philadelphia, was born on July 4, 1816. It is not certain where he obtained his education. (407) As a young man he made two voyages to China in a clipper ship and in 1848 he made a trip to California. He was engaged in business in his native city at the outbreak of the Civil War. Seventeen days after the firing on Fort Sumter he was commissioned colonel of the 10th Pennsylvania Infantry (a militia organization), perhaps receiving the appointment through the

influence of his elder brother, William M., who was a prominent Pennsylvania Whig politician and had served as Zachary Taylor's Secretary of the Treasury. In any event Meredith discharged his duties diligently and faithfully and is credited with having superintended the drilling and equipping of over thirty thousand men in the early days of the war. He subsequently took part in the ill-starred campaign under General Robert Patterson which permitted Joseph Johnston's forces to slip away and join P. G. T. Beauregard at First Manassas. After duty in the defenses of Washington during the winter of 1861, he organized the 56th Pennsylvania Infantry, became its colonel, and was assigned to McDowell's III Corps. While engaged at the battle of Second Manassas (Bull Run) in Doubleday's brigade of King's division, he was badly wounded and on November 29, 1862, was promoted brigadier general of volunteers. Upon his partial recovery in July, 1863, he was ordered to Fort Monroe as "agent for exchange of prisoners," (408) but was relieved the following January by General Benjamin F. Butler, the department commander, and ordered to report to the adjutant general for orders. (409) In 1864 he was sent to St. Louis to report to General W. S. Rosecrans, who was then commanding the Department of the Missouri. He seems to have been put on the shelf for the balance of the war. He was mustered out on August 24, 1865, and resided in St. Louis for one year, where he held the office of commissioner of exchanged prisoners. (410) In 1866 he moved to Buffalo, New York, and entered the wholesale drug business with his brother-in-law. General Meredith died in Buffalo on December 26, 1874, and was buried in Forest Lawn Cemetery.

Wesley Merritt, one of eleven children of an impecunious attorney, was born in New York City on June 16, 1834. (411) The family moved to a farm in St. Clair County, Illinois, when he was seven, and his father subsequently was a farmer, newspaper editor, and member of the legislature. Wesley pointed toward a legal career, but in 1855 accepted an appointment to West Point. He was graduated in the class of 1860, ranking twenty-second out of forty-one members in what was the most distinguished of classes to pass into the regular service immediately before secession. (412) After some routine frontier service in Utah as a lieutenant of dragoons, Merritt was recalled to Washington, and in February,

1862, became aide-de-camp first to General Philip Cooke, who was then commanding the cavalry of the Army of the Potomac, and later to his successor, General George Stoneman. His first important service was as commander of the reserve cavalry brigade during Stoneman's

abortive raid in the Chancellorsville campaign, although he ranked as only a captain of the 2nd (Regular) Cavalry. On June 29, 1863, he was promoted brigadier general of volunteers and led his brigade, mostly Regulars, in John Buford's division during the Gettysburg campaign. From then until the end of the war General Merritt was with the Army of the Potomac, commanding a brigade and then a division in the campaigns which followed Gettysburg. He was brevetted repeatedly in both the regular and volunteer services, and as of April 1, 1865, was made a full rank major general of volunteers. During the Appomattox campaign Merritt was second in command to Philip Sheridan and acted as one of the three Federal commissioners to receive the Confederates' formal capitulation. After the war he became lieutenant colonel of the 9th Cavalry, colonel of the 5th Cavalry in 1876, brigadier general, U. S. Army, in 1887 and in 1895 major general. During these thirty years he discharged much duty on the Indian frontier, was superintendent at West Point, and commanded various military departments. At the outbreak of the war with Spain, he was in command of the Department of the East, with headquarters at Governors Island, New York. Although now past his sixty-fourth birthday (he was carried on the rolls as sixty-two), he was given command of the first Philippine expedition. Upon his arrival there he assumed command of the United States forces investing Manila, and in the weeks that followed, he performed, in cooperation with Admiral George Dewey, the unprecedented feat of forcing the surrender of the defending Spaniards, while at the same time preventing the entrance of the Philippine insurgents under Emilio Aguinaldo, who were also besieging the city. With the islands under American control, General Merritt was ordered to Paris to confer with the peace commission there. After his return to the States, he reassumed command of the Department of the East and was retired by operation of law on what was supposedly his sixty-fourth birthday, June 16, 1900. During his last years General Merritt divided his time between his residences in Washington and Natural Bridge, Virginia, where he

died, December 3, 1910. His remains were taken to West Point for burial.

Nelson Appleton Miles was born on his father's farm near Westminster, Massachusetts, August 8, 1839. After receiving a rudimentary education in a local academy, he went

to Boston at the age of seventeen to work in a store, meanwhile attending night school, as well as taking instruction in military matters from a former French army colonel. When the Civil War came, the records exhibit (contrary in some instances to Miles's recollections in later life) that on September 9, 1861, he was commissioned first lieutenant in the 22nd Massachusetts Volunteers. During the first part of George B. McClellan's Peninsular campaign, Miles served on General Oliver O. Howard's staff; and at Seven Pines, where he sustained a wound in the foot, he distinguished himself while temporarily commanding a portion of the 81st Pennsylvania. He was appointed lieutenant colonel of the 61st New York as of the day of the battle and, thereafter, inscribed on the annals of American military history a record seldom if ever equaled by a volunteer soldier. After Francis C. Barlow was disabled at Sharpsburg, Miles succeeded to command of the regiment and the same month was officially advanced to colonel. At the battle of Fredericksburg in December, 1862, he sustained his second wound and was commended by Winfield S. Hancock, his brigade leader. For his conduct at Chancellorsville, where he was again wounded, he was made a brevet brigadier general of the Regular Army in 1867 and awarded the Medal of Honor in 1892. Not present at Gettysburg because of his wound, he returned to duty in time to take part in Grant's Overland campaign of 1864. He fought gallantly at the Wilderness and Spotsylvania while commanding a brigade of Barlow's division of Hancock's II Army Corps, and was commissioned brigadier general of volunteers on June 9, 1864, to rank from May 12. In the course of the siege of Petersburg, Miles attained command of a division, sustained his fourth wound of the war, and was brevetted major general of volunteers for outstanding conduct at the affair of Reams' Station. Miles's division also played an important part in the Appomattox campaign. On October 21, 1865, he was made major general of volunteers, temporarily in command of the II Corps, which numbered twenty-six thousand officers and men. At this time he determined to make the army

his career and upon the reorganization of the Regular Army in July, 1866, was appointed colonel of the newly constituted 40th U. S. Infantry (Colored Troops). In the meantime, he had served for a while as jailor of Jeffrson Davis at Fort Monroe, putting in irons the defenseless ex-Confederate president upon War Department orders, but without apparent protest upon his own part. In 1868 Miles married a niece of W. T. Sherman. Eleven days after Grant's inauguration Miles was transferred to command of the 5th Infantry, in 1880 was made brigadier, and ten years later major general in the regular service. During this time he compiled an unequaled record in the pacification of the western Indians, including the celebrated surrender of the Apache chief Geronimo, who was immediately betrayed by Miles or his superiors, and sent to Alabama. (413) In 1895 Miles by seniority became general-in-chief of the army and directed recruitment and training during the Spanish-American War. He also commanded in person the forces which took the territory of Puerto Rico. President McKinley advanced him to the grade of lieutenant general in 1901; the following year he became involved in the Dewey-Schley controversy, an imbroglio which won him an official reprimand from President Theodore Roosevelt, and in 1903 he was retired. More than two decades of life remained to him, during which he expanded his writings and served as head of a number of patriotic organizations. When he died while attending a circus performance in Washington on May 15, 1925, he was the last survivor of the full rank major generals of Civil War vintage and was survived by only two Union brigadiers, John R. Brooke and Adelbert Ames. General Miles was buried in Arlington National Cemetery in a mausoleum, the construction of which he had directed himself, years before.

John Franklin Miller, a native of South Bend, Indiana, was born on November 21, 1831. He was educated in South Bend, Chicago, and at Ballston Spa, New York, where he received his law degree

at the age of twenty-one. He began his practice in South Bend, but went to Napa, California, in 1853, where he continued his practice and served as county treasurer. He returned to South Bend in 1855 and was elected to the state senate in 1861. On August 27 of that year Miller was commissioned colonel of the 29th Indiana Volunteer Infantry, a regiment whose first impor-

tant service was in Kirk's brigade of Alexander McD. McCook's division of Buell's Army of the Ohio on the second day at Shiloh. It moved to Corinth, then through northern Alabama and Tennessee, and followed Braxton Bragg through Kentucky. At Murfreesboro where it is said he was wounded, Miller commanded a brigade in Negley's division under George Thomas, who directed the Union center. (414) In the course of the Tullahoma campaign, by which W. S. Rosecrans maneuvered Bragg out of Tennessee, Miller commanded a brigade of the XX Corps, again under McCook, and was wounded in a skirmish at Liberty Gap on June 27, 1863. (415) He was apparently not on duty again until May, 1864, when he was assigned to command of the city and post of Nashville. In the meantime, he had been appointed a brigadier general on April 10, 1864, to rank from January 5. At the battle of Nashville in December, Miller had under his command all or portions of twelve regiments of infantry, five of which were brigaded, as well as fourteen batteries. He was brevetted major general for his services there on March 13, 1865. The war over, General Miller resigned on September 25, 1865, declined a colonelcy in the Regular Army, and returned to California, where until 1869 he was collector of the port of San Francisco under appointment of President Johnson. For the next twelve years he was president of the Alaska Commercial Company, which controlled the fur industry in the newly acquired Pribilof Islands. In 1880 Miller was elected by the California legislature to a seat in the U. S. Senate, after having served in 1878-79 as a member of the state constitutional convention. In Washington he was chiefly known as a leading exponent of anti-Chinese legislation. He died, while in office, on March 8, 1886, and was buried in Laurel Hill Cemetery, San Francisco, but was reburied in Arlington National Cemetery in 1913.

Stephen Miller was born January 7, 1816, in Carroll, Pennsylvania, a crossroads in Clinton County. He was educated in the local school and, as he grew older, drifted into politics, serving as court clerk of Dauphin County and "flour inspec-

tor" in Philadelphia. From 1853 until 1855 he edited a Whig newspaper in Harrisburg; in 1858 he removed to St. Cloud, Minnesota, where he engaged in business and was both a delegate to the Republican convention in Chicago and a Lincoln elector in 1860. The following year, losing no time in get-

ting into the fight, Miller was mustered into service as lieutenant colonel of the 1st Minnesota two weeks after the fall of Sumter. The regiment reenlisted for three years on May 10, 1861. At First Manassas, where its historian claims for it "the heaviest percentage of loss . . . in that battle," it was a part of Franklin's brigade of Heintzelman's division. (416) It took part in the affair at Ball's Bluff, or Leesburg, where it acted as rear guard in the retreat of the Federals across the Potomac. After some duty in the Shenandoah in the spring of 1862, the regiment was sent to the Peninsula where it took part in the battle of Seven Pines and the battles of the Seven Days, where it was assigned to Sumner's II Corps. On August 24, 1862, Miller was made colonel of the newly organized 7th Minnesota, a unit brought into being primarily to combat the Sioux unrest in the state. He took command at Mankato in November; was prominent in suppressing the Indian outbreak of 1863; presided at the executions of thirty-eight Sioux, naïvely described as "disloyal"; and on October 26, 1863, was made a brigadier general. On January 18, 1864, having been elected governor of Minnesota, he resigned his army commission. General Miller occupied the governor's chair from 1864 to 1865—a period when little could be done constructively other than keep the Sioux at bay and contribute to the war effort. After 1871 he was an employee of the St. Paul and Sioux City Railroad, now a part of the Chicago and North Western system. He died in Worthington, Minnesota, August 18, 1881, and is buried there.

325

Robert Huston Milroy was born June 11, 1816, on a farm near Salem, Indiana, but the family moved to Carroll County in 1826. At the age of twenty-four he matriculated at Captain Partridge's Academy in Norwich, Vermont, and was graduated in 1843 with the de-

grees of Bachelor of Arts and Master of Military Science. From 1846 to 1847 he served as captain of a company of the 1st Indiana Volunteers. Then he studied law, was admitted to the bar, was a member of the constitutional convention of 1850, was appointed to the bench and resigned, and in 1854 took up the practice of law in Rensselaer, Indiana, where the outbreak of the Civil War found him. Milroy had recruited a company in and about Rensselaer before Lincoln's inauguration, and two weeks after Sumter he was mustered into Federal service as colonel of the 9th Indiana (a three-month unit which he reen-

listed for three years after the expiration of its original term of service). After taking part in George B. McClellan's western Virginia campaign, Milroy was promoted brigadier general of volunteers on September 3, 1861, and major general on March 10, 1863, to rank from November 29, 1862. He commanded the Cheat Mountain district for a time and then was engaged in the Shenandoah Valley campaign of 1862. He later commanded an "Independent Brigade," attached to Sigel's corps, at the battle of Second Manassas. The following June, in command of some 6,000 to 8,000 men at Winchester, he was outmaneuvered, outfought, and virtually "gobbled up" by Ewell's 2nd Corps of the Army of Northern Virginia while en route to Gettysburg. He lost thirty-four hundred prisoners, all twenty-three pieces of his artillery, and many dead and wounded. Milroy himself, with two hundred or three hundred cavalry, made good his escape to Harpers Ferry. (417) He held no further command in the field; however, after being hailed before a court of inquiry and being subjected to ten months of inactivity, he was at length formally "exonerated" of culpability and toward the end of the war served under G. H. Thomas at Nashville, organizing and assigning militia regiments. Postbellum General Milroy was a trustee of the Wabash and Erie Canal Company and after 1872 Indian agent in Olympia, Washington, where he died, March 29, 1890, and was buried in the Masonic Cemetery. Years later the people of Rensselaer erected a bronze statue of heroic size to his memory.

Ormsby MacKnight Mitchel was born July 28, 1809, in a log cabin on the site of the present town of Morganfield, Kentucky. When Mitchel was an infant, his father died and his widowed mother moved to Lebanon, Ohio, where he

obtained his early education and in turn began to support himself by clerking in a store in nearby Xenia. Mitchel would have been accounted an exceptionally bright student in any contemporary high school, and in 1825 secured an appointment to West Point from which he was graduated in 1829. In the next seven years he served as an instructor at West Point, was married, studied law, was admitted to the bar, resigned from the army, moved to Cincinnati, and became a member of the faculty of Cincinnati College, where he taught astronomy, philosophy, and mathematics, and devoted some time to railroad projects. But it was as a popularizer and dedicated student

of astronomy that Mitchel's main claim to fame rests. He was compellingly articulate on his favorite subject, arousing enthusiasm throughout the nation. Largely responsible for establishing the Naval Observatory and the Harvard Observatory, he also directed the Cincinnati Observatory and the Dudley Observatory at Albany. On August 9, 1861, President Lincoln appointed him a brigadier general of volunteers and he was assigned to command of the Department of the Ohio, which would soon be absorbed into Buell's Army of the Cumberland. Thereafter General Mitchel fought in no battle, but in March, 1862, seized the Memphis and Charleston Railroad at Huntsville, Alabama, and sent raiding expeditions to Stevenson and Decatur, Alabama, which temporarily secured the track to the Union forces. For this exploit he was made a major general to rank from April 11, 1862, but differences soon became apparent between himself and General D. C. Buell, who pronounced the management and control of his division as highly wanting in discipline. Mitchel tendered his resignation, but it was not accepted, and on September 17, 1862, he was transferred to command of the miniscule Department of the South and the X Corps, with headquarters at Hilton Head, South Carolina. There he came down with yellow fever and died at Beaufort, October 30, 1862. He was buried in Green-Wood Cemetery in Brooklyn, New York.

John Grant Mitchell, one of the youngest civilians to attain the full rank of general officer during the

Civil War, was born November 6, 1838, in Piqua, Ohio. He was graduated from Kenyon College in 1859 and then studied law in Columbus, Ohio. On June 27, 1861, he enlisted in the first battalion of Ohio reserves, and on July 30 was

appointed first lieutenant and adjutant of the 3rd Ohio Infantry, whose colonel was John Beatty. His early service was under General W. S. Rosecrans in West Virginia; then his regiment served in General O. M. Mitchel's campaign in Tennessee and Alabama, and he was promoted to captain and commander of Company C. In the summer of 1862 he went back to Ohio on recruiting service, was made lieutenant colonel of the 113th Ohio on September 2 and colonel on May 6, 1863. At Chickamauga, Mitchell commanded a brigade of Steedman's division of Granger's corps, whose heroic defense of the celebrated "Horseshoe Ridge" helped to make possible the re-

tirement of the remnant of the Federal army commanded by G. H. Thomas which got off in reasonably good order toward Chattanooga. He seems not to have been present at the battles of Chattanooga, when his brigade reverted to Beatty's command and his regiment was under its major. However, during the subsequent Atlanta campaign, Mitchell reassumed brigade command, directing the second brigade of Jefferson C. Davis' division of the XIV Corps, Army of the Cumberland. The brigade formed the right of the assaulting column at Kennesaw where it suffered frightful losses. Mitchell accompanied General Thomas back to Tennessee, was present at the decisive battle of Nashville, and later took part in the campaign of the Carolinas. (418) He was appointed a brigadier general of volunteers on January 12, 1865, and on March 13 was promoted major general by brevet "for gallant and meritorious services in the war, especially at the battle of Averysboro and Bentonville, North Carolina." General Mitchell resigned on July 3, 1865, and returned to Columbus to practice law. He served several terms on the city council and upon the accession of Benjamin Harrison to the presidency was appointed pension commissioner for Ohio at the instance of ex-President Hayes, who was his wife's uncle. (419) He died in Columbus on November 7, 1894, and was buried in Green Lawn Cemetery.

Robert Byington Mitchell was born in Mansfield, Ohio, April 4, 1823. For some reason it has been recorded that he graduated from both Kenyon College, Ohio, and Wash-

ington College, Pennsylvania, although neither school has a record of his attendance. (420) After studying law in Mount Vernon, he started a practice in Mansfield, served in the Mexican War as a lieutenant in the 2nd Ohio, and in 1855 was elected mayor of Mount Gilead, Ohio. The following year he moved to Linn County in the Kansas Territory, where he espoused the Free State cause although a Democrat; he served in the territorial legislature, as a delegate to the Leavenworth constitutional convention, as treasurer of the territory, and as delegate to the Democratic National Convention of 1860 in Charleston. With the outbreak of the Civil War Mitchell was commissioned colonel of the 2nd Kansas Infantry and was badly wounded at the battle of Wilson's Creek in August. The following year Lincoln appointed him a brigadier general to rank from April 8, 1862, and he was given command of a mixed brigade at Fort Riley. At the battle of Perryville, Kentucky, in October he commanded the 9th Division of Gilbert's corps. He was then stationed at Nashville for a number of months and during the Chickamauga campaign acted as chief of cavalry of Thomas' Army of the Cumberland. Just before the battle of Chattanooga he was ordered to Washington for court-martial duty. (421) During the years 1864 and 1865 General Mitchell commanded the district of Nebraska, then the district of North Kansas, and finally the district of Kansas. The same day he was honorably mustered out of the army (January 15, 1866) his nomination to be governor of New Mexico Territory was approved by the Senate, and he took the oath of office on June 6, 1866. "He failed to take his duties either seriously or with dignity . . . affronted the [legislature] by leaving Santa Fe . . . and absenting himself for . . . months without . . . explanation." (422) The legislature was forced to the expedient of forwarding bills which it had passed to Washington for approval by Congress. After substantial other friction had developed he resigned in 1869 and returned to Kansas. After an unsuccessful bid for a Congressional seat in 1872, he moved to Washington, where he died on January 26, 1882. General Mitchell is buried in Arlington National Cemetery.

William Reading Montgomery was born on July 10, 1801, in Monmouth County, New Jersey. He entered West Point at the age of twenty and was graduated in 1825, ranking near the bottom of the class. Subsequently he served at

its colonel, although at the time he seems to have been a resident of Pennsylvania. At First Manassas the regiment formed a part of the Fourth (Reserve) Division of McDowell's army and was not on the field of battle. Shortly thereafter (August 9, 1861) Montgomery was appointed a brigadier general of volunteers to rank from May 17. His subsequent service was either administrative or spent in awaiting orders: he was military governor of Alexandria, Virginia, in the autumn of 1861, then commanded at Annapolis for a time, and from April, 1862, until March, 1863, was stationed at Philadelphia. For the last five months preceding the tender of his resignation (said to have been caused by failing health), General Montgomery was a member of a military commission which sat at Memphis. His resignation having been accepted as of April 4, 1864, he returned to private life. After a brief interval in which he dealt in wood mouldings in Philadelphia, he retired to his home in Bristol, Pennsylvania, where he died about midnight on the night of May 31–June 1, 1871. (423) He is buried in St. James Churchyard, Bristol.

George Webb Morell was born in Cooperstown, New York, on January 8, 1815. His grandfather, on his mother's side, was a general officer of the Revolution; his father was a major general in the New York State militia and at the time of his death was chief justice of the Michigan supreme court. George was graduated from the Military Academy, ranking first in the fifty-six member class of 1835. After two years in the Corps of Engineers he

various times on the Canadian border during the disturbances of 1838-46, in the Florida War of 1840-42, and in the occupation of Texas prior to the war with Mexico. He greatly distinguished himself as a captain of the 8th Infantry in the Mexican War and was brevetted major and lieutenant colonel for gallantry at Palo Alto, Resaca de la Palma, and Molino del Rey. In 1852 he received the full rank of major. In 1854-55 Montgomery was stationed at Fort Riley, Kansas, where he seems to have favored to some extent the Free State cause, thus rendering himself *persona non grata* to the proslavery faction. The latter are alleged to have procured his dismissal from the service on the charge of "appropriating a portion of the Military Reserve at Fort Riley, Kansas, to the uses of the Pawnee Association for a town site, he being interested in that Association." At the beginning of the Civil War he organized the 1st New Jersey Volunteers and became

resigned (June 30, 1837) to engage in railroad construction, but in 1840 moved to New York City to study law. He was admitted to the bar in 1842 and practiced law until the outbreak of the Civil War with a brief interlude during the Mexican War when he was commissioned major of a regiment which was not mustered. In the early part of 1861 Morell served as colonel and quartermaster on the staff of the major general commanding the New York militia, organizing and forwarding regiments to the theater of war. He subsequently served in the defenses of Washington and on August 9, 1861, was made a brigadier general of volunteers. He commanded a brigade of Porter's division of the V Corps during the early part of the Peninsular campaign, and when Fitz John Porter succeeded to command of the corps in May, 1862, Morell advanced to divisional command. He fought gallantly and skillfully in the bat-

tles of the Seven Days, was with Porter at Second Manassas and Sharpsburg, and on July 25, 1862, was promoted to major general to rank from July 4. The court-martial of Porter for alleged dereliction at Second Manassas also destroyed Morell's career. It has been said that Porter was ruined by his devotion to McClellan, (424) it could as well be said that Morell was ruined by his devotion to Porter—or at least, his devotion to principle. His testimony was to say the least inimical to the interests of the cabal dedicated to the downfall of Porter, and after Sharpsburg Morell saw no further field service. (425) He commanded the defenses of the upper Potomac for a time, was awaiting orders for several months in 1863, and then had charge of the draft rendezvous at Indianapolis until he was mustered out of service on December 15, 1864. He then engaged in farming at Scarborough, New York, until his death there on February 11, 1883. He is buried under the chancel of St. Mary's Episcopal Church where for five years he conducted the services in the absence of a rector. (426)

Charles Hale Morgan, a graduate of the class of 1857 at West Point, was born at Manlius, New York, on November 6, 1834. He distinguished himself during the Civil War as chief of artillery and later chief of staff to General Winfield S. Hancock, and also by virtue of a talent for profanity exceeded only by that possessed by his chief. (427) After leaving the Military Academy as a brevet second lieutenant of artillery, he served at Fort Monroe, Virginia, for a time and then took part in the expedition of 1859 under Albert Sidney Johnston which stilled a potential Mormon uprising against the authority of the United States. Morgan arrived in the East in December, 1861, and after some duty in the defenses of Washington, went to the Virginia Peninsula in the spring of 1862,

where his battery of the 4th U. S. Artillery was attached to the artillery reserve of the army during the Seven Days battles. He was promoted to captain in the Regular Army on August 5 but was on sick leave until after the battle of Sharpsburg. On October 1 Morgan became chief of artillery of the II Corps and from then until the end of the war was closely associated with General Hancock, becoming the latter's chief of staff on January 1, 1863, at which time he was appointed a staff lieutenant colonel of volunteers. He was brevetted repeatedly in both the regular and volunteer services during the war,

and on May 21, 1865, was made a full brigadier general of volunteers. In the meantime he rendered yeoman's service to his chief on all the fields and during all the campaigns of the Army of the Potomac from Fredericksburg to the siege of Petersburg, after which he assisted Hancock in organizing the so-called "Veterans Reserve Corps," an organization which actually never came into being. When the war ended he was serving as chief of staff of the Middle Military Division commanded by Hancock. He was mustered out of the volunteer service on January 15, 1866, and reverted to his regular rank of captain, 4th Artillery, but was promoted major on February 5, 1867. Postbellum he had duty at a number of artillery garrisons: Fort Delaware, Fort Monroe, and Alcatraz Island in San Francisco Bay. He died at the latter post December 20, 1875, and was buried in the military cemetery on nearby Angel Island. In 1947 his remains were removed to Golden Gate National Cemetery at San Bruno, California.

Edwin Denison Morgan, better remembered as merchant, financier, philanthropist, and statesman than as a Civil War major general, was born February 8, 1811, in the Berkshire Hills village of Washington, Massachusetts, but at the age of eleven moved with his parents to Windsor, Connecticut. Here he received his early education while working on his father's farm. He began clerking for an uncle in Hartford, Connecticut when he was seventeen; was elected a city councilman at twenty-one; moved to New York at twenty-five; and by the age of thirty was one of the leading merchants of the metropolis. Subsequently he added security underwriting and banking to his wholesale grocery business, enlarging still further his fortune. Elected to the city board of alder-

men in 1849, he went to the state senate the following year and served until 1855; he was the first chairman of the Republican National Committee, a post which he continued to hold until 1864. In 1858 Thurlow Weed, the political "boss" of New York State, chose Morgan as his candidate for governor. He was elected and reelected in 1860 by the largest majority ever given a gubernatorial candidate up to that time. His first term was marked by constructive legislation and freedom from subservience to Weed; his second by his successful efforts in behalf of the Federal cause, during which he enrolled, armed, equipped, and forwarded no less than 223,000 men. Lincoln made him a major general of vol-

unteers on September 28, 1861, in order to give him military as well as civil authority, and placed him in command of the Department of New York. Toward the expiration of his second term as governor, the legislature elected him to the U. S. Senate, where he took his seat on March 4, 1863, having resigned his military commission on January 1. In the postbellum years he was not so successful politically and was defeated for reelection to the Senate in 1869 and for the governorship in 1876. Nevertheless, he twice declined the Treasury portfolio proffered him by President Johnson in 1865 and President Arthur in 1881, the last time after his nomination had been unanimously confirmed by the Senate. In the later years of his life he made large gifts to various educational, religious, and medical institutions; his total contributions were estimated at more than a million dollars—an enormous sum in an era when a penny bought what a dollar does today. Governor Morgan died in New York City on February 14, 1883, and was buried in Cedar Hill Cemetery, Hartford, Connecticut.

George Washington Morgan was born in Washington County, Pennsylvania, September 20, 1820. A born leader, he was a mercurial figure from his early youth. At the age of sixteen he deserted a college career to espouse the cause of Texas independence and was appointed an officer in the Texas army by Sam Houston. He entered the U. S. Army Military Academy in the class of 1845, but withdrew because of scholastic difficulties in his third-class year. Thereafter he studied law and became prosecutor of Knox

County, Ohio. In 1846 he was elected colonel of the 2nd Ohio Volunteers for the Mexican War (he was only twenty-six years old at the time). He commanded the regiment under Zachary Taylor until March 3, 1847, when he was commissioned colonel of the 15th U. S. Infantry. In this capacity, in the army under Winfield Scott, he was twice wounded and as of August 20, 1847, was brevetted brigadier general for gallantry at Contreras and Churubusco—a promotion not equalled during that war by a man so young. Honorably discharged in 1848, he occupied the next thirteen years in farming and practicing law at Mount Vernon, Ohio, meanwhile serving as United States consul at Marseilles and minister to Portugal. Morgan resigned from the latter post in 1861 and on November 12 of that year was commissioned a brigadier general of volunteers in the Federal army. His principal Civil War contribution was the expulsion of the Confederates from Cumberland Gap in 1862. He commanded a division under W. T. Sherman at Chickasaw Bayou and the XIII Corps at the capture of Arkansas Post, where he and Sherman, under John McClernand's orders, each commanded a corps. Friction between the two, which had developed when Sherman found fault with Morgan's handling of his division during the assault on the bluffs at Chickasaw, continued; and prior to the surrender of Vicksburg, Morgan, who was no abolitionist nor believer in Negro equality, became dissatisfied with the employment of Negro troops and tendered his resignation. He supported George B. McClellan in the Presidential election of 1864 and was defeated for governor of Ohio in 1865, but in the years following the war was elected to Congress three times on the Democratic ticket. As a Congressman, he was a vigorous opponent of radical Reconstruction measures. General Morgan died at Fort Monroe, Virginia, July 26, 1893, and was buried in Mount Vernon.

James Dada Morgan was born August 1, 1810, in Boston, Massachusetts. In 1826 he went to sea, supposedly on a three-year cruise, but after a month at sea mutiny occurred, the ship was burned, and after two weeks in a lifeboat he reached the coast of South America from whence he made his way home. At the age of twenty-four he moved to Quincy, Illinois, which was his residence for the rest of his life. In addition to flourishing as a merchant in the town, Morgan found time to devote to the local militia, serving with the "Quincy Riflemen" during the Mormon disturbances of the middle 1840's and as a captain of the 1st Illinois Infantry in Mexico. (428) Upon muster out in 1847 he returned to Quincy and his business. On April 29, 1861, he was commissioned lieu-

tenant colonel of the 10th Illinois, a three-month regiment of which he became colonel on May 20, 1861, and of which he continued as colonel when the command was remustered for three years on July 29. He directed a brigade of John Pope's forces at Island No. 10 and in the "siege" of Corinth following the battle of Shiloh, and was promoted brigadier general to rank from July 17, 1862. During the battles and campaigns of Chickamauga and Chattanooga, he seems to have been stationed with his command at Bridgeport, Alabama, where the great bridge over the Tennessee River on the Nashville & Chattanooga Railroad was positioned.

During the Atlanta campaign he commanded a brigade and at times Jefferson C. Davis' division of the XIV Corps. In the famous "March to the Sea" and the subsequent Carolina campaign, General Morgan commanded the 2nd Division of the XIV Corps and as of March 19, 1865, in the omnibus brevet promotions which followed the war's end, was made a major general of volunteers—an advancement which he seems to have richly deserved. He was mustered out in August and again returned to Quincy where he continued to prosper as a banker and businessman. In the forty years of his life after the war, he served as treasurer of the Illinois Soldiers and Sailors Home and as vice-president of the Society of the Army of the Cumberland, in whose annual reunions he took great interest and derived much pleasure until his death in Quincy on September 12, 1896. He was buried there in Woodland Cemetery.

William Hopkins Morris, born April 22, 1827, (429) in New York City, was the son of George Pope Morris, who wrote "Woodman, Spare that Tree" and other popular songs of the day. Young Morris was educated in the public schools and in 1846 entered West Point from which he was graduated five years later. After some garrison and recruiting duty, he resigned in 1854 to assist his father (a noted editor and poet as well as songwriter) with the *Home Journal*, a periodical owned by the elder Morris. William possessed not only a talent for invention but also a flair for the "soft sell": he secured a patent on his brainchild, a repeating

carbine, in 1859 and publicized it in later years through treatises on the subject aimed at the military. (430) In August, 1861, he was appointed assistant adjutant general of volunteers with rank of captain and served on the staff of his Hudson River neighbor, General John J. Peck, during the first winter of the war. Subsequent to the Peninsular campaign he was commissioned colonel of the 135th New York Infantry—a regiment which was quickly converted into the 6th New York Heavy Artillery and installed in the Washington defenses in deference to the War Department thinking at the time. (431) On March 16, 1863, he was appointed a brigadier general of volunteers to rank from the preceding November 29 and was stationed with his brigade on Maryland Heights. In the Gettysburg campaign he was attached to the command of General W. H. French, which constituted the III Corps

in the Bristoe and Mine Run campaigns. At the beginning of U. S. Grant's Richmond offensive, Morris' brigade was transferred to Ricketts' division of the VI Corps. He fought most capably at the Wilderness and was brevetted major general at the end of the war for his conduct, but he was wounded on May 9, 1864, at Spotsylvania and saw no further field service. In the postwar years General Morris resided on his estate, Briarcliff (named after one of his father's poems), in Putnam County, New York; was active in the National Guard, of which he became a brigadier and brevet major general; took part in local politics; and, as noted above, was something of a military essayist. He died August 26, 1900, while vacationing at Long Branch, New Jersey, and was buried at Cold Spring, New York.

James St. Clair Morton, certainly the only Civil War figure who at his own request forfeited a brigadier generalcy of volunteers in order to revert to a regular majority, was born September 24, 1829, in Philadelphia. A brilliant student, he entered the University of Pennsylvania at the age of fourteen and after four years there was appointed to West Point where he was graduated second in the class of 1851. Posted to the Corps of Engineers, as were all the top graduates in those days, Morton displayed great ability on a number of assignments, including Charleston Harbor, Fort Delaware, Fort Hancock, New Jersey, the Washington Aqueduct, and Fort Jefferson in the Dry Tortugas, where the Lincoln conspirators would later serve their sentences. Morton did not enter

Corps of Engineers. In this capacity he served as supervising engineer of the defenses of Nashville and nearby towns, and in January, 1864, he became assistant to the chief engineer in Washington. On May 18 he was assigned to Ambrose Burnside's IX Corps as chief engineer. After taking part in this corps' movements and actions at the North Anna River, Totopotomoy Creek, and Bethesda Church, he was killed in action in front of Petersburg on June 17, 1864, while reconnoitering the ground in front of Willcox's division in preparation for the assault of that day. Posthumously promoted brevet brigadier general, U. S. Army, General Morton lies buried in Laurel Hill Cemetery, Philadelphia.

the active theater of operations until June, 1862, when he became chief engineer of D. C. Buell's Army of the Ohio. This field was his forte and he had written several treatises on the subject; (432) consequently his promotion to the rank of brigadier general of volunteers on April 4, 1863, to rank from November 29, 1862, is not readily understandable. In any event, he continued in his chosen avocation, serving as chief engineer of G. H. Thomas' Army of the Cumberland in the fortification of Nashville and Chattanooga and as commander of the "Pioneer Brigade" of W. S. Rosecrans' forces. In the meantime he was present at the battle of Stone's River and at Chickamauga where he was brevetted for gallantry. At this juncture, just before the battles at Chattanooga which forced Braxton Bragg out of Tennessee, he was mustered out of the volunteer service and reverted to his Regular Army grade of major,

Gershom Mott was born in Lamberton, New Jersey (now a part of Trenton), on April 7, 1822. After attending a local academy, he became a drygoods clerk in New York

City at the age of fourteen. In the second year of the Mexican War he was appointed to a lieutenancy in the 10th U. S. Infantry—a regiment which saw no foreign service. Following his muster-out in 1848, he served for a time as collector of the port at Lamberton and then engaged in business in Bordentown. In 1861 he was a natural choice for lieutenant colonel of the 5th New Jersey, a regiment organized on August 17 at Trenton. His entire service was with the Army of the Potomac. Early in George B. McClellan's campaign up the Virginia Peninsula, Mott became colonel of the 6th New Jersey, which he led at Seven Pines and during the battle of the Seven Days. He was wounded at Second Manassas; was appointed brigadier general of volunteers on September 7, 1862; and at the bloody battle of Chancellorsville, where he was again wounded, he commanded a brigade of Berry's division of Sickles' III Corps. He was back on duty to exercise direction of his brigade in the fall of 1863 during the campaign of Mine Run, and the following spring was elevated to command of the 4th Division of Hancock's II Corps. At Spotsylvania it was charged that Mott's men had failed to support Upton's division of the VI Corps during the attack of May 10 against the Confederate works. (433) As a result, when George G. Meade proposed to Mott that his decimated division become a brigade of D. B. Birney's division, Mott bridled, but being assured that he would be mustered out of service otherwise, he accepted the demotion and went on to win new laurels. (434) After Birney was sent to Butler's Army of the James to assume command of

the X Corps, Mott took command of the 3rd Division, which included his own old troops, and led them in gallant style through the campaigns of Richmond and Appomattox. He was made a brevet major general of volunteers as of August 1, 1864, for services at the battle of the Petersburg Crater and on December 1, 1865, was appointed to the full rank, to date from May 26. General Mott declined a colonelcy in the regular service in 1868; meanwhile he secured a position as paymaster of the Camden & Amboy Railroad (now part of the Pennsylvania). He subsequently occupied a number of state offices, including that of commander of the New Jersey National Guard, until his death in New York City on November 29, 1884. He was buried in Riverview Cemetery, Trenton.

Joseph Anthony Mower was born on August 22, 1827, in Woodstock, Vermont. The family moved to Lowell, Massachusetts, however, when he was six. He was educated in the public schools of Lowell and at Norwich Academy in his native state. He worked as a carpenter for a brief time until he entered the army during the Mexican War as a private, serving until 1848. Seven years later, Mower, who had always desired a military career, was appointed a second lieutenant of the 1st U. S. Infantry. During the Civil War he made a magnificent record as regimental, brigade, divisional, and corps commander successively. Elected colonel of the 11th Missouri (Union) Infantry in May, 1862 (a state in which he had served since the beginning of the war), he was promoted to brigadier general on March 16, 1863, and to major general on August 12, 1864. By the end of the war he had been brevetted for gallantry through all grades to that of major general in the regular service. In the meantime, he fought at the battle of Iuka and at Corinth where he was

wounded, captured, escaped, and recaptured. Next he directed a brigade of W. T. Sherman's XV Corps in the Vicksburg campaign. He accompanied N. P. Banks on the ill-fated campaign up Red River, led the attacking column into Fort De Russy, and commanded the rear guard at Yellow Bayou during the retreat. Soon after he was given command of a division, Sherman stated that he was "the boldest young soldier we have." (435) At this time Sherman was forty-four, Mower thirty-six. Mower served with Sherman in Georgia and the Carolina campaign after taking part against Sterling Price in the latter's "invasion of Missouri" in the early part of 1864. After join-

ing Sherman in November, 1864, during the "March to the Sea," Mower commanded a division; during the long march northward from Savannah, which would terminate on Pennsylvania Avenue in Washington, he had charge of the XX Corps, directing them with great distinction in Slocum's Army of Georgia. Upon the reorganization of the regular service in July, 1866, Mower was given command of the newly authorized 39th Regiment of colored troops and was transferred in 1869 to the 25th Infantry, another colored regiment. He died of pneumonia in New Orleans on January 6, 1870, while commanding the Department of Louisiana. He was buried in Arlington National Cemetery.

James Nagle, colonel of four different Pennsylvania regiments and twice a brigadier general, was born in Reading, Pennsylvania, April 5, 1822. After receiving the

rudiments of an education in the Reading schools, he moved with his parents to Pottsville in 1835. Here he followed his father's trade of painter and paperhanger, at the same time participating in the state militia. In 1842 he organized the "Washington Artillery," which he led to the Mexican War as a captain of the 1st Pennsylvania. He served with Winfield Scott's army from Vera Cruz to Mexico City, was mustered out in 1848, and upon his return home was presented with a sword by the citizens of Schuylkill County. Early in 1861 Nagle became colonel of the 6th Pennsylvania Volunteers, a regiment not mustered into Federal service but which took part in Robert Patterson's unfortunate campaign in the Shenandoah. After his muster-out following the battle of First Manassas, he recruited and organized the 48th Pennsylvania Infantry. At the battle of Groveton on August 29, 1862, Nagle commanded a brigade of three regiments, including his own, in Reno's detachment of the IX Corps; he lost 531 men killed, wounded, and missing. (436) He was appointed brigadier general on September 10 and fought at South Mountain and Sharpsburg. At the latter battle his brigade, increased to four regiments, took part in the assault on Burnside's Bridge. At Fredericksburg the brigade, now counting six regiments, lost 522 of 2,700 effectives. (437) Nagle's appointment as brigadier expired on March 4, 1863, for want of Senate confirmation; he was reappointed, however, on March 23 to rank from March 13. He served with his brigade in Kentucky until failing health compelled his resignation on May 9, 1863. During the Get-

tysburg campaign he organized a regiment of ninety-day Pennsylvania militia, named the 39th Pennsylvania Infantry, which served from July 4 until August 2, 1863; then in 1864 he organized another regiment of hundred-day militia, the 194th Pennsylvania, which guarded the approaches to Baltimore during Jubal Early's raid on Washington; he was mustered out for the last time on November 5, 1864. Less than two years later, August 22, 1866, General Nagle died in Pottsville at the age of forty-four. He was buried there in Presbyterian Cemetery.

Henry Morris Naglee, born in Philadelphia on January 15, 1815, was graduated from West Point in the class of 1835. He submitted his resignation from the army soon after and engaged in civil engineering in New York State until the beginning of the Mexican War when he led a company of the 1st New York Volunteers for more than two years in

California and Lower California. Thereafter, he made his home in San Francisco where he was in the banking business. When the Civil War broke out, Naglee was reappointed in the Regular Army as lieutenant colonel of the newly authorized 16th Infantry, but resigned on January 10, 1862, before joining his regiment, in order to accept an appointment as brigadier general of volunteers on February 12, 1862. During the first winter of the war he served in the Washington defenses, and in George B. McClellan's Peninsular campaign he directed a brigade of Keyes's IV Corps. Upon the retirement of the Army of the Potomac from the vicinity of Richmond, Naglee was retained in the departments of North and South Carolina, and Virginia and North Carolina. In the summer of 1863 Naglee was in command of the District of Virginia at Norfolk, his superior being General John G. Foster at Fort Monroe. At this juncture it appears that General Naglee fell out with Governor Francis Harrison Pierpont of the "Restored Government of Virginia," (438) who demanded that all property owned by persons who should be unwilling to take the oath of allegiance not only to the United States but to the restored government should be forfeited and confiscated. This extreme measure Naglee refused to countenance. Accordingly, he was relieved from his command on September 23, 1863, and ordered to Cincinnati to await orders to join U. S. Grant's Army of Tennessee. The orders, of course, never came; and on April 4, 1864, General Naglee was honorably mustered out of service. In the years thereafter the general contin-

ued in the banking business and became interested in the growing of wine grapes at San Jose where he lived in his later years. He died in the Occidental Hotel in San Francisco, March 5, 1886, while paying a visit to his doctor; he was buried in Laurel Hill Cemetery.

James Scott Negley was born in a hamlet near Pittsburgh on December 22, 1826. He was educated in public schools and at Pitt University, then known as the Western

University of Pennsylvania, from which he was graduated in 1846. The same year he went to the Mexican War as a private in Company K, 1st Pennsylvania, serving for more than eighteen months. Soon after he became well known in the field of gardening, meantime maintaining an interest in military affairs by a continuing association with the local militia. He rose to brigadier general of the 18th Division and in 1861 was put in charge

341

of organizing and equipping volunteers in the Pittsburgh area. That summer he served under the unlucky Robert Patterson as a brigadier general of Pennsylvania volunteers, and on February 6, 1862, Negley was appointed a brigadier general of U. S. Volunteers to rank from the preceding October 1. Meanwhile he had been sent to Kentucky and served with D. C. Buell's army until the fall of 1862, when Braxton Bragg invaded Kentucky. Buell marched northward, leaving Negley to defend Nashville. At the battle of Murfreesboro, or Stone's River, Negley commanded a division under G. H. Thomas and was promoted major general for his able services. His capabilities were again demonstrated during W. S. Rosecrans' brilliant maneuvers which drove Bragg's men from the state of Tennessee. At the critical battle of Chickamauga, however, on September 19 and 20, 1863, he became the center of a controversy which would all but end his military career. Negley was bitterly castigated by his fellow division commanders, John M. Brannan of his own corps and Thomas J. Wood of the XXI Corps, for his performance while commanding the 2nd Division of Thomas' XIV Corps. (439) Although he was subsequently cleared by a board of inquiry of the charges of cowardice and desertion of his command leveled against him, he was never again assigned to the direction of troops in the field. After many months of inactivity, he resigned in January, 1865, declaring for the rest of his life that the treatment accorded him sprang from discrimination practiced by West Pointers against civilian officers.

Following his resignation, General Negley returned to Pittsburgh, and in 1868 was elected to Congress on the Republican ticket. In the years which followed he was reelected three times and defeated twice. In the interval he became associated with various utility, traction, and railroad interests in the New York area. He died in Plainfield, New Jersey, August 7, 1901, and was buried in Allegheny Cemetery, Pittsburgh.

Thomas Hewson Neill, a native of Philadelphia, was born April 9, 1826. He received his early education in the local public schools and then spent two years at the Univer-

sity of Pennsylvania, leaving at the end of his sophomore year to accept an appointment to West Point. He was graduated in the class of 1847, ranking twenty-seventh out of thirty-eight members. Neill did not take part in the Mexican War and until the outbreak of the Civil War was mainly employed on frontier duty with the 5th Infantry, except for three years he served as an instructor at the Military Academy. During the early months of the war he served on the upper Potomac as adjutant to Major General George Cadwalader, but in February, 1862, was commissioned colonel of the 23rd Pennsylvania, a command which he led throughout the Peninsular campaign in Darius N. Couch's division of Keyes's IV Corps. He was advanced to brigade command after Sharpsburg (a battle in which his regiment did not participate), directed the 3rd Brigade of Howe's VI Corps's division at Fredericksburg, and was appointed brigadier general of volunteers on April 15, 1863, to rank from November 29 1862. In the campaign of Chancellorsville he took part in John Sedgwick's operations against Marye's Heights and distinguished himself the next day at Salem Church. The VI Corps was in reserve at Gettysburg and saw little action, but the following autumn his brigade was engaged at Rappahannock Station and in the Mine Run campaign. At the battle of the Wilderness, which inaugurated U. S. Grant's campaign against Richmond, Neill, after the wounding of George W. Getty, succeeded to the command of the 2nd Division of the corps which he directed at Spotsylvania, the crossing of the North Anna, Cold Harbor, and the initial actions in front of Petersburg. After a short tour on the staff of the XVIII Corps, he joined Philip Sheridan in the Shenandoah early in September, serving as acting inspector general on the latter's staff until December, after which he seems to have been unemployed. (440) Brevetted major general in the volunteers and brigadier general in the Regulars, Neill reverted to the grade of major of infantry in the latter service in 1866. He transferred to the cavalry in 1870 and after four years as commandant of cadets at West Point was appointed colonel of the 8th Cavalry in 1879. He was then stationed at various points in Texas until his retirement "for disability contracted in line of duty" in 1883. General Neill died in Philadelphia March 12, 1885, and was buried at West Point.

William Nelson, member of an old Kentucky family intimate with the Clays, the Crittendens, and the Breckinridges, was born near Maysville, Kentucky, September 27, 1824. He attended Norwich Academy (now Norwich University) in Vermont from 1837 to 1839. Aside from the tragic circumstances which surrounded his death, his chief distinction lies in the fact that he was

the only naval officer, Union or Confederate, to become a full-rank Civil War major general. Nelson was appointed midshipman in 1840, served in the fleet which supported Winfield Scott's landing at Vera Cruz in 1847, and by 1855 had reached the grade of lieutenant. This was a relatively much higher grade than it is today, since he was then ranked only by the 164 men ahead of him on the lieutenants' roster, by 97 commanders and by 68 captains. (441) In early 1861 Nelson, whose brother Thomas had just been appointed United States minister to Chile by his old friend President Lincoln, made several surveys of political sentiment in Kentucky and reported his findings directly to the President. In April Lincoln sent him into the state to recruit for the Union, and he established Camp Dick Robinson in Garrard County, a rallying place for loyal Kentuckians. He was made brigadier general of volunteers on September 16, 1861. Nelson's first important field service came at Shiloh in April, 1862, when the leading brigades of his division of D. C. Buell's Army of the Ohio arrived on the field in the nick of time to repel the almost victorious Confederates and to participate in the Union counterattack of the next day. He then took part in the snail-like advance upon Corinth under Henry W. Halleck and in Buell's advance upon Chattanooga; he was promoted major general on July 19, 1862, to rank from the seventeenth. The same month he was detached from Buell's column and sent to Nashville and then into Kentucky to oppose the invading Confederates under Braxton Bragg and E. Kirby Smith. At

Richmond, Kentucky, August 30, 1862, Nelson was badly defeated by Kirby Smith's forces: he was slightly wounded himself and lost over 5,300 men, his trains, nine pieces of artillery, and 10,000 stand of small arms, whereas the Confederate loss numbered only 451 killed, wounded, and missing. (442) A month later Nelson was shot down in the Galt House in Louisville by a fellow-officer, Brigadier General Jefferson C. Davis, who felt he had been insulted on a prior occasion and whose face had been slapped a few moments before by Nelson. (443) He expired in a few minutes, and his remains now lie in Maysville. (444)

John Newton, whose ancestors had lived in Norfolk, Virginia, for almost two centuries, was born there August 25, 1822. (445) He was the son of Thomas Newton, who represented his district in Congress for twenty-nine years. He was graduated second in the class of 1842,

which included such illustrious names as W. S. Rosecrans, G. W. Smith, Mansfield Lovell, A. P. Stewart, John Pope, Seth Williams, Abner Doubleday, D. H. Hill, George Sykes, R. H. Anderson, Lafayette McLaws, Earl Van Dorn, and James Longstreet—to name only the more prominent. Assigned to the Corps of Engineers, his antebellum service was entirely in that branch. His only field service was in the Mormon Expedition of 1858. Newton was made a brigadier general of volunteers on September 23, 1861, and during the ensuing winter employed his acknowledged talents on the Washington defenses. As George B. McClellan's Peninsular campaign got under way, Newton transferred from staff to line and commanded a brigade of Slocum's division of the VI Corps there and in the Maryland campaign, which culminated in the drawn battle of Sharpsburg. Shortly afterward Newton was assigned to divisional command and at Fredericksburg suffered only nominal losses in the course of a fight which was a bloody repulse for the Federals. At this juncture he took it upon himself, along with others, to express directly to President Lincoln his distrust of Ambrose E. Burnside, who was commanding the Army of the Potomac. As a result of this he was included in the list of seven generals whom Burnside wished dismissed as a condition of his remaining in command. Lincoln relieved Burnside instead, but Newton's subsequent testimony before the Joint Congressional Committee on the Conduct of the War on this matter seems to have militated against the confirmation of his appointment as

major general of volunteers, a grade to which he was advanced on March 30, 1863. (446) Certainly his accomplishments on the field of battle left little to be desired. He was conspicuous in storming Marye's Heights at Fredericksburg during the campaign of Chancellorsville, and at Gettysburg he was selected by George G. Meade to direct the I Corps after the death of John F. Reynolds, even though he belonged to a different corps. After the corps was broken up and reassigned, he went to the western army under Sherman and served with distinction in the Atlanta campaign in command of a division in Howard's IV Corps of the Army of the Cumberland. After the fall of Atlanta proper Newton commanded the District of West Florida until war's end. His substantive grade of major general of volunteers was revoked as of April 18, 1864; at the end of the war, however, he was brevetted major general in both the regular and volunteer services. In the postbellum years he had a most distinguished career in the Corps of Engineers, becoming Chief of Engineers with rank of brigadier general on March 6, 1884. During this period his most notable exploit was the removal by blasting of two of the major hazards to navigation in New York's East River—a project in which he was aided by the ex-Confederate major general, Mansfield Lovell. General Newton was retired in 1886 and died at his New York residence May 1, 1895. He was buried at West Point.

Franklin Stillman Nickerson was born in Swanville, Maine, August 27, 1826. He was educated at the

345

academy in East Corinth, Maine, and thereafter studied law. This led him into a career in the U. S. Customs Service of which he became an official prior to the Civil War. When the 4th Maine Infantry was organized at Rockland on June 15, 1861, he was elected its major and in September was made lieutenant colonel. Meanwhile, he had been cited for his conduct at First Manassas by Colonel (later General) O. O. Howard, his brigade commander. On November 25, 1861, Nickerson was appointed colonel of the 14th Maine, a regiment which was organized during the winter and which was at once sent to the Department of the Gulf under General Benjamin F. Butler. In August, 1862, he aided in repulsing John C. Breckinridge's attack on Baton Rouge and was commended in effusive terms by Butler. The following March 16 he was promoted to brigadier general to rank from November 29, 1862. During the balance of the war General Nickerson's service was entirely in Louisiana under a succession of commanders. In the Red River campaign his brigade of Grover's division was a part of Franklin's XIX Corps, but two of his regiments were on veteran furlough, and the brigade seems to have been used in support in the neighborhood of Alexandria, Louisiana. Next, N. P. Banks ordered him to report to General Edward R. S. Canby. A few days later on July 22, 1864, by order of Canby, Nickerson was relieved from duty in the Department of the Gulf and ordered to report to the adjutant general in Washington for duty. At this juncture General Nickerson's name disappears from the *Official Records,* and it must be assumed that he was either on leave awaiting orders until the end of the war or was performing desk duty in Washington. In 1865 he tendered his resignation which was accepted as of May 13, 1865. Afterwards he took up residence in Boston, where he was to live for another half-century. Until 1905 he engaged in active practice as a lawyer; after this he seems to have resided with a son, in whose home he died on January 23, 1917, at the age of ninety-one. He was entombed in Forest Hills Crematory in Jamaica Plain, a Boston suburb. Only nine general officers of full rank in the Union army survived him, yet General Nickerson's death notices were obscured in the press by the news of events leading up to the entry of the United States into World War I.

Richard James "Uncle Dick" Oglesby was born in Oldham County, Kentucky, July 25, 1824. Orphaned at the age of nine, he later averred that the sale of the family slaves at that time made him an abolitionist. He then went to Decatur, Illinois, to live with an uncle. His early education was of the most rudimentary sort, and he was soon occupied as farmhand, rope-

maker, and carpenter. Savings from the earnings of these occupations enabled him to study law in Springfield. He gained admission to the bar just before the Mexican War in which he served as a lieutenant of Illinois volunteers. After the war Oglesby resumed his law practice, joined the California gold rush, spent almost two years in travel abroad, joined the Republican party at its formation, ran for Congress in 1858, and was elected to the Illinois senate in 1860. The following spring he resigned to accept a commission as colonel of the 8th Illinois Infantry and distinguished himself in command of a brigade of McClernand's division at

Forts Henry and Donelson. He was made brigadier general on March 22, 1862, and in October at the battle of Corinth, where his brigade was a part of T. A. Davies' division of the Army of West Tennessee, he was so severely wounded that he was unfit for duty until April, 1863. In the meantime he was promoted major general on March 10, 1863, to rank from the preceding November 29. He commanded a division and at times the left wing of the XVI Corps in west Tennessee and north Mississippi until he resigned from the service on May 26, 1864, in order to run for governor of Illinois on the Republican ticket. He was duly elected by a large majority in November. An ardent supporter of Lincoln's war policies, he later supported the Radical faction against Andrew Johnson. After his term ended in 1869, he practiced law until 1872 when a bargain was struck whereby Oglesby ran again for governor, but turned the office over to the lieutenant governor immediately after inauguration in return for a seat in the U. S. Senate. He declined reelection to the Senate in 1879, but in 1884 was reelected governor for the third time, becoming the first man in Illinois history to serve three times as governor. Failing in a bid for reelection to the Senate in 1891, General Oglesby spent his remaining years in retirement at his home, Oglehurst, in Elkhart, Illinois, where he died April 24, 1899. He was buried in Elkhart Cemetery.

John Morrison Oliver was born September 6, 1828, in Penn Yan, New York. He was educated at St. John's College on Long Island, and

campaign Oliver commanded the 3rd Brigade of Harrow's division of the XV Corps until, on August 4, 1864, it was discontinued and its troops transferred to the 1st Brigade. On the celebrated "March to the Sea" from Atlanta to Savannah, Oliver was again in brigade command, this time directing the 3rd Brigade of Hazen's division of the corps. He continued in this duty throughout the Carolina campaign and was officially promoted brigadier general of volunteers on January 12, 1865. After the termination of hostilities he commanded the division of which his brigade had been a part, first at Louisville and then at Little Rock, and was mustered out on August 24, 1865, with the brevet of major general for "faithful, efficient, and gallant service during the war." General Oliver then practiced law in Little Rock for a time prior to his appointment as assessor of internal revenue there. Later President Grant made him superintendent of postal service in the Southwest, and he moved to Washington. He resigned this position in 1871 because of ill health and for the same reason declined an appointment as associate justice of the District of Columbia supreme court. He died in Washington, March 30, 1872, and is buried in Lake View Cemetery, Penn Yan.

subsequently moved to Monroe, Michigan, where he engaged in business as a pharmacist and, when court was in session, served as recorder. On April 17, 1861, he enlisted as a private and was promoted first lieutenant in the 4th Michigan Infantry on June 20, captain on September 25, and colonel of the 15th Michigan on March 13, 1862. He was cited for "conspicuous gallantry" at Shiloh by General Alexander McD. McCook, where the 15th Michigan, although belonging to the "Unassigned Troops" of U. S. Grant's Army of the Tennessee, fought, at Oliver's request, in Rouseau's brigade of McCook's division of D. C. Buell's Army of the Ohio. (447) He commanded a brigade of the Army of West Tennessee at the battle of Corinth, but reverted to regimental command during the Vicksburg campaign in which the 15th Michigan served in Washburn's detachment of the XVI Corps. During the Atlanta

Emerson Opdycke, whose baptismal name seems to have been Samuel Emerson Opdycke, (448) was born on his father's farm in Hubbard township, Trumbull County, Ohio, January 7, 1830. His father had served in the War of 1812, whereas his grandfather was a captain of New Jersey militia in the

348

Revolutionary War. In 1837 the family moved to Williams County, Ohio; Opdycke himself, however, returned to Trumbull County in 1847 and made his home with a married sister in Warren. During the gold-rush days he twice went to California, but ultimately settled in Warren where he engaged in the mercantile business and became thoroughly indoctrinated with abolitionist teachings. He enlisted immediately after First Manassas and was mustered in on August 26, 1861, as a first lieutenant of the 41st Ohio. Opdycke proved to be one of those rare volunteer officers plucked from civilian life who worked at his new profession. His colonel was William B. Hazen, a Regular Army officer who conducted a class of instruction for his regimental subordinates; Opdycke consistently stood first in this class. He was soon detailed to instruct other officers in his brigade and was promoted captain on January 9, 1862. After serv-

ice at Shiloh, where his conduct was favorably noticed, he resigned in September, 1862, in order to help recruit the 125th Ohio of which he became lieutenant colonel on October 1, 1862, and colonel on January 14, 1863. The 125th Ohio was a tower of strength at Chickamauga on the famous Horseshoe Ridge; and at Chattanooga, Opdycke commanded a half-brigade which was one of the first commands to reach the summit of Missionary Ridge. During the Atlanta campaign Opdycke rendered distinguished service at Rocky Face Ridge, at Resaca where he was badly wounded, and at Kennesaw Mountain where he led an assault of a IV Corps brigade on the rocky and wooded heights. He commanded another brigade of the same corps from August, 1864, until the close of the war, especially distinguishing himself at the battle of Franklin, Tennessee, where his brigade, in reserve behind the Carter house, threw back the penetration of the Federal line made by the Confederates under P. R. Cleburne and J. C. Brown. For his services here he received the brevet of major general of volunteers and tardily on July 26, 1865, was given the full rank of brigadier. After the war General Opdycke lived in New York, where he engaged in the wholesale dry goods business. On April 22, 1884, he accidentally shot himself in the abdomen while cleaning a pistol; he died three days later of peritonitis. His remains were sent to Warren for burial in Oakwood Cemetery.

Edward Otho Cresap Ord was born in Cumberland, Maryland, October 18, 1818, but when he was a year old, his parents moved to Washington where he received his early education, much of it from his father. (449) He demonstrated great proficiency in mathematics and at the early age of sixteen received an appointment to West Point from which he was graduated in 1839.

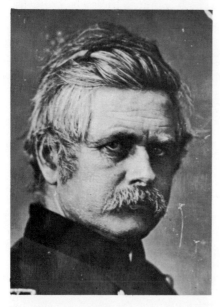

His first field service was against the perennially troublesome Florida Seminoles; then he was on duty in California during the Mexican War and in the meantime was advanced in rank from second lieutenant to captain. In the interval before the Civil War, Ord was on Indian duty in the Pacific Northwest; in 1859, however, chancing to be stationed at Fort Monroe, he participated in the expedition which suppressed John Brown's raid on Harpers Ferry. In 1861 he was again in California, where he was appointed a brigadier general of volunteers on September 14, 1861, and ordered East. During the first winter of the war he commanded a brigade on the right of the Washington defenses and saw his first action at Dranesville against Jeb Stuart. On May 3, 1862, Ord was appointed major general and ordered to the Western theater, where he won the regular brevet of colonel for "gallant and meritorious services" at Iuka—even though he was not present at the battle, not even within the sound of it. (450) A few days later, however, he performed good service by roughing up Van Dorn's Confederates who were falling back after their abortive assault on Corinth. He was severely wounded in this encounter and did not return to field duty until June, 1863, when he took part in the Vicksburg campaign as commander of the XIII Corps. Subsequently, he had commands in Louisiana and in the Shenandoah, was assigned the VIII Corps, and finally the XVIII Corps in the operations before Richmond. During the successful attack on Fort Harrison in September, 1864, Ord was again seriously wounded and did not resume command until January, 1865, when he took charge of the Army of the James and the Department of North Carolina, both formerly under Benjamin F. Butler. After the surrender at Appomattox, General Ord commanded various military departments, was made a brigadier general in the Regular Army as of July 26, 1866, and was retired as a major general in 1881. While on a ship bound from New York to Vera Cruz, he was stricken with yellow fever and died in Havana on July 22, 1883. He was buried in Arlington National Cemetery.

William Ward Orme was born in Washington, D. C., February 17, 1832, and was educated at Mount

St. Mary's College in Emmittsburg, Maryland. He went west in 1849 and after a short stay in Chicago, where he worked as a bank messenger, he moved to Bloomington, Illinois. At the age of twenty Orme was admitted to the bar and in 1853 became a partner of Leonard Swett, one of Lincoln's intimates. (By virtue of this partnership he became a favorite of Lincoln, who is said to have regarded him as the most promising young lawyer in the state.) In 1861 he was a delegate to the Illinois constitutional convention, and when the 94th Illinois Infantry was organized at Bloomington on August 20, 1862, Orme was elected its colonel. His first fight was at Prairie Grove, Arkansas, in December, where he led a brigade of Herron's division and was extolled by his superior for being "in the thickest of the fight, performing his duties with great gallantry." On March 13, 1863, he was promoted brigadier general to

rank from November 29, 1862, and with his command joined U. S. Grant's army in front of Vicksburg on June 11, 1863, along with the other brigade of Herron's division. In this unhealthy clime he contracted the tubercular condition which would ultimately cause his death. In November, General Orme was detailed to the inspection of various prison camps in New York, Pennsylvania, Ohio, Indiana, and Illinois and the following month was assigned to command of the post of Chicago, which carried with it supervision of Camp Douglas and its thousands of Confederate prisoners-of-war. A steady decline in his physical condition finally compelled his resignation from the army on April 20, 1864. At this juncture Lincoln arranged for Orme's appointment as supervising special agent of the Treasury Department at Memphis, a post which he held until his resignation in November, 1865. He went home to Bloomington, and after lingering for ten months, died on September 13, 1866. He was buried in Bloomington Cemetery. (451)

Thomas Ogden Osborn was born in the central Ohio hamlet of Jersey on August 11, 1832. He was graduated from Ohio University at Athens (not to be confused with Ohio State University at Columbus) in 1854, and then read law in the Crawfordsville, Indiana, office of the future Union general, Lew Wallace. Osborn began his law practice in Chicago in 1858, but with the outbreak of war in 1861 turned his attenton to recruiting the 39th Illinois Infantry, grandiosely styled the "Yates Phalanx" in honor of the governor.

He was appointed lieutenant colonel of this regiment on October 11, 1861, and colonel the following January 1. It was his fortune in the first years of the war to take a rather limited part in a series of relatively unimportant theaters, much of the time in command of his regiment but also directing a brigade of the XVIII Corps. However, in May, 1864, he lost the use of his right arm in Benjamin F. Butler's attack on Drewry's Bluff, and in the course of the siege of Petersburg he commanded a brigade of the XXIV Corps, Army of the James. On April 2, 1865, as the Federals finally penetrated R. E. Lee's lines, Osborn's brigade played an important part in the capture of Fort Gregg. He was brevetted brigadier and major general of volunteers and on May 1, 1865, was given the full rank of brigadier general. He then returned to his Chicago law practice; was Cook County treasurer from 1867 until 1869; served on the board of the National Home for Disabled Volunteers; spent a year in Texas investigating depredations committed by Indian and white renegades based on the Mexican side of the Rio Grande, and in 1874 was appointed minister to Argentina. Six years later his efforts and those of his opposite number in Santiago, Thomas Andrew Osborn (no relation), brought about a settlement of the long-standing Patagonian boundary dispute between Argentina and Chile. (The treaty was negotiated and ratified entirely by telegraph since no railroad existed at the time over the Andes.) Osborn received the official thanks of the Argentine government for his services. He resigned his post in 1885, but remained in South America, interesting himself in various railroad projects, one of which linked Paraguay and Bolivia. In 1890 General Osborn returned to Chicago and at the same time retired from business. He died on a visit to Washington, March 27, 1904, and was buried in Arlington National Cemetery.

Peter Joseph Osterhaus, certainly the most distinguished of the foreign-born officers who served the Union, was born in Coblenz, Germany (then Prussia) on January 4, 1823. Ninety-four years later, on January 2, 1917, just three months before the United States declared war on Germany and while Osterhaus was the recipient of a pension as a brigadier general in the United States Army, he died in nearby Duisburg. In the intervening years he had a notable and romantic career. After receiving a military education he became embroiled in the revolutions which swept Europe in 1848 and the following year was forced to flee to the United States. He settled first in Belleville, Illinois, where he was employed as a clerk. Later he removed to Lebanon, Illinois, and then to St. Louis, Missouri, whose large German population not only made him welcome but provided a springboard for his later military

career. Osterhaus entered the Civil War April 27, 1861, as a major of a Missouri battalion mustered into Federal service. He fought at Wilson's Creek in August with this battalion and in December was made colonel of the 12th Missouri (Union) Infantry. His next important encounter was at the battle of Elkhorn Tavern, or Pea Ridge, Arkansas, where he commanded a division of Curtis' forces. In June, 1862, he was appointed a brigadier general of volunteers, and during the Vicksburg campaign under U. S. Grant and W. T. Sherman he directed a division and was wounded at Big Black River. At Chatta-

nooga, Osterhaus served under Joseph Hooker and on the day of the assault upon Missionary Ridge performed magnificently as his command drove Braxton Bragg's men from the southern end of the ridge. In the subsequent Atlanta campaign he was made a major general on July 23, 1864, despite Sherman's opposition, the latter alleging Osterhaus' absence from the army seeking rank. He went through Georgia with Sherman and in the campaign of the Carolinas commanded for a time Logan's XV Corps. After the Civil War Osterhaus alternated his residence between France, where he served as United States consul in Lyons, and St. Louis, where he engaged in the wholesale hardware business. In his later years he again served in the United States consular service in Germany, and by act of Congress on March 17, 1905, he was placed on the retired list of the army as a brigadier general. He was buried in Coblenz.

Joshua Thomas Owen, nicknamed "Paddy" despite his birth in Caermarthen, Wales, on March 29, 1821, was brought to the United States by his parents at the age of nine. In 1845 he was graduated from Jefferson College in Canonsburg, Pennsylvania; he then engaged in teaching with his brother in the Chestnut Hill Academy and in the practice of law. He was a member of the Pennsylvania legislature from 1857 until 1859 and of the militia as a private in the 1st City Troop of Philadelphia. On May 8, 1861, he became colonel of the 24th Pennsylvania Volunteers—a ninety-day organization which was mustered into Federal service and stationed on the Potomac during the campaign of First Bull Run. He became colonel of the 69th Pennsylvania upon the muster-out of the 24th Pennsylvania and then "served in all the battles of the Army of the Potomac from Fair Oaks to Cold Harbor,

commanding a brigade part of the time and winning by gallant and meritorious conduct at Glendale promotion to the rank of brigadier general of volunteers, November 29, 1862." (452) That Owen took part in all the fights embraced by this eulogistic account is beyond cavil; however, the records exhibit that he was placed in arrest while the army was en route to Pennsylvania, (453) that his appointment as brigadier general on November 29, 1862, expired for want of confirmation, (454) and that his failure to support the brigade on his right at Cold Harbor in June, 1864, resulted in charges being placed against him for "disobedi-

ence of orders" by his division commander, John Gibbon. (455) In any event the affair was closed when he was honorably mustered out of service a month later. He returned to his home in Philadelphia, resumed his law practice, and acted as recorder of deeds there until 1871. In this year he founded the New York *Daily Register,* a law journal which became the official publication of the New York courts in 1873. He served as a member of the journal's editorial staff until his death at his home in Chestnut Hill (Philadelphia) on November 7, 1887. General Owen was buried in Laurel Hill Cemetery.

Charles Jackson Paine, great-grandson of a signer of the Declaration of Independence, was born August 26, 1833, in Boston. His early career was in the tradition of a New England scion of means: a primary education obtained at the Boston Latin School, graduation from

Harvard in 1853, the study of law in the office of the eminent Rufus Choate, admission to the bar, and extensive travel abroad. From 1858 until 1861 he practiced his profession in Boston; in September, 1861, he recruited a company of the 22nd Massachusetts Infantry with which he was mustered into service as captain on October 5, 1861. The regiment trained in the defenses of Washington that winter, and in January Paine served as major of the 30th Massachusetts for a couple of months until he was mustered out in March. (456) For the next two years he was in the Department of the Gulf and became colonel of the 2nd Louisiana, a Negro regiment recruited in New Orleans, on October 23, 1862. The following spring he fought most creditably at Port Hudson under the command of General N. P. Banks and led one of the assaults on the place. By the end of May, 1863, he was directing a brigade of the XIX Corps, and in November he assumed charge of a cavalry brigade in A. L. Lee's division. On March 8, 1864, Paine resigned his colonel's commission to accept a position on the staff of General Benjamin F. Butler, who secured his appointment as brigadier general of volunteers to rank from July 4, 1864. Paine took part in the attack on Drewry's Bluff; commanded a Negro division at New Market in September; was with Butler in his abortive attack on Fort Fisher; and served with W. T. Sherman in North Carolina as commander of the 3rd Division (Negro troops) of Terry's X Corps and later of the District of New Bern. He returned to civilian life with the brevet promotion of major general in 1866. Thereafter, he was

an important, if unheralded, power in the development of the United States railroad network: he was a director of the Santa Fe, the Burlington, and the Mexican Central railroads. In 1897 he was one of a three-member commission appointed by President McKinley to secure the international remonetization of silver. From the seventies until his death he was prominent in yachting circles, taking part on several occasions in defending the "America's Cup" and twice assuming the entire cost of the United States entries. He died in Weston, Massachusetts, August 12, 1916, and was buried in Mt. Auburn Cemetery, Cambridge.

Eleazer Arthur Paine, (457) a cousin of General Halbert E. Paine, was born September 10, 1815, in Parkman (a hamlet in Geauga County), Ohio. He was graduated from West Point in the class of 1839, and then served briefly on the staff of General Zachary Taylor in

the Seminole War before resigning his commission in 1840 to study law. After admission to the bar he practiced at Painesville, Ohio, from 1843 until 1848 and then at Monmouth, Illinois, until the outbreak of war in 1861. During his residence in Ohio he served as deputy United States marshal and as lieutenant colonel and brigadier general of militia. Paine, a personal friend of Lincoln, was appointed colonel of the 9th Illinois on July 26, 1861, and brigadier general of volunteers on September 3. He commanded a brigade at Paducah, Kentucky, in the fall of that year, and at Cairo, Illinois, in January and February, 1862, and the 4th Division of Pope's army in the operations against New Madrid, Island No. 10, Fort Pillow, and Memphis during March and April. In the course of the advance on Corinth after the battle of Shiloh, he continued to lead a division of the Army of the Mississippi; but seems to have rendered something less than entire satisfaction, since the balance of his duty was confined to rear echelons. General Paine was engaged in guarding the Louisville & Nashville Railroad from Mitchellville to Nashville from November, 1862, until May, 1864, and was in command of the District of Western Kentucky from July to September of 1864. Thereafter he was "awaiting orders" until he finally submitted his resignation, which was accepted to date from April 5, 1865. He returned to Monmouth and resumed his law practice. In his last years the General and his wife alternated their residence between their two daughters. While staying with the one who lived in Jersey City, New Jersey,

whose husband had died shortly before, Paine contracted pneumonia and died on December 16, 1882. He was interred, according to the local paper, in the same grave with his son-in-law in the burial ground of The Old Bergen Church in Jersey City. Because the grave is unmarked and the cemetery records have disappeared, the exact location is unknown. (458)

Halbert Eleazer Paine, was born in Chardon (Geauga County), Ohio, on February 4, 1826. Unlike his older cousin, Eleazer A. Paine, he did not attend West Point but was

graduated from Western Reserve University at Cleveland in 1845 and for a time taught school in Mississippi. He soon returned to Ohio, however, studied law, and after admission to the bar in 1848, began his practice in Cleveland. After moving to Milwaukee he formed, in 1857, a partnership with Carl Schurz, but left the practice to become colonel of the 4th Wisconsin Cavalry on July 2, 1861. Paine had a most distinguished military career even though he lost a leg in 1863 in one of the assaults upon Port Hudson during the campaign to open the Mississippi River. He offered the paradox of a dedicated abolitionist who on the one hand refused to return fugitive slaves to their masters, but on the other would not burn Baton Rouge, although expressly ordered to do so by his superior, Benjamin F. Butler. He was promoted to brigadier general on April 9, 1863; and after recuperating from his wound, he performed much valuable service, particularly during Jubal Early's raid on Washington in 1864. Paine had charge of the forces stationed between Forts Totten and Stevens at this time. Toward the end of the war he commanded the District of Illinois, and, after being brevetted major general for gallantry, he resigned his volunteer commission on May 15, 1865. He was immediately elected to Congress as a Republican and served three terms in support of the Radical faction. In his last term he was chairman of the powerful committee on elections which decreed the seating of representatives from the ex-Confederate states. In 1871 General Paine started a Washington law practice instead of standing for reelection. General Schurz, his old law partner who was now Secretary of the Interior, wished him to become his assistant; Paine declined but finally accepted appointment as Commissioner of Patents in 1878. In this capacity he introduced the use of typewriters into the Federal bureaucracy—a marked achievement for the time. After his resignation from this office in 1880 he compiled *A Treatise on the Law of Elections to Public Office,* presumably written to justify his own previous determinations while in Congress; it is now regarded as the authoritative work on the subject. General Paine died in Washington on April 14, 1905, and was buried in Arlington National Cemetery.

Innis Newton Palmer, a direct descendant of an Englishman who came to America in 1621, was born March 30, 1824, in Buffalo, New York. After attending the local schools he was appointed to West

Point and was graduated in 1846 along with George B. McClellan, Darius N. Couch, Stonewall Jackson, and George E. Pickett. Palmer served for nearly two years in Mexico as a lieutenant of mounted rifles and was twice brevetted for gallantry in action. Following the Mexican War his duty stations were almost entirely on the western frontier. When the 2nd Cavalry was authorized in 1855, Palmer became one of its captains and served under three officers who were to become celebrated figures in the Confederacy—A. S. Johnston, R. E. Lee, and W. J. Hardee. At the outbreak of the Civil War, Palmer succeeded to a majority in the 2nd Cavalry (changed to the 5th Cavalry in August, 1861) and was in command of the Regular Cavalry in the campaign of First Manassas; he was made a brigadier general of volunteers to rank from September 23, 1861. During the Peninsular campaign Palmer commanded a brigade of infantry in Couch's division of Keyes's IV Corps and fought creditably at Williamsburg, Seven Pines, Glendale, and Malvern Hill. That autumn he was engaged in organizing and sending to the front volunteer regiments from New Jersey and Delaware and in supervising the Philadelphia draft rendezvous. From December, 1862, until the end of the war he discharged various duties in the state of North Carolina—commanding at times a division of the XVIII Corps as well as the entire corps, the Department and District of North Carolina, the New Bern defenses, and the District of Beaufort. In 1865 he was awarded all the brevet ranks through brigadier in the Regular Army and major general in the volunteers. During the war General Palmer had become lieutenant colonel of the 2nd Cavalry and in 1868 succeeded to its colonelcy. The remaining years of his military life were spent primarily in the area now constituting the states of Wyoming and Nebraska; he also served on several cavalry boards. From 1876 until 1879 he was on

sick leave, and on March 20, 1879, was retired on his own application. More than twenty years of life remained to him, and these he spent in retirement in and near Washington. He died at Chevy Chase, Maryland, on September 9, 1900, and was buried in Arlington National Cemetery.

John McCauley Palmer—governor, Senator, major general, and presidential candidate—was born in Scott County, Kentucky, on September 13, 1817, but at the age of

fourteen moved to Illinois with his father, an antislavery Jacksonian Democrat. He attended Shurtleff College in Alton for two years before moving to Carlinville in 1839, where he read law and was admitted to the bar. Palmer's long and tortuous political career began in 1840 when he stumped for Martin Van Buren. In the years before the Civil War he consistently opposed the extension of slavery and served in the state senate as both a regular Democrat and an independent Democrat. In 1856, however, he was instrumental in the formation of the Illinois Republican party and ran for Congress in 1859 on the Republican ticket, but was defeated. The next year he was a delegate to the Chicago convention which nominated Abraham Lincoln. During the Civil War, Palmer was successively colonel of the 14th Illinois Infantry (May 25, 1861), brigadier general of volunteers (December 20, 1861), and major general (March 16, 1863 to rank from November 29, 1862). He commanded a division under John Pope at New Madrid and Island No. 10, a brigade during the advance on Corinth, and a division of Crittenden's Left Wing at Murfreesboro. Palmer was then promoted to the command of the XIV Corps which he led at Chattanooga and in the Atlanta campaign. In August, 1864, he was relieved from command at his own request by General W. T. Sherman as the result of a quibble over relative rank, an incident which did not reflect particularly favorably on him. (459) Later he had command of the Department of Kentucky. In 1868 Palmer was elected governor of Illinois on the Republican ticket, but in his inaugural address declared himself in favor of states' rights and the curtailment of Federal powers. By 1872 he was supporting Horace Greeley and the liberals against U. S. Grant and soon was back in the Democratic fold. In 1884 he was a delegate to the convention which nominated Grover Cleveland, in 1888 was defeated in a bid for the governorship, but in 1891 went to the U. S. Senate as a

Democrat. In 1896 he and ex-Confederate Lieutenant General Simon B. Buckner teamed up to run for president and vice-president as the candidates of the Gold Democrats who repudiated the free-silver doctrine of William Jennings Bryan. General Palmer died in Springfield on September 25, 1900, and was buried in Carlinville.

John Grubb Parke was born September 22, 1827, near Coatesville, Pennsylvania, but at the age of eight moved with his parents to Philadelphia. He attended the

academy of Samuel Crawford and the University of Pennsylvania and in 1845 entered West Point from which he was graduated in 1849, ranking second in the class. Parke's entire Regular Army career was in the Corps of Topographical Engineers and the Corps of Engineers (into which the former was merged in 1863), largely in survey work on the United States–Canada northwest boundary. During the Civil War, however, he demonstrated that he was an extremely competent troop commander. Returning from the Washington Territory to the East in October, 1861, he was made a brigadier general of volunteers on November 23 and assigned to the command of a brigade in Ambrose E. Burnside's North Carolina expedition. For his services in this first large-scale Union success, he was promoted major general on August 20, 1862, to rank from July 18. Meantime Parke served as Burnside's chief of staff in the Maryland campaign and at Fredericksburg. He commanded the IX Corps while Burnside was in charge of the Department of the Ohio and directed his men skillfully at Vicksburg and in the course of W. T. Sherman's subsequent capture of Jackson. He then took part in the Knoxville campaign against James Longstreet. In the spring of 1864 he again reported to Burnside as his chief of staff—Burnside's IX Corps at this time constituted an entity apart from the Army of the Potomac and reported directly to U. S. Grant by virtue of Burnside's seniority over George G. Meade. This awkward arrangement was terminated during the bloody Overland campaign against Richmond in which Parke did yeoman's work. After the debacle at the battle of The Crater, where Burnside's men failed to penetrate a huge gap in the Petersburg lines caused by the explosion of a mine, Burnside was relieved from command and succeeded by Parke. During the attack on Fort Stedman, March 25, 1865, Parke commanded the army in the temporary absence of Meade and moved quickly and

capably to repel the last tactical assault by Robert E. Lee's Army of Northern Virginia. For this service he was brevetted major general in the Regular Army. After the war he rose to the rank of colonel of engineers, and from 1887 until his retirement in 1889 he was superintendent of the Military Academy. He died in Washington, December 16, 1900, and was buried in the churchyard of St. James the Less in Philadelphia.

Lewis Baldwin Parsons was born April 5, 1818, in Perry in western New York State. When he was ten the family moved to St. Lawrence County. After he was graduated

from Yale in 1840, he conducted a school in Mississippi for a time, but returned North in order to study law at Harvard. He began his practice in Alton, Illinois, but moved to St. Louis in 1854, where he soon became chief executive officer of the Ohio & Mississippi Railroad (now a segment of the Baltimore and Ohio system). He resided in Cincinnati for several years as a consequence of this position, returning to St. Louis in 1860. The following year he served as volunteer aide to Frank Blair upon the occasion of the capture of the pro-Confederate Missouri militia camp under General D. M. Frost, and in October he was made an assistant quartermaster of volunteers with rank of captain. Parsons' entire contribution to the Union cause, and it was a most significant one, was as a master of transportation. Initially he had charge of all military river and rail transport in the vast Department of the Mississippi, which stretched from Montana to Pittsburgh and south to New Orleans. He remained in St. Louis until in August, 1864, he was given charge of all river and rail transportation in the armies of the United States with headquarters in Washington. Parson's services were invaluable—one of his exploits was the transfer of John M. Schofield's entire Army of the Ohio, with its artillery and trains, in January, 1864, from Mississippi to Washington in an average time of eleven days in an era when railroading was in its infancy. On May 11, 1865, he was commissioned brigadier general of volunteers, and on April 30, 1866—the day he was mustered out—he was brevetted major general. In 1875 General Parsons took up residence on a farm near Flora, Illinois, but in the next quarter-century was active as a director of several railroads and industrial corporations and as president of a bank in St. Louis. In 1880 he was the Democratic candidate for lieutenant governor of Illinois. General Parsons died in Flora on

March 16, 1907, and was buried in Bellefontaine Cemetery, St. Louis.

Marsena Rudolph Patrick, whose family arrived in America in the 1700's, was born near Watertown, New York, March 11, 1811. He ran away from home at an early age

and became successively, a canalboat driver, schoolteacher, medical student, and finally protégé of General Stephen van Renssalaer, who secured his admission to the Military Academy. He was graduated in 1835, ranked toward the bottom of a large class which included George Gordon Meade, and was posted to the 2nd Infantry. Patrick served for five years in the difficult and unrewarding Florida war against the Seminoles and for two years in the Mexican War. He was advanced to the rank of brevet major while he functioned as chief commissary to General John E. Wool's column in Chihuahua. He

361

resigned his commission in 1850 to engage in scientific farming at Geneva, New York. During the next decade he was instrumental in the promotion of the New York State Agricultural Society and the New York State Agricultural College, an antecedent of Cornell University. At the outbreak of the Civil War, Patrick became inspector general of the state of New York; he served in this position until March 20, 1862, when he was commissioned brigadier general of volunteers at the express request of General George B. McClellan. In the meantime he had served on the latter's staff as inspector general of New York volunteers. He commanded a brigade of Rufus King's division of McDowell's III Corps during the campaign of Second Manassas; then the division was transferred to Hooker's I Corps and engaged at South Mountain and Antietam. Soon thereafter McClellan, recognizing Patrick's outstanding capacity as a disciplinarian, appointed him provost marshal general of the Army of the Potomac— an office in which he was maintained by every successive army commander, including Ambrose E. Burnside, Joseph Hooker, and Meade. U. S. Grant ultimately made him provost marshal general of all the armies operating against Richmond, and on March 13, 1865, he received the brevet of major general. Despite a stern manner and a voice reminiscent of the proverbial bull of Bashan, General Patrick's kindheartedness toward the helpless and impoverished white Southerners in the District of Henrico (Richmond), which he commanded after the surrender, led to his relief. So obnoxious to him were

the Radical Republican policies that he was induced to run for office on the Democratic ticket. In his last years he was governor of the Soldiers' Home at Dayton, Ohio, where he died July 27, 1888. He was buried there in the Home Cemetery.

Francis Engle Patterson was born on May 7, 1821, in Philadelphia. (460) He was a son of General Robert Patterson, distinguished in the Mexican War but criticized for his activity during his brief appear-

ance in the Civil War, (461) and was a brother-in-law of General J. J. Abercrombie. Much overshadowed by his father in the war with Mexico, Francis Patterson nevertheless served as second lieutenant of the 1st (U. S.) Artillery; was promoted to first lieutenant in 1848; and, remaining in the regular service after the war, was promoted to be captain of the 9th Infantry on March 3, 1855. Two years later on May 1, 1857, he resigned his commission to return to civilian life. With the outbreak of the Civil War, however, he returned to the army as colonel of the 17th Pennsylvania, a ninety-day militia regiment. After some service as river guards on the Potomac line, the regiment was detailed to join General Robert Patterson's forces at Martinsburg, (West) Virginia, just prior to the battle of First Manassas and was mustered out on August 2. On April 15, 1862, Patterson was made a brigadier general of volunteers to rank from April 11. He commanded the 3rd Brigade of Hooker's division of Heintzelman's III Corps at Williamsburg and Seven Pines, although illness compelled him to relinquish his command during the fighting on June 1. The following November, Patterson was commanding his brigade of the same division, now under Daniel E. Sickles, stationed at Catlett's Station on the Orange & Alexandria Railroad. At this juncture he is said to have executed an unauthorized retreat because of a rumor, which proved groundless, of the presence of Confederate forces at Warrenton Junction. (462) Sickles' report is dated November 9, Heintzelman's endorsement recommending that "the matter be investigated" on November 11, and Ambrose E. Burnside's (commander of the army) on November 24. Meantime, on November 22, 1862, General Patterson "was found dead in his tent . . . killed by the accidental discharge of his own pistol." (463) The place of death is usually fixed at "Fairfax Court House" or "near Occoquan, Virginia." He was buried in Laurel Hill Cemetery, Philadelphia, on the lot with his father.

Gabriel René Paul, grandson of a Napoleonic officer who is said to have built the first house in St. Louis, (464) was born in that city on March 22, 1813. He was graduated from the Military Academy in the class of 1834. Most of his duty, preceding the Mexican War, was in the Southwest and against the Seminoles in Florida. During the war with Mexico he won the

brevet of major for gallant service at the storming of Chapultepec, a feat for which he was later presented with a sword by the citizens of St. Louis. Next he was stationed on the Indian frontier and was regularly promoted major of the 8th Infantry on April 22, 1861, while stationed at Albuquerque as acting inspector general of the Department of New Mexico. In December he was appointed colonel of the 4th New Mexico Infantry, a battalion which was later merged into the 1st New Mexico Cavalry. (465) The following spring, while Paul was in command of Fort Union and the District of Southern New Mexico, he backed up the field commanders who repelled the invasion led by Henry Sibley in his abortive attempt to win the territory for the Confederacy. In April he was promoted to lieutenant colonel, 8th Infantry, and on September 5, brigadier general of volunteers, an appointment which expired the following March for lack of confirmation by the Senate. He was reappointed April 18, 1863, and duly confirmed. (466) Paul commanded a brigade of four New York regiments in Doubleday's division of the I Corps at Fredericksburg and five New Jersey regiments of the same corps at Chancellorsville. On the first day of the crucial battle of Gettysburg, when the I Corps was all but destroyed and its commander killed, Paul, who was commanding a brigade of John C. Robinson's division, was severely wounded by a rifle ball which entered his right temple and passed out through his left eye. He was totally blinded and his senses of smell and hearing were greatly impaired. For his gallantry in attempting to rally a fragment of his command on this occasion, the 29th New Jersey presented him, blind and disabled though he was, with a "magnificent jeweled sword." After a partial recovery he attempted to discharge some nominal administrative duties, but was placed on the retired list as a brigadier general, U. S. Army, as of February 16, 1865. General Paul lived twenty more years; he died in Washington, May 5, 1886, and was buried in Arlington National Cemetery.

John James Peck was born in Manlius, New York, on January 4, 1821; received his elementary education in the local schools; and was graduated from West Point in 1843.

Exactly one-third of this class's thirty-nine members, including U. S. Grant, later became general officers in either the Federal or Confederate armies. After some garrison duty Peck served with great distinction in the Mexican War and was brevetted both captain and major for gallant and meritorious conduct. He resigned from the army in 1853 and at once commenced upon a financially rewarding business career in Syracuse, his wife's home. In the interval before the outbreak of the Civil War, Peck promoted a railroad, organized and managed a bank, served as president of the board of education, was twice nominated for Congress, and was a delegate to the Democratic

National Conventions of 1856 and 1860. On August 9, 1861, President Lincoln appointed him a brigadier general of volunteers, and in the course of the Peninsular campaign of the following spring he directed the 2nd Division of Keyes's IV Corps. On July 25, 1862, he was promoted to major general to rank from July 4, and commanded all Union troops in Virginia south of James River until September. The following spring, while commanding at Suffolk, Peck rendered his finest service to the Union cause by beating off the two Confederate divisions of John B. Hood and George E. Pickett, who were under the command of the celebrated General James Longstreet, in their attempt to envelop and capture the town. He was badly injured in this encounter, and after his recovery he directed affairs for a time in North Carolina, where little of consequence in a military sense occurred. On July 5, 1864, General Peck was assigned to the command of the Canadian frontier in the Department of the East and regulated intercourse with the British provinces until he was mustered out of service on August 24, 1865. He then returned to Syracuse and in 1867 organized the New York State Life Insurance Company, serving as its president for the remaining years of his life. Peck's health had been much undermined by illness and injuries received in two wars, and on April 21, 1878, he died at the comparatively early age of fifty-seven. He was buried in Oakwood Cemetery, Syracuse.

Galusha Pennypacker, the only general officer in the history of the U. S. Army who was not old enough to vote for or against the President who appointed him, was born near the site of the Revolutionary War encampment of Valley Forge in Chester County, Pennsylvania June 1, 1844. Both his father and grandfather had fought for their country, the former in Mexico, the latter against the British during the Revolution. Galusha was well educated in the private schools of the area in which he was born. When he was only sixteen he enlisted in the 9th Pennsylvania, a ninety-day

regiment of which he became quartermaster sergeant. He then recruited a company of the 97th Pennsylvania and was commissioned its captain on August 22, 1861, at the age of seventeen. He was promoted to major in October, and for some time thereafter served in the Department of the South, taking part in some minor operations in Florida and against the defenses of Charleston, South Carolina. In 1864 Pennypacker's regiment was transferred to Benjamin F. Butler's Army of the James. In this theater as a twenty-year-old colonel of volunteers he continued to demonstrate why he would one day be not only the youngest general officer ever appointed in the United States service but also the youngest colonel ever to command a regiment of the Regular Army. In the course of the various engagements in front of Petersburg, Pennypacker commanded a brigade of the XXIV Corps, was wounded four times, and took part in Butler's unsuccessful attempt to capture Fort Fisher in December and in its ultimate capture on January, 1865. General Alfred H. Terry called Pennypacker "the real hero of Fort Fisher" and stated that without his bravery the fort would not have been taken. He was desperately wounded in the assault and was hospitalized at Fort Monroe for ten months. On April 28, 1865, a month before his twenty-first birthday, Pennypacker was made brigadier general of volunteers to rank from February 18 and was brevetted major general as of March 13, 1865, and major general, U. S. Army in 1867. Upon the reorganization of the army in 1866 he became colonel of the 34th Infantry but transferred in 1869 to the 16th Infantry, which he commanded until his retirement in 1883. He served in the South until 1877 and then primarily on the western frontier until his retirement. In his later years he lived in Philadelphia, where he died on October 1, 1916. General Pennypacker was buried in the Philadelphia National Cemetery.

William Henry Penrose, son of an officer of the Regular Army, was born at Madison Barracks, Sacket's Harbor, New York, March 10, 1832. He took an irregular two-year course at Dickinson College,

Carlisle, Pennsylvania, and then moved to Michigan where he engaged in the profession of civil and mechanical engineering. At the outbreak of the Civil War in 1861, no doubt by virtue of his father's connection with the army, Penrose was appointed a second lieutenant of the 3rd U. S. Infantry. With promotion to first lieutenant on May 14, 1861, he served with his regiment until he was commissioned colonel of the 15th New Jersey Volunteers on April 18, 1863. In the interval he fought on the Peninsula, at Second Manassas in the brigade of Regulars, and at Fredericksburg and was favorably mentioned by his superiors for his conduct. At Chancellorsville, as colonel of the 15th New Jersey, he commanded his regiment and for a time the 1st Brigade of W. T. H. Brooks's division of the VI Corps in the assault and capture of Marye's Heights. He again directed his regiment at Gettysburg where the VI Corps was not heavily engaged. When the spring campaign of 1864 opened, Penrose was at the head of his regiment in the bloody battles of the Wilderness and Spotsylvania Court House where he succeeded to brigade command. In the Shenandoah Valley campaign directed by Philip Sheridan, Penrose again rendered distinguished service and received several brevet promotions for his conduct. He continued in command of the 1st Brigade of Wheaton's 2nd Division of the VI Corps until the surrender of the Army of Northern Virginia at Appomattox, and on June 27, 1865, was made a full brigadier general of volunteers. Penrose was mustered out of volunteer service in 1866 and languished as a captain of the 3rd Infantry for seventeen years. He was promoted to major in 1883, lieutenant colonel in 1888, and colonel of the 20th Infantry in 1893—thirty years after his accession to this rank as a volunteer. He transferred to the 16th Infantry the following year and was retired in 1896. He died of typhoid fever in Salt Lake City, Utah, on August 29, 1903, and is now buried in Arlington National Cemetery. (467)

John Smith Phelps, Congressman and governor of Missouri, is celebrated for his political acumen rather than for the brief period during which he occupied the rank of brigadier general of United

States volunteers. He was born in Simsbury, Connecticut, on December 22, 1814; was educated at what is now Trinity College in Hartford; studied law and was admitted to the bar. In 1838 Phelps moved to Springfield, Missouri, where he at once became not only financially successful but politically prominent. In 1844 he was elected to Congress, where he served continuously for eighteen years; he might have been speaker of the house in the late 1850's were it not for his Northern birth and his Union political convictions. Among his legislative achievements was the passage of the bill which introduced the three-cent stamp for first-class letter postage. Upon the outbreak of Civil War Phelps went home to Springfield and recruited "Colonel Phelps' Regiment," a six-month command which he led at the battle of Pea Ridge, or Elkhorn Tavern, in March, 1862. In July of that year President Lincoln appointed him military governor of Arkansas, and he was made brigadier general of volunteers on November 29 to rank from July 19. This appointment expired by law, however, on March 4, 1863, for lack of confirmation by the Senate. Prior to this time Phelps was addressed as and referred to as "Honorable John S. Phelps, Military Governor of Arkansas," rather than by his military title. (468) He resumed his law practice in 1864 and ran as a Democratic candidate for governor of Missouri in 1868, but was defeated mainly because of the wholesale proscription of Southern sympathizers under Missouri's recently adopted "Drake constitution." Eight years later, when the franchise had been substantially liberalized, Phelps unified the Northern and Southern factions of the party and was elected by a commanding majority. As his term ended four years later, the St. Louis *Globe Democrat* remarked on January 12, 1881, that "it will hardly be disputed that Missouri never had a better governor than John S. Phelps." Governor Phelps returned again to his law practice; he died in St. Louis on November 20, 1886. He was buried in Hazelwood Cemetery, Springfield, Missouri.

John Wolcott Phelps, who seems to have made a career of espousing either the right cause at the wrong time or vice versa, was born November 13, 1813, at Guilford, Vermont. After attending local schools, he was appointed to West Point in 1832 and was graduated in 1836. He took part in the Florida War of 1836-39 against the Creeks and Seminoles; was on duty on the Canadian frontier during

the border disturbances; and served at a number of garrison posts. He participated in the Mexican War and declined (for reasons not specified) the brevet commission of captain for his services, perhaps the only man ever to do so. (469) After a decade of further service on the Indian frontier he resigned in 1859 and devoted the next two years to inveighing in print against the institution of slavery and the Masonic order—both of which he abhorred with the zeal of a Crusader. He became colonel of the 1st Vermont on May 9, 1861, and brigadier general of volunteers on August 9, to rank from May 17. Phelps's regiment took and held Newport News for the defense of Hampton Roads and then was transferred to the Department of the Gulf under the command of General Benjamin F. Butler. Phelps commanded at Ship Island, the rendezvous for the Union army forces collected to force the opening of the Lower Mississippi. Subsequently, while in garrison at Camp Parapet on the outskirts of New Orleans, he organized the first Negro troops, an action promptly disavowed by the administration. He resigned in disgust on August 21, 1862, the same day that the Confederate government declared him an outlaw for having "organized and armed Negro slaves for military service against their masters. . . ." When the United States government finally came to a determination to enlist Negroes, it is said that Phelps declined a commission as a major general to command colored troops. (470)

He spent the rest of his life in Brattleboro, Vermont, where he continued to crusade for and against the causes near and dear to him. He was active in the Vermont Historical Society and the Vermont teachers' association until his death; wrote prolifically on a variety of subjects; and in 1880 ran for President on the Antimason ticket. He died in Guilford, February 2, 1885, and was buried there.

Abram Sanders Piatt, whose first name appeared as "Abraham" in the records of the War Department, was born in Cincinnati, on May 2, 1821. He was a brother of Donn Piatt, well-known journalist and author, and of Jacob Piatt, who as a Cincinnati councilman was the original advocate of the paid fire department. Abram received a classical education in the local academies and then devoted himself to farming in the Macacheek Valley, an occupation which he followed, with few interruptions, until his death. In 1846 he studied law for a time and edited the *Macacheek Press.*

At the beginning of the Civil War he recruited and became colonel of the 13th Ohio, a ninety-day regiment which did not leave the state, but on September 2 he was made colonel of the 34th Ohio, which spent the first winter of the war in the snowy mountains of West Virginia guarding the rear of W. S. Rosecrans' forces. Promoted brigadier general on April 30, 1862, Piatt commanded the only brigade of Sturgis' division to reach the front at Second Manassas and was warmly commended by John Pope in his report of the battle. This was something of a dubious honor in view of Pope's subsequent effort to discredit virtually everyone previously connected with George B. McClellan. During the Maryland campaign which followed, Piatt's brigade was detached in the Washington defenses. On December 13, 1862, at the battle of Fredericksburg, Piatt's horse fell with him, and the resulting back injury

369

caused him to turn over command of his brigade of Whipple's III Corps to his senior colonel. Presumably this injury brought about his resignation from the service, which was accepted as of February 17, 1863. He returned to his Ohio home and resumed farming. In 1877 labor unrest helped to create support for the Greenbackers who pressed for the free coinage of silver —a program irresistible to hard-pressed middle-western farmers. The Greenback-Labor ticket of 1878 polled more than a million votes in the presidential election and the following year narrowly missed electing Piatt governor of Ohio. He was for years a member of the Granger movement which advocated many of the reforms now existing in the Interstate Commerce Commission regulations and the antitrust laws. General Piatt died at his home, Mac-a-cheek, Logan County, Ohio, March 16, 1908, and was buried in nearby Piatt Cemetery.

Byron Root Pierce, a native of New York State, was born September 20, 1829, in East Bloomfield, Ontario County. His grandfather Root was a veteran of the Revolution. Pierce was educated in Rochester and following his father's trade, began his business life in a woolen mill. He finally became a dentist, however, and in 1856 moved to Grand Rapids, Michigan, where he practiced until the outbreak of the Civil War. Prior to 1861 Pierce had been captain of the "Valley City Light Guards" and was mustered into Federal service June 10, 1861, as captain of Company K, 3rd Michigan. He was promoted to major in October, lieutenant colonel in July,

1862, colonel the following January, and brigadier general of volunteers on June 7, 1864. The 3rd Michigan was engaged at First Manassas (Bull Run); on the Peninsula at Seven Pines and the Seven Days' battles; at Groveton and Chantilly during the campaign of Second Bull Run; at Fredericksburg, where Pierce commanded the regiment; at Chancellorsville, where General H. G. Berry, his brigade commander, pointed him out as "distinguished for gallantry"; and at Gettysburg, where Pierce sustained a wound—the third of five he received during the war— that would ultimately cost him his left leg. During the Overland campaign of 1864 which took the Army of the Potomac from the Rappahannock to Petersburg, Pierce commanded a brigade, and sometimes the 3rd Division, in Hancock's II Army Corps. He was present at Appomattox, and for his services a few days earlier at Sayler's Creek, he was brevetted major general. Honorably mustered out on August 24, 1865, General Pierce returned to Grand Rapids and "for some time he was connected with the U. S. post office department." (471) He was active in both the Grand Army of the Republic and the Military Order of the Loyal Legion. From 1887 until 1891 he was commandant of the Michigan Soldiers' Home, which was located in Grand Rapids because of his efforts, and in the late 1890's he successfully operated a Grand Rapids hotel. He retired in 1899 but lived for another quarter-century. At the time of his death on July 10, 1924, at the age of ninety-five, he was Michigan's last surviving Civil War general officer. General Pierce is buried in Fulton Street Cemetery, Grand Rapids. His passing was barely noted in the newspapers, reflecting the complete disinterest of the American press with Civil War figures in the decade immediately following World War I.

William Anderson Pile was born near Indianapolis, Indiana, on February 11, 1829, but his parents moved to Missouri when he was a small child, ultimately settling in St. Louis. After preparatory studies he became a minister of the Methodist Episcopal Church and a member of that denomination's Missouri conference. At the beginning of the Civil War he enlisted in the Union army as chaplain of the 1st Missouri Light Artillery and was commissioned on June 12, 1861. In the course of the next eleven months Chaplain Pile became Captain Pile, for on July 31, 1862, he was in command of Battery I of the 1st Missouri near Corinth, Missis-

sippi. (472) A month later he became lieutenant colonel of the 33rd Missouri Infantry, a command known as the "Merchants' Regiment" because it had been enlisted under the auspices of the Union Merchants' Exchange of St. Louis. Pile became its colonel December 23, 1862, and moved with it into

Arkansas. The regiment was chiefly occupied with garrison duty, but did take part in the expedition which sought to discover a back door to Vicksburg via the Yazoo River in March, 1863. It was then in garrison at Helena until January, 1864. Meantime Pile, who had been made a brigadier general of volunteers on December 26, 1863, was assigned to the command of a brigade of Negro troops at Benton Barracks, St. Louis. His most significant contribution to the war effort was in the campaign against Mobile, where, in command of the 1st Brigade of John P. Hawkins'

Negro division, he was brevetted major general "for gallant and meritorious services in the siege and capture of Fort Blakely, Alabama" in April, 1865. General Pile was mustered out of service in August and the next year was elected to Congress as a Republican. He was declared to be "thoroughly radical in politics," advocating "death to all supporters of the South, past or present." (473) Defeated for reelection to Congress in 1868, he was made territorial governor of New Mexico by President Grant; he served in this position until 1871, when he became Minister Resident to Venezuela. After 1876 General Pile operated in Philadelphia as an agent of the Venezuelan government. Later he moved to Monrovia, California, near Los Angeles, where he died July 7, 1889, and was buried in Live Oak Cemetery.

Thomas Gamble Pitcher was born in the river town of Rockport, Indiana, October 23, 1824. At the age of seventeen he was appointed to the Military Academy and was graduated in 1845, ranking next to the last in the class. Posted to the 5th Infantry as a brevet second lieutenant, he served in the military occupation of Texas which immediately preceded the Mexican War and was brevetted for gallantry in battle during the war. He became first lieutenant of the 8th Infantry in 1849 and captain in 1858. When the Civil War began Pitcher was depot commissary at Fort Bliss near El Paso, Texas. His only active field service was at the battle of Cedar Mountain, a preliminary to Second Manassas, where he commanded a battalion of skirmishers in Prince's brigade of Augur's divi-

sion. During the battle he received a severe wound in the knee which made him an invalid for a number of months. On March 20, 1863, he was promoted to brigadier general of volunteers to rank from the preceding November 29. From June, 1863, until the end of the war he was on duty as state provost marshal general, first in Vermont and subsequently in Indiana for the Federal government. While stationed in Vermont, Pitcher's subordinates were literally driven out of the town of Rutland, Vermont, by a force of five hundred Irishmen who refused to register to fight for their adopted country. (474) Eventually the authority of the United States prevailed, however, and Pitcher was able to move to Indianapolis, where he directed affairs of the bureau until his muster-out of the volunteer service in 1866. At this juncture he became simultaneously colonel of the 44th Infantry and superintendent of West Point, the latter an honor accorded to few and never previously to one who had graduated so low in his class, which is a testimonial either to Pitcher's ability or to the state of affairs in the War Department at the time. (475) From 1870 until 1877 he was governor of the Soldiers' Home at Washington, and the following year he was retired "for disability contracted in the line of duty." Seventeen years later General Pitcher died, probably of tuberculosis, at Fort Bayard, New Mexico, on October 21, 1895. He was buried in Arlington National Cemetery.

Alfred Pleasonton was born in the city of Washington on July 7, 1824, and attended the local schools before receiving an appointment to West Point in 1840. He was graduated from the Military Academy in 1844, ranking seventh in a class of twenty-five members. In 1846 he won the brevet of first lieutenant

for gallantry in the Mexican War and served on the Indian frontier and in Florida against the Seminoles as an officer of dragoons, part of the time as adjutant to General William S. Harney. As captain of the 2nd Dragoons (renamed 2nd Cavalry in 1861 upon the reorganization of the army), Pleasonton commanded the regiment on its march from Utah to Washington in September and October. He served in the capital's defenses that winter, was promoted to major on February 15, 1862, was distinguished in the Peninsular campaign, and soon after was made a brigadier in the volunteers (July 18 to rank from the sixteenth). He directed a division of the Cavalry Corps in the Maryland campaign, at Fredericksburg, and at Chancellorsville. At the latter fight he assumed the entire credit for saving the Union army by magnifying the repulse of a Confederate patrol into the defeat of Stonewall Jackson's entire corps. (476) He was, however, promoted to major general on June 22, 1863, after replacing General George Stoneman in command of the Cavalry Corps on June 7 upon the orders of Joseph Hooker. (477) Subsequently, he directed ten thousand Union horsemen at Brandy Station, Virginia, in the biggest cavalry fight of the war— an encounter which was said to have "made the Federal cavalry." But Pleasonton did not distinguish himself during the Gettysburg campaign. In February, 1864, he disapproved of the Kilpatrick-Dahlgren raid against Richmond—an abortive affair which accomplished nothing save a long casualty list, including Ulrich Dahlgren, but which was enthusiastically supported by the administration. This lukewarmness, coupled with the fact that the new general-in-chief, U. S. Grant, intended Philip Sheridan to command the Cavalry Corps, resulted in Pleasonton's relief from command on March 25, 1864, and banishment to the Department of the Missouri under the command of the recently exiled W. S. Rosecrans. Although again some of his claims were disputed, he performed creditably during Confederate General Sterling Price's Missouri raid in October. (478) At the end of the war Pleasonton was brevetted major general, U. S. Army; his regular rank, however, continued to be that of major of the 2nd Cavalry. When the Regular Army was reorganized in 1866, he was offered the lieutenant colonelcy of the 20th Infantry, which he declined, presumably wishing to remain in the cavalry. This refusal left him subordinate to both his colonel, T. J. Wood, and lieutenant colonel, I. N. Palmer. Pleasonton had been a year ahead of Wood at West Point and two ahead of Palmer, and he had ranked Wood by seniority on the list of volunteer major generals, while Palmer had made major general by brevet only. Accordingly, Pleasonton resigned and applied for retirement at his old volunteer rank, but was refused. He occupied some minor Federal posts, and finally, in 1888 was placed on the retired list as a major. He died in Washington on February 17, 1897, and was buried in the Congressional Cemetery.

Joseph Bennett Plummer was born, according to the vital records of Barre, Massachusetts, on November 15, 1816. He seems to have taken a

few years off his age, however, so as not to endanger an appointment to the Military Academy which he sought for at least two years. (479) He attended the local high school and was apparently a universal favorite, since virtually all the prominent citizens and ex-citizens of the area, including Governor William L. Marcy, united in recommending him for appointment to the Academy. After teaching school for a time, he finally entered West Point in 1837 and was graduated in 1841 with a host of others who would become Civil War generals. Plummer's military career prior to the outbreak of the Civil War was unexceptionable: he stood garrison duty as an infantry subaltern at various middle-western posts, spent the first year of the Mexican War on sick leave, and did quartermaster duty on the Texas frontier from 1848 until 1861. Promoted captain of the 1st Infantry in 1852, he was advanced to major, 8th Infantry, in April, 1862. Meantime he was wounded in the battle of Wilson's Creek while commanding a battalion of Regulars; the following month on September 25, 1861, he was commissioned colonel of the 11th Missouri Infantry. In the latter capacity he commanded the post of Cape Girardeau, Missouri, until March, 1862; and on March 11 was appointed brigadier general of volunteers to rank from October 22, 1861. Plummer commanded the 5th Division of John Pope's forces during the capture of New Madrid and was in command of a brigade of Stanley's division in the "siege of Corinth." Soon after, on August 9, 1862, while in camp near Corinth, he died "Of Wound And Exposure In The Active Field" and was ultimately buried in Arlington National Cemetery. (480)

Orlando Metcalfe Poe was born March 7, 1832, at Navarre, Ohio. He was graduated from West Point in 1856, standing sixth in his class, and was appointed to the Corps of Topographical Engineers (merged into the Corps of Engineers in 1863). During the interval before the Civil War, Poe was in the field on the survey of the northern lakes and was promoted first lieutenant in 1860. The following year he became one of George B. McClellan's principal subordinates, first in Ohio and subsequently in West Virginia and the Washington defenses. He was appointed colonel of the 2nd Michigan in September, commanded his regiment during the initial stages of the Peninsular campaign, was absent on sick leave during the Seven Days battles, but during the campaign of Second Manassas was given direction of a

brigade of Kearny's III Corps division. After this Union debacle his troops were retained in Washington until after the battle of Sharpsburg, but in December at Fredericksburg he was again in the field, as commander of a brigade of the IX Corps which was lightly engaged in the battle. Meantime he was appointed a brigadier general of volunteers on November 29, 1862, but the appointment was not confirmed by the Senate, and on March 4, 1863, he reverted to his Regular Army rank of captain of engineers. (481) He later served successively as chief engineer of the XXIII Corps and of the Army of the Ohio; in this position he was responsible for the defenses of Knoxville which repelled James Longstreet's assaults in November. In April, 1864, General W. T. Sherman made him chief engineer of the military Division of the Mississippi, and he rendered distinguished service in the Atlanta campaign, the "March to the Sea," and the Carolinas campaign. He was brevetted brigadier general, U. S. Army, at war's end. In 1873 he became a staff colonel and aide-de-camp to Sherman, then general-in-chief of the army, a position which he occupied until Sherman's retirement in 1884. Both before and after his association with Sherman, Poe had a distinguished peacetime career as a military engineer and was promoted through grades to colonel of engineers in 1888. He served on the lighthouse board, as supervisor of numerous projects in the Great Lakes, and in protecting the construction of the transcontinental railroads. While inspecting the Soo locks in Michigan he suffered an injury which resulted in his death on October 2, 1895. General Poe was buried in Arlington National Cemetery.

John Pope, one of the Civil War's more controversial figures, was born of distinguished ancestry on March 16, 1822, in Louisville, Kentucky. He was a collateral descendant of George Washington; his father was territorial secretary and delegate from the Illinois Territory and later a Federal judge; and his uncle was a United States Senator from Kentucky. More importantly, he was connected by marriage to the family of Mary Todd Lincoln. (482) Pope was graduated from West Point in 1842 in a class which furnished seventeen full-rank general officers to the opposing armies in the Civil War. After four years of survey duty, Pope won the brevets of lieutenant and captain for gallantry in the Mexican War. Following the war he discharged various assignments in the Topogra-

phical Engineers and was regularly promoted captain in 1856. Perhaps because of his connections, he was appointed a brigadier general of volunteers on June 14, 1861, to rank from May 17. His early war service seemed to amply justify his selection, as he opened the upper Mississippi River almost to Memphis by capturing Madrid and Island No. 10 in a series of well-executed movements in March and April, 1862. In the meantime he was promoted to major general on March 22. During the advance upon Corinth in May his army constituted the left wing of the forces under Henry W. Halleck. Pope was now at the apogee of his military career, and in June he was given command of all the forces in the East except for those under George B. McClellan on the Peninsula. These troops were designated the Army of Virginia and were designed to protect Washington and to demonstrate on the line of the

Orange & Alexandria Railroad in order to ease the pressure on McClellan. At this point Pope began to get in over his depth. He now commanded his former superiors (John C. Frémont, who had been his commander in Missouri, asked for relief); he tactlessly published a series of bombastic general orders which not only reflected unfavorably on his new command but also earned him the undying hatred and contempt of his opponents; and subsequent to the Union disaster at Second Manassas, he committed the cardinal military sin of blaming others for his own errors of judgment. Entirely misapprehending the situation on the Manassas plains, Pope allowed R. E. Lee to first divide and then reunite his two wings under Stonewall Jackson and James Longstreet. The latter virtually swept Pope back into the Washington defenses on August 30, 1862. Nevertheless Pope succeeded in having Fitz John Porter cashiered for disobedience of orders impossible of execution and displaying the grossest ignorance of the situation at the time they were issued. (483) McClellan was restored to command of all the forces in the East and Pope was put on the shelf in the Department of the Northwest where he served creditably during the Sioux uprising in Minnesota. From then until his retirement in 1886 he had various departmental commands, the last being the Division of the Pacific. He had been made a brigadier in the regular service to rank from July 14, 1862, and on October 26, 1882, was promoted to major general, proving, if nothing else, that seniority in that era would win out over all imaginable obstacles. The

sister of Pope's wife had married General Manning F. Force, and it was in the latter's quarters at the Ohio Soldiers' and Sailors' Home in Sandusky, Ohio, that Pope died on September 23, 1892. He was buried in Bellefontaine Cemetery, St. Louis.

Andrew Porter, grandson of the Revolutionary General Andrew Porter and a first cousin of the mother of Mary Todd Lincoln, was born in Lancaster, Pennsylvania,

July 10, 1820. He was also a first cousin of Brevet Brigadier General Horace Porter, U. S. Grant's Secretary of War and intimate friend. Andrew Porter attended West Point for six months in 1836 and at the beginning of the Mexican War was appointed a first lieutenant in the newly authorized Regiment of Mounted Riflemen. A year later he was made captain, and for gallantry in battle was brevetted major and lieutenant colonel. For the next fourteen years he did duty in Texas and the Southwest. On May 14, 1861, he became colonel of the new 16th U. S. Infantry and three days later fourth-ranking brigadier in the volunteer organization, although the appointment was not made until August 6, 1861. At the battle of First Manassas in July he commanded the 1st Brigade of Hunter's division which sustained 464 casualties; after the wounding of Hunter, Porter commanded the division itself. During McClellan's Peninsular campaign Porter was provost marshal general of the Army of the Potomac. At the close of this he was relieved from duty and that fall was ordered to Harrisburg, Pennsylvania, to aid in organizing and forwarding recruits. In October he was charged with enforcing the draft in Pennsylvania and appointed provost marshal general of the state, but on January 24, 1863, was relieved and ordered to report to the adjutant general in Washington. (484) In July of that year he served briefly as commander of "the depot for drafted men at Philadelphia," a post from which he was relieved on July 18. (485) Porter's health had been badly undermined by his service on the Indian frontier and his absences on sick leave were frequent; finally on April 4, 1864, he was mustered out of the volunteer service, resigning his regular commission of colonel sixteen days later. He then went abroad in order to travel for his health, making his permanent residence in Paris. He died there at his home on Rue du Colisée January 3, 1872. His remains were returned to the United States and buried in Elmwood Cemetery, Detroit. Porter's father,

George Bryan Porter, territorial governor of Michigan, is also buried there, as is his father-in-law, Major John Biddle, U. S. Army, a former Philadelphian and early-day settler of Michigan.

Fitz John Porter, "the most magnificent soldier in the Army of the Potomac, ruined by his devotion to McClellan," (486) was born August 31, 1822, in Ports-

mouth, New Hampshire. All his relations were in the navy: his father was a captain; the flamboyant Commodore David Porter was his uncle; and the latter's son was Admiral David Dixon Porter of Civil War fame. Fitz John attended Exeter until his appointment to West Point in 1841. He was graduated in 1845, ranking eighth in the class. Especially distinguished in the Mexican War, he won the brevets of captain and major for gallantry while with the army under

Winfield Scott. From 1849 until 1855 Porter was assistant instructor of artillery at the Military Academy, and from 1857 until 1860 he served as Albert Sidney Johnston's adjutant in the Utah expedition. The outbreak of the Civil War found him in Washington, and he was immediately commissioned colonel of the newly authorized 15th Regular Infantry, and on August 7 to rank from May 17, 1861, he was made brigadier general of volunteers. He was, at the time, eighth ranking officer in the entire volunteer establishment. After some service as chief of staff to General Robert Patterson in the Shenandoah, General George B. McClellan ordered Porter to Washington to assist him in transforming raw recruits into the fighting force which would become the Army of the Potomac. At this time began the never-waning loyalty of Porter to McClellan. (487) In the Peninsular campaign of 1862 Porter led first a division of the III Corps and during the battle of the Seven Days, the V Corps. The latter under his direction while isolated on the north bank of the Chickahominy, demonstrated some of the finest defensive fighting of the war at Mechanicsville and Gaines's Mill. After skillfully extricating his corps, he posted it at Malvern Hill during the army's withdrawal to the James River—a position which enabled the Federals to inflict a sanguinary repulse upon the Army of Northern Virginia on July 1, 1862. For his services Porter was made both major general of volunteers and brigadier by brevet in the Regulars. At this juncture the administration judged that the Peninsular campaign was a failure. Accordingly,

McClellan's troops were withdrawn, corps by corps, from Harrison's Landing and were attached to John Pope's Army of Virginia as they came within range and as the campaign of Second Manassas (or Bull Run) got under way. Porter loathed Pope, as did most of McClellan's officers, and spoke and wrote most intemperately about the man who was about to become his superior—these utterances would shortly come back to haunt him. As an aftermath of the Manassas campaign, during which he was ordered to execute impossible movements as a consequence of Pope's complete misapprehension of the circumstances, Porter was brought to trial by court-martial charged by Pope with disloyalty, disobedience, and misconduct in the face of the enemy. Porter had meanwhile served with McClellan during the Maryland campaign which culminated in the bloody battle of Sharpsburg where the V Corps was in reserve. He was relieved from command in November, placed in arrest, and tried by a military commission—all of whose members were in one way or another under obligation to Secretary of War Edwin Stanton to victimize McClellan at the expense of Porter. A combination of defective maps, perjured and hearsay testimony, Porter's indiscreet strictures upon Pope, and the Radicals' determination to unhorse McClellan were sufficient to warrant a guilty verdict and dismissal from the army on January 21, 1863. Porter spent the rest of his life in an effort to vindicate his name and have it reinstated on the army roster. Sixteen years later a board headed by General John M. Schofield (whom Porter had voted to expel from West Point for disciplinary reasons) completely exonerated Porter from the charges brought in 1863, cited him as the savior of the Army of Virginia at Second Manassas, and recommended that he be restored to his former rank. By this time the case had become a political issue ranking with the "bloody shirt," and it was not until 1886 that President Cleveland signed a bill which again placed his name upon the roll as colonel of infantry to rank from May 14, 1861. General Porter died at his home in Morristown, New Jersey, on May 21, 1901, and was buried in Green-Wood Cemetery, Brooklyn.

Edward Elmer Potter was born in New York City on June 21, 1823. He was educated in the local

schools, was graduated from Columbia in 1842, and then studied law. After a trip to California he returned to New York and turned his attention to farming. On February 3, 1862, he was commissioned a captain in the commissary department and accompanied Ambrose E. Burnside's expedition to the Carolina coast as chief commissary of John G. Foster's brigade. In May, 1862, Burnside authorized Potter to recruit the 1st North Carolina (Union) Infantry from disaffected citizens living in and about Washington, North Carolina, and appointed him acting colonel. (488) He subsequently was confirmed as lieutenant colonel of the regiment and on December 24, 1862, was appointed brigadier general of volunteers, ranking from November 29. He served under Foster during the balance of the war, sometimes as post and district commander but primarily as the latter's chief of staff. When Foster, now a major general, was assigned to the command of the Department of the Ohio in December, 1863, Potter accompanied him to the Western theater. When John M. Schofield superseded Foster in command of the department in February, 1864, due to an injury to the latter, Potter remained on inspection duty until he was transferred to the Charleston area to take part in the siege. Thereafter General Potter occupied various regional commands in the Department of the South, again under General Foster. At this time operations in the department consisted principally of establishing and maintaining liaison with W. T. Sherman's advancing legions and harassing the retreating Confederates, whose ultimate destination would be their place of parole at Greensboro, North Carolina. Potter was brevetted major general to rank from

March 13, 1865, in the omnibus promotions which marked the war's end, and on July 24, 1865, resigned his commission. He then alternated his residence between New York City and Madison, New Jersey. Having never married, he died of pneumonia alone in a boarding house on 21st Street, New York City, on June 1, 1889, and was buried in Marble Cemetery, at 2nd Avenue and 2nd Street on the lower end of Manhattan.

Joseph Haydn Potter, a career officer for nearly half a century, was born October 12, 1822, in Concord, New Hampshire. He was appointed to West Point, where he

was ranked immediately below U. S. Grant in the graduating class of 1843. Potter was wounded during the Mexican War at the battle of Monterey in 1846, meanwhile winning a brevet for gallantry. Subsequently he was employed on recruiting service and garrison duty

until he accompanied his regiment, the 7th Infantry, on the Utah expedition. At the beginning of the Civil War he was stationed in New Mexico and was involved, although innocently, in the disgraceful surrender of Regulars at San Augustine Pass on July 27, 1861. (489) After his exchange a year later, he was appointed colonel of the 12th New Hampshire Infantry. At the battle of Fredericksburg in December, 1862, Potter's regiment was unattached (490) and sustained nominal losses; however, at Chancellorsville, his command in Whipple's division of Sickles' corps lost heavily and Potter himself was again wounded and captured and not formally exchanged until autumn. The following year Potter served as assistant provost marshal general of Ohio until, in September, he was assigned to the command of a brigade of the XVIII Corps, Army of the James, on the Bermuda Hundred line. Soon after, he was given a brigade of the XXIV Corps, which he commanded until January, 1865, when he became chief of staff of the corps; he remained in this capacity until the end of the war. Potter had been promoted major in the regular service in 1863, and he was rewarded with the full commission of brigadier general of volunteers on May 1, 1865, and the brevet of brigadier general, U. S. Army, to rank from March 13, 1865. For the next twenty-five years General Potter, a veteran of many Indian outposts, served on the western frontier as lieutenant colonel of the 30th Infantry and 4th Infantry and as colonel of the 24th Infantry. He was also governor of the Washington Soldiers' Home for four years. On

April 1, 1886, he was promoted to brigadier general in the Regular Army, a rare distinction in that era, and the following October 12 was retired for age. General Potter died in Columbus, Ohio, December 1, 1892, and was buried there in Greenlawn Cemetery.

Robert Brown Potter, the son of an Episcopal bishop, was born in Schenectady, New York, July 16, 1829. (491) He attended Union College (where his maternal grandfather was president) for a time but he did not graduate. After studying law he was admitted to the bar and

practiced in New York City until the outbreak of the Civil War. He first enlisted as a private in the militia, was promoted to lieutenant, and on October 14, 1861, was commissioned major of the 51st New York —a regiment whose service during the entire war would be in the IX Corps, as would Potter's. He was promoted lieutenant colonel in November; accompanied Ambrose E. Burnside's North Carolina expedition in January, 1862; was distinguished in the Roanoke Island assault; and was wounded at New Bern in March. After receiving a promotion to colonel on September 10, Potter fought at Cedar Mountain, in the campaign of Second Manassas, and in Maryland, where he was mainly responsible for getting troops over Burnside's bridge at Sharpsburg, after several previous attacks had bogged down. After the battle of Fredericksburg he accompanied Burnside to Cincinnati and was made a brigadier general of volunteers to rank from March 13, 1863. Shortly after he was given divisional command and participated in the siege of Vicksburg, the capture of Jackson two weeks later, and the Knoxville campaign in November. Potter's division was present with the rest of the IX Corps during U. S. Grant's Overland campaign against Richmond in 1864. They sustained more than twenty-four hundred casualties from the Wilderness to Petersburg. At the battle of The Crater, it was the 48th Pennsylvania of his division which drove the shaft and exploded the mine, and it was Potter, alone of Burnside's division commanders, who was present with his men during the subsequent abortive assault on the Confederate works. In the final assault which shattered Robert E. Lee's attenuated lines on the morning of April 2, 1865, Potter was severely wounded. He had been brevetted major general to rank from August 1, 1864, and on September 29, 1865, was given the full rank. Mustered out of service the following January, General Potter acted as receiver for the Atlantic & Great Western Railroad until 1869. He went abroad in 1869 and remained in England until 1873 when he returned to the United States. He resided at Newport, Rhode Island, until his death on February 19, 1887. He was buried in Woodlawn Cemetery, New York City.

Benjamin Franklin Potts was born January 29, 1836, and grew up on a farm in Carroll County, Ohio. He secured the rudiments of an education in a local school, clerked in a

store, attended a small college in nearby Pennsylvania for a year, and taught school. After reading law in Carrollton, Ohio, he was admitted to the bar in 1859. Potts was a Democrat and attended the 1860 conventions in Charleston and Baltimore, as a staunch supporter of Stephen A. Douglas. After having raised a company in his own neighborhood, he entered the Union service as captain of the 32nd Ohio on August 20, 1861. Potts was in the West Virginia campaign in the spring of 1862 and was subsequently with General John C. Frémont at Cross Keys and Port Republic during Stonewall Jackson's celebrated Shenandoah Valley campaign. Upon the reorganization of the 32nd Ohio, Potts was advanced to lieutenant colonel on November 21, 1862, and colonel on December 28. From then until the end of the war he served in the Western theater, joining U. S. Grant's army at Memphis and serving under John A. Logan during the Vicksburg campaign. In the Atlanta campaign, the "March to the Sea," and the Carolina campaign under General W. T. Sherman, Potts was usually in command of a brigade of the XVII Corps, which fought at Big Shanty, Kennesaw, the battles around Atlanta, Jonesboro, and Lovejoy's Station. On the march through the Carolinas, Potts directed a brigade of Giles Smith's division of the XVII Corps under Frank Blair. He was made a full brigadier general on January 12, 1865, and major general by brevet to rank from March 13. After the war, having failed to obtain a colonelcy in the Regular Army, Potts resumed his Ohio law practice and was elected as a Republican representative to the state senate. In 1870 President Grant appointed him governor of the Montana Territory, a post in which he served until 1883, when he was removed by President Arthur, who had come to distrust Potts' ability to carry water on both shoulders, as between the Democratic territorial legislature and the Republican administration.

Shortly after leaving the governorship, Potts was elected to the legislature and, thereafter, devoted himself mainly to ranching near Helena, where he died on June 17, 1887, and was buried. (492)

William Henry Powell was born at the village of Pontypool, in Monmouthshire, South Wales, May 10, 1825. His parents came to the United States when he was five and he obtained his early education in the Nashville schools. In the years

before the Civil War Powell attained a considerable reputation as an engineer in various ironworks and in 1861 was manager of one at Ironton, Ohio. In August of that year he recruited a company of cavalry in southern Ohio which was mustered into Federal service as a unit of the 2nd (West) Virginia Cavalry on November 8, 1861, with Powell as company commander. He was promoted to major, lieutenant colonel, and colonel of this regi-

ment which served mainly in the state of its adoption in 1862 and 1863. On July 18, 1863, Powell was wounded and captured in an affair at Wytheville, Virginia; he was not exchanged until February, 1864. That summer and autumn Powell was attached to Philip Sheridan's cavalry in the Shenandoah campaign, and at the battle of Cedar Creek he commanded the 2nd Division of the cavalry, his command of two brigades and a battery having been detached from the Department of West Virginia. For his deportment in this engagement he was made a brigadier general of volunteers on the day of the battle and was brevetted major general of volunteers in the omnibus promotions at the end of the war, despite the fact that his resignation was accepted by the War Department on January 5, 1865. On January 13 Powell published a farewell address to his division wherein he alludes to "the cause that necessitates the act [of his resignation]" but does not elucidate further. (493) In any event he returned to his prewar occupation at Ironton; then in 1867 he moved to Mason County, West Virginia, where he was injured while superintending the erection of a nail factory. Moving again, he resided successively in Kansas City, St. Louis, Chattanooga, and Belleville, Illinois, where he established the Western Nail Company, which he managed until 1891. General Powell was active in the Grand Army of the Republic and was elected department commander in 1895. He was also prominent in Republican circles and was appointed collector of internal revenue by President McKinley in 1898. In his later years he lived in both Belleville and Chicago; he died on December 26, 1904, in Belleville and was buried in Graceland Cemetery, Chicago. (494)

Calvin Edward Pratt was born January 23, 1828, in Shrewsbury, Massachusetts. (495) As a young man he taught school in the neighborhood, meanwhile studying law

and taking an interest in the Worcester militia which he joined in 1852. In 1853 Pratt was elected justice of the peace in Worcester, but in 1859 he moved to Brooklyn, New York. In 1861 he and a colleague, at their own expense, recruited and organized the 31st New York Infantry; Pratt was officially mustered in as its colonel on August 14, 1861. In the meantime, however, the regiment participated to a limited extent in the battle of First Manassas: as a part of Dixon Miles's 5th Division it was in reserve at Centreville and helped cover the retreat of Irvin McDowell's army. (496) During the Peninsular campaign Pratt and his command were in Slocum's division of the VI Corps, and at Mechanicsville he was wounded in the face by a rifle ball which was not removed for some thirty years. On September 13, 1862, he was appointed a brigadier general of volunteers, and at Fredericksburg he commanded the 1st Brigade of Howe's division of the VI Corps, which was only lightly engaged. Pratt's resignation from the service dates from April 25, 1863; however, reports indicate that he was concerned with the ferry operation across the Rappahannock at Falmouth on April 29 and 30 which preceded the VI Corps assault on Marye's Heights in the campaign of Chancellorsville. (497) He probably had not yet received notice that his resignation had been accepted, but seems to have left the army on or before May 1, as he makes no further appearance in the *Official Records*. General Pratt resumed his Brooklyn law practice; was for a time collector of internal revenue; and in 1869 was elected to the appellate division of the court upon its creation. He died on August 3, 1896, at his farm in Rochester, Massachusetts, on Buzzard's Bay. He was buried in Rochester.

Benjamin Mayberry Prentiss, direct descendant of one of the settlers who came over on the *Mayflower,* was born in the Ohio River village of Belleville, Virginia (now West Virginia), November 23, 1819. At the age of seventeen he went with his parents to Marion County, Missouri, where for five years he was engaged in the operation of a ropewalk. He then moved to Quincy,

385

Illinois. Next he served as a subaltern of militia during the Mormon troubles and led a company of the 1st Illinois Volunteers in the Mexican War. After the war he studied law and in 1860 was a candidate for Congress on the Republican ticket. On April 29, 1861, he was commissioned colonel of the 10th Illinois Infantry, a regiment which was organized at Cairo to serve three months. On August 9, 1861, Prentiss was appointed brigadier general of volunteers to rank from May 17; the following month he was assigned to the command of "that section of the State of Missouri . . . lying north of the Hannibal and Saint Joseph Railroad" with orders to keep the railroad and telegraph open and "to prevent the secessionists from meeting . . . for camp and drill . . . as has been their custom. . . ." (498) He commanded the 6th Division of U. S. Grant's Army of the Tennessee on April 1, 1862, at Shiloh where he gallantly defended the celebrated

Hornets Nest. After holding off the Confederates for six hours, his position, an eroded lane with a field of brambles in front, was overrun and he was compelled to surrender. Exchanged in October, he served as a member of the Fitz John Porter court-martial and on March 13, 1863, was made a major general to rank from the preceding November 29. Meantime he was in command of the District of Eastern Arkansas, with headquarters at Helena, which he successfully defended against the attack of Confederate Commander T. H. Holmes on July 4, 1863. His resignation was accepted by the War Department on October 28, ostensibly "on the grounds of his . . . health and the situation of his family . . . ," but presumably because he felt he had been shelved. (499) He returned to Quincy and resumed his law practice, until President Grant appointed him a pension agent. He again returned to Missouri and practiced law in Kirksville for a time. Then, in 1881 he moved to Bethany, Missouri, where he was postmaster at the time of his death on February 8, 1901; he was buried in Miriam Cemetery, Bethany.

Henry Prince, one of the older general officers of the Union army, was born in Eastport, Maine, June 19, 1811, and was graduated from the Military Academy in the class of 1835. During the late thirties and early forties he fought in the Florida wars against the Seminoles and Creeks and was wounded at Camp Izard in 1836. During the war with Mexico, Prince was brevetted captain and major for gallantry as an officer of the 4th Infantry; he was so badly wounded at Molino del Rey that he was disabled for the next three years. In 1855 he accepted the staff appointment of major and paymaster; then after some years on frontier duty and another year on leave of absence because of his wounds, he was stationed in Wash-

ington until the outbreak of the Civil War. He was made a brigadier general of volunteers April 20, 1862, and commanded first a brigade and then Augur's division of Banks's corps. He was captured at Cedar Mountain on August 9 and held a prisoner until December. His principal field service after exchange was in the Rapidan campaign which followed R. E. Lee's retreat from Pennsylvania. Prince directed a division of French's III Corps in this campaign and at the affair of Mine Run was compelled to bear some of the onus for his commander's failure to engage the enemy. (500) In 1864 and 1865 he was employed primarily in garrison command in Tennessee, Alabama, and South Carolina. At the end of the war he was brevetted brigadier general in the regular service; in the following years he served in the pay department, rising to the position of deputy paymaster general with rank of lieutenant colonel in 1877. On December 31, 1879, he was retired for age. Thirteen years later, on August 19, 1892, in a hotel on Trafalgar Square in London, Prince, then eighty-one-years-old and racked by his old wounds, committed suicide. His body was brought home and interred in Hillside Cemetery, Eastport, the town of his birth.

Issac Ferdinand Quinby, a descendant of an old New England family, was born on a farm near Morristown, New Jersey, on January 29, 1821. He entered West Point in 1839 and was graduated in the class of 1843; he ranked sixth in the class whereas his lifelong friend U. S. Grant ranked twenty-first.

Quinby's early army service was spent in various garrisons and as an assistant professor of "natural philosophy" (physics) at the Military Academy. In 1852 he resigned his commission in order to teach mathematics and science at the University of Rochester, where he remained until the outbreak of the Civil War. In May, 1861, Quinby raised the "Rochester regiment," which was mustered into the service as the 13th New York for ninety days, although it had been accepted by the state as a two-year regiment. (501) With Quinby as its colonel, the 13th New York fought at First Manassas in Sherman's brigade and was swept from the field along with the other demoralized Federal commands. Quinby resigned the following month and returned to his scholastic pursuits, but on March 20, 1862, he accepted a commission as brigadier general of volunteers (to rank from March 17) and was assigned to the command of the District of Mississippi. In September he was assigned the 7th Division of the Army of the Tennessee. In the course of the operations against Vicksburg in the spring of 1863, Quinby and his division, under Grant's orders, unsuccessfully attempted to reach Vicksburg by the Yazoo Pass. Although General Quinby was plagued by illness, he took part in the battles of Champion's Hill and Big Black River and the first assaults on Vicksburg proper. He finally resigned on December 31, 1863, and resumed his academic career, remaining connected with the University of Rochester until 1884. Meanwhile he served as provost marshal of the 28th (New York) Congressional District in 1865 and as United

States marshal for the northern district of New York by appointment of Grant from 1869 until 1877. From 1885 to 1890 he was city surveyor of Rochester. General Quinby died at his home in Rochester on September 18, 1891, and was buried in Mount Hope Cemetery.

George Douglas Ramsay, one of the oldest officers to serve the Union in active service, was born in Dumfries, Virginia, February 21, 1802; he was the son of a Scotsman who

had established himself as a merchant in Alexandria. The family later moved to Washington. George was graduated from West Point in the class of 1820 and was commissioned a second lieutenant of artillery. In 1835 he transferred to the staff and was made captain in the Ordnance Department—a grade in which he would languish for more than a quarter-century, despite distinguished service in the command of a dozen arsenals. Ramsay was finally promoted major a few days after the fall of Fort Sumter and lieutenant colonel on August 3, 1861. He commanded the Washington arsenal from 1861 to 1863; during this time he became a favorite of President Lincoln because of his rectitude, breadth of intellect, and experience. Shortly after his promotion to colonel on June 1, 1863, a controversy developed concerning the appointment of a successor to Chief of Ordnance General James W. Ripley, who was about to retire after a half-century in the service of the United States. Lincoln favored Ramsay, but Secretary of War Edwin Stanton, who had been irritated previously by Ramsay's independence (an attitude impossible for Stanton to tolerate), urged the appointment of a certain Captain George T. Balch. A compromise was eventually struck by the two without Ramsay's knowledge: he was installed as brigadier general and chief of ordnance to rank from September 15, 1863, but Balch called the signals. This humiliating arrangement came to an end a year later on September 12, 1864, when Ramsay was retired "for age." (502) He continued to serve by special appointment, however, as inspector of arsenals and on other related duties until 1870, and was brevetted major general, U. S. Army, on March 13, 1865, for "long and faithful services in the army." After his retirement General Ramsay continued to make his home in Washington and was an active church member until his death on May 23, 1882. He was buried in Oak Hill Cemetery, Georgetown.

One of his sons, a graduate of the Naval Academy, rose to rear admiral, and two other sons were officers of the army.

Thomas Edward Greenfield Ransom was born November 29, 1834, in Norwich, Vermont. His father Truman B. Ransom was president of Norwich University, the cele-

brated military school (now located at Northfield, Vermont), and was colonel of the 9th U. S. Infantry when he was killed at the storming of Chapultepec in 1847. Thomas was educated at Norwich and received a degree in civil engineering in 1851. As a youngster he had acquired some practical experience in his chosen profession by working on the Rutland & Burlington Railroad. After his graduation he went to Illinois where he pursued an engineering career and engaged in the real estate business. He was living in Vandalia, south of Springfield, in 1861 and with the advent of the Civil War recruited a company of the 11th Illinois, a ninety-day regiment which was remustered in July for three years. From February 15, 1862, Ransom served successively as major, lieutenant colonel, and colonel. He was wounded in an affair at Charleston, Missouri, in August, 1861, again at Fort Donelson, and a third time at Shiloh—each time he refused to leave the field, and each time he was cited by his superiors for gallant conduct. In June, 1862, Ransom became chief of staff to General John A. McClernand and inspector general of the Army of the Tennessee, and later he commanded a brigade of the XIII Corps. He was made a brigadier general of volunteers on April 15, 1863, to rank from November 29, 1862, and during the Vicksburg campaign won encomiums from all his superiors for his performance while commanding a brigade of McArthur's division of McPherson's XVII Corps. He was sent subsequently on a foraging expedition to the vicinity of Natchez, in the course of which he captured five thousand head of cattle, a number of teams, and a large supply of ordnance stores. In January, 1864, U. S. Grant asked that Ransom succeed James Harrison Wilson in command of his cavalry after Wilson was ordered to Washington to take charge of the Cavalry Bureau. Grant termed him "the best man I ever had to send on expeditions." (503) Unfortunately, Ransom was already a part of N. P. Banks's ill-fated Red River campaign, directing a detachment of the XIII Corps. At Sabine Cross Roads while commanding the advance, his position was overrun and he was

again severely wounded. On August 2, 1864, he took charge of a division of the XVI Corps in front of Atlanta; and after the wounding of Grenville Dodge, he commanded the corps in the movement which forced John B. Hood to evacuate Atlanta after the decisive battle of Jonesboro. Ransom was next assigned to command of the XVII Corps which pursued the retreating Confederates through North Georgia and into Alabama. Despite illness and an aggravation of his partly healed wound, he accompanied his corps on the return from Alabama, dying near Rome, Georgia, October 29, 1864. For his services he was brevetted major general as of September 1, 1864, the date of the battle of Jonesboro. He was buried in Rosehill Cemetery, Chicago.

Green Berry Raum was born at Golconda, Illinois, an Ohio River town at the tip of the state, on December 3, 1829. His father was an officer in the War of 1812 and in the Black Hawk War, a member of the state senate, and clerk of the county and circuit courts. After receiving a public school education and making three trips to New Orleans by flatboat, Raum studied law and was admitted to the Illinois bar in 1853. After a short residence in the Kansas Territory he settled in Harrisburg, Illinois. In 1860 he was an alternate delegate to the Democratic National Convention as a Stephen A. Douglas supporter. When the 56th Illinois Infantry was organized at Camp Mather, near Shawneetown, Raum became successively its major, lieutenant colonel, and colonel. At the battle of Corinth in October, 1862, he led

a successful bayonet charge; next he commanded a brigade of McPherson's XVII Corps in the Vicksburg campaign and at the battle of Chattanooga, where he was badly wounded during the assault on Missionary Ridge. Returning to duty in February, 1864, Raum protected W. T. Sherman's communications northward to Dalton during the Atlanta campaign, and after John B. Hood's evacuation of Atlanta and movement northwestward, he reinforced the Resaca defenses, thereby compelling the Confederate commander to bypass the town. During the "March to the Sea" he directed a brigade of the XV Corps, now under Peter J. Osterhaus, and on January 16, 1865, was granted leave of absence; (504) he makes no further appearance in the *Official Records*. (505) He had been made a brigadier by brevet as of September 19, 1864, and on February 28, 1865, was given the full rank to date from

February 15; he resigned on May 6. General Raum had a varied postbellum career: he was builder and first president of the Cairo and Vincennes Railroad, Radical Republican member of Congress from Illinois (1867-69), commissioner of internal revenue (1876-83), practicing attorney in Washington (1883-89), and pension commissioner (1889-93). He was accused of using his position as pension commissioner to further his personal interests; however, two Congressional committees failed to agree on the censurability of his acts. For the last sixteen years of his life he practiced law in Chicago, where he died December 18, 1909. General Raum was buried in Arlington National Cemetery.

John Aaron Rawlins was born February 13, 1831, at Galena, Illinois; his family had originated in Virginia and had come to Illinois by way of Kentucky. When his father went to California for the gold rush of 1849, young Rawlins maintained the family, at the same time obtaining a law education and admission to the state bar in 1854. He served as city attorney of Galena in 1857 and like thousands of his Midwestern contemporaries was a Douglas Democrat in 1860. With the outbreak of war, Rawlins, the successful politician with a passion for the military life, teamed up with the unassuming ex-captain of the army who clerked in his brother's leather store, U. S. Grant. Within eight years Grant would be President of the United States, and Rawlins his Secretary of War. Grant asked Rawlins to become his aide-de-camp, and on August 30, 1861, he was commissioned captain and assistant adjutant general on the staff of Grant, who was then brigadier general. From that time until the end of his brief life, Rawlins was Grant's alter ego, discharging with objectivity the duties and responsibilities of intimate friend,

military and political adviser, editor, and, on perhaps a few occasions, those of apostle of sobriety, although it would seem that he played this role far less than is popularly believed. In any event Grant referred to him as "the most nearly indispensable" man he had around him. (506) As Grant attained fame and promotion, he secured for Rawlins appropriate advances in grade: he was made major on May 14, 1862; lieutenant colonel November 1, 1862; brigadier general of volunteers August 11, 1863; and brigadier general, chief of staff, U. S. Army, to rank from March 3, 1865 (this was the last appointment of a brigadier in the regular service made during the Civil War).

Rawlins was also brevetted major general in both the volunteer and regular services. His first wife had died of tuberculosis in 1861, and it was determined that he himself was suffering from the disease. Recommended travel on the high plains over the proposed route of the Union Pacific Railroad failed to improve his health, and when Grant made him him Secretary of War in March, 1869, he had only five months to live. He died in Washington, September 6, 1869, and is buried in Arlington National Cemetery.

Hugh Thompson Reid was born of South Carolina parentage on a farm in Union County, Indiana, on October 18, 1811. After acquiring a primary education in the local schools, he was graduated from Bloomington (Indiana) College, studied law, and was admitted to the bar. In 1839 he moved to Fort Madison, Iowa, where he practiced until 1849 when he moved to Keokuk. In 1840-42 he was prosecutor for the five counties comprising the southeast corner of the state, and after moving to Keokuk, he served for four years as president of the Des Moines Valley Railroad. On February 22, 1862, Reid entered the Union army as colonel of the 15th Iowa, a Keokuk regiment. His first service was in April at Shiloh where his command was employed by U. S. Grant to prevent stragglers from leaving the field and where he was badly wounded. (507) At the battle of Corinth the 15th Iowa was in Crocker's brigade of McKean's division; however, Reid himself was ill during the principal action and unable to exercise command. During the Vicksburg campaign

Reid, who had been promoted to brigadier general on April 9, 1863, to rank from March 13, commanded

a brigade of Negro and white troops of the XVII Corps around Lake Providence, Louisiana. An early proponent of the enlistment of colored troops, he offered the interesting observation that "every colored soldier who stops a rebel bullet saves a white man's life." He was ordered to the command of the post at Cairo, Illinois, in October. On March 16, 1864, he was relieved from this command, and at the time his resignation was accepted (April 4, 1864), he seems to have been in command of the District of Cairo with headquarters at Columbus, Kentucky. (508) General Reid returned to Des Moines after his resignation and again devoted himself to the interests of the Des Moines Valley Railroad Company. He was also a pioneer advocate of building the railroad and passen-

ger bridge over the Mississippi River at Keokuk, Iowa. He died of Bright's disease on August 21, 1874, and was buried in Oakland Cemetery. (509)

James William Reilly was born May 20, 1828, in Akron, Ohio. He was educated at Mount St. Mary's College (Emmittsburg, Maryland), studied law, was admitted to the bar, and in 1861 was elected to the Ohio legislature from Columbiana County. It is said that in the early years of his law practice in Wellsville, Ohio, it was not uncommon for him to walk from there to Lisbon, the county seat, a distance of some fifteen miles. (510) Reilly was appointed colonel of the 104th Ohio upon its organization on August 30, 1862. This regiment garrisoned various points in Kentucky until the summer of 1863 when it

joined Ambrose E. Burnside's army in East Tennessee. In the siege of Knoxville, Reilly commanded a brigade of Hascall's division of the XXIII Corps. The following spring his brigade took part in the Atlanta campaign, and at one point, although still a colonel, Reilly commanded the 3rd Division of the XXIII Corps. Reilly was promoted to brigadier general of volunteers on July 30, 1864, and after the Confederate evacuation of Atlanta accompanied G. H. Thomas' forces back to Tennessee to oppose John B. Hood's invasion of the state. At the bloody battle of Franklin which cost the Confederacy twelve general officers, Reilly distinguished himself again in temporary command of the 3rd Division of his corps—his men claimed one thousand prisoners and twenty-two battle flags. (511) He was not present at the battle of Nashville, (512) but directed the division during the movement which brought John M. Schofield's forces together with William T. Sherman's in the Carolinas. He served until his resignation was accepted on April 20, 1865, only a few days before the capitulation of J. E. Johnston and his army. This no doubt militated against his brevet promotion to major general. General Reilly then returned to Wellsville and resumed his law practice. A lifelong bachelor, he discharged innumerable duties of public trust including membership in the state constitutional convention of 1873, trustee of the Soldiers' Home at Xenia, counselor to young lawyers in the courts of eastern Ohio; and for many years the presidency of the First National Bank of Wellsville. He died at his home on November 6, 1905, and was buried in St. Elizabeth's Cemetery, Wellsville.

Jesse Lee Reno, whose surname was originally Renault, was born June 20, 1823, in the Ohio River town of Wheeling, Virginia (now West Virginia); however, his parents moved to Venango County, Pennsylvania around 1832. He was graduated from the Military Academy in 1846, ranking eighth in the class which included George B. McClellan, Stonewall Jackson, and George Pickett. Although he was an ordnance officer from his graduation until the early months of the Civil War, Reno won the brevets of first lieutenant and captain for gallantry at Cerro Gordo and Chapultepec. In the course of the next fifteen years his duties were varied: they included teaching at West Point, membership on ordnance boards, participation in topographical surveys, chief of ordnance on the Utah expedition under Albert Sidney Johnston, and the successive commands of the Mount Vernon, Alabama, and Leavenworth, Kansas, arsenals. He was forced to surrender the Mount Vernon arsenal to the state forces of Alabama in January, 1861. On November 12 of that year Reno was commissioned brigadier general of volunteers and subsequently commanded a brigade of Ambrose E. Burnside's expedition against the Carolina coast that winter, fighting at Roanoke Island, New Bern, and Camden. From April until his recall north in August, 1862, he directed a division in the newly established Federal Department of North Carolina. Reno was appointed major general on August 20 to rank from July 18, 1862, and during the campaign of Second Manassas, directed Burnside's IX Corps while the latter was in charge of the right wing of John Pope's army which was advancing northward from the line of the Rappahannock. Reno's corps sustained itself well at the battle of Second Manassas and again the following day (September 1, 1862) at Chantilly; then, the IX Corps retired to the Washington defenses along with the rest of Pope's forces. It remained in the capital until it was led out a few days later under the banner of George B. McClellan, who had been restored to command of the Army of the Potomac. In the subsequent Maryland campaign against R. E. Lee's Confederate invaders, Reno was mortally wounded while leading his men into Fox's Gap in South Mountain on September 14, 1862. The field where he was injured is now marked by a seldom-seen monument to his memory. His body was first taken to Boston, where his wife was residing, and placed in a vault in Trinity Church. On April 9, 1867, his remains were removed to Oak Hill Cemetery, Georgetown, D. C.

Joseph Warren Revere, grandson of Paul Revere, was born May 17, 1812, in Boston. He was named for one of his grandfather's dental patients, the patriot Dr. Joseph Warren who was killed at Bunker Hill.

(513) Revere entered the navy as a midshipman at the age of sixteen and during the next twenty-two years served all over the globe, receiving a promotion to lieutenant in 1841. After resigning from the navy in 1850 he lived for a time in California and subsequently served in the Mexican army as a colonel, charged with organizing the artillery arm. From 1852 until 1861 he resided in Morristown, New Jersey, when not traveling abroad. First volunteering for the navy, Revere finally entered the Federal service as colonel of the 7th New Jersey Infantry on September 19, 1861.

During the Peninsular campaign this regiment was in Hooker's division of Heintzelman's III Corps; however, Revere himself seems to have been present only during he Seven Days battles, when the brigade was directed by Joseph B. Carr. Commissioned brigadier general on October 25, 1862, he commanded the 3rd Brigade of Sickles' division of the III Corps at Fredericksburg, losing only one killed and one wounded. The battle of Chancellorsville, however, was Revere's Waterloo. After Howard's XI Corps had been overrun by Stonewall Jackson's celebrated flank march to the Union right, Berry's division of the III Corps was hurried forward to retrieve disaster. But Berry was mortally wounded; so the command devolved upon the senior brigadier Revere, who, instead of throwing everything he had at the onrushing Confederates, marched that portion of his command within reach to the rear "for the purpose of reorganizing and bringing them back to the field comparatively fresh." (514) This solicitude earned for him a court-martial and dismissal from the service—a sentence which was mitigated by the President who permitted the unfortunate commander to resign, effective August 10, 1863. In his remaining seventeen years of life, General Revere, although suffering from declining health, traveled extensively abroad and wrote a couple of memoirs. He died in Hoboken, New Jersey, April 20, 1880, and was buried in Morristown.

John Fulton Reynolds was born in Lancaster, Pennsylvania, September 20, 1820, only fifty-odd miles

from the point where he would meet his death. Prior to entering the Military Academy in 1837, he attended school in nearby Lititz, in Longgreen, Maryland, and at the Lancaster County Academy. Reynolds was graduated from West Point in 1841. After four years of garrison duty on the Atlantic coast as an artillery officer, he was ordered to the Texas frontier and was awarded the brevet promotions of captain and major for gallant and meritorious conduct in the Mexican War. In the next fourteen years he performed garrison duty at various points, twice crossed the plains, and in September, 1860, was named Commandant of Cadets and instructor of tactics at West Point—the position he held when war broke out the following spring. Reynolds was made lieutenant colonel of the newly reactivated 14th U. S. Infantry on May 14, 1861, and brigadier general of volunteers on August 26 to rank from the twentieth. On June 27, 1862, Reynolds was directing a brigade of McCall's division of Porter's V Corps behind Boatswain's Swamp on the Virginia Peninsula. The brigade was covering the retirement of George B. McClellan's right wing, when the Confederates overran the position and routed McCall's entire division, which included the brigades of George G. Meade and Truman Seymour. Reynolds and his adjutant were cut off and captured early the next morning by a Rebel picket detail and were not exchanged until August 8. (515) Upon rejoining the army he was assigned to command the 3rd Division, Pennsylvania Reserves, which was temporarily attached to McDowell's III Corps during the battle of Second Manassas. During the Maryland campaign he was in charge of the Pennsylvania militia which was mustered against the anticipated invasion of the state. Subsequently he was made commander of the I Corps, which he led at Fredericksburg in Franklin's "Left Grand Division." One of his divisions which was under Meade effected the only lodgment in the Confederate lines on that ill-starred December day. A few days before on November 29, 1862, Reynolds had been made major general. According to many authorities, Reynolds is said to have been offered, after Chancellorsville, command of the Army of the Potomac, replacing Joseph Hooker; but he declined the honor because he felt Washington would not give him a free hand. (516) At all events his junior, Meade was named, and Reynolds uncomplainingly took up the direction of the left wing of the army under his former subordinate. Or-

dered to occupy the strategically located village of Gettysburg (a name as unknown at the time as was Iwo Jima), Reynolds put his three corps—his own under Doubleday, the III Corps under Sickles, and Howard's XI Corps—on the road. By midmorning of July 1, 1863, he arrived on the field northwest of the town and on the south side of the Cashtown Road. While bringing up the 2nd Wisconsin, the leading regiment of the three corps, to aid the hard-pressed cavalry under John Buford, Reynolds was shot from his horse and killed instantly by a Rebel marksman who was firing from a barn on the edge of a nearby woodland. Three days later Reynolds was buried in Lancaster.

Joseph Jones Reynolds was born in Flemingsburg, Kentucky, on January 4, 1822, but when he was fifteen his parents moved across the Ohio River to Lafayette, Indiana. The next year he entered Wabash Col-

lege at Crawfordsville; a year thereafter, however, he was appointed to West Point. He was graduated in the class of 1843, which included U. S. Grant, with whom Reynolds remained on friendly terms. After some garrison duty and serving in the military occupation of Texas just prior to the war with Mexico, he was assigned as an instructor at the Academy, where he taught for eight years. He then did frontier duty in the Indian Territory until he submitted his resignation as first lieutenant, 3rd Artillery, in 1857. In the next four years he taught engineering at Washington University, St. Louis, and engaged in the grocery business in Lafayette. Immediately upon the outbreak of hostilities in 1861, Reynolds was appointed colonel of the 10th Indiana (militia), then brigadier general of Indiana volunteers, and on June 14, 1861, to rank from May 17, brigadier general, U. S. Volunteers. (517) He commanded at Cheat Mountain under W. S. Rosecrans in September, but resigned the following January because of the death of a brother with whom he was in partnership. While out of the service he aided in organizing Indiana troops and was again appointed a brigadier on September 17, 1862, and a major general of volunteers on November 29. He commanded a division of the XIV Corps at Chickamauga, and on October 10, 1863, was made chief of staff of G. H. Thomas' Army of the Cumberland, a position he held until after the battle of Chattanooga. In January, 1864, Reynolds was put in charge of the New Orleans defenses, and in July he took command of the XIX Corps and organized the campaign against Mobile. From November, 1864, until April, 1866, he commanded the Department of Arkansas; he became colonel of the 26th Infantry upon the expansion of the Army in July, 1866, and was brevetted brigadier and major general, U. S. Army, on March 2, 1867. He transferred to the 3rd Cavalry in 1870 and commanded occupation forces in the southwest, including the Department of Texas, until he was relieved of command in 1872 and ordered to rejoin his regiment. In 1871 he was elected U. S. Senator by the carpetbag legislature in Texas, but his seat was successfully contested by a brother of General A. J. Hamilton. He next commanded at various points in Nebraska and Wyoming. Reynolds was commanding the advance of Crook's expedition when it attacked and captured a Sioux village on the Powder River on March 17, 1876. He prematurely ordered a retreat, leaving his dead and a wounded private in the hands of the Indians who "promptly cut the [private] limb from limb." Some time later Reynolds' conduct, along with that of certain other officers, was the subject of a general court-martial. Subsequently, he resigned, his army career wrecked. After his retirement he established a residence in Washington, where he died on February 25, 1899; he was buried in Arlington National Cemetery.

Americus Vespucius Rice was born November 18, 1835, in Perryville, Ohio. He attended Antioch College for a time but was graduated from Union College, Schenectady, New York, in 1860. Rice was studying law when, two weeks after the fall of Sumter, he was mustered

into the service of the United States as a captain of the 21st Ohio, a three-month regiment which saw some service in western Virginia. It was mustered out in August, and the following month he was re-mustered as a captain of the 57th Ohio which was enlisted for three years or the duration of the war. At Shiloh as a part of Sherman's division, the regiment numbered only 450 for duty because of illness; it then sustained 187 casualties while defending the little meetinghouse, which gave its name to the battle. Rice had been promoted to lieutenant colonel of the regiment in February and led it at Shiloh as well as at Chickasaw Bayou. In the successful attack on Arkansas Post, he was warmly commended for his services by Giles Smith, who commanded the brigade on Rice's left. (518) On May 24, 1863, he became colonel of the 57th Ohio and served during the Vicksburg and the Atlanta campaigns. While in command of his regiment he was wounded on June 27, 1864, at Kennesaw Mountain and was unable to rejoin the army until June 23, 1865, when, as a brigadier general of volunteers appointed on May 31, he took command of the 3rd Brigade, 2nd Division, of the XV Corps. (519) Rice, one of the youngest general officers recruited from civilian life, was neither a Radical, nor even a Republican. After being mustered out in 1866, he became a banker in Ottawa, Ohio, was a delegate to the 1872 National Democratic Convention, and served as a Democratic member of Congress from 1875 to 1879 (he did not stand for reelection in 1878). In the later years of his life General Rice engaged in business in his home town, acted as state pension agent, and in 1898 moved to Washington where he was appointed purchasing agent of the U. S. Census Bureau—a position which he held at the time of his death, April 4, 1904. He was buried in Arlington National Cemetery.

Elliott Warren Rice, a younger brother of General Samuel A. Rice, was born in Allegheny City (now part of Pittsburgh), Pennsylvania, on November 16, 1835; the next year his parents moved to Belmont County, Ohio. After attending school in Wheeling, (West) Virginia, he entered Franklin College (now Ohio University), at Athens, Ohio, and in 1855 went to Oskaloosa, Iowa, to study law with his brother. He was graduated from the law school of the University of Albany in 1858, and he returned to Oskaloosa, where he practiced law in partnership with his brother. He entered the Union army as a private in Company C, 7th Iowa, was made corporal on July 24, 1861, major on August 30, and colonel April 7; 1862. At the battle of Belmont he commanded the regiment after his colonel was wounded and

lieutenant colonel killed; Rice himself was badly wounded. He was still on crutches at Fort Donelson but fought at Shiloh in W. H. L. Wallace's division; at the battle of Corinth in October, 1862, he commanded his regiment in T. A. Davies' division of the Army of West Tennessee. After pursuing the Confederates to Rienzi, Mississippi, Rice was sent to Bethel, Tennessee, to take charge of the post and district and then on to La-Grange to protect the Memphis & Charleston Railroad between Memphis and Corinth. During the Atlanta campaign Rice commanded the 1st Brigade, 2nd Division, XVI Corps, and for a time the division itself, taking part in all the battles which led up the investment of

Atlanta. He was promoted to brigadier general of volunteers on June 22, 1864, and during the Atlanta campaign, W. T. Sherman's celebrated "March to the Sea," and the campaign of the Carolinas, he directed his brigade which was now in Corse's division of Logan's XV Corps, Army of the Tennessee. His last encounter was at Bentonville; shortly after this the Confederate forces under Joseph E. Johnston surrendered at Durham Station. Rice was brevetted major general in the omnibus promotions of March, 1865, and after being mustered out in August, 1865, practiced law in Washington for twenty years. In 1885 declining health compelled him to move to the home of a sister in Sioux City, Iowa, where he died June 22, 1887, and was buried in Floyd Cemetery. General Rice was wounded seven times during the war and carried the bullet he received at Belmont the rest of his life.

James Clay Rice was born December 27, 1829, in the western Massachusetts hamlet of Worthington. With little formal education he entered Yale University where he was graduated in 1854. For a time he engaged in teaching at Natchez, Mississippi, meanwhile conducting the literary department of a local newspaper and studying law. In 1855 he went to New York and the following year was admitted to the practice of law. He was made a lieutenant of the 39th New York as early as May 10, 1861, captain in August, and lieutenant colonel of the 44th New York on September 13. After becoming colonel of the 44th New York in July, 1862, he led

it throughout George B. McClellan's Peninsular campaign. This regiment formed a part of Morell's division of the V Corps with which Rice was thereafter connected. For a time at Second Manassas, he was in command of his brigade. But during the Confederate invasion of Maryland the 44th New York is shown under the command of its major, and at Fredericksburg under the command of its lieutenant colonel. Rice rejoined his men, however, in time to be reported in command on December 31, 1862, and took part in the battle of Chancellorsville in May, 1863, although the brigade to which he was attached sustained only nominal losses. At Gettysburg, Rice performed heroic service on Little Round Top, when the command of the brigade devolved upon him. It is not too much to say that this little band of four regiments, numbering scarcely a thousand muskets, saved the Union cause from disaster on that memorable second of July, while sustaining 352 casualties. For his services at this engagement Rice was made a brigadier general of volunteers on August 17, 1863, and assigned to permanent command of a brigade in Cutler's division of the I Corps. When the I Corps was broken up, Rice rejoined the V Corps and at the beginning of the Wilderness campaign directed a brigade of Wadsworth's division. At Spotsylvania on May 10, 1864, his thigh was shattered by a rifle ball, necessitating amputation of his leg. He failed to rally from the operation and died shortly after. (520) When the surgeon had asked him on which side he would rest more comfortably, he had replied, "Turn my face to the enemy." He was buried in Rural Cemetery, Albany, New York.

Samuel Allen Rice, brother of General Elliott W. Rice, was born in Cattaraugus County, New York, on January 27, 1828; the family moved, however, to western Pennsylvania and then to Belmont County, Ohio. Rice was educated at what is now Ohio University at Athens, and at Union College, Schenectady, New York. During his youth he made a number of merchandising trips on his father's flatboat down the Ohio and Mississippi rivers to New Orleans. After graduation from Union College in 1849 and a year of study at its law school, Rice went to Iowa, locating finally in 1851 in Oskaloosa where he established his law practice. His legal career in this pioneer state was outstanding: he was elected county attorney in 1853, attorney general of the state three years later, and reelected in 1858. During

the summer of 1862 he organized the 33rd Iowa and was commissioned its colonel by Governor Samuel J. Kirkwood on August 10, though the regiment was not mustered into Federal service until October 1, 1862. Rice's entire military service took place in the states of Missouri and Arkansas—a theater of little note at the time, imperfectly understood since, and in general relegated to the background by historians. However, the peripheral operations undertaken in the area played an important part in the final outcome of the war. In the spring of 1863 Rice went to Helena, Arkansas, and with his command opened the Yazoo Pass for navigation. After this he took a gallant part in the battle of Helena, during which the Confederate T. H. Holmes unsuccessfully attempted to recapture the town while half of the Federal troops in the department were away sustaining U. S. Grant in his effort to take Vicksburg. On August 4, 1863,

Rice was elevated to brigadier general of volunteers and was with General Frederick Steele when the latter captured the capital of Arkansas. In the spring of 1864 Banks and Steele were supposed to launch a two-pronged attack which would effectively clear the Rebels out of North Louisiana and Arkansas— Banks moving up Red River and Steele applying a pincer toward Camden. At the battle of Jenkins' Ferry, April 30, 1864, in what was essentially a rear-guard action, fragments of Rice's spur were carried by a bullet into his right ankle, shattering the bone. He was transported home to Oskaloosa where the primitive surgical procedures of the day virtually condemned him to death on July 6, 1864. He was buried in Forest Cemetery.

Israel Bush Richardson, whose nicknames "Fighting Dick" and "Greasy Dick" were equally well earned, (521) was born in Fairfax, Vermont, December 26, 1815. A descendant of Revolutionary War General Israel Putnam, he was appointed to West Point in 1836 and was graduated five years later, ranking thirty-eighth in the celebrated class of 1841 which contributed twenty-three generals to the Civil War out of its fifty-two members, fourteen members having died prior to 1861. Richardson served against the Florida Seminoles immediately following his graduation, but it was not until the war with Mexico that he especially distinguished himself, winning the brevets of captain and major for gallantry at Contreras, Churubusco, and Chapultepec. After some further service on the southwestern frontier, he resigned in 1855 to take up farming in Pon-

tion of the Peninsula by the Army of the Potomac. The apogee of his career came at Sharpsburg, where his division of Sumner's II Corps aided to some extent by W. H. French's division, drove D. H. Hill's Confederates from "Bloody Lane," in a savagely fought battle. While directing the fire of one of his supporting batteries of artillery, Richardson was wounded by a ball from a spherical case shot fired from a Confederate battery enfilading his line. (523) He was taken to the Pry House, George B. McClellan's headquarters, where he died on November 3, 1862. His remains were taken to Pontiac for burial.

tiac, Michigan. (522) On May 25, 1861, Richardson, who had recruited and organized the 2nd Michigan Infantry, was mustered into Federal service as its colonel. At the battle of First Manassas he commanded a brigade which was only slightly engaged while covering Blackburn's Ford of Bull Run. Nevertheless, he brought his command off the field in good order in the midst of a general rout and was made brigadier general on August 9. After making a reputation as an organizer and disciplinarian during the winter, he was assigned to a division of Sumner's corps for the campaign on the Virginia Peninsula in the spring and summer of 1862. Throughout this campaign he displayed the iron courage which endeared him to the rowdy Irish of Meagher's brigade. On July 5, 1862, he was promoted to major general to rank from July 4 and was assigned to a division of Hooker's I Corps after the evacua-

James Brewerton Ricketts, born June 21, 1817, was a native of New York City. He was appointed to

West Point in 1835 and was graduated in the class of 1839. Ricketts pre-Civil War career as an officer of artillery was unexcep-

403

tionable, and he received no brevet promotions in the Mexican War, although he took part in the battles of Monterey and Buena Vista. He was made captain in 1852, and at First Manassas on July 21, 1861, he commanded a battery attached to Franklin's brigade of Heintzelman's division. During this battle he was shot four times and was taken prisoner by the Confederates; he was not exchanged until January, 1862. Ricketts was promoted to brigadier general of volunteers on April 30, 1862, to rank from the day of the battle "for gallant and meritorious conduct" and was assigned to the command of a division of McDowell's corps, which he commanded at Cedar Mountain (where he covered N. P. Banks's withdrawal) and at Second Manassas. (524) At Sharpsburg, Ricketts had two horses killed and was badly injured when the second one fell on him. When he recovered sufficiently for duty, he was appointed to the Fitz John Porter court-martial, and as a result his reputation has suffered as has that of certain of the other members who were patently self-servers. (525) He did not return to the field until March, 1864, when he was assigned to a division of Sedgwick's VI Corps, which he led through Grant's Overland campaign against Richmond. In July, 1864, his command, numbering 3,350 muskets, was hurried North to oppose Jubal Early's raid on Washington. Ricketts arrived at the Monocacy River in time to bear the brunt of the Confederate assault and to delay Early for a vital twenty-four hours. Lew Wallace, his superior on the field, recorded that the division "fought magnificently"; of the total Union loss of 677 men, Ricketts' division lost 595. He then engaged in Philip Sheridan's Shenandoah campaign; and at Cedar Creek in October, while temporarily commanding the corps, Ricketts was wounded by a bullet through his chest which disabled him for life. Nonetheless, he returned to command of his division two days before R. E. Lee's surrender at Appomattox. Ricketts was brevetted major general of volunteers on August 1, 1864, and in the Regular Army as of March 13, 1865. On January 3, 1867, he was retired from active service as a major general for disability from wounds received in battle; however, he continued to do court-martial duty until 1869. He lived in Washington until his death on September 22, 1887; he was buried in Arlington National Cemetery.

James Wolfe Ripley was one of a handful of Civil War officers born in the eighteenth century. A native of Windham County, Connecticut, he was born December 10, 1794. Only 101 men preceded him at West Point, where, like most of his classmates of 1814, he was commissioned after little more than a year of study due to the exigencies of the War of 1812. Ripley served his country continuously for fifty-five years. For the first eighteen years of his army career he was an artillery officer, serving at Sackett's Harbor, New York, in 1814-15, under Andrew Jackson against the Seminoles and during the invasion of Florida. He transferred to the staff in 1832 and a year later was placed in charge of the Kennebec arsenal, which he directed until 1842. He then served as superintendent of the

Springfield armory for twelve years; on the Pacific Coast as chief of ordnance of the department; and as inspector of arsenals until 1860. Abroad on inspection duty in 1861 when the news of secession reached him, he immediately took a ship for home. When a friend observed that his country needed the sixty-six-year-old veteran, Ripley stoutly replied, "It can have me and every drop of blood in me." Ironically, he was the uncle of Ohio-born Confederate brigadier Roswell S. Ripley. He assumed direction of the Ordnance Department on April 23, 1861, succeeding the seventy-year-old Colonel H. K. Craig, who had been its chief for ten years. As a zealous and incorruptible, if not always imaginative, head of the Ordnance Department, his honesty, devotion to duty, and unbending principles were never seriously questioned; however, his notions about advances in the science of ordnance were no less inflexible, causing him to oppose virtually every innova-

tion suggested to the War Department. Although his position may to some extent be justified by the multiplicity of existing weapons for which he was expected to supply ammunition, his last-ditch fight against the introduction of breech-loaders ultimately caused his replacement on September 15, 1863, "under the Law of July 17, 1842, having been borne on the Army Register more than forty-five years." On August 3, 1861, he had been commissioned brigadier in the Regular Army, and until 1869 he continued to serve as "Inspector of Armament of Forts on the New England Coast." Brevetted major general, U. S. Army, in 1865, General Ripley died in Hartford, Connecticut, on March 15, 1870, and was buried in Springfield.

Benjamin Stone Roberts, a descendant of an old New England family of Welsh extraction, was born in Manchester, Vermont, on November 18, 1810. He graduated from

West Point, ranking near the bottom of the class of 1835, but resigned his commission four years later in order to become chief civil engineer of a New York railroad which is now a part of the Rutland. He was appointed geologist of New York State in 1841 and the following year aided in the construction of the railroad line from St. Petersburg (now Leningrad) to Moscow. After returning to the United States he studied law and began a practice in Des Moines, Iowa. With the outbreak of the Mexican War, Roberts was reappointed in the army with the rank of first lieutenant of Mounted Rifles. He was promoted to the regular rank of captain and the brevet ranks of major and lieutenant colonel and received a sword from his adopted state of Iowa—all for his distinguished service in this war. Remaining in the army, he discharged frontier duty at various stations in the Southwest and was promoted to major of his regiment on May 13, 1861 (the regiment's name was changed to 3rd Cavalry under the act of August 3, 1861). Roberts took part under Edward Canby in opposing Confederate General Henry Sibley's New Mexico invasion and was brevetted colonel for his services at the battle of Valverde. Soon after, he was summoned East and during the campaign of Second Manassas served as John Pope's inspector general as well as his chief of cavalry, thus becoming embroiled in the celebrated case of Fitz John Porter in which he officially preferred the charges which brought Porter to ruin. (526) After the trial he was shelved along with Pope and sent to Minnesota where he remained until recalled to Washington in February, 1863, to briefly command the upper defenses of the capital. He then held a series of minor commands until the end of the war. Nevertheless, his efforts in behalf of the clique pledged to oust George B. McClellan from command of the army were not unnoticed: he had received the full rank of brigadier general of volunteers to rank from July 16, 1862, and was awarded the brevets of brigadier in the regular service and major general of volunteers at the close of the war. Roberts became lieutenant colonel of his regiment in 1866 and was assigned as Professor of Military Science at Yale in 1868. He retired in 1870 so he could prosecute claims against the United States. He died in Washington, January 29, 1875, and was buried in Oak Hill Cemetery, his remains later being removed to his birthplace.

James Sidney Robinson was born October 14, 1827, on a farm near Mansfield, Ohio. After attending the local schools he learned the printer's trade and moved in 1845 to Kenton, Ohio, where he edited and published the Kenton *Republican* from 1847 until he entered the Union army in 1861. His name, however, was not removed from the paper's masthead until 1865. From 1856 to 1858 he was also chief clerk of the Ohio house of representatives. Robinson enlisted five days after the bombardment of Sumter, was elected first lieutenant the following day, captain on May 4, and led his company of the 4th Ohio—a ninety-day regiment—at Rich Mountain under George B. McClellan. He became major of the 82nd Ohio on December 31,

1861, lieutenant colonel April 9, 1862, and colonel August 29, 1862. He served with John C. Frémont in the Shenandoah that summer, and at the battle of Second Manassas he was in Milroy's "Independent Brigade" of Sigel's I Corps, Army of Virginia, taking charge of the 82nd Ohio after his colonel was killed. At Chancellorsville, the regiment was "unattached," although serving with Schurz' division of Howard's ill-fated XI Corps and sustaining eighty-one casualties when Howard's position was overrun by Stonewall Jackson's famous flank attack. At Gettysburg, Robinson's command was again involved in the defeat of the XI Corps, and he was severely wounded. Upon his return to duty, the XI and XII Corps had been consolidated into the XX Corps and sent west under Joseph Hooker and were poised to jump off against Joseph E. Johnston in W. T. Sherman's campaign against Atlanta. Robinson was assigned to

the command of the 3rd Brigade, 1st Division, of the XX Corps, which he led with sufficient distinction to be brevetted brigadier general of volunteers in December, 1864, and appointed a full brigadier on January 12, 1865. Meantime he had taken his command through Georgia and the Carolinas to Johnston's surrender at Durham Station and the grand review of the armies in Washington. In the postwar years General Robinson's career was hardly less distinguished: he served as commissioner of railroads and telegraphs in Ohio, occupied a seat in Congress from 1881 until his resignation in 1885, and was secretary of state of Ohio from 1885 until 1889. He died at his home in Kenton, January 14, 1892, and was buried in Grove Cemetery there.

John Cleveland Robinson, "the hairiest general . . . in a much-bearded army," (527) was born April 10, 1817, in Binghamton, New York. He also became known during the Civil War as a "salty old regular" (528) and as one of the Army of the Potomac's bravest and most distinguished division commanders. Robinson matriculated at the Military Academy in 1835, but in his second class year was dismissed for a violation of regulations. (529) On October 27, 1839, however, he was commissioned directly into the army as a second lieutenant of the 5th Infantry. During the Mexican War he served as a quartermaster and took part in the battles of Palo Alto, Resaca de la Palma, Monterrey, and the capture of Mexico City. He became captain in 1850 and in the next decade saw duty in Florida, Texas, and Utah. The outbreak of the Civil War found him in command of storied Fort McHenry in Baltimore Harbor, where he bluffed the local pro-Southern authorities into leaving the fort alone during the riots of April 19, 1861, which attended the passage of loyal regiments through the city. Later he engaged in recruiting volunteers in Ohio and Michigan and on September 1, 1861, was commissioned colonel of the 1st Michigan Infantry. The following spring he was promoted to brigadier general of volunteers to rank from April 28 and fought throughout George B. McClellan's Peninsular campaign in command of a brigade in Kearny's division of the III Corps. He directed the same command at Second Manassas and at Fredericksburg, whereupon he was elevated to division commander in Reynolds' I Corps. His troops were only lightly engaged during the campaign of Chancellorsville,

but on the first day at Gettysburg they formed the extension of the Union right on Oak Knoll. After Howard's XI Corps was swept from the field, the division fought savagely for hours, sustaining 1,685 casualties out of 2,500 men brought into action. Robinson retired the survivors in good order, and upon the reorganization which saw the I Corps's remnants consolidated with other units, he was given a division of Warren's V Corps. As the first Federal infantry to come upon the field of Spotsylvania early in the morning of May 8, 1864, he was ordered to assault the Confederate position without waiting to even mass his men. Putting himself at the head of his leading brigade, he made the attack but failed; Robinson himself received a ball in the left knee which necessitated the amputation of his leg and his removal from field duty. (530) He commanded various military districts in New York until the close of hostilities, when he directed the Freedmen's Bureau in North Carolina for a time. In 1867 and 1868 he successively commanded the departments of the South and the Lakes, after receiving the brevet of major general in both the regular and volunteer forces. On May 6, 1869, he was placed as a major general on the retired list because of disabilities arising from wounds received in battle while in divisional command. General Robinson was lieutenant governor of New York from 1872 to 1874 and thereafter devoted much time to veterans' activities, serving at various times as commander-in-chief of the Grand Army of the Republic and president of the Society of the Army of the Potomac. For his "most distinguished gallantry while at the head of his leading brigade" in the attack at Spotsylvania, he received the Congressional medal on March 28, 1894. The last years of his life, totally blind, he lived in Binghamton, where he died on February 18, 1897, and was buried in Spring Forest Cemetery.

Isaac Peace Rodman was born August 18, 1822, in South Kingstown, Rhode Island. (531) After receiving a basic education in the local schools, he became an outstanding

citizen of the area: he engaged in business with his father, became a prominent merchant, and served on the town council and in both branches of the Rhode Island legislature. In 1861 he was serving as a member of the state senate, but as a Quaker he was torn between the precepts of religion and loyalty. Unhesitatingly, however, he accepted a captaincy in the 2nd Rhode Island on June 6, 1861,

a three-year regiment which in conjunction with the rest of Ambrose E. Burnside's brigade lost its colonel and 362 members at First Bull Run. Rodman resigned October 25, 1861, in order to accept the colonelcy of the 4th Rhode Island on October 30. The following winter he accompanied Burnside's expedition to the Carolinas and took a gallant part in the reduction of Roanoke Island, the battle of New Bern, and the capture of Fort Macon, which guarded the harbor of Beaufort, North Carolina. On April 30, 1862, Rodman, upon the recommendation of Burnside, was made a brigadier general of volunteers to rank from April 28. Meantime he had contracted what was supposed to be typhoid fever and was sent home to Rhode Island to recuperate. Immediately before the critical battle of Sharpsburg, Rodman joined the Army of the Potomac and was assigned to command a division of the IX Corps under the ill-fated Jesse L. Reno, while Burnside was directing the left of the Army of the Potomac. George B. McClellan's strategy to overpower R. E. Lee was strongly dependent upon the ability of Burnside's corps to cross Antietam Creek and come in on the Confederate right. After a number of futile and ill-directed assaults in the vicinity of "Burnside's Bridge," Rodman got his men over an upper ford just in time to be assailed by Powell Hill's men arriving from the capitulation at Harpers Ferry. Rodman's men responded magnificently, but their left, the untried 16th Connecticut, caved in just as General Rodman was bringing up the 4th Rhode Island in support. At this moment he was struck down by a ball in the chest. Taken to a battlefield hospital, he survived until September 30, 1862; he was buried in a family cemetery at Peace Dale, Rhode Island.

William Starke Rosecrans, "Old Rosy," was born September 6, 1819, in his father's farmhouse on Little Taylor Run, Delaware County, Ohio. (532) As a boy he had little formal education but was

studiously inclined and an avid reader. He went to work at the age of fourteen and in 1838 secured an appointment to the Military Academy where he was graduated in 1842, ranking fifth in the class. In the next ten years his career in the Engineer Corps was unexceptionable: he took no part in the Mexican War; was promoted first lieutenant in 1853, and resigned in 1854. None of his civilian pursuits was particularly remunerative, and the outbreak of the war in 1861 found him head of an unsuccess-ful kerosine refinery in Cincinnati. Seven days after Sumter, Rosecrans became an aide on the staff of General George B. McClellan with the state rank of colonel of engineers. In June, 1861, he became simultaneously colonel of the 23rd Ohio Infantry and a brigadier general in the Regular Army to rank from May 16. During McClellan's campaign in western Virginia, he commanded a brigade at Rich Mountain, and after McClellan's departure to assume command of the Union army, Rosecrans opposed General Robert E. Lee in the campaign which drove Confederate troops from the area and resulted in the erection of the state of West Virginia. The following May, Rosecrans directed the left wing of John Pope's Army of the Mississippi which, under overall command of Henry Halleck, performed the tortoise-like advance upon the railroad junction of Corinth after the battle of Shiloh. He then succeeded Pope in command after the latter was summoned to the Eastern theater. Rosecrans was now under the command of U. S. Grant, successor to Halleck; and in October the indecisive battles of Iuka and Corinth were fought, wherein the Confederates Sterling Price and Earl Van Dorn sought to strike decisively at the railroad in combination, while the Union forces were striving to defeat them in detail. On September 17, 1862, Rosecrans had been appointed a major general of volunteers to rank from date, but, upon complaining of this date and of his relative rank, he was reappointed October 25, 1862, to rank from March 21, 1862. (533) He was then ordered to relieve Don Carlos Buell in Kentucky and his

410

troops, composed of three corps, were designated the Army of the Cumberland; he took command on October 27, 1862. At year's end he repulsed Braxton Bragg's Army of Tennessee at Murfreesboro—an engagement in which losses of almost twenty-five thousand approximated one-third of the effectives engaged on both sides. (534) On January 3, 1863, Bragg drew back to a line along Duck River with headquarters at Tullahoma; Confederates W. J. Hardee's corps were at Wartrace and Leonidas Polk's at Shelbyville. After a six-month lull in operations, Rosecrans, toward the end of June, 1863, inaugurated a campaign of maneuver—as brilliant as any in American military annals—which forced the Confederates from their position into the fortified railroad center of Chattanooga and then by a skillful feint up the Tennessee, out of the town. Rosecrans and Bragg had both been calling loudly for reinforcements from their respective governments; and Bragg received them in substantial measure, with the result that for one of the few times in the war the Confederates outnumbered their adversaries. (535) At Chickamauga, a meandering creek whose name means "River of Death," the casualties numbered almost thirty-five thousand in a battle which lasted only two days (September 19 and 20, 1863) but which inflicted a crushing defeat upon the Union and virtually wrote finis to Rosecrans' military career. Upon the retirement of the Federal forces to Chattanooga, he was supplanted in command by Grant on October 19, 1863. He commanded the Department of Missouri during 1864 and then was either awaiting orders or

on leave until he resigned his Regular Army commission on March 28, 1867. In 1868 President Johnson made him minister to Mexico, a post from which Grant, upon taking office in 1869, removed him. During the rest of his life he resided mainly in California on his ranch near present-day Redondo Beach, where he was wont to comment on oil seepage into his water wells. He was elected to Congress in 1880 and served until 1885, rising to chairman of the Committee on Military Affairs. From 1885 until 1893 he was register of the Treasury. General Rosecrans died at his ranch March 11, 1898, and was first buried in Rosedale Cemetery, Los Angeles. On May 17, 1902, his remains were reinterred in Arlington National Cemetery.

Leonard Fulton Ross, the son of one of Illinois' earliest settlers, was born at Lewistown, where his father was the proprietor, on July 18, 1823. After a year at Jacksonville College, he read law and was admitted to the bar in 1845. During the Mexican War he served with distinction as a lieutenant in the 4th Illinois Volunteers, whose colonel was Edward D. Baker, Lincoln's friend. He was later probate judge of Fulton County, county clerk, local Democratic leader, and stockbreeder of wide reputation. Upon the outbreak of the Civil War, Ross was appointed colonel of the 17th Illinois to rank from May 25, 1861. He served in Missouri and Kentucky, taking part in a number of minor engagements during the summer of 1861, including the expedition to Fredericktown, Missouri, in October. At Fort Donelson he commanded the 3rd Bri-

gade of McClernand's division and on April 26, 1862, was promoted brigadier general of volunteers. Absent at Shiloh, he participated in the "siege" of Corinth and in July, 1862, was stationed in command of a division at Bolivar, Tennessee, to protect the Mississippi Central Railroad (now the Illinois Central) and the surrounding country. For a time he was also in command of the District of Jackson. In December, 1862, Ross was in charge of a division in U. S. Grant's movement into Mississippi, which was frustrated by Earl Van Dorn's celebrated raid on Holly Springs. During the Vicksburg campaign he commanded the infantry forces engaged in the Yazoo Pass expedition—the third attempt by Grant to get his forces in the rear of Vicksburg from above the town. After this expedition he was assigned to the post of Helena, Arkansas. Ostensibly for business reasons but "believing that the war was near its close," General Ross

resigned his commission on July 22, 1863, and returned to civilian life. After the war he operated stock farms at Avon, Illinois, and Iowa City, Iowa. He was appointed collector of internal revenue for the ninth Illinois district in 1867; was three times a delegate to Republican national conventions; and in 1868 and 1872 was an unsuccessful candidate for Congress. For many years he was widely known in agricultural circles as an importer and breeder of fine livestock and as an officer in various organizations dedicated to progressive agriculture and breed improvement. General Ross died at his old home in Lewiston on January 17, 1901, and was buried there in Oakhill Cemetery. (536)

Lovell Harrison Rousseau, a descendant of one of four Huguenot brothers who came to America from France in 1689 after the revocation of the Edict of Nantes, was born

August 4, 1818, near Stanford, Lincoln County, Kentucky. (537) When his father died in a cholera epidemic when he was fifteen, Lovell terminated his formal education and became a common laborer in the construction of a turnpike road. Later he settled in Lexington and studied law, and in 1840 he moved to Bloomfield, Indiana, where he was admitted to the bar. In 1844 he was elected to the Indiana legislature and during the Mexican War served with gallantry as a captain of the 2nd Indiana Volunteers. He was a member of the state senate from 1847 to 1849; then he returned to Kentucky to practice law in Louisville. In 1860 he was elected to the Kentucky senate, but, a dedicated opponent of secession, he resigned in 1861 in order to recruit volunteers for the Union The declared "neutrality" of the state delayed his muster-in as colonel of the 3rd Kentucky (Union) Infantry until September 9, 1861. He was promoted to brigadier general on October 1 and major general on October 22, 1862, to rank from the eighth. At Shiloh he commanded a brigade of D. C. Buell's Army of the Ohio and at Perryville gallantly led a division of Alexander McD. McCook's corps. Subsequently, he succeeded to divisional command in G. H. Thomas' Army of the Cumberland, serving with distinction at the battle of Murfreesboro (Stone's River) in the Tullahoma campaign and at the end of the Chickamauga campaign. Although he was not present at the battle of Chickamauga itself, he rejoined his command the day after. (538) From November, 1863, until November, 1865, General Rousseau had commanded of the districts of Nashville and of Tennessee, the latter with headquarters at Murfreesboro. He resigned in 1865 to take the seat in Congress to which he had been elected from Kentucky as a full-blown Republican Radical. However, he foreswore these extreme tenets and soon found himself an avowed exponent of moderation and a supporter of Andrew Johnson. After caning the Radical Josiah B. Grinnell of Iowa in a Capitol corridor, he was censured by the House and resigned his seat, but was triumphantly reelected by his Kentucky constituency. Johnson made him a brigadier and brevet major general in the Regular Army on March 28, 1867, and he was sent to Alaska to formally receive that territory from the Russians. In 1868 he succeeded Philip Sheridan in command of the department of Louisiana; he died in New Orleans, January 7, 1869. General Rousseau was buried in Arlington National Cemetery. He was the father-in-law of General Louis D. Watkins, who died nine months earlier than Rousseau, also in New Orleans.

Thomas Algeo Rowley, a lifelong resident of Pittsburgh except for his service in two wars, was born there on October 5, 1808. He learned the cabinetmaker's trade, but subsequently was elected a justice of the peace. When war was declared with Mexico, he served as captain of a company of Pennsylvania volunteers from 1847 until 1848 known as the "Jackson Blues." On his return he did work for the city as a contractor, was active in politics, and from 1857 to 1860 was clerk of courts of Allegheny

County. On April 25, 1861, Rowley was commissioned colonel of the 13th Pennsylvania, a three-month regiment which was designated the 102nd Pennsylvania upon reenlistment. The 13th was mainly employed in garrison duty on the Potomac line. The 102nd was present throughout the war from the Peninsula to Appomattox, reenlisting almost to a man at the end of 1863. Rowley and his command fought at Yorktown, Williamsburg, Seven Pines, and Malvern Hill in Couch's division of Keyes's IV Corps. The brigade, first under John J. Peck and subsequently under Albion P. Howe, was detached from the IV Corps and helped cover the withdrawal of the Union army after Second Manassas, acting as support to a battery at Chantilly. At Sharpsburg it was in reserve, and upon Ambrose E. Burnside's taking command of the army, it was assigned permanently to the VI Corps. Rowley, who had been

slightly wounded at Seven Pines, was promoted brigadier general on November 29, 1862. At Fredericksburg he was briefly in command of a brigade of Newton's division of the VI Corps, but for reasons not made apparent in the records was superseded by Frank Wheaton who was in command of the 2nd Rhode Island of Devens' brigade of the same division. (539) During the campaign of Chancellorsville, Rowley directed a I Corps brigade in Doubleday's division; and at Gettysburg he was for a time in command of the division while Abner Doubleday directed the corps. When the decimated I Corps was broken up, Rowley was assigned to the draft rendezvous at Portland, Maine. (540) Prior to the opening of the spring campaign of 1864, Rowley returned to the Army of the Potomac and was court-martialed at Culpeper, Virginia, on April 23, 1864. (541) However, Secretary of War Edwin Stanton disapproved the sentence and ordered Rowley restored to duty. As a result, he was given the command of the District of the Monongahela, with headquarters in Pittsburgh, where he remained for the balance of the year. He resigned on December 29, 1864. After the war he practiced law and served as United States marshal from 1866 to 1870. He died May 14, 1892, and was buried in Allegheny Cemetery. (542)

Daniel Henry Rucker, whose army career spanned forty-five years and whose life spanned nearly a century, was born on April 28, 1812, in Belleville, New Jersey. As a young man he moved to Grosse Isle, Michigan, a village near Detroit, and it was from Michigan that he was

commissioned directly into the army as a second lieutenant of the 1st Dragoons on October 13, 1837. He was promoted first lieutenant in 1844, captain in 1847, and for gallantry at Buena Vista in the Mexican War won the brevet of major. In 1849 Rucker transferred from line to staff and was thereafter associated with the Quartermaster's Department. He was promoted to major in August, 1861, and during the Civil War was brevetted major general in both the volunteers and the Regular Army for "diligent and faithful service" and "faithful and meritorious service." The procurement and distribution of wagons, ambulances, horses, mules, harness, forage, and the thousand other items needed for the transportation of an army do not afford a potential for heroics; nevertheless, the Quartermaster's Department was one of the most, if not the most, efficiently operated of the War Department bureaus, and

Rucker seems to have ably seconded his chief, General Montgomery C. Meigs. Upon the reorganization of the army in July, 1866, General Rucker was named assistant quartermaster general with rank of colonel, a post which he occupied until 1882, when Meigs, who had headed the bureau since 1861, retired. On February 13, 1882, Rucker was made quartermaster general with rank of brigadier general and ten days later was himself placed on the retired list. He continued to make his residence in Washington, where he lived for another twenty-eight years. On January 6, 1910, less than four months before his ninety-eighth birthday, he died in his home. Only one other full-rank general officer of the Civil War lived to an older age than Rucker, and only 30 of the 583 who won such rank survived him. He was buried in Arlington National Cemetery. (543)

Thomas Howard Ruger, the son of an Episcopal minister, was born April 2, 1833, in Lima, New York, but the family moved to Janesville, Wisconsin, when he was thirteen. In 1850 he was appointed to the Military Academy and was graduated in 1854, ranking third in his class. (544) A year later he resigned his commission to become a lawyer in Janesville. Ruger reentered the service as lieutenant colonel of the 3rd Wisconsin on June 29, 1861, and became colonel on September 1. After "preventing the assemblage of a Rebel Legislature at Frederick, Maryland" in the same month, he had the misfortune to be associated with N. P. Banks in the Shenandoah Valley and again at Cedar Mountain, where Stone-

415

wall Jackson drove the Union forces helter-skelter. During the Maryland campaign Ruger's regiment was a part of the XII Corps; he was commissioned a brigadier general of volunteers to rank from November 29, 1862. In the meantime he was wounded during the fight at Sharpsburg while in brigade command. In the campaign of Chancellorsville he commanded a brigade of Alpheus Williams' division; and at Gettysburg he directed the division while Williams was temporarily in command of the XII Corps, and Henry W. Slocum of the right wing of the army. When the XI and XII Corps were sent to the western theater and consolidated as the XX Corps, Ruger again commanded a brigade in Williams' division. After the fall of Atlanta he accompanied General G. H. Thomas' detachment back to Tennessee, and was in command of a division of the XXIII Corps at the savage battle of Franklin, where his

heroism later earned him the brevet of major general of volunteers. (545) In the Carolina campaign which terminated with the surrender of Joseph E. Johnston's army at Durham Station, North Carolina, Ruger's 1st Division, along with the balance of John M. Schofield's corps, joined W. T. Sherman in time to participate in the closing scenes of the war in the East. Following the war he commanded the Department of North Carolina for a year and then was made colonel of the 33rd Infantry, one of the newly authorized regular regiments. General Ruger served as superintendent of West Point in the seventies, was advanced to brigadier general in 1886 and major general in 1895. His postbellum career embraced the command of various military departments as well as active duty in the field. Retired at the statutory age of sixty-four, he spent his last years in Stamford, Connecticut, where he died on June 3, 1907. He was buried at West Point.

David Allen Russell was born December 10, 1820, in Salem, New York. His father David Abel Russell was a Congressman from 1835 to 1841 and during his last year in Congress secured for his son an appointment to West Point. Young Allen was graduated near the bottom of the class of 1845, more than a third of whose members attained the full rank of general officer on one side or the other during the Civil War. (546) Russell was posted to the infantry and won the brevet of first lieutenant for gallantry in the Mexican War. He subsequently served in garrison and on frontier duty in the Pacific Northwest and

was promoted captain, 4th Infantry, in 1854. Returning to the East in November, 1861, he served in the Washington defenses during the first winter of the war. He was made colonel of the 7th Massachusetts Volunteer Infantry on January 31, 1862, and engaged in the Peninsular campaign, his regiment constituting a part of Couch's division of Keyes's IV Corps. This division was the only IV Corps unit which fought in the Maryland campaign, during which it was attached to Franklin's VI Corps. On November 29 Russell was promoted brigadier general and at Fredericksburg directed a brigade of the VI Corps which was only lightly engaged. The following May, however, the VI Corps, now under John Sedgwick, stormed Marye's Heights during the campaign of Chancellorsville, and Russell's brigade sustained 368 casualties. At Gettysburg the 1st Division's total casualties amounted to only one killed and seventeen wounded; two

of the wounded were in Russell's brigade. At Rappahannock Station in November, Russell, temporarily in command of a division, greatly distinguished himself by personally leading a charge which overran the Confederate bridgehead on the north side of the river—a position supposedly so strong that one of Jubal Early's brigade commanders stated he could hold it against the whole Federal army. (547) Rebel casualties numbered 1,674 and the Union trophys included four pieces of artillery and eight battle flags which Russell personally escorted to Washington at George G. Meade's behest. Prior to the launching of U. S. Grant's Richmond campaign the following spring, Russell was assigned to permanent divisional command in the VI Corps and fought with distinction from the Wilderness to Petersburg. In July, 1864, his division was hurried north along with the rest of the VI Corps to resist Early's raid on Washington and later to pursue the Confederate leader in the Shenandoah Valley. At the battle of Winchester on September 19, 1864, while leading one of his brigades, Russell was killed instantly by a shell fragment which tore through his heart. He was buried in Evergreen Cemetery, Salem.

Friedrich (Frederick) Salomon was born on April 7, 1826, probably in the village of Strobeck in Saxony, then a part of Prussia. (548) He obtained a good education in the local gymnasium, became a surveyor, rose to the rank of lieutenant during his army service, and was a student of architecture in Berlin when the revolutions which swept

throughout the war in an area which was seldom in the spotlight. On July 4, 1863, Salomon, commanding a division of the XIII Corps, fought off a determined attack by a Confederate force under Lieutenant General T. H. Holmes on the defenses of Helena and earned high praise from his district commander General Benjamin M. Prentiss, who stated that "the thanks . . . of the nation . . . are due . . . General . . . Salomon." (549) He commanded the 3rd Division at the Battle of Jenkins' Ferry where his command's stout defense enabled Frederick Steele's battered troops to cross the Saline River. He was brevetted major general on March 13, 1865, for meritorious service and was honorably mustered out on August 25. After the war General Salomon was appointed surveyor general of Missouri. Upon the accession of Rutherford B. Hayes to the presidency, he was made United States surveyor general of the Territory of Utah, an office which he continued to fill during the terms of Presidents Garfield and Arthur. He died in Salt Lake City, on March 8, 1897, and was buried there in Mt. Olivet Cemetery.

Europe broke out. He was the eldest of four brothers who emigrated to America in 1848; two were brevetted brigadier general during the Civil War and another was governor of Wisconsin in 1862-63. He settled in Manitowoc, Wisconsin, where he became prominent as surveyor, register of deeds, and engineer in the location of the Manitowoc & Wisconsin Railroad (today a part of the Chicago & Northwestern Railroad). Salomon entered the volunteer army on May 19, 1861, as a captain of the 5th Missouri, a three-month regiment whose colonel was one of his brothers; this regiment fought at Wilson's Creek in Sigel's brigade. On November 26, 1861, Salomon was appointed colonel of the 9th Wisconsin which he commanded in Missouri and Arkansas until he was made brigadier general on July 18, 1862, to rank from July 16, and was assigned to the command of a brigade in Kansas. He served

John Benjamin Sanborn was born in the New Hampshire village of Epsom on December 5, 1826. He entered Dartmouth College with the class of 1855 but remained only one year. He then seems to have studied law, for he was admitted to the bar in 1854. The same year he moved to St. Paul, Minnesota, where he resided the rest of his life. When Fort Sumter fell he was the state's quartermaster general and a few days later became its adjutant general as well. As such he sent five regiments, a battalion, and two batteries to the war in 1861. Late that year he became colonel of the 4th Minnesota, which joined Henry W. Halleck's forces after Shiloh. At the battle of Iuka in September, 1861, Sanborn led one of W. S. Rosecrans' brigades of the Army of

Mississippi which sustained 588 casualties out of the 2,200 present in a bloody little fight regarded as indecisive by both sides. At the battle of Corinth the following month he returned to command of his regiment; however, during the Vicksburg campaign he was in charge of the 1st Brigade of Crocker's division, McPherson's XVII Corps, and won the honor of leading the advance into the Confederate fortress after the surrender. He was commissioned brigadier general on August 4, 1863, and brevetted major general from February 10, 1865. In the autumn of 1863 he took command of the Dis-

trict of Southwest Missouri and, under the general command of General S. R. Curtis, led his men with considerable distinction during Sterling Price's raid into the state in 1864; Sanborn's command bore the brunt of the fighting at Independence. In the summer of 1865 General Sanborn conducted a campaign against the southwestern Indian tribes which resulted in the signing of treaties (ultimately valueless) at the mouth of the Little Arkansas River in October. Subsequently, under the direction of President Johnson in 1865-66, Sanborn smoothed out the difficulties which arose between the Five Civilized Tribes (Cherokee, Choctaw, Chickasaw, Creek, and Seminole) and their slaves who had been freed by treaty rather than by the Emancipation Proclamation. Later General Sanborn was again an outstanding member of the St. Paul bar and served in the Minnesota legislature, in the House in 1872 and in the Senate from 1891 until 1893. He died in St. Paul on May 16, 1904, and was buried in Oakland Cemetery.

William Price Sanders was born August 12, 1833, in Kentucky, probably in Frankfort or nearby Forks of Elkhorn. (550) When he was about seven years old, his father, a well-known lawyer, moved with his family to Natchez, Mississippi. Young Sanders profited from his father's political connections: Aaron G. Brown, postmaster general under James Buchanan, secured William's appointment to West Point in 1852, and Jefferson Davis interceded in his behalf when he was about to be dismissed the following year for deficiency in languages. (551) After his graduation in 1856, he served on the frontier as an officer of dragoons and in the Utah expedition. During the first winter of the war Sanders was on duty in the Washington defenses as a captain of the 6th Cavalry, a regiment which served on

the Peninsula the following summer and in the Maryland campaign in September, 1862. Sanders was on sick leave until February, 1863, when he was made colonel of the 5th Kentucky (Union) Cavalry to rank from March 4. He took part in the pursuit of John Hunt Morgan and his raiders through Kentucky, Indiana, and Ohio in July; served as chief of cavalry, Department of the Ohio, in September and October; and in the Knoxville campaign commanded a brigade of the XXIII Corps and subsequently the 1st Division of the cavalry corps under James M. Shackelford. On November 18, 1863, Sanders was engaged in checking James Long-street's advance as Ambrose E. Burnside's army got in position in the rear; he was fighting dismounted on Kingston Road, a mile in advance of the defenses of Knoxville, when he was mortally wounded. Sanders died the next day in the bridal suite of the Lamar Hotel in Knoxville. He had been promoted to the rank of brigadier general of volunteers exactly a month before he received his fatal wound, and his loss was "keenly felt" by his associates, men and officers alike. (552) General Sanders was probably first buried in the yard of the Episcopal Church in Knoxville. Sometime subsequently, on a date unknown to Knoxville historians as well as the Quartermaster's Department, he was reinterred in a most obscure manner in the National Cemetery at Chattanooga. The overlooked grave is identifiable only by a simple government headstone bearing his name and volunteer rank, singular enough when it is considered that two of his sisters were the wives of James Ben Ali Haggin and Lloyd Tevis, the California Croesuses. (553)

Rufus Saxton was born on October 19, 1824, in Greenfield, Massachusetts. He attended nearby Deerfield Academy and worked on a farm until, at the age of twenty, he received an appointment to West Point from which he was graduated in the class of 1849. Saxton's appointment was to the artillery with which he served against the Florida Seminoles, on the Northern Pacific Railroad survey, in garrison at various points, on coast survey in the East, as an instructor of artillery tactics at West Point, and on Euro-

pean duty. During this period he patented a self-registering thermometer for deep-sea soundings. When war came in 1861 Saxton was in command of an artillery detachment at the St. Louis arsenal, but after assisting General Nathaniel Lyon in dispersing the disloyal Missouri State Guard at Camp Jackson, he became Lyon's chief quartermaster. He then joined George McClellan's staff in West Virginia and later accompanied the Port Royal expedition as quartermaster. He was appointed a brigadier general of volunteers as of April 15, 1862, and commanded the defenses of Harpers Ferry in May and June. During the balance of the war he commanded at various points in the South under a multiplicity of formal titles; however, his principal occupation was the enlistment and organization of Negroes, principally ex-slaves, into the Federal army. At the end of hostilities he passed naturally into the newly

created Freedmen's Bureau, acting as its assistant commissioner for the states of South Carolina, Georgia, and Florida until January, 1866, when he was mustered out of the volunteers. He had been brevetted major general in the volunteers and brigadier general in the Regular Army. He returned, with grade of major, to the Quartermaster's Department, where he served faithfully and competently in various districts and departments across the nation for twenty-two years. He became lieutenant colonel and deputy quartermaster general in 1872, and colonel and assistant quartermaster general in 1882. For the last five years of his service he headed the q u a r t e r m a s t e r depot in Jeffersonville, Kentucky. After his retirement on October 19, 1888, General Saxton made his home in Washington. He died there on February 23, 1908, and was buried in Arlington National Cemetery.

Eliakim Parker Scammon, who attended the Military Academy as E. Parker Scammon, was born December 27, 1816, in the village of Whitefield, Maine. (554) He entered the Military Academy at the age of sixteen and was graduated in ninth place in the class of 1837, whose most celebrated members were Braxton Bragg, John Sedgwick, and Joseph Hooker. As an officer of Topographical Engineers he served at West Point, in the Florida War against the Seminoles, and in 1847 became a member of General Winfield Scott's staff at Vera Cruz. Thereafter, he performed survey duty on the northern lakes for eight years. In 1856, while detailed to construct military roads in the New Mexico Territory, he

[Confederate] guerillas," (555) while sleeping aboard a steamboat on the Kanawha River, (556) and held as a prisoner of war until August 3, 1864. In the last months of the war he commanded the District of Florida. Scammon was mustered out of service on August 24, 1865, and from 1866 until 1870 was United States consul on Prince Edward Island. In 1875 he became professor of mathematics at Seaton Hall College, South Orange, New Jersey, where he remained for a decade. During the last six years of his life General Scammon made his home in New York City where he died on December 7, 1894. He was buried in Calvary Cemetery, Long Island City.

was dismissed from the service for "Conduct to the Prejudice of Good Order and Military Discipline," and "Disobedience of Orders." He then taught parochial school in Cincinnati until June 14, 1861, when he was commissioned colonel of the 23rd Ohio Volunteer Infantry, succeeding General W. S. Rosecrans. The regiment skirmished at Carnifix Ferry, West Virginia, in September, 1861, and was engaged in discipline and drill until May, 1862, when it fought a series of minor actions in the District of the Kanawha, with Scammon commanding a brigade. In the Maryland campaign he commanded the 1st Brigade of the "Kanawha Division" of Burnside's IX Corps and, for a time, the division; he was promoted to brigadier general to rank from October 15, 1862. He was then placed in charge of the District of Kanawha, which he commanded until February 3, 1864, when he was "gobbled up by

Robert Cumming Schenck, a celebrated nineteenth-century figure almost unknown today, was born on October 4, 1809, in the Ohio River village of Franklin which his father is said to have founded. Aside from his connection with the Civil War,

422

in which he attained the rank of major general, his talents won him eight terms in Congress, eight years as principal diplomatic representative of the United States in South America and to the Court of St. James, membership on the Alabama Claims Commission, and a reputation for being an authority on draw poker. He was graduated from Miami University in 1827, began the practice of law in Dayton, was elected to the Ohio legislature in 1840, and to Congress in 1842, as a Whig. After serving four terms in Congress, Schenck was made minister to Brazil by President Filmore; he held this position until 1853. At the outbreak of the Civil War, Schenck, who had campaigned enthusiastically for Abraham Lincoln, was made a brigadier general of volunteers on June 5, 1861, to rank from May 17. He commanded a brigade of General Daniel Tyler's division at First Manassas and saw service in the Shenandoah Valley the following spring during Stonewall Jackson's famous campaign. At Second Manassas he led the 1st Division of Sigel's I Corps of the Army of Virginia and was disabled for further field service by a wound in the arm. He was made major general to rank from August 30, 1862, and commanded the Middle Department and VIII Corps at Baltimore until he resigned on December 5, 1863, to sit again in Congress. In the ensuing eight years Schenck occupied the powerful chairmanship of the committee on military affairs, and later of ways and means. Failing of reelection in 1870, he was sent by President Grant as minister to London, where he took part in settling the claims arising from the exploits of Raphael Semmes and his Confederate raider. In 1876 Schenck gave permission for the use of his name in the sale of stock in England for a Utah silver mine of which he was a director; this brought about his resignation and return to the States. He resumed the practice of law in Washington, meanwhile acquiring the reputation of being an authority on draw poker—a subject about which he wrote a treatise. General Schenck died in Washington on March 23, 1890, and was buried in Woodland Cemetery, Dayton, Ohio.

Alexander Schimmelfennig was born in Lithauen, Prussia, on July 20, 1824. He served as an engineer officer in the Prussian army during the Schleswig-Holstein war and later in the revolution in Baden, which was crushed by the intervention of Prussia. He came to the United States in 1853, taking up

residence in Philadelphia where the following year he published a book which forecast the Crimean War. He made his living as an engineer and draftsman and by 1860 seems to have been working for the War Department in Washington in this capacity. Schimmelfennig offered his services to the government immediately after the outbreak of hostilities in 1861 and in September was mustered in as colonel of the 74th Pennsylvania Infantry; because of an injury suffered when his horse fell with him and a bout with smallpox, he saw no active service in the field until the campaign of Second Manassas in which he succeeded to the command of the 1st Brigade of Schurz's division of Sigel's corps after General Henry Bohlen was killed at Freeman's Ford on August 22, 1862. His next important battle was that of Chancellorsville where he was caught up in the rout of the XI Corps, now commanded by Oliver O. Howard. At Gettysburg, on the first day of the battle, Schimmelfennig was briefly in command of Schurz's division when he was "struck down by the blow of a gun" (557) during the retirement of the XI Corps to Cemetery Ridge; he sought shelter in a nearby pigsty where he remained for two days. (558) After this battle he sought transfer to South Carolina, since he no longer wished to serve in the XI Corps, but an attack of malaria took him out of action again for an extended period. He recovered in time to be present at the capitulation of Charleston on February 18, 1865, and for some time thereafter was in command of the city. On April 8, 1865, he was granted sick leave for thirty days after becoming a victim

of a most virulent type of tuberculosis. He sought relief at Dr. Aaron Smith's Living Springs Water Cure Establishment near Wernersville, Pennsylvania, but died there suddenly on September 5, 1865, and was buried in Charles Evans Cemetery, Reading, Pennsylvania. (559)

Albin Francisco Schoepf was born in Podgorz, Poland, then a part of Austria, on March 1, 1822, of an Austrian father and a Polish mother. Schoepf was educated in Vienna and had risen to a captaincy

in the Austrian army by 1848 when he defected to the Hungarian revolutionists. After the suppression of the revolt he escaped to Syria, subsequently making his way to the United States in 1851. While working as a porter in a Washington hotel he attracted the attention of Joseph Holt, then Commissioner of Patents, who obtained a clerkship for him. He followed Holt to the War Department and on September

424

30, 1861, was commissioned a brigadier general of volunteers. He was sent to Kentucky, Holt's home state, and inflicted a repulse on the Confederate General F. K. Zollicoffer, who attacked his fortified camp in Rock Castle County in October, 1861. But he was later driven out by the same general in a panicky retreat which came to be known as the "Wild Cat Stampede." Schoepf took part in the battle of Fishing Creek, or Mill Springs, at which Zollicoffer met his death, and Schoepf's brigade was the advance of G. H. Thomas' forces in pursuit of the retiring Rebels. At Perryville he commanded a division of General C. C. Gilbert's III Corps of D. C. Buell's army, a command in which he won no laurels through no particular fault of his own. When Gilbert's head rolled, Schoepf's rolled with it, and he seems to have served out the balance of the war in a position of little importance, commanding the Federal prison at Fort Delaware, near New Castle. At the end of hostilities, Schoepf's name did not appear on the list of brevet promotions and he was honorably mustered out of service on January 15, 1866. It has been said that his principal shortcoming was his inflexible belief in the rigid discipline which characterized European armies of the day and which was not well adapted to democratic volunteers. He returned to the patent office and in time rose to be chief examiner, a position which he filled for the remainder of his life. General Schoepf died at his home in Hyattsville, Maryland, on May 10, 1886, and was buried in the Congressional Cemetery in Washington. (560)

John McAllister Schofield was born in the western New York State hamlet of Gerry on September 29, 1831. At the age of twelve he was taken by his father, a Baptist preacher, to Freeport, Illinois. At

the age of sixteen young Schofield worked as a surveyor in Wisconsin and at seventeen taught school there. Although he had determined to be a lawyer, he accepted an appointment to West Point in 1849 and was graduated in 1853, ranking seventh in the class. In the years before the Civil War he served in Florida and as an instructor at the Military Academy. In 1860 he became professor of physics at Washington University, St. Louis, under a leave of absence from the army. During the early part of the war Schofield served as mustering officer for the state of Missouri, as major of the 1st Missouri Infantry, which he subsequently reorganized as artillery, and as chief of staff to General Nathaniel Lyon at the battle of Wilson's Creek. On November 21, 1861, he was made a brigadier general of volunteers and charged with the command of all of the Union militia of the state of Missouri. From October, 1862, until April, 1863, he commanded the Army of the Frontier, which was operating in southwest Missouri and northwest Arkansas. He was promoted major general on November 29, 1862, but this appointment expired on March 4, 1863, for lack of Senate confirmation; however, on May 12, 1863, he was again appointed with the same date of rank and was duly confirmed. (561) Meanwhile he commanded a division of the XIV Corps in Tennessee, and from May, 1863, until January, 1864, he commanded the Department of the Missouri. During the Atlanta campaign Schofield commanded the Army of the Ohio (XXIII Corps). After W. T. Sherman started on his "March to the Sea," Schofield was left under the general direction of G. H. Thomas to oppose John B. Hood's invasion of Tennessee. With the XXIII Corps and two divisions of the IV Corps he inflicted a bloody and crippling repulse on Hood at Franklin, although he was compelled to evacuate the field and leave his dead and wounded in the hands of the enemy. At Nashville two weeks later, where Hood was virtually destroyed, Schofield again directed the XXIII Corps. (562) For his services in Tennessee he was made brigadier in the Regular Army to rank from November 30, 1864, the date of the battle of Franklin. His command was then moved by rail and water to North Carolina, where he effected a junction with Sherman

at Goldsboro on March 23, 1865. While commanding the newly created Department of North Carolina, he participated in Sherman's closing operations which terminated in the surrender of Joseph E. Johnston at Durham Station. Schofield was brevetted major general, U. S. Army, again for services at Franklin, and then went to France to negotiate for the withdrawal of French troops from Mexico. In 1868 he served as Secretary of War in the cabinet of President Johnson, but resigned soon after U. S. Grant's inauguration. At this time he became major general, U. S. Army, to fill the vacancy caused by the promotion of Philip Sheridan to the grade of lieutenant general. Perhaps his most notable postwar contribution to the nation's welfare was his recommendation that Pearl Harbor be acquired for a naval base. From 1876 to 1881 he was superintendent at West Point, where he acted as president of the board which exonerated Fitz John Porter from the accusations which had caused Porter's dismissal from the army in 1863. After commanding various military departments and divisions, General Schofield succeeded to the command of the army upon the death of General Sheridan in 1888. He was promoted to lieutenant general in February, 1895, and retired on his sixty-fourth birthday in September. He died in St. Augustine, Florida, March 4, 1906, and was buried in Arlington National Cemetery.

Carl Schurz—revolutionary, orator, ambassador, senator, editor, polemicist, and major general of United States volunteers—was born

in the Rhenish village of Liblar, near Cologne, Prussia, on March 2, 1829. He received a superior education at Cologne and at the University of Bonn. When the revolutions of 1848 swept across Europe, Schurz served as a subaltern for a few months against the Prussian forces and then made his way to Switzerland. Expelled from France as an undesirable in 1851, he lived in England before coming to the United States in 1852. He resided in Philadelphia for three years. Schurz, who possessed a remarkable oratorical talent, soon mastered the English language and for the rest of his life was greatly in demand as a bilingual speechmaker on a wide range of subjects. He settled in Wisconsin in 1856 and, having taken up the antislavery cause, campaigned vigorously and effectively, first for John C. Frémont and in 1860 for Abraham Lincoln. He was rewarded with the Spanish legation by Lincoln, but returned to the United States in January,

1862, to press for immediate abolition of slavery. Lincoln would not be hurried; and it may be inferred that his commissioning of Schurz as a brigadier general of volunteers (to rank from April 15, 1862) rid him, at least temporarily, of a sometimes troublesome adviser, as well as having a happy effect on many thousands of loyal German-Americans. That Schurz was virtually without military experience seems to have mattered little. He was immediately assigned to command of a division of Frémont's army, then in the Shenandoah. Upon the formation of John Pope's Army of Virginia, Frémont was supplanted by Franz Sigel, in whose corps Schurz fought at Second Manassas in creditable fashion in spite of the fact that the battle constituted a Union disaster. In the campaigns of Chancellorsville and Gettysburg he was less fortunate. On both battlefields his division was thrown into headlong rout, and the so-called Dutch units were execrated throughout the rest of the Army of the Potomac. How much of this obloquy was deserved by Schurz and his men and how much was deserved by his corps commander Oliver O. Howard has been debated for almost a century. (563) In any event, Schurz, who had been promoted to major general on March 17, 1863, proceeded to the western theater with the XI and XII Corps under General Joseph Hooker. After the battle of Chattanooga, Schurz, having fallen out with Hooker, was assigned to command a recruit depot in Nashville. He spoke throughout the North in behalf of Lincoln's reelection in 1864 and, after the election, served as chief of staff to General Henry W. Slocum in the campaign of the Carolinas. For forty years after the end of hostilities, as lecturer, Senator, and editor of five different nationally known publications, Schurz was a tireless advocate of equal rights for the Negro, the suppression of the spoils system, anti-imperialism, and the preservation of the public domain. Although he served only one term in the Senate (1869-1875, from Missouri), he exercised a large influence on every presidential election from 1860 to 1904. The last years of his life were devoted mainly to literary pursuits, pronouncements on public questions, and occasional addresses. Toward the end he became regarded as the dean of elder statesmen and was consulted on virtually every question of national importance. Alternating his residence between the Pocantico Hills, Lake George, New York, Augusta, Georgia, and New York City, he died at his residence on 91st Street on May 14, 1906, and was buried in Sleepy Hollow Cemetery, Tarrytown. At his death he had completed his autobiography to the year 1869; with an added sketch of his later career by Frederic Bancroft and William Dunning, it was posthumously published in three volumes (1907-1909), as *The Reminiscences of Carl Schurz.*

Robert Kingston Scott, as unique a mixture of hero and rogue as ever wore a United States uniform, was born in Armstrong County, Pennsylvania, on July 8, 1826. He studied medicine, worked as a miner in the California gold rush, visited Mexico and South America, and ultimately began the practice

of his profession in Henry County, Ohio, where he also amassed a competence by profitable real estate investments. He entered the war as major of the 68th Ohio, was made lieutenant colonel in November, 1861, and colonel the following July. The regiment performed

guard duty at various points until the Vicksburg campaign, during which it fought at Port Gibson, Raymond, Champion's Hill, and at the city itself in Logan's division of the XVII Corps. During the Atlanta campaign Scott commanded the brigade of which his regiment had been a part and continued in this capacity (with advancement to brigadier general on April 21, 1865, to rank from January 12) in W. T. Sherman's march through the Carolinas. Up to this point Scott seems to have been a thorough soldier, lacking neither courage nor ability; he was brevetted major general in December, 1865. Soon after he was made head of the South Carolina branch of the Freedman's Bureau, still retaining his military rank which he did not relinquish until he was elected governor of the state in 1868 by the Negro-carpetbagger alliance. At this time the helpless state was being plundered by such corrupt political figures as "Honest John" Patterson, later U. S. Senator, Frank Moses, speaker of the overwhelmingly Negro legislature (80 per cent of whose members were illiterate), and the subversive intellectual Robert Brown Elliott, who would sit in Congress. Governor Scott quickly succumbed to the venality which surrounded him and assumed a leading part in its continuance. "Subject alike to alcoholic and female allurements," at the high point of his career he was seduced while drunk by the notorious burlesque actress Pauline Markham into signing a fraudulent issue of state bonds. (564) Fleeing the state after the restoration of white rule in 1877, he returned to Ohio where he celebrated Christmas Day, 1880, by committing a homicide. (565) He died in Henry County, August 12, 1900, and was buried in Napoleon.

Winfield Scott, one of America's most distinguished soldiers, was born on his father's farm Laurel Branch near Petersburg, Virginia, on June 13, 1786. To include him in a compendium of Civil War generals emphasizes only the smallest facet of his brilliant career. Standing six feet five inches, he was a natural leader even as an undergraduate at William and Mary and as a law student in Petersburg. In the War of 1812, Scott, who had been appointed to the army by President Jefferson in 1808, was greatly distinguished on the Canadian frontier. At Lundy's Lane where he was badly wounded, he became an international hero. Already a brigadier of Regulars, he was brevetted major general as well. By the time of the Civil War in 1861 General Scott had been involved in not only a score of successful military campaigns but also an equal number of political skirmishes in which he had not fared so well. He became commander-in-chief of the army in 1841 and was the acknowledged genius of the Mexican War; nevertheless, the animosity of President Polk toward him prevented to some degree the honors which he had fairly won. In 1852 he was the Whig nominee for President, but was overwhelmingly defeated by Franklin Pierce. In 1857 he opposed the Mormon aggression in Utah, which was perpetrated nevertheless by troops of the U. S. Army under Albert Sidney Johnston. General Scott was particularly distinguished as a moderator between warring factions, including the settlement in South Carolina of the nullification question during Jackson's administration, the settlement of the Canadian frontier problems in 1838, and the translation of the Cherokees of South Carolina and Tennessee to Oklahoma. Upon the outbreak of the Civil War Scott found himself in command of a small professional army scattered over the continental United States. He alone envisaged a four-year war and the number of men which would be required to subdue the South. When solicited by a lifelong friend to defect to the Confederacy, he resoundingly declared his loyalty to the Union: "I have served my country, under the flag of the Union, for more than fifty years, and so long as God permits me to live, I will defend that flag with my sword, even if my native State assails it." (566) He conceived the "Anaconda Plan," which in essence became overall Federal strategy in 1864-65. However, at the outbreak of war "Old Fuss and Feathers," a brevet lieutenant general since 1847, was nearly seventy-five years of age, afflicted with dropsy, unable to sit a horse, proud and irascible. He was blamed for the errors of his subordinate General Robert Patterson, which enabled Joseph E. Johnston to effect a junction with P. G. T. Beauregard and resulted in the Union rout at First Manassas. After George B. McClellan had been made commander of the Army of the Potomac, Scott requested retirement on October 31, 1861. He went abroad for a time but soon returned to America. He died at

West Point on May 29, 1866, and was buried there in the Post Cemetery.

John Sedgwick, one of the most beloved soldiers in the Army of the Potomac, was born September 13, 1813, at Cornwall Hollow in the Connecticut Berkshires. He ob-

tained his early education in the local school, spent a few months in the Sharon Academy, and for two winters taught school himself. Shortly before his twentieth birthday he entered West Point and was graduated in 1837 along with Braxton Bragg, Jubal Early, John C. Pemberton, and Joseph Hooker. During the next decade he served against the Seminoles, in moving the Cherokees from Georgia to Oklahoma, and at various garrison points. He served under both Generals Zachary Taylor and Winfield Scott in the Mexican War and won the brevets of captain and major. Upon the expansion of the army in

1855, Sedgwick, an artillerist by profession, became major of the newly authorized 1st Cavalry, whose colonel and lieutenant colonel in 1861 were Robert E. Lee and William J. Hardee. Upon their defection to the Confederacy, Sedgwick become the regiment's colonel and was commissioned brigadier general of volunteers to rank from August 31, 1861. In George B. McClellan's campaign on the Virginia Peninsula, Sedgwick directed a division of Sumner's II Corps until he was wounded and disabled at the battle of Glendale or Frayser's Farm on June 30, 1862. He was promoted to major general on July 25 to rank from July 4. At Sharpsburg he was again distinguished for gallantry and was wounded three times, finally being carried unconscious from the field. Within ninety days he reported for duty and, after a short tour in command of the IX Corps, was put in command of the VI Corps. In the Chancellorsville campaign Sedgwick was directed by Hooker to cross the Rappahannock, storm Early's position on Marye's Heights, and then advance upriver to a junction with the rest of the army—a movement impossible of execution after the collapse of Hooker's right wing under Oliver O. Howard. After the sharp fight at Salem Church, Sedgwick prudently got his command back to the left bank in good order. At Gettysburg the VI Corps was used as a reserve and sustained comparatively few casualties. At the battle of Rappahannock Bridge in November, he commanded the V and VI Corps in an operation which gained the Union 1,700 prisoners, eight flags, and four pieces of artillery. In U. S. Grant's Rich-mond campaign the following spring, General Sedgwick commanded his corps with his customary skill at the Wilderness. At Spotsylvania a few days later, on May 9, 1864, his aides cautioned him about exposing himself unnecessarily while delineating his line and indicating where he wished his batteries placed. His reply, "they couldn't hit an elephant at this distance," was soon followed by the whistle and thump of a sharpshooter's bullet which struck him below the left eye and killed him almost instantly. (567) General Sedgwick was buried in his native village of Cornwall Hollow.

William Henry Seward, Jr., the youngest son of Abraham Lincoln's Secretary of State, was born at Auburn, New York, on June 18, 1839. At the age of eighteen he began clerking in an Albany hardware store, but in 1859 went to Washington to become private secretary to his father, who was then a United

States Senator. The following year he organized the banking house of William H. Seward and Company, in Auburn. During the early months of 1862, as secretary of the war committee of his congressional district, he was engaged in recruiting and forwarding troops to the front. In August of that year Seward became lieutenant colonel of the 138th New York, an infantry regiment which was changed to artillery in December and named the 9th New York Heavy Artillery. The regiment served in the Washington defenses until the spring of 1864 when U. S. Grant's heavy losses in the Wilderness caused its reconversion to infanty duty and assignment to Ricketts' division of the VI Corps. In the spring of 1863 Seward is said to have undertaken "a delicate secret mission" to General N. P. Banks in Louisiana at the behest of Lincoln. (568) Seward fought at Cold Harbor and was promoted colonel on June 10, 1864. The following month his command was hurried north to oppose Jubal Early at the Monocacy, where he sustained an arm wound and a broken leg when his horse was shot from under him. On September 13, 1864, he became one of the youngest general officers of the army. (569) After recovery from his injuries he was sent to Martinsburg in command of a brigade of the Department of West Virginia and for a time, after the capture of General George Crook by Confederate partisan rangers, commanded the 3rd Division. He resigned his commission in the volunteer service effective June 1, 1865, and returned to Auburn to resume his place at the head of his banking house. For more than half a century thereafter he was one of the most prominent men in western New York, taking a leading part in political affairs, charitable ventures, and patriotic and historical societies. He was also a director of several corporations and member of a number of clubs. When he died in Auburn on April 26, 1920, only six full-rank general officers of the Union army survived him. General Seward was buried in Fox Hill Cemetery, Auburn.

Truman Seymour, the son of a Methodist preacher, was born in Burlington, Vermont, on September 24, 1824. He spent two years at Norwich University (then in Nor-

wich, Vermont, but now located in Northfield, Vermont) and then accepted an appointment to West Point, where he was graduated in 1846. As a young artillery officer he fought with distinction in the Mexican War, gaining the brevets of first lieutenant and captain. A three-year tour at the Academy was followed by serving in action against the Florida Seminoles in 1856-58. The outbreak of war found him stationed in Charleston Harbor and he was brevetted major for gallant conduct in the defense of Fort Sumter. After some recruiting duty and service in the Washington defenses he was made a brigadier general of volunteers on April 28, 1862, and assigned to a brigade in McCall's division of Fitz John Porter's V Corps on the Peninsula. After the capture of McCall at the battle of Glendale (or Frayser's Farm) on June 30, Seymour commanded the division at Malvern Hill. At Second Manassas the division, now under John F. Reynolds, was temporarily attached to Irvin McDowell's corps of the Army of Virginia. (570) Seymour and his brigade distinguished themselves at the battle of South Mountain by forcing Turner's Gap, a feat for which he was brevetted lieutenant colonel in the Regular Army. His command also did well at Sharpsburg where he won the brevet of colonel. In November, 1862, he was transferred to Charleston Harbor and led the abortive attack on Battery Wagner in July, 1863; Seymour was severely wounded in this encounter. After returning to duty in December, General Seymour was detailed to the Florida expedition, where his troops were roughly handled at the battle of Olustee, or Ocean Pond—the sole major engagement fought on Florida soil during the war. Relieved and ordered again to the Army of the Potomac, he was taken prisoner at the Wilderness in May and was not exchanged until August. (571) After his release he commanded a division of the VI Corps in the Shenandoah Valley, at the siege of Petersburg, and in the Appomattox campaign. Upon the termination of hostilities Seymour was brevetted major general in both the Regular Army and the volunteers. In 1866 he was promoted to the substantive rank of major of the 5th Artillery, a position he occupied until his retirement, at his own request, in 1876. Thereafter, he lived in Florence, Italy, where he died on October 30, 1891. His remains were interred in the Cimitero degli Allori there. Curiously enough, his wife, who survived until 1919, was buried at West Point. (572)

James Murrell Shackelford was born on a farm in Lincoln County, Kentucky, on July 7, 1827. He was educated in the schools of nearby Springfield and Stanford; at the age of twenty he enlisted in Company I, 4th Kentucky Volunteers, and was soon elected first lieutenant of his

company. Mustered out in 1848, he studied law and was admitted to the Kentucky bar in 1853; he practiced his profession in Louisville until the outbreak of the Civil War. In the fall of 1861 he recruited the 25th Kentucky (Union) Infantry and was commissioned its colonel on January 1, 1862. The regiment fought at Fort Donelson in Cruft's brigade of Lew Wallace's division, sustaining eighty-four casualties. Contrary to published sources, it does not appear that Shackelford was present at Shiloh; the records indicate that he had resigned his commission shortly before the battle. (573) In August he raised the 8th Kentucky Cavalry, was made its colonel on September 13, 1862, and on March 17, 1863, was promoted to brigadier general of volunteers to rank from January 2. The 8th Kentucky Cavalry was organized into three battalions (which frequently saw service separately) to serve for twelve months. In September he was slightly wounded in the foot during a skirmish with Adam Johnson's Kentucky Confederates at Geiger's Lake; the 1st Battalion which he was directing personally, then moved to Bowling Green. The principal service of the regiment was its participation in the pursuit and capture of the celebrated Confederate raider John Hunt Morgan, during his expedition across the Ohio in July, 1863. Shackelford himself, now a brigadier, was nominally in command of the 1st Brigade, 2nd Division, XXIII Corps, a mixed force of infantry and cavalry. Morgan's forces were broken up piecemeal day by day, and their leader finally surrendered to Shackelford near Wellsville, Ohio, after a chase through three states. The balance of Shackelford's military service was marked by his participation in the capture of Cumberland Gap during the campaign in East Tennessee, where he commanded a cavalry division of the XXIII Corps, and at Knoxville the Cavalry Corps of the Department of the Ohio. Shackelford resigned from the army in January, 1864, (574) and returned to his law practice. In 1889 he was made United States judge for the Indian Territory and after 1893 practiced law at Muskogee (now Oklahoma) where he became attorney for the Choctaw nation. He died at his summer home in Port Huron, Michigan, on September 7, 1909, and was buried in Cave Hill Cemetery, Louisville.

Alexander Shaler was born March 19, 1827, in Haddam, Connecticut, but was brought to New York City at the age of seven. He was educated in private schools and seems

to have inherited a private income, since his principal avocations before and after the war were the New York National Guard and various non-remunerative positions of public trust. At the age of eighteen he joined the "Washington Grays," later the 8th New York Militia, and subsequently rose to be major of the famous 7th New York Militia, which was brought to Washington a few days after the fall of Fort Sumter and remained about six weeks. On June 11 he was commissioned lieutenant colonel of the 65th New York Volunteer Infantry, originally called the 1st U. S. Chasseurs. Shaler served continuously with the Army of the Potomac and was engaged in every important battle of that army until the spring of 1864; he received promotion to colonel after the battle of Malvern Hill and to brigadier general on May 26, 1863. After Sharpsburg the division of the IV Corps in which he had been serving was attached to the VI Corps, and after Fredericksburg he succeeded to command of the 1st Brigade, 3rd Division of the corps. During the winter of 1863 Shaler was in charge of the Confederate prison on Johnson's Island in Sandusky Bay, but returned to the army in time to take part in the battle of the Wilderness on May 6, 1864, where he was captured. He was probably the only officer who had commanded a Union stockade for Confederate prisoners to find himself an inmate of a Confederate stockade for Union prisoners. After his exchange he was ordered to report to Edward R. S. Canby in New Orleans, and in the last months of the war he was in charge of a division of the VII Corps and

of the White River District in Arkansas. He was mustered out in August, 1865, with the brevet of major general and in 1893 was awarded the Medal of Honor for gallantry in storming Marye's Heights at Fredericksburg during the campaign of Chancellorsville. After the war General Shaler held a multiplicity of public offices, including the presidency of the New York City fire department and the health department. He also belonged to innumerable clubs and societies and was active in the Military Order of the Loyal Legion, serving as head of the New York commandery. During his last years he made his residence in Ridgefield, New Jersey. He died in New York City, December 28, 1911, and was buried in Ridgefield.

Isaac Fitzgerald Shepard was born in Natick, Massachusetts, on July 7, 1816, and was educated at Harvard, where he was graduated in 1842.

From 1844 until 1857 he was principal of a Boston grammar school and in 1859-60 was a member of the Massachusetts legislature. He also was editor of the Boston *Daily Bee* in 1846-48. Shepard went to St. Louis early in 1861; an avowed antisecessionist and abolitionist, he soon found a place for himself on the staff of General Nathaniel Lyon with rank of major and assistant adjutant general of the state militia. He was Lyon's principal aide at Wilson's Creek and after the latter's death became lieutenant colonel of the 19th Missouri Infantry and colonel of the 3rd Missouri, when the two regiments were consolidated in January, 1862. A year later he was warmly commended for his conduct in the capture of Arkansas Post by both Generals A. P. Hovey and W. T. Sherman. (575) Shepard was ever zealous for the cause of the Negro and in May, 1863, accepted the colonelcy of the 51st U. S. Colored Infantry, which was recruited largely in the wake of the advancing Federals from runaway slaves and contrabands. The uniformed Negroes were used mainly for garrison and fortification duty; consequently, Shepard's later Civil War service involved little combat duty. He was promoted brigadier general of volunteers on November 17, 1863, to rank from October 27. The following year found him stationed at Vicksburg with his brigade of three Negro regiments in General John P. Hawkins' Negro division of the District of West Tennessee. (576) At this juncture Shepard's nomination to be a brigadier general failed to obtain Senate approval and his commission expired by action of law. He returned to Missouri and

lived a challenging and interesting life for another twenty-five years. He was at various times adjutant general of Missouri, United States consul in Swatow and Hankow, China, chairman of the Republican state committee, department commander of the Grand Army of the Republic, editor of the Missouri *Democrat* and of the "Missouri State Atlas." After returning from China in 1886 General Shepard made his home in Massachusetts. He died in Bellingham, on August 25, 1889, and was buried in Ashland Cemetery, Middlesex County, Massachusetts. (577)

George Foster Shepley was born on January 1, 1819, in Saco, Maine. His father Ether Shepley was a pi-

oneer in the state and served as United States Senator and Chief Justice of the Supreme Court at various times. Young Shepley was graduated from Dartmouth at the age of eighteen; he studied law and started a practice at Bangor when he was only twenty. In 1848 he was appointed United States district attorney for the state (a position which his father had also held), but was ousted by the Whigs upon the accession of Zachary Taylor the following March. He was reappointed by Franklin Pierce in 1853 and served until the outbreak of the Civil War in 1861. Meantime Shepley had formed a close friendship with Benjamin F. Butler while attending the 1860 Democratic National Convention at Charleston where both were delegates, Shepley supporting Stephen A. Douglas, and Butler, Jefferson Davis. Shepley was commissioned colonel of the 12th Maine Infantry in November, 1861, and accompanied Butler's forces in the expedition against New Orleans the following spring. After the capture of the city on May 1, 1862, Butler made Shepley post commander at New Orleans, military governor of Louisiana in June, and effected his promotion to brigadier general in July to rank from the eighteenth. Shepley continued in this capacity until the spring of 1864, when the "reorganized electorate of the state," comprising the Union minority, elected Governor Michael Hahn. Meanwhile, it must be admitted that a fair share of the blame for the excesses charged to Butler's rule should be born by Shepley, who was his right-hand man. At the beginning of the spring campaign of 1864 in Virginia, Shepley was assigned to the supervision of the District of Eastern Virginia, under his old superior. At the close of the war he operated as chief of staff to General Godfrey Weitzel, who recommended him for promotion

(which he did not receive), and became military governor of Richmond upon its occupation by the XXV Corps in April, 1865. He resigned his commission in July and returned to his law practice. In 1869 General Shepley was appointed United States circuit court judge for the state of Maine by President Grant. He died in Portland, Maine, reportedly of Asiatic cholera, on July 20, 1878, and was buried there in Evergreen Cemetery.

Philip Henry Sheridan, one of the three Union generals who won the greatest fame in the Civil War, may have been born in any one of several locations on a date which he himself occasionally reestablished. According to his memoirs, he was born in Albany, New York, on March 6, 1831. (578) When he was an infant the family moved to the frontier village of Somerset, Ohio, where the future general secured a basic education, clerked in a country store, and received an appointment to West Point in the class of 1852 by virtue of the failure of the original appointee to pass the entrance examination. A year before his expected graduation, "a quarrel of a belligerent character" with a fellow-cadet (later General William R. Terrill) resulted in his suspension from the Academy for a year. (579) Accordingly he was graduated in 1853, ranking in the bottom third of his class. After eight years of service on the frontier his advance in rank from the grade of second lieutenant, 4th Infantry, was not achieved until the defection of superiors to the Confederate cause created vacancies in the line of promotion in 1861. Sheridan's first active field service was as chief quartermaster and commissary of the Army of Southwest Missouri; next he served as General Henry W. Halleck's headquarters quartermaster during the tortoise-like advance on Corinth subsequent to Shiloh. On May 25, 1862, however, he was appointed colonel of the

2nd Michigan Cavalry; thereafter his rise in rank and responsibility was meteoric and is comparable only to that of John B. Hood, Sheridan's classmate who rose from first lieutenant to full general in the Confederate hierarchy. Sheridan was made a brigadier general of volunteers on September 13, 1862, to rank from July 1; fought stubbornly at Perryville and Murfreesboro; and on March 16, 1863, was promoted major general to rank from the date of the battle of Murfreesboro. At Chickamauga Sheridan commanded the 3rd Division of Alexander McD. McCook's XX Corps, losing 1,500 out of 4,000

men brought into action as well as two of his three brigade commanders. Some two months later at Missionary Ridge during the various encounters which made up the battle of Chattanooga, Sheridan's men, without orders from anybody, clawed up the height and wrested it from their Confederate opponents. The position was considered impregnable by the Southern commander, Braxton Bragg, and its loss occasioned his relief from command at his own request. Sheridan, on the other hand, made a reputation which immediately attracted the attention of U. S. Grant, who assigned him to the supervision of all of the cavalry of the Army of the Potomac the following spring. At this time Sheridan, a relatively obscure division commander of infantry, sprang into world prominence. Coincident with the beginning of Grant's Overland campaign against Richmond in May, 1864, Sheridan's 10,000 Federal troopers began to make themselves felt in opposition to the depleted and poorly horsed legions of the legendary Jeb Stuart. His men killed Stuart at Yellow Tavern in May, but were not so successful at Hawes' Shop and Trevilian Station. Nevertheless, a constant flow of propaganda magnified Sheridan's successes along with those of Grant, while minimizing the reverses and attendant casualties. After Jubal Early's raid on the environs of Washington in July, 1864, Sheridan was placed in command of the VI and XIX Corps, three divisions of cavalry, and a plentiful supply of artillery (the whole numbering some 43,000 effectives) and ordered to close the "back door on Washington," Virginia's fertile

Shenandoah Valley, by destroying everything which could lend support to the Confederate war effort. He defeated and drove back Early at Winchester and Fisher's Hill in September, but in October, while he was absent, his Army of the Shenandoah was surprised and temporarily routed by the numerically inferior Rebels. Only Early's dilatoriness—a consequence of his indulging in the fond hope that the defeated Federals would dissolve into retreat—saved Sheridan, who was en route from Winchester "twenty miles away," from disaster. Arriving on the field after passing a stream of fugitives, Sheridan, a battlefield tactician of the first order, found only Getty's division of the VI Corps and the cavalry in line of battle and resisting the enemy. In a matter of hours and in the absence of further Confederate pressure, Sheridan reformed his army and retrieved victory from defeat. For this exploit he was made a major general in the Regular Army on November 14, 1864, to rank from November 8, and received the thanks of Congress. Having made of the Shenandoah a wasteland where "a crow would be compelled to carry his own rations," Sheridan rejoined the Army of the Potomac in front of Petersburg in time to take a leading part in the operations which culminated in Robert E. Lee's capitulation at Appomattox Court House on April 9, 1865. At Five Forks Sheridan smashed the weakened Confederate right flank; at Sayler's Creek he compelled the surrender of a large segment of what remained of the renowned Army of Northern Virginia; and near Appomattox he got the leading elements of his men astride Lee's line of retreat. After the conclusion of hostilities in Virginia, Sheridan was instrumental in forcing the government of Napoleon III to withdraw its military support of the Mexican Emperor Maximilian of Austria. The nadir of Sheridan's career was reached in 1867 when he occupied the post of commander of the Fifth Military District, an area embracing Louisiana and Texas which was established by the oppressive Reconstruction acts. Sheridan's administrative policies were so stringent and severe that his removal by President Johnson after six months met with only slight protest from the Radicals in Congress. Upon the accession of Grant to the presidency in 1869, W. T. Sherman became a full general and Sheridan, lieutenant general. Until 1883 Sheridan occupied a number of posts including command of the Division of the Missouri in a period when troubles with the Plains Indians were an everyday occurrence. In 1870-71 he witnessed at first hand the Franco-Prussian War which resulted in the unification of Germany. In 1884 upon the retirement of Sherman he became commanding general of the army and a few months before his death was elevated to the rank of full general to rank from June 1, 1888. General Sheridan died on August 5, 1888, at Nonquitt, Massachusetts, and was buried in Arlington National Cemetery. His wife was a daughter of General Daniel H. Rucker.

Francis Trowbridge Sherman was born in Newtown, Connecticut, on December 31, 1825. When he was nine years old, the family moved to Chicago (then a town of 350 population) where the elder Sherman commenced the manufacture of brick, an enterprise in which he was aided by his son. Sherman's father later became one of Chicago's early mayors. Young Sherman pursued various occupations, including a

clerkship in the Chicago post office; he also spent a year in California at the height of the gold rush. On October 30, 1861, he was commissioned lieutenant colonel of the 56th Illinois, the "Mechanic Fusileers," a regiment which was mustered out in February, 1862. (580) The following month he was remustered as major of the 12th Illinois Cavalry, a position he held until September 4, 1862, when Governor Richard Yates appointed him colonel of the 88th Illinois, which was also called the "Second Board-of-Trade Regiment." Sherman's command fought at Murfreesboro as part of Joshua W. Sill's brigade of Philip Sheridan's division; Sill was killed and the brigade sustained nearly seven hundred casualties. Shorly thereafter Sherman became a brigade commander in the XX Corps and although not present at Chickamauga was one of the leaders of Sheridan's division of the IV Corps who stormed up Missionary Ridge and drove Braxton Bragg's Confederates from their supposedly impregnable position. When the Atlanta campaign opened Sherman was attached to IV Corps' headquarters as chief of staff to General Oliver O. Howard, and on July 7, 1864, while conducting a reconnaissance, was captured. After a series of adventures he was exchanged in October, 1864, and joined Sheridan's staff in the Shenandoah Valley as inspector general. He was present at Waynesboro, Dinwiddie Court House, Five Forks, Sayler's Creek, and Appomattox and was brevetted brigadier general on March 13, 1865. On July 21, 1865, he was belatedly accorded the full rank while serving as provost marshal general of the Military Division of the Gulf under Sheridan at New Orleans. Mustered out in February, 1866, he returned to Louisiana where he lost heavily by investing in a sugar plantation. In 1867 he began manufacturing barbed wire in Chicago and the same year was appointed postmaster of the city by President Johnson. Sherman also served a term in the Illinois legislature in 1873. In 1890 he moved his residence to Waukegan, Illinois, where he died on November 9, 1905. He was buried in Graceland Cemetery, Chicago. (581)

Thomas West Sherman was born in Newport, Rhode Island, on March 26, 1813. When he was eighteen

years old he walked to Washington to secure from President Andrew Jackson an appointment to West Point. After his graduation from the Academy in 1836, he became an officer of artillery and took part in the transfer of the Cherokees from Georgia to Indian Territory, served in the Florida War, was garrisoned at Fort Moultrie in Charleston Harbor, and fought in the war with Mexico, winning the brevet of major for gallantry at the battle of Buena Vista. He later served on frontier duty in Minnesota, in the Kansas Free-State controversy, and in Dakota Territory. At the outbreak of the Civil War, Sherman was quickly advanced to lieutenant colonel in the Regular Army and was one of the first group of volunteer brigadiers appointed (August 6 to rank from May 17, 1861). His first important service was in command of the land forces of the Port Royal (South Carolina) expedition. On April 30, 1862, Sherman was as-

signed to command a division of the Army of the Ohio in the advance upon Corinth after the battle of Shiloh. In August he was ordered to report to the Department of the Gulf for duty and, after some service in the defenses of New Orleans, commanded a division under N. P. Banks in the operations against Port Hudson. On May 27, 1863, while leading an assault on the Confederate works at Port Hudson, he sustained a wound which cost him his right leg. He returned to duty in March, 1864, and occupied various district commands in and about New Orleans until the end of the war. He had been promoted colonel, 3rd Artillery, in the Regular Army in 1863 and in 1865 was brevetted major general in both the regular and volunteer services. From 1866 until 1870 General Sherman commanded his regiment at various points on the Atlantic Coast, including Fort Adams at Newport and the post of Key West. For a time in 1868 he was in charge of the Department of the East. Invalided out of the Army in 1870 with the rank of major general, General Sherman died in Newport, on March 16, 1879, and was buried there in Island Cemetery.

William Tecumseh "Cump" Sherman, the most widely renowned of the Union's military leaders next to U. S. Grant, was born February 8, 1820, in Lancaster, Ohio, one of eleven children. When his father, a justice of the Ohio supreme court, died suddenly in 1829, the family was taken in by various friends and relatives. Young Sherman found a home with Thomas Ewing, United States Senator and cabinet officer, whose daughter he later married.

He thus became the brother-in-law of Generals Charles, Hugh, and Thomas Ewing, Jr. (Sherman's brother John served almost fifty years in Congress, Senate, and Cabinet.) Notwithstanding Cump's brilliant qualifications, it must be acknowledged that this imposing array of relatives and political connections did nothing to retard his rise from impecunious ex-officer in 1861 to full general commanding the army in 1869. Senator Ewing obtained for Sherman an appointment to West Point, where he was graduated sixth in the class of

1840. His army career for the next thirteen years was unexceptionable, although he won the brevet of captain "for meritorious services in California during the War with Mexico." In 1853 Sherman resigned his commission to enter the banking business in San Francisco as representative of a St. Louis firm. Both the San Francisco branch and the main office in St.

Louis ultimately failed, and Sherman turned to the practice of law, also unsuccessfully, in Leavenworth, Kansas, with two of his brothers-in-law. In 1859 he secured the superintendency of the Louisiana State Seminary of Learning and Military Academy at Pineville (now Louisiana State University at Baton Rouge). In January, 1861, Sherman was required to receipt for a portion of the arms surrendered by the United States arsenal in Baton Rouge a few days before; promptly he submitted his resignation to the governor with the ringing declaration, "On no earthly account will I do any act or think any thought hostile . . . to the . . . United States." (582) For a few months he headed a St. Louis streetcar company, but on May 14, 1861, was reappointed to the army as colonel of the newly authorized 13th U. S. Infantry. Prior to the first battle of Manassas, Sherman was assigned to command of a brigade of Tyler's division (the division's 605 casualties exceeded that of any other Federal brigade engaged in this battle). On August 7, 1861, Sherman became the seventh-ranking brigadier general of volunteers in the service, standing eleven numbers ahead of U. S. Grant on the list as arranged by the War Department. (583) The following month he was sent to Kentucky to assist in holding the state. At this stage of the war Sherman's volatile temperament was strained by the insufficiencies of the volunteers, the ingrained knowledge that the war was not going to be a picnic, and the constant probing of news correspondents into affairs which he deemed to be the exclusive province of the military. Outraged re-

442

porters portrayed him as a visionary, unstable and even mentally deranged. Relieved by Don Carlos Buell, Sherman went to St. Louis and reported to Henry W. Halleck; soon after, he took part in the bloody battle of Shiloh, where he commanded a division on the defense perimeter which was surprised and overrun by Albert Sidney Johnston's Confederates. Despite this, the battle eventually resulted in a Federal triumph, and Sherman was made major general of volunteers to rank from May 1, 1862. During the course of the several operations to open the Mississippi River, Sherman was in the forefront with his command. He was unsuccessful in the initial assault at Chickasaw Bluffs; served under John McClernand in the capture of Arkansas Post; and in the campaign which resulted in the surrender of Vicksburg directed the XV Corps. In the campaign which relieved W. S. Rosecrans' beleaguered army at Chattanooga after the battle of Chickamauga, Sherman's corps assaulted the Confederate right under P. R. Cleburne at the end of Missionary Ridge and were roughly handled "in a bayonet-to-bayonet combat of a savagery unexcelled in the war's annals." (584) After Grant's promotion to chief command of the armies of the United States, Sherman assumed command of all troops in the western theater and entered upon a series of operations which would not only constitute the apogee of his career but would inaugurate the theory of "modern warfare" by which total destruction would be visited upon the civilian population in the path of the advancing columns. During the campaign which culminated in the capture of the city of Atlanta, Sherman utilized his superior numbers to flank his opponent Joseph E. Johnston out of one defensive position after another. Ultimately the latter was relieved; whereupon Sherman inflicted a series of bloody repulses upon the combative John B. Hood. Leaving two army corps under the direction of G. H. Thomas to take care of the Confederate Army of Tennessee, Sherman then cut loose from his communications and began the celebrated "March to the Sea." He turned up in Savannah at Christmas time, having cut a swath of desolation forty-miles wide through the heart of Georgia. The march northward through the Carolinas followed, and two weeks after Appomattox, Johnston, again in command, capitulated at a way station near Durham, North Carolina. Sherman had been made a brigadier general in the Regular Army after Vicksburg, and major general after Atlanta. He twice received the thanks of Congress during the war. With the army reorganization in 1866 he was advanced to Grant's old grade of lieutenant general, and when the latter was inaugurated President in 1869 Sherman became full general and commander-in-chief of the army. His tenure as head of the army was not always serene, and in 1874 he moved his headquarters to St. Louis, distrusting the political maelstrom which was Washington, although he returned there in 1876. One of his most important contributions during this period was the establishment of the Command School at Fort Leavenworth. On February 8, 1884, upon his own application, he was placed on the retired list.

From then until his death seven years later he was continuously in demand as a speaker and commentator and in 1884 was besieged with importunities to run for President. After 1886 he made his home in New York City, where he died on February 14, 1891. He was buried in Calvary Cemetery, St. Louis. His Confederate opponent, the venerable Joseph E. Johnston, marched bareheaded in his funeral procession and was himself dead of pneumonia within five weeks. That Sherman was a military genius can hardly be disputed. He possessed an extraordinary mind, grasped major problems with uncanny rapidity, and understood the art of war perhaps to a greater degree than any one of his contemporaries on either side. Unlike some other masters of the military art, however, he was only a mediocre battlefield tactician: at Shiloh he failed to take the most elementary precautions against surprise, at Missionary Ridge was misled by the terrain, and at Kennesaw Mountain sacrificed three thousand men in a frontal assault on a position easily turned a few days later.

James Shields, reportedly the only man to represent three different states in the U. S. Senate, was born May 10, 1810, in County Tyrone, Ireland. (585) He reached America in 1826, and settled first in Kaskaskia, Illinois. Shields had received an excellent classical education and spoke English and three other languages fluently. He soon was immersed in Democratic politics and the practice of law; he became a member of the Illinois legislature in 1836, served as state auditor thereafter, became a justice of the state supreme court, and was commissioner of the land office in Washington in 1845. In the course of his political career, he almost fought a duel with Abraham Lincoln. During the Mexican War he was a brigadier general of Illinois volunteers, was brevetted major general, and received the commendation of Winfield Scott. He was elected to the Senate from Illinois 1849-55, but failed of reelection. Shields now settled on a Minnesota land grant and was elected Senator upon the admission of the state to the Union in 1858, but was not reelected the following year. After a short residence on the West Coast, Shields was commissioned a brigadier general of U. S. Volunteers on August 19, 1861, by his old antagonist (and later close friend) Lincoln. Despite efforts on the part of Irish and other foreign societies and journals to magnify Shields's military reputation, his career in the Civil War could hardly be considered successful. Opposed to

Stonewall Jackson in the Shenandoah Valley, where he was expected to act in concert with John C. Frémont, Shields was defeated along with Frémont. Although a division commander at this time, Shields fades from the *Official Records* after the retreat across the Potomac and it is difficult to determine what duties he discharged until his resignation from the service was accepted on March 28, 1863. (586) He went back to San Francisco for a time, but by 1866 was living in Carrollton, Missouri, where he reentered the political arena. Losing an election to the U. S. House of Representatives by a very small margin in 1872, he was chosen to fill an unexpired term in the Senate in 1879. Poor health compelled him to forsake reelection. Shields had been a formidable speaker for a variety of causes for nearly fifty years, and it was while on a lecture tour that he died in Ottumwa, Iowa, on June 1, 1879. He was buried in St. Mary's Cemetery, Carrollton, Missouri.

Henry Hastings Sibley, a distant cousin of General Henry Hopkins Sibley of the Confederacy, was born in Detroit, Michigan, on February 29, 1811, when the area was virtually a wilderness. He received a superior education for the place and time and in 1829 entered the employ of the American Fur Company as a clerk. Five years later he began to actively engage in the fur trade itself and in 1835 built the first private residence in Minnesota at Fort Snelling. In 1848 Sibley was elected territorial delegate to Congress from the part of Wisconsin Territory not embraced by the state of Wisconsin, and the next year was

instrumental in the establishment of the Minnesota Territory. When the territory achieved statehood in 1858, he was elected its first governor. During the Sioux uprising in 1862, Sibley, who had enjoyed much prestige among the tribes for many years, was placed in com-

mand of the state forces sent against them. He was commissioned a brigadier general of U. S. Volunteers on September 29, 1862, but was not confirmed by the Senate and the appointment expired by law the following March 4. However, on March 20, 1863, he was reappointed and duly confirmed. Although he performed admirably against the Sioux and in 1865-66 was one of the commissioners to negotiate treaties with the various warlike tribes, it is probable that General Sibley never saw an armed Confederate. He was brevetted major general on November 29, 1865, for "efficient and meritorious service" and was mustered out on April 30, 1866. At this time

445

he changed his residence to St. Paul where he spent the balance of his life. He headed, at various times, a gas company, an insurance company, and a bank. He was elected to the state legislature in 1871 and while serving in this body delivered a speech opposing the repudiation of the state railroad bonds which resulted in the maintaining of Minnesota's credit. For many years he was president of the St. Paul Chamber of Commerce and was active on the Board of Regents of the University of Minnesota. He received an honorary LL.D. from Princeton University in 1888. During the later years of his life he wrote a number of articles for the collections of the state historical society, meanwhile, serving as the society's president. General Sibley died on February 18, 1891, in St. Paul and was buried there in Oakland Cemetery.

Daniel Edgar Sickles, always a controversial figure, was born October 20, 1819, in New York City. After attending New York University and studying law, he appraised the chances of advancement in various fields and quickly chose politics. As a Tammany stalwart he became corporation counsel of the city at the age of twenty-eight, but resigned the same year to be secretary of legation in London. He then served as a New York State senator and was a representative in Congress from 1857 to 1861. Sickles first achieved national notoriety in 1859 when he shot down, in the shadow of the White House, his young wife's paramour, son of the author of "The Star Spangled Banner." During a lurid trial, in which the defense counsel was headed by Edwin M. Stanton,

Sickles for the first time in American jurisprudence pleaded the "unwritten law" and was acquitted. Subsequently he enraged both critics and admirers by publicly forgiving his errant spouse. As a War Democrat in 1861, Sickles' offer of his services was eagerly accepted by the

administration and he soon found himself a brigadier general of volunteers, ranking from September 3, 1861. He was assigned the command of New York's Excelsior Brigade, which he had been instrumental in recruiting. His later career as division and corps commander, with promotion to the grade of major general to rank from November 29, 1862, found him frequently at odds with his superiors. Nonetheless, he demonstrated many soldierly qualities and was utterly fearless in combat. He fought on the Peninsula and at Sharpsburg in Joseph Hooker's division of the III Corps; commanded the division at Fredericksburg; and in the campaign of Chancellorsville commanded the III Corps. In the latter battle elements of his command reported Stonewall Jackson's celebrated flank march, while it was in progress, as a retreat. The subsequent advance of two-thirds of the corps to pursue the flying Rebels left Oliver O. Howard's XI Corps on its right completely isolated and contributed largely to the ensuing debacle. At Gettysburg Sickles' men were supposed to cover the Federal left in the vicinity of the Round Tops. Not liking the position and in defiance of direct orders to the contrary, he advanced the corps line into the famous Peach Orchard, creating a salient which was subsequently overrun by James Longstreet's assault. The end results were the virtual destruction and subsequent disappearance of the III Corps, the termination of Sickles' command in the field by virtue of a wound which cost him his right leg, and a controversy with George G. Meade. (587) After his recovery President Lincoln dispatched him on a tour of Union-held Southern territory for an appraisal of the effects of amnesty, Negro progress, and Reconstruction. (588) Next, he performed a diplomatic mission to Colombia; served as military governor of South Carolina; and in 1869 was retired with rank of major general in the Regular Army, a position which he would hold for forty-five years. At this time Grant appointed him minister to Spain, where he was chiefly distinguished diplomatically by becoming the intimate friend of Isabella, former Queen of Spain. He served a term in Congress in 1893-95 and for many years

was chairman of the New York State Monuments Commission, a position from which he was removed in 1912 by reason of alleged peculation. An octogenerian relic of a bygone age, General Sickles became separated not only from his family but from reality and died, "irresponsible and cantankerous," (589) on May 3, 1914, at his residence in New York. He was buried in Arlington National Cemetery.

Franz Sigel was born November 18, 1824, at Sinsheim in the grand duchy of Baden, Germany. Like many of the young German revolu-

tionaries, he graduated from a military academy (at Karlsruhe) in 1843 and became a subaltern in the service of Grand Duke Leopold. During the 1848 insurrections he acted as minister of war for the revolutionary forces which were overthrown by the Prussians. He fled first to Switzerland, then to England, and finally to New York in

447

1852. In the years before the Civil War he taught school in both New York and St. Louis and held a major's commission in the 5th New York Militia. By 1861 he was director of śchools in St. Louis, a community with a large minority of German-born citizens. By virtue of the administration's policy of wooing all immigrants whose affections were Union and antislavery, Sigel became a brigadier general on August 7, 1861, to rank from May 17 and a major general on March 22, 1862. Despite his military shortcomings, he did much to unify the large German population of the Northern states and contributed thousands of recruits to the Union ranks. "I fights mit Sigel" became almost a password among the Dutch and his influence with them never waned. He performed well at the capture of the secessionist Camp Jackson in St. Louis under Nathaniel Lyon and at the engagement at Carthage, Missouri—both minor skirmishes which served mainly the purpose of reestablishing Federal authority. At Elkhorn Tavern (Pea Ridge) in Arkansas he contributed greatly to the Union victory. His career thereafter was not as successful. Acceding to the command of John C. Frémont's corps during the campaign of Second Manassas, his troops were not engaged at Sharpsburg or Fredericksburg; and, while in command of the Department of West Virginia in 1864, he had the misfortune to fight the battle of New Market against the cadets of the Virginia Military Institute, by whom he was soundly trounced. (590) Subsequently he was removed from field duty and on May 4, 1865, resigned his commission as major general.

General Sigel lived for nearly forty more years, during which he ran for public office, changed his party allegiance from Republican to Democratic, and ultimately served as United States pension agent at New York by appointment of President Cleveland. He died at his residence in New York City, on August 21, 1902, and was buried in Woodlawn Cemetery.

Joshua Woodrow Sill, after whom Fort Sill, Oklahoma, was named, was born on December 6, 1831, in Chillicothe, Ohio. His early educa-

tion was in large measure secured from his father, a prominent attorney of the town. He was appointed to West Point in 1839 and was graduated third in the class of 1853, whose members included Philip Sheridan, James B. McPherson, John M. Schofield, and John B. Hood. Sill was brevetted an ordnance subaltern and served for a year at the Watervliet arsenal. He was then an instructor at West Point for three years and from 1857 until 1860 was on duty at a succession of arsenals. On January 25, 1861, he resigned his commission to become professor of mathematics and civil engineering in the Brooklyn (New York) Collegiate and Polytechnic Institute. Upon the bombardment of Fort Sumter, he immediately offered his services to the governor of Ohio and was appointed assistant adjutant general of the state. He fought at Rich Mountain, West Virginia, in July with the 33rd Ohio and on August 27, 1861, became colonel of the regiment. By November he was commanding a brigade in D. C. Buell's Department of the Ohio, and it was a contingent from his command which in April, 1862, took part in the "Locomotive Raid" into Georgia which has been celebrated in song, story, and motion picture. During Buell's advance into Kentucky to intercept Braxton Bragg's Confederate invaders, Sill, who had been made brigadier general of volunteers on July 16, 1862, commanded the 2nd Division of Alexander McD. McCook's I Corps. Sill was not present at Perryville, a battle fought by segments of the armies of both commanders on October 19, 1862. At Murfreesboro, however, he was in charge of a brigade in Sheridan's division. The night before the opening of the battle he dropped into his former classmate's tent and upon leaving picked up Sheridan's uniform coat instead of his own. The following morning Bragg's daylight assault forced back the Union right and center, reminiscent of the forcing shut of a jackknife blade with the hinge being

the connection of T. L. Crittenden's right and the left of G. H. Thomas. Farther to the Federal right Sheridan's division which composed the left element of McCook's corps fought desperately after its right was overwhelmed. While at the head of his command, repulsing a Confederate assault, Sill, wearing Sheridan's tunic, was killed instantly. He was buried in Grand View Cemetery near Chillicothe. (591)

James Richard Slack was born September 28, 1818, in Bucks County, Pennsylvania. He was educated in an academy at Newton, Pennsyl-

vania, but at the age of nineteen moved with his parents to Delaware County, Indiana. He then worked on his father's farm, taught school, studied law, and was admitted to the bar on his twenty-second birthday. A few weeks later he settled in Huntington, Indiana, possessing only six dollars in cash and the

449

clothes he was wearing. In 1842 Slack was elected county auditor, a position he held for nine years. He served seven terms in the state senate and in 1854 was defeated as a candidate for Congress. On December 13, 1861, Slack was commissioned colonel of the 47th Indiana Infantry and at New Madrid and Island No. 10 commanded a brigade under John Pope. He subsequently was in district and post command at various points, took part in the White River expedition and the engagement at Yazoo Pass, and during the Vicksburg campaign commanded a brigade of Hovey's division of McClernand's XIII Corps. Soon after, he was transferred to the Department. of the Gulf where he was stationed for the remainder of the war: he took a minor part in the Red River expedition; was in command at Thibodeaux, Louisiana, for a time heading a division of the XIII Corps; was present at all the engagements in the campaign against Mobile, including the capture of Spanish Fort, Fort Blakely, and the city itself. Slack had been promoted to brigadier general of volunteers on November 10, 1864, and as of March 13, 1865, was brevetted major general. He was mustered out early in 1866 and returned to Huntington, where he resumed his law practice. When the Twenty-eighth Judicial Circuit was created, General Slack was appointed to the bench by the governor and was elected thereto in 1872 and re-elected in 1878. He again ran unsuccessfully for Congress in 1880. The following year on July 28, he died of a heart attack while visiting in Chicago and was buried in Mt. Hope Cemetery, Huntington. (592)

Adam Jacoby Slemmer, was born on January 24, 1829, in Montgomery County, Pennsylvania. He received his early education in the local country schools and at the age of seventeen entered West Point, where he was graduated in the class

of 1850. Slemmer's first active service was against the Florida Seminoles; he was then stationed in southern California for four years; and from 1855 to 1859 taught a variety of subjects at the Military Academy. At the beginning of hostilities he was a first lieutenant, 1st Artillery, commanding Fort Barrancas and the barracks on Pensacola Bay. On January 10, 1861, the day Florida seceded from the Union, he contributed a key bit of strategy to the Union cause by moving his little command to Fort Pickens on Santa Rosa Island. This position remained from first to last in the hands of the Federal forces and ensured control of the Gulf of Mexico. On May 14 he was promoted directly to major of the newly authorized 16th Infantry, which he aided in recruiting and organizing. He soon became acting inspector general of the Department of the Ohio and served under General D. C. Buell in 1862 in his operations in Mississippi, North Alabama, Tennessee, and Kentucky, taking part in the siege of Corinth and the advance into Kentucky to oppose Braxton Bragg's Confederates. At the battle of Murfreesboro, Slemmer commanded, as major, the 1st Battalion and one company of the 2nd Battalion of the 16th Infantry in a brigade of Regulars assigned to L. H. Rousseau's division of G. H. Thomas' XIV Corps of the Federal forces under W. S. Rosecrans. In the course of this battle on December 31, 1862, Slemmer was so badly wounded that his active field service was brought to a close. During convalescence from his wound he was promoted brigadier general of volunteers on April 4, 1863, to rank from November 29, 1862. From July, 1863, until the end of the war General Slemmer served as president of a board for examination of sick and wounded officers at Columbus and Cincinnati. He was promoted lieutenant colonel in the regular service in 1864 and brevet brigadier general in 1865; after the war he served in garrison and as a member of a board for examination of candidates for promotion. While in command of Fort Laramie, Wyoming (then Dakota Territory), a post to which he had been assigned in 1867, he died on October 7, 1868, of heart disease at the age of thirty-nine and was buried in Montgomery Cemetery, Norristown, Pennsylvania, in the county of his birth.

Henry Warner Slocum was born September 24, 1827, at Delphi (also called Delphi Falls), a hamlet in Onondaga County, New York. He was the direct descendant of an Englishman who came to America in 1637. He attended nearby Cazenovia Seminary, taught school for several years, and in 1848 secured

an appointment to the Military Academy, where he was graduated in 1852. After some service against the Florida Seminoles and garrison duty in Charleston Harbor, he resigned in 1856 to begin the practice of law for which he had fitted himself while in the army. He took up residence in Syracuse, New York, and served as county treasurer, as a state legislator, and as an instructor in artillery in the New York State militia with rank of colonel. As of May 21, 1861, Slocum became colonel of the 27th New York, a two-year regiment which was mustered in at Elmira on July 9; the regiment fought in Andrew Porter's brigade of David Hunter's division at First Bull Run (Manassas), where it sustained 130 casualties and its commander was wounded in the thigh. Upon his return to duty Slocum was given a brigade of William B. Franklin's division, and, when Franklin became commander of the VI Corps, Slocum succeeded him in divisional command. He had been made a brigadier general of volunteers on August 9, 1861, and on July 25, 1862, was promoted major general to rank from July 4, the next-to-youngest of this rank in the army at this time. (593) He led his division through the Peninsular campaign, aided in covering John Pope's retreat from the battlefield of Second Manassas, and rendered valuable service during the campaign in Maryland. After the bloody battle of Sharpsburg, Slocum was appointed to lead the XII Corps, an organization created the month before from N. P. Banks's II Corps of Pope's Army of Virginia. (594) The XII Corps was not employed at the battle of Fredericksburg, but in the ensuing campaign of Chancellorsville was heavily engaged, losing 2,755 men from its six brigades of infantry. Of all those who became disenchanted with the leadership of Joseph Hooker during this battle, Slocum and Darius N. Couch of the II Corps were the most articulate, each expressing his opinion unreservedly. (595) At the crucial battle of Gettysburg the XII Corps held the extreme right of the Union line, stretching southward from Culp's Hill across the Baltimore Pike; Slocum was the senior major general present on the field. After this battle and the debacle at Chickamauga in September, the XI

and XII Corps were moved, under the general command of Hooker, to the west to succor the beleaguered Federals in Chattanooga. Slocum promptly submitted his resignation to President Lincoln (596), but it was refused. A compromise was ultimately reached whereby one division of the corps, under Slocum, was charged with the protection of the Nashville & Chattanooga Railroad while the other division served directly under Hooker. Just prior to the inception of the Atlanta campaign he was assigned to the District of Vicksburg, where he served until August, 1864. Meantime the XI and XII Corps were consolidated into the XX Corps, with Hooker as commander. After the death of James B. McPherson in July the command of his Army of the Tennessee was given to Oliver O. Howard; whereupon Hooker huffily asked to be relieved, because he considered himself overslaughed by a junior. At this juncture Slocum was called from Vicksburg to succeed to the command of the XX Corps, which was the first Federal command to enter Atlanta on September 2, 1864. In the subsequent "March to the Sea" and the campaign of the Carolinas, Slocum commanded the left wing of W. T. Sherman's forces (XIV and XX Corps), while Howard commanded the right (XV and XVII); toward the end these forces were respectively designated the Army of Georgia and the Army of the Tennessee. On September 28, 1865, Slocum resigned his commission and returned to Syracuse. He ran that year for New York secretary of state on the Democratic ticket but was defeated by General Francis C. Barlow. The following spring he moved to Brooklyn where he practiced law and the same year declined a colonel's commission in the Regular Army. He was a Democratic presidential elector in 1868 and was elected to Congress for three terms as a Democrat (from 1869 to 1873 and from 1883 to 1885). As a Congressman he was one of the staunchest adherents of General Fitz John Porter in his battle to win vindication from his unjust court-martial sentence. Slocum was also a member of the Board of Gettysburg Monument Commissioners. He died in Brooklyn, on April 14, 1894, and was buried in Green-Wood Cemetery.

John Potts Slough was born in Cincinnati, on February 1, 1829. At the age of twenty-one he became a member of the Ohio legislature but was expelled from that body for having struck another member with his fists during a political altercation. He subsequently moved to

Kansas Territory and from there to Denver in 1860. A year after the war broke out, Slough, whose Union allegiance seems to have originally been in some question, (597) became colonel of the 1st Colorado Infantry, which was "intensively drilled at Denver during the opening months of 1862." During Confederate General Henry H. Sibley's invasion of New Mexico, Slough's command, theoretically under Edward R. S. Canby, won the day at Glorieta Pass in direct defiance of Canby's explicit orders. Slough promptly repaired to Washington, where President Lincoln found it expedient to appoint him a brigadier general of volunteers on August 25, 1862. From then until the close of the war General Slough served as military governor of Alexandria, an office which frequently brought him into conflict with the army commanders within his sphere of influence. (598) He was a member of Fitz John Porter's court-martial, a detail which reflected no credit on any members of the court but rather emphasized the willingness of its members to succumb to the convictions of Secretary of War Edwin M. Stanton. Slough was honorably mustered out of volunteer service on August 24, 1865, and was appointed chief justice of New Mexico Territory, where "his imperious temper rendered him very unpopular." (599) On December 15, 1867, Slough had an affray in the billiard room of La Fonda in Santa Fe with a member of the territorial legislature who had introduced a resolution censuring Slough for unprofessional conduct. (600) He received a mortal wound from which he died on the seventeenth. (601) Temporarily buried in Santa Fe, his remains were taken the following summer to Spring Grove Cemetery in Cincinnati, where they now lie.

Andrew Jackson Smith, whose father fought twice in wars against Great Britain, was born on a farm in Bucks County, Pennsylvania, on April 28, 1815. After his graduation from West Point in the class of

1838 he was commissioned into the 1st Dragoons with which he served all over the west during the next twenty-three years. He was promoted first lieutenant in 1845, captain in 1847, and major on May 13, 1861. At the beginning of the Civil War, Smith was commissioned colonel of the 2nd California Cavalry, but resigned his volunteer commission on November 3 to become chief of cavalry under General Henry W. Halleck, serving as such until after the evacuation of Corinth by P. G. T. Beauregard's Confederates. On March 20, 1862, he

was appointed a brigadier general of volunteers to rank from the seventeenth and on May 14, 1864, was advanced to major general. He commanded one of W. T. Sherman's four divisions at Chickasaw Bluffs in December, 1862, and a division of the XIII Corps the following month in the attack on Arkansas Post and during the Vicksburg campaign. In N. P. Banks's campaign up Red River during the spring of 1864 he directed elements of the XVI and XVII Corps detached from the Army of the Tennessee. He then served successively in Tennessee, Mississippi (defeating Nathan B. Forrest at Tupelo, July 14, 1864), Missouri, and back to Tennessee to take part in the battle of Nashville against John B. Hood. By this time the wanderings of his troops had become so extensive that he referred to them as the "lost tribes of Israel." During the campaign against Mobile in 1865 Smith commanded the reorganized XVI Corps of two divisions. At the close of the war he was brevetted major general in the Regular Army and in 1866 became colonel of the 7th Regular Cavalry. After receiving an appointment as postmaster of St. Louis (his wife's home) in 1869 from President Grant, General Smith resigned his army commission. He was city auditor of St. Louis from 1877 to 1889 and commanded a brigade of Missouri militia during the strikes of 1877. Under an act of Congress approved on December 24, 1888, Smith was reappointed in the army on January 22, 1889, and retired with rank of colonel of cavalry the same day. He died at his home in St. Louis on January 30, 1897, and was buried in Bellefontaine

Cemetery. His career attracted little notoriety compared to that of many of his colleagues; nevertheless, he was one of the most competent division and corps commanders in the service.

Charles Ferguson Smith, son of an army surgeon, was born on April 24, 1807, in Philadelphia. He entered the Military Academy only nineteen years after its doors were opened and was graduated in 1825. Four years later he returned to the Academy to serve in various capaci-

ties, including that of commandant of cadets, until 1842. During this period both U. S. Grant and W. T. Sherman were cadets; Grant later revered Smith as his beau ideal of a soldier, and Sherman went so far as to state that neither Grant nor he would have ever been heard of had it not been for Smith's untimely death. (602) During the Mexican War Smith achieved an outstanding reputation in both Zachary Taylor's and Winfield Scott's armies and was brevetted major, lieutenant colonel, and colonel for gallant and meritorious conduct at Palo Alto, Resaca de la Palma, Monterey, Contreras, and Churubusco. After the city of Mexico was taken, he was in charge of the police guard there until 1848. He was advanced to the full rank of major in 1854 and to that of lieutenant colonel the following year. In 1856 he led an expedition into the Red River country of northern Idaho and the next year took part in Albert Sidney Johnston's campaign against the Mormons. From February, 1860, until February, 1861, he commanded the Department of Utah. For two weeks in April, 1861, he commanded the Department of Washington, but a soldier rather than a politician, he was shunted into recruiting duty in New York until August. He was appointed brigadier general of volunteers on August 31 and colonel of the 3rd Regular Infantry on September 9, 1861. In the course of the operations against Forts Henry and Donelson he came under the command of his former pupils, Grant and Sherman, both of whom felt a good deal of diffidence in giving him an order. During the investment of Fort Donelson, where he commanded a division of Grant's forces, Smith led in person a charge which was largely responsible for the subsequent surrender of the place—an exploit which earned for Grant the nickname of "Unconditional Surrender." Smith was advanced to major general on March 22, 1862. At this juncture, due to what was euphemistically referred to as a "misunderstanding" (603) among Grant, Henry W. Halleck, and George B. McClellan, Smith was assigned to the command of the forces sent up the Tennessee River to locate Johnston's Rebels, who were known to be concentrating at Corinth. The contretemps was resolved when Smith abraded his shin, while jumping into a rowboat; he, subsequently, developed an infection which, aggravated by dysentery, caused his death at Grant's headquarters in Savannah, Tennessee, on April 25, 1862. He was buried in Laurel Hill Cemetery, Philadelphia. There has been much conjecture as to what "might have been" had Smith commanded at Shiloh instead of his former pupil. However, Smith himself, lying in his sickbed and hearing the thunder and crash of battle a few miles to the north, was as bemused as were Grant and his principal lieutenant Sherman. (604)

Giles Alexander Smith, a brother of General Morgan L. Smith, was born in Jefferson County, New York, on September 29, 1829. When he was about eighteen years old he moved to Ohio, living first in London and later engaging in business for about ten years in Cincinnati. He next moved to Bloomington, Illinois, where he was occupied as proprietor of a hotel at the outbreak of the Civil War. On June 14, 1861, he became captain of a company of the 8th Missouri Infantry, a regiment of which his brother was colonel. His first action was at the capture of Fort Donelson where he was commended in the report of his major. (605) He was in some of the heaviest fighting at Shiloh, took part in the advance on Corinth, and succeeded his brother as colonel in June, 1862. In

the attack on Chickasaw Bluffs in December and the capture of Arkansas Post in January, 1863, he commanded a brigade, first in the XIII Corps and then in the XV Corps. Smith served throughout the ensuing Vicksburg campaign and the subsequent expulsion of Joseph E. Johnston from Jackson; he was made a brigadier general of volunteers to rank from August 4, 1863. During the Chattanooga campaign he was severely wounded in the course of W. T. Sherman's assault on the north end of Missionary Ridge. In the Atlanta campaign he was assigned to command a division of the XVII Corps and at the battle of Atlanta sustained William J. Hardee's assault on the Union left—an assault which came within a hair's breadth of rolling up James B. McPherson's entire command. Smith was brevetted major general of volunteers on September 1, 1864, and then led his division in the "March to the Sea" and throughout the campaign of the Carolinas. On November 24, 1865, he was advanced to the full rank of major general of volunteers, the last such appointment on the basis of seniority made in the Civil War. (606) Mustered out in 1866, he returned to his home in Bloomington. He was appointed Second Assistant Postmaster General by President Grant in 1869, but resigned in 1872 because of failing health. He moved to California in 1874 in an attempt to improve his health but returned to Bloomington two months before his death on November 5, 1876. He was buried in Bloomington Cemetery.

Green Clay Smith, whose uncle was General Cassius M. Clay, was born July 4, 1826, in Richmond, Kentucky. (607) Before serving a year during the Mexican War as a second lieutenant of infantry, he entered Transylvania University from which he was graduated at the age

of eighteen. Three years later he took his degree from the Lexington Law School and commenced practice with his father, a prominent Kentucky politician and member of Congress. Young Smith moved to Covington in 1858 and in 1860 was a member of the legislature and a staunch supporter of the Union. He is said to have enlisted in the army as a private, but in any case was made colonel of the 4th Kentucky (Union) Cavalry on March 15, 1862, and brigadier general of volunteers to rank from June 11. On May 5, 1862, his regiment and two others under the command of General Ebenezer Dumont took part in the rout of the celebrated Confederate John Hunt Morgan at Lebanon, Tennessee. Later, he was not as successful in resisting the incursions of the dauntless raider, moving his superior General Jeremiah T. Boyle at one point to query Don Carlos Buell, "Don't you want General G. Clay Smith?" (608) Smith was elected to Congress in the fall of 1862 and resigned his army commission on December 4, 1863. He was a congressman until 1866, when he resigned to accept the post of territorial governor of Montana. Meantime he had been brevetted major general of volunteers "for meritorious service during the war." A few years later he entered the ministry, was ordained in 1869, and the same year became pastor of the Baptist church in Frankfort, Kentucky. The Reverend Smith was of an evangelical bent and many of the succeeding years of his life were devoted to this cause. An ardent temperance advocate, he was the candidate of the National Prohibition party in 1876, attracting 9,522 votes in the presidential election of that year. From 1890 until his death on June 29, 1895, he was pastor of the Metropolitan Baptist Church of Washington, D. C. His death occurred in Washington, and he was buried in Arlington National Cemetery.

Gustavus Adolphus Smith was born December 26, 1820, in Philadelphia. He lived in both Maryland and Ohio, finally settling in 1837 in Decatur, Illinois, where for years he

manufactured carriages, "enjoying a lucrative trade that extended far into the south." (609) When the news of the fall of Fort Sumter reached Decatur, Smith was among the first to volunteer and for several months was engaged in drilling recruits both in Illinois and in Missouri. On September 1, 1861, he became colonel of the 35th Illinois Infantry, which was known as "Gus Smith's Independent Regiment."

At the battle of Elkhorn Tavern (Pea Ridge), Smith was directing the fire of the 1st Iowa Battery when "[his] horse was shot from under him. While awaiting another horse . . . a bullet struck his sword in his hand; his belt was shot from his waist; he received a shot in the right shoulder and was struck on the right side of the head with a piece of shell which fractured his skull . . . he was then taken from the field [supposedly] mortally wounded." (610) His wounds did not fully heal until 1868. In July, 1862, he was authorized to recruit a brigade and as a result was made a brigadier general of volunteers to rank from September 19, 1862, but because he was unable to stand field duty the Senate failed to act on his nomination which expired by law March 4, 1863. He then reverted to colonel of the 35th Illinois. F. B. Heitman states in his *Register* that he was "dismissed" on September 22, 1863. (611) However, he was remustered as colonel of the 155th Illinois on February 28, 1865, and with this regiment performed guard duty on the Nashville & Chattanooga Railroad until the end of the war when he was brevetted brigadier general of volunteers. He was honorably mustered out of service on December 14, 1865. After residing temporarily in Alabama, Smith was appointed collector of internal revenue for the District of New Mexico in 1870 by his friend President Grant. He lived in Santa Fe from the time of his appointment until his death. For more than thirty-five years he took a great interest in the Odd Fellows lodge, serving in a number of executive and honorary capacities. General Smith died in Santa

Fe on December 11, 1885, and was buried in Fairview Cemetery; his remains were later removed to the U. S. National Cemetery in Santa Fe.

John Eugene Smith, the son of a Napoleonic officer who had fought at Waterloo, was born in Berne, Switzerland, on August 3, 1816.

(612) His parents came to America while he was a small child and established their residence in Philadelphia, where young Smith was educated and learned the trade of jeweler and goldsmith. He moved to St. Louis and then to Galena, Illinois, in 1836. In 1860 he was elected county treasurer and the following year may have been instrumental in rescuing U. S. Grant from obscurity by recommending to Governor Richard Yates that Grant ought to know how to organize a regiment. (613) After serving on the governor's staff for a time, Smith recruited and organized the 45th Illinois and was commissioned its colonel on July 23, 1861. He was successively engaged at the capture of Forts Henry and Donelson and the battle of Shiloh, part of the time in command of a brigade. At Shiloh, McClernand's division, to which he was attached, sustained 1,740 casualties. Smith was made a brigadier general on November 29, 1862, and during the Vicksburg campaign directed a brigade of Logan's division of McPherson's XVII Corps, and in the final stages of the siege the so-called 7th Division of the corps itself. At Chattanooga in November his was the only XVII Corps's division present to take part in the defeat of Braxton Bragg's army. In the advance on Atlanta his division was stationed at Cartersville and other points in rear of W. T. Sherman's advancing forces. He then led his command throughout the "March to the Sea" and the campaign of the Carolinas and especially distinguished himself at the capture of the city of Savannah. Before the close of hostilities he was brevetted major general and in the closing months of 1865 commanded the District of Western Tennessee. Smith was mustered out of the volunteer service in April, 1866, but upon the reorganization and enlargement of the Regular Army in July he was appointed colonel of the 27th Infantry. The following year he was brevetted brigadier and major general, U. S. Army. He served at various points on the Indian frontier until his retirement on May 19, 1881. General Smith then made his residence in Chicago, where he died on January 29, 1897. He was buried in Greenwood Cemetery, Galena.

Morgan Lewis Smith, the elder brother of General Giles A. Smith, was born March 8, 1821, in Mexico, New York, but as an infant was taken by his parents to Jefferson County, New York. He left home

when he was twenty-one and became something of a wanderer, occupying himself successively as schoolteacher (in New Albany, Indiana), professional soldier in the Regular Army for five years under an assumed name, and riverboatman on the Ohio and Mississippi from 1850 until the outbreak of war. At this point he recruited and organized the 8th Missouri Infantry, composed largely of rowdies from the St. Louis waterfront whom he turned into excellent soldiers. He was the regiment's first colonel and served as such until he was assigned to brigade command in the assault on Fort Donelson. His brigade of Lew Wallace's division was heavily engaged at Shiloh; its only casualties were dead and wounded men—

a testimonial to his ability on a field where thousands of skulkers went to the rear. Smith was advanced to brigadier general on July 16, 1862, and at year's end was so badly wounded at Chickasaw Bluffs that he was unable to return to duty until October, 1863. At the battle of Chattanooga in November he commanded the 2nd Division of the XV Corps and during the Atlanta campaign the next year was in temporary command of the corps itself while John A. Logan was commanding the Army of the Tennessee after the death of James B. McPherson. Soon after, Smith became incapacitated for further active service in the field because of the aggravation of the wound received at Chickasaw Bluffs. After returning from sick leave he was assigned to the command of the District of Vicksburg, where he remained until the end of the war. Not waiting for muster out, General Smith resigned his commission on July 12, 1865, which probably accounts for his failure to receive a brevet promotion to major general. President Johnson appointed him United States consul general in Honolulu, where he served until U. S. Grant took office. He then engaged in business in Washington: he acted as counsel for claimants against the government, bid on mail routes in the South and West, and was connected with a building association. He died suddenly on December 28, 1874, while on a trip to Jersey City, New Jersey, and was buried in Arlington National Cemetery.

Thomas Church Haskell Smith was born March 24, 1819, in Acushnet, Massachusetts. He was graduated from Harvard in 1841, ranking second in his class. He then went west to Marietta, Ohio, where he commenced a study of law which he completed back in Cambridge. He then practiced in Cincinnati until 1848 when he embarked upon the construction of telegraph lines linking North and South. In 1851 he returned to Cincinnati. A Douglas Democrat of strong convic-

tions prior to the outbreak of war, Smith boldly went all out for the Union cause and on September 5, 1861, was made lieutenant colonel of the 1st Ohio Cavalry. During the advance upon Corinth following the battle of Shiloh, Smith became attached to the headquarters of John Pope, who appointed him his aide-de-camp in July, 1862, and took him east when he was summoned to head the Army of Virginia. Smith's testimony against Fitz John Porter during the latter's court-martial upon charges preferred by Pope's inspector general

(B. S. Roberts) after the fiasco at Second Manassas was not only highly damaging to Porter but also imaginative, visionary, and adhering more rigidly to prejudice than fact, as was brought out seventeen years later when Porter was exonerated. (614) Nevertheless Smith was rewarded by the War Department for his zeal by promotion to the grade of brigadier general on March 16, 1863, and accompanied Pope to Minnesota. Smith commanded the District of Wisconsin that year and at war's end accompanied Pope to the Department of Missouri when the latter took over that command. Smith was mustered out of service in 1866 and began raising livestock in southwest Missouri. The Chicago Fire of 1871, however, destroyed his sources of independent income and he was compelled to accept government service, first in the Treasury Department, and subsequently (1878) as paymaster with rank of major in the Regular Army. He was retired for age in 1883; thereafter, he made his home in the Ojai Valley of southern California. He died April 8, 1897, at Nordhoff (now Ojai), California, and was buried in Santa Barbara Cemetery. Smith was a controversial figure who to the end of his days, despite all evidence to the contrary, insisted that Pope was a military genius, brought to ruin by the jealousy of George B. McClellan's supporters, chief of whom was, of course, Porter. (615)

Thomas Kilby Smith was born in Dorchester, Massachusetts, on September 23, 1820. When he was about eight years old, his parents moved to Hamilton County, Ohio,

where they settled on a farm. Young Smith pursued a law career and was graduated from Cincinnati College in 1837; he then studied under Salmon P. Chase, who would later become Lincoln's Secretary of the Treasury and Chief Justice of the U. S. Supreme Court. Smith's antebellum career ranged from a clerkship in the Post Office Department in Washington to the post of United States marshal for Ohio's southern district. On September 9, 1861, he was mustered into service as lieutenant colonel of the 54th Ohio, a regiment of which he was made colonel the month following. Although Smith (one of many by that name who followed U. S. Grant and W. T. Sherman in the western theater of war) achieved no sensational successes, he performed most capably in a long series of campaigns which began with Shiloh and ended with command of a large segment of the Gulf Coast. He was promoted brigadier general on August 11, 1863; in the mean-

time he had served on Grant's staff during the Vicksburg campaign and also had commanded a brigade of the XV Corps. The following year he was sent up the Red River, with N. P. Banks, in command of a mixed force of infantry, cavalry, and artillery which was designed to protect the navy vessels accompanying the expedition—an assignment which he discharged with fidelity and good judgment. The campaign, however, was adjudged a failure and the officers involved were shunted off either to oblivion or to other posts. Smith, arriving from Red River with only eight hundred effectives in his command of eighteen hundred men, was assigned by his superior C. C. Washburn to a chase of Nathan B. Forrest—an expedition fraught with interest if not with military results. Shortly thereafter, Smith was compelled to relinquish field service because of his health, but he was brevetted major general of volunteers March 13, 1865, in the omnibus promotions which closed the war. General Smith was made consul at Panama in 1866 but soon returned to his home in Torresdale, Pennsylvania, then a Philadelphia suburb. In 1887 he took up residence in New York, where he died on December 14, 1887. His remains were returned to Torresdale for burial.

William Farrar Smith, known in the army as "Baldy," was born in St. Albans, Vermont, on February 17, 1824, and was graduated from West Point in 1845, ranking fourth in his class. As an engineer officer, he spent the years before the outbreak of the Civil War in a variety of surveys and exploration duties, as an instructor at the Military

Academy, and as member and secretary of the lighthouse board. With rank of colonel of the 3rd Vermont (from July 16), he took part in the battle of First Manassas on the staff of General Irvin McDowell, and on August 13, 1861, was promoted to brigadier general of volunteers. He commanded a division of the VI Corps on the Peninsula and in the Maryland campaign and headed

the VI Corps at Fredericksburg, receiving promotion to major general to rank from July 4, 1862. After Fredericksburg, Smith and William B. Franklin, the commander of the "Left Grand Division," wrote a letter to President Lincoln unsparingly criticizing Ambrose E. Burnside's plan of campaign for the future. (616) This indiscretion, compounded by the fact that Smith was a close friend of George B. McClellan, resulted in his losing both his corps command and his promotion (the Senate failing to confirm his nomination to major

general). This would not be the last time Smith would be at odds with his superiors. After a series of unimportant commands in Pennsylvania and West Virginia, he turned up in Chattanooga as chief engineer of the Department of the Cumberland and later served in this position in the Military Division of the Mississippi. While in Mississippi he had a disagreement with W. S. Rosecrans over who was due the credit for opening the supply line which brought commissary supplies and forage to Rosecrans' starving men and animals after Bragg's investment of Chattanooga. But he was praised by U. S. Grant, W. T. Sherman, and G. H. Thomas for his unquestioned engineering genius, and he made a valuable contribution to the assault on Missionary Ridge. He was accordingly reappointed major general to rank from March 9, 1864, and was duly confirmed. Grant now brought him east and gave him command of the XVIII Corps of Benjamin F. Butler's Army of the James. Although Butler's fitness for military command was questionable, he wielded enormous political influence, and Smith might have restrained his impulse to state that Butler was "as helpless as a child on the field of battle and as visionary as an opium eater in council." Smith's corps was attached to the Army of the Potomac in time to take part in the bloody repulse at Cold Harbor, where he found time to bitterly criticize George G. Meade. Next, Smith's corps and a division of colored troops were ordered to take Petersburg. His fatal hesitation here, perhaps because of the formidable character of the Confederate works or perhaps because of a bout with malaria from which he had suffered for a decade, may have lost him the opportunity to shorten the war by nearly a year. On July 19, 1864, he was relieved from command of the XVIII Corps, seemingly to placate Butler, for Smith was brevetted major general, U. S. Army, in the omnibus promotions of March, 1865. He resigned his volunteer commission in 1865 and his regular commission of major of engineers in 1867. In his remaining years he acted as president of a cable telegraph company, as president of the board of police commissioners of New York City, and from 1881 to 1901 as a civilian engineer in government employ on various river and harbor improvements. He made numerous literary contributions to the history of the war, including several articles for *Battles and Leaders of the Civil War*. He died in Philadelphia (his home for the last ten years of his life) on February 28, 1903, and was buried in Arlington National Cemetery.

William Sooy Smith was born in the central Ohio hamlet of Tarlton, on July 22, 1830. He worked his way through Ohio University at Athens and was graduated in 1849. He then procured an appointment to the Military Academy, where he was graduated in 1853, ranking sixth in the class which included James B. McPherson, John M. Schofield, Philip Sheridan, and John B. Hood of the Confederacy. Smith resigned his commission a year after graduation to associate himself with the Illinois Central Railroad as a construction engineer. He subsequently organized an engineering firm with which he

was employed in 1861. At this time Smith returned to Ohio and on June 26 was commissioned colonel of the 13th Ohio Infantry. He took part in the West Virginia campaign and then fought at Shiloh and Perryville in Don Carlos Buell's Army of the Ohio. He had been made a brigadier general of volunteers in April, 1862, and at Perryville directed a division of T. L. Crittenden's corps, most of which did not get into the battle. During the Vicksburg campaign he commanded a division of the XVI Corps. He was then made chief of cavalry of the forces in the West under U. S. Grant and subsequently W. T. Sherman; in March, 1864, with seven thousand troops, he embarked upon his celebrated raid from Memphis to West Point, Mississippi, where in a series of engagements he was badly defeated and driven back to Memphis by the Confederate Nathan B. Forrest who had less than half as many effectives. (617) He resigned July 15,

1864, because of ill health and re-tired to a farm at Oak Park, Illinois. Regaining his former vigor, General Smith made monumental contributions to the science of engineering, particularly as related to the underpinning of bridges and skyscrapers. He built the first all-steel bridge in the world over the Missouri River at Glasgow, Missouri, and about 1890 devoted his attention to the construction of buildings in Chicago, where, unlike New York, bedrock lies far below the surface. Until 1910 he had a hand in the construction of virtually every tall building constructed in the city. General Smith retired to the quiet of the country village of Medford, Oregon, where he spent his last years, active in his profession to the end. He died in Medford on March 4, 1916 (in his eighty-sixth year), and was buried in Forest Home Cemetery, Riverside, Illinois.

Thomas Alfred Smyth, an unsung Irish hero of the Civil War, was born on December 25, 1832, in the parish of Ballyhooley, county of Cork. (618) Obtaining the rudiments of an education, he worked upon his father's farm until 1854, when he came to the United States and "followed a business of carving in Philadelphia." (619) The lure of excitement then caused him to join the revolutionary expedition of William Walker to Nicaragua. In 1858 he settled in Wilmington, Delaware, as a coachmaker. When the shooting began in 1861, Smyth was ready with a company of infantry which he vainly offered to the Delaware authorities. It ultimately became part of the 24th Pennsylvania along with other companies

which were recruited in and about Philadelphia; this all-Irish regiment served for only three months. Soon after its muster out, Smyth was appointed major of the 1st Delaware Infantry, an outfit enlisted for three years; he became its lieutenant colonel in December, 1862,

and colonel the following February. He accompanied this regiment to Suffolk, Virginia, in July, 1862, and then in September back to the field of Sharpsburg (Antietam), where it lost almost one third of its effectives present for duty. The 1st Delaware was present at Fredericksburg, Chancellorsville, and Gettysburg. In the latter battle Smyth commanded a brigade of Hays's division of Hancock's II Corps which did its share in breaking the back of George E. Pickett's celebrated charge on July 3. Smyth continued to render distinguished service during the campaign on the Rappahannock that autumn and in the course of the advance upon Petersburg and Richmond in 1864. On October 1, 1864, he was promoted to brigadier general of volunteers; soon after this promotion he took part in the encounters at Deep Bottom, Gravelly Run, and Hatcher's Run. While in pursuit of the Army of Northern Virginia during the Appomattox campaign, Smyth, serving in divisional command, was riding on his skirmish line in the course of the action near Farmville on April 7, 1865, when he was shot through the mouth by a Confederate sharpshooter, the ball shattering a cervical vertebra. Taken to the nearby residence of Colonel S. D. Burke (for whom Burkeville was named), Smyth lived for two days, finally succumbing on the day of R. E. Lee's surrender. Posthumously promoted major general by brevet to rank from the date he was wounded, Smyth became the last Federal general to be killed in the war. He was buried in the Wilmington and Brandywine Cemetery in Wilmington. (620)

James Gallant Spears was born in Bledsoe County, Tennessee, on March 29, 1816. After he became of age he acquired a meager education by his own efforts, studied law, and located at Pikeville, Tennessee, to practice his profession. In 1848 he was elected clerk of the circuit court and by 1851 had acquired both land and slaves. Spears, a Douglas Democrat and an uncompromising Unionist, was a delegate to the Knoxville convention in May, 1861, and to the meeting of the same body in Greeneville in June. In the summer of 1861 he learned that he was to be arrested for disloyalty to the Confederate govern-

ment; whereupon he fled to Kentucky, aided in organizing the 1st Tennessee (Union) Infantry, and was appointed its lieutenant colonel on September 1, 1861. The following March 5 he was promoted to brigadier general. The 1st Tennessee was in reality a battalion, with Spears its senior officer; he led it at Wild Cat Mountain and Mill Springs. In June, 1862, he was in charge of a brigade of the Army of the Ohio which took part in the capture of Cumberland Gap, as well as in the subsequent retreat to the Ohio River in the fall of the year; with another brigade he arrived on the field of Murfreesboro in time to take part in the action on January 3, 1863. At Chickamauga his brigade was a part of Granger's reserve corps but was not actually engaged in the battle. He later took part in the relief of Knoxville. In spite of his staunch Union sympathies Spears felt that the Emancipation Proclamation, which deprived him of his Negroes, was illegal and unconstitutional. He expressed himself on the matter in such violent language that his sentiments were communicated to Washington. This resulted in an investigation authorized by President Lincoln and on February 6, 1864, his arrest. (621) By the verdict of a court-martial Spears was dismissed from the service on August 30, 1864, after disdaining an offer which would have permitted him to resign. "He was brave in battle, but hot-headed, impulsive, and obstinate in what he thought was right. . . ." (622) He then returned to his home and set about retrieving his fortune, which had been considerable. On July 22, 1869, he died at his summer home at Braden's Knob in Bledsoe County, and was buried in Pikeville.

Francis Barretto Spinola was born on March 19, 1821, at Stony Brook, on the north shore of Long Island, New York. After attending an academy in Dutchess County, he studied law, was admitted to the bar in 1844, and immediately plunged into Democratic politics. He served five years as a Brooklyn alderman, six years as a member of the state assembly, and four as state senator; in 1860 he was a delegate to the Democratic National Convention in Charleston, South Carolina. Spinola was appointed a brigadier general on October 2, 1862, "for meritorious conduct in recruiting and organizing a brigade of four regiments and accompanying them to the field." During the following winter and spring he took part in a number of minor operations in southeast Virginia and North Carolina while commanding several

regiments of Pennsylvania militia. These regiments were recalled to take part in the pursuit of Robert E. Lee's army after the battle of Gettysburg, and Spinola was wounded near Manassas Gap during the operation. In March, 1864, prior to the opening of Grant's Overland campaign against Richmond, the number of army corps in the Army of the Potomac was reduced to three, and the troops of the I and III Corps, which had been badly decimated at Gettysburg and in the campaigns of the fall of 1863, were ordered distributed among the II, V, and VI Corps. One of the officers declared supernumerary by George G. Meade (623) and subsequently relieved from duty with the Army of the Potomac was General Spinola. After a tour of recruiting duty in New York City, he was court-martialed for "conniving with bounty brokers to defraud and swindle recruits" and sentenced to dismissal. (624) The sentence apparently was not approved, for his resignation from the service was accepted on June 8, 1865. Returning home, he engaged in banking and in the insurance business and resumed his political activities. In 1886, 1888, and 1890 he was elected to Congress as a Democrat and appropriately served as a member of the Committee on Military Affairs and the Committee on War Claims. He was also an alternate delegate to the Democratic National Convention at Chicago in 1884. General Spinola died in Washington soon after the commencement of his third Congressional term and was buried in Green-Wood Cemetery, Brooklyn.

John Wilson Sprague was born April 4, 1817, in the village of White Creek, New York, close to the Vermont border. At the age of thirteen, after receiving a primary education in local schools, he entered Rensselaer Polytechnic Institute at

Troy but left before his graduation in order to enter business. In 1845 he went to Ohio where he lived successively in Milan and Sandusky. In 1851-52 he served a term as treasurer of Erie County. Soon after the outbreak of war in 1861, Sprague recruited a company which became a part of the 7th Ohio Infantry, a three-month regiment which reenlisted for three years in June. (625) On January 23, 1862, he became colonel of the 63rd Ohio, which he led at New Madrid and Island No. 10 in John Pope's Army of the Mississippi. At the battle of Corinth in October, 1862, nine of his thirteen line officers and 45 per cent of his total force were killed or wounded. Thereafter and until the beginning of W. T. Sherman's campaign against Atlanta, the XVI Corps, to which Sprague's regiment was attached, served mainly in garrison at various points in West Tennessee. In April, 1864, Sprague was assigned to command a brigade of the 4th Division of the corps and on July 30, 1864, he was promoted to the rank of brigadier general. Years later he was awarded the Congressional medal for having saved the corps' trains at Decatur, Georgia, on July 22, 1864 (the day of the battle of Atlanta proper). During the operations incident to the withdrawal of Hood northeastward into Alabama and Tennessee, the 4th Divison of the XVI Corps became the 1st Division of the XVII Corps and was briefly commanded by Sprague. (626) Again in brigade command, he accompanied Sherman in the "March to the Sea" and through the Carolinas and was brevetted major general of volunteers to rank from March 13, 1865. (627) After the war General

Sprague engaged in railroad construction, in 1870 was general manager of the western division of the Northern Pacific Railroad, and became one of the founders of the city of Tacoma. He resigned from the railroad about 1883 but remained in Tacoma, where he was one of the leading business figures of the city, until his death on December 24, 1893. General Sprague was buried in Tacoma Cemetery.

Julius Stahel, whose Hungarian surname was Számvald, was born in Szeged, Hungary, on November 5, 1825. After attending school in

Szeged and Budapest he entered the Austrian army as a private and rose to lieutenant, but in the struggle for Hungarian independence he cast his lot with the revolutionary cause and, after the movement was suppressed with the aid of Prussia in 1849, fled the country. He lived in London and Berlin as a teacher and journalist before he came to America in 1859. For the next two years he was employed by a German-language weekly in New York City. In 1861 he and Louis Blenker recruited the 8th New York (1st German Rifles), becoming lieutenant colonel and colonel respectively; at the first battle of Manassas (Bull Run) the regiment aided in covering the fleeing Union forces from that celebrated debacle. (628) On August 11, 1861, Stahel succeeded Blenker as colonel, and on November 12 was advanced to brigadier general. He fought under John C. Frémont in the Shenandoah in the spring of 1862, opposing Stonewall Jackson. At Second Manassas he commanded the 1st Division of Franz Sigel's corps after the wounding of General Robert C. Schenck and then was in reserve under Schenck and Sigel until he was assigned to command of the cavalry in the Washington defenses in the spring of 1863. When he was promoted to major general of volunteers on March 17, 1863 (for a reason obscure to most military observers), he ranked immediately after General Philip Sheridan. In the spring of 1864 General Stahel led a division of cavalry under General David Hunter, again in the Shenandoah and in West Virginia, in the course of which both men were virtually forced out of the active theater of war. However, at the battle of Piedmont on June 5, 1864, he was greatly distinguished in an action which subsequently (in 1893) led to the award of the Congressional medal. Thereafter, he served on court-martial duty until he resigned his commission on February 8, 1865. After the war he served for years in the consular service in Japan and

China. Upon returning to the United States, he became connected with the Equitable Insurance Company of New York. A lifelong bachelor, he died in a New York hotel on December 4, 1912, at the age of eighty-seven and was buried in Arlington National Cemetery.

David Sloane Stanley was born in the Ohio hamlet of Cedar Valley on June 1, 1828. He was a direct descendant of one Thomas Stanley who came to Massachusetts from

England in 1634. Intending to be a doctor, he was apprenticed to study medicine, but in 1848 he received an appointment to the Military Academy. He was graduated in 1852 and posted to the cavalry. All his antebellum service was on the Indian frontier and in 1861 he was stationed at Fort Washita in what is now Oklahoma. Spurning a Confederate commission which was offered to him, he led his men back to Fort Leavenworth, Kansas, and

took part in the Missouri campaign of that summer, including the battle of Wilson's Creek, where he was employed in guarding the Federal trains. On September 28, 1861, he was appointed a brigadier general of volunteers, but was out of action with a broken leg during the winter. The following March, Stanley commanded a division of the Army of the Mississippi at New Madrid and Island No. 10, in the tortuous advance upon Corinth after Shiloh, and at the battles of Iuka and Corinth. From November, 1862, to September, 1863, he was chief of cavalry of W. S. Rosecrans' Army of the Cumberland and was engaged at Murfreesboro and in the Tullahoma campaign which maneuvered Braxton Bragg out of Tennessee, but he was on sick leave during the Chickamauga campaign. Meantime he was advanced to major general to rank from November 29, 1862. Upon his return he commanded first a division and then the IV Corps near Chattanooga and in the Atlanta campaign, and he was privately blamed by W. T. Sherman for permitting William J. Hardee to escape annihilation at Jonesboro. (629) His corps was then detached, along with John M. Schofield's XXIII Corps, to oppose John B. Hood in Tennessee. Stanley was wounded at the battle of Franklin and remained in camp near Nashville until the end of the war. He was brevetted major general, U. S. Army, in 1865 and on July 28, 1866, was commissioned colonel of the 22nd Infantry and returned to the Indian frontier. He served throughout the West in the postbellum years and was advanced to the grade of brigadier general, U. S.

Army, on March 24, 1884, upon the retirement of General R. S. Mackenzie. He then commanded the Department of Texas until he was retired for age in 1892. From 1893 until 1898 he was governor of the Soldiers' Home in Washington; he died in this city on March 13, 1902, and was buried in the home's cemetery.

George Jerrison Stannard was born October 20, 1820, in Georgia, Vermont. Between the ages of fifteen and twenty he worked on his father's farm in summer and taught

in the neighborhood school during the winter. In 1845 he became a clerk in a St. Albans foundry and by 1860 had become a partner in the firm. Meantime he had taken an interest in militia affairs and, when the Civil War came, was colonel of the 4th Regiment. His first duty was in recruiting and organizing volunteers for the field, but in June, 1861, he became lieutenant colonel of the 2nd Vermont and in July, 1862, colonel of the 9th Vermont. He was advanced to brigadier general on March 11, 1863, and was brevetted major general on October 28, 1864, for his gallant part in the attack on Fort Harrison on the outer line of the Richmond defenses, an exploit which cost him his right arm (his fourth wound of the war) and terminated his active service. Meanwhile he had fought at First Manassas, on the Peninsula, and in covering the retreat of John Pope's men from the battlefield of Second Manassas. During the Maryland campaign he and his regiment were surrendered to Stonewall Jackson as a part of the garrison of Harpers Ferry. After he was exchanged, Stannard was given command of the 2nd Vermont brigade with which he fought in Doubleday's division of the I Corps at Gettysburg, where he was badly wounded by the explosion of a shell. In the Richmond campaign of May and June, 1864, Stannard commanded first a brigade and then a division of the XVIII Corps, Army of the James, which was attached to the Army of the Potomac in the movement against Petersburg. He received his second wound at Cold Harbor and his third while leading the advance on the Petersburg fortifications. After he had partially recovered from the loss of his arm in the Fort Harrison encounter, he was assigned to duty on the Vermont border and continued to serve in the Department of the East until the close of the war. In February, 1866, he was on duty in Baltimore in connection with the Freedmen's Bureau. Upon his resignation from the army in 1867 General Stannard was appointed collector of customs for the District of Vermont, a post which he held until 1872. From 1881 until his death in Washington on June 1, 1886, he was doorkeeper of the House of Representatives. He was buried in Lake View Cemetery, Burlington, Vermont.

John Converse Starkweather was born in Cooperstown, New York, on May 11, 1830. After attending local schools and Union College, Schenectady, from which he was

graduated in 1850, he studied law and was admitted to the bar. Shortly thereafter he moved to Milwaukee where he practiced until 1861. In May, 1861, Starkweather was designated colonel of the 1st Wisconsin Infantry, a regiment enlisted originally for three months but which was reenlisted and remustered for three years in October. Starkweather took part in the affair at Edwards' Ferry and after reenlistment was sent to Kentucky.

At Perryville in October he commanded a brigade of L. H. Rousseau's division of Alexander McD. McCook's corps and continued in command of the same brigade at Murfreesboro, Chickamauga, and Chattanooga, receiving the promotion to brigadier general on July 17, 1863. Although it is sometimes stated that he "participated . . . in the capture of Atlanta," (630) he was in fact assigned to command of the post of Pulaski, Tennessee, on May 16, 1864, (631) and remained in that vicinity until he ran afoul of Nathan B. Forrest, who captured or dispersed a large part of his command during the celebrated Confederate cavalryman's raid into northern Alabama and Middle Tennessee in the autumn of 1864. (632) In December, Starkweather applied for duty with Philip Sheridan, who bluntly rejected the application. (633) Earlier that year Starkweather had been a member of the court-martial which tried and dismissed Surgeon General W. A. Hammond, which accounts for Edwin M. Stanton's supplicating Sheridan to accept Starkweather for assignment. A further command not forthcoming, General Starkweather resigned his commission on May 11, 1865, and returned to Milwaukee. He combined farming and the practice of law there for a time, but ascertaining that prospects were brighter in the vicinity of the capital, moved to Washington, where attorneys with the title of General, who could prosecute claims against the government for damages, pensions, and other matters, were greatly in demand. He practiced law there until his death on November 14, 1890. His body was returned to Milwaukee for interment in Forest Home Cemetery.

James Blair Steedman was born in Northumberland County, Pennsylvania, on July 29, 1817. A giant of a man, Steedman was a civilian general who inspired the instant

confidence of the raw farm boys whom he took into a score of bloody actions. He had almost no formal education but learned the trade of printer, and in 1857 was designated public printer of the United States government. Meantime he had occupied himself with service in the Texas army during the Mexican War, in the Ohio legislature, as a forty-niner in the California gold rush, and as owner of the Toledo *Times*. He was an avowed Douglas Democrat and in 1860 was a delegate to the National Democratic Convention in Charleston as well as an unsuccessful can-

didate for Congress. Steedman became colonel of the 14th Ohio on April 27, 1861, a ninety-day regiment which was reenlisted for three years upon the expiration of its original term of service. With this regiment he took part in the battle of Philippi in West Virginia and then was sent to the western theater. He was advanced to brigadier general as of July 17, 1862, rendered most distinguished service in command of a brigade of Gilbert's corps at the battle of Perryville and at Murfreesboro. During the Tullahoma campaign which maneuvered Braxton Bragg's Confederates out of Tennessee, Steedman had charge of a division of Granger's reserve corps. At the Union reverse at Chickamauga, "General Steedman [performed] the most conspicuous act of personal courage recorded of any general officer on the Federal side. . . ." (634) His heroism was virtually the salvation of the Union forces left on the field, but his Democratic leanings postponed his promotion to major general until April 20, 1864. (635) During the Atlanta campaign he performed duty in the rear echelons, but after G. H. Thomas was detached from W. T. Sherman's forces to oppose John B. Hood's advance into Tennessee, he commanded a "provisional detachment" of about eleven regiments of mixed troops (numbering some fifty-two hundred for duty) at the battle of Nashville. He resigned from the army on August 18, 1866, to become collector of internal revenue at New Orleans. In later years he edited a paper in Toledo, served in the state senate, and became chief of police of Toledo in May, 1883. On October 18, 1883, General

Steedman died in Toledo and was buried in Woodlawn Cemetery.

Frederick Steele, a descendant of one of the founders of Hartford, Connecticut, was born on January 14, 1819, in Delhi, New York. He was graduated from West Point in 1843 in the class which included

U. S. Grant. After some garrison duty in New York and Michigan he took part with distinction in the Mexican War, winning the brevets of first lieutenant and captain. With promotion to captain in 1855 and major in 1861, Steele served routinely as an infantry officer in the years before the Civil War in California, Minnesota, Nebraska, and Kansas. He was stationed at Fort Leavenworth in 1861, and his first important activity was as commander of a battalion of Regulars at Wilson's Creek. (636) He was appointed colonel of the 8th Iowa Volunteers on September 23, 1861, and advanced to brigadier general on January 29, 1862. Commanding a division of Curtis' Army of the Southwest, he took part in the campaign in Arkansas in 1862, which resulted in the occupation of Helena. Steele was promoted to major general on March 17, 1863, to rank from the preceding November 29, meanwhile commanding a division of W. T. Sherman's forces in the attack on Chickasaw Bluffs, or "First Vicksburg," and in the capture of Arkansas Post. During the Vicksburg campaign proper he directed a division of the XV Corps. After the surrender of the Confederacy's Mississippi stronghold he was placed in command of the United States forces in Arkansas and ordered to clear the state of organized Rebels who might aid Confederate operations east of the Mississippi River. He drove down through the state, captured Little Rock in September, 1863, and the following spring was directed to collaborate with N. P. Banks in his ill-fated Red River campaign. The overall strategy contemplated the advance of Banks up Red River to Alexandria, Louisiana, with a fleet of gunboats in support, while Steele essayed a movement overland from Little Rock to divert the Confederate defenders and/or support Banks's column. Both operations, through no fault of Steele, eventuated disastrously despite the fact that Steele was able to return his badly decimated troops to Little Rock, after a number of hard-fought engagements. In 1865 he commanded a division under Edward R. S. Canby in the campaign against Mobile. At the end of hostilities he was sent to Texas and was not mustered out of volunteer service until 1867, meanwhile having been appointed colonel of the 20th Infantry. A year later, while in command of the Department of Columbia, he was on leave at San Mateo, California, when he fell from a buggy which he was driving and died on January 12, 1868. He is now buried in Woodlawn Memorial Park, Colma, California. (637)

Isaac Ingalls Stevens, a descendant of one John Stevens who was living in Andover as early as 1641, was born at Andover, Massachusetts, on March 25, 1818. After sixteen months at Phillips-Andover Academy, he entered West Point

in 1835 and was graduated in 1839, ranking first in the class, "Old Brains" Halleck standing third. Commissioned into the Corps of Engineers, Stevens spent the next seven years repairing and constructing New England fortifications. A swarthy little man standing only an inch over five feet, he served throughout the Mexican War with Winfield Scott's army, was severely wounded in the assault on Mexico City, and was brevetted captain and major for gallantry. In 1853, thirteen years after receiving the promotion to first lieutenant, he resigned his commission in order to accept the governorship of Washington Territory; at the same time he secured the appointment of director of exploration for the Northern Pacific Railroad survey, which he conducted en route to his post. In his effort to open 100,000 square miles of land to white settlement, he made some rather arbitrary decisions which led to controversy with the Federal judiciary, the Attorney General, and the commander of the army in the Pacific area. Nevertheless, he was elected territorial delegate to Congress in 1856, reelected in 1858, but defeated in 1860, when he assumed the chairmanship of the extreme proslavery national ticket of John C. Breckinridge and Joseph Lane who was his close friend. There was accordingly some reluctance to accept his services when he tendered them to the Federal government at the outbreak of war, and it was July 30, 1861, before he was appointed colonel of the 79th New York (the "Highlanders"), a regiment whose first colonel had been killed at First Manassas and which was on the brink of mutiny. Stevens promptly restored order in the ranks, and so won the esteem of his men that when he was promoted brigadier general of volunteers on September 28, 1861, they requested transfer to his brigade. Stevens took part in the Port Royal expedition and was in command of Beaufort, South Carolina, for a time. He made an unsuccessful attack (under protest) on the enemy works at Secessionville and in July, 1862, returned to Virginia. He took part in the campaign of Second Manassas, commanding a division of the IX Corps (then under Jesse L. Reno) and was killed instantly by a bullet through the temple at the battle of Chantilly on September 1, 1862. On March 12, 1863, he was posthumously confirmed major general to rank from July 18, 1862. General Stevens was buried in Island Cemetery, Newport, Rhode Island, his wife's home.

John Dunlap Stevenson was born in the Shenandoah Valley town of Staunton, Virginia, on June 8, 1821. He attended South Carolina

College, studied law in his hometown, and was admitted to the bar there, but he soon moved to Missouri where he began practice. In 1846 he organized and was elected captain of a battalion of the 1st Missouri Mounted Volunteers which saw service with S. W. Kearny's troops in the invasion of New Mexico. After the war he moved to St. Louis and in the interval before the Civil War was several times a member of the state legislature and for one term president of the senate. Stevenson became colonel of the 7th Missouri (Union) Infantry on June 1, 1861, and after the battle of Shiloh commanded at Jackson, Tennessee. He headed a brigade under James B. McPherson during the battle of Corinth and in the pursuit of the retiring Confederates; he was promoted to brigadier general on March 13, 1863, to rank from the preceding November 29. During the Vicksburg campaign his brigade was in Logan's division of the XVII Corps. He then led an expedition into northern Louisiana to clear the area of Confederates, commanding a division and one brigade of infantry, two batteries and a section of a third, and a battalion of cavalry. During the Chickamauga and Chattanooga campaigns he was in charge of the post of Corinth. When the Atlanta campaign began he was posted, with twenty-five hundred men, at Decatur, Alabama, and along the Tennessee & Alabama Railroad northward to Pulaski, Tennessee. This assignment seems to have been unsatisfactory for on April 22, 1864, his resignation was accepted. (638) He was, however, reappointed brigadier general on August 8, 1864, with his original date of rank and assigned to command of the District of Harpers Ferry, West Virginia, where he remained until the end of the war. For a few days in February, 1865, he was temporarily in

476

command of the Department of West Virginia. He was brevetted major general of volunteers and upon the expansion of the Regular Army in 1866 was made colonel of the 30th Infantry. He was awarded the brevet of brigadier general, U. S. Army, in 1867 but for several months in 1869 was unassigned due to the reduction of the army effected that year. On December 31, 1870, General Stevenson was honorably discharged at his own request and resumed his law practice in St. Louis. He died there on January 22, 1897, and was buried in Bellefontaine Cemetery.

Thomas Greely Stevenson was born February 3, 1836, in Boston. From early childhood he was interested in military affairs and joined the state militia as soon as his age would permit, rising from the ranks to major of the 4th Battalion of Infantry. Meanwhile he had acquired a reputation as a drillmaster, and

upon the outbreak of the Civil War many of his former enlisted men became officers in other Massachusetts volunteer regiments. Stevenson himself recruited the 24th Massachusetts, the nucleus of which was his old militia battalion, and was mustered in as its colonel on December 3, 1861. The regiment immediately was assigned to accompany Ambrose E. Burnside's expedition against the Carolina coast and was attached to John G. Foster's brigade during the operations against Roanoke Island and New Bern. Stevenson took part in the defense of Washington, North Carolina, in September and directed a brigade in the movements on Goldsboro and Kinston. Foster applied for Stevenson's promotion to brigadier and he was duly appointed on December 24, 1862, but the nomination was not confirmed by the Senate and he was reappointed and confirmed on April 9, 1863, to rank from March 14. In the summer of 1863 General Stevenson saw much active service in Charleston Harbor, where his brigade was attached to Naglee's division. He was present at the initial reduction of Morris Island, a key point in the Confederate defenses, and commanded the troops held in reserve during the assault on Battery Wagner, a fort on the northern extremity of the island at the base of Cumming's Point. Stevenson was on sick leave during the winter of 1863-64, suffering from malarial fevers contracted in the swampy approaches to Charleston, but in the spring of 1864 was assigned to the command of a division of Burnside's IX Corps during the initial phases of U. S. Grant's Overland campaign against Richmond. On the morning of May 10, 1864, while at the head of his command, General Stevenson was killed instantly by a Confederate sharpshooter. His body was taken back to Boston for burial in Mount Auburn Cemetery, Cambridge.

James Hughes Stokes was born probably in Hagerstown, Maryland, in June, 1815. (639) At the time of his appointment to West Point in 1831, he was a resident of

Baltimore. He was graduated from the Academy, ranking just ahead of Montgomery Blair and George G. Meade in the class of 1835, and was posted to the artillery. After much arduous duty against the Creeks and Seminoles and participation in the transfer of the Cherokees to Indian Territory (now Oklahoma), Stokes accepted a commission as captain in the Quartermaster's Department, but resigned in 1843 to engage in business. From 1858 until 1861 he was an executive of the

Illinois Central Railroad, residing in the North Shore suburb of Lake Forest, where he had built a home in 1859. Stokes's principal Civil War exploit was his removal of a stand of twenty-thousand small arms from the St. Louis armory to Springfield, Illinois, after duping by a clever ruse a secessionist mob. The transfer deprived the Rebel party in Missouri of sorely needed munitions, and the arms were delivered to Governor Richard Yates of Illinois for issuance to loyal recruits. (640) Stokes received the thanks of the Illinois legislature for this feat and was then employed as state commissioner to purchase arms for Illinois volunteers. In 1862 Stokes recruited the "Chicago Board of Trade Battery," of which he was elected captain. He was once more mustered into United States service on July 31, 1862. Although nominally only a volunteer battery commander, Stokes took an important part in every fight of the western army from Perryville to Chattanooga, commanding a division of artillery at the time of the storming of Missionary Ridge in November, 1863. The following February he again moved from line to staff and returned to quartermaster duty in the Military Division of the Mississippi, as an inspector with rank of lieutenant colonel. Due to unknown reasons Stokes was mustered out of service on August 22, 1864, as a lieutenant colonel and reappointed the same day as a captain and assistant adjutant general. On July 22, 1865, after the war was over, he was appointed brigadier general of volunteers and was mustered out for the last time a month later. After the war General Stokes became progressively blind, but he still engaged in real estate business in Chicago until he moved to New York in 1880. He died there on December 27, 1890, and is buried in an unmarked grave in Washington Street Cemetery, Geneva, New York, the home of his second wife.

Charles John Stolbrand (641) was born near Kristianstad, Sweden, on May 11, 1821. At the age of eighteen he entered the Royal Vendes

Artillery as a cadet and during the Schleswig-Holstein campaign of 1848-50 took part with some members of his regiment in the successful defense of Denmark against the armed intervention of Prussia. At the termination of the war Stolbrand emigrated to the United States and settled in Chicago, where he became prominent in Swedish affairs. When the Civil War broke out he organized an artillery company which could not be accepted since the quota was filled, but in the summer he organized another (from nearby Sycamore and De Kalb), "Battery De Kalb," which was accepted with Stolbrand as its captain. He was promoted to major on December 3, 1861, and commenced a most distinguished career as an officer of artillery of the post of Jackson, Tennessee, in September, 1862. He directed Logan's division artillery during the Vicksburg and Chattanooga campaigns and was chief of artillery of the XV Corps at the beginning of the Atlanta campaign. While reconnoitering in the vicinity of Kingston, Georgia, on May 19, 1864, he was captured by a Confederate patrol but escaped and rejoined his command in October. At this time he was directing a full brigade of artillery, comprising ten batteries with almost a thousand men and forty-six guns. He continued on the "March to the Sea" and in the campaign of the Carolinas, but at the end of January, 1865, despondent because of his failure to obtain promotion, asked to be mustered out. W. T. Sherman, who did not wish to lose his services, asked him to carry some dispatches to Washington for delivery to President Lincoln on his way home. One of the dispatches was a recommendation for Stolbrand's promotion and Lincoln, upon reading it, made him a brigadier general on the spot. (642) During the last weeks of the war he commanded a brigade composed of three Illinois infantry regiments in the XVII Corps. Stolbrand was mustered out in January, 1866, and settled in Columbia, South Carolina, where he immediately engaged in politics. He was secretary of the carpetbagger-dominated constitutional convention of 1868, delegate to the Republican National Convention the same year, and presidential elector for U. S. Grant. He also served as superintendent of the state penitentiary. During the administration of Benjamin Harrison, General Stolbrand was superintendent of the new Federal courthouse and post office building in Charleston. (643) He died there on February 3, 1894, and was buried in Arlington National Cemetery.

Charles Pomeroy Stone, descendant of Puritan ancestors who had fought in every war in which the American people had been engaged, was born on September 30, 1824, in Greenfield, Massachusetts.

He was graduated from West Point in 1845 and served as an ordnance officer with Winfield Scott's army, winning the brevets of first lieutenant and captain in Mexico. Prior to his resignation from the service

in 1856 he spent five years as chief of ordnance of the Pacific department, locating sites for forts and arsenals. He was then employed by the Mexican government on a survey of the state of Sonora. Early in 1861 Stone, under orders from Scott, served as inspector general of the District of Columbia militia and secured the safety of the capital and of the President-elect, President Lincoln coming to trust him implicitly. Stone was appointed colonel of the 14th Regular Infantry on May 14, 1861, and brigadier general of volunteers on August 6 to rank from May 17, standing eighth in seniority of all those appointed. After command of a brigade of Robert Patterson's Army of the Shenandoah during the ill-fated campaign of First Bull Run, Stone was assigned to the command of a division of three brigades, a "corps of observation" on the Upper Potomac. At this juncture, through the rashness of a subordinate, Colonel (and Senator) Edward D. Baker, who was killed in the action, Stone was made to bear the burden of the Union disaster at Ball's Bluff. The Radicals in Congress, who already believed Stone "unsound" on the question of slavery, demanded his removal. (644) On February 8, 1862, at midnight, without charges being then or ever preferred, Stone was arrested and subsequently confined for 189 days in Forts Lafayette and Hamilton. (645) He was grudgingly released on August 6 without reparation or even acknowledgment of error. In 1863, after nine months of unemployment, he was assigned to the Department of the Gulf at the request of General N. P. Banks and served with gallantry at Port Hudson and in the Red River campaign. On April 4, 1864, Secretary of War Stanton caused him to be mustered out of his volunteer commission (as brigadier general), and, as a colonel of the Regular Army, he was again without employment. He finally resigned on September 13, 1864. After the war he served thirteen years as chief of staff of the Army of the Khedive of Egypt, where he was greatly distinguished. Later he was engineer for the foundations of the Statue of Liberty. He died in New York City, on January 24, 1887, and was buried at West Point.

George Stoneman was born in the western New York hamlet of Busti on August 22, 1822. After attending nearby Jamestown Academy he procured an appointment to the Military Academy and was graduated there in 1846. (Two of his classmates were George B. McClellan and Stonewall Jackson.) Although commissioned into the 1st Dragoons, he was detailed as quartermaster of the celebrated "Mormon Battalion" which marched from Leavenworth, Kansas, to San Diego during the Mexican War. He then served on the southwestern frontier until the opening of the Civil War, at which time he was third ranking captain of the 2nd (later 5th) Cavalry. He was immediately promoted to major and, after serving on George B. McClellan's staff in West Virginia, was made chief of cavalry of the Army of the Potomac when McClellan took over its command, receiving the rank of brigadier general of volunteers from August 13, 1861. He was advanced to major general on March 16, 1863, to rank from No-

vember 29, 1862. Meantime, after the Peninsular campaign of 1862 Stoneman commanded the 1st Division of the III Corps and at the battle of Fredericksburg, the corps itself. When Joseph Hooker took command of the Army of the Potomac prior to the campaign of Chancellorsville, Stoneman was again installed as chief of cavalry. With most of the entire Cavalry Corps of over ten thousand men, he was sent to operate in Robert E. Lee's rear while the infantry attacked in front. "Stoneman's Raid" as it was called caused great consternation in Richmond, but effected nothing concrete and deprived Hooker of his mounted arm when he could have put it to good use. Stoneman was replaced by Alfred Pleasonton after the battle, served as chief of the cavalry bureau in Washington for a time, and the following winter commanded the XXIII Corps in the West. During the Atlanta campaign he directed the Cavalry Corps of the Army of the Ohio until he was captured on July 31, 1864, while on a raid designed to free the prisoners at Andersonville. After his exchange in October he operated in southwestern Virginia, East Tennessee, and North Carolina in cooperation with W. T. Sherman's advancing armies. He was brevetted major general, U. S. Army, appointed colonel of the 21st Infantry in 1866, and commanded the Department of Arizona until he was retired for disability in 1871. Stoneman then settled on an estate which he owned in the heart of present-day San Marino, California. He served as railroad commissioner of California and in 1882 was elected governor of the state for a four-year term. He died in Buffalo, New York, on September 5, 1894, and was buried in Lakewood, New York, a few miles from his birthplace.

Edwin Henry Stoughton was born in the village of Chester, Windsor County, Vermont, on June 23, 1838. He was descended from one Thomas Stoughton, who arrived in Massachusetts in 1630, and was the nephew and namesake of Edwin Wallace Stoughton, later minister to Russia. The younger Stoughton was a member of the first five-year class at West Point, graduating in 1859. (646) After some routine garrison duty in New York Harbor, he was on leave of absence and resigned his commission on March 4, 1861. On September 25 of that year he was appointed colonel of the 4th Vermont by Governor Frederic Holbrook. This regiment was stationed in the defenses of Washington during the first winter of the war and then took part in George B. McClellan's Peninsular campaign in W. T. H. Brooks's division of the VI Corps. From July until November, 1862, Stoughton was on leave of absence, whereupon he was advanced to brigadier general of volunteers with rank from November 5—Stoughton was only twenty-four years of age at the time and the youngest general officer in the service. That winter he commanded a brigade of Vermont regiments on the outer perimeter of the defenses of the capital and in March, 1863, made his headquarters at Fairfax Court House. The Confederate partisan John S. Mosby, who was at this time harrying the Federal patrols and outposts in the vicinity, learned of a break in the picket line between Chantilly and Centreville and on the night of March 8, 1863, stole through it with twenty-nine of his men. In the midst of thousands of Union troops he took Stoughton from his bed and rode out of town with thirty-two other prisoners and fifty-eight horses. As Jeb Stuart later characterized it, this was a "feat, unparalleled in the war. . . ." (647) It also blasted Stoughton's career as a soldier. Four days previously his commission as brigadier had expired by operation of law, the Senate failing to act on his nomination. When he was exchanged in May, no move was made to reappoint him in the army or give him another command. He subsequently made his residence in New York City and engaged in the practice of law with his uncle. He died in New York on Christmas Day, 1868, and was buried in Immanuel Cemetery, Rockingham, Vermont, a few miles from his birthplace.

George Crockett Strong was born on October 16, 1832, in Stockbridge, Vermont, but lost his father at an early age, was adopted by an uncle, and as a consequence grew up in Easthampton, Massachusetts. He

was appointed to the Military Academy in 1853 and was graduated in the class of 1857 with the brevet of second lieutenant of ordnance. Prior to the outbreak of the Civil War, Strong was stationed at a succession of United States arsenals in Pennsylvania, Virginia, Alabama, and New York. He was Irvin McDowell's ordnance officer during the campaign of First Manassas and then served for a time as assistant ordnance officer on George B. McClellan's staff. In September, 1861, he transferred to Benjamin F. Butler's staff and was appointed assistant adjutant general of volunteers with the rank of major. He aided in organizing the expedition which occupied New Orleans and subsequently became Butler's chief of staff as well as chief of ordnance. Strong seems to have suffered poor health, as he was absent on sick leave from June to September, 1862, and again from December, 1862, to June, 1863. In the interval between these two leaves he commanded an expedition to Ponchatoula, Louisiana (headquarters of General M. Jeff. Thompson of the Confederate Missouri State Guard), where he destroyed a large train of supplies. In the operations against Charleston, South Carolina, in 1863, Strong, who had been promoted brigadier general of volunteers on March 23, 1863, to rank from the previous November 29, commanded a brigade which was the first to land on Morris Island on July 10. At the assault on Fort Wagner (sometimes known as Battery Wagner) on July 18, while he was leading the storming column, Strong was struck in the thigh by a rifle ball. The wound resulted in lockjaw which caused his death twelve days later in New York City, where he had been taken for treatment. (648) He was buried in Green-Wood Cemetery, in Brooklyn, New York. The day after his death he was nominated, confirmed, and duly appointed major general of volunteers to rank from July 18, 1863, the day he was wounded.

William Kerley Strong was born on April 30, 1805, in Duanesburg, New York. He became a prominent wool merchant in New York City, but, after amassing a fortune at a

comparatively early age, retired to his estate at Geneva, New York. When the Civil War broke out he was traveling in Egypt, but at once set out for France where he was instrumental in purchasing arms for the Union cause. Prior to the war he had taken an active part in politics as a member of the Democratic party and his subsequent patriotic addresses on behalf of the govern-

ment induced President Lincoln to commission him a brigadier general of volunteers on September 28, 1861. He first commanded Benton Barracks at St. Louis under John C. Frémont; then in March, 1862, he was put in charge of the District of Cairo, where he remained for several months until he seemingly was detailed for duty in New York. He was relieved of duty on December 15, 1862, and ordered to report to General Samuel R. Curtis at St. Louis for duty. (649) The latter apparently assigned Strong to duty as president of a commission ordered to investigate the evacuation of New Madrid, Missouri, during December; the commission convened at St. Louis in February, 1863. On June 16, 1863, he was assigned to the command of the District of St. Louis by John M. Schofield, who was then in charge of the Department of the Missouri. (650) On October 20, 1863, General Strong's resignation was accepted at his own request, whereupon he returned to New York City. In November of that year he was in communication with Secretary of War Stanton relative to the enlistment of colored troops in New York with appropriate credit to the state's draft quota. (651) Shortly thereafter while driving in Central Park, he was thrown from his carriage and so severely injured that he was paralyzed for the remainder of his life. He died in New York City on March 16, 1867, and was buried in Green-Wood Cemetery, Brooklyn.

David Stuart was born on March 12, 1816, in Brooklyn, New York, but as a young man he accompanied his father to Michigan, finally settling in Detroit. He studied law and began his practice. Then, in 1852 he was elected to Congress as a Democrat, but was defeated for re-election in 1854. He moved to Chicago and became solicitor for the Illinois Central Railroad. On July

22, 1861, Stuart was commissioned lieutenant colonel of the 42nd Illinois Infantry and on October 31, colonel of the 55th Illinois. During the spring of 1862 he commanded a brigade of W. T. Sherman's division and at Shiloh held the extreme left of the Federal line—his brigade suffered heavily, was driven back, and he himself was wounded. However, he was able to take part in the subsequent capture of Corinth, again in regimental command, and was next stationed in the vicinity of Memphis after its evacuation by the Confederates. On November 29, 1862, Stuart was appointed brigadier general (the Senate was not in session) and took part in the fight at Chickasaw

Bluffs, sometimes known as First Vicksburg, commanding a brigade of Morgan L. Smith's division of Sherman's XV Corps. When Smith was wounded, Stuart assumed command of the division and led it in the assault and capture of Arkansas Post in January, 1863. He continued to direct the division until the news reached the army that the Senate had rejected his appointment as brigadier general on March 11, 1863; he was, of necessity, relieved from command by Sherman. (652) Nothing in the records explains the Senate's action: Stuart seems to have done well and had been esteemed by his colleagues, and Sherman issued a laudatory order when relieving him, expressing the hope that he would soon "return to the colors." Stuart resigned from the service on April 3, returned to Detroit, and resumed his legal practice. After the war he practiced law in New Orleans until the spring of 1868 when he once more returned to Detroit. He died on September 11, 1868, and was buried in Elmwood Cemetery, Detroit. (653)

Frederick Shearer Stumbaugh was born near Shippensburg, Pennsylvania, on April 14, 1817. After receiving an education in the neighborhood schools, he studied law, was admitted to the bar on January 17, 1854, and commenced practice in Chambersburg. (654) He was also much interested in the militia and at the outbreak of war in 1861 was commanding officer of the Franklin County forces, which he enlisted in the 2nd Pennsylvania Infantry (a three-month regiment), becoming its colonel on April 20, 1861. Upon the muster out of this command

(which had performed guard duty on the Potomac fords), Stumbaugh was appointed colonel of the 77th Pennsylvania as of October 26, 1861. His army service did not focus the particular attention of his superiors upon either him or his regiment. He was attached to D. C. Buell's Army of the Ohio at Shiloh on the second day of that encounter and in the advance upon Corinth; he participated in a number of minor engagements during Braxton Bragg's invasion of Kentucky and was in the detachment of Sill's division in the rear during the battle of Perryville. "Soon after that battle [his regiment] returned to Nashville, where it rested until the opening of the winter campaign." (655) At this juncture Stumbaugh, who had not been in brigade command for two successive days in his career, was appointed a brigadier general of volunteers, ranking from November 29, 1862. He had, however, led his regiment for a number of months with industry, ability, and fidelity. Nevertheless, for a reason not defined in the records, his appointment was revoked, on January 22, 1863. At his own request General Stumbaugh was honorably discharged as colonel of the 77th Pennsylvania on May 15, 1863. (656) He then returned to Chambersburg to practice law. Some years later he moved to Iowa, first locating in Rush County, but later moving to Topeka, where he died on February 25, 1897, and was buried in Topeka Cemetery. (657)

Samuel Davis Sturgis was born in Shippensburg, Pennsylvania, on June 11, 1822. He entered the Military Academy at the age of twenty and was graduated in the class of 1846. During the Mexican War he served as a lieutenant of dragoons and was captured and held prisoner for eight days while making a reconnaissance near Buena Vista. After that war he served in the

West, was promoted to first lieutenant and captain, and took part in a number of Indian campaigns. The outbreak of the Civil War found him in command at Fort Smith, Arkansas, with a part of his regiment, the 1st Cavalry. Many of his officers defected to the Confederacy; however, Sturgis refused to surrender and managed to march his troops with much of the government property to Fort Leavenworth. He was promoted to major and at Wilson's Creek in August succeeded to command of the Federal forces after the fall of Nathaniel Lyon. The following March Sturgis was appointed brigadier general to rank from August 10, 1861, the day of the battle. After a tour of duty in the Washington defenses he was ordered to the front to support John Pope's Army of Virginia just prior to the battle of Second Manassas. While attempting to secure priority for the movement of his division on the railroad, he was told that he must wait his turn as other troops and supplies were going forward to support Pope; his reaction was the now famous observation, "I don't care for John Pope one pinch of owl dung!" (658) He fought in the Maryland campaign, at Fredericksburg in charge of a IX Corps division, and at Sharpsburg, where Ferrero's brigade of his division finally carried Burnside's Bridge. Sturgis went west with the IX Corps in 1863 and later had a number of relatively unimportant commands in Tennessee and Mississippi. He also served as chief of cavalry of the Department of the Ohio. In June, 1864, he was routed by Nathan B. Forrest at the battle of Brice's Cross Roads, Mississippi—an encounter which terminated Sturgis' Civil War service. He was brevetted brigadier and major general, U. S. Army, in March, 1865, and was mustered out of the volunteers in August; whereupon he reverted to his regular rank of lieutenant colonel of the 6th Cavalry. On May 6, 1869, he became colonel of the 7th Cavalry, whose lieutenant colonel was George Custer. Sturgis was stationed at a number of western forts during the two decades following the war and for four years was governor of the Soldiers' Home in Washington. He was retired for age in 1886 and died in St. Paul, Minnesota, on September 28, 1889. He was buried in Arlington National Cemetery.

Jeremiah Cutler Sullivan, son of a Virginia-born lawyer who became a justice of the Indiana supreme court, was born on October 1, 1830, in Madison, Indiana. He entered the navy in 1848 and was commissioned a midshipman, serving at sea on four different vessels before resigning his commission in 1854 to study law. (659) At the beginning of the Civil War he helped recruit and organize the 6th Indiana Volunteers and as a captain took part in the action at Philippi, (West) Virginia on June 3. When the 6th Indiana (a three-month regiment) was mustered out, Sullivan became colonel of the 13th Indiana, which enlisted for three years, and fought at Rich Mountain. During the Shenandoah Valley campaign of 1862, he commanded a brigade of Shields's division at Kernstown and was commissioned a brigadier general to rank from April 28. Soon after, he was sent west and assigned to command of a brigade in W. S. Rosecrans' Army of the Mississippi, which he led at the battles of Iuka and Corinth. Later that fall he was put in charge of the District of Jackson, Tennessee, where he had the unenviable job of pitting scattered garrison troops against the forces of Nathan B. Forrest. Sullivan served as acting inspector general on U. S. Grant's staff for a

time early in the Vicksburg campaign and after the capitulation became James B. McPherson's chief of staff. In September, 1863, he was relieved in the west and returned to duty in the Department of West Virginia under General Benjamin F. Kelley, his father-in-law, who assigned him a division with which to guard the line of the Baltimore and Ohio Railroad from the Monocacy River west to Sleepy Creek. After Philip Sheridan took charge of the Middle Military Division which embracd the Department of West Virginia, in the summer of 1864, Sullivan seems to have been awaiting orders for a time. In March,

1865, Winfield S. Hancock stated in an official communication that he wished no officer on duty with him who had been sent to the rear by his predecessor Sheridan. (660) General Sullivan's resignation was accepted by the War Department on May 11, 1865, and, perhaps significantly, he did not receive the brevet of major general, despite the fact that he was in divisional command for many months. After the war he resided in Oakland, Maryland, for a time, moving to California about 1878. Although a lawyer by profession, he did not practice and was employed, when employed at all, in minor clerical jobs. He died in Oakland, California, on October 21, 1890, and was buried in Mountain View Cemetery. (661)

Alfred Sully, a son of the painter Thomas Sully, was born in Philadelphia, on May 22, 1820. After his graduation from West Point in the class of 1841, he took part in the warfare against the Florida Seminoles and in the siege of Vera Cruz in 1847 during the Mexican War. He also served on frontier duty at a number of widely separated points and was operating against the rebellious Cheyennes when civil war broke out. Sully, after some preliminary duty in north Missouri and in the Washington defenses, was appointed colonel of the 1st Minnesota on March 4, 1862, and in the course of George B. McClellan's Peninsular campaign rose to brigade command in Sedgwick's division of the II Corps. He returned to command of his regiment at Sharpsburg, but was commissioned brigadier general of volunteers on September 26, 1862, and at Fredericksburg and in the campaign of

Chancellorsville once again directed a brigade. Soon after the battle of Chancellorsville, Sully, who was perhaps more esteemed as an Indian fighter than as a brigade commander of infantry in the Army of the Potomac, was assigned to the command of the District of Dakota. In this position, under the nominal command of General John Pope, he executed a number of successful forays against the hostile Sioux in Minnesota and the Dakotas. Toward the close of the Civil War, Sully was brevetted major general of volunteers and brigadier general, U. S. Army. Upon muster out of the volunteer service he reverted to his regular rank of major of infantry, but was soon advanced to lieutenant colonel of the 3rd Infantry. In December, 1873, he became colonel of the 21st Infantry. Meanwhile, General Sully had discharged duty on the Indian frontier all over the West. During the last years of his life, his health permitting, he was intermittently in com-

mand of Fort Vancouver, Washington. He died there on April 27, 1879, and was buried ultimately in Laurel Hill Cemetery, Philadelphia.

Edwin Vose Sumner, the oldest active corps commander in the Civil War, was born on January 30, 1797, in Boston. His antecedents date back to the very beginning of settlement in Massachusetts. He was commissioned directly into the army in 1819 and adhered to his oath of allegiance until his death, despite the fact that one son-in-law would command Stonewall Jackson's Second Corps artillery in the Army of Northern Virginia and become Robert E. Lee's secretary, and another was a relative of General Joseph E. Johnston. On the

other hand, two of his sons became general officers in the U. S. Army: both were appointed in the regular service in 1861 and fought throughout the Civil War with marked dis-

489

tinction. Sumner, who was known as "Bull Head" in the old army because a musket ball was alleged to have once bounced off his head, (662) had a long and distinguished army career which began soon after the close of America's second war with Britain at which time he was appointed a lieutenant of the 2nd Infantry. He became captain of dragoons in 1833 and major in 1846, meantime serving chiefly on the Indian frontier. Sumner was greatly distinguished in Mexico, receiving the brevets of lieutenant colonel and colonel and a regular promotion to lieutenant colonel in 1848. He continued to serve in the West and became colonel of the 1st Cavalry in 1855. The following year he was involved in the Kansas troubles as commanding officer at Fort Leavenworth. In 1861 upon the dismissal of General David E. Twiggs from the service, Sumner was appointed to succeed him as one of the three Regular Army brigadiers. He had previously been Lieutenant General Winfield Scott's choice to accompany President-elect Lincoln from Springfield to Washington. When the corps organizations were established in the Army of the Potomac, Sumner was given command of the II Corps, which he led in the Peninsular campaign of 1862. He was wounded twice and extolled by George B. McClellan for "extreme gallantry" as well as "judgment and energy" during this campaign. He was brevetted major general, U. S. Army, for services at the battle of Seven Pines on May 31, 1862, and advanced to major general of volunteers on July 16 to rank from May 5. At the battle of Sharpsburg in September he was subjected to some criticism for not having put all his men into action and for having been at the head of his leading division, like a colonel of cavalry, instead of in the rear where he could properly supervise operations. (663) At Fredericksburg he commanded the "Left Grand Division" of the army, consisting of his own and the IX Corps, but upon the accession of Joseph Hooker to command of the army, Sumner asked to be relieved. Assigned to the Department of Missouri, he died while en route there at Syracuse, New York, on March 21, 1863, and was buried in Oakwood Cemetery, Syracuse.

Wager Swayne, a son of U. S. Supreme Court Justice Noah Haynes Swayne, was born in Columbus, Ohio, on November 10, 1834. Both his mother and father were natives of Virginia who had moved to free territory because of their opposition to slavery. Young Swayne was

graduated from Yale in 1856 and from the Cincinnati Law School in 1859. He began practice in Columbus with his father, who was elevated to the Supreme Court in 1862. On August 31, 1861, Swayne entered the army as major of the 43rd Ohio, a regiment which took part in the operations against New Madrid and Island No. 10 under John Pope. It also took part in the advance upon Corinth after the battle of Shiloh and at the battle of Corinth proper in October, 1862; Swayne later won the Congressional medal for gallantry displayed in the battle. The same month he was promoted to colonel. From that time until the opening of the Atlanta campaign in May, 1864, Swayne and his regiment performed garrison duty at various points in Tennessee. When W. T. Sherman pushed south toward Atlanta, however, the 43rd Ohio, attached to the XVI Corps, fought at Resaca, Dallas, Kenesaw Mountain, and in the battles around Atlanta. When Sherman's forces were regrouped for the "March to the Sea" and the campaign of the Carolinas, Swayne's regiment became part of the XVII Corps. On February 2, 1865, at the crossing of the Salkehatchie River in South Carolina, he was struck by a shell fragment which necessitated the amputation of his right leg above the knee. He was brevetted brigadier general of volunteers as of February 5 and on March 13 was given the full rank, although the records do not exhibit that he ever exercised brigade command for so much as a day (published statements to the contrary). (664) Later that year he was selected by General Oliver O. Howard, head of the Freedmen's Bureau, to direct bureau operations in Alabama, and since he would also be exercising military command he was advanced to major general of volunteers on May 1, 1866 (to rank June 20, 1865), the last such appointment made during the Civil War period. As a further mark of favor he was commissioned colonel of the newly authorized 45th Regular Infantry and in 1867 was brevetted brigadier and major general, U. S. Army. When the army was reorganized in 1869, Swayne's regiment was consolidated with the 14th Infantry, and he was without a command until he was placed on the retired list the following year. He then took up the practice of law in Toledo, but moved to New York in 1881, where he had a large and lucrative corporate practice. He died there December 18, 1902, and was buried in Arlington National Cemetery.

Thomas William Sweeny was born in County Cork, Ireland, on Christmas Day, 1820. At the age of twelve he followed his widowed mother to America; she had already come to survey the prospects of the new country. Sweeny secured employment in a law-publishing firm and interested himself in the militia, joining the "Independent Tompkins Blues," later called the "Baxter Blues," which served in the Mexican War as Company A of the 1st New York Volunteers. He lost his right arm at the battle of Churubusco and in 1848 was commissioned a lieutenant of the 2nd U. S. Infantry, with which he served until 1861. He was promoted to captain in January of the latter year. After serving under Nathaniel Lyon in St. Louis, Sweeny was with

491

Franz Sigel at Carthage in command of the ninety-day Missouri militia, and at Wilson's Creek he was wounded and carried from the field. In January, 1862, he became colonel of the 52nd Illinois Infantry. He served at Fort Donelson, and at Shiloh he commanded a brigade of W. H. L. Wallace's division, which sustained 1,247 casualties in its six regiments—with Sweeny numbered among the wounded. At the battle of Corinth in October, 1862, he succeeded to brigade command after the death of General Pleasant A. Hackleman, and was advanced to brigadier general on March 16, 1863, to rank from November 29, 1862. The year 1863 he spent mainly in garrison duty in Tennessee and Mississippi, during which time he was advanced to the command of a division of the XVI Corps, which he led in the Atlanta campaign. After the battle of Atlanta he was arrested and court-martialed on charges preferred by Grenville M. Dodge, commander of the XVI Corps, but was acquitted after a lengthy trial. Significantly, he was not restored to command, and Oliver O. Howard, commander of the Army of the Tennessee, commented to W. T. Sherman in January, 1865, that "Sweeny has been cleared, but I don't want him. . . . [He] might be mustered out, with a view to the interest of the service . . . ." (665) In December, 1865, Sweeny was dismissed from the Regular Army for being absent without leave, but political considerations apparently dictated his restoration on November 8, 1866. In the meantime he became involved in the Fenian movement of that year which contemplated conquering Canada as a first step in freeing Ireland from the British. Their "invasion" of Canadian soil was a fiasco and Sweeny was arrested by the United States but released. Despite all these incidents he was placed on the retired list of the army with the rank of brigadier general on May 11, 1870. Thereafter he made his home in Astoria, on Long Island, where he died on April 10, 1892. He was buried in Green-Wood Cemetery, Brooklyn.

George Sykes was born October 9, 1822, at Dover, Delaware. After preliminary studies in the local schools he was appointed to West Point in 1838 and was graduated four years later in a class which was to contribute no less than twelve corps and army commanders to the Union and Confederate causes. Following his graduation he served in the Florida War, in barracks at various points in the South and West, in the Mexican War (where he won a captain's brevet for gallantry), and on the Indian frontier in New Mexico and Texas. Sykes was promoted major, 14th Infantry, in 1861 and at the battle of First Manassas (Bull Run) commanded a battalion of Regulars which gave the best performance on the Union side, covering the panic-stricken re-

treat of the volunteers. Sykes became a brigadier general of volunteers on September 28, 1861, and during George B. McClellan's campaign on the Peninsula directed first a brigade and then a division of Porter's V Corps—nine of the eleven regiments of his division were Regular troops. His command fought hard in the second battle of Bull Run, but was only lightly engaged at Sharpsburg, where Porter was held in reserve, and at Fredericksburg. Sykes was advanced to the grade of major general on November 29, 1862. At Chancellorsville, he was not involved in the rout of the Federal

right and his casualties were less than three hundred men. He succeeded George G. Meade in command of the V Corps, after Meade was named commander of the Army of the Potomac, and at Gettysburg he played a crucial part in support of Sickles' III Corps position and the left of the Union line. Later that year he took part in the Rappahannock and Mine Run campaigns, where Meade found him too slow when aggressive action was demanded. (666) Sykes was relieved in December, 1863, and in the spring went to the Department of Kansas, where he remained until the close of the war. In 1866 he reverted to his regular rank of lieutenant colonel, 5th Infantry, becoming colonel, 20th Infantry, in 1868. He then commanded his regiment at a number of duty stations from Minnesota to Texas. General Sykes died at Fort Brown (Brownsville), Texas, on February 8, 1880, and was buried at West Point. Although a bulldog on defense, he seems to have been uninspired and uninspiring when initiative and boldness were called for; hence his nickname in the Old Army, "Tardy George."

George William Taylor was born in Hunterdon County, New Jersey, on November 22, 1808; he had a varied career in and out of both the army and navy. He was graduated from Captain Partridge's Military Academy at Middletown, Connecticut, in 1827 and the same year entered the navy as a midshipman. He resigned in 1831 to become a farmer in New Jersey. During the Mexican War he served as lieutenant and captain in the 10th U. S. Infantry and was honorably discharged in 1848. He then spent three years in California, but returned to New Jersey to engage in mining and the manufacture of iron. When the Civil War began Taylor became colonel of the 3rd

New Jersey, a three-year regiment which was assigned to Kearny's 1st New Jersey Brigade. When Philip Kearny was advanced to division command in the III Corps, Taylor, who had been made a brigadier general to rank from May 9, 1862, succeeded to command of the brigade (which was in Slocum's division of the IV Corps) and led it most creditably during the battle of the Seven Days on the Peninsula. A few weeks later his command was one of the first to be ferried northward from the Army of the Potomac when the scene of action shifted from the Peninsula to the Manassas plains during the campaign of Second Bull Run. At this juncture Confederate General Stonewall Jackson was bearing

down on the Federal storehouses and freight cars at Manassas Junction. In response to the attendant alarms and rumors Taylor's brigade was put on the cars and dispatched on the Orange & Alexandria Railroad to defend the railroad bridge over Bull Run. Forced to detrain a quarter of a mile north of the bridge because of the debris of a former collision on the line, Taylor deployed his little brigade, without a piece of artillery, in line of battle against the powerful Confederate division of Isaac R. Trimble, who was supported by two veteran batteries firing shell and canister at short range. Taylor was mortally wounded; his brigade dissolved; and on September 1, 1862, he died in Alexandria of his wounds. He was buried in Rock Church Cemetery, Hunterdon County, New Jersey.

Joseph Pannell Taylor, whose brother Zachary was twelfth President of the United States, was born

494

at Springfields, a family estate near Louisville, Kentucky, on May 4, 1796. He enlisted in the ranks on the Canadian border during the United States' second war with Great Britain and was subsequently appointed a second lieutenant of the 28th Infantry on May 20, 1813. Discharged at the close of the war, he was shortly reinstated in the army and during the next forty-five years pursued the painfully slow advance in rank which fell to the lot of those officers who found themselves in staff positions. However, in the course of the Mexican War, Taylor served as chief commissary of the army in the northern theater of war and was brevetted colonel in 1848 for "meritorious conduct particularly in performing his duties in prosecuting the war with Mexico." From November, 1841, until September, 1861, he was assistant commissary general of subsistence with the rank of lieutenant colonel. When Colonel George Gibson died in September, after forty-three years in office, Taylor succeeded him as commissary general. On February 9, 1863, the office of commissary general was changed to provide for the rank of staff brigadier general and Taylor was accordingly commissioned as such. He discharged the duties of his department until his death on June 29, 1864. His nephew Richard was a lieutenant general in the Confederate Army and his niece Sara Knox was the first wife of Jefferson Davis. General Taylor was buried in Oak Hill Cemetery, Georgetown.

Nelson Taylor was born in South Norwalk, Connecticut, on June 8, 1821. He was educated in the local public schools and in 1846 enlisted for the Mexican War as a captain of the 1st New York Infantry. He was stationed in California during the entire war, and after muster-out in 1848 he remained there, settling in Stockton. He became state senator in 1849, was president of the board of trustees of the insane asylum in 1850, and was elected sheriff of San Joaquin County in 1855. Soon after, he returned to New York and was graduated from Harvard Law School in 1860; the same year he ran for Congress, unsuccessfully, on the Democratic ticket. At the beginning of the Civil War, he again entered the army, this time as colonel of the 72nd New York, and on September 7, 1862, was advanced to brigadier general. When his regiment was organized it was assigned to Sickles' Excelsior brigade. Taylor successively led the regiment and the brigade during George B. McClellan's campaign on the Virginia Peninsula and in the campaign of Second Manassas. In the latter battle his command was in a division of Hooker's III Corps and suffered severely. The III Corps was not present at Sharpsburg, but shortly after the battle Taylor was ordered to report to McClellan, who assigned him to command a brigade of Gibbon's division of the I Corps, which he led at the battle of Fredericksburg. Despite the fact that Gibbon's report called "special attention to [Taylor's] services" at Fredericksburg, his resignation was accepted by the War Department on January 19, 1863, whereupon he returned to his New York law practice. (667) That summer, during the draft riots, General Taylor took command of some troops in Harlem. In 1864 he was elected to Congress as a Democrat and served from 1865 to 1867; he was unsuccessful in his campaign for reelection. In 1869 he returned to South Norwalk, where he practiced law for many years and was city attorney several times. He died on January 16, 1894, and was buried in Riverside Cemetery, South Norwalk.

William Rufus Terrill was born April 21, 1834, in Covington, Virginia, but he grew up in Warm Springs, Virginia, where his father was a prominent lawyer and member of the Virginia legislature both before and during the Civil War. His brother James Barbour Terrill was a Confederate brigadier who was killed in action near Cold Harbor in 1864. William Rufus was appointed to West Point in 1849, was graduated in 1853, and was subsequently posted to the artillery. He served in garrison, against the Seminoles in Florida, on re-

cruiting duty, at the Academy as a mathematics instructor, in the Kansas border disturbances, and on coastal surveys. According to family tradition, when civil war threatened he went to his father's home to discuss what course he should take and ultimately determined to adhere to the Union so long as he

did not have to serve in Virginia. (668) On May 14, 1861, he was commissioned a captain of the newly authorized 5th Regular Artillery and was employed in recruiting and organizing his battery at Washington. He then was sent to Kentucky as commandant of the camp of instruction near Louisville. During the first six months of 1862, Terrill was chief of artillery of the 2nd Division (McCook's) of D. C. Buell's Army of the Ohio. At Shiloh, "Terrill's Battery was a host in itself. Its fire was terrific. It was handled superbly. Wherever [he] turned his guns, silence prevailed. . . ." (669) He took part in the siege of Corinth which followed and then was attached to General William Nelson's forces, whose mission was to oppose Braxton Bragg's invasion of Kentucky. After the debacle at Richmond, Kentucky, Terrill was made a brigadier general of volunteers to rank from September 9, 1862, upon the recommendation of General H. G. Wright, who was commanding the Department of the Ohio. (670) At the battle of Perryville on October 8, 1862, Terrill was in command of one of the two brigades of James S. Jackson's division of Alex. McD. McCook's corps. Both brigade commanders as well as Jackson lost their lives, Terrill "while in the act of rallying his broken troops." About 4:00 P.M. he was struck in the side by a shell fragment and he died at 11:00 P.M. in a field hospital. (671) General Terrill is now buried at West Point. (672)

Alfred Howe Terry, descendant of a long line of New Englanders, was born in Hartford, Connecticut, on November 10, 1827. He spent a brief time at the Yale Law School in 1848, but upon his admission to the bar in 1849, withdrew. From 1854 to 1860 he was clerk of the New Haven County superior court. Terry was one of those rare militia officers who rose to eminence in the volunteer ranks during the Civil War and remained in the Regular Army to win the rank of major general. He was present at Bull Run (First Manassas) as colonel of the 2nd Connecticut, a ninety-day militia regiment in Keyes's brigade, and then recruited the 7th Connecticut for three years or the war. With the latter he took part in the capture of Port Royal, South Caro-

lina, in November and in the siege and reduction of Fort Pulaski, Georgia, guarding the mouth of the Savannah River, the following April. Terry was appointed brigadier general of volunteers on the twenty-sixth of April. He served in the various operations against Charleston until the autumn of 1863 when he was transferred to Benjamin F. Butler's Army of the James and assumed command of the X Corps. During 1864 he was occupied mainly in operations against Richmond and Petersburg. In December, 1864, he took part in Butler's failure to seize Fort Fisher at the mouth of Cape Fear River. The following month Terry was put in command of virtually the identical forces, which took the huge earthwork in two days, thus sealing off the Confederacy's last port, Wilmington, North Carolina. For this exploit he received the thanks of Congress as well as his brigadier's commission in the Regular Army.

497

He had been promoted to major general of volunteers on January 16, 1865, four days earlier. (673) His corps was then attached to John M. Schofield's Army of the Ohio, with which it operated in conjunction with the oncoming forces of W. T. Sherman until the surrender. During the postwar years Terry exercised departmental command, mainly in the Indian country, and was in charge of the Department of Dakota at the time of the Little Big Horn battle in 1876. During this encounter he was in personal command of the various columns engaged in the field, including that of George Custer. Much controversy arose at the time as to whether Custer had exceeded Terry's orders; Terry, however, refused all comment on the matter. In 1886 he was advanced to major general, one of three authorized by the table of organization, and in 1888 was placed on the retired list. He was the first nongraduate of the Military Academy in many years to hold a general officer's commission in the Regulars, and he was the first Civil War volunteer officer to attain the grade of major general, U. S. Army. General Terry died December 16, 1890, in New Haven, Connecticut, and was buried there in Grove Street Cemetery.

Henry Dwight Terry was born in Hartford, Connecticut, on March 16, 1812. As a young man he moved to the state of Michigan, where he studied law and began his practice in Detroit. He also took an active interest in military matters; accordingly, with the outbreak of the Civil War, he recruited and organized the 5th Michigan Infan-

try, which was mustered into service on August 28, 1861. F. B. Heitman exhibits that Terry himself was commissioned colonel of the regiment on June 10, 1861. He served in the Washington defenses during the first winter of the war. In the Peninsular campaign Terry and his men were attached to Berry's brigade of Kearny's III Corps division and sustained heavy losses at Williamsburg and Seven Pines (Fair Oaks). He was not present during the Seven Days battles nor thereafter until he was ordered to report at Fort Monroe on December 26, 1862, meantime receiving promotion to brigadier general to rank from July 17, 1862. He commanded a brigade of Corcoran's division at Suffolk, Virginia, during its investment by James Longstreet in the spring of 1863. Subsequent to the Gettysburg campaign, Terry returned to the Army of the Potomac as commander of a division of the VI Corps, which he led during the fall campaign on the line of the Rappahannock. In January, 1864, he and his division were sent to Sandusky and Johnson's Island to take charge of the prison there, (674) but he was superseded in command in May, 1864, (675) and at this point disappears from the *Official Records*. His resignation was accepted on February 7, 1865, whereupon he resumed the practice of law in Washington. He died there on June 22, 1869, and was buried in Clinton Grove Cemetery, Mt. Clemens, Michigan, near Detroit.

John Milton Thayer, whose Massachusetts forebears date back to 1647, was born on January 24, 1820, in Bellingham. He secured his early education in the district school while working on his father's farm, taught school himself, and in 1841 was graduated from Brown University in Providence, Rhode Island. He then studied law and began practice in Worcester, Massachusetts, where he remained

until 1854, meanwhile serving as a lieutenant of the "Worcester Light Infantry," the local militia company. Thayer then moved with his family to Nebraska Territory and acquired farm land near Omaha. When the Pawnees became troublesome, he was commissioned the first brigadier general of the territorial militia and soon demonstrated adeptness as an Indian fighter. With the outbreak of the Civil War, he was made colonel of the 1st Nebraska, a regiment recruited as infantry but designated cavalry in 1863. (676) He took a creditable part in the capture of Fort Donelson and the battle of Shiloh, commanding a brigade of Lew Wallace's division on both occasions, and on October 4, 1862, was advanced to brigadier general of volunteers. However, the Senate failed to act on his nomination and it expired by law on March 4, 1863, whereupon he was reappointed to rank from March 13 and was duly confirmed. In the Vicksburg campaign he commanded the 1st Division of the XV Corps and then accompanied General Frederick Steele west of the Mississippi, assuming command of the District of the Frontier with headquarters at Fort Smith, Arkansas, on February 22, 1864. He took part in Steele's Camden campaign, which was designed to support N. P. Banks's advance up Red River, and remained in Arkansas during the balance of the war. On February 27, 1865, Thayer was relieved at Fort Smith and assigned to command of the post at Saint Charles, Arkansas, (677) his troops consisting of a single regiment of Kansas cavalry and a battery. In the omnibus promotions at the end of hostilities,

Thayer was made a brevet major general and on July 19, 1865, his resignation was accepted by the War Department. When Nebraska became a state in 1867, he became one of its first two Senators, serving as an ardent Radical Republican and supporter of U. S. Grant. Failing of reelection in 1871, he was appointed governor of Wyoming Territory by Grant. In 1886 Thayer was elected governor of Nebraska and was reelected in 1888. In 1890, although not a candidate for reelection, he filed a suit against his successor, claiming the latter was not a United States citizen; this enabled him to occupy the governor's chair until 1892, when he was dispossessed by the Supreme Court. Thereafter he retired to private life in Lincoln, where he died at the age of eighty-six on March 19, 1906. He was buried in Wyuka Cemetery.

George Henry Thomas, third of the triumvirate who won the war for the Union, was born in the middle of slave territory in Southampton County, Virginia, on July 31, 1816. Curiously enough, he and his sisters (who disavowed him until the end of their days after he adhered to the cause of the Union in 1861) were in the center of Nat Turner's slave rebellion in 1831 and were compelled with their widowed mother to flee their home and hide in the nearby woods. (678) In 1836 he was appointed to the Military Academy on the recommendation of a family friend and Congressman from his district. (679) Thomas was graduated in 1840, ranking twelfth in the class in which W. T. Sherman stood sixth and Paul O. Hébert, later an obscure Confederate brig-

adier, was first. Thomas served in the artillery for fifteen years, was stationed at various coastal forts, and took part in operations against the Seminoles and in the Mexican War. In the latter he was brevetted captain and major for gallantry at

the battles of Monterey and Buena Vista. When the 2nd Cavalry (later denominated the 5th) was authorized in 1855, he became one of its first majors and until the outbreak of the Civil War was stationed almost constantly on the Indian frontier in Texas. During most of this period his colonel was Albert Sidney Johnston, his lieutenant colonel Robert E. Lee, and his senior major William J. Hardee. Much has been written about Thomas when he approached his moment of decision in 1861, mainly because he had applied for the position of commandant of cadets at Virginia Military Institute on January 18, 1861; his enemies asserted that at the time he was mani-

500

festly pro-secessionist. However, two months later he flatly turned down the offer of Virginia's Governor John Letcher to become chief of ordnance of the state's forces. (680) By virtue of Johnston and Lee's joining the Confederacy, Major Thomas was advanced to lieutenant colonel and colonel three weeks after the bombardment of Fort Sumter. He commanded a brigade under General Robert Patterson in the Shenandoah during the campaign of First Manassas and was made a brigadier general of volunteers on August 17, 1861. Thereafter his service was in the western theater of war. Transferred to Kentucky, he commanded the Union forces which dispersed the Confederates under F. K. Zollicoffer at Mill Springs in January, 1862, and was present at Shiloh in D. C. Buell's Army of the Ohio in April. Thomas was promoted to major general of volunteers to rank from April 25; and first under Henry W. Halleck, then under Buell, and later under W. S. Rosecrans, he rendered service at the siege of Corinth, the battles of Perryville and Stone's River, and the disaster at Chickamauga. His performance in these battles was not surpassed by any subordinate commander in this nation's history. On the crest of Horseshoe Ridge at Chickamauga, with three-fifths of the Union army streaming to the rear along with its commander, Thomas planted himself and a decimated array of broken regiments, brigades, and divisions, and held his ground until late afternoon, when he retired, without serious molestation, to Chattanooga. For this heroic stand, the "Rock of Chickamauga" was made a brigadier general in the

Regular Army on October 27, 1863. The following month the battle of Chattanooga was fought, during which Thomas' men, without orders, stormed the heights of Missionary Ridge and drove Braxton Bragg's Confederates from their position. In the Atlanta campaign Thomas' Army of the Cumberland, containing nine infantry and three cavalry divisions, plus artillery and some unattached troops, constituted more than half of W. T. Sherman's entire force. After the Federal occupation of Atlanta and the movement of John B. Hood northwestward to Alabama and Tennessee, Thomas was detached with some 35,000 men to Nashville, where another 35,000 were brought from commands in other theaters. At Franklin, Tennessee, on November 20, 1864, Hood's Army of the Tennessee was badly used up in a frontal assault on the Federal breastworks and in December was virtually cancelled out as an organization by the results of the two-day battle of Nashville. This action earned for Thomas the nickname of the "Sledge of Nashville." On January 16, 1865, he was promoted to major general, U. S. Army, to rank from the date of the battle of Nashville and in March received the thanks of Congress by a resolution dated the third. He continued in command of the Department of the Tennessee until 1867, during which time President Johnson attempted, without success, to exploit him for political reasons by using his name to supersede U. S. Grant in command of the army, a ploy which Thomas refused to go along with. He was assigned at his own request in 1869 to the command of the

Division of the Pacific and the next year, while in command there, with headquarters at San Francisco, died of a stroke in his office on March 28, 1870. He was buried in Oakwood Cemetery, Troy, New York, his wife's home.

Henry Goddard Thomas was born in Portland, Maine, on April 4, 1837. At the age of twenty-one he was graduated from Amherst and then studied law and was admitted to the Maine bar. He enlisted in

the 5th Maine as a private in April, 1861, and was commissioned captain in June. This command fought at the battle of First Manassas, after which, on August 5, 1861, Thomas accepted a commission as a captain in the newly authorized 11th U. S. Infantry. He was on recruiting duty until the summer of 1862 and did not join his regiment until autumn. Thereafter his principal contribution to the war effort was the

recruitment and organization of Negro troops, with whom he was associated until the end of the war. He was commissioned colonel first of the 79th U. S. Colored Infantry and then of the 19th Colored Infantry, taking command of the latter on January 16, 1864. Thomas is said to have been the first officer of the Regular Army to accept a colonelcy of colored troops. (681) He was assigned to Ferrero's IX Corps's division of Negro troops at the beginning of U. S. Grant's Overland campaign and was present during all of the battles incident thereto, including the battle of The Crater. On November 30, 1864, Thomas was made a brigadier general of volunteers and transferred to Benjamin F. Butler's Army of the James, where he commanded a brigade of four colored regiments in the XXV Corps. At the end of the war he was brevetted through all ranks to that of brigadier general, U. S. Army, and major general of volunteers, but he was mustered out of volunteer service in January, 1866, as a captain of the 11th Infantry, a grade which he occupied for the next decade. He became major of the 4th Infantry in 1876 and two years later transferred to the paymaster's department with the same rank. On July 2, 1891, he went on the retired list, and on January 23, 1897, he died in Oklahoma City. His remains were returned to Portland for burial.

Lorenzo Thomas, adjutant general of the army from 1861 until his retirement in 1869, was born October 26, 1804, in New Castle, Delaware. He was graduated from West Point in 1823. He served twice in the intermittent campaigns against the

Florida Seminoles, once in the Quartermaster's Department, and once as chief of staff. During the Mexican War, he acted as chief of staff to General William O. Butler, and from 1853 until 1861 he served as chief of staff to the commander-in-chief, Winfield Scott, with the staff rank of lieutenant colonel. In August, 1861, Thomas became adjutant general with rank of brigadier general from the third of that month. He seemingly did not rise to the tremendous demands of a vastly expanded department and, more fatally, incurred the displeasure of Secretary of War Stanton, who virtually banished him from Washington in 1863 to organize colored regiments in the Military Division of the Mississippi. He was kept busy with this and other minor duties until the end of the war, when he received the routine brevet promotion to major general, U. S. Army. While General E. D. Townsend directed the adjutant general's office in Washington,

Stanton kept Thomas on the move, inspecting such facilities as the newly created national cemeteries. In 1868, President Johnson attempted to supersede Stanton by the appointment of Thomas as Secretary of War ad interim. But Thomas defeated the President's purpose by boasting of his ability and determination to oust Stanton from office by force, if necessary. Such was his ingenuousness that his later testimony at Johnson's impeachment may have aided in acquitting the President. General Thomas was retired in 1869, ten days before Johnson left office, and died in Washington on March 2, 1875. He was buried in Oak Hill Cemetery, Georgetown.

Stephen Thomas was born in Bethel, Vermont, on December 6, 1809. He received a grammar-school education and then was apprenticed to a woolen manufacturer. He became successful and prominent at a comparatively early age: he was in the legislature three different times, state senator for one term, delegate to the constitutional conventions of 1844 and 1851, and served as both register and judge of the probate court of Orange County, Vermont. On February 18, 1862, Thomas was mustered into service as colonel of the 8th Vermont, a regiment recruited to take part in Benjamin F. Butler's New Orleans expedition. While in the area he took part in a number of skirmishes and as a part of Weitzel's brigade aided in opening and guarding the Opelousas railroad. In the spring and summer of 1863 he commanded a brigade under N. P. Banks in the operations which terminated in the surrender of Port

503

Hudson, the last point on the Mississippi held by the Confederacy. Thomas led two assaults and was wounded in one. His regiment then took part in William B. Franklin's abortive expedition to Sabine Pass, Banks's first attempt to penetrate Texas territory. In July, 1864, the regiment went by steamer to Fort Monroe and then proceeded to Washington to oppose the enterprising Jubal Early, who had all but swept up Lincoln, his Cabinet, and the Federal Treasury. During the subsequent campaign in the Shenandoah Valley, in which two divisions of the XIX Corps under William H. Emory were involved, Thomas was for a time in command of a brigade; in 1892 he was awarded the Medal of Honor for distinguished conduct at Cedar Creek. He was honorably mustered out as colonel on January 21, 1865, and presumably returned to his home in Vermont. However, on April 21, 1865, he was appointed a brigadier general of volunteers to

rank from February 1. During 1867-68 General Thomas was lieutenant governor of the state and from 1870 until 1877 was United States pension agent; thereafter he engaged in farming. In his last years he lived in Montpelier, where he died on December 18, 1903. He was buried in Green Mount Cemetery.

Charles Mynn Thruston, a son of Senator Buckner Thruston of Kentucky, was born in Lexington on February 22, 1798. (682) He was appointed to the Military Academy during the War of 1812, when he was only fifteen years old, and was graduated a year later in the era when class rank was unrecorded. (683) During the war, Thruston

served on Governors Island, New York, as an engineer constructing defenses. With the peace of Ghent he returned to routine garrison duty as an officer of artillery, receiving the promotion to captain in

1827, relieved only by field service against the Florida Seminoles in the 1830's. He resigned his commission on August 31, 1836, to become a farmer in Cumberland, Maryland. In 1838 he assumed the presidency of a local bank and in 1861-62 was mayor of Cumberland. The town was a division point on the vital east and west link of the Baltimore & Ohio Railroad and on September 7, 1861, Thruston was appointed a brigadier general of volunteers for the purpose of protecting it and insuring the movement of trains both ways. Confederate forays soon demonstrated that the right-of-way could not be protected, and throughout the war the railroad had its track regularly torn up, its bridges demolished, and its trains derailed. (Confederate commanders would telegraph impertinent messages to Washington as a preliminary to cutting the line.) No blame can be attached to General Thruston; one of his successors, George Crook, was snatched from his bed in Cumberland and marched to Richmond as a prisoner in 1864. Nevertheless Thruston felt that the command should be in younger hands and accordingly resigned on April 17, 1862. He returned to working his farm near Cumberland, where he died on February 18, 1873. He was buried in Rose Hill Cemetery.

William Badger Tibbits was born March 31, 1837, in Hoosick Falls, New York. He was graduated from Union College in Schenectady in 1859 and then began the study of law and engaged in manufacturing. Upon President Lincoln's first call for seventy-five thousand volunteers, Tibbits recruited a com-

pany of the 2nd New York Infantry, a two-year regiment, and was commissioned its captain on May 14, 1861. The command's first action was at the battle of Big Bethel near Fort Monroe, where the Federals were beaten by the Confederate Carolinians of D. H. Hill. With promotion to major in October, 1862, Tibbits took part successively in George B. McClellan's Peninsular campaign, the campaign of Second Manassas, battle of Fredericksburg, and campaign of Chancellorsville. The 2nd New York was then mustered out upon the expiration of its term of service. Tibbits reentered the army on February 5, 1864, as colonel of the 21st New York Cavalry, also known as the "Griswold Light Cavalry," which he took to West Virginia. He engaged in the battle of New Market, commanding a brigade of cavalry of Stahel's division of Franz Sigel's forces who were beaten and sent North in retreat by

505

the Confederates under John C. Breckinridge. The bitterest pill to swallow in this defeat was the fact that the most celebrated Rebel unit on the field was the cadet battalion of the Virginia Military Institute, theretofore deemed too young for service in an army notable for the youth of its personnel. (684) After the accession of David Hunter to command of the Department of West Virginia, Tibbits was present at the battle of Piedmont and was highly recommended for promotion by General Hunter in August. (685) Tibbits was brevetted brigadier general of volunteers on October 21, 1864, and, after the bulk of Philip Sheridan's Army of the Shenandoah was brought to the. Petersburg theater, he remained in the Middle Military Division commanding a division of cavalry. He was brevetted major general of volunteers in March, 1865, and on October 18 of that year was commissioned a full-rank brigadier general, one of the last such promotions made by the War Department during the Civil War. General Tibbits was mustered out of service in 1866 and returned to Troy, New York, where he resided until his death on February 10, 1880. He was buried in Oakwood Cemetery.

Davis Tillson was born in Rockland, Maine, on April 14, 1830. He attended West Point from July, 1849, until September, 1851, when he suffered an accident which resulted in the amputation of one of his legs and compelled his resignation. In 1857 he was elected to the Maine legislature, the following year was made adjutant general of the state, and in 1861 was appointed collector of customs for the

Waldoboro district. On November 30, 1861, Tillson was mustered into the national service as captain of the 2nd Maine Battery, a unit of the 1st Mounted Artillery Regiment. He was advanced to major in May, 1862, and to lieutenant colonel in December. The seven batteries of the regiment fought in

widely separated areas, and Tillson was soon serving in a succession of posts as chief of artillery to various commanders; during this time he took a most creditable part in the battles of Cedar Mountain and Second Manassas. On March 21, 1863, he was commissioned brigadier general of volunteers to rank from November 29, 1862. In April he was ordered to Cincinnati as chief of artillery for fortifications in the Department of the Ohio and subsequent to the siege of Knoxville was charged with supervision of the defensive works there, meantime commanding a brigade of infantry in Jacob Ammen's division of the

XXIII Corps. In January, 1865, he became commander of the District of East Tennessee by virtue of General Ammen's resignation and as such was also commander of the 4th Division of the XXIII Corps. In March he took over a division of the Army of the Cumberland and served in this position until the end of the war. Tillson had been active in recruiting Negro soldiers and was retained in the army until December 1, 1866, while he directed branches of the Freedmen's Bureau in Tennessee and Georgia. He then engaged as a cotton planter for a year in Georgia, but returned to his home state in 1868 and became interested in the lime and granite business. He died in Rockland on April 30, 1895, and was buried there. (686)

John Blair Smith Todd, reportedly connected by marriage to both Abraham Lincoln and John Cabell Breckinridge, (687) was born April 4, 1814, in Lexington, Kentucky. When he was thirteen years old, his parents took him to Illinois and he was appointed to the Military Academy in 1832 from this state. He was graduated five years later, ranking toward the bottom of a class which numbered Jubal Early, John Sedgwick, John C. Pemberton, and Joseph Hooker among its members. Todd served in Florida against the Seminoles on two occasions, performed frontier duty in the Indian Territory and in Arkansas, took part in the Mexican War, and thereafter was stationed in garrison and at various frontier posts with the rank of captain, 6th Infantry. He was serving at Fort Pierre, (South) Dakota, when he resigned in 1856 to become sutler at Fort

Randall. Meantime he studied law, was admitted to the bar in 1861, and began his practice at Yankton. On September 19, 1861, he was commissioned a brigadier general of volunteers and commanded the North Missouri District for a time and from June 3, 1862, until July 17, 1862, when his appointment expired, the 6th Division of the Army of the Tennessee. The previous December, when the Territory of Dakota was formed with Yankton as the capital, Todd became a delegate to Congress. (688) He served until March, 1863, and then successfully contested the election of his opponent, serving again from June, 1864, until March 3, 1865, but was an unsuccessful candidate for reelection another time. In 1866 and 1867 he was speaker of the territorial house of representatives and the following year again sought unsuccessfully to be returned to Congress. It is claimed by some sources that he was territorial governor in 1869-71; (689) however, this is not verifiable. (690) He retired from public life following his defeat for reelection in 1868 and died in Yankton County, (South) Dakota, on January 5, 1872. He was buried in Yankton City Cemetery.

Alfred Thomas Archimedes Torbert, who was an officer in both the Union and Confederate armies at one and the same time, was born on July 1, 1833, in Georgetown, Delaware. He was educated in the

neighborhood schools, was appointed to West Point in 1851 and was graduated with the class of 1855. From then until the beginning of the Civil War, Torbert creditably discharged routine duties as a subaltern of the 5th Infantry in Texas, Florida, Missouri, Utah, and New Mexico, and on February 25, 1861, was promoted to first lieutenant. The records indi-

cate that he was on leave of absence until April 17, 1861, during which period he was nominated and confirmed as a first lieutenant of artillery in the Army of the Confederate States, ranking from March 16, 1861. (691) From April to September he was on duty mustering in New Jersey recruits and on September 16 became colonel of the 1st New Jersey, succeeding General William R. Montgomery. On the twenty-fifth he was advanced to captain of the 5th U. S. Infantry, his last full-rank promotion in the Regular Army. (692) During the first three years of the war Torbert acted as an infantry commander, fighting in the campaign of 1862 on the Virginia Peninsula as commander of his regiment in the VI Corps, in the campaigns of Second Manassas, South Mountain, and Sharpsburg where he was in brigade command, and at Fredericksburg, Chancellorsville, and Gettysburg. In all of these actions he was commended warmly by his superiors for meritorious conduct and on November 29, 1862, was made a brigadier general of volunteers. In April, 1864, incident to the reorganization of the Army of the Potomac prior to U. S. Grant's advance upon Richmond, Torbert and D. M. Gregg were assigned to command the two cavalry divisions under Philip Sheridan which covered the left flank of the army as it moved south. Torbert took part in the several cavalry actions of that summer and in August became chief of cavalry of the Middle Military Division in the Shenandoah Valley. He inflicted a severe defeat on the Confederate cavalrymen T. L. Rosser and L. L. Lomax at Tom's Brook in early October, capturing eleven pieces of artillery and "everything else carried on wheels." (693) Later that month at Cedar Creek, Torbert's troopers and Getty's division of the VI Corps were the only organized Federal units in line of battle when Sheridan completed his famous ride from Winchester. Torbert continued in this assignment until the end of the war, although with a greatly diminished command after Sheridan returned to the Petersburg theater. During the war Torbert received every brevet through that of major general in both the regular and volunteer services; however, when he was mustered out as brigadier general of volunteers on January 15, 1866, he once again found himself a mere captain of the 5th U. S. Infantry and apparently was offered no promotion when the army was reorganized and expanded in July. He finally resigned on October 31, 1866. From 1869 until 1878 he held a succession of minor diplomatic posts, resigning as consul general in Paris in 1878 to engage in business in Mexico. While en route there from New York on August 29, 1880, he lost his life when the steamer *Vera Cruz* on which he was traveling was wrecked off Cape Canaveral. General Torbert's remains were recovered and buried in the Methodist Episcopal Cemetery in Milford, Delaware.

Joseph Gilbert Totten, the tenth graduate of the U. S. Military Academy, was born in New Haven, Connecticut, on April 17, 1788. (694) (His uncle Jared Mansfield was the first professor of mathematics at West Point.) Young Totten entered the Academy almost as

soon as its doors were open and was commissioned second lieutenant, Corps of Engineers, on July 1, 1805. Including his attendance at West Point, his military career spanned sixty-two years, for the last

twenty-six of which he was chief engineer of the army. This period of service was interrupted only once, from 1806 to 1808, when he acted as his uncle's secretary while Mansfield made the first formal survey of the newly admitted states of the Northwest Territory. Totten was a captain of engineers before most of the Civil War generals were born. During the War of 1812, he won the brevets of major and lieutenant colonel for services on the Canadian frontier and in 1818 became major of engineers. After a score of years of distinguished engineering service in many areas and fields, he became chief engineer of the army and also inspector of the Military Academy. In the Mexican War he operated as Winfield

Scott's chief engineer during the siege of Vera Cruz and was brevetted brigadier general, U. S. Army for gallant and meritorious conduct on March 29, 1847. During the years before the Civil War, Totten was a prominent contributor to a number of areas of scientific advancement, including the lighting of the navigational hazards of the eastern seaboard, the investigation of the effect of the firing of newly perfected heavy ordnance in outmoded gun positions, and the study of the New York, Boston, and San Francisco harbors. Meanwhile he wrote a number of reports bearing on the country's defenses. He continued as chief engineer of the army after the outbreak of the Civil War; in 1863 was elevated to the grade of brigadier general, U. S. Army; and following his sudden death from pneumonia in Washington on April 22, 1864, was posthumously brevetted major general. General Totten was buried in the Congressional Cemetery.

Zealous Bates Tower, born in Cohasset, Massachusetts, on January 12, 1819, was a lineal descendant of one John Tower who emigrated from Hingham, England, to Hingham, Massachusetts, in 1637. Young Tower entered the Military Academy in 1837 and was graduated in 1841, ranking first in the class. Twenty-one of the thirty-seven members of this class surviving in 1861 became general officers in either the Union or Confederate armies. Tower was commissioned an engineer officer and during the Mexican War won the brevets of first lieutenant, captain, and major for gallantry while serving on the staff of General Winfield Scott. In

the years preceding the Civil War he performed engineering duty on both the Atlantic and Pacific coasts. His first wartime service was as chief engineer for the defenses of Fort Pickens, Florida, during 1861. He was made a brigadier general of volunteers on June 12, 1862, to rank from November 23, 1861, and during the campaign of Second Manassas directed a brigade of Ricketts' division of McDowell's corps, fighting at Cedar Mountain, Thoroughfare Gap, and the battle of Second Manassas. He was "particularly distinguished by the long marches which he made, by his incessant activity, and by the distinguished gallantry he displayed in the action of the 30th of August, in which action he was severely wounded [while] at the head of his brigade." (695) This wound incapacitated Tower for further field service. In July, 1864, he returned to duty and was assigned as superintendent at West Point. In September, however, he was sent to

Nashville to strengthen the defenses and he remained there until the end of the war. He was then brevetted major general in both the regular and volunteer forces. Tower was promoted to lieutenant colonel of engineers in November, 1865, and colonel in January, 1874. After retiring in 1883, he returned to the city of his birth to live. He died there on March 20, 1900, and was buried in Central Cemetery.

John Basil Turchin (Ivan Vasilovitch Turchinoff), Russia's only contribution to the ranks of Civil War general officers, was born in the Province of the Don on January

30, 1822. He was graduated from the Imperial Military School at St. Petersburg (now Leningrad) in 1841, and rose to be a colonel of the Imperial Guard. During the Crimean War, he served on the personal staff of the crown prince, later Czar Alexander II. Turchin also planned and erected the Finnish coastal defenses, which were hailed as among the most elaborate and scientific in Europe. In 1856 Turchin emigrated to the United States, settling in Chicago where he secured employment in the engineering department of the Illinois Central Railroad. He was commissioned colonel of the 19th Illinois Infantry on June 17, 1861, and, utilizing European methods of discipline, soon had his command whipped into shape. Turchin was a thorough soldier; however, he advocated the Continental theory that to the victor belong the spoils. Accordingly, his regiment and later his brigade were notorious for their disregard of the persons and property, regardless of sex, of enemy civilians. In February, 1862, D. C. Buell placed him in command of a brigade of O. M. Mitchel's division, with which he captured the town of Huntsville, Alabama, in April. The next month, after taking the town of Athens, Alabama, he encouraged his men to rob and pillage indiscriminately—allegedly in reprisal for the townspeople having stoned and fired on his leading regiment, the 18th Ohio. For this and the offense of having allowed his wife to accompany him in the field in violation of orders, he was relieved from command, court-martialed, and recommended for dismissal. His wife, however, prevailed upon President Lincoln to set the verdict aside and, further, to commission him a brigadier general of volunteers to rank from July 17, 1862. Turchin's subsequent battle record fully justified Lincoln's confidence. He fought gallantly at Chickamauga, commanding a brigade of J. J. Reynolds' division of

Thomas' XIV Corps and earning the nickname "The Russian Thunderbolt." Two months later at the assault on Missionary Ridge, one of his regiments was the first to scale the Confederate works, and during the Atlanta campaign his division commander Absalom Baird eulogized his soldierly and patriotic qualities. Turchin went on sick leave on July 15, 1864, and on October 4, 1864, was compelled to resign because of his health. (696) After the war he became solicitor of patents in Chicago and in 1873 established a Polish colony at Radom in southern Illinois. Late in life he became mentally deranged and died on June 19, 1901, in the Southern Hospital for the Insane, Anna, Illinois. He was buried in the National Cemetery at Mound City.

John Wesley Turner was born July 19, 1833, near Saratoga, New York, but his parents moved to Chicago

when he was ten years old. At the age of eighteen he received an appointment to West Point and was graduated in the class of 1855. In the years before the Civil War he served in Oregon as an artillery subaltern, against the Florida Seminoles, and in garrison duty at various points. In August, 1861, Turner moved from line to staff and served as General David Hunter's chief commissary in Kansas and later as General Benjamin F. Butler's in New Orleans. When Quincy A Gillmore succeeded Hunter as commander of the Department of the South in 1863, Turner, who had again been serving under Hunter, was made chief of staff and chief of artillery of the department and took part in the operations in Charleston Harbor that summer. He was made a brigadier general of volunteers to rank from September 7, 1863, and the year following directed a division of "Baldy" Smith's XVIII Corps of the Army of the James in the operations against Petersburg. In the final operations of U. S. Grant's forces which led up to Robert E. Lee's surrender at Appomattox, Turner commanded a division of nine regiments (the other divisions had upwards of fifteen regiments) in Gibbon's XXIV Corps. He had been brevetted a major general of volunteers for services "in the campaign of 1864, on several occasions before the enemy" and in the omnibus promotions of March, 1865, was awarded the brevets of brigadier and major general, U. S. Army. From June, 1865, until April, 1866, he commanded the District of Henrico, which included the city of Richmond. After he was mustered out of the volunteers in 1866, he reverted to his regular staff rank of colonel and additional aide-de-camp and served for five years as depot commissary at St. Louis. General Turner resigned from the army in 1871 but remained in St. Louis. He was prominent in both business and public affairs during the remainder of his life, serving as street commissioner for a number of years as well as president and director of several corporate enterprises, including a gas company and two banks. He died of pneumonia at his residence on April 8, 1899, and was buried in Calvary Cemetery.

James Madison Tuttle was born on September 24, 1823, in Summerfield, Ohio. After receiving a public-school education he moved

to Farmington, Iowa, about 1846, where he engaged in farming and operated a store. He was elected sheriff of Van Buren County in 1855, county treasurer in 1857, and recorder two years later. On May 31, 1861, he went into the army as lieutenant colonel of the 2nd Iowa and, upon the promotion of S. R. Curtis, became its colonel on September 6. Tuttle was present at Fort Donelson with his regiment, the first to occupy the enemy works after the capitulation. At the battle of Shiloh he was in command of a brigade of W. H. L. Wallace's division and, after Wallace's death, of the division itself. He did yeoman's service at the "Hornet's Nest," an eroded lane which ran parallel to the Confederate line of attack on the first day of the battle, a position which if carried might well have resulted in the ultimate disaster for U. S. Grant's forces. During the siege of Vicksburg he commanded one of Sherman's XV Corps's divisions, and during the first capture of the capital of Mississippi he compelled Joseph Johnston's Confederates to evacuate the city so hurriedly that he was able to capture a part of their artillery. Tuttle was prone to mix soldiering with politics and in 1863 ran for governor of Iowa on the Democratic ticket. He was defeated but, nothing daunted, ran again the following year and was again defeated. He seemingly was not averse to capitalizing on his rank and position to line his own pockets if the opportunity arose; this may have resulted in the acceptance of his resignation by the War Department on June 14, 1864. (697) He returned to Iowa, served several terms in the legislature, and engaged in farming, real estate operations, and pork packing. In 1877 he became interested in mining in the Southwest. He had an interest in the Jack Rabbit Mine, south of

Casa Grande, Arizona, where he died of a stroke during the night of October 24, 1892. General Tuttle's body was taken east for burial in Woodland Cemetery, Des Moines, Iowa.

Daniel Tyler, son of a veteran of the battle of Bunker Hill and uncle of General Robert O. Tyler, was born January 7, 1799, in Brooklyn, Connecticut. He prepared for Yale,

but in 1816 went to the Military Academy, where he was graduated in 1819. He became an outstanding authority on artillery and ordnance, studying at the artillery school in Metz and translating the French systems into English. Later he was superintendent of inspectors of arms made by private contractors for the army. His rigid honesty in this position militated against his promotion, and he resigned in 1834, still ranked as a first lieutenant. (698) During the next quarter-century he engaged unsuc-

cessfully in the manufacture of pig iron and then was markedly successful in the promotion of a series of railroad and canal companies. His forte was taking over virtually bankrupt concerns and placing them on a profitable basis. For five years he was president of the Macon & Western Railroad in Georgia. When the Civil War came, Tyler became colonel of the 1st Connecticut Infantry, a ninety-day regiment, and brigadier general of Connecticut Volunteers. He commanded a division of Irvin McDowell's army at the battle of First Manassas and, because of exceeding his orders and undistinguished troop handling, was responsible for part of the Federal defeat, despite the fact that he later claimed the campaign "was gotten up by General McDowell . . . to make him the hero of a short war." Tyler was mustered out August 11, 1861, but the following March was appointed a brigadier general of U. S. Volunteers to rank from the thirteenth. He took part in the siege of Corinth, commanding a brigade of Stanley's division; was one of the commission which investigated General D. C. Buell's campaign in Kentucky and Tennessee; and in 1863 commanded the posts of Harpers Ferry and Baltimore, and later the District of Delaware. He resigned April 6, 1864, then past the retirement age of sixty-five. In the 1870's General Tyler founded the town of Anniston, Alabama (named for his daughter-in-law), which soon became an industrial complex including an iron works, a cotton mill, a water works, and a car factory—all exploiting the iron deposits of eastern Alabama. He subsequently acquired large tracts of land in Guadalupe County, Texas, and served as president of an Alabama railroad which he had rescued from financial difficulties. He died while on a visit to New York City on November 30, 1882, and was buried in Hillside Cemetery, Anniston.

Erastus Barnard Tyler was born April 24, 1822, in West Bloomfield, New York, but when he was still young his parents moved to Ohio, settling first at New Castle and subsequently at Ravenna. He was educated at Granville College (now

Denison University), and then went into the fur business. He hunted for fur-bearing animals in the mountains of West Virginia and also purchased furs and skins from others which he prepared for market. At the outbreak of the Civil War he helped raise the 7th Ohio Volunteers and was elected its colonel over James A. Garfield. The regiment's first service was in West Virginia, where on August 28, 1861, it was surprised, while eating breakfast, and dispersed by John B. Floyd's Confederates. (699) The following spring Tyler commanded a brigade of Shields's division at Kernstown and Port Republic and on May 14 was commissioned a brigadier general. In August he was given a brigade of the V Corps, which was in reserve at Sharpsburg but which was heavily engaged at Fredericksburg and Chancellorsville. Soon afterward, these Pennsylvania regiments were mustered out by virtue of expiration of their terms of service, and General Tyler was assigned to a command in the Baltimore defenses on June 30, 1863. He remained on duty in and near Baltimore until the end of the war, discharging various functions, and in the omnibus promotions of March, 1865, was brevetted major general. Meantime, he married (for the second time) into a Baltimore family and continued to live there after he was mustered out of the army in August, 1865. He was active in the Masons, in the Grand Army of the Republic, and in 1877 was appointed postmaster of the city by President Hayes. On January 9, 1891, he died at his suburban home in Calverton, now a part of Baltimore, and was buried in Greenmount Cemetery.

Robert Ogden Tyler, a nephew of General Daniel Tyler, was born in the hamlet of Hunter, New York, on December 22, 1831, but as a boy of seven was taken by his parents to Hartford, Connecticut. He was appointed to the Military Academy in 1849 and was graduated in 1853, a classmate of James B. McPherson and of John M. Schofield. Posted

November 29, 1862, he commanded the artillery of Joseph Hooker's "Center Grand Division" at Fredericksburg. He was in charge of the artillery reserve of the Army of the Potomac at Chancellorsville and at Gettysburg where his 130 guns pounded George E. Pickett's advancing columns as they attempted to storm Cemetery Ridge on the third day of the battle. When the Virginia campaign of 1864 opened, U. S. Grant's heavy losses at the Wilderness resulted in the reconversion of heavy artillery regiments in the Washington defenses to infantry regiments which were sent to the front. Tyler commanded a brigade of Gibbon's division, II Corps, at Spotsylvania; at Cold Harbor he was struck in the ankle by a ball which not only lamed him permanently but brought about his death a decade later. At the end of the war he was brevetted major general in the Regular Army; he had already received the same brevet in the volunteers "for great gallantry at the Battle of Cold Harbor." When the army was reorganized in 1866, General Tyler was made deputy quartermaster general with rank of lieutenant colonel, but his presence at his various duty stations was interrupted by a number of trips abroad in an effort to improve his declining health. He died in Boston, Massachusetts, on December 1, 1874, and was buried in Cedar Hill Cemetery, Hartford.

to the artillery, he saw service in such widely separated parts of the country as Florida, Arizona, Washington, and Minnesota. In April, 1861, he became an unwilling spectator at the bombardment of Fort Sumter, as a member of the expedition sent to relieve the place. The next month he transferred to the staff in the Quartermaster's Department, acting as depot quartermaster at Alexandria. In September, Tyler was commissioned colonel of the demoralized 4th Connecticut Infantry Volunteers, a regiment which had been badly handled in the Shenandoah. He soon whipped it into shape and in January, 1862, it was renamed the 1st Connecticut Heavy Artillery. In the spring of that year Tyler took part in the Peninsular campaign in command of George B. McClellan's siege train. Despite the most trying difficulties in moving heavy ordnance from place to place, he lost but one gun during the whole campaign. Promoted to brigadier general of volunteers on

Hector Tyndale, whose full name seems to have been George Hector Tyndale according to his death certificate, was born in Philadelphia on March 24, 1821. He was the son of an Irish emigrant who had become successful as an importer of glass and china, and, reportedly, he declined an appointment to West Point at the request of his mother in order to enter his father's business. At all events, upon the death of the elder Tyndale in 1845, he and his brother-in-law became large importers of glass

and ceramics; Tyndale established himself as an authority on ceramics. When the abolitionist John Brown was awaiting the scaffold at Charlestown, Virginia, Tyndale in an excess of quixotic zeal accompanied Mrs. Brown south to see her husband in his last moments and to escort his body north. The outbreak of Civil War in 1861 found him in Paris on business, but he hurried home and was commissioned major of the 28th Pennsylvania on June 28, 1861, and lieutenant colonel the following April 25. The regiment's first important action was at Front Royal, Virginia, in May, 1862, under N. P. Banks; it

next took part in the battles of Cedar Mountain and Second Manassas. At the battle of Sharpsburg, Tyndale, although still a lieutenant colonel, commanded with conspicuous gallantry a brigade of the XII Corps, had three horses shot from under him, and was wounded twice. He was made a brigadier general on April 9, 1863, and returned to duty in May, but was not actively engaged until the XI and XII Corps were sent to the Western theater after the Federal reverse at Chickamauga. At the battle of Chattanooga, Tyndale commanded a brigade of Howard's XI Corps. During the following winter, he commanded the 3rd Division of the corps stationed at Shellmound, Tennessee. On May 2, 1864, just as the Atlanta campaign was about to be launched, General Tyndale was given a leave of absence because of illness. (700) He resigned on August 26, 1864, but was brevetted major general of volunteers in the promotions of March, 1865, in recognition of his past services. After the war he was again one of Philadelphia's prominent merchants, civic leaders, and philanthropists. He died there on March 19, 1880, and was buried in Laurel Hill Cemetery.

Daniel Ullmann was born in Wilmington, Delaware, on April 28, 1810, and was graduated from Yale in 1829. After studying law, he was admitted to the bar in New York City, where he maintained a large practice and was for several years a master in chancery. In 1851 he was the Whig candidate for state attorney general, and three years later ran for governor on the Know-Nothing ticket. When the Civil

War broke out Ullmann aided in recruiting the 78th New York ("78th Highlanders") and was commissioned its colonel on April 28, 1862. After some preliminary garrison duty, the command took part in the campaign of Second Manassas in Augur's division of

Banks's corps. In the course of the retreat from Cedar Mountain, prior to which Ullmann had been prostrated by typhoid, he was captured and imprisoned in Richmond until October when he was released on parole. On January 13, 1863, he was advanced to brigadier general and sent to New Orleans to organize five Negro regiments, which formed the nucleus of the "Corps d'Afrique." He was present with a part of his command at the siege of Port Hudson, (701) and until November, 1864, he remained at Port Hudson, a large part of the time acting as commander of the post. He was then assigned to com-

mand of the post at Morganza, Louisiana, where he was on duty until February 26, 1865, when he was relieved and ordered to Cairo, Illinois, to await orders. From there he was ordered home and saw no further service. Despite this somewhat unimpressive record he was awarded the brevet of major general for "meritorious service during the war." Upon his muster out of the army in August, 1865, General Ullmann retired from public life, and made his home near Nyack, New York. He traveled extensively and devoted much time to scientific and literary studies. He died on September 20, 1892, at his Nyack residence and was buried in Oakhill Cemetery, Nyack.

Adin Ballou Underwood, descendant of a colonial Massachusetts family, was born May 19, 1828, in Milford, Massachusetts. After he was graduated from Brown University in 1849, he studied law at Harvard, was admitted to the bar in 1 8 5 3, and in 1 8 5 5 settled in Boston. His father had been a militia brigadier and at the beginning of the Civil War young Underwood was active in recruiting volunteers for the Union cause. On May 25, 1861, he became captain of the 2nd Massachusetts Infantry, the second regiment from the state to enlist for three years; it took part in the Shenandoah Valley campaign of 1862. On August 13, 1862, Underwood was commissioned lieutenant colonel of the 33rd Massachusetts and the following April, colonel. His command was in Barlow's brigade of von Steinwehr's division of the ill-fated XI Corps at the battle of Chancellorsville, but sustained only nominal losses in the rout there. At

Gettysburg his regiment was involved in the events of the first day which virtually put the XI Corps out of action. When the XI and XII corps were sent to the support

of the beleaguered Federals at Chattanooga, under the overall command of Joseph Hooker, Underwood's regiment was in the thick of the fight which reopened the Tennessee River. On October 29, 1863, his upper leg was shattered by a ball which left him a cripple for life. (702) He was appointed a brigadier general on November 19, 1863, to rank from the sixth, and was awarded the brevet of major general in August, 1865, but saw no further service during the war. General Underwood was mustered out of the army on August 24, 1865, and returned to Boston, where he was surveyor of the port for almost twenty years. He died on January 24, 1888, and was buried in Newton Cemetery, Newton,Massachusetts.

Emory Upton was born August 27, 1839, on a farm near Batavia, New York. After a semester or two at Oberlin College, Ohio, he· was appointed to the Academy and was graduated in May, 1861, ranking eighth in the class. He was at once assigned to help drill the untutored Federal volunteers who flooded Washington in the early months of the Civil War. As a commander in all three branches of the army (artillery, infantry, and cavalry), Upton has seldom, if ever, had his record equaled. He was advanced from a subaltern (at the age of twenty-one) to a brevet major general of both Regulars and volunteers in the short space of the war (he lacked four months of being twenty-six). The interval was marked by extraordinarily valuable service on a score of battlefields. His most outstanding hour of combat came, probably in the morning of May 10, 1864, when with twelve regiments he smashed into the

"Bloody Angle" at Spotsylvania and might have overrun the position if he had been properly supported. Two days later it took Winfield S. Hancock's entire II Corps to chew off the Confederate salient in the war's most brutal struggle, at a cost of seven thousand Federal casualties. Upton had been colonel of the 121st New York since October 23, 1862, and was commissioned brigadier general to rank from May 12, 1864. He had previously distinguished himself in the campaigns of Sharpsburg, Fredericksburg, and Chancellorsville and, in the course of Philip Sheridan's Shenandoah Valley campaign in 1864, commanded first a brigade and then the mortally wounded Russell's division of the VI Corps at Winchester, where Upton, himself wounded, maintained command while being carried about on a stretcher. After his recovery, General James H. Wilson asked for his services in 1865 and he commanded the 4th Division in Wilson's celebrated cavalry raid through Alabama and Georgia which ended the war. Although Upton came out of the war a brevet major general in both the Regulars and volunteers, his regular rank was captain, 5th Artillery. When the army was expanded in 1866 he became lieutenant colonel of the newly authorized 25th Infantry. For the next fifteen years his duties were mainly of an instructional nature, and from 1870 until 1875 he served as commandant of cadets at West Point. In 1880 he was assigned to command at the Presidio in San Francisco. For some years General Upton suffered intolerably from an affliction which may have been migraine headache (703) and

which necessitated numerous leaves for his health. On March 15, 1881, he shot himself in his quarters in the Presidio. He was buried in Fort Hill Cemetery, Auburn, New York, by the side of his young wife who had died eleven years before. Upton was the author of numerous military treatises of great value; some were not published until years after his death.

James Henry Van Alen, son of a wealthy New York merchant, was born on August 17, 1819, at Kinderhook, New York. He was educated by private tutors and never devoted himself to any particular

business other than managing his affairs. At the outbreak of the Civil War he was residing in New York City and, at his own expense, recruited and completely equipped the 3rd New York Cavalry. He was mustered into service as its colonel on August 28, 1861. This regiment was on duty in the defenses of

Washington during the first winter of the war; on April 15, 1862, Van Alen was promoted to brigadier general of volunteers. During the Peninsular campaign George B. McClellan placed him in command of Yorktown and Gloucester, where he remained until relieved in October. From November, 1862, until February, 1863, he was one of the members of the court of inquiry investigating General Irvin McDowell's conduct at Second Manassas. (704) In the battle of Chancellorsville, Van Alen was assigned to duty as General Joseph Hooker's aide-de-camp, but on May 7, 1863, was placed in command of the defenses of Aquia Creek and vicinity, including the adjacent Richmond, Fredericksburg, & Potomac Railroad. He resigned his commission on July 14, 1863, and returned to civilian life. From then until his death General Van Alen traveled extensively, meantime making his home at residences which he maintained in Newport and London. His only son, who at the age of sixteen had run away to war to join his father and who was subsequently wounded, married a daughter of William Astor. General Van Alen was returning from a visit to England with his three grandchildren when he either fell or jumped overboard from the Cunard liner *Umbria* in the early morning of July 22, 1886. His body was never recovered. (705)

Horatio Phillips Van Cleve was born in Princeton, New Jersey, on November 23, 1809. He was educated at the College of New Jersey (now Princeton) and at West Point, graduating from the latter in

1831. He served in garrison in Wisconsin until 1836 when he resigned. During the next twenty-five years he was a farmer near Monroe, Michigan, a teacher in Cincinnati, a farmer again near Ann Arbor, Michigan, a civil engineer in the employ of the state of Michigan, U. S. surveyor of public lands in Minnesota, and from 1856 to 1861 a stockman in Minnesota. On July 22, 1861, Van Cleve was commissioned colonel of the 2nd Minnesota Infantry, a regiment which first saw action in January, 1862, at the battle of Fishing Creek, Kentucky, fighting in the brigade commanded by R. L. McCook. During the siege of Corinth following the battle of Shiloh, Van Cleve, who had been promoted to brigadier general on March 21, 1862, directed a brigade of D. C. Buell's Army of the Ohio. At the battle of Murfreesboro he was wounded while in command of a division in T. L. Crittenden's left wing of W. S.

Rosecrans' army. At Chickamauga his division became involved in the famous Confederate breakthrough of September 20 and was shattered, losing 962 men. The XXI Corps went out of existence the following month, and although the other two division commanders, Thomas J. Wood and John M. Palmer, were retained in the new table of organization, General Van Cleve was relegated to command of the post and forces at Murfreesboro, Tennessee, where he served for the balance of the war. Nevertheless, in the omnibus promotions of March, 1865, he was brevetted major general of volunteers and was honorably mustered out in August. In the postwar years he was adjutant general of the state of Minnesota from 1866 to 1870 and again from 1876 to 1882; he was also postmaster at St. Anthony, Minnesota, from 1871 to 1873. During the last years of his life General Van Cleve resided in Minneapolis, where he died on April 24, 1891. He was buried in Lakewood Cemetery.

Ferdinand Van Derveer was a lifelong resident of Butler County, Ohio, where he was born, in Middletown, on February 27, 1823. He was educated locally, studied law, and had begun practice when the Mexican War broke out. He served successively as first sergeant, first lieutenant, and captain of the 1st Ohio Volunteers and headed one of the storming columns in the capture of Monterrey. In the interval before the Civil War, Van Derveer resumed his law practice and also served as county sheriff. He became colonel of the 35th Ohio on September 24, 1861, and served continuously with this regiment until

he was honorably mustered out of service on August 26, 1864. Meanwhile he participated in the siege of Corinth and the battles of Perryville and Murfreesboro, was in brigade command at Chickamauga, and was at the head of his command when it was among the first to scale the heights of Missionary Ridge. During the Atlanta campaign of 1864, Van Derveer's brigade of Baird's XIV Corps division was engaged in all the battles up to and including that of Peachtree Creek in July although Van Derveer himself was on sick leave after June 27. The following month he was mustered out at Chattanooga, along with his regiment. On October 4, 1864, he was reappointed in the army with the rank of brigadier general of volunteers, but did not rejoin the forces under W. T. Sherman. Instead, in January, 1865, he was assigned to command a brigade of Stanley's IV Corps in the vicinity of Huntsville, Alabama. He served in this position until an order dated June 7, 1865, reduced the corps to three divisions of two brigades each, whereupon he was rendered supernumerary and resigned. General Van Derveer then returned to his home in Hamilton, Ohio, and once again resumed his law practice. He was judge of the court of common pleas of Butler County for many years. He died in Hamilton on November 5, 1892, and was buried in Greenwood Cemetery.

William Vandever was born March 31, 1817, in Baltimore, Maryland. He attended the local schools, but moved to Illinois in 1839 and to Iowa in 1851. He commenced the

study of law in Iowa and, after admission to the bar in 1852, started a practice in Dubuque. In 1858 he was elected to Congress as a Republican and reelected in 1860, serving until September 24, 1861, when he was mustered into the Union army as colonel of the 9th Iowa Volunteers. Meantime he had been a member of the peace convention in the summer of 1861. He commanded a brigade of Curtis' forces at the battle of Pea Ridge (Elkhorn Tavern) in March, 1862, and was promoted to brigadier general on November 29. He then took part in the capture of Arkansas Post, and during the Vicksburg campaign on June 11, 1863, joined McPherson's XVII Corps, his brigade becoming a part of Herron's division. From then until the opening of the Atlanta campaign, Vandever was stationed in the vicinity of Vicksburg. On June 20, 1864, he assumed command of a brigade of the XVI Corps at Rome, Georgia, and on August 2 command at Marietta. (706) In November he was sent to Louisville as a member of General T. W. Sweeny's court-martial but in January, 1865, he took charge of a brigade of Jefferson C. Davis' XIV Corps at Savannah; he lead this brigade throughout the campaign of the Carolinas and until the surrender of the Confederate army under General Joseph E. Johnston at Greensboro, North Carolina, in April. Vandever was brevetted major general in June, was mustered out in August, and returned to his law practice in Dubuque. He was appointed United States Indian inspector by President Grant in 1873 and served in this position until 1877. Seven years later he moved to Ventura, California (officially San Buenaventura, by which it was then known), and in 1886 was reelected to Congress after a lapse of twenty-four years, serving until 1891; he was not a candidate for reelection in 1890. General Vandever retired upon the conclusion of his term and died in Ventura on July 23, 1893. He was buried in Ventura Cemetery.

Stewart Van Vliet was born in Ferrisburg, Vermont, on July 21, 1815. He was appointed to the Military Academy at the age of twenty-one and was graduated in 1840, ranking ninth in the class. He served in the

artillery until 1847, when he became a staff captain in the Quartermaster's Department. In the course of the Mexican War, he was present at Monterrey and Vera Cruz. Van Vliet was in charge of building posts on the Oregon Trail in the late 1840's and 1850's and aided in fitting out the Utah expedition of 1857. The beginning of the Civil War found him stationed at Fort Leavenworth. He was promoted to major in August, 1861, and acted as chief quartermaster of the Army of the Potomac, from the twentieth of August to July 10,

1862, when he was relieved at his own request. He had been appointed a brigadier general of volunteers on September 23, 1861, but this appointment expired July 17, 1862, a week after his relief. (707) For the remainder of the war, he was on duty in New York City furnishing transportation and supplies. In October, 1864, he was brevetted through all grades to brigadier general in the Regular Army and in 1865 was brevetted major general, U. S. Army. On November 23, 1865, he was again appointed brigadier general of volunteers to rank from March 13, and was brevetted major general to rank from the same date. He became deputy quartermaster general with rank of lieutenant colonel in 1866 and assistant quartermaster general, with rank of colonel six years later; meanwhile he served as chief quartermaster of various military departments and divisions until his retirement for age in 1881. From 1875-81 he was inspector of the Quartermaster's Department. General Van Vliet remained in Washington after his retirement and died there on March 28, 1901; he was buried in Arlington National Cemetery.

Charles Henry Van Wyck, descendant of an old Dutch Long Island family, was born May 10, 1824, in Poughkeepsie, New York, but grew up in Bloomingburg where his father was a physician. He was graduated first in the class of 1843 from Rutgers, studied law, was admitted to the bar in 1847, and in 1850 was elected district attorney of Sullivan County, serving by reelection until 1856. Originally a Democrat of the Barnburner persuasion, he subsequently embraced Repub-

licanism and in 1858 was elected to Congress, where he remained until March 3, 1863. Meantime, he recruited the 56th New York Infantry (also known as the "Tenth Legion") and was commissioned its colonel on September 4, 1861. Van Wyck was not present with his command during the early battles on the Virginia Peninsula in 1862, and in the battles of the Seven Days, when Van Wyck was shown to be present, the regiment's chronicler reports it was "not closely engaged." (708) In December, 1862, he and his regiment were sent to South. Carolina, where they were stationed at various points in the vicinity of Charleston during the balance of the war, first under General Henry M. Naglee in the XVIII Corps and later in the X Corps. In January, 1865, he was given command of a brigade in the Department of the South (709) and, after the evacuation of Charleston by the Confederates, remained with the Union occupation forces until Au-

gust, 1865. On September 27, 1865, he was appointed a full-rank brigadier general of volunteers, one of the last four made in the course of the war. General Van Wyck was again elected to Congress from New York in 1866 and in 1868, but in 1874 he moved to Nebraska City, Nebraska, where he had acquired property in 1857. He immediately became engaged in politics: he was a member of the constitutional convention of 1875, a three-term member of the state senate (1876-80), and the following year was sent to the U. S. Senate by the legislature. An early advocate of the direct election of Senators, he introduced a constitutional amendment to make this possible during his term in office. His interest therein became marked when, although an overwhelming favorite on the Nebraska senatorial preferential ballot for reelection to the Senate, he was rejected by the legislature, which elected a conservative party hack to succeed him. Subsequently General Van Wyck espoused the cause of Populism, but was unsuccessful in successive campaigns for governor and the state senate. He died in Washington, D. C., on October 24, 1895, and was buried in Milford, Pennsylvania, the home of his wife.

James Clifford Veatch was born on December 19, 1819, in the village of Elizabethtown, Indiana, but by 1841 was living in Rockport on the Ohio River. He was admitted to the Indiana bar in 1840, practiced law for many years, and from 1841 to 1855 was auditor of Spencer County. He was a member of the state legislature during the 1861-62 term, but had already entered the army as colonel of the 25th Indiana Infantry on August 19, 1861. This regiment's first important service was performed at the capture of Fort Donelson. At Shiloh, Veatch commanded a brigade of Hurlbut's division and sustained 630 casualties in his four regiments. He was

made a brigadier general of volunteers on April 28, 1862, and, after taking part in the siege of Corinth, moved on Memphis with the balance of Hurlbut's division. He was in command of the District of Memphis for many months and engaged in numerous minor operations near there, including an engagement at the Hatchie River with the forces of Sterling Price and Earl Van Dorn after the battle of Corinth. From the beginning of the Atlanta campaign until July 17, 1864, when he went on sick leave, Veatch commanded the 4th Division of the XVI Corps, Army of the Tennessee. During this period he seems to have incurred the dis-

pleasure of Oliver O. Howard, who ordered Veatch to remain in Memphis and await orders after his return from leave in September. (710) He was without a command for a time, discharged the duties of minor posts in Tennessee, Mississippi, and Arkansas, and in February, 1865, was sent to the Department of the Gulf. During the campaign which resulted in the capture of Mobile in April, he commanded a division of Granger's XIII Corps and was subsequently brevetted major general of volunteers, specifically for his services in Mobile from March 26 to April 12, 1865. He was then in command of a district in West Louisiana until he was honorably mustered out in August. General Veatch returned to his home in Rockport, was adjutant general of Indiana in 1869, and from 1870 until 1883 was United States collector of internal revenue for his district. He died in Rockport on December 22, 1895, and was buried in Sun Set Hill Cemetery.

Egbert Ludovicus Viele, whose family in America was keeping a tavern in New Amsterdam at least as early as 1639, was born on June 17, 1825, in 'Waterford, New York. (711) He was educated in the public school at Lansingburg and was graduated from Albany Academy. He was appointed to West Point and was graduated in 1847. Immediately sent to Mexico City as an infantry subaltern, he was stationed there during the occupation. Following some routine frontier duty, he resigned his commission in 1853 to engage in civil engineering and the next year was appointed state topographical engineer of New Jer-

sey. For a time he was also chief engineer of New York City's Central Park, but his plan for development of the park was ultimately rejected in favor of that submitted by Frederick Law Olmsted, and in 1860 he became chief engineer of Prospect Park in Brooklyn. Viele's Civil War career is largely overshadowed by his accomplishments as an engineer and author of engineering monographs, although his *Handbook for Active Service,* published in 1861, was released not only in New York but also in Richmond for the benefit of budding Confederate officers. He was an engineer captain in the 7th New York Militia in the Washington defenses during the early months of the war, and on August 17, 1861, was appointed brigadier general of U. S. Volunteers. In the expedition which effected the reduction of Fort Pulaski on the Savannah River in April, 1862, Viele won high praise for his "incessant watchfulness and arduous labors." (712) After the capture of Norfolk, Virginia, in May, 1862, he served as military governor until October, 1863, when he was transferred to direct the draft in northern Ohio; he resigned on October 20, 1863, and returned to his engineering practice in New York. General Viele had a most distinguished postbellum career, serving as New York City Park Commissioner in 1883-84, as a Democratic representative in Congress 1885-87 (he was defeated for reelection), and as a spokesman for sundry societies and associations interested in engineering and history. His treatises on the topography of Manhattan Island, exhibiting the original water courses and filled land, proved of great value to the later builders of skyscrapers. He died in New York on April 22, 1902, and was buried at West Point.

Strong Vincent was born in Waterford, Pennsylvania, on June 17, 1837. He was educated at Erie Academy (Pennsylvania), Trinity College (Hartford, Connecticut), and Harvard College, from which he was graduated in 1859. He then studied law and was admitted to the bar within a year, commencing practice in Erie, where his father owned an iron foundry. With the firing on Fort Sumter in April, 1861, Vincent at once volunteered for service and from April 21, to July 25 was first lieutenant and adjutant of a regiment of Pennsylvania militia enrolled for three months. He reenlisted for three years and on September 21, 1861, was commissioned lieutenant colonel of the 83rd Pennsylvania. He fought in the siege of Yorktown

527

L. Chamberlain's 20th Maine. As John B. Hood's sinewy Rebels came up the valley between the Round Tops on the afternoon of July 2, 1863, Vincent's four regiments were diverted by General G. K. Warren to the southern slope of Little Round Top and deployed in the very nick of time to oppose them. Chamberlain's desperate bayonet assault on the left came at the moment that the 16th Michigan on the right caved in. Vincent ran down into the smoke and confusion to rally his men and was shot down. He died on July 7 in a field hospital within sight of the battlefield (a few weeks after his twenty-sixth birthday) and was buried in Erie Cemetery. Probably because the date of his wounding was incorrectly reported in Washington, he was commissioned brigadier general of volunteers on July 3, 1863, to rank from date; however, it is doubtful that he knew of his promotion. (713)

Francis Laurens Vinton, whose father was an officer of the Regular Army and was killed at the siege of Vera Cruz in 1847, was born at Fort Preble, Maine, on June 1, 1835. His father and two of his uncles were West Point graduates, (714) and young Vinton was graduated from the Academy in the class of 1856, but resigned during his graduation leave to study mining engineering in Paris. He was graduated from the École des Mines in 1860 and became an instructor of mechanical drawing at Cooper Union in New York. At the outbreak of the Civil War he was reappointed in the Regular Army with the rank of captain and in October, 1861, was commissioned colonel of the

during the Peninsular campaign, but soon after the engagement at Hanover Court House was stricken with malaria. He became colonel of the 83rd Pennsylvania on June 27, 1862, upon the death of Colonel J. W. McLane at Gaines's Mill, but apparently did not rejoin his command until the battle of Fredericksburg, where his regiment had a casualty list of some two hundred. The 83rd Pennsylvania was only lightly engaged at Chancellorsville, where it was in reserve as part of Meade's V Corps. When the Army of the Potomac was reorganized to oppose Robert E. Lee's second invasion of the North, Vincent was assigned to the command of the 3rd Brigade, 1st Division, V Corps, now under George Sykes. If any one brigade saved George G. Meade's army at Gettysburg, it was Vincent's; and if any one regiment, the honor must go to the left element of the command, Colonel (later Brevet Major General) Joshua

43rd New York Infantry. With this regiment he took part in George B. McClellan's campaign on the Virginia Peninsula in the spring of 1862 in Winfield S. Hancock's brigade of "Baldy" Smith's division of the VI Corps. This corps had no active part in the campaign of Second Manassas, and, during Robert E. Lee's invasion of Maryland which culminated in the battle of Sharpsburg, Vinton seemingly was not present for duty. (715) At the battle of Fredericksburg, however, he was in command of the 3rd Brigade of Howe's division of the corps and was so badly wounded that he saw no further service. He had been appointed a brigadier general on September 19, 1862, but the Senate failed to act on his nomination and it expired on March 4, 1863. On April 9 he was reappointed to rank from March 13 and was duly confirmed. However, on May 5 he resigned both his regular and volunteer commissions, pre-

sumably because of his health. In 1864 he became the first professor of civil and mining engineering at the newly opened Columbia College School of Mines in New York, where he remained until 1877, when he resigned, moved to Denver, Colorado, and became a consulting mining engineer. He died of erysipelas in Leadville, Colorado, on October 6, 1879, and was buried in Evergreen Cemetery. Some time later General Vinton's remains were brought East for reburial in Swan Point Cemetery, Providence, Rhode Island.

Israel Vogdes was born on August 4, 1816, in Willistown, a hamlet in Chester County, Pennsylvania. He was appointed to West Point at the age of seventeen and was graduated in 1837, ranking eleventh in the class which included Braxton Bragg, Jubal Early, John Sedgwick, and Joseph Hooker. For twelve years he taught mathematics at the

Academy and then he saw some service against the Florida Seminoles as an officer of artillery. He was subsequently stationed in Charleston Harbor and at the Artillery School for Practice at Fort Monroe. In 1861 Vogdes held the rank of captain, 1st Artillery; when the resignations of Southern officers began to come in, he was advanced to major on May 14. He took part in the defense of Fort Pickens in Pensacola Harbor and on October 9, 1861, was taken prisoner in the course of a Confederate attack designed to reduce Santa Rosa Island and the fort. Finally exchanged in August, 1862, (716) he played an important part in designing and building artillery positions in the Charleston, South Carolina perimeter, including Light-House Inlet, Morris Island, and Folly Island. Meantime he had been made a brigadier general of volunteers on November 29, 1862. During the last year of the war he was in command of the defenses of Norfolk and Portsmouth, Virginia. General Vogdes emerged from the war as colonel of the 1st Artillery—a rank to which he had been appointed in 1863—and as a brevet brigadier general, U. S. Army, "for Gallant and Meritorious Services in the Field during the Rebellion." From the close of the war until fall of 1865, he was in command of a district in Florida. Thereafter, as colonel of his regiment, he was post commander successively at Fort Hamilton, New York, Charleston, South Carolina, and Fort Adams in Newport Harbor, Rhode Island. General Vogdes was retired at his own request on January 2, 1881. He established his residence in New York City, where he died on December 7, 1889. He was buried at West Point.

Adolph Wilhelm August Friedrich, Baron von Steinwehr (717) was born on September 25, 1822, at Blankenburg in the Duchy of Brunswick. His father was an officer in the service of the duke and

his grandfather had been a lieutenant general in the Prussian army. Young von Steinwehr was reared to be a soldier and, after attending the Brunswick military academy, became a lieutenant in the ducal service. In 1847 he took a year's leave of absence, came to America, and endeavored to obtain a Regular Army commission for service in the Mexican War. Failing in this, he obtained an appointment in the coast survey and while in Mobile married into an Alabama family. In 1849 he took his wife back to Brunswick but five years later returned to the United States and settled on a farm near Wallingford,

Connecticut. When the Civil War broke out, he was appointed colonel of the 29th New York, which took part in the campaign of First Manassas (Bull Run) as a part of Blenker's brigade of Miles's division but was in reserve at Centreville and not actively engaged. He was assigned to the command of the 2nd Brigade of Blenker's division, which was attached to John C. Frémont's Mountain Department in the Shenandoah Valley campaign of 1862; however, von Steinwehr is not shown to have been present at Cross Keys. When Franz Sigel replaced Frémont in corps command, after the organization of John Pope's Army of Virginia, von Steinwehr was given the 2nd Division—one brigade of his division lost over four hundred men at Second Manassas. At Chancellorsville and Gettysburg the corps, now called the XI Corps of the Army of the Potomac, was commanded by Oliver O. Howard and was routed at both battles, with the German elements therein taking most of the blame. In point of fact, von Steinwehr made an important contribution to what little opposition was offered by the Federal right at Chancellorsville by constructing earthworks which were held beyond the call of duty by Buschbeck's brigade of his division. After the disaster at Chickamauga, the XI and XII Corps were sent west. Von Steinwehr participated in clearing the Tennessee River and in the battle of Chattanooga in command of his division. However, upon the consolidation of the XI and XII Corps into the XX Corps the following April, he was demoted to command of a brigade of the XIV Corps, while a man his junior (Brig-adier General John W. Geary) was given command of one of the four divisions of the XX Corps. (718) Apparently feeling that he had been overslaughed, he seems to have declined the assignment, for he makes no further appearance in the *Official Records*. (719) His resignation was accepted July 3, 1865. After the war he became quite celebrated as a geographer and cartographer, teaching at Yale, working for the Federal government, and publishing a number of works. He resided successively in New Haven, Washington, and Cincinnati. Von Steinwehr died in Buffalo, New York, on February 25, 1877, and was buried in Albany Rural Cemetery, Albany, New York. (720)

Melancthon Smith Wade, whose father was one of the first settlers in Ohio, was born in Cincinnati on December 2, 1802. He was educated in the local schools and subsequently engaged in the dry-goods

531

business, but retired when he was only thirty-eight years of age. He was active in the Ohio militia for many years and held the successive grades of captain, colonel, and brigadier general. With the outbreak of the Civil War he devoted himself as far as he was able to the recruitment and organization of Ohio volunteers and on October 1, 1861, was mustered into the U. S. Army as a brigadier general of volunteers. He was the first post commander at Camp Dennison, which was located about twenty miles northeast of Cincinnati on the Little Miami River, but both his age and poor health militated against his making an important contribution to the Union war effort, and on March 18, 1862, his resignation was accepted by the War Department. His service was so obscure that his name does not appear in the index to the *Official Records*. In his last years General Wade was interested in the cultivation of fruit and was an active member of the Cincinnati horticultural society. He died at his estate in Avondale, now a part of Cincinnati, on August 11, 1868, and was buried in Spring Grove Cemetery, Cincinnati.

James Samuel Wadsworth was born on October 30, 1807, in Geneseo, New York. His father was becoming one of the largest owners of cultivated lands in the state, and young Wadsworth's life was dedicated from boyhood to the private and public responsibilities which he would inherit. He spent two years at Harvard, studied law, and was admitted to the bar, although he had no intention of practicing. He went into politics because he

felt it incumbent upon him to do so and, although first a Democrat, was one of the organizers of the Free-Soil party which joined the Republican fold in 1856. In 1861 he was a member of the Washington peace conference, an unofficial gathering

of Northern and Southern moderates whose aim was to avert war. When conflict became inevitable, he immediately offered himself and his fortune to the Union cause. Having no pretensions, he served as a volunteer aide to Irvin McDowell at First Manassas. McDowell then recommended his appointment as brigadier general and his commission as such was forthcoming on August 9, 1861. Wadsworth had neither formal military training nor any illusions about himself, but, on the other hand, he had the habit of command and the experience of a lifetime on the frontier and the farm to draw on. He became military governor of the District of Columbia in March, 1862, and because he saw no prospect of field duty with George B. McClellan in the Peninsular campaign he allowed his supporters to run him for governor of New York on the Republican ticket. The Democrats scored large gains in this off-year election, and Wadsworth was one of the casualties. Following the battle of Fredericksburg in December, 1862, Wadsworth was assigned to the command of the 1st Division of John F. Reynolds' I Corps. The command was not significantly engaged at Chancellorsville, but at Gettysburg, Wadsworth's division, as well as the remainder of the corps, fought like heroes to stave off disaster while the rest of the Army of the Potomac was being brought into action. Reynolds was killed, and the I Corps itself was so decimated that its regiments were subsequently distributed, along with those of the III Corps, to other units when the Army of the Potomac was reconstituted for Grant's Overland campaign in the spring of 1864. At this juncture Wadsworth was assigned to the command of a division of Warren's V Corps—a tribute to his soldierly qualities considering the number of brigade and division commanders rendered supernumerary by the reorganization of the army. At the Wilderness on May 6, 1864, while leading his men in an attempt to repel an assault, he was shot off his horse, a bullet entering the back of his head and lodging in his brain. He was taken to a Confederate field hospital where he died two days later without regaining consciousness. (721) General Wadsworth's remains were later recovered under a flag of truce and are now buried in Temple Hill Cemetery, Geneseo.

(722) He was posthumously promoted to major general to rank from the day he was mortally wounded.

George Day Wagner was born on September 22, 1829, in Ross County, Ohio, but at the age of four was taken by his parents to Warren County, Indiana, where the family settled on a farm. Young

Wagner was raised on the farm and received his education in the country schools. In 1856 he was elected to the lower house of the Indiana legislature as a Republican, two years later to the state senate, and in 1860 campaigned vigorously for Abraham Lincoln. When the Civil War broke out Wagner immediately offered his services and was commissioned colonel of the 15th Indiana on June 14, 1861. After some service in West Virginia he commanded a brigade of D. C. Buell's Army of the Ohio at Shiloh

533

and was commended by his division commander T. J. Wood. He again rendered good service at the battle of Murfreesboro and during the battle of Chickamauga was commander of the post of Chattanooga. On April 4, 1863, he was commissioned brigadier general to rank from November 29, 1862. In the assault on the heights of Missionary Ridge in November, 1863, Wagner's brigade (a part of Sheridan's division of Granger's corps) suffered seven hundred casualties while sweeping Braxton Bragg's Confederates off the mountain. Wagner continued as a brigade commander in the IV Corps in the Atlanta campaign and was sent back to Tennessee with G. H. Thomas and the Army of the Cumberland to oppose John B. Hood's invasion of the state in the autumn of 1864. At Franklin on November 30 Wagner was in command of a division of the IV Corps which formed the rear guard of John M. Schofield's retiring forces; a part of this division was entrenched a half-mile in advance of the main Union position with orders to retire whenever Hood evidenced a disposition to advance in force. In what was claimed to be disobedience of orders, Wagner elected to make a stand, and, when the position was overrun, the assaulting Rebels very nearly followed the remnants of Wagner's two brigades into the Federal works. On December 9, 1864, he was relieved from further duty with the Army of the Cumberland at his own request, allegedly because of his wife's illness, and ordered to Indianapolis to await orders. He was honorably mustered out on August 24, 1865, without brevet promotion. After

the death of his wife that year, General Wagner began a law practice in Williamsport, Indiana. He had been president of the state agricultural society just before the war and once again served in this position. He died suddenly in Indianapolis on February 13, 1869, and was buried in Armstrong Cemetery, near Greenhill, Warren County, Indiana, a few miles from the farm where he grew to manhood. (723)

Charles Carroll Walcutt was born on February 12, 1838, in Columbus, Ohio. His father was a veteran of the War of 1812 and his grandfather of the Revolution. Young

Walcutt was educated in the Columbus schools and at Kentucky Military Institute (near Frankfort), where he was graduated in 1858. The following year he was elected surveyor of Franklin County, Ohio. In April, 1861, he raised a company in response to President Lincoln's first call for 75,-

000 volunteers, but it was not accepted for service because Ohio's quota was already filled. He was commissioned a major in state service in June and on October 1, 1861, was appointed major of the 46th Ohio in Federal service. The next spring at Shiloh, where the regiment saw its first action, Walcutt was wounded in the left shoulder. (He carried the bullet for the remainder of his life.) Walcutt served under W. T. Sherman from that time until the end of the war, rising to colonel of his regiment on October 16, 1862, brigadier general of volunteers on July 30, 1864, and brevet major general "for special gallantry" in March, 1865. On the celebrated "March to the Sea," during which he was again wounded, the commander of the Army of the Tennessee Oliver O. Howard gave him the accolade, "there is not a braver or better officer." (724) Walcutt took part in the siege of Vicksburg, the capture of Jackson, the battle of Chattanooga, the relief of Knoxville, and the principal battles of the Atlanta campaign. On July 22, 1864, at the battle of Atlanta proper, he was instrumental in saving Frank Blair's XVII Corps from disaster by disobeying an order to retire. He was advanced to command of a brigade of Logan's XV Corps, just before the assault on Missionary Ridge in November, 1863, and to divisional command at the close of the war, marching in the grand review at Washington at the head of the 1st Division of the XIV Corps. He was mustered out in January, 1866, and returned home to become warden of the Ohio penitentiary, but in July accepted the lieutenant colonelcy of

the 10th Regular Cavalry. He resigned this commission, however, four months later and resumed his position at the prison, serving until 1869, when he was appointed collector of internal revenue by President Grant. He had been an elector for Grant the previous November and was active in Republican politics as well as state and local government until the end of his life. General Walcutt served as mayor of Columbus from 1883 to 1887; he was also prominent in the Loyal Legion and the Masonic order. He died while on a visit to Omaha, Nebraska, on May 2, 1898, and was buried in Greenlawn Cemetery, Columbus.

Lewis "Lew" Wallace, celebrated as the author of *Ben Hur : A Tale of the. Christ* and other literary works, was born in Brookville, Indiana, on April 10, 1827, but moved to Indianapolis as a small boy when his father was elected governor of

the state. Wallace was a precocious youth and interested himself early in a number of fields of endeavor ranging from clerical duties through politics, history, and law to service as a first lieutenant of the 1st Indiana in the Mexican War. He was admitted to the bar in 1849 and in 1856 was elected to the state senate, meantime moving his residence to Crawfordsville. Upon the bombardment of Fort Sumter he was appointed state adjutant general by Governor Oliver P. Morton and on April 25, 1861, was made colonel of the 11th Indiana, a three-month regiment which was re-enlisted in August for three years. After some preliminary service in West Virginia, Wallace, who had been advanced to brigadier general of volunteers on September 3, 1861, took part in the capture of Fort Donelson and was made a major general to rank from March 21, 1862. At Shiloh a few days later the military opportunity of his life was handed him by U. S. Grant, who told him to march his division upstream from Crump's Landing to the battlefield. For some reason, Wallace lost his way, was compelled to make a circuitous countermarch, and, instead of smashing in the Confederate left at a crucial point of the battle, limped upon the field hours too late to do more than assist the day following. In the summer of 1864, however, with greatly inferior numbers, he checked Jubal Early's Washington-bound Confederates at the Monocacy River long enough for elements detached by Grant from the Army of the Potomac to prevent the capture of the capital. In 1865 he was a member of the military commission which tried the Lincoln conspirators, and

he was president of the court-martial which tried and condemned Henry Wirz, commandant at Andersonville. After the war General Wallace once unsuccessfully sought public office by election, but twice won it by appointment, serving as governor of New Mexico Territory and United States minister to Turkey. In the meantime he wrote prolifically and was greatly in demand as a lecturer and speaker. He died in Crawfordsville on February 15, 1905, and was buried there in Oak Hill Cemetery.

William Harvey Lamb Wallace was born in Urbana, Ohio, on July 8, 1821. As a small boy he moved with his father to Illinois, where the family settled in La Salle

County. In 1846 he was admitted to the state bar, but the following year volunteered as a private in the 1st Illinois Volunteers for service in the Mexican War. He rose to be first lieutenant and regimental adjutant and fought in a number of engagements under General Zachary Taylor. In the years following he served by election as district attorney and practiced law until the outbreak of the Civil War, when he reentered the army as colonel of the 11th Illinois. This was a ninety-day command which reenlisted for three years' service upon expiration of its original term and was commanded by Wallace during the early months of the war. In the course of the siege and capture of Fort Donelson he commanded a brigade of McClernand's division so ably that he was appointed a brigadier general of volunteers on March 21, 1862. At the crucial battle of Shiloh in April, Wallace was given command of one of the six divisions of U. S. Grant's Army of the Tennessee, which he directed with bravery and circumspection until he was compelled to fall back on the position of Benjamin M. Prentiss' division in the "Hornets' Nest." Prentiss was ultimately forced to surrender his position after standing off repeated Confederate assaults. The ultimate surrender reflected in no way upon Wallace's gallantry; while pulling his command out of a hopeless situation and taking his men to the rear, he was mortally wounded. He died at Savannah, Tennessee (Grant's headquarters), on April 10, 1862, and was buried in a private cemetery near Ottawa, Illinois.

John Henry Hobart Ward, whose father and grandfather both ultimately died of wounds received in defending their country, was born on June 17, 1823, in New York City. He was educated at Trinity Collegiate School and at the age of

eighteen enlisted in the army. From April, 1842, until April, 1847, he served successively as private, corporal, sergeant, and sergeant major in the 7th Infantry, took part in the siege of Fort Brown, was wounded at Monterrey, and was present at the capture of Vera Cruz, where he subsequently was wed to one of the belles of the town. For nine years during the 1850's, he was the assistant to the state commissary general and then commissary general. When the Civil War broke out Ward was commissioned colonel of the 38th New York, which he led at the battle of First Manassas, in all of the battles of the Peninsular campaign, at Second Manassas, and at Chantilly. In the latter campaign he temporarily commanded David Birney's brigade of the III Corps and on October 4, 1862, was made a brigadier general of volunteers and placed in permanent command of the brigade. He fought at Fredericksburg,

Chancellorsville, and Gettysburg (where he was wounded) and in the II Corps at the Wilderness and Spotsylvania (where he was wounded again); meanwhile he occasionally commanded Birney's division, which went from the III to the II Corps in the post-Gettysburg consolidation. Up until the battle of the Wilderness in May, 1864, Ward had been almost universally eulogized by his superiors for bravery and ability. (725) Thus, it was a distinct shock to many of his associates when he was relieved from command on May 12, 1864, "for misbehavior and intoxication in the presence of the enemy during the Battle of the Wilderness." (726) He was, however, honorably mustered out of service on July 18, 1864. Many prominent persons asked that Ward be restored to rank and then brought to trial so that his guilt could be ascertained, but as late as October 2, 1864, the Secretary of War refused to revoke the dismissal order. For thirty-two years after the war General Ward served as clerk of the superior and supreme courts of New York. On July 24, 1903, while vacationing in Monroe, New York (where one of his daughters was buried), he was run over by a train and killed. After a Masonic funeral in Brooklyn, New York, his body was brought back to Monroe for burial in Community Cemetery.

William Thomas Ward was born in Amelia County, Virginia, on August 9, 1808. But his parents moved to Kentucky when he was quite young, and he was educated at St. Mary's College, near Lebanon. He then studied law and commenced practice in Greensburg, Kentucky.

In 1847 he became major of the 4th Kentucky Volunteer Infantry and was stationed in Mexico until he was mustered out in 1848. He then served successively in the Kentucky legislature and as a representative in Congress from 1851 to 1853. With the official adherence of Kentucky to the Federal cause, Ward was commissioned a brigadier general of volunteers on September 18, 1861. He compiled a very creditable record from that time until the surrender of Joseph E. Johnston in North Carolina in 1865, when he was in command of the 3rd Division of the XX Corps and was brevetted a major general of volunteers to rank from February 24, 1865. Ward's first service was in Kentucky, under the command of General Jeremiah Boyle, and consequently he was a victim of John Hunt Morgan's raid in 1862. In November, 1862, he was attached to the Army of the Ohio and was made post commander at Gallatin, Tennessee. General Ward occupied a succession of garrison commands, protecting various towns and railroad junctions in Tennessee, and early in 1864 was assigned to command of the 1st Division of Howard's XI Corps, Army of the Cumberland. Upon the consolidation of the XI and XII Corps into the XX Corps immediately prior to the opening of the Atlanta campaign, Ward assumed command of a brigade of the 3rd Division; and when General Daniel Butterfield, the division's commander, went on sick leave, Ward took over and led the division from Atlanta to Savannah and in the campaign of the Carolinas. He was twice wounded at Resaca, Georgia, but would not leave the field and continued in service until he was mustered out on August 24, 1865. After the war General Ward practiced law in Louisville, Kentucky, until his death on October 12, 1878. He was buried in Cave Hill Cemetery.

James Meech Warner, whose earliest direct ancestor came to Massachusetts Bay from England in 1630, was born January 29, 1836, in Middlebury, Vermont. He attended Middlebury College from 1851 to 1855, when he accepted an appointment to the Military Academy (then offering a five-year course); he was graduated in 1860, ranking next to the bottom of the class—a scholastic level which came to be something of a trademark of successful combat officers in the 1861-65 period. Posted originally as a subaltern to the 10th Infantry, he performed most of his antebellum duty at Fort Wise (later Fort Lyon), Colorado, near the site of Bent's Old Fort on the Arkansas

River, and during the first six months of 1862 he was in command of the station. In July he was relieved and ordered east, becoming colonel of the 11th Vermont Infantry to rank from September 1, 1862, by commission of Governor Fred-

eric Holbrook. The 11th Vermont was installed in the defenses of Washington and, in keeping with the War Department policy of the time, was made into a heavy artillery regiment of twelve companies numbering nearly two thousand men. When U. S. Grant called for reenforcements following his heavy losses in the Wilderness, the 11th Vermont was sent to Belle Plain as infantry and joined the decimated Vermont brigade with fifteen hundred men in line, outnumbering the rest of the brigade by several hundred. Accordingly, it was divided into battalions, commanded by its three majors, and was maneuvered like three regiments. Soon after the command was brought into line at Spotsylvania on May 12, 1864, it was subjected to a severe fire by Confederate artillery. Warner, while walking up and down on the earthworks to encourage his men, was struck by a ball through his neck. He returned to action in time to command a segment of the Washington defenses during Jubal Early's raid in July, 1864 and, thereafter, performed distinguished service in the Shenandoah Valley under Philip Sheridan. Besides his contribution to the success of the Union cause at Fisher's Hill (following the battle of Winchester), which his brigade carried by a bayonet charge, his conduct was outstanding at Cedar Creek where the 1st Brigade formed the extreme right of the army and, along with the rest of Getty's division of the VI Corps, was the only organized infantry in line of battle when Sheridan arrived on the field. At Petersburg on the morning of April 2, 1865, he was said to be the first mounted man inside the Confederate works. He had been brevetted a brigadier general of volunteers to rank from August 1, 1864, and at the end of the war was advanced to the full rank (from May 8, 1865) and was also brevetted brigadier general, U. S. Army. General Warner resigned from the army early in 1866 to engage in business in Albany, New York. He was postmaster of the city during Benjamin Harrison's administration and was an unsuccessful candidate for mayor on the Republican ticket. He died of a stroke on March 16, 1897, while attending the theater in New York City; he was buried in Middlebury. (727)

Fitz-Henry Warren was born on January 11, 1816, in Brimfield, Massachusetts. He seems to have been

educated locally and gainfully employed in the area until 1844, when he moved to Burlington, Iowa, and became connected with the Burlington *Hawkeye,* meanwhile interesting himself in politics. He was second assistant postmaster general in 1849 and subsequently first assistant. With the outbreak of the Civil War he was named colonel of the 1st Iowa Cavalry on June 13, 1861, and for more than a year was actively employed against Confederate recruits and sympathizers in middle and western Missouri. He was advanced to brigadier general of volunteers on July 16, 1862, and on December 31 of this year was in command of the post of Houston, Missouri. During the Gettysburg crisis he was on duty in Pennsylvania, but in September, 1863, was ordered to the Department of the Gulf. After some service on the

Texas Gulf Coast, he took a minor part in N. P. Banks's Red River campaign, briefly commanding the XIII Corps. He was later posted at Baton Rouge, Louisiana, and then at Brownsville, Texas, where he commanded the United States forces on the Rio Grande River. Seemingly he suffered from ill health, since on September 30, 1864, he was ordered to report to "the commanding general Department of the East, for assignment to such duty as he may be able to perform." (728) Warren was brevetted major general of volunteers as of August 24, 1865, and mustered out the same day. Following the war he served in the Iowa state senate (1866), as United States minister to Guatemala (1867-68), and as Democratic presidential elector from Iowa (1872). He was then associated with the New York *Tribune* and with the New York *Sun* for a short time. Shortly before his death he returned to Brimfield, where he died on June 21, 1878, and is buried.

Gouverneur Kemble Warren was born in Cold Spring, New York, on the Hudson River across from West Point on January 8, 1830. He was appointed to the Military Academy at the age of sixteen and was graduated in 1850, ranking second in the class. From then until the outbreak of the Civil War he served in the topographical engineers and as an instructor of mathematics at his alma mater. On May 14, 1861, he was appointed a lieutenant colonel of the 5th New York and with it saw some action at the first battle of the war, Bethel Church, Virginia, on June 10. In August he became colonel of the regiment, and on the

Peninsula he was wounded at Gaines's Mill, while directing a brigade of Sykes's division of Porter's V Corps. He continued to command a brigade under Fitz John Porter at Second Manassas and at Sharpsburg in the Maryland campaign; subsequently he was promoted to brigadier general of volunteers on September 26, 1862, and major general on August 8 to rank from May 3. Warren possessed an eye for ground as good as any in the Army of the Potomac, and on the second day at Gettysburg, while observing the lay of the land from a signal station on Little Round Top which overlooked the Confederate right, he noted the threat to the entire Federal position on Cemetery Ridge by John B. Hood's onrushing Confederates who were already in the little interval between Big and Little Round Top. At this point Warren was chief engineer of the Army of the Potomac and was not exercising line command; however, in a matter of minutes he had Vincent's and Weed's brigades of Sykes's V Corps, which was coming to the front, hurrying to the southern slope of the knoll where the signal station stood, in the nick of time to deploy a line of defense. Today a bronze statue of Warren, field glasses in hand, marks the spot where the second day of the battle of Gettysburg was won. Had it not been won there and then, there would have been no need for Pickett's famous charge the next day, for there would have been no Federal army on Cemetery Ridge. From August, 1863, until March, 1864, Warren was in temporary charge of the II Corps in the absence of the wounded Winfield S. Hancock; he was then assigned to permanent command of the V Corps when the Army of the Potomac was reshuffled for the Overland campaign against Richmond. Warren's handling of his corps in the bloody operations which led up to the siege of Petersburg could hardly be taken exception to; however, there seems to have been a personality clash among him, U. S. Grant, and Philip Sheridan. When Sheridan was put in command of all of the forces ordered to break the Confederate defenses at Five Forks and to seize the Southside Railroad (the last artery connecting Petersburg and the South), he was authorized by Grant to relieve Warren at his discretion. Sheridan grasped the first opportunity to do so, despite the fact that Warren had handled his three divisions as well as perhaps anyone in the same job could have done. (729) In any event, his military career was destroyed: he spent his remaining years in the army in the Engineer

Corps and did not become a lieutenant colonel until 1879, when a court of inquiry not only exonerated him completely of culpability at Five Forks but criticized the manner of his relief. In the meantime, he wrote prolifically in matters relating to his profession and boasted several signal accomplishments in the field, including the railroad bridge over the Mississippi at Rock Island, Illinois. General Warren died at his home in Newport, Rhode Island, on August 8, 1882, and was buried in Island Cemetery.

Cadwallader Colden Washburn, whose civilian career far outshone his tour of duty as a volunteer ma-

jor general during the Civil War, was born on April 22, 1818, in Livermore, Maine, where his father had moved from Massachusetts in 1806. His first American ancestor had settled in Duxbury in 1632 and both of his grandfathers had been officers of the Revolutionary Army. Three of his six brothers served in Congress or the Senate, and at one point he and two of his brothers were simultaneously members of the House of Representatives. (730) Driven by necessity, Washburn went west at the age of twenty-one and in 1842 began a law practice in Mineral Point, Wisconsin, some thirty-odd miles from where his brother Elihu had settled in Galena, Illinois. Washburn amassed an enormous fortune in the rapidly developing country from land speculation, banking, railroading, lumbering, supplying water power, and flour milling. He was elected to Congress as a Republican representative from Wisconsin in 1854 and served for three terms by reelection; he was also a member of the Washington peace conference of 1861. His brother Elihu was not only Abraham Lincoln's intimate but also U. S. Grant's principal sponsor—these connections may have had something to do with his phenomenal rise in rank from colonel, 2nd Wisconsin Cavalry (February 6, 1862), to brigadier general of volunteers (July 16, 1862), and to major general (March 13, 1863 to rank from November 29, 1862). Nevertheless, he seems to have rendered good service while on active duty, first in Missouri under Eugene Carr in the Army of the Southwest and finally in command of the Department of West Tennessee, with headquarters at Memphis. In the meantime he commanded the Yazoo Pass expedition during Grant's initial attempts to take Vicksburg on the land side, and, during the final siege and capture of the city itself, Washburn directed a detachment of three divisions of the XVI Corps. General Washburn resigned from the army on May 25, 1865, and returned home. In the years following the war he served two more terms in Congress (1867-71) and was governor of Wisconsin from 1871 to 1873. At the same time he was instrumental in organizing Washburn, Crosby, and Company (now General Mills) in Minneapolis and invested in a number of other enterprises which brought him one of the great fortunes of the Midwest. He died at Eureka Springs, Arkansas, on May 14, 1882, while on a health pilgrimage, and was buried in Oak Grove Cemetery, La Crosse, Wisconsin.

Louis Douglass Watkins, who was born near Tallahassee, Florida, probably on November 29, 1833, (731) was taken early in life by his parents to the District of Columbia, where he was educated. During the 1850's he became affiliated with a

Washington militia company known as the "National Rifles," but when the company entertained treasonable designs against the Federal government, Watkins resigned and joined the 3rd Battalion, District of Columbia Infantry—a loyal outfit. On May 14, 1861, he was commissioned a first lieutenant in the Regular Army and served with the 5th Cavalry in the Peninsular campaign, during which he was severely wounded at Gaines's Mill. In July, 1862, he was advanced to captain and sent to Kentucky, where he acted as aide-de-camp on the staff of A. J. Smith during Braxton Bragg's invasion of the state; in October he was appointed chief of cavalry of the Army of Kentucky and accompanied S. P. Carter on the latter's raid into East Tennessee. Becoming colonel of the 6th Kentucky (Union) Cavalry in February, 1863, he engaged in a number of skirmishes in the neighborhood of Nashville and commanded a brigade of the 1st Cavalry Division, Army of the Cumberland, in the Chickamauga and Chattanooga campaigns. During the Atlanta campaign Watkins' brigade as a part of E. M. McCook's division was engaged in guarding the railroad in W. T. Sherman's rear. Subsequently, Watkins took part in the Tennessee campaign of November and December, 1864, and the pursuit of John B. Hood after the battle of Nashville. His brigade was broken up late in January, 1865, and in April he was made post commander at Louisville, Kentucky, where he did duty until the end of the war. Watkins had been brevetted a brigadier general of volunteers on June 24, 1864, and on September

25, 1865, was accorded the full rank. When the Regular Army was reorganized in 1866, he was appointed lieutenant colonel of the 20th Infantry and was stationed at Richmond until January, 1867, when the regiment was ordered to Baton Rouge. Watkins had married a daughter of General Lovell H. Rousseau in 1864 and, when ordered to Baton Rouge, seems to have established his wife and two children in New Orleans. He died there, while visiting them on March 29, 1868; and after temporary burial in the old Girod Street Cemetery his remains were ultimately interred in Arlington National Cemetery, next to those of his father-in-law, who by coincidence died nine months later in New Orleans. (732)

Alexander Stewart Webb, son of the well-known newspaper proprietor and diplomat James Watson Webb, was born on February 15, 1835, in New York City. He at-

tended private schools until he received an appointment to West Point in 1851. He was commissioned in the artillery upon his graduation in 1855, fought against the Florida Seminoles in 1856, and the next year returned to the Military Academy as an instructor in mathematics. At the beginning of the Civil War, he took part in the defense of Fort Pickens, was present at First Manassas, was assistant to General W. F. Barry, Chief of Artillery of the Army of the Potomac from July, 1861, to April, 1862, and during the Peninsular campaign was Barry's acting inspector general. During Robert E. Lee's invasion of Maryland, Webb acted as chief of staff for Porter's V Corps; after this campaign he was assigned to the camp of instruction in Washington as inspector of artillery. In January, 1863, he became assistant inspector general of the V Corps and, a few days prior to Gettysburg, took command of the 2nd Brigade of John Gibbon's division of Winfield S. Hancock's II Corps; on the same day (June 23, 1863) he was promoted to brigadier general of volunteers. On the third day of this battle, Webb's four Pennsylvania regiments were posted in the immediate vicinity of "the little clump of trees" which was the focal point of George Pickett's charge; the command lost 451 men killed and wounded in the encounter, Webb was among the wounded and was later awarded the Congressional medal for his conduct. During the subsequent campaign on the Rappahannock he was in charge of Gibbon's division in the absence of both Gibbon and Hancock, but in the spring of 1864 reverted to command of his old brigade. He was gravely wounded at Spotsylvania and did not return to duty until January, 1865, when he became chief of staff to General George G. Meade, a position he held until the end of the war. Webb received the brevet of major general in both the regular and volunteer services. In 1866 he was appointed lieutenant colonel of the 44th Infantry. He again taught at the Military Academy, and in 1870 was honorably discharged from the army at his own request, presumably so that he could accept the presidency of the College of the City of New York. He remained as president for thirty-three years. General Webb died at his home in Riverdale, New York, on February 12, 1911, and was buried at West Point.

Max Weber (sometimes listed as Von Weber) was born on August 27, 1824, in the village of Achern, a few miles south of Baden-Baden, in the Grand Duchy of Baden. He

was graduated from the military school at Karlsruhe in 1843, became a lieutenant in the Grand Duke's army, but defected to the rebels during the revolutions of 1848. After the revolt was crushed by the army of Prussia, Weber emigrated to New York and for many years conducted the Hotel Konstanz at William and Frankfort streets—a rendezvous for refugees from southern Germany. At the outbreak of war in 1861, Weber organized the "Turner Rifles" which was mustered into Federal service as the 20th New York Infantry on May 9, 1861. On April 28, 1862, he was made a brigadier general of volunteers. He was commandant at Fort Monroe for a time and discharged a number of other minor assignments; however, at the battle of Sharpsburg he was greatly distinguished as commander of a brigade of French's division of Sumner's II Corps. (733) In this battle he was badly wounded, losing permanently the use of his right arm. At the end of 1863 he returned to limited duty in Washington and in April, 1864, was assigned to command of the post at Harpers Ferry and of the troops between Sleepy Creek and the Monocacy River. During Jubal Early's raid on Washington, Weber was dislodged from his station but was able to reoccupy it a few days later when the Confederates withdrew from the area. At the end of the war he was unassigned and on May 13, 1865, resigned his commission. After the war he was appointed American consul at Nantes, France, and later served as tax assessor in New York. Subsequently, President Grant appointed him collector of internal revenue for New York.

General Weber had been retired for a number of years when he died at his residence in Brooklyn on June 15, 1901; he was buried in Evergreen Cemetery.

Joseph Dana Webster, military confidant of U. S. Grant and W. T. Sherman, was born on August 25, 1811, in Hampton, New Hampshire. He was graduated from Dartmouth College in 1832 and began the study of law, but in 1835 he became a civil engineer in the employ of the government and in 1838 accepted a commission in the Regular Army's topographical engineers. He served in the Mexican War and, resigning as a captain in 1854, settled in Chicago, the home of his wife. He was a member of the body which arranged the early sewerage system and raised the downtown level of the city above the encroaching waters of Lake Michigan. When the storm of civil conflict was at hand, Webster was one of a delegation of Chicago cit-

izens who in January, 1861, signed an uncompromising manifesto against extremists in both the North and South. He was reappointed in the army on July 1, 1861, as a staff paymaster, but was sent immediately to Cairo, Illinois, where he superintended the construction of defenses. On February 1, 1862, he received the token appointment of colonel of the 1st Illinois Light Artillery (none of whose batteries ever served together), which afforded him the necessary rank to discharge the duties of Grant's chief of staff at Belmont, Forts Henry and Donelson, and Shiloh. In the course of the opening day of Shiloh, when the possibility that the Union forces would be completely overwhelmed and driven into the Tennessee River was strong, Webster, on Grant's orders, maneuvered fifty-odd pieces of artillery into line on the bluff almost overlooking Pittsburg Landing, where thousands of skulkers and wounded milled about. The last Confederate attack sputtered out; the Federals were victorious the following day, and Webster returned to his staff duties. He was commissioned brigadier general of volunteers to rank from November 29, 1862, and during the Vicksburg campaign was in charge of all the railroads supplying Grant's forces. Thereafter, he became chief of staff to Sherman and during the Atlanta campaign remained in Nashville, where he operated as an administrator backing up Sherman's gigantic column as it advanced on the line of the Western & Atlantic Railroad toward Atlanta. He acted in the same capacity for G. H. Thomas at Nashville, where he was posted by orders of Sherman and

discharged his duties and responsibilities in exemplary fashion. At the end of the war he was brevetted major general and returned to the Chicago area. From 1869 to 1872 he was city assessor of internal revenue, and in July, 1872, was appointed collector of internal revenue. He died at the Palmer House in Chicago on March 12, 1876, and was buried in Rosehill Cemetery. (734)

Stephen Hinsdale Weed was born on November 17, 1831, in Potsdam, New York, but his family moved to New York City when he was young. (735) He obtained his primary education in the city and in 1850 was appointed to West Point, where he was graduated in 1854. In the antebellum years, as an officer of artillery, he served on frontier duty, against the Florida Seminoles, in the Kansas disturbances, and in the 1858-61 expedition to Salt Lake City. He was promoted to captain of the 5th Artillery on May 14,

1861, and was stationed near Harrisburg, Pennsylvania, during the following winter. He took part in the Peninsular campaign as commander of a battery, fought at Second Manassas as chief of artillery for Sykes's division of the V Corps, and during the Maryland campaign again in charge of his own battery. At Fredericksburg and Chancellorsville, he commanded all the artillery of the V Corps and on June 6, 1863, was promoted from captain to brigadier general of volunteers and assigned to the direction of a brigade of infantry in Ayres's division of the corps. At Gettysburg, Weed and one of his regimental commanders, Patrick H. O'Rorke of the 140th New York, were as distinguished in saving the Union left on July 2 as were Strong Vincent and J. L. Chamberlain. After the right of Vincent's brigade on Little Round Top gave way, Weed's brigade, with O'Rorke's men in the lead, was thrown into the breach by G. K. Warren. (736) The 140th New York charged the victorious Confederates with unloaded guns and unfixed bayonets, by sheer elan making them pause and draw back. Weed also got a battery of six three-inch rifles to the top of the hill by sheer muscle strength, for there was no road—not even a semblance of one. While directing their fire he was shot down, the bullet passing through his arm and into his chest. He died a few hours later and was buried in the Moravian Cemetery at New Dorp, Staten Island, New York.

Godfrey Weitzel, the son of German immigrants, was born on November 1, 1835, in Cincinnati, Ohio. His early education was obtained in the local schools, but he was appointed to the Military Academy and was graduated in 1855, ranking second in the class. Commissioned in the Engineer Corps, he was detailed, for the next four

years, to the construction and repair of the fortifications guarding the approaches to New Orleans. From 1859 until 1861 he was on duty at West Point as assistant professor of engineering. After discharging some relatively minor responsibilities, he was appointed chief engineer of General Benjamin F. Butler's expedition against New Orleans in the spring of 1862. After the occupation of the city, Butler made Weitzel his second in command and acting mayor, and on August 29, 1862, he was promoted to brigadier general of volunteers. Weitzel commanded a division under N. P. Banks at the siege of Port Hudson in 1863 and the following year returned to the East to become chief engineer of Butler's Army of the James operating against Petersburg. He was brevetted a major general of volunteers (August 29, 1864) and subsequently was assigned to the successive commands of the XVIII and XXV Corps—the latter was composed of entirely Negro infantry. On November 17, 1864, he was made a full-rank major general. In December he again acted as second in command to Butler, this time in the first attack on Fort Fisher. The failure of this encounter could hardly be charged to Weitzel, but it did link him to a certain extent with Butler, who was shortly relieved. Nevertheless, during the final operations of the war which culminated in the breaking of R. E. Lee's line on April 2, 1865, Weitzel commanded all the troops north of the Appomattox River and on April 3 electrified the nation with his brief telegram: "We entered Richmond at eight o'clock this morning." After he was mustered out of volunteer service in March, 1866, Weitzel reverted for a time to his regular rank of captain of engineers, but was promoted to major in August, a grade which he would occupy for sixteen years. General Weitzel's most notable engineering accomplishments in the years following the war were the construction of the ship canal at the Falls of the Ohio, the great lock at Sault Sainte Marie, and the lighthouse on Stannard's Rock in Lake Superior, thirty miles off the Upper Michigan shore. He was promoted to lieutenant colonel in 1882, but declining health dictated his assignment to less arduous duties in Philadelphia, where he died on March 19, 1884. He was buried in Spring Grove Cemetery, Cincinnati.

William Wells was born in Waterbury, Vermont, on December 14, 1837. He was educated in academies in Vermont and New Hampshire and then became a merchant in Burlington, Vermont. At the outbreak of the Civil War, contrary to Southern tradition which de-

nominated all Yankees "mudsills," Wells enlisted as a private in the only cavalry regiment raised in Vermont during the war. He ultimately became the sixth colonel (of seven) of the regiment and enjoyed a notable career, despite the fact that his New England farm boys were roughly handled initially by the Confederates. The regiment's first active service was in the Shenandoah Valley under the command of General N. P. Banks; later it participated in the Second Bull Run campaign—in neither operation did the Federal cavalry distinguish itself. The 1st Vermont Cavalry was in the field during the

Gettysburg campaign as part of Farnsworth's brigade; thereafter, it was attached to the Army of the Potomac. By this time Wells had risen to major. The next action seen by the command was in Judson Kilpatrick's Richmond raid which gave rise to the celebrated Dahlgren controversy. (737) Wells succeeded to the command of the regiment after its previous leader had been killed at Salem Church on June 3, 1864, in the course of U. S. Grant's Richmond campaign. From the beginning of this campaign until the end of the war, Wells followed the fortunes of Philip Sheridan, accompanying the latter into the Shenandoah Valley in August and fighting at Winchester and Cedar Creek, where he commanded the 2nd Brigade of Custer's division. Wells continued on this duty throughout the closing operations at the Petersburg front and in the Appomattox campaign. He was brevetted both brigadier and major general toward the end of the war and on May 19 was appointed a full-rank brigadier general of volunteers. Mustered out early in 1866, he served as adjutant general of Vermont until 1872, then was collector of internal revenue for thirteen years, and was a member of the state senate in 1886-87. General Wells died in New York City on April 29, 1892, and was buried in Lake View Cemetery, Burlington.

Thomas Welsh was born on May 5, 1824, in Columbia, Pennsylvania. He was educated in the town's public schools and soon became interested in the lumber business of which Columbia was then an important center. (738) He entered the Mexican War as a private in the

2nd Kentucky Regiment, was promoted to first sergeant, was severely wounded at Buena Vista while serving under Zachary Taylor, subsequently took part in Winfield Scott's campaign against the city of Mexico as a second lieutenant of the 11th U. S. Infantry, and was discharged in 1848. In the years before the Civil War, Welsh had prospered as a merchant, canalboat owner, justice of the peace, and lock superintendent at Columbia. He recruited a company of the 11th Pennsylvania (a ninety-day command) in a matter of hours one evening in April, 1861, became its lieutenant colonel, and, after its muster out in July, was appointed colonel of the 45th Pennsylvania on October 21, 1861. He went to Charleston Harbor in 1862, commanding a brigade of H. G. Wright's division there in June, but he soon was returned to the Army of the Potomac, and at South Mountain and Sharpsburg Welsh commanded the 2nd Brigade of Orlando B. Willcox's division of Ambrose E. Burnside's IX Corps (the brigade had little to do with the storming of "Burnside's Bridge" over Antietam Creek, however). At Fredericksburg, Welsh was again in command of the 45th Pennsylvania, despite the fact that he had been promoted brigadier general of volunteers on November 29, 1862. He went to Cincinnati the following April for assignment by Burnside, who was then commanding in the Department of the Ohio, but in the meantime Welsh's appointment as brigadier had expired for want of Senate confirmation. He was reappointed, however, on March 23 to rank from March 13, 1863, and appears to have been duly confirmed. In the operations incidental to Burnside's defense of his far-flung department, Welsh was assigned to command of the 1st Division of the IX Corps, but in the course of the Vicksburg campaign contracted some form of malarial fever which caused his death in Cincinnati on August 14, 1863. He was buried in Mount Bethel Cemetery, Columbia.

Henry Walton Wessells was born on February 20, 1809, in the Berkshire village of Litchfield, Connecticut. He was graduated from West Point at the age of twenty-four, and then served for three years against the Florida Seminoles. In the Mexican War he was brevetted major and later was presented with a jeweled sword by his state for gallantry at the battles of Contreras and Churubusco. During the next fourteen years he served without promotion on the Pacific Coast and in the Dakotas and Kansas. His first Civil

War duty was as colonel of the 8th Kansas Infantry on the Missouri border, but in March, 1862, he was transferred east to the Army of the Potomac and on April 25 became a brigadier general of volunteers. In the Peninsular campaign, where he was wounded slightly at Seven Pines, he commanded a brigade of Keyes's IV Corps. He was stationed at Suffolk that autumn and then took part in the operations in North Carolina. On May 3, 1863, he became commander of the District of the Albemarle and a year later had the misfortune to be garrisoning the town of Plymouth, North Carolina, when he was assailed and forced to surrender by the Rebel forces of General Robert F. Hoke. This action resulted in Hoke's becoming one of the youngest major generals in Confederate service, (739) and Wessells' becoming a prisoner of war for four months. After his exchange General Wessells acted for a time as commissary of prisoners and then as commandant of a New York draft rendezvous. At the end of the war he was brevetted brigadier general in the Regular Army and later in 1865 became lieutenant colonel of the 18th U. S. Infantry. Stationed on the Indian frontier for a time, he was on retirement and recruiting service until he was retired at his own request in 1871. He returned to the town of his birth and died on January 12, 1889, in Dover, Delaware. He was buried in the cemetery at Litchfield.

Joseph Rodman West was born on September 19, 1822, in New Orleans, Louisiana, but in early childhood was taken by his parents to

Philadelphia, where he was educated in private schools and attended the University of Pennsylvania in 1836-37. He returned to New Orleans in 1841, but during the Mexican War was a captain of the Maryland and District of Columbia volunteers. In 1849 he went to California and engaged in newspaper work, becoming proprietor of the San Francisco *Price Current*. With the outbreak of the Civil War, West was commissioned lieutenant colonel of James Henry Carleton's 1st California Volunteers and took part in the recapture of Arizona and New Mexico from the Confederates. He succeeded Carleton as colonel of the regiment in June, 1862, and was promoted to brigadier general on October 25, 1862. The following January he led an expedition against a group of the Apache nation in which one of its most celebrated chiefs Mangas Coloradas was killed. He commanded the District of Arizona in 1863 and during the Red River campaign was in charge of a division of the VII Corps in Arkansas. He continued on duty in Arkansas under the command of General Frederick Steele and took a minor part in the operations against Confederate General Sterling Price in the autumn of 1864. (740) The end of the war found him in command of all the cavalry in the Department of the Gulf stationed at New Orleans and Baton Rouge. He was brevetted major general of volunteers on January 4, 1866, the same day that he was mustered out of military service at San Antonio, Texas. General West then returned to New Orleans, was a deputy United States marshal, auditor for customs 1867-71, and in the latter year was elected to the U. S. Senate as a Republican. After home rule was restored in the state, "he was not a candidate for reelection" in 1876. (741) From 1882 to 1885 he was a member of the board of commissioners of the District of Columbia. He died on October 31, 1898, in Washington and was buried in Arlington National Cemetery.

Frank Wheaton, whose father-in-law was ranking general of the Confederacy Samuel Cooper, was born on May 8, 1833, at Providence, Rhode Island. He left

Brown University at the age of seventeen in order to take a job with the Mexican-American Boundary Commission, where he worked for five years. In 1855 he was commissioned directly into the 1st U. S. Cavalry (now 4th Cavalry) as a first lieutenant and saw considerable service on the Indian frontier. The outbreak of the Civil War found the family impossibly divided in sentiment: Wheaton's father-in-law, a native of Dutchess County, New York, was adjutant general of the army; his mother-in-law was a sister of Senator James

Murray Mason of Virginia, who as a Confederate commissioner would become even more celebrated as the Mason of the Mason and Slidell affair which brought England and the United States to the brink of war. Cooper sided with his wife's family; his daughter sided with her husband. The die being cast, Wheaton became lieutenant colonel of the 2nd Rhode Island Infantry, which fought at First Manassas and lost its colonel, Wheaton succeeding to command as of July 21, 1861. In the campaign on the Virginia Peninsula, the 2nd Rhode Island was in Keyes's IV Corps; and at Williamsburg, Wheaton was commended for his conduct. On November 29, 1862, he was promoted to brigadier general of volunteers and assigned to a brigade of the VI Corps with which he was connected until the war's end. He was present at Fredericksburg in December, 1862, and again the following May when John Sedgwick carried Marye's Heights during the campaign of Chancellorsville. Wheaton remained in command of his brigade while U. S. Grant slugged his way through the Wilderness to the defenses of Petersburg, and then, in command of a division, Wheaton was hurried to Washington to repel the attack of Jubal Early's raiders on the capital. During the ensuing operations in the Shenandoah under Philip Sheridan and after the return of the VI Corps to the Petersburg front, Wheaton earned the brevets of major general in the volunteer and regular services. He was mustered out of the volunteers in 1866, becoming lieutenant colonel of the 39th Infantry the same year. In 1873 he commanded the expedition against the Modocs in the Lava Beds of northern California. (This expedition later resulted in the assassination of General Edward R. S. Canby, who had gone there to negotiate with them.) (742) Wheaton was appointed colonel of the 2nd Infantry in 1874; brigadier general, U. S. Army, in 1892; and major general in 1897. He died in Washington on June 18, 1903, and was buried in Arlington National Cemetery.

Amiel Weeks Whipple was born on October 15, 1816, in Greenwich, Massachusetts, a village subsequently inundated by the construction of the Quabbin Reservoir in

the 1930's. He sought appointment to the Military Academy as early as 1834, meantime teaching school and studying at Amherst as an undergraduate. He was eventually appointed to West Point in 1837 and was graduated in 1841,

ranking fifth in the class which contributed twenty-two general officers to the contending armies in the Civil War. Whipple, as an officer of topographical engineers in the years before 1861, was occupied in the survey of the United States-Canadian boundary and subsequently with that of the boundary between the United States and Mexico. In the 1850's he surveyed a railroad route to California through Arizona Territory, and, when the territory was formally established in 1863, its seat of government was named Fort Whipple, or Whipple Barracks, in his honor. In the late 1850's Whipple was employed in removing obstacles to navigation in the Great Lakes, particularly in the St. Mary's River. When the war came, he served on Irvin McDowell's staff as chief topographical engineer at the battle of First Manassas and subsequently commanded a brigade and division in the defenses of Washington. He was commissioned brigadier general of volunteers on April 14, 1862. In October, 1862, preparatory to the campaign of Fredericksburg, Whipple was assigned to the direction of the 3rd Division of the III Corps in Joseph Hooker's "Center Grand Division," but the division was not closely engaged, one of its brigades sustaining only nominal losses. During the fighting in the tangled woodland around Chancellorsville on May 4, 1863, Whipple was sitting on his horse, writing an order to dislodge a Rebel sharpshooter who was annoying nearby officers, when a ball from the same marksman's rifle struck him in the stomach and passed out near his spine. (743) He died in Washington on May 7, and was buried in South Cemetery, Portsmouth, New Hampshire, the home of his wife. He was appointed major general on the day of his death to rank from May 3.

William Denison Whipple was born in the Madison County, New York, hamlet of Nelson on August 2, 1826. He was appointed to West Point in 1847 and was graduated in

1851, ranking toward the bottom of the class (a low standing belied by his future assignments). He performed routine duty on the Indian frontier in New Mexico and Texas and in 1861 was on quartermaster duty at Indianola, Texas, when that post was captured by the Texas insurgents. He escaped through the enemy's lines and made his way east in time to participate in the battle of First Manassas as assistant adjutant general of Hunter's division. Whipple served as a staff officer during and after the Civil War and was successively promoted to captain, major, brigadier general of volunteers (on July 17, 1863), and colonel. He also won the brevet of major general, U. S. Army, for gallant and meritorious services in the field during the rebellion. He discharged duty in the Departments of Pennsylvania and Virginia, the Middle Military Department, the VIII Corps, and sundry other posts. On November 12, 1863, he became assistant adjutant general of the army and Department of the Cumberland and the following month was appointed G. H. Thomas' chief of staff. In the latter capacity he took part in all the operations of the Chattanooga and Atlanta campaigns and the movements which arrested John B. Hood's invasion of Tennessee at Franklin and Nashville. He continued with Thomas after the war, until the latter's death in San Francisco in 1870, when Whipple returned to Washington to take a post in the adjutant general's office. On January 1, 1873, General Whipple was appointed aide-de-camp to General-in-Chief of the army W. T. Sherman, a capacity in which he served for five years. From 1878 until his retirement in 1890 he was adjutant general of the Division of the Missouri, the Division of the Atlantic, and the Department of the East. Thereafter he took up residence in New York City, where he died on April 1, 1902. He was buried in Arlington National Cemetery.

Walter Chiles Whitaker was born on August 8, 1823, in Shelbyville, Kentucky. He was educated at Bethany College, (West) Virginia, and had begun to study law when

hostilities with Mexico caused his enlistment in the 3rd Kentucky Infantry with which he served as second lieutenant. After the war he practiced criminal law in Shelbyville, operated a large farm, and, like virtually all lawyers of the day, engaged in politics. As a member of the state senate in 1861, he offered the resolution which put the state on the side of the Federal government and terminated Kentucky's posture of "neutrality" between North and South. In December, 1861, he entered the Union army as colonel of the 6th Kentucky (Union) Infantry and fought at Shiloh the following spring as a part of D. C. Buell's Army of the Ohio, which arrived in time to turn the tide of battle in favor of the Union on the second day. Whitaker and his regiment were not present at Perryville, but at Murfreesboro in December, 1862, were heavily engaged. He was advanced to brigadier general of volunteers

on June 25, 1863, and at the battle of Chickamauga commanded the 1st Brigade of Steedman's division of Granger's Reserve Corps, which by marching to the sound of the guns preserved a large part of W. S. Rosecrans' forces from destruction. He continued in command of a brigade at Chattanooga and during the Atlanta campaign in Stanley's division of the IV Corps. Whitaker was wounded at Chattanooga and, after John B. Hood's repulse in the battles around Atlanta and withdrawal toward Tennessee, his command accompanied G. H. Thomas northwestward. Whitaker fought at Franklin and Nashville, commanding a brigade of the IV Corps, and in August, 1865, was mustered out of service, meantime having been brevetted major general of volunteers for services in the Atlanta campaign to rank from March 13, 1865. At the end of the war he resumed the practice of law in Louisville and was connected with a number of criminal trials which added little to his legal reputation. He seems to have been a "man of ardent spirit" who also sought solace in "ardent spirits." (744) During some of his postbellum years he was confined to a mental institution. However, he is said to have died in full possession of his faculties in Lyndon, Kentucky, on July 9, 1887, and was buried in Grove Hill Cemetery, Shelbyville.

Julius White was born on September 23, 1816, in Cazenovia, New York. He moved to Illinois at the age of twenty and seems to have engaged in a variety of commercial pursuits both in Illinois and Wisconsin. In 1849 he was a member of the Wisconsin legislature, and,

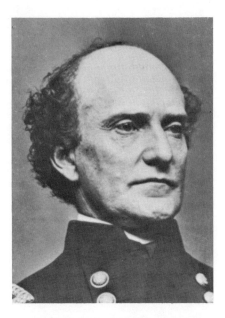

upon the inauguration of Abraham Lincoln in 1861, White was appointed collector of customs in Chicago, where he was then living. He resigned this post to become colonel of the 37th Illinois Infantry, a regiment which he had recruited in the Chicago area, called the "Frémont Rifles." At the battle of Elkhorn Tavern (Pea Ridge) he commanded a brigade in Jefferson C. Davis' division and on June 9, 1862, was promoted to brigadier general. The following September he was involved in the surrender of Harpers Ferry during Robert E. Lee's invasion of Maryland. White, ignorant of the terrain and its defenders, had offered to waive rank so that Colonel Dixon Miles, an old Regular, could continue in command. The latter's defense of the position was substandard, according to any critique, and freed Stonewall Jackson's troops to turn the tide at Sharpsburg in the nick of time to avert a Confederate catastrophe. White was subsequently put in arrest, but, when the examining commission published their findings, was not only exonerated but commended for "decided capability and courage." (745) In January, 1863, he was assigned to duty in the Department of the Ohio and under General Ambrose E. Burnside commanded a division of the XXIII Corps at Knoxville in the autumn of 1863. After Burnside's recall to the Army of the Potomac in the spring of 1864, White served as his chief of staff until the Petersburg Mine disaster. When Burnside left the army, White was given command of the 1st Division of the IX Corps (this division was later broken up and its regiments distributed to the 2nd and 3rd Divisions). Shortly after, General White went on sick leave and apparently did not rejoin the army. His resignation was accepted by the War Department on November 19, 1864; however, as of March 13, 1865, he was brevetted major general—a rather unusual circumstance and a testimonial to the esteem in which he must have been held by his superiors. In the years after the war White seems to have enjoyed only modest financial success; however, he was active in the Military Order of the Loyal Legion and for a time served as its Illinois commander. He died in Evanston, Illinois, on May 12, 1890, and was buried in Rosehill Cemetery, Chicago. (746)

Edward Augustus Wild was born on November 25, 1825, in Brookline, Massachusetts. He was graduated from Harvard in 1844 and from the Jefferson Medical College soon after; he then took a course of med-

557

ical lectures in Paris and during the Crimean War served as a surgeon in the Sultan's forces. He returned to Brookline and practiced his profession until the outbreak of the Civil War. At this juncture, foregoing medical duty, he enlisted in the 1st Massachusetts Infantry and became

captain of one of its companies on May 23, 1861. He was present at First Bull Run, although his brigade (Richardson's) was only slightly engaged at Blackburn's Ford and sustained but one casualty; however, in George B. McClellan's Peninsular campaign Wild was severely wounded at Seven Pines. He was honorably mustered out of the 1st Massachusetts and on August 21, 1862, was remustered as colonel of the 35th Massachusetts, which he led in September at South Mountain where he lost his left arm. On April 24, 1863, he was commissioned brigadier general of volunteers. After recovering from his wound, Wild, who was a zealous abolitionist, assisted in recruiting the regiments of Negro troops known as "Wild's African Brigade," which he commanded until the close of the war. These troops were recruited and organized at New Bern, North Carolina, and on June 30, 1863, numbered 950. They joined Quincy Gillmore in Charleston Harbor in September but subsequently were sent to the Norfolk and Portsmouth area, where Wild commanded all the Negro troops in the vicinity. His brigade fought at Cold Harbor in Hinks's division of "Baldy" Smith's XVIII Corps, but later rejoined the X Corps and performed picket duty on the Appomattox River. At the end of the war his brigade occupied Richmond as part of Kautz's division of Weitzel's XXV Corps. Wild was mustered out in January, 1866. He became interested in silver mining and was superintendent of a Nevada mine for a time before going to South America. General Wild died August 28, 1891, in Medellín, Colombia, and was buried there in the Cementerio de San Pedro.

Orlando Bolivar Willcox was born in Detroit, Michigan, on April 16, 1823. Destined for a career in the army, he was graduated from West Point in 1847. He was briefly detailed to garrison duty in Mexico City and Cuernavaca at the close of the Mexican War and then was on duty at various points including stations in New Mexico, Massachusetts, and Florida. Willcox resigned his commission in 1857 to practice law in Detroit, but returned to the army in 1861 as colonel of the 1st Michigan Infantry. At the battle of First Manassas he was

wounded and captured while in command of a brigade of Heintzelman's division; he remained a prisoner for more than a year, part of the time as a hostage for Rebel privateersmen whom the Federal authorities had threatened to hang as pirates. On the day of his release (August 19, 1862), he was commissioned a brigadier general of volunteers to rank from the date of the battle in which he had been captured the previous year and given command of the 1st Division to Ambrose E. Burnside's IX Corps. He led a division, and sometimes the corps itself, at Sharpsburg, Fredericksburg, Knoxville, and during Grant's Overland campaign against Richmond in the summer of 1864. When Burnside left the Army of the Potomac after the debacle at The Crater in August, Willcox might presumedly have been his logical successor in command of the corps, but John G. Parke, who was chief of staff of the

corps and a major general, received the post, and Willcox continued to command his division until the close of the war. (747) He was brevetted major general in both the Regulars and volunteers and in 1895 was awarded the Congressional medal for "most distinguished gallantry" at the battle of Manassas thirty-four years before. He was mustered out of service in January, 1866, and returned to Detroit to resume his law practice, but upon the enlargement of the Regular Army in July was reappointed as colonel of the 29th Infantry. He transferred to the 12th Infantry in 1869 and served at San Francisco almost continuously until 1878, when he assumed command of the Department of Arizona during a period when the Apache warfare was at its height. He remained in this post until 1882 and as a consequence of his service here the town of Willcox, Arizona, was named for him (748) In 1886 he was promoted to brigadier general, U. S. Army, and in 1887 was retired. Two years later he did a tour of duty as governor of the Soldiers' Home at Washington. General Willcox remained in Washington for a time, but in 1905 moved to Coburg, Ontario, where he died on May 10, 1907, at the age of eighty-four; he was buried in Arlington National Cemetery. He was the author of two novels published under the pseudonym "Major Walter March."

Alpheus Starkey Williams was born on September 20, 1810, in Saybrook, Connecticut. He was graduated from Yale University in 1831 and studied law for three years, meantime traveling extensively throughout the United States.

From 1834 until 1836 he traveled abroad and then he opened a law office in Detroit. In the 1840's he was successively probate judge, newspaper owner, lieutenant colonel of a Michigan regiment in the Mexican War, and postmaster of Detroit. Upon the outbreak of the

Civil War, he was president of the state military board and brigadier general of state volunteers. He was commissioned as brigadier general in the United States service on August 9, 1861, to rank from May 17, and during the Shenandoah Valley campaign of 1862 and the battle of Cedar Mountain he commanded a division of N. P. Banks's troops, which became the II Corps of John Pope's Army of Virginia. After Second Manassas, in which the corps was not actively engaged, it was renamed the XII Corps of the Army of the Potomac and assigned to the direction of J. K. F. Mansfield. When the latter was killed at Sharpsburg, Williams was

in command for a time but was soon superseded by Henry Slocum— apparently the intention of the authorities was to give corps direction only to Regular Army officers. Williams did well at Chancellorsville and Gettysburg, went to the West after Chickamauga, and when the XI and XII Corps were consolidated into the XX Corps, received a division in this corps which was now in the Army of the Cumberland. He fought in command of his division and the corps throughout the Atlanta campaign, in the "March to the Sea," and the campaign of the Carolinas, but seems always to have been eventually superseded in corps command, first by Slocum and later by Joseph A. Mower. He was never accorded the substantive grade of major general, although he was brevetted as such to take rank from January 12, 1866. In 1866 he was appointed minister resident to the Republic of Salvador, a position he held for three years. In 1870 he ran unsuccessfully for governor of Michigan as a Democrat, but in 1874 was elected to Congress and in 1876 reelected. He died in Washington during his second term on December 21, 1878, and was buried in Elmwood Cemetery, Detroit. His collected letters, *From the Cannon's Mouth: The Civil War Letters of General Alpheus S. Williams,* edited by M. M. Quaife, were published in 1959.

David Henry Williams was born on a farm in Otsego County, New York, (749) March 19, 1819. After obtaining a rudimentary education in the schools of the neighborhood, he studied civil engineering and at the age of eighteen went to Detroit, where he was a railroad surveyor for the next decade. According to his obituary he took part in the Mexican War, although he does not appear in F. B. Heitman's *Histori-*

cal Register as an officer. He later moved to Pittsburgh, where he practiced his profession and became interested in militia matters, for, soon after the outbreak of the Civil War, he was commissioned colonel of the 82nd Pennsylvania, a regiment called the 31st Pennsylvania until the termination of the campaign of 1862 on the Peninsula. (750) The regiment was engaged at Seven Pines and lost quite heavily at Malvern Hill, where it was in Couch's division of Keyes's IV Corps. Williams' command sustained nominal losses in the course of the Maryland campaign, which culminated in the battle of Sharpsburg (the most savage, single day fight of the Civil War); after this battle Darius

N. Couch's old division was assigned to the VI Corps. At Fredericksburg in December, Williams' regiment was in Cochrane's brigade of Newton's division—the brigade sustaining only twenty-four casualties in its six regiments. Meantime he had been promoted to brigadier general of volunteers on November 29, 1862, but apparently the commission was not forwarded, since on January 31, 1863, he was commander of the 82nd Pennsylvania in the division now commanded by Charles Devens. (751) This was his last appearance in the *Official Records,* and as of March 4, 1863, his appointment expired by law, the Senate failing to act upon his nomination. He then returned to Pittsburgh and resumed his profession of engineer, a career which was soon terminated by the failure of his health. For many years an invalid, he wrote prolifically for magazines and newspapers. He died in Allegheny (now Pittsburgh) on June 1, 1891, and was buried in Allegheny Cemetery.

Nelson Grosvenor Williams was born in Bainbridge, New York, a village near the headwaters of the Susquehanna River, on May 4, 1823. While a small boy he moved with his parents to Utica, where he grew up. He entered the Military Academy in 1839, but withdrew in July, 1840, "for deficiency in mathematics." (752) He later engaged in the importing business in New York City, but in 1855 moved to Dubuque, Iowa, where he conducted a general store for a time; then he settled on a farm in Dyersville, Iowa. Williams was commissioned colonel of the 3rd Iowa Infantry on June 26, 1861, and served

under Stephen A. Hurlbut that summer in Missouri, taking part in several unimportant movements in the northern part of the state. At Shiloh he directed a brigade of Hurlbut's division and was severely injured when a cannonball struck his horse, hurling the animal to the ground on top of him. He was paralyzed for a number of weeks, and consequently resigned his commission on November 27, 1862. Meantime Hurlbut had applied for his promotion to brigadier general, and he was appointed on November 29, 1862. Because he was no longer in service, the Senate refused the appointment on March 9, 1863. In the interim Williams had returned to his Iowa farm, where he continued to reside until 1869, when President Grant, a former classmate at West Point, appointed him a deputy collector of customs in New York City. He continued in this position until his death twenty-eight years later, at which time "he had charge of the public stores in

Laight St." (753) General Williams died at his residence in Brooklyn on November 30, 1897, and was buried in Green-Wood Cemetery. (754)

Seth Williams was born on March 22, 1822 in Augusta, Maine. After obtaining his early education at the local academy, he received an appointment to West Point and was graduated in 1842. After some routine garrison duty, he served through the entire Mexican War as aide-de-camp to General Robert Patterson and was brevetted captain for gallantry at Cerro Gordo. He was the "efficient and favorite" adjutant of the Military Academy from 1850 to 1853, and in the latter year formally transferred to the adjutant general's department, where he served the rest of his life. He became major in August, 1861, and brigadier general of volunteers on September 23. From then until March, 1864, Williams was adjutant general of the Army of the Po-

tomac, performing his duties in an eminently satisfactory manner on the successive staffs of such opposed personalities as George B. McClellan, Ambrose E. Burnside, Joseph Hooker, and George G. Meade. When U. S. Grant as general-in-chief chose to make his headquarters with the Army of the Potomac, shortly before the commencement of the Richmond campaign, he selected Williams to be his inspector general, a capacity in which he served until February 9, 1866. He was then assigned as adjutant general of the Military Division of the Atlantic, with headquarters at Philadelphia. Meantime he had been brevetted through grades to that of major general in both the regular and volunteer services. (He won the brevet of major general of volunteers as early as August, 1864.) Toward the end of February, 1866, he became ill and went to his sister's home in Boston, where he died on March 23 of "congestion of the brain." (755) His body was taken to Augusta for interment in Forest Grove Cemetery.

Thomas Williams was born on January 10, 1815, in Albany, New York. His father, one of Detroit's earliest settlers, had moved his family to Albany during the troubles incident to the War of 1812. The elder Williams was a militia general and during the Black Hawk War his son served as a private under him. In 1833 young Williams was appointed to West Point and in 1837 was graduated as an artillery subaltern. During the next seven years Williams discharged a variety of tasks which included service against the Florida Seminoles, gar-

rison duty, and a tour at the Military Academy as an instructor. From 1844 to 1850 he was aide-de-camp to General-in-Chief Winfield Scott and was brevetted captain and major for gallantry in the Mexican War. During the next decade he

was stationed in garrison at several points and also saw further service against the Seminoles and in the West. He was at the Artillery School for Practice at Fort Monroe, when the Civil War broke out in 1861. On May 14 he became major of the 5th Artillery and on September 28 brigadier general of volunteers. After briefly acting as inspector general of the Department of Virginia and commanding his old regiment in Philadelphia, he took part in Ambrose E. Burnside's North Carolina expedition in October, 1861, and was in command of Fort Hatteras until March, 1862. He was then assigned to a brigade of Benjamin F. Butler's forces for the land operations against New Orleans. After the Lower Mississippi was opened and New Orleans occupied, Williams and his brigade were detailed to the occupation of Baton Rouge. Under orders from Butler he made an abortive effort to isolate Vicksburg from the Mississippi by digging a canal across the neck of land opposite. (756) On August 5, 1862, he was back in Baton Rouge, where he was assailed by the forces of John C. Breckinridge, who was endeavoring to recapture the town. While conducting a most competent and successful defense of his position with greatly inferior numbers, Williams was killed by a rifle ball in the chest. Some three weeks later he was buried in the family lot in Elmwood Cemetery, Detroit. (757)

James Alexander Williamson was born on February 8, 1829, in Adair County, Kentucky, but was taken to Indiana at the age of three, and to Keokuk County, Iowa, when he was fifteen. He was graduated from

Knox College in Galesburg, Illinois, and then returned to Lancaster, Iowa, where he studied law and began a practice. About 1854 he went to Des Moines and the next year was one of the leaders in the movement which moved the state capital from Iowa City to Des Moines. Until the Civil War, Williamson was a staunch Democrat, serving as chairman of the State Democratic Committee and as a delegate to the 1860 Baltimore convention which nominated Stephen A. Douglas for the presidency. During the war he rose from first lieutenant to brevet major general of volunteers, despite the fact that he had no previous military experience of any kind. (His promotions were a result of his fearlessness and eagerness to learn.) After a few months service as adjutant of the 4th Iowa, whose colonel was Grenville M. Dodge, Williamson was elected lieutenant colonel of the regiment in April, 1862, and became its colonel in July. He was appointed brigadier general on April 1, 1865, to rank from January 13 and brevetted major general as of March 13, 1865. Meanwhile, he fought at Elkhorn Tavern under Samuel R. Curtis; garrisoned Helena, Arkansas, during the summer and fall of 1862; and participated in the hard fighting at Chickasaw Bayou under W. T. Sherman, the subsequent capture of Arkansas Post under John A. McClernand, and the Vicksburg campaign, where his regiment was part of Steele's division of Sherman's XV Corps. Before the surrender of Vicksburg, Williamson was compelled to take a leave of absence because of his health, but upon return to duty was assigned to the command of a brigade, which he led in the Chattanooga campaign including the engagement on Lookout Mountain and the storming of Missionary Ridge. During the Atlanta and Savannah campaigns he directed the 2nd Brigade of Osterhaus' division. Soon after the capture of Savannah Williamson returned to Iowa and, during the summer of 1865, served under General Grenville M. Dodge in command of the District of Missouri and in fighting Indians. He was mustered out in November, 1865. Williamson was wounded five times during the war, was repeatedly recommended for promotion, and won the universal approbation of his superiors. By the end of hostilities he had become an active Republican and in 1868 was a delegate to the Republican National Convention. The same year he became associated with the promotion of the Union Pacific Railroad and subsequently interested himself in western lands. From 1876 to 1881 he was commissioner of the General Land Office and in the latter year became land commissioner of the Atlantic & Pacific Railroad (predecessor of the Santa Fe). He was president of this railway when he retired in 1892. General Williamson died at his summer home in Jamestown, Rhode Island, on September 7, 1902, and was buried in Rock Creek Cemetery, Georgetown, D. C. (758)

August (von) Willich was born in the Prussian city of Braunsberg on November 19, 1810. His father had fought in the Napoleonic Wars, and young Willich entered the cadet house at Potsdam at the age of twelve and the military academy at Berlin at fifteen. He was a first

lieutenant in the Prussian army at eighteen and a captain at twenty-one. When the disorders of 1846-48 swept Europe, Willich eagerly embraced the teachings of Karl Marx, was permitted to resign from the army after a court-martial, learned the trade of carpenter, and in 1848 after fighting in Baden fled Germany with the collapse of the revolt against the monarchy. He came to the United States in 1853 and secured employment as a carpenter in the Brooklyn Navy Yard. An ardent communist, he was appointed editor of a German-language labor newspaper in Cincinnati in 1858 by the workers' party for whom he fronted. Paradoxically enough, after his induction into the Federal army in 1861, he became one of the premier officers and disciplinarians in the service and in 1870 would offer his services to the King of Prussia, whom he had attempted to overthrow in 1848, to fight the French of Napoleon III.

Willich recruited a great number of Germans (reportedly fifteen hundred) in a matter of days after the outbreak of the Civil War, and, after some service with the 9th Ohio, he was commissioned colonel of the 32nd Indiana by Governor Oliver P. Morton, who was seeking a commander for a German regiment raised in that state. Virtually every one of his associates agreed that Willich was daft: he was elderly, spoke English with a strong East Prussian accent, and expected that his men would perform the evolutions of drill in answer to bugle calls. To the surprise of everyone, they did this, not only on the parade ground but also on the battlefield, where their commander was invariably found in front of his line of battle. Willich distinguished himself at Shiloh and Perryville and at Murfreesboro was captured on the first day of the battle after his horse was killed under him. By this time he was a brigadier general, ranking from July 17, 1862. He was paroled and exchanged in time to take part in the fight at Chickamauga, commanding a brigade of Alexander McD. McCook's XX Corps. At the commencement of W. T. Sherman's campaign against Atlanta, Willich was wounded by a rifle ball in the shoulder at Resaca, but upon his recovery was assigned to command of the combined post of Cincinnati, Covington (Kentucky), and Newport Barracks, Kentucky, where he served until the end of the war. (759) He was brevetted major general to rank from October 21, 1865. Thereafter, General Willich was county auditor at Cincinnati for three years, but he was unable to resist the patriotic lure of a war be-

tween his mother country and France and crossed the Atlantic to offer his services to William I of Germany (they were politely declined on the grounds of age). He remained in Berlin for a time, attending lectures by Karl Marx. General Willich later returned to the United States and took up residence in St. Mary's, Ohio, his final home. He died there on January 22, 1878, and was buried in Elmwood Cemetery.

James Harrison Wilson, perhaps the most distinguished of the "boy generals" of the Civil War, was born on September 2, 1837, on his father's farm near Shawneetown,

Illinois. (The elder Wilson was a native of Virginia and a relative of the James River Harrisons.) After a year at McKendree College in St. Clair County, young Wilson matriculated at West Point in 1855, then a five-year course, and was graduated in 1860 ranking sixth in

the class. Three of its members, Wilson, Wesley Merritt, and Stephen D. Ramseur, would become major generals within the next five years and a fourth, James M. Warner, brigadier general. Until the outbreak of the Civil War, Wilson served as assistant topographical engineer of the Department of Oregon at Fort Vancouver. During the winter of 1861-62 he was chief topographical engineer of the Port Royal expedition and of the Department of the South; in the latter capacity he took part in the reduction of Fort Pulaski at the mouth of the Savannah River. He acted as aide-de-camp to General George B. McClellan during the Maryland campaign in the fall of 1862 and was present at South Mountain and Sharpsburg. Soon after, Wilson joined U. S. Grant's headquarters in the West with rank of staff lieutenant colonel, but with primarily engineering duties. In the Vicksburg campaign he was inspector general of the Army of Tennessee and as such took part in all the battles before and after the siege and capitulation of the city. On October 30, 1863, he was made brigadier general of volunteers—the only officer ever promoted to troop command from Grant's regular staff. Wilson continued on staff duty during the battle of Chattanooga; was chief engineer of the force, under W. T. Sherman, which was sent to relieve Knoxville; and on February 17, 1864, was assigned as chief of the cavalry bureau in Washington. In this position he displayed his outstanding talent for organization and administration which, coupled with the tactical sense he was later to demonstrate, made him one of the war's foremost

figures. At the outset of the Richmond campaign, Grant had him assigned to command a division of Philip Sheridan's cavalry, which he led with boldness and skill in the numerous fights of that summer en route to Petersburg and in the Shenandoah Valley. Just before the battle of Cedar Creek in October, he was detached and ordered west again as chief of cavalry of Sherman's Military Division of the Mississippi, a post which placed him virtually on a par with Sheridan in the East. He prepared Judson Kilpatrick's men for the campaign from Atlanta to Savannah and then recruited, equipped, drilled, and organized the rest ot the cavalry in the western theater into a corps of seventeen thousand troops, which he commanded during the virtual destruction of John B. Hood's Army of Tennessee at Franklin and Nashville in November and December, 1864. The following spring Wilson overwhelmed Nathan B. Forrest at Selma, Alabama, dispersing the latter's forces, and then Wilson turned east, sweeping through the remnant of the Confederacy and whirling away its defenders in the greatest independent cavalry movement of the Civil War. He reached Macon, Georgia, on April 20, 1865, where hostilities virtually terminated. He was made a major general of volunteers on June 21 to rank from May 6 and was also brevetted major general in the Regular Army. With the army's reorganization of 1866 he became lieutenant colonel of the newly created 35th Infantry, but his duty assignments continued to be in the Corps of Engineers. He was honorably discharged at his own request in 1870 in order to engage in the construction and management of various railroad enterprises, and in 1883 he established a residence in Wilmington. During the next fifteen years he devoted his time to business, travel, and public affairs, meantime writing prolifically on a number of subjects. When the war with Spain broke out in 1898, Wilson immediately volunteered and served as a major general of volunteers in Puerto Rico and Cuba. He also took part in the Boxer Rebellion in China and in 1901 was placed on the retired list of the army as a brigadier general by special act of Congress. The following year he represented President Theodore Roosevelt at the coronation of Edward VII. General Wilson lived through the administrations of four more presidents; he died in Wilmington on February 23, 1925, and was buried in Old Swedes Churchyard. Only Generals Nelson A. Miles, John R. Brooke, and Adelbert Ames survived him of the 583 who held full-rank commissions during the Civil War.

Isaac Jones Wistar was born on November 14, 1827, in Philadelphia. He was educated at Haverford College, studied law, and commenced practice in his native city. At the outbreak of the Civil War he recruited a company of volunteers of which he was elected captain. This unit became a part of the 71st Pennsylvania, dubbed the "California Regiment" because former California Senator Edward D. Baker of Oregon had raised the force in Philadelphia by special authority of President Lincoln. Wistar was made its lieutenant colonel and was commanding it at Ball's Bluff in October, 1861, when Baker,

who was commanding the "Philadelphia brigade," was killed in one of the more abortive actions of the war. Wistar succeeded Baker as colonel, with commission from November 11, 1861, and reportedly took part in the Peninsular campaign of 1862 in Sedgwick's division of Sumner's II Corps, although at Seven Pines the regiment was recorded under the command of its major and during the Seven Days battles its lieutenant colonel. (760) At Sharpsburg the 71st Pennsylvania was in Howard's brigade, and the latter states in his report of the battle that Wistar "with his right arm nearly useless from a former wound, had his left disabled." (761) In May, 1863, he was assigned to command of the reserve brigade of Getty's division at Suffolk, having been commissioned brigadier general on March 16 to rank from the preceding November 29. He remained in this general area, participating in a series of minor operations, until the beginning of the Richmond campaign. In early May, 1864, he was in command of a brigade of W. F. Smith's XVIII Corps, Army of the James, (762) which took part in the unfortunate movement that resulted in the bottling up of Benjamin F. Butler on the Bermuda Hundred Neck, but on May 18 Wistar was succeeded in command by Colonel Griffin Stedman (after whom the famous Fort Stedman was later named). (763) At this juncture Wistar disappears from the *Official Records* and on September 15, 1864, his resignation was accepted by the War Department. In the years after the war he again practiced law and became prominent in the coal business. He also won distinction as a writer and speaker on penology. General Wistar died in Claymont, Delaware, on September 18, 1905, and was buried in Laurel Hill Cemetery, Philadelphia.

Thomas John Wood, whose second cousin was General Ben Hardin Helm of the Confederate Army, was born on September 25, 1823, in Munfordville, Kentucky. He obtained his early education in the village schools and then went to West Point, where he was graduated in the class of 1845. During the Mexican War he won a brevet for gallantry at Buena Vista and later was stationed in Mexico City. Although originally commissioned in the Corps of Topographical Engineers, he transferred to the cavalry in 1846 and accordingly saw much service on the Indian frontier. He became captain of the 1st Cavalry in 1855 and from 1859 to 1861 was on leave of absence in Europe. At the beginning of the Civil War he was engaged in mustering Indiana troops into Federal service and on October 11, 1861, was commissioned brigadier general of volunteers. Meantime a fortuitous series of resignations in the several cavalry regiments by officers "going South" propelled Wood from captain to colonel of the 2nd Cavalry in less than eight months. (764) He commanded a division of D. C. Buell's Army of the Ohio at Shiloh and Perryville; and at Murfreesboro in the last days of 1862 he especially distinguished himself while his three brigades of T. L. Crittenden's corps shored up the apex of a Federal line which at this point resembled an almost closed jackknife after the forcing back of Alexander McD. McCook's and G. H. Thomas' corps on the right. Wood was wounded on December 31, but refused to leave the field until the fighting for the day was over. At Chickamauga in September, 1863, the most controversial incident of his military career occurred. At the height of this furious and sanguinary battle one of W. S. Rosecrans' staff officers thought he detected a gap between the divisions of Wood and J. J. Reynolds (which belonged to different corps), although in fact John M. Brannan's division was in the interval, partially screened by woods. When the report was communicated to Rosecrans, he ordered Wood to close up on Reynolds and support him—an order which more than anything else doomed the Federal cause to disaster on that fatal day. Wood, who had been criticized earlier the same day by Rosecrans for not moving rapidly enough, failed to notify the army commander that Brannan was between him and Reynolds and, instead, pulled his division out of the line around the rear of Brannan, leaving a gap of more than a quarter mile into which the alert James Longstreet quickly hurled six Confederate divisions which all but demolished the Army of the Cumberland. Only Thomas' stout defense on Horseshoe Ridge to the north prevented an irretrievable catastrophe. Nevertheless, Rosecrans was removed and Wood was not held responsible for his alacrity to obey what must have struck him as a peculiar order. (765) Despite all this, his subsequent contribution to the Union cause was outstanding. His men were the first over the Confederate defenses on Missionary Ridge in November; and during the Atlanta campaign, at Lovejoy's Station on September 2, 1864, he went about the battlefield with a shattered leg, encouraging his men. In the later stages of John B. Hood's Tennessee campaign,

Wood was temporarily in command of the IV Corps and after the battle of Nashville pressed Hood's fleeing remnants. On February 22, 1865, Wood was made major general to rank from January 27. After the war he was on duty in Mississippi for a time, winning the approbation of its citizens for his humane administration. On June 9, 1868, he was retired from active service, for disability from wounds received in battle, as a major general He then took up a residence in Dayton, Ohio, his wife's home, and became a member of the Military Academy's Board of Visitors. The last survivor of the Academy's class of 1845, he died on February 25, 1906, in Dayton. General Wood was buried at West Point.

Daniel Phineas Woodbury was born on December 16, 1812, in New London, New Hampshire. He studied at nearby Hopkinton Academy and Dartmouth College, but left the latter in 1832 to enter West

Point. Upon his graduation in 1836, he was assigned to the 3rd Artillery but soon transferred to the engineer corps. For the next quarter-century he was engaged with a multiplicity of engineering projects, including the construction of the Cumberland Road in Ohio, Fort Warren in Boston Harbor, Forts Kearny and Laramie on the Oregon Trail, Fort Jefferson in the Dry Tortugas, and Fort Taylor at Key West. Meantime he became first lieutenant in 1838 and captain in 1853. The firing upon Fort Sumter in 1861 placed Woodbury in a most difficult position. He had married into a family with unbroken Southern antecedents on the maternal side and had, himself, invested heavily in property in Wilmington, North Carolina, where his wife's family was residing at the time of President Lincoln's call for volunteers. (766) He was besieged on all sides by pleas to resign from the Federal service and accept greatly augmented rank with the Confederacy. To all of this he turned a deaf ear and, by virtue of a special pass from Jefferson Davis, proceeded northward with his wife and children, his loyalty unshaken. In the campaign of First Manassas, Woodbury made the reconnaissance which determined Irvin McDowell's line of advance against the Confederate left flank and subsequently guided the divisions of Samuel P. Heintzelman and David Hunter to Sudley Springs Ford. He was promoted brigadier general of volunteers to rank from March 19, 1862, and in the Peninsular campaign directed George B. McClellan's brigade of engineer troops. At Fredericksburg he was in charge of laying the pontoon bridges across Rappahannock River and the following March was assigned to command of the District of Key West and Tortugas in the Department of the Gulf. He continued on this duty for the next eighteen months, succumbing to yellow fever at Key West on August 15, 1864. First buried there, his remains were later removed to Fort Barrancas National Cemetery, Pensacola. He was awarded the brevets of brigadier and major general, U. S. Army, as of December 13, 1862, and August 15, 1864.

Charles Robert Woods, a brother of General William B. Woods, was born on February 19, 1827, at Newark, Ohio. He spent his boyhood

on the family farm and received a limited education from a tutor. Appointed to the Military Academy in 1848, he was graduated four years later and subsequently performed routine duty in Texas and Washington as an infantry officer until 1860. His first Civil War service was as commander of the troops sent on the *Star of the West* to relieve Fort Sumter, an unsuccessful attempt during which the first hostile shot of the war was actually fired. (767) As colonel of the 76th Ohio, Woods took part briefly in operations in West Virginia in the fall of 1861 and was present at the capture of Fort Donelson and at the battle of Shiloh in Lew Wallace's division of U. S. Grant's army. During the advance on Corinth which followed, he was advanced to brigade command. In W. T. Sherman's Chickasaw Bluffs expedition and the ensuing movement to Arkansas Post, Woods was again in charge of his old regiment, but in the Vicksburg campaign proper he directed a brigade of Sherman's XV Corps and on August 4, 1863, was formally promoted to brigadier general of volunteers. He won the brevet of colonel in the Regular Army for gallant conduct at Chattanooga in November, 1863, and in the Atlanta campaign commanded a division of the XV Corps, now under John A. Logan. His troops took part in the pursuit of John B. Hood, and then embarked upon the celebrated "March to the Sea" and the campaign of the Carolinas which followed. He was brevetted major general of volunteers as of November 22, 1864, and was awarded the same rank in the regular service at the close of the war. With the reorganization of the army in July, 1866, he became lieutenant colonel of the 33rd Infantry, but his health began to fail a few years later and he was retired in 1874 as colonel of the 2nd Infantry, a rank to which he had been promoted earlier the same year. He spent the remaining years of his life on his estate Woodside near Newark, where he died on February 26, 1885 and was buried in Cedar Hill Cemetery.

William Burnham Woods, elder brother of General Charles R. Woods, was born on the family farm at Newark, Ohio, on August 3, 1824. He spent three years at Western Reserve College and then attended Yale, where he was graduated in 1845. He was admitted to the Ohio bar in 1847 and became interested in politics as a Democrat in the 1850's, becoming mayor of Newark and member and speaker of the Ohio house of representatives. Although at first violently at odds with the measures taken by the Lincoln administration, he later became a Republican stalwart. In February, 1862, Woods became lieutenant colonel of the 76th Ohio, his brother's regiment, and succeeded to the colonelcy in September,

1863, after the latter's promotion to brigadier general. Beginning with the battle of Shiloh, his Civil War career virtually paralleled that of his younger brother, whom he followed to Corinth, Chickasaw Bayou, Arkansas Post, the campaign in North Georgia, the "March to the Sea," and the Carolina campaign where he commanded the 1st Brigade of the 1st Division which was commanded by his brother. At the end of the war Woods was commissioned brigadier general of volunteers (May 31, 1865) and was also brevetted major general, although evidence is lacking that he had ever exercised divisional command for so much as a day. Curiously, his brother's ultimate volunteer rank, both full and brevet, was no higher than his own, although the younger Woods directed a division for months. After the war he settled in Alabama, taking full advantage of the opportunities presented by the prostrate white landowners; in 1869 President Grant appointed him a United States circuit court judge for the area which embraced Georgia and the Gulf States. Residing in Atlanta for the next eleven years, he was distinguished for moderation while adjudicating the vexing problems of the era arising from Reconstruction and the newly freed Negroes. In 1880 President Hayes appointed him associate justice of the U. S. Supreme Court. He died in Washington on May 14, 1887, and was buried in Cedar Hill Cemetery, Newark, near his brother who had died two years before.

John Ellis Wool, born on February 29, 1784, at Newburgh, New York, less than three years after Lord

Cornwallis' surrender at Yorktown, was the oldest officer to exercise active command on either side during the Civil War. Orphaned at an early age, he had little formal education and pursued a variety of occupations until the War of 1812. Reputations were made swiftly in that day, and Wool emerged from the war as colonel and inspector general of the army, at the same time retaining the lineal rank of lieutenant colonel of the 6th Infantry. In 1826 he was brevetted brigadier general for faithful service and in 1841 was promoted to a full brigadier general of the line. Meanwhile, he had visited Europe to inspect foreign military establishments and had aided in moving the unfortunate Cherokees from their tribal lands in Georgia and Tennessee to what is now eastern Oklahoma. In the war with Mexico, Wool was greatly distinguished at the victory of Buena Vista—he was voted a sword and the thanks of

573

Congress some years later for his services here. He was meantime brevetted major general to rank from February 23, 1847. From then until the beginning of the Civil War, General Wool commanded the Department of the East and the Department of the Pacific. As commander of the former in 1861 he sent reinforcements into Fort Monroe in time to save it for the Union; the ensuing bastion established on the Virginia capes operated to the disadvantage of the Confederacy from the very beginning of the war. On May 17, 1862, General Wool was made a major general in the regular service to rank from the preceding day and continued in command of the Department of Virginia until he was retired on August 1, 1863. For fifty years, he had rendered signal service to his country. He died in Troy, New York, on November 10, 1869, aged eighty-five, and was buried in Oakwood Cemetery.

George Wright was born in Norwich, Vermont, on October 21, 1801 or 1803 (both years are cited by various authorities). Stationed on the Pacific Coast for the duration of the Civil War, he is remembered as the general who had almost nothing to do with the conflict. He obtained his early education at Captain Partridge's Military School at Norwich (now Norwich University at Northfield, Vermont) and in 1818 was appointed to West Point, where he was graduated in 1822. Wright had a long and eminently distinguished record in the army, dating from his graduation. During many years on garrison and recruiting duty, he was brevetted major for service against the Florida

Seminoles, lieutenant colonel for gallantry at Contreras and Churubusco in the Mexican War, and colonel for his services at Molino del Rey, where he was in charge of the assault on the Mexican works and was wounded. He became colonel of the 9th Infantry in 1855 after

having been in garrison for several years at duty stations primarily on the Pacific Coast. So valuable were his services felt to be in California and the Pacific Northwest at the outbreak of civil war that he was promoted from command of the Department of Oregon to that of the Department of the Pacific, and on September 28, 1861, he was made a brigadier general of volunteers to comport with his command. He served throughout the Civil War in a department virtually stripped of troops, improvising "with sleepless vigilance, unflagging energy, and uncompromising patriotism" the means to sustain the authority of the

United States government on the sparsely settled Pacific slope. On his way to assume command of the Department of the Columbia at the close of the war, General Wright lost his life in the wreck of the steamer *Brother Jonathan,* which broke up off the coast of northern California on July 30, 1865. His body was recovered six weeks later and was interred in the City Cemetery at Sacramento.

Horatio Gouverneur Wright was born on March 6, 1820, in the village of Clinton, Connecticut. He attended the local schools and was appointed to West Point in 1837. He was graduated second in the

Academy's class of 1841 and was posted to the Corps of Engineers. His duties until the beginning of the Civil War were all connected with this department and included ten years service in Florida and in the Dry Tortugas where he assisted in the construction of Forts Taylor

and Jefferson. His first wartime service was an abortive effort to destroy the Norfolk Navy Yard dry dock before its evacuation by the Federals on April 20, 1861; he was captured during the operation by the Virginia state forces but was soon released. He acted as chief engineer of Samuel P. Heintzelman's division at the battle of First Manassas and joined the Port Royal expedition in the same capacity. He was made brigadier general of volunteers on September 16, 1861. In February, 1862, he led an expedition against the Florida coast and in June directed one of Henry W. Benham's two divisions at the disastrous repulse at Secessionville, South Carolina (although he remonstrated with his superior against making the assault). He was then assigned to command of the Department of the Ohio with headquarters in Cincinnati, remaining there until ordered east in May, 1863. Wright had been advanced to major general to rank from July 18, 1862, but the appointment was refused by the Senate on March 12, 1863, and revoked on the twenty-fourth. He was reappointed a year later on May 12, 1864, and confirmed. (768) He led a division of Sedgwick's VI Corps at Gettysburg (where his casualties were nominal), at Rappahannock Bridge, and in the Mine Run campaign; then in May, 1864, he led his command into the Wilderness. Upon the death of John Sedgwick at Spotsylvania, Wright succeeded to command of the corps, remaining commander to the end of the campaign. In July he was sent with his corps to Washington to oppose Jubal Early's raid and that autumn took part in the famous Shenandoah campaign under Philip Sheridan. Wright was a steady and dependable subordinate, but, when an opportunity for greatness was thrust upon him at Cedar Creek as commander of the disorganized Union army during Sheridan's absence there was something lacking. When the guns were silent and the smoke had drifted away, it was Sheridan who had come upon the scene, revitalized the troops, and turned defeat into victory. Elements of Wright's corps were first over the Confederate works at Petersburg in April, 1865, and were present at Appomattox a week later. For a year after the war he commanded the Department of Texas, then returning to engineering duty. He was brevetted major general, U. S. Army, in March, 1865, and after muster out of the volunteer service reverted to his regular rank of lieutenant colonel of engineers. He was advanced to colonel in 1879 and the same year became brigadier general and chief engineer of the army. Meantime he had charge of a number of projects, including numerous river and harbor improvements and the completion of the Washington Monument. General Wright was retired for age on his sixty-fourth birthday, but continued to reside in Washington, where he died on July 2, 1899. He was buried in Arlington National Cemetery.

Samuel Kosciuszko Zook was born on March 27, 1821, in Chester County, Pennsylvania. When very young he was taken by his parents to the home of his maternal grandparents on the old campground of Valley Forge, where he grew up. As a boy he became associated with the militia of Chester, Delaware, and Montgomery counties and at the age of nineteen became adjutant of the 100th Pennsylvania. In 1842 he entered the Philadelphia office of the Washington and New York Telegraph Company and was sub-

sequently appointed superintendent. As a consequence of this promotion he moved to New York City, where he continued his interest in military affairs and rose to the lieutenant colonelcy of the 6th New York Militia. At the outbreak of the Civil War he accompanied his regiment to Annapolis and served as military governor of the town during the campaign of First Manassas. On July 31, 1861, the enlistment period of his regiment expired, but he recruited the 57th New York and was commissioned its colonel on October 19, 1861. The following spring and summer he took part in George B. McClellan's Peninsular campaign in French's brigade of Richardson's division of Sumner's II Corps. This command was not present at Second Manassas and Zook himself was not present at Sharpsburg, where the 57th New York was under the command of its lieutenant colonel. However, at the battle of Fredericksburg, Zook commanded a brigade of Hancock's division and lost 527 men while assaulting the "Sunken Road" on Marye's Heights. Wounded himself in this encounter, he was warmly commended by Winfield S. Hancock and on March 23, 1863, was promoted to brigadier general to rank from November 29, 1862. He was with his brigade at Chancellorsville and again at Gettysburg on July 2, 1863, when the Union cause teetered on the very brink of disaster. In one of the myriad crises which erupted on that sultry afternoon, Zook and his command were rushed to the support of the III Corps which had been broken and driven by James Longstreet's men. In one of the gallant incidents of the war, Zook ordered his men to march over the disordered troops of Barnes's V Corps brigade and take their place in the line. While leading them, he was fatally wounded in the abdomen; he died soon after midnight in a field hospital on the Baltimore Pike, and was buried in Montgomery Cemetery, Norristown, Pennsylvania. (769)

APPENDICES

NOTES

BIBLIOGRAPHY

APPENDIX I

Abbot, Henry L.
Abbott, Ira C.
Abbott, Joseph C.
Abert, William S.
Acker, George S.
Adams, Alonzo W.
Adams, Charles F., Jr.
Adams, Charles P.
Adams, Charles W.
Adams, Robert N.
Adams, Will A.
Agnus, Felix
Albright, Charles
Alden, Alonzo
Alexander, Andrew J.
Alexander, Barton S.
Alexander, Edmund B.
Alger, Russell A.
Allaire, Anthony J.
Allcock, Thomas
Allen, Harrison
Allen, Thomas S.
Ames, John W.
Ames, William
Amory, Thomas J. C.
Anderson, Allen L.
Anderson, John F.
Anderson, Nicholas L.

Anderson, William B.
Ankeny, Rollin V.
Anthony, DeWitt C.
Appleton, John F.
Armstrong, Samuel C.
Askew, Frank
Astor, John Jacob
Atkins, Smith D.
Averill, John T.
Avery, Matthew H.
Avery, Robert
Babbitt, Edwin B.
Babcock, Orville E.
Babcock, Willoughby
Bache, Hartman
Badeau, Adam
Baily, Silas M.
Baker, Benjamin F.
Baker, James H.
Balch, Joseph P.
Baldey, George
Baldwin, Charles P.
Baldwin, William H.
Ball, William H.
Ballier, John F.
Balloch, George W.
Bangs, Isaac S.
Bankhead, Henry C.

Banning, Henry B.
Barber, Gershom M.
Barnes, Charles
Barnett, James
Barney, Albert M.
Barney, Benjamin G.
Barney, Lewis T.
Barrett, Theodore H.
Barrett, Wallace W.
Barriger, John W.
Barry, Henry W.
Barstow, Simon F.
Barstow, Wilson
Bartholomew, Orion A.
Bartlett, Charles G.
Bartlett, William C.
Barton, William B.
Bassett, Isaac C.
Batchelder, Richard N.
Bates, Delevan
Bates, Erastus N.
Baxter, DeWitt C.
Beadle, William H. H.
Beaver, James A.
Beckwith, Amos
Beckwith, Edward G.
Bedel, John
Beecher, James C.
Bell, George
Bell, John H.
Bell, Joseph W.
Bendix, John E.
Benedict, Lewis
Benjamin, William H.
Bennett, John E.
Bennett, Thomas W.
Bennett, William T.
Bentley, Richard C.
Bentley, Robert H.
Benton, Thomas H.
Berdan, Hiram
Bertram, Henry
Beveridge, John L.
Biddle, James
Biggs, Herman
Biggs, Jonathan
Biles, Edwin R.
Bingham, Henry H.

Bingham, Judson D.
Bintliff, James
Bishop, Judson W.
Black, John C.
Blackman, Albert M.
Blair, Charles W.
Blair, Lewis J.
Blair, William H.
Blaisdell, William
Blake, George A. H.
Blakeslee, Erastus
Blanchard, Justus W.
Blanden, Leander
Bloomfield, Ira J.
Blunt, Asa P.
Bodine, Robert L.
Bolinger, Henry C.
Bolles, John A.
Bolton, William J.
Bomford, James V.
Bond, John R.
Bonham, Edward
Bonneville, Benjamin L. E.
Boughton, Horace
Bouton, Edward
Bowen, Thomas M.
Bowerman, Richard N.
Bowers, Theodore S.
Bowie, George W.
Bowman, Samuel M.
Bowyer, Eli
Boyd, Joseph F.
Boynton, Henry
Boynton, Henry V.
Bradshaw, Robert C.
Brady, Thomas J.
Brailey, Moses R.
Brayton, Charles R.
Breck, Samuel
Brewerton, Henry
Brewster, William R.
Brice, Benjamin W.
Brinkerhoff, Roeliff
Briscoe, James C.
Brodhead, Thornton F.
Bronson, Stephen
Brooks, Horace
Brown, Charles E.

Brown, Harvey
Brown, Hiram L.
Brown, John M.
Brown, Lewis G.
Brown, Nathan W.
Brown, Orlando
Brown, Philip P.
Brown, S. Lockwood
Brown, Simeon B.
Brown, Theodore F.
Brown, William R.
Browne, Thomas M.
Browne, William H.
Brownlow, James P.
Bruce, John
Brumback, Jefferson
Brush, Daniel H.
Buell, George P.
Bukey, Van H.
Burbank, Sidney
Burke, Joseph W.
Burke, Martin
Burling, George C.
Burnett, Henry L.
Burton, Henry S.
Busey, Samuel T.
Butler, Thomas H.
Byrne, James J.
Cady, Albemarle
Callender, Franklin D.
Callis, John B.
Cameron, Daniel
Cameron, Hugh
Campbell, Cleaveland J.
Campbell, Edward L.
Campbell, Jacob M.
Campbell, John A.
Candy, Charles
Capehart, Henry
Capron, Horace
Card, Benjamin C.
Carle, James
Carleton, Charles A.
Carman, Ezra A.
Carnahan, Robert H.
Carruth, Sumner
Carson, Christopher
Case, Henry

Casement, John S.
Cassidy, Ambrose S.
Catlin, Isaac S.
Cavender, John S.
Chamberlain, Samuel E.
Champion, Thomas E.
Chaplin, Daniel
Chickering, Thomas E.
Chipman, Henry L.
Chipman, Norton P.
Christ, Benjamin C.
Christensen, Christian T.
Christian, William H.
Churchill, Mendal
Cilley, Jonathan P.
Cist, Henry M.
Clapp, Dexter E.
Clark, George W.
Clark, Gideon
Clark, John S.
Clark, William H.
Clarke, Henry F.
Clary, Robert E.
Clay, Cecil
Clendenin, David R.
Clitz, Henry B.
Clough, Joseph M.
Coates, Benjamin F.
Coates, James H.
Cobb, Amasa
Cobham, George A.
Coburn, John
Cockerill, Joseph R.
Cogswell, William
Coit, James B.
Cole, George W.
Colgrove, Silas
Collier, Frederick H.
Collis, Charles H. T.
Colvill, William, Jr.
Comly, James M.
Commager, Henry S.
Comstock, Cyrus B.
Congdon, James A.
Conklin, James T.
Conrad, Joseph
Cooke, Edwin F.
Coon, Datus E.

Corbin, Henry C.
Coughlin, John
Coulter, Richard
Gowen, Benjamin R.
Cox, John C.
Cox, Robert C.
Craig, Henry K.
Cram, George H.
Cram, Thomas J.
Cramer, Francis L.
Crandal, Frederick M.
Crane; Charles H.
Crane, Nirom M.
Cranor, Jonathan
Crawford, Samuel J.
Crocker, John S.
Crosman, George H.
Cross, Nelson
Cross, Osborn
Crowninshield, Caspar
Cumming, Gilbert W.
Cummings, Alexander
Cummins, John E.
Cunningham, James A.
Curly, Thomas
Curtin, John I.
Curtis, Arthur R.
Curtis, Greely S.
Curtis, James F.
Curtis, William B.
Curtiss, James E.
Cutcheon, Byron M.
Cutting, William
Cutts, Richard D.
Cuyler, John M.
Daggett, Aaron S.
Daggett, Rufus
Dana, Edmund L.
Dana, James J.
Dandy, George B.
Darr, Francis
Davis, Edwin P.
Davis, Hasbrouck
Davis, Henry G.
Davis, Nelson H.
Davis, William W. H.
Dawes, Rufus R.
Dawson, Andrew R. Z.

Dawson, Samuel K.
Day, Hannibal
Day, Henry M.
Day, Nicholas W.
Dayton, Oscar V.
Deems, James M.
De Groat, Charles H.
De Hart, Richard P.
De Lacy, William
De Land, Charles V.
Denison, Andrew W.
Dennis, John B.
De Russy, Rene E.
Devereux, Arthur F.
Devol, Hiram F.
De Witt, David P.
Dick, George F.
Dickerson, Christopher J.
Dickey, William H.
Dickinson, Joseph
Dilworth, Caleb J.
Dimick, Justin
Dimon, Charles A. R.
Diven, Alexander S.
Diven, Charles W.
Dixon, William D.
Doan, Azariah W.
Dodd, Levi A.
Dodge, George S.
Donaldson, James L.
Donohoe, Michael T.
Dornblaser, Benjamin
Doster, William E.
Doubleday, Ulysses
Dox, Hamilton B.
Drake, Francis M.
Drake, George B.
Draper, Alonzo G.
Draper, William F.
Drew, Charles W.
Drum, Richard C.
Duane, James C.
Ducat, Arthur C.
Dudley, Nathan A. M.
Dudley, William W.
Duer, John O.
Duff, William L.
Duncan, Samuel A.

Duncan, Thomas
Dunham, Thomas H.
Dunlap, Henry C.
Dunlap, James
Dunn, William McK.
Duryea, Hiram
Duryee, Jacob E.
Dustin, Daniel
Dutton, Arthur H.
Dutton, Everell F.
Dye, William McE.
Dyer, Isaac
Eastman, Seth
Easton, Langdon C.
Eaton, Charles G.
Eaton, John, Jr.
Eaton, Joseph H.
Eckert, Thomas T.
Edgerton, Alonzo J.
Edmands, J. Cushing
Edwards, Clark S.
Eggleston, Beroth B.
Egloffstein, Baron Fred W.
Ekin, James A.
Eldridge, Hamilton N.
Elliott, Isaac H.
Elliott, Samuel M.
Ellis, Augustus Van H.
Ellis, Theodore G.
Elstner, George R.
Elwell, John J.
Ely, John
Ely, Ralph
Ely, William G.
Engelmann, Adolph
Enochs, William H.
Ent, Wellington H.
Enyart, David A.
Erskine, Albert
Estes, Lewellyn G.
Evans, George S.
Everett, Charles
Fairchild, Cassius
Fairchild, Harrison S.
Fallows, Samuel
Fardella, Enrico
Farnsworth, Addison
Farnum, John E.

Farrar, Bernard G.
Fearing, Benjamin D.
Finley, Clement A.
Fisher, Benjamin F.
Fisher, Joseph W.
Fisk, Henry C.
Fiske, Francis S.
Fiske, William O.
Fitzhugh, Charles L.
Fitz Simmons, Charles
Flanigan, Mark
Fleming, Rufus E.
Fletcher, Thomas C.
Flood, Martin
Flynn, John
Fonda, John G.
Ford, James H.
Forsyth, George A.
Foster, George P.
Foster, John A.
Foust, Benezet F.
Fowler, Edward B.
Franchot, Richard
Francine, Louis R.
Frank, Paul
Frankle, Jones
Fraser, John
Frazar, Douglas
Frederick, Calvin H.
French, Winsor B.
Frink, Henry A.
Frisbie, Henry N.
Fritz, Peter, Jr.
Frizell, Joseph W.
Frohock, William T.
Fry, Cary H.
Fuller, Henry W.
Fullerton, Joseph S.
Funke, Otto
Fyffe, Edward P.
Gage, Joseph S.
Gallagher, Thomas F.
Gallup, George W.
Gansevoort, Henry S.
Gardiner, Alexander
Gardner, John L.
Garrard, Israel
Garrard, Jeptha

Gates, Theodore B.
Gates, William
Geddes, James L.
Gerhardt, Joseph
Gibson, Horatio G.
Gibson, William H.
Giesy, Henry H.
Gilbert, Samuel A.
Gilchrist, Charles A.
Gile, George W.
Ginty, George C.
Given, Josiah
Given, William
Glasgow, Samuel L.
Gleason, John H.
Gleason, Newell
Glenny, William
Gobin, John P. S.
Goddard, William
Godman, James H.
Goff, Nathan, Jr.
Goodell, Arthur A.
Gooding, Oliver P.
Goodyear, Ellsworth D. S.
Gowen, George W.
Graham, Harvey
Graham, Samuel
Graham, William M.
Granger, George F.
Greeley, Edwin S.
Green, William N.
Greene, James D.
Greene, Oliver D.
Gregg, John I.
Gregg, William M.
Gregory, Edgar M.
Grier, David P.
Grier, William N.
Griffin, Daniel F.
Grindlay, James G.
Grosvenor, Charles H.
Grosvenor, Thomas W.
Grover, Ira G.
Grubb, Edward B.
Guiney, Patrick R.
Guppey, Joshua J.
Gurney, William
Guss, Henry R.

Gwyn, James
Hagner, Peter V.
Haines, Thomas J.
Hall, Caldwell K.
Hall, Cyrus
Hall, Henry S.
Hall, Jairus W.
Hall, James A.
Hall, James F.
Hall, Robert M.
Hallowell, Edward N.
Halpine, Charles G.
Hambright, Henry A.
Hamilton, William D.
Hamlin, Charles
Hammell, John S.
Hammond, John
Hammond, John H.
Hanna, William
Hardenbergh, Jacob B.
Harding, Chester
Harlan, Emory B.
Harnden, Henry
Harriman, Samuel
Harriman, Walter
Harris, Andrew L.
Harris, Benjamin F.
Harris, Charles L.
Harrison, Benjamin
Harrison, Marcus L.
Harrison, Thomas J.
Hart, James H.
Hart, Orson H.
Hartshorne, William R.
Hartsuff, William
Hartwell, Alfred S.
Hartwell, Charles A.
Haskell, Llewellyn F.
Hastings, Russell
Haughton, Nathaniel
Hawkes, George P.
Hawkins, Rush C.
Hawley, William
Hayden, Julius
Hayes, Edwin L.
Hayes, Joseph
Hayes, Philip C.
Hayman, Samuel B.

Hazard, John G.
Healy, Robert W.
Heath, Francis E.
Heath, Herman H.
Heath, Thomas T.
Hedrick, John M.
Heine, Wilhelm
Heinrichs, Gustav
Henderson, Robert M.
Henderson, Thomas J.
Hendrickson, John
Hennessy, John A.
Henry, Guy V.
Henry, William W.
Herrick, Walter F.
Herring, Charles P.
Hickenlooper, Andrew
Hill, Bennett H.
Hill, Charles W.
Hill, Jonathan A.
Hill, Sylvester G.
Hillis, David B.
Hillyer, William S.
Hitchcock, George H.
Hobart, Harrison C.
Hobson, William
Hoffman, Henry C.
Hoffman, William
Hofmann, John W.
Hoge, George B.
Hoge, George W.
Holabird, Samuel B.
Holbrook, Mellen T.
Holloway, Ephraim S.
Holman, John H.
Holt, Thomas
Holter, Marcellus J. W.
Hooker, Ambrose E.
Horn, John W.
Hotchkiss, Charles T.
Hough, John
Houghtaling, Charles
Houghton, Moses B.
Howard, Charles H.
Howe, John H.
Howland, Horace N.
Howland, Joseph
Hoyt, Charles H.

Hoyt, George H.
Hoyt, Henry M.
Hubbard, James
Hubbard, Lucius F.
Hubbard, Thomas H.
Hudnutt, Joseph O.
Hudson, John G.
Huey, Pennock
Hugunin, James R.
Humphrey, Thomas W.
Humphrey, William
Hunter, Morton C.
Hurd, John R.
Hurst, Samuel H.
Hutchins, Rue P.
Hutchinson, Frederick S.
Hyde, Thomas W.
Ihrie, George P.
Ingraham, Timothy
Innes, William P.
Irvine, William
Irwin, William H.
Ives, Brayton
Jackson, Joseph C.
Jackson, Samuel M.
Jacobs, Ferris
James, William L.
Jardine, Edward
Jarvis, Dwight
Jeffries, Noah L.
Jenkins, Horatio
Jennison, Samuel P.
Johns, Thomas D.
Johnson, Charles A.
Johnson, Gilbert M. L.
Johnson, James M.
Johnson, Lewis
Johnson, Robert
Jones, Edward F.
Jones, Fielder A.
Jones, John S.
Jones, Joseph B.
Jones, Samuel B.
Jones, Theodore
Jones, Wells S.
Jones, William P.
Jordan, Thomas J.
Jourdan, James

Judson, Roscius W.
Judson, William R.
Karge, Joseph
Keifer, Joseph W.
Keily, Daniel J.
Kellogg, John A.
Kelly, John H.
Kelton, John C.
Kennedy, Robert P.
Kennett, Henry G.
Kent, Loren
Ketner, James
Kidd, James H.
Kiddoo, Joseph B.
Kilburn, Charles L.
Kilgour, William M.
Kimball, John W.
Kimball, William K.
Kimberly, Robert L.
King, Adam E.
King, John F.
King, William S.
Kingsbury, Charles P.
Kingsbury, Henry D.
Kinney, Thomas J.
Kinsey, William B.
Kinsman, Josiah B.
Kirby, Byron
Kirby, Dennis T.
Kirby, Isaac M.
Kirkman, Ralph W.
Kise, Reuben C.
Kitchell, Edward
Kitching, John H.
Knefler, Frederick
Knowles, Oliver B.
Kozlay, Eugene A.
Krez, Conrad
Kueffner, William C.
Laflin, Byron
Lagow, Clark B.
La Grange, Oscar H.
La Motte, Charles E.
Landram, William J.
Lane, John Q.
Langdon, Elisha B.
Lansing, Henry S.
Lasselle, William P.

Latham, George R.
Laughlin, Rankin G.
Lawrence, Albert G.
Lawrence, William Henry
Lawrence, William Hudson
Leake, Joseph B.
Le Duc, William G.
Lee, Edward M.
Lee, Horace C.
Lee, John C.
Lee, William R.
Leech, William A.
Le Favour, Heber
Le Gendre, Charles W.
Leiper, Charles L.
Leonard, Hiram
Leslie, Thomas J.
Lewis, Charles W.
Lewis, John R.
Lewis, William D.
Lieb, Herman
Lincoln, William S.
Lindley, John M.
Lippincott, Charles E.
Lippitt, Francis J.
Lister, Frederick W.
Litchfield, Allyne C.
Littell, John S.
Littlefield, Milton S.
Littlejohn, De Witt C.
Livingston, Robert R.
Locke, Frederick T.
Lockman, John T.
Loomis, Cyrus O.
Loomis, Gustavus
Lord, Therndon E.
Loring, Charles G.
Love, George M.
Lovell, Charles S.
Lovell, Frederick S.
Lowe, William W.
Ludington, Marshall I.
Ludlow, Benjamin C.
Ludlow, William H.
Lyle, Peter
Lyman, Luke
Lynch, James C.
Lynch, William F.

Lyon, William P.
McAlester, Miles D.
McAllister, Robert
McArthur, William M.
Macauley, Daniel
McBride, James D.
McCall, William H. H.
McCallum, Daniel C.
McCalmont, Alfred B.
McCleery, James
McClennan, Matthew R.
McClurg, Alexander C.
McConihe, John
McConihe, Samuel
McConnell, Henry K.
McConnell, John
McCook, Anson G.
McCook, Edwin S.
McCormick, Charles C.
McCoy, Daniel
McCoy, Robert A.
McCoy, Thomas F.
McCreary, David B.
McCrillis, Lafayette
McDougall, Charles
McDougall, Clinton D.
McEwen, Matthew
McFerran, John C.
McGarry, Edward
McGowan, John E.
McGregor, John D.
McGroarty, Stephen J.
McIvor, James P.
Mackay, Andrew J.
McKeever, Chauncey
McKenny, Thomas I.
McKibbin, David B.
McKibbin, Gilbert H.
McLaren, Robert N.
McLaughlen, Napoleon B.
McMahon, John
McMahon, Martin T.
McMillen, William L.
McNary, William H.
McNaught, Thomas A.
McNett, Andrew J.
McNulta, John
McQuade, James

McQueen, Alexander G.
McQuiston, John C.
MacThompson, James
Macy, George N.
Madill, Henry J.
Magee, David W.
Malloy, Adam G.
Manderson, Charles F.
Mank, William G.
Mann, Orrin L.
Manning, Stephen H.
Mansfield, John
Markoe, John
Marple, William W.
Marshall, Elisha G.
Marshall, William R.
Martin, James S.
Martin, John A.
Martin, William H.
Mason, Edwin C.
Mather, Thomas S.
Mathews, Joseph A.
Mathews, Salmon S.
Mattocks, Charles P.
Maxwell, Norman J.
Maxwell, Obediah C.
May, Dwight
Maynadier, Henry E.
Maynadier, William
Mehringer, John
Merchant, Charles S.
Merrill, Lewis
Mersy, August
Messer, John
Meyer, Edward S.
Michie, Peter S.
Michler, Nathaniel
Miller, Abram O.
Miller, Madison
Miller, Morris S.
Mills, James K.
Mills, Madison
Mindil, George W.
Minty, Robert H. G.
Mintzer, William M.
Mitchell, Greenville M.
Mitchell, William G.
Mix, Elisha

Mizner, Henry R.
Mizner, John K.
Moffitt, Stephen
Molineux, Edward L.
Monroe, George W.
Montgomery, Milton
Moody, Granville
Moon, John C.
Moonlight, Thomas
Moor, August
Moore, David
Moore, Frederick W.
Moore, Jesse H.
Moore, Jonathan B.
Moore, Marshall F.
Moore, Timothy C.
Moore, Tredwell
Morehead, Turner G.
Morgan, George N.
Morgan, Michael R.
Morgan, Thomas J.
Morgan, William H. (Ind.)
Morgan, William H. (Wis.)
Morrill, John
Morris, William W.
Morrison, David
Morrison, Joseph J.
Morrison, Pitcairn
Morrow, Henry A.
Morse, Henry B.
Mott, Samuel R.
Mudgett, William S.
Mulcahy, Thomas
Mulford, John E.
Mulholland, St. Clair A.
Mulligan, James A.
Mundee, Charles
Murphy, John K.
Murray, Benjamin B.
Murray, Edward
Murray, Eli H.
Murray, John B.
Mussey, Reuben D.
Myer, Albert J.
Myers, Frederick
Myers, George R.
Myers, William
Nase, Adam

Neafie, Alfred
Neff, Andrew J.
Neff, George W.
Neide, Horace
Nettleton, Allured B.
Newberry, Walter C.
Newport, Reece M.
Nichols, George F.
Nichols, George S.
Nichols, William A.
Niles, Nathaniel
Noble, John W.
Noble, William H.
Northcott, Robert S.
Norton, Charles B.
Noyes, Edward F.
Nugent, Robert
Nye, George H.
Oakes, James
O'Beirne, James R.
O'Brien, George M.
O'Dowd, John
Oley, John H.
Oliphant, Samuel D.
Oliver, Paul A.
Olmsted, William A.
Ordway, Albert
Osband, Embury D.
Osborn, Francis A.
Otis, Calvin N.
Otis, Elwell S.
Otis, John L.
Packard, Jasper
Painter, William
Palfrey, Francis W.
Palfrey, John C.
Palmer, Oliver H.
Palmer, William J.
Pardee, Ario, Jr.
Pardee, Don A.
Park, Sidney W.
Parker, Ely S.
Parkhurst, John G.
Parrish, Charles S.
Parrott, James C.
Parry, Augustus C.
Partridge, Benjamin F.
Partridge, Frederick W.

Pattee, John
Pattee, Joseph B.
Patten, Henry L.
Patterson, Joab N.
Patterson, Robert E.
Patterson, Robert F.
Payne, Eugene B.
Payne, Oliver H.
Pearce, John S.
Pearsall, Uri B.
Pearson, Alfred L.
Pearson, Robert N.
Pease, Phineas
Pease, William R.
Peck, Frank H.
Peck, Lewis M.
Peirson, Charles L.
Pelouze, Louis H.
Pennington, Alexander C. M.
Perkins, Henry W.
Per Lee, Samuel R.
Perry, Alexander J.
Phelps, Charles E.
Phelps, John E.
Phelps, Walter, Jr.
Phillips, Jesse J.
Pickett, Josiah
Pierce, Francis E.
Pierson, John F.
Pierson, William S.
Pinckney, Joseph C.
Pinto, Francis E.
Plaisted, Harris M.
Platner, John S.
Pleasants, Henry
Pollock, Samuel M.
Pomutz, George
Pope, Edmund M.
Porter, Horace
Porter, Samuel A.
Post, Philip S.
Potter, Carroll H.
Potter, Joseph A.
Powell, Eugene
Powers, Charles J.
Pratt, Benjamin F.
Prescott, George L.
Preston, Simon M.

Prevost, Charles M.
Price, Francis
Price, Richard B.
Price, Samuel W.
Price, William R.
Prime, Frederick E.
Pritchard, Benjamin D.
Proudfit, James K.
Pugh, Isaac C.
Pulford, John
Quincy, Samuel M.
Ramsey, John
Randall, George W.
Randol, Alanson M.
Ratliff, Robert W.
Raynolds, William F.
Raynor, William H.
Read, Samuel T.
Read, Theodore
Reese, Chauncey B.
Reeve, Isaac V. D.
Remick, David
Reno, Marcus A.
Revere, Paul J.
Revere, William H. Jr.
Reynolds, Joseph S.
Richardson, Hollon
Richardson, William P.
Richmond, Lewis
Riggin, John, Jr.
Rinaker, John I.
Ripley, Edward H.
Ripley, Theodore A.
Risdon, Orlando C.
Ritchie, John
Robbins, Walter R.
Roberts, Charles W.
Roberts, Joseph
Roberts, Samuel H.
Robertson, James M.
Robeson, William P.
Robinson, George D.
Robinson, Henry L.
Robinson, Milton S.
Robinson, William A.
Robison, John K.
Rockwell, Alfred P.
Rodenbough, Theophilus F.

Rodgers, Hiram C.
Rodman, Thomas J.
Rogers, George
Rogers, George C.
Rogers, Horatio, Jr.
Rogers, James C.
Rogers, William F.
Roome, Charles
Root, Adrian R.
Rose, Thomas E.
Ross, Samuel
Ross, William E. W.
Rowett, Richard
Rowley, William R.
Ruff, Charles F.
Ruggles, George D.
Ruggles, James M.
Runkle, Benjamin P.
Rusk, Jeremiah M.
Rusling, James F.
Russell, Charles S.
Russell, Henry S.
Rust, Henry
Rust, John D.
Rutherford, George V.
Rutherford, Reuben C.
Sacket, Delos B.
Sackett, William
Salm, Felix Prince
Salomon, Charles E.
Salomon, Edward S.
Sanborn, William
Sanders, Addison H.
Sanders, Horace T.
Sanderson, Thomas W.
Sanford, Edward S.
Sargent, Horace B.
Satterlee, Richard S.
Sawtelle, Charles G.
Sawyer, Franklin
Scates, Walter B.
Schmitt, William A.
Schneider, Edward F.
Schofield, George W.
Schriver, Edmund
Schwenk, Samuel K.
Scofield, Hiram
Scott, George W.

Scott, Rufus
Scribner, Benjamin F.
Seaver, Joel J.
Seawell, Thomas D.
Seawell, Washington
Selfridge, James L.
Serrell, Edward W.
Sewall, Frederic D.
Sewall, William J.
Shaffer, George T.
Shaffer, John W.
Shafter, William R.
Shanks, John P. C.
Sharpe, George H.
Sharpe, Jacob
Shaurman, Nelson
Shaw, James
Shedd, Warren
Sheets, Benjamin F.
Sheetz, Josiah A.
Sheldon, Charles S.
Sheldon, Lionel A.
Shepherd, Oliver L.
Shepherd, Russell B.
Sherwin, Thomas
Sherwood, Isaac R.
Shiras, Alexander E.
Shoup, Samuel N.
Shunk, David
Shurtleff, Giles W.
Sibley, Caleb C.
Sickel, Horatio G.
Sickles, Hiram F.
Sidell, William H.
Sigfried, Joshua K.
Simonson, John S.
Simpson, James H.
Simpson, Marcus D. L.
Simpson, Samuel P.
Slevin, Patrick S.
Slocum, Willard
Small, Michael P.
Smith, Arthur A.
Smith, Benjamin F.
Smith, Charles E.
Smith, Charles H.
Smith, Edward W.
Smith, Franklin C.

Smith, George W.
Smith, Israel C.
Smith, James
Smith, John C.
Smith, Joseph R.
Smith, Joseph S.
Smith, Orland
Smith, Orlow
Smith, Robert F.
Smith, Robert W.
Smith, William J.
Sniper, Gustavus
Sowers, Edgar
Spalding, George
Spaulding, Ira
Spaulding, Oliver L.
Spear, Ellis
Spear, Samuel P.
Spencer, George E.
Spicely, William T.
Spofford, John P.
Spooner, Benjamin J.
Sprague, Augustus B. R.
Sprague, Ezra T.
Spurling, Andrew B.
Stafford, Joab A.
Stager, Anson
Stagg, Peter
Stanley, Timothy R.
Stanton, David L.
Starbird, Isaac W.
Starring, Frederick A.
Stedman, Griffin A., Jr.
Stedman, William
Steere, William H. P.
Steiner, John A.
Stephenson, Luther, Jr.
Stevens, Aaron F.
Stevens, Ambrose A.
Stevens, Hazard
Stevenson, Robert H.
Stewart, James, Jr.
Stewart, William S.
Stewart, William W.
Stibbs, John H.
Stiles, Israel N.
Stockton, Joseph
Stokes, William B.

Stone, George A.
Stone, Roy
Stone, William M.
Stough, William
Stoughton, Charles B.
Stoughton, William L.
Stout, Alexander M.
Stratton, Franklin A.
Streight, Abel D.
Strickland, Silas A.
Strong, James C.
Strong, Thomas J.
Strong, William E.
Strother, David H.
Sullivan, Peter J.
Sweet, Benjamin J.
Sweitzer, Jacob B.
Sweitzer, Nelson B.
Swift, Frederick W.
Switzler, Theodore A.
Swords, Thomas
Sypher, Jay H.
Talbot, Thomas H.
Talley, William C.
Tarbell, Jonathan
Taylor, Ezra
Taylor, Jacob E.
Taylor, John P.
Taylor, Thomas T.
Tevis, C. Carroll
Tew, George W.
Thayer, Sylvanus
Thom, George
Thomas, Charles
Thomas, De Witt C.
Thomas, Minor T.
Thomas, Samuel
Thompson, Charles R.
Thompson, Henry E.
Thompson, John L.
Thompson, Robert
Thompson, William
Thomson, David
Thornton, William A.
Thorp, Thomas J.
Throop, William A.
Thruston, Gates P.
Thurston, William H.

Tidball, John C.
Tilden, Charles W.
Tilghman, Benjamin C.
Tillson, John
Tilton, William S.
Titus, Herbert B.
Tompkins, Charles H.
Totten, James
Tourtellotte, John E.
Townsend, Edward D.
Townsend, Frederick
Tracy, Benjamin F.
Trauernicht, Theodore
Tremain, Henry E.
Tripler, Charles S.
Trotter, Frederick E.
Trowbridge, Luther S.
True, James M.
Truex, William S.
Trumbull, Matthew M.
Turley, John A.
Turner, Charles
Vail, Jacob G.
Van Antwerp, Verplanck
Van Buren, Daniel T.
Van Buren, James L.
Van Buren, Thomas B.
Van Petten, John B.
Varney, George
Vaughan, Samuel K.
Viall, Nelson
Vickers, David
Vifquain, Victor
Vincent, Thomas M.
Vinton, David H.
Von Blessingh, Louis
Von Schack, George
Von Schrader, Alexander
Von Vegesack, Ernest
Voris, Alvin Coe
Vreeland, Michael J.
Wade, James F.
Wagner, Louis
Wainwright, Charles S.
Waite, Carlos A.
Waite, Charles
Waite, John M.
Walcott, Charles F.

Walker, Duncan S.
Walker, Francis A.
Walker, Moses B.
Walker, Samuel
Walker, Thomas M.
Wallace, Martin R. M.
Wallen, Henry D.
Wangelin, Hugo
Ward, Durbin
Ward, George H.
Ward, Henry C.
Ward, Lyman
Warner, Adoniram J.
Warner, Darius B.
Warner, Edward R.
Warner, Willard
Warren, Lucius H.
Washburn, Francis
Washburn, Henry D.
Washburne, George A.
Wass, Ansel D.
Waters, Louis H.
Weaver, James B.
Webber, Alonzo W.
Webber, Jules C.
Weld, Stephen M.
Welles, George E.
Wells, George D.
Wells, Henry H.
Wells, Milton
Welsh, William
Wentworth, Mark F.
West, Francis H.
West, George W.
West, Henry R.
West, Robert M.
Wever, Clark R.
Wheelock, Charles
Wherry, William M.
Whistler, Joseph N. G.
Whitaker, Edward W.
Whitbeck, Horatio N.
White, Carr B.
White, Daniel
White, David B.
White, Frank
White, Frank J.
White, Harry

Whiteley, Robert H. K.
Whittelsey, Charles H.
Whittelsey, Henry M.
Whittier, Charles A.
Whittier, Francis H.
Whittlesey, Eliphalet
Wilcox, James A.
Wilcox, John S.
Wilder, John T.
Wildes, Thomas F.
Wildrick, Abram C.
Wiles, Greenberry F.
Wiley, Aquila
Wiley, Daniel D.
Williams, Adolphus W.
Williams, James M.
Williams, John
Williams, Reuben
Williams, Robert
Williams, Thomas J.
Willian, John
Willson, Lester S.
Wilson, James
Wilson, James G.
Wilson, Thomas
Wilson, William
Wilson, William T.
Winkler, Frederick C.
Winslow, Bradley
Winslow, Edward F.
Winslow, Robert E.
Winthrop, Frederick

Wise, George D.
Wisewell, Moses N.
Wister, Langhorne
Witcher, John S.
Withington, William H.
Wolfe, Edward H.
Wood, James, Jr.
Wood, Oliver
Wood, Robert C.
Wood, William D.
Woodall, Daniel
Woodford, Stewart L.
Woodhull, Maxwell V.
Woodruff, Israel C.
Woodward, Orpheus S.
Woolley, John
Wormer, Grover S.
Wright, Edward
Wright, Elias
Wright, John G.
Wright, Joseph J. B.
Wright, Thomas F.
Yates, Henry, Jr.
Yeoman, Stephen B.
Yorke, Louis E.
Young, Samuel B. M.
Young, Thomas L.
Zahm, Lewis
Ziegler, George M.
Zinn, George
Zulich, Samuel M.

APPENDIX II

STATES OR COUNTRIES OF BIRTH

Alabama (*4*)

Birney, D. B.
Birney, W.
Crittenden, T. T.
Hamilton, A. J.

Connecticut (*23*)

Birge
Bradley
Carrington
Clark
Ferry
Harding
Harland
Ketchum
Lyon
Mansfield
Phelps, J. S.
Ripley
Sedgwick
Shaler
Sherman, F. T.
Taylor, N.
Terry, A. H.
Terry, H. D.
Totten
Tyler, D.
Wessells
Williams, A. S.
Wright, H. G.

Delaware (*5*)

Lockwood
Sykes
Thomas, L.
Torbert
Ullmann

Florida (*3*)

Davis, E. J.
McIntosh
Watkins

Georgia (*2*)

Frémont
Meigs

Illinois (9)

Carlin
Cook
Fry, J. B.
Hardin
Logan

Raum
Rawlins
Ross
Wilson

Indiana (21)

Burnside
Catterson
Crocker
Cruft
Davis, J. C.
Dumont
Foster, R. S.
Gresham
Hackleman
Hawkins
Hovey, A. P.

Kimball
Lucas
Miller, J. F.
Milroy
Pile
Pitcher
Reid
Sullivan
Veatch
Wallace, L.

Kentucky (41)

Anderson
Blair
Boyle
Buford, J.
Buford, N. B.
Burbridge
Canby
Clay
Cooper, J. A.
Crittenden, T. L.
Croxton
Edwards, J.
Fry, S. S.
Garrard, K.
Garrard, T. T.
Gilbert, J. I.
Gorman
Harrow
Hobson
Holt
Jackson, J. S.

Johnson, R. W.
Long
McClernand
McMillan
Mitchel
Nelson
Oglesby
Palmer, J. M.
Pope
Reynolds, J. J.
Rousseau
Sanders
Shackelford
Smith, G. C.
Taylor, J. P.
Thruston
Todd
Whitaker
Williamson
Wood

Louisiana (1)

West

597

Maine (31)

Ames
Beal
Berry
Blunt
Burnham
Carleton
Chamberlain
Connor, S.
Copeland
Dana
Dow
Fessenden, F.
Fessenden, J. D.
Grover
Hamlin
Hatch, E.

Hayes, J.
Hinks
Howard
Howe
Ingalls
Jameson
Nickerson
Prince
Scammon
Shepley
Thomas, H. G.
Tillson
Vinton
Washburn
Williams, S.

Maryland and District of Columbia (20)

Abercrombie
Benton
Brannan
Buchanan
Carroll
Cooper, J.
Emory
Force
French
Getty

Hammond
Hunter
Judah
Kenley
Lauman
Ord
Orme
Pleasonton
Stokes
Vandever

Massachusetts (45)

Andrews, G. L.
Banks
Barnard
Barnes, J.
Bartlett, W. F.
Briggs
Buckland
Chapman
Cutler
Devens
Dodge, G. M.
Dwight
Edwards, O.
Eustis
Gordon
Hamblin

Hooker
Jackson, N. J.
Keyes
Lander
Lowell
McGinnis
Marcy
Miles
Morgan, E. D.
Morgan, J. D.
Paine, C. J.
Plummer
Pratt
Revere
Rice, J. C.
Saxton

Shepard
Smith, T. C. H.
Smith, T. K.
Stevens
Stevenson, T. G.
Stone
Sumner

Thayer
Tower
Underwood
Warren, F. H.
Whipple, A. W.
Wild

Michigan (4)

Farnsworth, E. J.
Hunt, H. J.

Sibley
Willcox

Missouri (3)

Chetlain
Dent

Paul

New Hampshire (13)

Andrews, C. C.
Butler
Dix
Estey
Foster, J. G.
Griffin, S. G.
Kelley

Marston
Porter, F. J.
Porter, J. H.
Sanborn
Webster
Woodbury

New Jersey (11)

Arnold, L. G.
Dodge, C. C.
Harker
Howell
Kilpatrick
Montgomery

Mott
Quimby
Rucker
Taylor, G. W.
Van Cleve

New York (113)

Augur
Averell
Ayres
Baker, L. C.
Barlow
Barnum
Barry
Bartlett, J. J.
Baxter
Bayard
Belknap
Bidwell
Bowen

Bragg
Brayman
Brown
Butterfield
Cameron
Carr, E. A.
Carr, J. B.
Chambers
Champlin
Chapin
Chrysler
Cochran
Couch

Cullum
Curtis, N. M.
Curtis, S. R.
Davies, H. E.
Davies, T. A.
Delafield
Dennis
De Russy
Devin
Doubleday
Duryee
Eaton
Egan
Fisk
Gibbs
Graham, C. K.
Granger, G.
Halleck
Hamilton, C. S.
Hamilton, S.
Hardie
Hartsuff
Hascall
Haskin
Hatch, J. P.
Kearny
Ketcham
King, J. H.
King, R.
Kirby
Ledlie
Lee
Leggett
Mackenzie
McKinstry
Martindale
Merritt
Morell
Morgan, C. H.
Morris
Oliver
Palmer, I. N.
Parsons
Patrick

Peck
Penrose
Pierce
Potter, E. E.
Potter, R. B.
Rice, S. A.
Ricketts
Robinson, J. C.
Ruger
Russell
Schofield
Seward
Sheridan (?)
Sickles
Slocum
Smith, G. A.
Smith, M. L.
Spinola
Sprague
Starkweather
Steele
Stoneman
Strong, W. K.
Stuart
Tibbits
Turner
Tyler, E. B.
Tyler, R. O.
Upton
Van Alen
Van Wyck
Viele
Wadsworth
Ward, J. H. H.
Warren, G. K.
Webb
Weed
Whipple, W. D.
White
Williams, D. H.
Williams, N. G.
Williams, T.
Wool

North Carolina (3)

Hawley
Johnson, A.

Meredith, S.

Ohio (64)

Allen
Bailey
Beatty, J.
Brooks
Buckingham
Buell
Burns
Bussey
Crook
Custer
Ewing, C.
Ewing, H. B.
Ewing, T.
Fairchild
Forsyth
Garfield
Gilbert, C. C.
Gillmore
Granger, R. S.
Grant, U. S.
Griffin, C.
Grose
Hayes, R. B.
Kirk
Lytle
McCook, A. McD.
McCook, D., Jr.
McCook, E. M.
McCook, R. L.
McDowell
McLean
McPherson
Maltby
Manson
Mason
Mitchell, J. G.
Mitchell, R. B.
Opdycke
Osborn
Paine, E. A.
Paine, H. E.
Piatt
Poe
Potts
Reilly
Rice, A. V.
Robinson, J. S.
Rosecrans
Schenck
Sherman, W. T.
Sill
Slough
Smith, W. S.
Stanley
Swayne
Tuttle
Van Derveer
Wade
Wagner
Walcutt
Wallace, W. H. L.
Weitzel
Woods, C. R.
Woods, W. B.

Pennsylvania (66)

Baird
Barnes, J. K.
Beatty, S.
Brisbin
Brooke
Cadwalader
Campbell, C. T.
Clayton
Corse
Craig
Crawford
Deitzler
Ellet
Elliott
Franklin
Geary
Gibbon
Gregg
Grierson
Hancock
Hartranft
Haupt
Hays, A.
Heckman

Heintzelman
Herron
Humphreys
Jackson, C. F.
Kane
Keim
Knipe
Lightburn
McCall
McClellan
McKean
Meredith, S. A.
Miller, S.
Morgan, G. W.
Morton
Nagle
Naglee
Negley
Neill
Parke
Patterson

Pennypacker
Porter, A.
Reynolds, J. F.
Rice, E. W.
Rowley
Scott, R. K.
Slack
Slemmer
Smith, A. J.
Smith, C. F.
Smith, G. A.
Steedman
Stumbaugh
Sturgis
Sully
Tyndale
Vincent
Vogdes
Welsh
Wistar
Zook

Rhode Island (6)

Arnold, R.
Casey
Greene

Rodman
Sherman, T. W.
Wheaton

South Carolina (1)

Hurlbut

Tennessee (6)

Campbell, W. B.
Carter
Gillem

Harney
Haynie
Spears

Vermont (24)

Alvord
Caldwell
Cowdin
Dewey
Doolittle
Grant, L. A.
Hazen
Hitchcock
Hovey, C. E.
Mower
Phelps, J. W.
Ransom

Richardson
Roberts
Seymour
Smith, W. F.
Stannard
Stoughton
Strong, G. C.
Thomas, S.
Van Vliet
Warner
Wells
Wright, G.

Virginia (18)

Ammen

Cooke

Davidson

Denver

Duval

Dyer

Graham, L. P.

Harris

Hays, W.

Newton

Prentiss

Ramsay

Reno

Scott, W.

Stevenson, J. D.

Terrill

Thomas, G. H.

Ward, W. T.

Wisconsin (1)

Hunt, L. C.

FOREIGN-BORN (45)

Canada (4)

Benham

Cox

Farnsworth, J. F.

McNeil

France (3)

Cluseret

De Trobriand

Duffié

Germany (12)

Blenker

Bohlen

Kautz

Matthies

Osterhaus

Salomon

Schimmelfennig

Schurz

Sigel

Von Steinwehr

Weber

Willich

Great Britain (5)

Baker, E. D.

Fuller

McArthur

Owen

Powell

Hungary (2)

Asboth

Stahel

Ireland (12)

Busteed

Connor, P. E.

Corcoran

Gamble

Jackson, R. H.

Jones

Kiernan

Lawler

Meagher

Shields

Smyth

Sweeny

Poland (2)

Krzyzanowski   Schoepf

Russia (1)

Turchin

Spain (2)

Ferrero   Meade

Sweden (1)

Stolbrand

Switzerland (1)

Smith, J. E.

APPENDIX III

Brownsville, Texas, last engagement of the war at, May 12, 1865 (skirmish)
Buckhead Creek, Georgia, November 28-29, 1864
Buckland Mills, Virginia, October 19, 1863
Buffington's Island, Ohio, July 19, 1863
Bull Run, *see* First and Second Manassas
Camden expedition, Arkansas, March 23-May 3, 1864
Carolinas campaign, January 1-April 26, 1865
Carthage, Missouri, July 5, 1861
Cedar Creek (Bell Grove), Virginia, October 19, 1864
Cedar Mountain (Cedar Run Mountain, Slaughter Mountain, Southwest Mountain), Virginia, August 9, 1862
Chambersburg, Pennsylvania, burned, July 30, 1864
Chancellorsville, Virginia, May 2-4, 1863
Chantilly (Ox Hill), Virginia, September 1, 1862
Charleston, South Carolina, bombardment of, August 21, 1863; December 31, 1863
Charlestown, West Virginia, October 18, 1863
Chattanooga, Tennessee, November 23-25, 1863
Chattanooga campaign, Tennessee, August-November, 1863
Cheat Mountain campaign, West Virginia, September 11-17, 1861
Chickahominy, *see* Cold Harbor
Chickamauga, Georgia, September 19-20, 1863
Chickamauga campaign, Georgia, August 16-September 22, 1863
Chickasaw Bayou, Mississippi, December 27-28, 1862
Chickasaw Bluffs, Mississippi, December 29, 1862
Cloyd's Mountain, Virginia, May 9, 1864
Cold Harbor (Gaines's Mill, Chickahominy), Virginia, June 27, 1862
Cold Harbor, Virginia, June 3, 1864; vicinity of, May 31-June 12, 1864
Columbia, Tennessee, in front of, November 24-27, 1864
Corinth, Mississippi, October 3-4, 1862
Corrick's Ford, West Virginia, July 13, 1861
Cosby Creek, Tennessee, January 14, 1864
Crampton's Gap, *see* South Mountain
The Crater, Virginia, July 30, 1864
Cross Keys, Virginia, June 8, 1862
Cumberland Gap, Tennessee, evacuated by Federals, September 17, 1862
Dalton, Georgia, May 9-13, 1864; surrendered, October 13, 1864
Devall's Bluff, Arkansas, July 6, 1862 (skirmish)
Dinwiddie Court House, Virginia, March 31, 1865
Dranesville, Virginia, November 26-27, 1861; December 20, 1861
Drewry's Bluff, Virginia, May 12-16, 1864
Dumfries (Quantico Creek), Virginia, October 11, 1861
Dumfries, Virginia, December 12, 1862; December 27, 1862

Durham Station, North Carolina, surrender of J. E. Johnston at, April 26, 1865

Egypt, Mississippi, December 28, 1864

Elkhorn (Pea Ridge), Arkansas, March 6-8, 1862

Elkhorn Tavern, *see* Elkhorn

Ezra Church, Georgia, July 28, 1864

Falling Waters, Maryland, July 14, 1863 (skirmish)

Farmington, Mississippi, May 9-10, 1862

Farmville, Virginia, April 7, 1865

Fisher's Hill, Virginia, September 22, 1864

Fishing Creek, *see* Mill Springs

Five Forks, Virginia, April 1, 1865

Fort Blakely, Alabama, April 2-9, 1865

Fort Donelson, Tennessee, siege and capture of, February 13-16, 1862

Fort Fisher, North Carolina, bombardment of, December 24-25, 1864; bombardment and capture of, January 13-15, 1865

Fort Gregg (Petersburg lines), Virginia, April 2, 1865

Fort Harrison, Virginia, September 29-30, 1864

Fort Hatteras, North Carolina, August 28-29, 1861

Fort Henry, Tennessee, January 17-22, 1862

Fort Hindman (Arkansas Post), Arkansas, January 4-17, 1863

Fort Jackson, Louisiana, bombardment and surrender of, April 18-28, 1862

Fort McRee, in Pensacola Harbor, Florida, November 22, 1861; January 1, 1862

Fort Morgan, Alabama, August 9-23, 1864

Fort Moultrie, South Carolina, occupied by Federals, February 18, 1865

Fort Pillow, Tennessee, April 14-June 5, 1862; captured by Confederates, April 12, 1864

Fort St. Philip, Louisiana, capture of, April 18-28, 1862

Fort Sanders, Tennessee, November 29, 1863

Fort Stedman, in front of Petersburg, Virginia, March 25, 1865

Fort Sumter, South Carolina, bombardment of, April 12-13, 1861

Fort Tyler, near West Point, Georgia, April 16, 1865

Fox's Gap, *see* South Mountain

Franklin, Tennessee, November 30, 1864

Frayser's Farm (White Oak Swamp), Virginia, June 30, 1862

Fredericksburg (Marye's Heights), Virginia, May 3-4, 1863

Fredericksburg, Virginia, December 13, 1862

Front Royal, Virginia, May 23, 30, 31, 1862

Fussell's Mill, Virginia, August 13-20, 1864

Gaines's Mill, *see* Cold Harbor

Galveston, Texas, attack on blockade fleet at, January 1, 1863

Gettysburg, Pennsylvania, July 1-3, 1863

Gettysburg campaign, Pennsylvania, June-July, 1863

Glorieta Cañon, New Mexico, March 26-28, 1862
Grand Gulf, Mississippi, March 31, 1863
Greensboro, North Carolina, J. E. Johnston surrendered at, April
  26, 1865
Groveton (Manassas Plains), Virginia, August 29, 1862
Grubbs Crossroads, Kentucky, August 21, 1864
Harpers Ferry, West Virginia, September 12-15, 1862
Harrisonburg, Pennsylvania, June 6, 1862 (skirmish)
Hatcher's Run, Virginia, February 5-7, 1865
Helena, Arkansas, January 1, 1863; July 4, 1863
High Bridge, Virginia, April 6-7, 1865 (skirmish)
Holly Springs, Mississippi, July 1, 1862; November 13, 28, 1862;
  December 20, 1862
Island No. 10, Tennessee, capture of, April 7-8, 1862
Iuka, Mississippi, September 19, 1862
Jackson, Mississippi, capture of, July 10, 1863
Jenkins' Ferry, Arkansas, April 30, 1864
Jonesboro, Georgia, August 31-September 1, 1864
Kelly's Ford (Fair Gardens), Tennessee, January 27, 1864
Kelly's Ford, Virginia, December 20-22, 1862; November 7, 1863
Kennesaw Mountain, Georgia, June 27, 1864
Kentucky campaign, August-October, 1862
Kernstown, *see* Winchester
Kinston, North Carolina, January 25, 1863; expedition, June
  20-23, 1864
Knoxville campaign, Tennessee, November 17-December 4, 1863
Laurel Hill, West Virginia, July 11, 1864
Lexington, Missouri, captured, September 20, 1861
Little Rock, Arkansas, capture of, September 10, 1863
Lookout Mountain, Tennessee, November 24, 1863
Loudon Heights, *see* Harpers Ferry
Lynchburg, Virginia, June 17-18, 1864
McDowell, Virginia, May 8, 1862
Malvern Hill, Virginia, July 1, 1862
Manassas, First (Bull Run), Virginia, July 21, 1861
Manassas, Second (Bull Run), Virginia, August 29-30, 1862
Manassas campaign, Virginia, July 16-22, 1861
Manassas Junction, Virginia, January 7, 1862
Mansfield, Louisiana, April 8, 1864
Marks' Mills, Arkansas, April 25, 1864
Martinsburg, West Virginia, September 18, 1864
Maryland campaign (Antietam campaign), September 10-19, 1862
Meadow Bridge (Beaver Dam Creek, Mechanicsville), Virginia,
  June 26, 1862
Mechanicsville, *see* Meadow Bridge
Meridian expedition, Mississippi, February 3-March 5, 1864
Mill Springs (Fishing Creek), Kentucky, January 19, 1862
Milliken's Bend, Louisiana, June 7, 1863

Mine Creek, Kansas, October 25, 1864 (skirmish)
Mine Run campaign, Virginia, November 26-December 2, 1863
Missionary Ridge, Tennessee, November 25, 1863
Mobile, Alabama, operations about, February 16-March 27, 1864;
    May 4, 1865; evacuated by Confederates, April 11, 1865
Monocacy, Maryland, July 9, 1864
Morgan's Raids, Kentucky: July 4-28, 1862; December 22, 1862-
    January 2, 1863; May 31-June 20, 1864; Ohio: July 13-26, 1863;
    Indiana: July 9-13, 1863
Murfreesboro, Tennessee, December 31, 1862-January 3, 1863
Nashville, Tennessee, December 15-16, 1864
New Bern, North Carolina, March 14, 1862
New Hope Church, Georgia, May 25-June 5, 1864
New Madrid, Missouri, capture of, March 3-14, 1862
New Market, Virginia, June 13, 1862; May 15, 1864
New Orleans, Louisiana, capture of, April 25, 1862
Newburgh, Indiana, capture of, July 18, 1862
Newtonia, Missouri, September 30, 1862
Olustee, Florida, February 20, 1864
Overland campaign, Virginia, Summer, 1864
Paducah, Kentucky, capture of, March 25, 1864
Payne's Farm, Virginia, November 27, 1863
Pea Ridge, *see* Elkhorn
Peach ·Orchard, Virginia, June 29, 1862
Peachtree Creek, Georgia, July 20, 1864
Peninsular campaign, Virginia, April-July, 1862
Pennsylvania campaign, *see* Gettysburg campaign
Pensacola, Florida, evacuated by Confederates, May 9-12, 1862;
    evacuated by Federals, March 20-24, 1863
Perryville, Kentucky, October 7-8, 1862
Petersburg, Virginia, assault on lines of, June 15-18, 1864
Petersburg, Virginia, siege of, June 15, 1864-April 2, 1865
Piedmont, Virginia, June 5, 1864
Pine Mountain, Georgia, June 14, 1864
Pittsburg Landing, *see* Shiloh
Pleasant Hill, Louisiana, April 9, 1864
Plymouth, North Carolina, April 17-20, 1864
Port Gibson, Mississippi, May 1, 1863
Port Hudson, Louisiana, siege of, May 21-July 9, 1863
Port Republic, Virginia, June 8-9, 1862
Port Royal (Port Royal Ferry), South Carolina, January 1, 1862;
    June 6, 1862; July 4, 1862
Port Royal Bay (Forts Walker and Beauregard), South Carolina,
    November 7, 1861
Port Walthall Junction, Virginia, May 6-7, 1864
Prairie Grove, Arkansas, December 7, 1862
Princeton, West Virginia, September 16, 1861; May 15-17, 1862
Rappahannock Bridge, Virginia, October 22, 1863

Reams' Station, Virginia, August 25, 1864
Red River campaign, Louisiana, March 10-May 22, 1864
Resaca, Georgia, May 14-15, 1864
Rich Mountain, West Virginia, July 11, 1861
Rich Mountain campaign, West Virginia, *see* Western Virginia campaign
Richmond, Kentucky, August 30, 1862
Richmond, Virginia, siege of, June 19, 1864-April 3, 1865
Romney, West Virginia, January 10, 1862
Romney expedition, West Virginia, December 1861-January 1862
Salem Church, Virginia, May 3-4, 1863
Savage's Station, Virginia, June 29, 1862
Savannah campaign, Georgia, November 15-December 21, 1864
Sayler's Creek, Virginia, April 6, 1865
Secessionville, South Carolina, June 16, 1862
Selma, Alabama, April 2, 1865
Seven Days battles, Virginia, June 26-July 2, 1862. *See* Cold Harbor, Frayser's Farm, Malvern Hill, Meadow Bridge, Peach Orchard, Savage's Station
Seven Pines (Fair Oaks), Virginia, May 31-June 1, 1862
Sharpsburg (Antietam), Maryland, September 17, 1862
Shenandoah Valley campaign, Virginia, Early's, June-November, 1864
Shenandoah Valley campaign, Virginia, Jackson's, April-June, 1862
Shiloh (Pittsburg Landing), Tennessee, April 6-7, 1862
Smithburg, Tennessee, July 4, 1863 (skirmish)
South Mountain, Maryland, September 14, 1862
Spanish Fort, Alabama, siege and capture of, March 27-April 8, 1865
Spotsylvania Court House, Virginia, May 8-21, 1864
Spring Hill (Thompson's Station), Tennessee, November 29, 1864
Springfield, *see* Wilson's Creek
Suffolk, Virginia, expedition against and siege of, April 11-May 4, 1863
Telford's Depot, Tennessee, September 8, 1863
Tennessee campaign, Hood's, November-December, 1864
Thoroughfare Gap, Virginia, August 28, 1862; October 17-18, 1862
Tullahoma campaign, Tennessee, June 23-July 7, 1863
Tupelo, Mississippi, May 5, 1863; July 14-15, 1864
Valverde, New Mexico, February 21, 1862
Vicksburg campaign, Mississippi, December 20, 1862-January 3, 1863; siege, May 19-July 4, 1863
Walthall's Junction, *see* Port Walthall Junction
Washington, D. C., Early at Fort Stevens near, July 11-12, 1864
Waynesboro Virginia, June 10, 1864; September 29, 1864; March 2, 1865

NOTES

Where an officer's career has been wholly reconstructed from published and generally accessible works, the sources are not given in these notes. In such cases the reader will understand that the subject's life is treated *in extenso* in one or more such standard reference biographies as *Dictionary of American Biography, Cyclopedia of American Biography,* and so on. However, newspapers, manuscripts, obscure books and information secured from descendants or other individuals are always cited. Notes are also given in those instances in which the author's research had led him to differ from previously published accounts. Complete citations for books included in the notes are included in the bibliography.

(1) In 1850 General Abercrombie gave his age as forty-six, and his wife gave hers as thirty-three. Twenty years later, in 1870, he admitted to sixty-eight, she to forty-six. (Federal Census, 1850, Bexar County, Texas; and 1870, Queens County, New York.) Neither his descendants nor research in the Washington records disclosed details of his family or early life.

(2) Date of birth from records of the Commune Chêne-Bougeries, a section of Geneva, Switzerland. (Courtesy of Rev. Gerald B. O'Grady, rector, American Church, Geneva.) Allen's parents emigrated from Ireland to the United States in 1805, locating in West Point. (Letter to author from Indiana State Library, February 7, 1957.)

(3) Exact place of birth on authority of New Jersey Historical Society.

(4) The retirement order read: "For Disability resulting from Long and Faithful Service and Disease contracted in the Line of Duty."

(5) The most complete sketch of Asboth's life is to be found in Vasvary, *Lincoln's Hungarian Heroes,* 44-47.

(6) Bruce Catton remarks that during this raid "Averell wandered over to Rapidan Station and went into bivouac there . . . as much out of the war as if he had been in Cuba. . . ." (*Glory*

Road, 228.) Averell was summarily relieved of his command by Hooker but was later reinstated.

(7) Some sources state that Bailey was born in Salem, Ohio, on April 28, 1827. The author has been unable to resolve the discrepancy. However, the year of his marriage (1846) makes the earlier date seem a little more likely.

(8) This regiment was to be credited to California's quota. However, California refused to recognize it, and for a time the regiment made its returns directly to the War Department, the same as the Regulars. Ultimately, Governor Andrew G. Curtin commissioned Baker and accepted the regiment as the 71st Pennsylvania.

(9) The question is not whether Baker should be treated as a general officer, for in a letter written September 22, 1861, the day of his appointment as major general, he says he will decline the commission. From then until his death he was universally referred to and signed himself Colonel.

(10) Baker, *The Secret Service in the Late War,* a book replete with misstatements, exaggerations, and omissions.

(11) The Carter Cemetery on October 25, 1957, advised the author that the graves in the Mutual Family Cemetery "were moved en masse to Forest Hills" and that "the burial records were never turned over to Forest Hills." Accordingly, General Baker "no doubt, is now here in an unmarked grave."

(12) Authority for the expedition seems to have been the responsibility of President Lincoln and Secretary of State Seward.

(13) According to the University of Pennsylvania School of Medicine, "—the 'K' was used as an identifying mark rather than an initial for a middle name." (Letter to author, May 23, 1957.)

(14) So says one of Barnes's biographers. However, Dr. George Worthington Adams, in his authoritative book, felt that Barnes's principal qualification was his friendship with Edwin M. Stanton; that the accomplishments of his regime were conceptions of William A. Hammond's; and that with his advent "there was an end of new ideas, and . . . a partial relapse into antebellum lethargy. The Department slumbered." (*Doctors in Blue,* 41-42.)

(15) Barnum's middle name was obtained from his death certificate, a copy of which is in the author's possession.

(16) New York *Times,* January 30, 1892.

(17) Day of birth was obtained from obituary in Washington *Post,* dated January 15, 1893, data for which was presumably given by his brother, Reverend W. A. Bartlett of Washington, D. C.

(18) *Official Records of the Union and Confederate Armies,* XXIX, Pt. 1, pp. 102-103. Hereinafter cited as *Official Records;* unless otherwise stated, all references will be to Series I.)

(19) Most published sources record his birth as January 6, 1840; however, his own memoirs cite June. (Letter to author from Pittsfield Public Library, August 1, 1957.)

(20) Much of the data regarding General Baxter was obtained from his great-granddaughter, Mrs. Robert Colby of Mason, Michigan.

(21) *Kansas Historical Quarterly,* XXIV (Spring, 1958), 4 n.

(22) Much of the data on General Beal was obtained by the courtesy of Mr. F. A. Towne, Norway, Maine.

(23) The author is indebted to the Stark County Historical Society of Ohio for data on General Beatty.

(24) Place of birth obtained from copy of birth certificate in author's possession. The same document records Benham's mother's birthplace as England; this does not comport with some sources which place both her and her son's birth at Quebec.

(25) T. A. Morris, an 1834 graduate of West Point who resigned his commission in 1836, was a brigadier general of Indiana volunteers, receiving this commission from the governor. He was not mustered into United States service and was honorably mustered out of state service July 27, 1861.

(26) *The Union Army,* VII, 31; however, *Official Records,* VIII, 249-50, exhibit that Colonel Thomas Patterson, 18th Indiana, commanded the brigade of Jefferson C. Davis' 3rd Division of which Benton's regiment was a part.

(27) The author's correspondence with Buxton L. Layton of New Orleans and personal research in the city have established that Benton's remains were removed from Greenwood at an unknown date and forwarded to the Masonic Cemetery. However, since the latter cemetery has no record of the burial, it is conjectural exactly where General Benton's remains now lie. There is no record of his burial in Richmond. (Letter to author from Morrison-Reeves Library, July 31, 1957, Richmond, Indiana.) A parallel case is that of the ex-Confederate brigadier Young M. Moody, who died under identical circumstances the year following and whose remains were also transferred in the 1880's to the Masonic Cemetery after being first buried in one of the vaults of the Louisiana Relief Lodge, Free and Accepted Masons, in Greenwood. (Much of the information on Benton's early career has been obtained from the *History of Wayne County, Indiana.*)

(28) *Official Records,* XXV, Pt. 1, p. 447.

(29) *Official Records,* XXXVI, Pt. 3, p. 709

(30) Place of birth on authority of Kentucky Historical Society, quoting from Frankfort (Kentucky) *Commonwealth,* August 4, 1871.

(31) The outline of Bradley's career outside the army was put together by the courtesy of the Chicago Historical Society and by the Connecticut Historical Society, quoting from the Hartford (Connecticut) *Times,* March 14, 1910.

(32) Although Brannan's middle name has been universally given as Milton, including the application of his widow for an increased pension in 1898, he himself gave it as Myer, when he accepted his commission as brevet major general at Nashville, Tennessee, on May 12, 1865. (Brannan file, National Archives.) His mother's maiden name was Myer, according to a copy of his death certificate in the author's possession.

(33) Unpublished correspondence in the National Archives.

(34) In 1876, Tilden's Democratic victory over Hayes was nullified by the disqualification of thousands of Democratic ballots in Florida and Louisiana by Republican election boards which were backed up by United States regular troops, mainly Negroes who were ex-bondsmen.

(35) Letter to author from Mrs. Donna D. Finger, Reference Depart-

ment, Kansas City Public Library, August 27, 1957, states that "a local historian believes him buried in Union Cemetery in an unmarked grave, although the cemetery itself has no such record." However, subsequent research has located Brayman's grave on a lot surmounted by a handsome monument in Ripon Cemetery, Ripon, Wisconsin. He purchased the lot upon the death of his wife in 1886.

(36) The author is grateful to Mrs. Janet Edwards, Local History Collection, The Berkshire Athenaeum, Pittsfield, Massachusetts, for data on General Briggs.

(37) See note 446 for a discussion of the reasons for Brooks's demotion.

(38) Letter to author from Huntsville Public Library, October 22, 1957.

(39) Date of birth courtesy Toledo Public Library from an article in the Toledo (Ohio) *Blade,* winter of 1926.

(40) *Appleton's Cyclopedia,* I, 398, states that Brown "obtained the rudiments of education in a log schoolhouse in Tecumseh, Michigan."

(41) Authority of an article in the Toledo (Ohio) *Blade,* winter of 1926, courtesy Toledo Public Library.

(42) Brown's wartime career can be found in the *Official Records.*

(43) According to a brief obituary in the St. Louis (Missouri) *Republic,* "After the war [Brown] engaged in the mercantile business in St. Louis and made a fortune, which he afterwards lost." The farm is supposed to have been at "Hastings, Calhoun County." (*Appleton's Cyclopedia,* I, 398.)

(44) No death notice appeared in the Toledo, Chicago, or New York papers.

(45) Letter to author from Mr. A. L. Chelf, Cuba, Missouri (n.d.).

(46) It is likely that the taint of Buchanan's previous association with Fitz John Porter resulted in the rejection of his appointment. Hell had no fury to match the vindictiveness of the Republican Radicals in their efforts to immolate the supporters of George B. McClellan and Porter.

(47) Buckingham's manuscript, "Recollections," in the possession of his grandson John R. Buckingham of Parkland, Pennsylvania, reveals that he and Lee were privileged to board at "a private house" (Mrs. Kinsley's) and "to sit up at night as long as we chose." This was for excellence in mathematics and as a reward for their being chosen assistant professors, although only third-class men.

(48) Extensive research and correspondence with many of General Burnham's collateral descendants, particularly Mr. Frank W. Nash, Cherryfield, Maine, have failed to reveal any more data than is set forth here. General Burnham seems to have died as he lived—heroically and unpretentiously.

(49) *Official Records,* XXVII, Pt. 3, pp. 458-59; see also Cleaves, *Meade of Gettysburg,* 133.

(50) Much of the data has been taken from Caldwell's obituary in the Topeka (Kansas) *Daily Capital,* courtesy Kansas State Historical Society.

(51) Information on General Campbell's postbellum career, courtesy South Dakota State Historical Society in a letter to author, January 6, 1910.

(52) Date and place of Canby's birth according to Heyman, *Prudent Soldier*, 16. However, Canby's brother-in-law General J. P. Hawkins in his reminiscences gives this data as East Bend, Kentucky, November 19.

(53) Exhaustive research into the history of the Canby and Sibley families by the author discloses no connection by marriage.

(54) Place and date of his birth from Hunt. *James H. Carleton*, 26.

(55) The author is indebted to Mr. Alfred H. Johnson, Carrollton, Illinois, for much data relative to General Carlin. See also Livingston (Montana) *Enterprise*, October 10, 1903.

(56) *Official Records*, XXXVI, Pt. 2, p. 346.

(57) Tucker, *Hancock the Superb*, 215, states that "His [Carroll's name] will always be associated with Hancock's and with some of the greatest moments of the II Corps . . . he was a soldier of great capacity and splendid fighting courage."

(58) Casey's Redoubt was also identified for all time with the court-martial of Fitz John Porter, who was cashiered for alleged misbehavior at Second Manassas. Casey was made a member of the court, despite the fact that a few months previously Porter had refused to accept him as a subordinate. (Eisenschiml, *The Celebrated Case of Fitz John Porter*, 78, 170.)

(59) Catterson's death certificate records his middle name as Frank.

(60) Place and date of birth and data on early life from Indianapolis (Indiana) *Star*, April 12, 1914.

(61) Indianapolis *Star*, April 12, 1914; Washington (Arkansas) *Telegraph*, September 3, 1871; Little Rock, Arkansas, *City Directories* 1872-73, 1873-74; Hempstead's *History of Arkansas*, 633-34; *Arkansas Historical Quarterly*, various volumes; copy of death certificate in the author's possession.

(62) This information according to Mrs. Ernest J. Stiefel of St. Paul Park, Minnesota, a niece to whom the author is indebted for much data. There was also a very full obituary in the San Antonio (Texas) *Express*, January 4, 1888.

(63) *Official Records*, XI, Pt. 1, pp. 865, 868.

(64) *Official Records*, XII, Pt. 2, pp. 417, 435-36.

(65) Much of the data on Chapin is taken from Clark's *The 116th Regiment of New York Volunteers*. For a report of the assault in which Chapin met his death, see *Official Records*, XXVI, Pt. 1, pp. 510-11.

(66) Information on General Chapman's antebellum and postbellum careers from *Biographical Sketches of Members of the Indiana Legislature*, courtesy Indiana State Library.

(67) Collier does not specify who the three others were.

(68) The last was Joel A. Dewey who was appointed nine days later.

(69) David Y. Thomas in *Dictionary of American Biography*, IV, 187.

(70) *Official Records*, XXIII, Pt. 2, pp. 11-12.

(71) No problem of research in connection with the Union generals presented more of a challenge than that of Cluseret. Aside from a brief obituary in the New York *Herald*, August 24, 1900,

which incorrectly recorded the day of his death, all background research was conducted abroad in the French language. The author is especially indebted to M. Maxime Serre of Toulon, Mrs. Roy O. Cook of Algiers, stepmother of Mrs. Carolyn Sutton of San Diego, and Mr. Kenneth Gardner of San Diego, whose fluent French supplemented the author's meager command of the language.

(72) Cf., note 446 for an explanation of Cochrane's resignation.

(73) The spelling of Connor's given name on authority of his daughter Miss Mabel Connor of Augusta, Maine, courtesy of Mrs. Ralph H. Conant, Augusta.

(74) Much of the data relating to General Copeland is by courtesy of the Michigan Historical Commission and the Michigan State Library and includes material from *Michigan Biographies,* I, 200, and Ward, *Orchard Lake and Its Island,* 22-25. Place of death and burial, authority of Mrs. Stuart Ralph, Town Clerk, Orange Park, Florida, in a letter to author, March 14, 1957.

(75) *Register of Graduates and Former Cadets,* 163.

(76) See Horn, *The Army of Tennessee,* 376.

(77) *Official Records,* XXXIX, Pt. 3, p. 113. This message was the sheerest nonsense, Corse having sustained a nick in the side of his face.

(78) Much of the data relating to General Cowdin is from Roberts, *The Ancient and Honorable Artillery Company of Massachusetts, 1637-1688,* courtesy Boston Public Library.

(79) Eisenschiml, *The Celebrated Case of Fitz John Porter.*

(80) Much of the data relating to General Craig, courtesy of the state Historical Society of Missouri.

(81) T. L. Crittenden was alleged to be a "kinsman" of Zachary Taylor by his biographer in *Dictionary of American Biography,* IV, 549.

(82) Very little data on T. T. Crittenden appears in published sources. Most of the information on his antebellum and postbellum careers was obtained from a grandson Thomas T. Crittenden of San Diego to whom the author is much indebted. The general was first buried in Rock Creek Cemetery, Georgetown; his remains were removed to Arlington National Cemetery in 1931.

(83) *Official Records,* XLV, Pt. 2, p. 388 and XLVI, Pt. 2, p. 628.

(84) *Official Records,* XLV, Pt. 2, p. 443 (dated December 31, 1864).

(85) However, Henry W. Halleck claimed winter may have prevented Crocker's eastward journey. (*Official Records,* XLVI, Pt. 2, p. 802.) On the other hand, Carleton, commanding the Department of New Mexico, refers to the order relieving Crocker (in an order of his own dated March 11, 1865) as "No. 477, Series of 1864." Did Carleton ignore the order or did it not get through? There was no telegraph or railroad from the Missouri River to Santa Fe at the time. All communication was by stage or horseback. On March 8, 1865, the War Department telegraphed Thomas at Nashville to have Crocker report to the adjutant general in Washington, "as soon as [he] reports to you." (*Official Records,* XLIX, Pt. 1, p. 860.) U. S. Grant evidently

was very "high" on Crocker, as his numerous communications to Edwin M. Stanton and Halleck attest. (*Official Records*, XLVI, XLVII, XLVIII, *passim*.)

(86) Secretary of War Stanton was so enraged by this event that U. S. Grant had to cool him off until an official investigation was made. Even then (and no investigation took place) there was talk of replacing Crook with Crocker. The latter, however, was in New Mexico and unavailable. All the details of this incident are in the *Official Records*, XLVI, *passim*.

(87) Place and date of Croxton's birth, authority of family Bible in possession of his niece Mrs. Harry S. Hill, Paris, Kentucky (letter to author, March, 1960).

(88) Much of the data on General Cruft, courtesy Indiana State Library, Indianapolis, quoting Terre Haute (Indiana) *Express*, March 23, 1883, and Daily, *Greater Terre Haute and Vigo County*, 297-98.

(89) Monaghan, *Custer*, 10-12.

(90) During the Peninsular campaign George B. McClellan rode up to a crossing of the Chickahominy and remarked he would like to know how deep the water was. His staff not responding, Custer plunged in, rode across and back, and called out, "That's how deep it is, General." (Monaghan, *Custer*, 80.)

(91) The *Official Records* index lists Davies as Henry E. Davies, Jr., although, according to his own memoir (cited by *Dictionary of American Biography*), his father was named Henry Ebenezer Davies. *Appleton's Cyclopedia*, II, 90, on the other hand, has a sketch of the father headed "Henry Eugene."

(92) Fry, *Military Miscellanies*, 486-505. Fry was at the time Don Carlos Buell's chief of staff and arrested Davis in Buell's name.

(93) Davis was first buried in the churchyard in Memphis, Indiana, but was moved to Crown Hill the following year.

(94) *Arizona Daily Star* (Tucson), April 11, 1884, which recites in a most detailed account that Deitzler was killed "this morning." *Dictionary of American Biography* erroneously records his death on the tenth.

(95) Of all 583 Federal generals of full rank, General Dennis had become the most obscure by the time of his death. Recreating his antecedents and career involved extensive research in original documents and friendly help from several dispersed localities. Among these were: Mr. Lewis B. Farr, Clerk, 6th District Court, Tallulah, Louisiana; Mrs. Dorothea Dennis (a granddaughter-in-law), East St. Louis, Illinois; Miss Mahala Saville, University of Mississippi Library, University, Mississippi; Mr. Michael M. Reynolds, Louisiana State University Library, Baton Rouge, Lousiana; Miss Helen Eldridge, Newburgh Free Library, Newburgh, New York; and Mr. Clyde O. Walton, Illinois State Historian, Springfield, Illinois.

(96) *Dictionary of American Biography* gives the dates of both Dent's birth and death incorrectly. Dates used here were taken from his grave marker in Arlington National Cemetery; also in Colorado *Sun*, December 24, 1892.

(97) Because of the many volunteer commissions issued from 1861

to 1865, many "old army" officers prized their regular commissions above their temporary commissions (of higher grade) in the volunteer service.

(98) Authority Mr. Sidney Forman, Librarian, U. S. Military Academy, West Point, letter to author, May 5, 1960.

(99) *Official Records,* XI, Pt. 1, p. 50.

(100) See Detroit (Michigan) *Free Press,* May 30, 1891, and June 2, 1891.

(101) Most Union writers of the campaign of Chancellorsville tend to deal briefly with what must be a painful subject, in view of the later prominence of the commanders involved. But see Catton, *Glory Road,* 199-205. The best fighting of the XI Corps was done by Buschbeck's brigade—and who has ever heard of Buschbeck? Despite his subsequent gallantry and ability when he commanded a brigade of Geary's division of the XX Corps, he was mustered out as colonel, without even a brevet promotion to brigadier general.

(102) *The Union Army,* II, 187.

(103) Authority of letter to author from Oberlin College, May 11, 1960.

(104) Much other data on Dewey, aside from the *Official Records,* courtesy of Mr. Robert T. Quarles, Jr., Director of Archives, Nashville, Tennessee.

(105) *Official Records,* XVIII, 541, 561.

(106) *Official Records,* XVIII, 560. The officer in question was Colonel Samuel P. Spear of the 11th Pennsylvania Cavalry.

(107) Spear had enlisted in the 2nd U. S. Dragoons two years before Dodge was born. (Heitman, *Historical Register,* 909.)

(108) For some details of Dodge's postbellum career, see the New York *Times,* November 5, 1910, p. 7, col. 4.

(109) James, *They Had Their Hour,* 257.

(110) Information as to General Doolittle's antebellum and postbellum careers from Toledo (Ohio) *Blade,* February 20, 1903, and from Mrs. Irene McCreery of the Toledo Public Library.

(111) Newton was Doubleday's junior in rank by some six months.

(112) W. Randall Waterman in *Dictionary of American Biography,* V, 411-12.

(113) *Official Records,* XLIII, Pt. 2, p. 429.

(114) *Official Records,* I, 35. In fairness to Duffie it should be pointed out that Philip Sheridan often spoke and acted upon impulse and not always without prejudice (cf. his relief of Warren at Five Forks). There may also have been a personality clash between Hibernia and Gaul. After his death the men of the 1st Rhode Island erected a monument to his memory in Providence, certainly a testimonial to his soldierly qualities. However, he was referred to as "a swaggering and flashy fellow" by one officer with whom he was imprisoned at Danville, Virginia, and bitterly criticized by another. Cf. Small, *The Road to Richmond,* 177, and Putnam, *A Prisoner of War in Virginia, 1864-65, passim.* Small was major of the 16th Maine; Putnam was first lieutenant and adjutant of the 176th New York.

(115) *Memorandum Relative to the General Officers . . .* erroneously

lists a Hiram Duryea as the officer to whom full rank as brigadier general was accorded instead of Hiram Duryée.

(116) *Biographical Directory of the American Congress 1774-1949* gives Duval's middle name as Harding, which is apparently an error, according to Mr. Boyd B. Stutler of Charleston, West Virginia, an authority on West Virginia history to whom the author is much indebted for information on General Duval's life.

(117) In 1860 the population of Virginia numbered 1,100,000 whites and 491,000 slaves. In the forty-eight counties which became West Virginia, the whites numbered 335,000 and the slaves less than 13,000. Thus in eastern Virginia there was a slave for each one and one-quarter white persons; whereas in the western part of the state there was one slave for approximately thirty-eight whites.

(118) Letter, from the U. S. Military Academy to the author, May 24, 1960.

(119) Johnson, *The Red River Campaign*, 57-59.

(120) *Official Records*, XLIII, Pt. 1, pp. 300-307.

(121) Bruce, *Lincoln and the Tools of War*, 168.

(122) New Haven (Connecticut) *Daily Morning Journal & Courier*, February 22, 1877. Also see New Haven *Evening Register*, February 22, 1877 and New Haven *Daily Palladium* and New Haven *Evening Union*, same date.

(123) Year of birth obtained from Edward's grave marker in Arlington National Cemetery. *Biographical Directory of the American Congress 1774-1949* gives 1805 apparently in error.

(124) General Egan's career before and after the war has been reconstructed with difficulty. For much of the data within, the author is indebted to his great-niece Miss Elsie Anderson of Washington, D. C., who is the authority for the statement that his middle name was Wilberforce, not Washington as rendered by Heitman, *Historical Register*. It is possible that the general adopted Washington as a patriotic cognomen later in life. The name Egan was misspelled Eagan on his New York City death certificate with the result that he was buried under the wrong name in the National Cemetery in Brooklyn, even though a stone later erected by the survivors of the 40th New York spelled the name correctly. In 1957 the matter was called to the attention of the War Department, and Cypress Hills was given permission to change its records from Eagan to Egan.

(125) Fisher, *Biographical Sketches of El Dorado Citizens*, courtesy Kansas State Historical Society, letter to author, June 14, 1960.

(126) In point of fact he resigned "for deficiency in Philosophy at the end of his Second Class Year." (Letter from U. S. Military Academy to the author, May 29, 1960.) In those days many cadets "resigned" for scholastic deficiencies, since it was popularly supposed one "lost face" by failing one or more courses.

(127) Published as *Senate Executive Document No. 7*, 30 Cong., 1st Sess.

(128) Although three men were reappointed after their original appointments lapsed, one officer had not accepted his appointment and a number had died or resigned. Nevertheless, 125 separate

appointments to the grade of major general of volunteers had been made prior to that of Emory and only five were made after his. Thus, as an example, Emory was junior to George Custer in the volunteer service, although Custer's regular rank was that of captain in the same regiment of which Emory was colonel.

(129) Authority of Mr. Leslie I. Harvey, Nashua Cemetery Association, Nashua, New Hampshire, letter to author, September 10, 1957.

(130) *Official Records,* XXXVI, Pt. 1, p. 96.

(131) *Quarterly Review* number of the *Michigan Alumnus,* December 5, 1959, reprinted in the winter 1959-60 issue of the *Purple and Gold,* organ of the Chi Psi Fraternity of which Farnsworth was a member.

(132) *Ibid.*

(133) Thus Sherman characterized Kilpatrick in November, 1864. (Lewis, *Sherman, Fighting Prophet,* 405.)

(134) Catton, *A Stillness at Appomattox,* 249.

(135) Place and date of birth authority of Office of Adjutant General of Ohio, January 12, 1957.

(136) See note 446 for a discussion of the circumstances which aroused the enmity of Ambrose E. Burnside.

(137) At this time "the corps was . . . commanded by bumbling, red-faced General W. H. French, who mishandled his troops so flagrantly that Hooker's and Kearney's veterans sardonically referred to their outfit as 'the III Corps as we understand it.'" (Catton, *Glory Road,* 353.)

(138) Virgin Bay, on the west shore of Lake Nicaragua, was an important point of transshipment on the Accessory Transit Company's interocean route across Nicaragua. The company in earlier days had been pioneered by Commodore Cornelius Vanderbilt.

(139) It is not to the credit of Garfield that until his death he publicly clung tenaciously to the view that Porter was honestly convicted. (Cf., Eisenschiml, *The Celebrated Case of Fitz John Porter, passim.*)

(140) *National Cyclopedia of American Biography,* XXIII, 258, makes this statement categorically, and it comports with his acknowledged age in years and months when he entered West Point. His younger brother's birth in May, 1829, renders impossible the birth date given in *Dictionary of American Biography.*

(141) According to W. T. Sherman, Garrard retreats "if he can see a horseman in the distance with a spyglass." (Lewis, *Sherman, Fighting Prophet,* 405.) Sherman supplanted Garrard with Judson Kilpatrick, whom he thought to be "a hell of a damned fool." (*Ibid.*)

(142) The author is indebted to Mr. T. T. Burchell of Manchester for considerable data relating to Garrard's grandfather.

(143) George W. Cullum erroneously records Gilbert's death as occurring on January 23, 1903. That he died on the seventeenth is testified to by his obituary in the Baltimore *Sun,* January 18, 1903, and by the inscription on his grave marker in Cave Hill Cemetery.

(144) Burlington (Iowa) *Hawkeye,* February 20, 1884. For other data on Gilbert the author is indebted to Mrs. M. C. Wheelwright, Des Moines, Iowa.

(145) Authority of Colonel Campbell Brown, Nashville, letter to author, July 25, 1961.

(146) General Graham's career, hitherto rather obscure, has been reconstructed from various sources, including an obituary in the Washington *Post,* September 15, 1905. His relationship to Colonel James Duncan Graham, West Point class of 1817, Corps of Engineers; Major Campbell Graham, West Point class of 1822, Corps of Topographical Engineers; and Lieutenant Colonel William Montrose Graham, West Point class of 1817, killed at the battle of Molino del Rey in 1847—who were his brothers—has been largely overlooked. Even Dr. D. S. Freeman completely ignored William D. Graham in Appendix II to Volume I of *Lee's Lieutenants,* entitled "Southern Resources of Command."

(147) Granger's classmate, General Thomas J. Wood, said of him: "Had Granger never rendered any other service to the nation than he did on that illustrious occasion, he would have been justly entitled to its lasting gratitude." This encomium is significant, since Granger's independence occasionally bordered on insubordination and in ordinary circumstances he lacked drive. Even though Granger was "great in battle," as William S. Rosecrans described him, U. S. Grant did not trust him and gave him no command of importance after 1863.

(148) Most published sources recite that L. A. Grant was born January 17, 1829. However, his death certificate records 1828 and further states he was aged "90 yrs. 2 mos. 3 days" when he died at 1:00 A.M. on the morning of March 20, 1918.

(149) *The Union Army,* I, 111.

(150) *Personal Memoirs of P. H. Sheridan,* I, 435. It may be further noted that although Gregg was brevetted major general of volunteers in August, 1864, he received no promotions whatever in the regular service (brevet or otherwise) after the beginning of the war, and his regular rank was captain of the 6th Cavalry when he resigned. In a strange parallel, his first cousin J. Irvin Gregg, who was not a West Pointer and was commissioned directly into the Regular Army in 1861, attained the brevet rank of major general of volunteers and brigadier general, U. S. Army, but was never given the full rank of brigadier general of volunteers and hence does not appear in these pages as the subject of a sketch. However, on July 28, 1866, when the Regular Army was reorganized, J. Irvin Gregg was made colonel of the 8th Cavalry, while such a luminary as George Custer, a full major general of volunteers and by brevet in the regular service, had to be content with the lieutenant colonelcy of the 7th Cavalry.

(151) Colonel Thomas M. Spaulding, U. S. Army, in his sketch of Griffin in *Dictionary of American Biography,* relates that on the battlefield of Second Manassas Griffin was heard to ask "what Pope had ever done that he should be made a major-general." In the face of this outburst, why Griffin's head did not roll along with Porter's is difficult to understand.

(152) Griffin was first buried in the Episcopal Cemetery, Galveston, but his body was removed to the vault of his wife's family on December 28, 1867. His son also died in the same epidemic. (*Army & Navy Journal,* V [January 4, 1868], 311, courtesy of

Thomas R. Hay.) Mrs. Griffin was a sister of General S. S. Carroll, who is also buried in Oak Hill Cemetery.

(153) This claim would not appear to be particularly well founded since the report of the brigade commander, Colonel Jacob Ammen, renders it explicit that two other regiments of his brigade, the 6th and 24th Ohio, also took part in the first day's action. (Cf., *Official Records,* X, Pt. 1, pp. 332 ff.)

(154) During 1876-77 Grover, then Democratic governor of Oregon, almost succeeded in electing Tilden over Hayes in the disputed presidential election of that time by attempting to certify one Democratic elector in place of a Republican who had been disqualified because of his occupancy of a postmaster ship. Had Grover's brief prevailed (disallowed by the electoral commission), Tilden would have won the election 185 to 184, instead of the other way around. It may be deemed a certainty that the elder Grover's labors on the part of Tilden did nothing to enhance his brother's prospects for promotion postbellum.

(155) The author has been unable to verify Grover's "brilliant forced march . . . to the Missouri River" after being summoned to surrender by the Confederate government—as related in the *Dictionary of American Biography,* VIII, 29—while he was stationed at Fort Union. At least, these documents do not appear in the *Official Records.*

(156) There is some discrepancy between published sources as to the date of General Hackleman's death. Most state he was "killed" on either the third or the fourth. However, the *Official Records* render it implicit that he was wounded sometime between 2:00 P.M. and 5:00 P.M. on the afternoon of the third and died that night. Davies states that he visited his wounded brigade commander that night and that Hackleman "breathed his last while [he] was with him. . . ." (*Official Records,* XVII, Pt. 1, p. 257.)

(157) Hassler, *General George B. McClellan,* 181-82.

(158) Horn, *The Army of Tennessee,* 160, quoting A. W. Alexander, *Grant as a Soldier,* 89.

(159) During the campaign of the fall of 1863, George G. Meade, goaded beyond endurance by Halleck's objurgations, replied, "If you have any orders to give me, I am prepared to . . . obey them, but I must insist on being spared the infliction of such truisms in the guise of opinions as you have recently honored me with, particularly as they were not asked for. . . ." (Meade to Halleck, October 18, 1863, in *Official Records,* XXIX, Pt. 2, p. 346.)

(160) This affair, which caused a tremendous sensation at the time, would have been called a skirmish a year later. Federal casualties numbered seventy-six, Confederate, eleven, as the latter repulsed some feeble, poorly handled assaults by Unionists who had already sustained losses by firing wildly at one another.

(161) *Official Records,* XI, Pt. 3, pp. 129, 185-86.

(162) Cf., Catton, *Grant Moves South,* 395-96, for a résumé of the events leading up to Hamilton's resignation. Also see Henry W. Halleck to U. S. Grant, December 9, 1863 (*Official Records,* XXIV, Pt. 1, p. 28): "Gen. C. S. Hamilton's resignation has been

received. . . . No doubt he resigns to get a higher command. This game sometimes succeeds, but it also sometimes fails."

(163) *Official Records*, XXVI, Pt. 1, p. 396.

(164) To illustrate the inequities of promotion: Colonel George Webster of the 98th Ohio was killed in action at Perryville while commanding a brigade of Alexander McD. McCook's corps. He never received so much as a posthumous brevet promotion.

(165) Adams, *Doctors in Blue,* 31. The author is indebted to this fine work for much information on Surgeon General Hammond.

(166) *Ibid.,* 39 ff.

(167) In 1878 Congress approved a bill authorizing Hammond's restoration to the service if justice so indicated. He was accordingly restored and placed on the retired list with the grade of brigadier general, thus making possible his eventual burial in Arlington National Cemetery.

(168) On June 15, 1861, Captain and Mrs. Hancock gave a farewell dinner in Los Angeles for a party of their old army friends which included General and Mrs. Albert Sidney Johnston, Major Lewis Armistead, and Captain R. B. Garnett. Years later she recalled that three of the guests were later killed in front of Hancock's lines at Gettysburg. Two were, of course, Armistead and Garnett, brigade commanders in Pickett's division who died in the famous charge; the identity of the third man cannot be determined. (Tucker, *Hancock the Superb,* 64-65.)

(169) Hancock mistook the source of the missile (which he pulled out of his thigh unaided), remarking, "They must be hard up for ammunition when they throw such shot as that." (*Ibid.,* 155-56.)

(170) Hancock's judge advocate, Captain Henry Harrison Bingham, in *ibid.,* 263.

(171) Curiously enough, George W. Cullum omits all mention of Hardie's appointment to the grade of brigadier general of volunteers in his summary of the latter's career, although the appended biographical sketch—the inclusion or noninclusion of which represents Cullum's opinion of the officer's professional standing —makes mention thereof and adds that Hardie "vacated [the] position" when he was made an assistant adjutant general in the regular service. This view is echoed by the *Dictionary of American Biography*. Both sources seem to ignore the fact that Hardie's appointment as assistant adjutant general, U. S. Army, followed by almost a month the revocation of his volunteer brigadier generalcy. (Cf., Cullum, *Biographical Register,* II, 162-65; *Dictionary of American Biography,* XII, 242; Heitman, *Historical Register,* 499-500; *Memorandum Relative to the General Officers,* 15.)

(172) This might seem to be a demotion; however, he was lieutenant colonel and aide-de-camp in the volunteer army, whereas his appointment as major and assistant adjutant general was in the Regulars.

(173) It is interesting to note that George W. Cullum in his *Biographical Register* accorded Hardie, whom hardly anyone has ever heard of, a biographical sketch extending to almost two pages. In the same volume, General Custer, who died the same

year in a blaze of newspaper publicity on the Little Big Horn, is disposed of in a sketch which barely exceeds a page.

(174) Hardin's death certificate lists his birthplace as, "Morgan County, Illinois," of which Jacksonville is the county seat, as does his obituary in *Annual Association of Graduates,* U. S. Military Academy, 1924.

(175) In 1854 it was determined by Secretary of War Jefferson Davis to lengthen the course at the Military Academy to five years. Accordingly, the plebes entering in that year were divided by age, the older group to graduate in 1858, the younger, in 1859. The exigencies of the Civil War ended the experiment, and the cadets who had entered in 1856 were graduated in May, 1861, and those who had entered in 1857, in June, 1861. Thus one-half of those who entered in 1854 and all of those who entered in 1855 and 1856 took the five-year course.

(176) The occasion of his death went virtually unnoticed both in Florida and Illinois, despite General Hardin's distinguished ancestry, his father's close friendship with Lincoln (who kept an avuncular eye on the younger man), the publication of several articles as well as a history of his old regiment, and his status as the youngest general officer on the retired list in the history of the service—to say nothing of his combat record. Perhaps eighty-six-year-old Civil War generals were out of style in 1923, an interesting contrast to the obsequies attending the death of Walter Williams in 1960, an aged Texan to whom the nation paid homage as the "last survivor of the Civil War"—despite the fact that it could (then and now) be readily demonstrated that Williams was the end product of the publicity agents who feed on the ignorance of the public.

(177) Cf., Dyer, *Fightin' Joe Wheeler,* 91-97. Anyone who drove off the combined forces of Wheeler and N. B. Forrest, even in the course of a minor operation, deserves substantial credit.

(178) There is a tradition in the Harding family that President Warren G. Harding was the great-grandson of one of General Harding's brothers. (Correspondence by the author with Mrs. C. D. Hetz, San Diego, California, April, 1961.) Although biologically possible, it would have required three successive generations to have had sons at the age of twenty, since General Harding's oldest brother was born in 1804, and President Harding in 1865.

(179) Published sources usually give 1837 as the year of Harker's birth; however, when he accepted his appointment to the Academy, he stated he was eighteen on December 2, 1853. (Letter, in Harker file, Adjutant Generals Office, National Archives.) His monument, erected by the officers and men of his command, bears the date 1835.

(180) Data on Harker is sketchy. The information on his early life has been derived from Cushing and Sheppard, *History of the Counties of Gloucester, Salem and Cumberland* and Foster, *New Jersey and the Rebellion.* Although he never married, Lewis in *Sherman, Fighting Prophet* recounts a romantic tale to the effect that the young general wooed and won a Tennessee belle while encamped upon the estate of her relative, brother of Confederate brigadier Gideon J. Pillow. Unfortunately, the story is not sup-

ported by a citation. (*Ibid.*, 377.) There are a number of references to Harker in Beatty's *Memoirs of a Volunteer* which would seem to demonstrate that Harker's talents as a soldier were no greater than his social charms, not the least of which was a discriminating taste for fine wines.

(181) See Keyes's report, "The gallantry with which . . . the Third Regiment of Connecticut Volunteers charged up the hill upon the enemy's artillery and infantry was never, in my opinion, surpassed." (*Official Records, II, 354.*) The command subsequently seems to have retired in good order, maintaining its regimental formation. (*The Union Army, I, 276.*)

(182) Other than the *Official Records,* most of the data on General Harland has been obtained from Beers, *Genealogical and Biographical Record of New London County, Connecticut,* 248-50, through the kindness of Mrs. Albert H. Chase of Norwich, who remembers the general as a delightful dancing partner.

(183) Authority of Stanley F. Horn, letter to author, January 31, 1961.

(184) Probably because Harney's appointment derived from a Louisiana Congressman, a common practice of the day.

(185) The others were Brevet Lieutenant General Winfield Scott and Brigadier Generals John E. Wool and Edwin V. Sumner, who had been appointed to fill the vacancy caused by the dismissal of D. E. Twiggs.

(186) The Confederate Brigadier General Daniel M. Frost was the husband of the niece of Harney's wife.

(187) The author is indebted to Mr. Boyd S. Stutler, Charleston, West Virginia, for certain facts of General Harris' career.

(188) Mrs. Frederick Pierce Leonard in *Indiana History Bulletin* (December, 1925), 18-24. This sketch, apparently written in 1923, is noncritical and contains some misstatements of fact. Harrow is represented as an intimate of Lincoln, to whom the latter frequently turned for advice and who offered Harrow a Cabinet post, which was declined. Significantly, perhaps, Harrow is not indexed in Carl Sandburg's six-volume biography of Lincoln. On the other hand, Harrow patently had considerable influence in highly placed quarters, as evidenced by his later military career.

(189) *Official Records,* XXXIX, Pt. 2, pp. 554-55, and *Battles and Leaders of the Civil War,* IV, 287.

(190) *Official Records,* XLVII, Pt. 2, pp. 70, 81; Howard commented blandly that he did not desire "to displace any of [his] present division or brigade commanders."

(191) Harrow must have been something of a stormy petrel. This occasion marked the third consecutive resignation of his military career. On July 29, 1862, he resigned as colonel of the 14th Indiana, but was reappointed by Governor Oliver P. Morton the following month. (Heitman, *Historical Register,* I, 506.) He apparently resigned his brigadier's commission after the battle of Gettysburg, possibly out of pique because he was supplanted by A. S. Webb as division commander, since the record shows that the acceptance of his resignation "was revoked . . . by direction of the President . . . ," October 5, 1863. (*Official Records,* XXIX, Pt. 2, p. 484.) As noted in his sketch he was several times relieved

from command of various units and contrary to the statement of his daughter (cf., note 188) was not brevetted major general in the omnibus promotions which accompanied the end of the war —although he served for many months in division command.

(192) Tyre does not appear in the *Encyclopaedia Britannica Atlas* index, but may be found on the map of New York State in Rand Mc-Nally's *Road Atlas,* just to the north of the New York State Thruway and some four miles east of Interchange 41.

(193) Hartsuff was not present at Second Manassas; he had been ordered to Alexandria by Irvin McDowell for treatment of a stomach ailment which had virtually prostrated him. Hartsuff himself refused to request relief from duty, even though his brigade surgeon reported that he was more than half-dead from lack of nourishment. (Cullum, *Biographical Register,* II, 487-88.)

(194) Apparently George W. Cullum regarded Hartsuff as the *beau ideal* of a soldier, for the eulogistic biographical sketch appended to his military career covers more than four pages. Grant himself earned but little more than five and one-half pages. (Cullum, *Biographical Register,* 486-90.)

(195) The index to the *Encyclopaedia Britannica Atlas* lists the village as Leroy; however, it is designated as Le Roy on Plate 172 of the *Atlas* itself. Other sources invariably cite Le Roy, hence the author's use of this spelling.

(196) *Official Records,* XXXIX, Pt. 2, p. 366.

(197) For details see *Official Records,* Pt. 1, pp. 489-90.

(198) Oswego (New York) *Daily Times,* August 3, 1874, courtesy Mr. Thomas A. Cloutier, business manager, Oswego *Palladium-Times.* It is interesting to note that his obituary, in the high-flown style of the day, omitted mention of the surrender of the Baton Rouge arsenal, certainly the most newsworthy event of Haskin's career. Even though there was nothing discreditable about the surrender and Haskin subsequently received several promotions and numerous stations of trust, the contemporary feeling was to sweep it under the rug lest it soil the reputation of "a hero of the war." This sort of approach to Civil War officers of both sides by their contemporaries has resulted in the whole affair being wrapped in a kind of rosy fog.

(199) *Official Records,* XXXII, Pt. 2, p. 98: Grierson to Stanton, January 14, 1864, also states that Hatch "is now slowly recovering from a wound through his lungs. . . ."

(200) *Official Records,* XXXIV, Pt. 4, p. 487.

(201) See Jack D. L. Holmes in *Tennessee Historical Quarterly,* December, 1959, 297: "Troops under General Edward Hatch occupied Oxford early in August [1864]. Mrs. Jacob Thompson . . . watched the soldiers ransack her beautiful mansion. When they heard the Confederates . . . were advancing . . . they retreated, Hatch loading [an] ambulance with pictures, china, glassware, and silver from Mrs. Thompson's house."

(202) The inscription on his monument confirms the day of birth as December 22.

(203) Haupt's first name found its way into the War Department records as Hermann.

(204) Catton, *Mr. Lincoln's Army,* 6. Haupt was the second lead in

the celebrated melodrama in which General Samuel D. Sturgis declaimed through a rosy haze to Haupt that he cared for General John Pope not "one pinch of owl dung" during a colloquy involving the transportation of Sturgis' division to the Manassas front just before Second Bull Run. For an entertaining recital of the latter incident, see *ibid.*, 6-8. Subsequently, Lincoln marveled publicly about the Aquia Creek bridge which Haupt had constructed "out of beanpoles and cornstalks." (*Ibid.*)

(205)   The author is indebted to Mr. Kimball C. Elkins, Harvard College Library, for this and other facts of General Hayes's career.

(206)   E. H. Abbott in *The Harvard Graduates' Magazine* (December, 1912), a sketch of Hayes's life which is inaccurate in some minor respects. Gouverneur K. Warren reported to George G. Meade on May 16, 1864, that Hayes had been wounded in the head but could return to duty "in a few days, if not at once." (*Official Records*, XXXVI, Pt. 2, p. 818.) It would not appear that the injury was so serious as to cause dipsomania in later years, although it might have served as a convenient excuse.

(207)   *Dictionary of American Biography*, VIII, 447.

(208)   Rhodes, *History of the United States from Hayes to McKinley*, 12, quoted in *Dictionary of American Biography*, VIII, 450.

(209)   Haynie's middle name is also given in published sources as Nichols and Nicholas. (Cf., Miller, *Photographic History of the Civil War*, X, 199, and *Cyclopedia of American Biography*, III, 146.)

(210)   *Battles and Leaders of the Civil War*, I, 429.

(211)   *Official Records*, XXIV, Pt. 3, p. 257. At this juncture Haynie wrote two expository letters to President Lincoln and the latter's private secretary, John G. Nicolay; both letters set forth controlling reasons for his resignation from the army. In the one to Nicolay, he wrote "to request a favor"—that his resignation might be accepted because of his wife's health. (Copies of letters in the author's possession: Haynie to Lincoln, February 7, 1863, and Haynie to Nicolay, March 14, 1863, courtesy Miss Margaret A. Flint, Illinois State Historical Library, Springfield, Illinois.)

(212)   Hays's father removed to Nashville in 1820 and for years was attorney general of Tennessee.

(213)   In the horse artillery the gunners were mounted, enabling the units to keep pace with cavalry.

(214)   *Official Records*, XXV, Pt. 1, *passim*, in which it is erroneously reported that Hays was wounded.

(215)   *Official Records*, Series II, V, 618.

(216)   *Official Records*, XLVI, Pt. 3, pp. 597-98. On June 19, 1865, he was relieved from duty with the Army of the Potomac by order of General U. S. Grant. (*Ibid.*, 1286.)

(217)   Hazen's censure earned him a general court headed by General Hancock which resulted in his being reprimanded by President Cleveland for "unwarranted and captious criticism" of his superior, a meaningless chastisement since experts were agreed that Hazen was right.

(218) *Appleton's Cyclopedia* spells Heckman's middle name as it is in this sketch; Heitman, *Historical Register,* spells it Adams.

(219) F. B. Heitman does not record Heckman's Mexican War service; however, it is described as within by *The Union Army,* VIII, 128; Powell, *Officers of the Army and Navy,* 401, and *Appleton's Cyclopedia.*

(220) According to F. B. Heitman, Heckman was mustered as stated within; *The Union Army,* VIII, 128, however, records that he became captain of the 1st Pennsylvania as early as April 20, 1861, and major of the 9th New Jersey on October 3.

(221) See Godfrey Weitzel's report, *Official Records,* XXXVI, Pt. 2, p. 152.

(222) This experience was something less than the "infamous and outrageous persecution" highlighted in the northern press, since the officers were well housed and fed, by their own admission, and were exposed to no more danger than the other residents of the city.

(223) Cf., Edward O. C. Ord's report in *Official Records,* XLII, Pt. 1, p. 794, and *passim.*

(224) Catton, *Mr. Lincoln's Army,* 32.

(225) *Dictionary of American Biography,* VIII, 593, is in error in stating that Herron was "the youngest major-general in the Civil War. . . ." Several other officers, younger than Herron, were subsequently made major general. Among them were W. H. F. Lee and R. F. Hoke of the Confederacy, and George A. Custer of the U. S. Army.

(226) *Dictionary of American Biography,* VIII, 593.

(227) Monaghan, *Civil War on the Western Border,* 261-73.

(228) Certified copy of death certificate in the author's possession. *The Union Army,* VIII, 129, relates that Herron practiced law in New York and was "a prominent member of the G.A.R. and the Loyal Legion."

(229) Apparently for purposes of simplification, Hincks dropped the *c* from his surname when he joined the army, for he is referred to in the *Official Records,* in Heitman, *Historical Register,* in *The Union Army,* and in other official publications as Hinks. However, his obituary in the Boston *Evening Globe* (February 19, 1894) spelled the name Hincks (letter to author from Boston Public Library, August 14, 1957), and both the burial permit and interment order clearly render it Edward Winslow Hincks (letter to author from Mount Auburn Cemetery, February 21, 1961). His grave marker reads General E. W. Hincks. It is conjectural from what source Heitman obtained the middle name Ward, which he employs. Heitman also errs as to the day of Hinck's death.

(230) Cullum, *Biographical Register,* I, 167-79.

(231) *Dictionary of American Biography,* IX, 96, recites in its sketch of Hobson, "He was promptly recognized in the call to arms, as colonel of the 2nd Kentucky Infantry. . . ." This regiment was recruited in Ohio, composed almost entirely of Ohio men, and mustered at Pendleton, Ohio. The author can find no record of General Hobson's connection with it.

(232) The details of this strange episode, which brought down the

wrath of Edwin M. Stanton and Henry W. Halleck upon Hobson, can be found in the *Official Records,* XXXIX, Pts. 1 and 2, *passim;* and *ibid.,* Series II, 370, 388, 397, 469. Had S. G. Burbridge not defended his conduct, it is likely his head would have rolled.

(233) *Official Records,* Series I, XLIX, Pt. 1, p. 511.

(234) According to the clerk of court, Hardinsburg, Kentucky, the cemetery is located on the Herman Dutschke farm. The *Encyclopaedia Britannica* locates Holt about three miles west of Stephensport, Kentucky, in Breckinridge County. Although not specifically located on the Rand McNally *Road Atlas* of Kentucky, Holt would appear to be on State Route 64, between Stephensport and Addison, Kentucky.

(235) Catton, *Glory Road,* 16. In 1861 Hooker was unable to pay his way to the Atlantic Coast and his friends subscribed a purse for his passage east. (Bigelow, *The Campaign of Chancellorsville,* 5.)

(236) Letter from Hooker to John B. Floyd, February 2, 1858, copy in the author's possession.

(237) Bigelow, *The Campaign of Chancellorsville,* 6.

(238) Horn, *The Army of Tennessee,* 297-98.

(239) Adams, *An Autobiography,* 161; Agassiz (ed.), *Meade's Headquarters 1863-1865,* 230.

(240) *Official Records,* XXXII, Pt. 2, p. 355.

(241) His taking of leave aroused the ire of W. T. Sherman, who stated that Hovey "left us in the midst of bullets to go to the rear in search of personal advancement." (*Official Records,* XXXVIII, Pt. 5, p. 247.)

(242) *Official Records,* XVII, Pt. 7, p. 758.

(243) *Dictionary of American Biography,* IX, 272.

(244) *Appleton's Cyclopedia,* III, 276.

(245) Of the ten who became general officers, eight did so in Confederate service; six of the eight died in action, as did Stephen Weed for the Union; only the two Lees for the Confederacy, Thomas H. Ruger, and Howard himself survived the war.

(246) Howard says he resigned "instead of asking for an enabling leave of absence" because "officials of the War Department were still obstructing such leaves," particularly those for ordnance officers. (Howard, *Autobiography,* I, 113.) The premise may be valid; the author, however, has encountered no other case of this nature.

(247) Franz Sigel asked to be relieved because the XI Corps was the smallest in the army and he felt it should be the largest, since he was the senior major general present. Howard, commanding a division of the II Corps, was irked because Daniel E. Sickles, technically his junior in rank (although both had been tendered their commissions on the same day), had been assigned to the command of the III Corps and, ever touchy regarding protocol, complained to Joseph Hooker that as the senior major general present—not in corps command—he was entitled to a corps. Howard's touchiness exhibited itself again at Gettysburg, when W. S. Hancock rode on the field with orders from George G. Meade to take command. Howard attempted to make an issue

of the fact that he was Hancock's senior since his name preceded Hancock's on the list of commissions as major general made out on November 29, 1862. It might be pointed out that Hancock subsequently became a Regular Army brigadier eight months before Howard and a major general twenty years before. (Bigelow, *The Campaign of Chancellorsville,* 40-42; Tucker, *Hancock, The Superb,* 131-34.)

(248) The family had been Quakers since the days of Penn, but both Howell's father and grandfather were expelled from the Society of Friends for taking up arms. (Powers, *History of the Eighty-fifth Regiment Pennsylvania Volunteer Infantry,* 425.)

(249) *Ibid.,* 422; *The Union Army,* VIII, 134; inscription on his marker in Eglington Memorial Gardens, Clarksboro, courtesy of Mr. J. G. Engle, letter to author, May 22, 1957. The *Official Records* are strangely silent in reference to Howell's accident and death; it is only stated therein that he was relieved from command of the 3rd division on September 13, the day after his accident and the day before his death, with no particularization being offered. At the same time Howell disappears from the *Official Records.* (Cf., *Official Records,* XLII, Pt. 2, p. 811.)

(250) *Memorandum Relative to the General Officers, 20.*

(251) Despite Hunt's brilliant contributions in many fields over a period of nearly a half-century, he was retired at the same grade which he had occupied for fourteen years, that of colonel. A subsequent bill to retire him with the rank of major general was passed by both houses of Congress but vetoed by President Arthur. It would truly seem that his "services were not adequately appreciated by his government" as set forth by his biographer, presumably upon the authority of Hunt's son, in *Dictionary of American Biography,* IX, 387.

(252) The renowned James Morris Morgan relates in his highly entertaining *Recollections of a Rebel Reefer,* 349-51, an incident which occurred while Hunt was in command in Charleston in 1876. In brief: Hunt protected a group of white carpetbaggers, at their own request, from a mob of disgruntled Negroes by asking the ex-Confederate general James Conner to call out his "rifle clubs" to support him (Hunt). The white Southerners appeared as if by magic; the Negroes melted away; and Hunt was in bad odor with the Congressional Radicals. Morgan goes so far as to claim that the "very carpetbaggers whose worthless lives he had saved flocked to Washington and protested his promotion on the ground that he was a rebel sympathizer and had on one occasion taken command of the rebel rifle clubs . . . to cow the loyal element in Charleston." (*Ibid.,* 351.)

(253) Various dates are given for Ingalls' birth in a number of published sources; the author has used the date on Ingalls' grave marker in Arlington National Cemetery. Ingalls' death certificate, however, records that he was "72 years 4 months 26 days" old, which would make his birth date either the nineteenth or twentieth of August, 1820.

(254) Ingalls ranked thirty-second in this class in which W. B. Franklin was first and U. S. Grant, twenty-first.

(255) J. Bennett Nolan in *The Historical Review of Berks County*

(Pennsylvania), XVI, 4, 115-16, courtesy the Historical Society of Berks County, Reading, Pennsylvania.

(256) *Official Records*, XII, Pt. 2, p. 395.

(257) *Appleton's Cyclopedia*, III, 385; *The Union Army*, VIII, 138.

(258) *Official Records*, I, 172.

(259) *Official Records*, XXI, 451. In the course of this forlorn hope, described by a contemporary foreigner as "the most wanton sacrifice of . . . human life in the history of modern warfare," General Jackson's horse was first shot from under him. He was "afterwards sitting on the railroad track" when his aide approached him with an order from General George G. Meade, then his division commander. Both Jackson and the aide were shot and killed instantly. Because of the exposed condition of the ground and the subsequent retirement of the Army of the Potomac across the Rappahannock, the bodies were not reclaimed for two days. (See J. Bennett Nolan in *The Historical Review of Berks County*, XVI, 4, 115-16.)

(260) Heitman, *Historical Register*, I, 567; *The Union Army*, VIII, 139.

(261) *Official Records*, X, Pt. 1, p. 107.

(262) *Official Records*, XVI, Pt. 1, p. 910.

(263) Brigadier General William R. Terrill and Colonel George Webster, 98th Ohio. Jackson and Webster were shot dead, Jackson while standing at the left of one of his batteries, Webster from his horse. Terrill lived for several hours after being mortally wounded.

(264) *Official Records*, XXV, Pt. 1, pp. 168, 176; his brigade of A. S. Williams' division was commanded by Colonel Samuel Ross, 20th Connecticut.

(265) Birth date according to the inscription on Jackson's grave marker.

(266) Norton, *Sketches of the "Town of Old Town,"* courtesy Old Town Public Library, Old Town, Maine.

(267) *Official Records*, XI, Pt. 1, p. 842; the regiments were the 63rd and 105th Pennsylvania.

(268) Extract from a letter from General Samuel P. Heintzelman, quoted in *Official Records*, XXV, Pt. 2, p. 141.

(269) Heintzelman records: "He died of typhoid fever, brought on, no doubt, by exposure and the excitement of the battles alluded to." (*Ibid.*) For the place of his death the writer is indebted to Mrs. Ralph H. Conant, Augusta, Maine, who was told by an old time resident of Orono that he died of tuberculosis en route from Boston.

(270) The oft-told canard that Johnson was illiterate at the time of his marriage has no basis in fact.

(271) Sandburg, *Lincoln The War Years*, IV, 91.

(272) W. A. Dunning, *Essays on the Civil War and Reconstruction*, 303. Incapacitated by a paralytic stroke, Grimes was carried into the Senate chamber to vote "Not guilty." A perfect storm of abuse broke upon his head, and after experiencing a second stroke he resigned from the Senate in 1869. He died in 1872.

(273) His son is authority for the fact that the *W* was merely a letter. (Cf., *Dictionary of American Biography*, X, 116.)

(274) There seems to be no concrete foundation for the statement that he was commissioned a lieutenant colonel of the 3rd Kentucky

(Union) Cavalry on August 28, 1861, as stated by George W. Cullum and others. On October 10, 1861, General W. T. Sherman at Louisville refers to Johnson as being "with Colonel (James S.) Jackson's cavalry regiment, in process of formation at Owensborough. . . ." This was the 3rd Kentucky, but the rolls of the command do not exhibit Johnson's name. (Cf., *Official Records,* IV, 300; *The Union Army,* IV, 346; and *Official Army Register of the Volunteer Force,* IV, 1218-19.)

(275) Cf., McCook's report, *Official Records,* X, Pt. 1, p. 306. Most biographical sketches of Johnson have him present at Shiloh, despite the fact that the *Official Records* make it plain he had become ill at Columbia, Tennessee, and was at home during the battle. (*Ibid.,* 317.) He rejoined his command during the operations against Corinth.

(276) Duke, *Morgan's Cavalry,* 151-52.

(277) Adolph von Steinwehr's division was stationed in the vicinity of Centerville on the line of the Orange & Alexandria Railroad in the fall of 1862.

(278) The regiment's casualties were only six men wounded; *The Union Army,* II, 160.

(279) The elder Judah was the great-grandson of an orthodox Jewish rabbi who came to the United States during the Revolution. Henry Moses' elder brother was Theodore Dehone Judah, "father of the Pacific railroad," whose surveys for Huntington, Crocker, *et al.,* laid the groundwork for the Central Pacific and the ultimate linking of east and west in 1869.

(280) "His personal intrepidity on the Battlefield amounted to absolute rashness, and . . . injured his usefulness as a . . . Commander, so eager was his impulse to pitch at the enemy, even when the odds were greatly against him." Plattsburgh (New York) *Republican,* January 20, 1866.

(281) Authority of Mr. Van Buren Lamb, Jr., Summit, New York.

(282) Kane evidently commanded the regiment here. Cf., his report to Edward O. C. Ord in *Official Records,* V, 481. However, it is elsewhere stated that he deferred to "the Mexican War veteran, Charles J. Biddle" as to the colonelcy, when the regiment was originally organized and mustered. Biddle is shown to have resigned on December 11, nine days before. (*Official Army Register of the Volunteer Force,* III, 836.)

(283) Kane was declared exchanged on August 27, 1862, for Lieutenant Colonel Williams C. Wickham, later a Confederate brigadier. *Official Records,* Series II, IV, 438.) Kane is stated to have been a "kinsman" of Wickham's wife. (Cf., *Confederate Military History,* III, 686.)

(284) The venerable George S. Greene's brigade of Geary's division bore the brunt of the Confederate attack, sustaining 303 casualties, compared with only 98 for Kane's and 139 for Candy's. (*Official Records,* XXVII, Pt. 1, p. 184-85.) It has been stated by Kane's biographers—no doubt copying from each other—that he was "entrusted with a message to General George G. Meade that the Confederates were in possession of the Union cipher." He was given a brevet promotion eighteen months after his resignation for getting this earth-shaking dispatch through to

army headquarters, having risen from a sickbed, "too weak to sit his horse." (*Dictionary of American Biography*, X, 258.) Aside from wondering how he negotiated the fifty-odd miles from Baltimore to Gettysburg if unable to ride, it is a matter of record that General Schenck, commanding at Baltimore, merely reported to Henry W. Halleck on July 1 that he had "sent up General Kane last evening to Westminster. . . ." (*Official Records*, XXVII, Pt. 3, p. 475.) Kane reports that he had to pass through Jeb Stuart's cavalry screen in civilian clothes to reach the army, but says nothing of his illness, nor of Meade; nor does Meade mention Kane. (*Official Records*, I, 846-48.) Aside from all this, however, there is abundant testimony to prove that General Kane was one of the most capable civilian officers.

(285)   Pforzheim is the capital of Baden; another source relates that he was born in Ispringen in the same province. Since Ispringen cannot be found in any contemporary gazetteer, the reader may at least relate Pforzheim to a map location; it is assumed that Ispringen was or is in the vicinity.

(286)   He had also resigned April 6, 1846, but was reinstated five weeks later upon the outbreak of the Mexican War.

(287)   Major General Robert Patterson was not mustered into the service of the United States during the Civil War; his commission was derived from the governor of Pennsylvania. For this reason his name does not appear in *Memorandum Relative to the General Officers in the Armies of the United States During the Civil War, 1861-1865*. For the same reason he is not accorded a biographical sketch within.

(288)   *Official Records*, XI, Pt. 1, pp. 561-62.

(289)   Probably dysentery, the great contemporary scourge for which no cure was known. See *The Union Army*, VIII, 144.

(290)   In the first year of the war the "loyal" regiments recruited in western Virginia were called 1st Virginia, 2nd Virginia, etc. After Congress admitted West Virginia as a state in 1862, the nomenclature was changed accordingly.

(291)   For the details of this daring raid by Confederate partisans, of whom Crook's future brother-in-law was one, and its aftermath see the sketch of General Crook within.

(292)   *The Union Army*, II, 270. This is a rather tall claim. Front Royal was an interesting fight in that it pitted the 1st Maryland (Confederate) Infantry under Colonel (later Brigadier General) George H. Steuart against Kenly's 1st Maryland Federals, the latter being marched to the rear as prisoners by the former. (See Freeman, *Lee's Lieutenants*, I, 381.)

(293)   *Official Records*, XXXIII, 722, 794.

(294)   There is some question as to whether he was born in Dover or Dover Plains, hamlets six or eight miles apart. His death record cites the latter.

(295)   *Official Records*, XXVII, Pt. 1, p. 165.

(296)   *Official Records*, XLIV, 237.

(297)   *Official Records*, XLVII, Pt. 2, p. 42.

(298)   *Official Army Register of the Volunteer Force*, II, 653; *Biographical Directory of the American Congress, 1774-1949, passim; Memorandum Relative to the General Officers*, 21, 37; *Official*

Records, XLIV, XLVII; and Heitman, *Historical Register.* Although Ketchum was roundly praised by his superiors for his soldierly qualities (mainly after his election to Congress, it must be confessed) and although he sustained two severe wounds while demonstrating great personal gallantry, the reader of today must wonder whether the rewards of his valor would have been so great had he not been so favorably situated politically.

(299) Singularly enough, although the trial of Mrs. Wharton was the occasion for a Roman holiday by the Baltimore and Washington, D. C., papers, the news of Ketchum's death on June 28, 1871, was completely suppressed or, at least, completely overlooked. Since his sister's husband Brigadier General Benjamin Brice was paymaster-general of the army and since he, himself, was a retired major general by brevet, it is difficult to credit the latter explanation, particularly as the funeral took place from the Brice residence in Washington. "The Wharton trial" became celebrated in both legal and medical circles, finding its way into such scholarly publications as the *American Journal of Medical Science* (April, 1872), the *Medical and Surgical Reporter of Philadelphia* (1872), and the *American Law Review* (July, 1872), reprinted in the *United States Law Review* (July, 1934). In addition proceedings of the trial were published in book form by the *Baltimore Gazette* in 1872, under the title *Trial of Mrs. Elizabeth G. Wharton, on the Charge of Poisoning General W. S. Ketchum. . . .*

(300) Then called Baltimore Store.

(301) It has escaped most notice that Kiernan was born and grew up in Ireland, because he seems to have stated he was a native American when he applied for commission into the army in 1861. Although his mother's maiden name was Monica Lawler Lynch, his name appears as James Louis Kiernan on a marriage certificate furnished the pension bureau after his death by his widow, who survived until 1928. (Pension Bureau Records, Adjutant Generals Office, National Archives.)

(302) Kiernan makes only three appearances in the *Official Records,* an all time record for a full-rank general officer appointed by the President and confirmed by the Senate. (*Official Records,* XXVI, Pt. 1, pp. 712, 829, and *ibid.,* Series III, III, 740.)

(303) The chief source of information on Kiernan is an obituary notice which appeared in *The Medical Register of New York and Vicinity,* for 1870/71, pp. 321-22, which does not accord in some instances with official sources. (Photocopy in the author's possession, courtesy the New York Academy of Medicine.)

(304) His birth in Ireland is corroborated by both his death certificate and the records of the Green-Wood Cemetery; the information for these was presumably furnished by his widow, the former Harriet Josepha Sands, daughter of Joseph Sands of Brooklyn, in whose lot Kiernan was buried.

(305) The alleged finding on Dahlgren's body of documents urging the assassination of Confederate officials and the burning of Richmond stirred up a contemporary furore. (For details see, Freeman, *Lee's Lieutenants,* III, 334, 334 n.; and Catton, *A Stillness at Appomattox,* 17-18.

(306) *Southern Historical Society Papers,* XII, 126-28. According to this eyewitness account, General M. C. Butler was in immediate command of the Confederate division engaged. Kilpatrick is described as "a sorry-looking figure in his shirt and drawers" as he bolted from the house, his companion as a "forlorn, forsaken damsel—one who was neither maid, wife, nor widow. . . ."

(307) According to his death certificate, Kimball died at age seventy-five; *The Union Army* gives his birth date as November 22, 1822, but *Dictionary of American Biography* cites November 22, 1823.

(308) Horn, *The Army of Tennessee,* 258.

(309) King's grandfather, of the same name, was a prominent Federalist Congressman and Senator and U. S. minister to England by appointment of George Washington.

(310) General King's culpability in quitting his assigned position at Gainesville, his fight with Stonewall Jackson at Groveton, his retirement from there, and the subsequent wanderings of his division—as well as the paradox of his sitting on the Porter court—have been argued endlessly. His son, Captain (later General) Charles King, defends his conduct in *Battles & Leaders of the Civil War,* II, 495. That he was obliquely censured by an official court of inquiry, however, is a matter of record and may be found in *Official Records,* XII, Pt. 1, p. 330. Eisenschiml (*The Celebrated Case of Fitz John Porter,* 51, 79) savagely assails the conduct of King at Manassas and his selection as a member of the court-martial. Porter makes the categorical statement therein that King "was drunk on the 29th and 30th and unable to attend to any duty."

(311) His family connections were not only endless but also hopelessly divided on the question of secession. More than a dozen cousins split their allegiance between North and South during the Civil War.

(312) *Official Records,* XXV, Pt. 1, p. 310.

(313) Walker, *History of the II Army Corps,* 245-46.

(314) G. K. Warren to Seth Williams, September 6, 1863. (*Official Records,* XXIX, Pt. 2, p. 160.)

(315) *Official Records,* XX, Pt. 1, p. 296. For a lucid and concise account of the assault of McCown, Cleburne, and Wharton on Johnson's division, see Horn, *The Army of Tennessee,* 200-201.

(316) Although every published source relates that Kirk died on July 29, 1863, the author was advised by the Illinois Veterans' Commission that the correct date is July 23. However, his grave marker and the records of Rosehill Cemetery have the date given within.

(317) The rebellion was the result of a movement headed by Thomas W. Dorr to extend the franchise in Rhode Island in 1841-42. At this time less than 1,800 propertied voters, operating under a charter granted by Charles II in 1663, could control a population in excess of 108,000. Ultimately what amounted to universal manhood suffrage was granted by the legislature, but not before the Regular Army was ordered into the state to support the militia and to quell the Dorrites.

(318) Schurz declared that the reason for Krzyzanowski's non-confirma-

tion by the Senate was the inability of any Senator to pronounce his name. (Lonn, *Foreigners in the Union Army and Navy*, 234.)

(319) See Jackson's report, *Official Records*, V, 389 ff., wherein he states his objective was Grafton and the taking of Hancock was not worth the potential casualty list.

(320) See Lander's report, *ibid.*, 405-406. Lander's biographers (probably copying from each other) misspell the name as "Blooming Gap," although it appears uniformly in the *Official Records* as within.

(321) *Ibid.*, 406.

(322) *Official Records*, LI, Pt. 1, pp. 544-46.

(323) The quotation is from Edward O. C. Ord's report in *Official Records*, II, 575. See *ibid., passim,* for the attendant circumstances and the views of others present. W. T. Sherman sustained Ord on the basis that a corps commander must be satisfied with his division commanders, as he wrote U. S. Grant. (See *ibid.*, 523, 525-26.) It is apparent from Sherman's various communications that he felt that a misunderstanding or misinterpretation of orders may have occurred. Nevertheless, Lauman's military career was ended.

(324) *Official Records*, LII, 413.

(325) For General Lawler's sketch the author is indebted to Professor J. T. Dorris, retired, of Eastern Kentucky State Teachers College, whose biography of General Lawler appeared in the *Journal of the Illinois State Historical Society*, XLVIII, No. 4 (Winter, 1955), 366-401.

(326) Professor Dorris describes the location of this cemetery as "not far from the road from Harrisburg to Shawneetown and not far from the Ohio River." (Letter to the author, August 22, 1957.)

(327) The testimony is abundant that Ledlie was an arrant physical coward. Aside from many other contemporary observations, U. S. Grant's simple statement that "Ledlie, besides being otherwise inefficient, proved also to possess disqualification less common among soldiers" tells all. (Cf., Catton, *A Stillness at Appomattox,* 240, 244-45, 415 n. 8; *Official Records*, XL, Pt. 1, p. 128.)

(328) *Official Records*, XLII, Pt. 3, pp. 896, 919.

(329) *Official Records*, XLVIII, Pt. 1, pp. 487, 513, and II, 12, and LIII, 593. Although nothing particularly indicative appears in the *Official Records,* the failure of Lee to be promoted a brevet major general of volunteers is significant, for such promotions were as liberally conferred as were Good Conduct Medals in World War II.

(330) *Official Records*, XXXIX, Pt. 1, p. 792.

(331) F. B. Heitman records that Leggett became lieutenant colonel of this regiment on December 18, 1861; however, neither *The Union Army* nor the *Official Army Register of the Volunteer Force* indicate that he served in this capacity.

(332) The author is greatly indebted to Dr. Roy Bird Cook, Charleston, West Virginia, for the sketch within, which could not have been composed without benefit of his splendid article in *West Virginia History*, XV, No. 1, pp. 5-57.

(333) Lightburn's own family was divided on the question of disunion, two of the brothers becoming captains in the Union army and a third serving in the Confederacy's 31st Virginia Infantry.

(334) Only Lightburn himself, who died at the age of seventy-six, and one sister who died at age fifty-eight, mar an otherwise immaculate family record for longevity. Two of his sisters lived to the ages of one hundred-two and one hundred-nine, another sister to ninety-seven, a brother to ninety-three, and five other brothers and sisters into their eighties.

(335) F. B. Heitman gives Lockwood's middle name as Hall. However, Hayes, the spelling given by other sources, is corroborated by his death record in the District of Columbia and is accordingly used herein.

(336) It is necessary to emphasize this point because Logan in later years was compelled on many occasions to "repel the calumny" that at the beginning of the war he had been disloyal "at heart."

(337) See Lewis, *Sherman, Fighting Prophet*, 388-89; and Eisenschiml, *The Celebrated Case of Fitz John Porter, passim*. Logan's untiring animosity toward General Fitz John Porter, whom he accused of being a traitor, amply demonstrates not only his own bias against West Point, but also perhaps a devotion to the clearing of his own name against the charge of original adherence to secession.

(338) "Waving the bloody shirt"—or attempts to appeal to election audiences on the basis of Civil War prejudices against the Democrats—was the stock in trade of Republican campaign orators for a generation after Appomattox.

(339) *The Union Army*, II, 454; Duke, *Morgan's Cavalry*, 198-201.

(340) During the capture of Selma and the defeat of Nathan B. Forrest, Long was struck in the head by a bullet which produced partial paralysis of his right side, including tongue, face, and right arm, from which he never fully recovered. He was retired under the Act of July 28, 1866, which authorized officers to be retired "at the rank of the command held by them when wounded." Since Long was exercising divisional command at Selma, he was placed on the retired list as major general, but was reduced to brigadier by the Act of March 3, 1875, when the retirement law was changed from "rank of the command" to "actual rank." (Unpublished records, Adjutant Generals Office, National Archives.)

(341) The author is much indebted to Mr. William W. Vanderhoof, Union County Supervisor of Veterans' Interment, Elizabeth, New Jersey, for locating the place of General Long's burial.

(342) Lincoln had repaired to Fort Stevens, on the Seventh Street Road, to observe Jubal Early's men coming down from Silver Spring and deploying in front of the Washington defences. As he surveyed the terrain, a Federal surgeon three feet away was killed by a rebel sharpshooter, which impelled a young aide, on the staff of General H. G. Wright, by the name of Oliver Wendell Holmes (later the venerated Supreme Court Justice), to shout out, "Get down, you fool." (Leech, *Reveille in Washington*, 343.)

(343) *Official Records,* XLIII, Pt. 1, p. 431.

(344) The author is greatly indebted to Mr. Harry Chase, Pomfret Center, Connecticut, for data on the place of birth and place of burial of General Lyon, as well as for a disquisition on the meaning of Connecticut "towns," "parishes," "societies," etc. A "town" was a geographical area rather than a defined community; thus Lyon was born near what is today the village of Eastford and is buried near the village of Phoenixville.

(345) Horn, *The Army of Tennessee,* 28, 432 n. 25.

(346) Rumor was rife at the time that Lyon was deliberately shot by one of his own men—a tale reenforced to some extent by the fact that he was a rigid disciplinarian, cordially hated by many of the Midwest farm boys of his command, and that the fatal bullet entered the small of his back. (Letter of Mr. Harry Chase to author, August 11, 1961; Chase's grandparents were neighbors of Lyon and attended his funeral.)

(347) Lytle is best known for his epic poem of love and battle "Anthony and Cleopatra," published in 1858, which begins: "I am dying, Egypt, dying . . ."

(348) Lytle's report in *Official Records,* V, 136.

(349) When W. S. Rosecrans came to write his report of the battle of Chickamauga some months after he had been relieved, he made it a point to write an almost extravagant praise of Lytle's services, who, it must be remembered, had been on Rosecrans' staff in West Virginia. (*Official Records,* XXX, Pt. 1, p. 82.)

(350) *Official Records,* Series II, IV, 437.

(351) The most notable graduate of the class, aside from McClellan himself, was the celebrated Confederate Lieutenant General T. J. ("Stonewall") Jackson. Others whose names became household words in the 1860's were Federal corps commanders Jesse L. Reno and Darius N. Couch, the rebel John Adams, the Union cavalry leader George Stoneman, and the Confederate division commanders D. R. Jones, Cadmus Wilcox, and George Pickett; the latter was translated into the Regular Army from the bottom position in the class rankings. (Cf., Cullum, *Biographical Register,* II, 249-305.)

(352) Allen, *The Army of Northern Virginia in 1862,* 440.

(353) On April 29, 1864, Henry W. Halleck wrote W. T. Sherman: "It seems little better than murder to give important commands to such men as . . . McClernand . . . , and yet it seems impossible to prevent it." (*Official Records,* XXXIV, Pt. 3, pp. 332-33.)

(354) This expedition, suggested by W. T. Sherman, unauthorized by U. S. Grant, and taken part in by D. D. Porter with his gunboats, is best described by Lloyd Lewis in his *Sherman, Fighting Prophet,* 259-62. Grant termed the raid "a wild goose-chase," when he first heard of it.

(355) *Dictionary of American Biography,* XI, 588.

(356) Alexander McCook's father Daniel, Sr., and the latter's brother John, whose families were known as the "tribe of Dan" and the "tribe of John," could add up one major general, three brigadier generals, four colonels, one major, one captain, and three lieutenants. Of the thirteen cousins, only one, Alexander's youngest brother Charles was not an officer. (He was killed at the

age of seventeen at First Manassas in 1861.) Daniel, Sr., a colonel of Ohio militia, was killed while opposing the Confederate John H. Morgan's raid. (James H. Rodabaugh, "The Fighting McCooks," *Civil War History,* III, No. 3 [September, 1957], 287-90.)

(357) On September 20, Alexander McCook's corps formed the right of W. S. Rosecrans' army at Chickamauga, G. H. Thomas was on the left, and Crittenden was in reserve, as a support to both. In the course of the confused shifting of troops on the right in order to answer Thomas' cries for help, an opening was created when T. J. Wood's division of Crittenden's forces pulled out of the line to support J. J. Reynolds' division of Thomas. Through the hole poured John B. Hood's division of James Longstreet's command, which by an accident of fate was ordered to charge at that very minute. Seizing his opportunity, the latter wheeled Hood's men to the right, in disregard of Braxton Bragg's orders, and gained one of the major Confederate successes of the war. Even though officially exculpated, neither McCook nor Crittenden quite measured up to their responsibilities. (Cf., Horn, *The Army of Tennessee,* 263-64; *Official Records,* XXX, Pt. 1, pp. 930-1053; and Gracie, *The Truth About Chickamauga, passim.*) John Beatty, who knew McCook well, regarded him as a "blockhead" and thought it "astonishing that he should be permitted to retain command of a corps for a single hour." (Ford [ed.], Beatty's *Memoirs of a Volunteer 1861-1863,* p. 218.)

(358) *Appleton's Cyclopedia,* IV, 92; however, on June 2, 1961, Mrs. Sarah A. Verner, Librarian, Rare Book Room, University of Alabama, advised the author that she could find no record that Daniel McCook, Jr., ever attended the University of Alabama and further stated that the University was never located at Florence.

(359) Lewis, *Sherman, Fighting Prophet,* 377.

(360) Curiously enough, although there is no question that Daniel McCook died on the seventeenth, his grave marker in Spring Grove Cemetery is inscribed "July 22, 1834-July 21, 1864."

(361) Edward McCook was of the "tribe of John." See note 356.

(362) Hoehling, *Last Train From Atlanta,* 189.

(363) Robert McCook was of the "tribe of Dan"; see note 356 for the McCook relationships.

(364) Also called Fishing Creek and Logan's Crossroads.

(365) For the particulars of the wounding of Robert L. McCook and the subsequent trial of his assailant Captain Frank Gurley, see *Official Records,* XVI, Pt. 1, pp. 838-41, and Series II, VI and VIII, *passim.* Judge Advocate General Joseph Holt's review of the findings of the military commission, unfavorable to Gurley as might have been expected and recommending to President Lincoln that sentence of death be carried out, found Gurley guilty of murder mainly because, according to Confederate law, Jefferson Davis alone was vested with the power to appoint officers of partisan rangers. Whether Gurley was later executed is not made apparent. Exchanged, apparently inadvertently, while still under sentence of death in March, 1865, he was ar-

rested in Huntsville after the war and ordered executed; however, on November 28, 1865, President Johnson suspended sentence "until further notice." At this point he disappears from the *Official Records.*

(366) McDowell's testimony against his former associate Porter consisted primarily of half-truths and answers to the effect, "I do not recollect." See Eisenschiml, *The Celebrated Case of Fitz John Porter,* 96-102. McDowell could have acquitted Porter in a matter of minutes; as it was, he attempted to acquit himself and John Pope before a court-martial organized to convict Porter. The verdict was not reversed until 1879, when during the inquiry which finally exonerated Porter, McDowell was made to look like a perjurer.

(367) Much of the sketch of McGinnis is taken from *Commemorative Biographical Record of Prominent and Representative Men of Indianapolis and Vicinity,* courtesy Indiana State Library.

(368) As early as 1924 one of the thirty-six known autographs of Gwinnett sold at public auction for $14,000. (*Dictionary of American Biography,* VIII, 66.)

(369) The year of Mackenzie's birth is in question; most sources, including his grave marker at West Point, give 1840. However, data given on his death record, upon the authority of "M. R. S. Mackenzie," indicates the year was 1841.

(370) See Warner, *Generals in Gray,* 22, and note 53.

(371) He was the only graduate of a class after 1861 to attain the full rank of general officer during the Civil War.

(372) *Personal Memoirs of U. S. Grant,* II, 541.

(373) "Custer fought only two major engagements with the Indians and met defeat and death in the second one. Mackenzie won five major victories and many skirmishes with the same enemies. . . . Custer is known to all. Mackenzie died insane, unwept and unsung except to the informed few." Edward S. Wallace, "The Mackenzie Raid," *The Westerners New York Posse Brand Book,* IV, No. 4, 73 ff.

(374) *Ibid., passim.* This is a splendid article on one of the least known episodes in the plains warfare of the seventies.

(375) Information as to place and date of McKinstry's birth, authority of Mr. F. Clever Bald, Assistant Director, Michigan Historical Collections, University of Michigan, Ann Arbor. (Letter to the author, January 30, 1957.)

(376) The appointment expired by law on July 17, 1862, because of nonconfirmation by the Senate.

(377) The story of McKinstry's peculations is ably set forth in Shannon, *Organization and Administration of the Union Army,* I, 64-65. In the year of his tribulation (1862) he caused to be published a pamphlet entitled the "Vindication of Brigadier General J. McKinstry," which, if it proves anything, determines that corruption in the service of supply in the frontier command extended everywhere.

(378) The year of McLean's birth is given in most published sources as 1815. However, a copy of his death record in the author's possession states that his age at death was eighty-six years,

eleven months, and two days, fixing the year of his birth as 1818. The later year is confirmed by Charles H. Whipple in his *Genealogy of the Whipple-Wright, Wager, Ward-Pell, McLean-Burnet Families,* 78.

(379) It must be confessed that Charles Devens in his official report (*Official Records,* XXV, Pt. 1, pp. 632-35), while "especially" commending Von Gilsa, failed to mention McLean among those officers deserving of praise for their conduct.

(380) Howard's report, *Official Records,* XXXVIII, Pt. 1, pp. 194-95.

(381) In February, 1863, this regiment was named the 1st Indiana Heavy Artillery.

(382) Brown's men felt that after the defence of Springfield in January, 1863, where he lost the use of an arm, he had also lost his nerve. (Monoghan, *Civil War on the Western Border,* 331.)

(383) *History of Sandusky County, Ohio,* 359-61. (William Bros., Cleveland, 1882.)

(384) Lewis, *Sherman, Fighting Prophet,* 385.

(385) Meek, *Twentieth Century History of Sandusky County, Ohio . . . ,* 283.

(386) Maltby's Mexican War service is not mentioned by F. B. Heitman, who gives his middle name as Adalmon and incorrectly states that he died March 20, 1868.

(387) Details of Maltby's Mexican War service, courtesy Adjutant General's Department, State of Ohio. (Letter to author, July 3, 1961.)

(388) Much of Maltby's career is derived from obituaries in the Galena *Illinois Weekly Gazette,* December 17, 1867; Galena City Directories; and Bateman and Selby (eds.), *Historical Encyclopedia of Illinois and History of Jo Daviess County.* These materials, courtesy of Miss Margaret A. Flint, Assistant State Historian, Illinois State Historical Library, Springfield. The author here would like to acknowledge his debt to Miss Flint for her faithful, continuous, and cheerful help in making this book possible.

(389) Cullum, *Biographical Register,* I, 278.

(390) This widely circulated guidebook became a virtual best-seller, for it contained notes relating to more than thirty overland trails.

(391) The mentioned acts provided for four inspectors general with rank of colonel and five assistant inspectors general with rank of major. Only three of the former were appointed; in a matter of weeks, however, Marcy became senior colonel and thus titular head of the department. Heitman, *Historical Register,* I, 39, indicates that Marcy was chief of the department from August 9, 1861 to January 2, 1881 with rank of "Brigadier General."

(392) The conclusion is inescapable that the hatred for George B. McClellan of such Senate radicals as Benjamin Franklin Wade of Ohio, Zachariah Chandler of Michigan, and Charles Sumner of Massachusetts must have dictated this snub to his father-in-law.

(393) Heitman, *Historical Register,* I, 694.

(394) *The Union Army,* VIII, 160.

(395) Matthies' report of the battle of Chattanooga, *Official Records,* XXXI, Pt. 1, p. 653.

(396) Certain facts of Matthies' career were obtained from the obituary in the Burlington (Iowa) *Hawkeye,* October 17, 1868, and Burlington City Directory for 1859, both courtesy of Burlington Free Library.

(397) See Cleaves, *Meade of Gettysburg,* for an exposition of this episode in early Spanish-American relations.

(398) The family was greatly divided in 1861-65. One of Meade's sisters lived on a Mississippi plantation and was a violent secessionist; another was the wife of Confederate Navy Captain Thomas B. Huger, who was killed at New Orleans in 1862; and Mrs. Meade's sister was the wife of Confederate Brigadier General Henry A. Wise, who as governor of Virginia had signed John Brown's death warrant in 1859. Three other sisters married United States officers, and a brother was a captain in the U. S. Navy. Numerous nephews served on both sides during the struggle.

(399) On November 29, 1862, thirteen men were appointed major generals of volunteers to rank from date. As finally arranged by the War Department, Reynolds' name immediately preceded that of Meade on the seniority list.

(400) Lincoln remarked at the time that Meade would fight well "on his own dunghill." (Cleaves, *Meade of Gettysburg,* 123; the author is much indebted to this valuable work.)

(401) Philip Sheridan was appointed November 14, 1864, to rank from November 8; Meade was not appointed until November 26, although his commission was subsequently made out to rank from August 18, 1864. Sheridan was subsequently promoted lieutenant general over Meade on March 4, 1869, when U. S. Grant became President and W. T. Sherman, general-in-chief.

(402) Lonn, *Foreigners in the Union Army and Navy,* 203.

(403) Lewis W. Hunt in *Montana,* XII, No. 1 (Winter, 1962), 23-35. General Meagher's "unfortunate habit" was known far and wide throughout the territory.

(404) At this stage of Meigs's career, surrounded as he was by blocks of stone and marble, lumber and building material, workmen's shacks, and the seemingly utter confusion which attends a major engineering project such as the extension of the Capitol, he was jokingly referred to as "Meigs among the ruins of Carthage." (Leech, *Reveille in Washington,* 13.)

(405) During this period of his life Meigs submitted an article to the editors of *Battles and Leaders of the Civil War,* concerning the relations of Lincoln with his generals, which bore heavily on George B. McClellan. It was not included in the publication of this Civil War work in 1888 and came to life only a generation later in the January, 1921, issue of the *American Historical Review* as a "document." (*Dictionary of American Biography,* XII, 508.)

(406) "There at close quarters was begun a bitter standup fight . . . [John] Gibbon's Brigade, of one Indiana [19th] and three Wisconsin regiments, was the tough bone Jackson attempted to

crack. . . . These regiments stood off Jackson's Division and half of Ewell's, and forced the Confederate artillery to shift its ground." Two other regiments from Abner Doubleday's brigade supported Gibbon here. (Freeman, *Lee's Lieutenants,* 108.)

(407) *Appleton's Cyclopedia* records that it was "William and Mary"; however, Mr. Herbert L. Ganter, Archivist, College of William and Mary, Williamsburg, Virginia, advised the author that the college has no record of his attendance, but that a biographical register of the matriculates of the University of Pennsylvania lists Meredith as having entered that institution in 1830 and having left in his sophomore year. (Letters to the author, August 16 and 25, 1961.)

(408) *Official Records,* Series II, VI, 141.

(409) *Ibid.,* 874.

(410) Buffalo (New York) *Express,* December 28, 1874. (Courtesy Miss Alice J. Pickup, Librarian, Buffalo and Erie County Historical Society, letter to author, August 1, 1961.)

(411) Most sources reflect that Merritt was born in 1836, the birth year of his younger brother Edward, whose appointment to West Point was declined by Edward and accepted by Wesley. Once recorded in the army records, such an error becomes immutable.

(412) Six became general officers and ten gave up their lives for either the Union or the Confederacy. Of the remaining twenty-six, only one failed to achieve substantial recognition during the war.

(413) Geronimo and his people made their last encampment on the author's New Mexico ranch under guard of Miles's troops, en route to the railroad at Willcox, Arizona, where the Indians were dispatched to exile—first in Alabama, subsequently in Florida, and lastly in Oklahoma. Perhaps as an additional rebuke to Miles, Geronimo rode in Roosevelt's inaugural parade in 1905, portraying a phase of the Old West which many settlers in the area no doubt failed to heartily endorse.

(414) *Dictionary of American Biography,* XII, 630. If Miller was wounded, it must have been very slightly, since he makes no mention of it in his report of the battle, dated January 6, 1863. (*Official Records,* XX, Pt. 1, pp. 431-36.) His command, however, lost 745 men out of 2,181 engaged, as well as 74 horses and 6 pieces of artillery. (See *ibid.*)

(415) This wound is at least partially vouched for by the fact that he is not shown in command of his brigade of R. W. Johnson's division three days after the fight and makes no further appearance in the *Official Records* for eleven months. (*Official Records,* XXIII, Pt. 1, p. 413.)

(416) *The Union Army,* IV, 98.

(417) At this juncture General Henry W. Halleck, the general-in-chief, remarked acidly in a telegram to General Robert C. Schenck, Milroy's department commander, "Do not give General Milroy any command. . . . We have had enough of that sort of military genius. . . ." (*Official Records,* XXVII, Pt. 3, p. 124.)

(418) At Nashville Mitchell commanded a brigade of James B. Steedman's provisional division, made up of detachments from the various corps serving with W. T. Sherman on the "March to the Sea," who had been unable to rejoin their proper commands.

(*Official Records,* XLV, Pt. 1, p. 94.) He resumed command of his regular XIV Corps brigade in the course of the Carolina campaign.

(419) Columbus (Ohio) *Evening Post-Press,* November 7, 1894.

(420) By what may be more than a coincidence, General John Grant Mitchell (*q.v.*), also born in Ohio, *was* a graduate of Kenyon College.

(421) *Dictionary of American Biography* states that this move was due to "severe wounds which incapacitated him for field duty," a condition of affairs not borne out by his own published correspondence in the *Official Records.*

(422) Keleher, *Violence in Lincoln County,* 5.

(423) Both dates are found in various sources.

(424) John Hay to John G. Nicolay, August, 1885, in Thayer, *Life and Letters of John Hay,* II, 31.

(425) For a complete exposé of this unprincipled conspiracy, see Eisenschiml, *The Celebrated Case of Fitz John Porter, passim.*

(426) The Reverend Leland B. Henry, D.D., Scarborough, New York, to the author, October 5, 1957.

(427) The title of "Master of Invective," however, must go to Major John A. Harman, Confederate General Stonewall Jackson's chief quartermaster, who was said to be able to "swear a six-mule team out of the mud," or "could start a mule train a mile long by his language at the back end." (Freeman, *Lee's Lieutenants,* II, 267.) Also cf., Tucker, *Hancock, The Superb, passim,* for Morgan's (and Hancock's) claim to fame in this realm.

(428) *Dictionary of American Biography* records that he "was promoted major for extreme gallantry at the battle of Buena Vista"; however, Heitman, *Historical Register,* discloses no such advance in rank.

(429) Various sources cite different years of birth: Morris' death certificate gives 1824; Cullum, *Biographical Register,* records 1827; this was adopted by *Dictionary of American Biography;* but *Appleton's Cyclopedia* sets forth 1826. According to his grave marker, however, the year was 1827, as used within.

(430) *Field Tactics for Infantry* (1864) and *Tactics for Infantry, Armed with Breechloading or Magazine Rifles* (1882).

(431) Multitudes of regiments, organized and mustered in the fall of 1862 as infantry, were converted to heavy artillery in order to man the elaborate system of forts surrounding Washington. These regiments remained there until the spring of 1864, when by U. S. Grant's attrition at the Wilderness they were reconverted to infantry and were sent to the front at Spotsylvania.

(432) *A Memoir on Fortification* (1858), *Memoir on the Dangers and Defenses of New York City* (1858), *Memoir on American Fortification* (1859), and *Memoir of the Life and Services of Captain and Brevet Major John Sanders, of the Corps of the Engineers, U. S. Army* (1860).

(433) Tucker, *Hancock, the Superb,* Chapter XIII, *passim.*

(434) Charles A. Dana to Stanton, May 16, 1864, *Official Records,* XXXVI, Pt. 1, p. 72.

(435) *Official Records,* XXXII, Pt. 3, p. 325.

(436) *Official Records,* XII, Pt. 2, p. 545.

(437)   *Official Records,* XXI, 320.

(438)   The reader is referred to Governor Pierpont's biography in *Dictionary of American Biography* to understand the confused circumstances which ultimately gave rise to the creation of the state of West Virginia. It may be noted that even in the oppressive reconstruction years Pierpont was forced to spend the last years of his life in Pittsburgh. Nevertheless, his statue appeared in Statuary Hall of the national Capitol in 1910 by vote of the West Virginia legislature. For the specific circumstances which embroiled Naglee, see *Official Records,* XXIX, Pt. 2, *passim.*

(439)   Gracie, *The Truth About Chickamauga,* 197-200, defends Negley's conduct, particularly against John M. Brannan, stating categorically that the latter's slurs were a cover-up for his own shortcomings.

(440)   Neill's name does not appear in the *Official Records* after December 2, 1864; and G. W. Cullum's outline of his career makes no mention of his activities, if any, between December, 1864, and September 6, 1865, when he went on leave of absence.

(441)   *Register of the Commissioned and Warrant Officers of the Navy of the United States, including Officers of the Marine Corps, and Others, for the Year 1856, passim.*

(442)   Horn, *The Army of Tennessee,* 164, quoting Nelson's own official report.

(443)   Dozens of versions of this celebrated encounter, mostly inaccurate and mainly fictitious, have appeared in print. The facts may be found in James B. Fry, *Military Miscellanies,* 486-505. A friend of both men, Fry, later provost marshal general of the army but then D. C. Buell's chief-of-staff with rank of colonel, placed Davis under arrest immediately following the shooting. That there was provocation on both sides, that Nelson was overbearing, and that Davis was quick to resent a fancied slight cannot be denied. It is curious, however, that the administration took no steps to bring the killer of the brother of one of Lincoln's foreign representatives and friends to trial. As related in the sketch of Davis (*q.v.*), the latter's punishment consisted of not receiving a promotion to full-rank major general of volunteers, to which his later distinguished command of a corps under W. T. Sherman richly entitled him.

(444)   Nelson's remains were buried, successively, in Cave Hill Cemetery, Louisville, at Camp Dick Robinson, and finally in Maysville. (Fry, *Military Miscellanies,* 500.)

(445)   The exact date of Newton's birth is in dispute. Previously published sources give it as August 24, 1823; however, his death certificate (a copy of which is in the author's possession), expressing his age at death in years, months, and days, gives the date as within.

(446)   This curious episode originated in a letter of December 20, 1862, to Lincoln signed by William B. Franklin, then commanding the "Left Grand Division" of the Army of the Potomac, and William F. Smith, commanding the VI Corps. The letter suggested an alternative plan for an advance on Richmond and stated categorically that "the plan of campaign . . . already . . . commenced cannot possibly be successful." (*Official Records,*

XXI, 868-70.) W. T. H. Brooks, commanding the 1st Division of the corps, Newton, commanding the 3rd Division, and John Cochrane, commanding Newton's 1st Brigade—all apparently subscribed to these sentiments. Newton and Cochrane urged them upon the President shortly afterward in a private interview. The results were disastrous for the careers of all four: Franklin was effectively shelved; Smith was transferred from the army and his appointment as major general not confirmed; Brooks's and Newton's appointments were revoked; and Cochrane resigned "because of his health," although he subsequently succeeded in living to be eighty-five. Also see Hooker to Stanton, February 25, 1864 (*Official Records*, XXXII, Pt. 2, p. 468), in which Hooker refers to Smith as "the evil genius of Franklin, Brooks, and Newton."

(447) *Official Records*, X, Pt. 1, pp. 305-306; *Battles and Leaders of the Civil War*, I, 538. It is not clear in the records to what command the 15th Michigan was attached on the first day of the battle. Apparently, it was defeated, driven in, and was among the horde of fugitives along the riverbank, through which D. C. Buell's men had to march in order to reach the front on the second day. It was at this juncture that Oliver stepped forward and volunteered his services and those of some 230 of his men to Alexander McD. McCook.

(448) Marriage Records, Trumbull County, Ohio, courtesy Miss Josephine B. Brown, Reference Librarian, Warren Public Library, which exhibit that "Samuel Emerson Opdycke and Lucy Wells Stevens married March 3, 1857 by James Marvin, M. G." Mrs. Opdycke died in 1922 in her ninety-first year and is buried next to her husband.

(449) Edward O. C. Ord's father James Ord is thought to have been a natural son of George IV of England by his morganatic marriage to Mrs. Fitzherbert. This is family tradition as verified for the author by a great-great-nephew of E. O. C. Ord, Ord Preston of La Jolla, California.

(450) Horn, *The Army of Tennessee*, 174.

(451) Much of the information on General Orme is from an article in the *Journal of the Illinois State Historical Society*, XXIII, No. 2 (July, 1930), 246-47.

(452) *The Union Army*, VIII, 190.

(453) Tucker, *Hancock, the Superb*, 127-28.

(454) Heitman, *Historical Register*, I, 763; *Memorandum Relative to the General Officers* . . . , 16, 18. Both sources show that General Owen was reappointed on March 30, 1863, as a brigadier general.

(455) *Official Records*, XXXVI, Pt. 1, pp. 435-36. Unofficial lines of communication were far more ruthless. Assistant Secretary of War Dana in a telegram to Edwin Stanton, June 12, 1864, stated: "General Owen is under arrest for misconduct in the face of the enemy and ordered to Fort Monroe. . . ." (*Ibid.*, 96.)

(456) There is substantial confusion in published sources regarding Paine's official capacities at various dates. The regimental record of the 30th Massachusetts does not exhibit his name in any grade (*The Union Army*, I, 197); he appears in the *Official Records*,

XXIV, Pt. 1, p. 158, as lieutenant colonel of the 9th Louisiana of the "African Brigade," a regiment which eventually was named the 5th U. S. Colored Heavy Artillery but whose roster, again, does not carry his name (*The Union Army,* VIII, 152); and his military career prior to his arrival in the Department of the Gulf amounts to hearsay. To complicate matters still further, he is frequently listed as Charles I. Paine. On the other hand, Heitman's *Historical Register,* confirms his majority in the 30th Massachusetts, implying, at least, that he was mustered and took the oath in this particular office.

(457)   There is considerable debate regarding Paine's middle name. According to G. W. Cullum he entered West Point as Eleazer A. Paine, but graduated as Eleazer Paine. According to Charles B. Scott, Esq., Oxford, Nebraska (a great-nephew who kindly consulted several of his relatives), the name was Arthur. Other members of the Paine family are of the opinion that the initial stood for nothing.

(458)   John R. Williams, Curator of Records, The Old Bergen Church, Jersey City, to the author, August 26, 1957: "Except for the very early years the record of burials was kept by morticians and have long since been lost."

(459)   Palmer had taken offense because he had been asked to take temporary orders from John M. Schofield, who, he claimed, was his junior in rank because he was confirmed by the Senate after Palmer was, although both ranked from the same date. On top of this, Schofield, a regular officer, was senior to Palmer as a brigadier by date of commission and technically ranked as an army commander (Army of the Ohio), although his command of three divisions was constituted as the XXIII Corps. In any event Palmer's objection was not valid and was not sustained by either G. H. Thomas or W. T. Sherman. (*Official Records,* XXXVIII, Pt. 5, *passim.*)

(460)   Published sources usually give the date of Patterson's birth as June 24, 1827; however, his tombstone inscription and death notices appearing contemporaneously in the Philadelphia papers upon the authority of his father fix the date as stated within.

(461)   The elder Patterson was accused at the beginning of the war of having permitted the Confederate Joseph E. Johnston to slip away from him and reenforce P. G. T. Beauregard at First Manassas, thus achieving a memorable victory for the South.

(462)   *Official Records,* XIX, Pt. 2, pp. 562-63.

(463)   Philadelphia *Public Ledger,* November 24, 1862; *The Union Army,* VIII, 194. The contemporary Philadelphia papers failed to print even a hint as to the cause of death, the *Public Ledger* stating that it "has not been ascertained."

(464)   Although G. W. Cullum makes this statement, it is difficult to credit, since St. Louis was settled fully a generation before Napoleon I achieved fame. (Cullum, *Biographical Register,* I, 576.)

(465)   *Official Army Register of the Volunteer Force* . . . , VII, 12.

(466)   An offhand remark by Lincoln in a note in his own handwriting, dated August 23, 1862, states: "Today Mrs. Major Paul . . . calls and urges the appointment of her husband as Brigadier. . . . She is a saucy woman and . . . will keep tormenting me until

I may have to do it." (Basler, *The Collected Works of Abraham Lincoln,* V, 390-91, courtesy of Bruce Catton, via Raymond McCoy, Santa Fe, New Mexico.) This traduces Paul and has caused historians to contend that Mrs. Paul's persistence rather than Paul's merit won him the promotion. The sketch of Paul refutes the calumny.

(467) Salt Lake (Utah) *Tribune,* August 30, 1903, recounts Penrose's army career. He was stationed at Camp Douglas near Salt Lake for years and made the city his home after 1896.

(468) *Dictionary of American Biography* states that Phelps "soon resigned the position on account of the failure of his health." His last appearance in the *Official Records* (XXII, Pt. 1, p. 78) reports him ill at the Planters' House in St. Louis on January 27, 1863.

(469) The author has never in years of research found another Regular Army officer who declined a brevet promotion under such circumstances.

(470) *The Union Army,* VIII, 197. There is no record of anyone being appointed a major general in order to command colored troops exclusively.

(471) *The Union Army,* III, 370.

(472) Heitman, *Historical Register,* I, 792; *The Union Army,* VIII, 198.

(473) Keleher, *Violence in Lincoln County 1869-1881,* p. 20. The author is greatly indebted to Mr. W. A. Keleher for various facets of General Pile's postbellum career.

(474) Of all the nationalities represented in the United States in 1861, the Irish were the most bitterly anti-Negro. Tending to settle in urban centers, they regarded Negroes as challengers to their own livelihoods. This situation is pointed up by the fact that Irish immigrants were employed North and South to clear and level forest land and to build the early railway grades. In the South an able-bodied Negro was worth far more than a hired Irishman; hence, scores of the latter died in the malarial swamps of Alabama and Mississippi. The Irish of New York and New England were something less than distinguished for patriotism in their opposition to the draft. For a description of the Rutland affair, see *Official Records,* Series III, III, 383-85.

(475) Pitcher served as superintendent of West Point from August 28, 1866, until September 1, 1870. His appointment to the position was at a time when the power struggle between President Johnson and the Republican Radicals was building up to its climax. It is probable that officers of greater reputation declined the position. Pitcher was succeeded by such illustrious names as T. H. Ruger, J. M. Schofield, O. O. Howard, Wesley Merritt, and John Parke. It may also be significant that when Pitcher relieved G. W. Cullum in command of the Academy, the latter subsequently found nothing to write about him in his *Biographical Register* except the bare facts of his career.

(476) Catton, *Glory Road,* 207.

(477) *Ibid.,* 229.

(478) Monaghan, *Civil War on the Western Border,* 340.

(479) Most sources, including Cullum's *Biographical Register,* imply or state that Plummer was born in either 1819 or 1820, and his

monument in Arlington National Cemetery records that he was "AETAT, 43 Years" at the time of his death. Plummer himself, however, in a letter dated March 7, 1836, stated that he was born in November, 1817. (Unpublished document, Adjutant General's Office, National Archives.)

(480) Quite obviously General Plummer's remains were not immediately interred in Arlington National Cemetery, since the latter did not become a shrine until the 1890's. The author has been unable to discover where Plummer was first buried or when his remains were removed to Arlington, despite the gracious assistance of Mr. J. Metzler, Superintendent of Arlington National Cemetery.

(481) One of Poe's biographers states that "the Senate failed to confirm his reappointment"; however, the author can find no evidence that he was appointed a brigadier in the volunteer army more than once. (Cf., *Dictionary of American Biography*, XV, 29.)

(482) Pope's second cousin Ninian W. Edwards was the husband of Mrs. Lincoln's elder sister Elizabeth Todd.

(483) Porter (*q.v.*) won a reversal of the verdict and reinstatement in the army years after the war. The case was a political football for twenty years mainly because of Porter's devotion to George B. McClellan.

(484) *Official Records*, XXI, 1003.

(485) *Official Records*, Series III, III, 468, 542-43.

(486) John Hay to John G. Nicolay, August, 1885, quoted in Eisenschiml, *The Celebrated Case of Fitz John Porter*, 240-41. The latter work is also authority for the correct spelling of Porter's first name which is sometimes found hyphenated.

(487) Specifically, *Ibid.*, 28.

(488) *Official Records*, IX, 385.

(489) For a full discussion of this "battle" of Fort Fillmore, see Kerby, *The Confederate Invasion of New Mexico and Arizona*, 34-35; *Official Records*, IV, 14, 16-20.

(490) *Official Records*, XXI, 398-99.

(491) F. B. Heitman records Potter's middle name as Barnwell and the state of his birth as Massachusetts. His father Alonzo Potter was rector of St. Paul's Church, Boston, from 1826 until 1831; his mother was a daughter of President Eliphalet Nott of Union College, Schenectady. Potter's biographer in *Dictionary of American Biography* cites a Potter genealogy and the general's obituary in the New York *Tribune*. Moreover, *Appleton's Cyclopedia* confirms both Brown as his middle name and Schenectady as his birthplace.

(492) Potts was first buried in the Benton Avenue Cemetery, but his remains were transferred to Forestvale Cemetery in 1892.

(493) *Official Records*, XLVI, Pt. 2, p. 125.

(494) Much detail on Powell's career has been obtained from *An Interesting Talk with General W. H. Powell*, 60, and from *Historical Encyclopedia of Illinois and History of St. Clair County*, 1094—both by courtesy of the Illinois State Historical Library, Springfield.

(495) Published sources usually record Pratt's birth in Princeton, Massa-

chusetts; however, Shrewsbury appears in his obituary in the Worcester *Evening Gazette,* August 4, 1896, which indicates that the information was supplied by his sister. (Courtesy of Paris Fletcher, Esq., Worcester.)

(496) *Battles and Leaders of the Civil War,* I, 194.

(497) *Official Records,* XXV, Pt. 1, pp. 206-207, 210, 212.

(498) *Official Records,* III, 499.

(499) *Official Records,* XXX, Pt. 4, p. 118. In this dispatch from Stephen A. Hurlbut, commanding the XVI Corps at Memphis, to Henry W. Halleck in Washington, the former makes plain his disapprobation of Prentiss for a position. He cannot give him an "adequate command . . . without displacing officers . . . better qualified. . . ." Hurlbut also advised Halleck that U. S. Grant "[has] no command for him below. . . ."

(500) *Official Records,* XXIX, Pt. 1, pp. 14, 15. Also cf., Catton, *Glory Road,* 353. The conclusion is more or less inescapable that in the situation which was presented at Mine Run on November 26, 1863, neither Prince nor French won imperishable glory. Since Prince's was the leading division of the III Corps during the operation, it is difficult not to conclude that he was the "division commander" referred to by French as being responsible for the failure of the corps. (Letter in the National Archives, cited by Colonel T. M. Spaulding in his sketch of French in *Dictionary of American Biography.*) Cf., sketch of W. H. French within.

(501) In August, 1861, the regiment was remustered into the United States service for the remainder of the two-year term for which it had been accepted into state service—a procedure which caused a virtual rebellion and resulted in some of the members of the unit receiving sentences to the Dry Tortugas for discipline. (*The Union Army,* II, 57.)

(502) Bruce, *Lincoln and the Tools of War, passim.*

(503) *Official Records,* XXXII, Pt. 2, p. 141.

(504) This leave was for thirty days, with permission to go North. (*Official Records,* XLVII, Pt. 2, p. 62.)

(505) Raum's sketch in *The Union Army,* VIII, 207, records that "his final service [was] as commander of a brigade in the veteran corps under Halleck [Hancock?] at Winchester, Virginia." This probably refers to the "Veterans' Corps," which Hancock had sought to recruit following his relief from duty with the Army of the Potomac. The effort was a signal failure since the men enlisted were not credited to the various state quotas. If Raum commanded such a "brigade," the attendant duties must have been negligible.

(506) Wilson, *The Life of John A. Rawlins.* . . .

(507) Catton, *Grant Moves South,* 226 (Reid is erroneously referred to here as James T. Reid).

(508) *Official Records,* Series III, IV, 179, 201.

(509) Much of the data on General Reid is by courtesy of the Keokuk Public Library, abstracted from a pamphlet entitled *History of the Fifteenth Regiment Iowa Veteran Volunteer Infantry* (author, place and date of publication not stated).

(510) East Liverpool (Ohio) *Review,* November 7, 1905, courtesy of

Miss E. Frances Jones, Librarian, Carnegie Public Library, East Liverpool, Ohio.

(511) *The Union Army,* VIII, 208. But see *Official Records,* XLV, Pt. 1, p. 413, and II, 33.

(512) Published sources usually state that he "commanded a brigade at Nashville on December 15-16." Actually Colonel (later General) C. C. Doolittle, chief of staff of the XXIII Corps, was assigned to the command of the 1st Brigade, 3rd Division, XXIII Corps, "during the temporary absence of Brigadier-General Reilly," on December 14, 1864 (*Official Records,* XLV, Pt. 2, p. 187). His report of the battle on December 22, 1864, states, "I assumed command of this brigade [Reilly's] on the morning of the 15th instant. . . ." (*Ibid.* I, 413.)

(513) James, *They Had Their Hour,* 71-72.

(514) *Official Records,* XXV, Pt. 1, p. 460.

(515) *Dictionary of American Biography* states that he was exchanged for Confederate Brigadier General William Barksdale; however, the author can find no record that the latter was captured before, during, or after the Peninsular campaign. Like Reynolds, he died at Gettysburg.

(516) Certainly Reynolds conferred with Lincoln at the White House in the weeks following the Chancellorsville debacle; it is equally to be inferred that the President sounded him out relative to the army command. (Cf., Sandburg, *Abraham Lincoln, The War Years,* II, 100, for one version of the episode.)

(517) May 17, 1861, was the earliest date of rank given any brigadier of U. S. Volunteers; however, no less than thirty-four officers, commissioned at various dates from May 17 to August 12, were accorded rank as of this date. Reynolds stood nineteenth on the list as finally arranged by the War Department. U. S. Grant's name immediately preceded Reynolds'. Curiously enough, with the exception of W. T. Sherman, who was ranked seventh, the others were either killed, cashiered (Fitz John Porter was fifth), or faded into relative obscurity.

(518) *Official Records,* XVII, Pt. 1, p. 776.

(519) *Official Records,* XLVII, Pt. 1, p. 81.

(520) Most sources record, without elaborating, that General Rice "met his death" on May 11, implying that he survived past midnight of the tenth. On the other hand, Colonel Lyman in his entry for May 10 states, "Poor General Rice . . . very daring . . . was to-day killed by a sharpshooter. The ball broke his thigh . . he never rallied. . . ." (Agassiz [ed.], *Meade's Headquarters 1863-1865,* 109.) The latter authority is borne out by the inscription on his monument in Rural Cemetery (courtesy of Mr. Earl G. Terko, Registrar), which recites in part: "Fell Mortally Wounded May 10, 1864. . . . Surviving Three Hours." Since the action in which he met his death began shortly after 2:00 P.M. on the tenth, it is manifest that he died the same day. (Cf., *Official Records,* XXXVI, Pt. 1, *passim.*)

(521) Richardson's utter disregard for danger gave rise to his nickname.

(522) Richardson's resignation was possibly a result of his not receiving a higher commission upon the organization of the new army regiments under the Act of March 3, 1855.

(523) The wound which ultimately killed Richardson has been variously assessed; no one, however, has stated its exact nature or locale. Catton in *Mr. Lincoln's Army*, 304, dismisses the matter with the comment that he was "hit by a rifle bullet and was carried off the field—only slightly wounded, it seemed, but in a few days an infection set in and the wound killed him." Contemporary accounts, however, range from Hancock's official report that he was "severely wounded" and compelled to be borne from the field, to that of the battery commander who stood next to him when he was struck and who officially reported on October 4, 1862, that Richardson "was mortally wounded." (Cf., *Official Records*, XIX, Pt. 1, p. 344.)

(524) During Second Manassas Ricketts' division was thrown forward by Irvin McDowell into Thoroughfare Gap in the Bull Run Mountains to bar the advance of James Longstreet, who was seeking to unite his wing of the Army of Northern Virginia with that of Stonewall Jackson. Rufus King's division was ordered to Gainesville in support, but King withdrew without orders, compelling Ricketts, who was being flanked and in danger of being cut off, to withdraw also. Some historians have criticized Ricketts' action and have attempted to infer from the findings of the subsequent "McDowell Board of Inquiry" that the board found Ricketts guilty of a "grave error." This writer feels that the "grave error" was charged to King and that Ricketts' subsequent retirement was a logical consequence thereof.

(525) With the exceptions of Prentiss, to whom no suspicion attaches, and Ricketts, every judge was beholden to Edwin M. Stanton for his tenure or impending promotion. The other judges, after the guilty verdict, were remunerated in a number of ways. Only Ricketts, significantly, "was not promoted after the verdict was rendered, nor one of the brigadiers who at the close of the war were made major-generals. . . ." (Cullum, *Biographical Register*, II, 4-5.) This suggests that Ricketts may have voted for acquittal, thus incurring the War Department's displeasure. For a full discussion see Eisenschiml, *The Celebrated Case of Fitz John Porter, passim;* and *Official Records*, XII, Pt. 1, pp. 323-32, and, XII, Supplement to Pt. 2, *passim.*

(526) Roberts, as did some of the judges themselves, served as a catspaw for Edwin M. Stanton; he not only brought the charges but also testified against Porter at the court-martial. Roberts' subsequent career is mute testimony to the regard in which he was held in army circles.

(527) Small, *The Road to Richmond*, 80.

(528) Catton, *Glory Road*, 297.

(529) The usually found euphemism that Robinson "resigned to study law" is untrue. He was dismissed after a general court-martial found him guilty of violating Paragraph 279 of the Academy regulations by addressing a fellow-cadet who had reported him for "inattention while marching," "on the subject of such report" without obtaining authority to do so and for further representing that he had obtained such authority, "such representation being contrary to truth." (Unpublished records of the Adjutant's Office, U. S. Military Academy, courtesy of Mr. Ken-

neth W. Rapp, Archives Assistant, U. S. Military Academy.)

(530) This little fire fight was known as the battle of Laurel Hill.

(531) Rodman was the eldest of sixteen children born to the first wife of his father; it is not recorded how many offspring Rodman's father was responsible for by subsequent marriages.

(532) The descendants of Harmon Henrick Rosenkrantz, who arrived in New Amsterdam in 1651, ultimately used twenty-three variants in spelling the family name. The future general acquired his nickname at West Point. (Lamers, *The Edge of Glory*, 8, 9, 13.)

(533) *Official Records*, XVII, Pt. 2, p. 239. If his first date of rank had been allowed to stand, he would have been junior to no less than thirty-nine major generals whom he subsequently ranked. As matters were finally adjusted, he stood tenth on the list of volunteer major generals, and on the roster of field commanders was ranked only by N. P. Banks, Benjamin F. Butler, David Hunter, U. S. Grant, Irvin McDowell, and Ambrose E. Burnside. (*Memorandum Relative to the General Officers*, 4-6.) Curiously, William M. Lamers, in his biography of Rosecrans, makes no mention of this promotion or of the attendant circumstances.

(534) Livermore, *Numbers and Losses in the Civil War in America*, 97.

(535) *Ibid.*, 105-106.

(536) The most useful sketch of Ross's life is in Powell (ed.), *Officers of the Army and Navy (Volunteer)*, 281. Place and date of death and place of burial courtesy Illinois State Historical Society.

(537) Although published sources recite Rousseau's birthplace as stated within, a collateral descendant gives Garrard County, Kentucky, as his birthplace. Since the family made several moves and Lovell was one of twelve children, there is probably confusion as to who was born where.

(538) *Official Records*, XXI, Pt. 1, p. 279. Rousseau had been absent from his command since the beginning of the movement against Chattanooga and did not rejoin until Rosecrans' shattered forces were falling back on that city.

(539) *Official Records*, XXI, 60, 142, 534-35, 935.

(540) *Official Records*, XXIX, Pt. 1, p. 322.

(541) *Official Records*, XXXVI, Pt. 2, p. 330. He reported for duty to the Army of the Potomac on or before June 21, 1864, on which date U. S. Grant issued Special Orders No. 40 (*Ibid.*, XL, Pt. 2, p. 270), in part as follows: "It being deemed unadvisable to place him on duty because of the feeling in the Army . . . of distrust of his fitness to command troops in the field, he will . . . report to the adjutant general . . . for orders." On the twenty-fourth Rowley was accordingly ordered to report to Darius N. Couch, commanding the Department of the Susquehanna at Harrisburg. (*Ibid.*, 375.) He was actually convicted of the charges, which ranged from "drunkenness on duty on the battlefield [of Gettysburg]" to "conduct to the prejudice of good order and military discipline" and "conduct unbecoming an officer and a gentleman," and was sentenced to be cashiered. (Unpublished documents, Adjutant General's Office, National Archives.)

(542) The marker at his grave is incorrect both as to the years of birth and of death

(543) George Sears Greene lived to be fourteen days older than Rucker.

(544) George Washington Custis Lee, son of Robert E. Lee, who would be a Confederate major general ranked first; Jeb Stuart stood thirteenth; Stephen D. Lee seventeenth; and Dorsey Pender nineteenth. Five other graduates in this class became Confederate brigadiers; only Otis Howard and Stephen Weed, who was killed at Gettysburg, would serve the Union as general officers.

(545) On March 2, 1867, Ruger was brevetted brigadier general, U. S. Army for gallant and meritorious service in the battle of Gettysburg.

(546) Sixteen of the forty-one graduates died or were killed prior to 1861; of the remaining twenty-five, fourteen became generals and three took no active part in the war.

(547) *Battles and Leaders of the Civil War*, IV, 87. The confident colonel was either Archibald C. Godwin, later brigadier general, who subsequently was killed in the same battle and in the same manner as Russell, or Colonel Davidson B. Penn, 7th Louisiana, Both took breakfast the following morning with one of their captors, Martin T. McMahon, lieutenant colonel and assistant adjutant general to General John Sedgwick at the time.

(548) *Appleton's Cyclopedia* records his birth as "near Halberstadt"; Lonn in *Foreigners in the Union Army and Navy*, 198, states that he "came from the village of Strobeck near Magdeburg, Germany." Halberstadt and Magdeburg, both in Saxony, are about thirty miles apart. Lonn also gives Salomon the middle initial S, for which the author has been unable to find verification. Her source appears to have been Wilhelm Kaufmann, *Die Deutschen im Amerikanischen Burgerkriege* (Munich and Berlin, 1910), a work devoted to inflating the reputations of Germans who fought for the Union.

(549) Lonn, *Foreigners in the Union Army and Navy*, 544, apparently relying on Kaufmann, makes the statement that Prentiss "later claimed the victory at Helena as his." This is doubtful in view not only of Prentiss' warm words of praise but also of the fact that it was due to Prentiss that the Federals were under arms every morning at 2:30 to resist the assault which he suspected was coming. (Cf. *Official Records*, XII, Pt. 1, pp. 387-90, 392-93.

(550) One source states that Sander's father sold the property at Forks of Elkhorn in 1823; another records his birth in Lexington, Kentucky; however, both Speed's *The Union Regiments of Kentucky* and Collins' *History of Kentucky* record Frankfort. (Cf., Darnell, *Forks of Elkhorn Church*, 246, and *Appleton's Cyclopedia*, V, 386. The author is greatly indebted to Mrs. Dorothy Thomas Cullen of The Filson Club, Louisville, and Mr. G. Glenn Clift of the Kentucky Historical Society for data on Sanders.

(551) Unpublished letters, Adjutant General's Office, National Archives.

(552) A. E. Burnside to Abraham Lincoln, November 21, 1863, in *Official Records*, XXXI, Pt. 1, p. 269.

(553) Still more singular is the fact that Sanders' mother later applied,

as a needy person, for a pension which was denied her. (Unpublished records, Adjutant General's Office, National Archives.) The reason for the denial may lie in the fact that Sanders' three brothers fought spiritedly for the Confederacy as members respectively of the 1st, 2nd, and 28th Mississippi Cavalry Regiments. (In the latter connection the author wishes to express his gratitude to Miss Mahala Saville of the University of Mississippi Library, whose research casts some doubt on his burial in the Second Presbyterian Church indicating that it may have been in the yard of the Episcopal Church instead.)

(554)   His death certificate, expressing his age in years, months, and days, indicates he was born January 27, 1817, in Lincoln County, Maine. Whitefield is in Lincoln County.

(555)   *Harper's Weekly,* February 27, 1864, p. 131, col. 4.

(556)   *Official Records,* XXXIII, 109.

(557)   Lonn, *Foreigners in the Union Army and Navy,* 197.

(558)   *The Reminiscences of Carl Schurz,* III, 35-36.

(559)   The author is especially indebted to Dr. Alfred C. Raphelson, University of Michigan, Flint College, Flint, Michigan, for data from his manuscript on the life of General Schimmelfennig. It may be noted in passing that Miss Lonn records Schimmelfennig as von Schimmelfennig, implying a title of nobility. His surname is also sometimes rendered as Schimmelpfennig.

(560)   The facts of Schoepf's early life are difficult to establish. There seems to be no question that his father was an official Austrian resident in what was an Austrian town when Schoepf was born. Schoepf enlisted in a Polish legion dedicated to the cause of Hungarian independence in 1848, despite the fact that he had been lately an officer in the army of the Austrian emperor. For this act he is claimed by the Hungarians as one of their own. The references are numerous and, beside the standard works, in clude Lonn, *Foreigners in the Union Army and Navy;* Vasvary, *Lincoln's Hungarian Heroes;* and Horn, *The Army of Tennessee.*

(561)   Curiously, neither Cullum, *Biographical Register* nor *Memorandum Relative to the General Officers* make mention of the Senate's failure to confirm Schofield's first nomination to the grade of major general of volunteers, although Schofield himself discusses the matter at length in his *Forty-Six Years in the Army.* The nomination was bottled up in the Military Affairs Committee by a small minority who were inimical to Schofield's handling of the touchy Missouri problem.

(562)   At this time he was accused by partisans of G. H. Thomas of intriguing with U. S. Grant to obtain chief command of the forces in the west, an allegation vehemently denied by Schofield in his autobiography and by his own adherents. But see O'Connor, *Thomas: Rock of Chickamauga,* 301, 306, 311, 312, 359-66, 376-78.

(563)   Major John Bigelow, Jr., in his definitive *The Campaign of Chancellorsville* thoughtfully analyzes the Federal debacle on the Rapidan-Rappahannock; there are scores of works on Gettysburg, many treating the battle of the first day with great particularity.

(564) See Bowers, *The Tragic Era,* 348-60 for an exposé of conditions in South Carolina during Scott's regime.

(565) He killed a young drug clerk whom he believed responsible for making his son drunk and was acquitted on a plea of accidental homicide. (*Dictionary of American Biography,* XVI, 499.)

(566) Freeman, *Lee's Lieutenants,* I, 712 n.

(567) *Battles and Leaders of the Civil War,* IV, 175.

(568) *Who's Who in New York.*

(569) He was 25 years, 2 months, and 26 days old at the time he was appointed.

(570) George G. Meade's principal biographer indicates that Meade, who did not like Seymour, felt he had not fought well at either Glendale or Second Manassas. (Cleaves, *Meade of Gettysburg,* 77.)

(571) During this period he is alleged to have been "inhumanly exposed" to the fire of Federal batteries, while a prisoner in Charleston. (Cullum, *Biographical Register,* II, 271.) The accusation is refuted by the testimony of Seymour and his four fellow-captives, Generals Henry W. Wessells, E. P. Scammon, Charles A. Hackman, and Alexander Shaler. (*Official Records,* XXXV, Pt. 2, p. 163.)

(572) Letter of William Dale Fisher, American Consul, Florence, to author, November 25, 1957; letter of Lt. Col. Earl K. Buchanan, Quartermaster, West Point, New York, to author, November 1, 1957.

(573) The 25th Kentucky was commanded at Shiloh by its lieutenant colonel and subsequently by the colonel of the 17th Kentucky, with which it was consolidated soon after the battle. According to Heitman, *Historical Register,* 876, Shackelford resigned March 24, 1862; *The Union Army,* IV, 1268, states March 22. After the capture of Fort Donelson in February, 1862, "he was . . . obliged to retire for a time because of ill health. . . ." (Mrs. Carolyn Thomas Foreman in *The Chronicles of Oklahoma,* XII, No. 1 [March, 1934], pp. 103-104.)

(574) His letter of resignation set forth that he had recently lost his wife and had "four very small children and a widowed helpless mother. . . ." Foreman in *The Chronicles of Oklahoma,* XII, No. 1, p. 109.

(575) One account of his life states that he brought four companies of the 3rd Missouri to Pea Ridge and "was in the battle. . . ." (*The Union Army,* VIII, 231.) The records exhibit, on the other hand, that the portion of the 3rd Missouri present, "unattached," was commanded by Major Joseph Conrad. (*Battles and Leaders of the Civil War,* I, 337.)

(576) *Official Records,* XXXIX, Pt. 2, p. 69.

(577) Place of burial, courtesy of Mrs. Mary E. Holmes, Librarian, Franklin Library, Franklin, Massachusetts.

(578) Sheridan stated at times that he was born in Massachusetts and at other times, in Somerset, Ohio. When he entered West Point he indicated that he was born in 1830, but, in 1864 when he accepted his commission as brigadier general in the Regular Army, he moved the year of his birth to 1832. Some historians believe he was born at sea en route to America on a vessel fly-

ing the British flag, others, that he was born in Ireland. Perhaps Sheridan himself did not know, but for obvious reasons wished it to be known that he was native-born. The author is indebted to Mr. Thomas R. Hay of Locust Valley, New York, for data relating to Sheridan's birth.

(579) *Personal Memoirs of P. H. Sheridan,* I, 11.

(580) The number fifty-six was subsequently given to another Illinois regiment organized in February, 1862, with Green B. Raum (*q.v.*) as its colonel. The reasons for the disbanding of the "Mechanic Fusileers" are not readily apparent. (*Official Army Register of the Volunteer Force,* VI, 309-10.)

(581) General Francis (Frank) Sherman's biography appears in none of the general references. The sketch within was compiled with the assistance of Miss Margaret A. Flint, Research Librarian of the Illinois State Historical Library, Springfield, to whom the author is indebted for many favors. Sources consulted by Miss Flint included: *History of Chicago 1857-1871,* II, 242-43; *Chicago: Pictorial and Biographical,* VI, 165-68; and the Waukegan (Ill.) *Daily Sun,* November 9, 1905. In addition, extensive use was made of the *Official Records,* Heitman, *Historical Register,* and *The Union Army.*

(582) Lewis, *Sherman, Fighting Prophet,* 136. This volume is the best biography of Sherman.

(583) *Memorandum Relative to the General Officers,* 8.

(584) Horn, *The Army of Tennessee,* 299.

(585) Various dates of birth are advanced for Shields; the one used within is inscribed on his grave marker in St. Mary's Cemetery, Carrollton, Missouri.

(586) It is an inescapable conclusion that General Shields resigned because his services had not been recognized.

(587) Cf., *Battles and Leaders of the Civil War,* III, *passim;* Swanberg, *Sickles the Incredible*; Cleaves, *Meade of Gettysburg*; and Pinchon, *Dan Sickles* . . . , for various viewpoints and conclusions.

(588) But he was admonished not to command any of the officers of the army and navy who were to consult with him and facilitate his trip. (Pinchon, *Dan Sickles,* 208.)

(589) *Literary Digest,* May 16, 1914, quoted in *Dictionary of American Biography.* In his old age Sickles advanced the year of his birth by six years, and the incorrect date appears in *Dictionary of American Biography* and other authoritative sources. However, both of his biographers, Edgcumb Pinchon and W. A. Swanberg, give the date as within. Pinchon asserts that the date is verified "by the family archives and is indubitably correct."

(590) Sigel's opponents on this day consisted of the infantry brigades of John Echols and Gabriel Wharton, the cadet corps of the institute numbering about 225 boys between the ages of fourteen and sixteen, and John D. Imboden's cavalry—the whole under John C. Breckinridge did not amount to more than 3,600 all told. Sigel admitted to having 5,500 men on the field. (*Official Records,* XXXVII, Pt. 1, p. 76.) He was relieved from command on May 19, 1864, U. S. Grant commenting to Henry W. Halleck, "By all means I would say appoint . . . anyone else to the command of West Virginia." (*Ibid.,* 492.)

(591) The author is indebted to Kent Castor and R. E. Pairan of Chillicothe for data on General Sill.

(592) Much of Slack's life has been reconstructed from *Memorial Record of Northeastern Indiana,* 478-82, courtesy of Miss Louise Wood, Indiana State Library, Indianapolis.

(593) The youngest at the time was Major General Alexander McD. McCook, who was born April 22, 1831, and appointed July 19, 1862, to rank July 17. He was appointed six days before Slocum, although ranking several numbers below by date of commission.

(594) Following the battle of Second Manassas, Pope's three corps were transmitted into the Army of the Potomac: Franz Sigel's I becoming the XI; N. P. Banks's II becoming the XII; and Irvin McDowell's III becoming the I.

(595) Darius N. Couch refused to serve any longer under Joseph Hooker and was relieved from command of his corps, at his own request, prior to the Pennsylvania campaign. He was succeeded by Winfield S. Hancock.

(596) *Official Records,* XXIX, Pt. 1, p. 156. "My opinion of General Hooker both as an officer and a gentleman is too well known . . . for me to refer to it. . . . The public service cannot be promoted by placing under his command an officer [Slocum] who has so little confidence in his ability. . . . It would be degrading in me [*sic*] to accept any position under him. . . ."

(597) Eisenschiml, *The Celebrated Case of Fitz John Porter,* 80, 81.

(598) Hooker wanted Slough arrested for obstruction of orders in June, 1863, a request which expired upon the relief from command a few days later of Hooker himself. (*Official Records,* XXVII, Pt. 1, p. 56.)

(599) *The Union Army,* VIII, 242.

(600) Keleher, *Turmoil in New Mexico,* 204.

(601) The *New Mexican* (Santa Fe), December 17, 24, 1867, courtesy of Mrs. Elma A. Medearis, Museum of New Mexico Library.

(602) James Harrison Wilson, *Under the Old Flag,* I, 323.

(603) It was reported that U. S. Grant was drinking again and, moreover, committing the greater sin of not reporting regularly enough to Henry W. Halleck. (Cf., Catton, *Grant Moves South,* 197-99.)

(604) Smith at first refused to believe that a major battle was in progress, preferring to believe that it was a "picket-line skirmish." Some hours later he owned that "a part of the army" might be engaged. (*Ibid.,* 328.)

(605) *Official Records,* VII, 235.

(606) Smith was appointed November 24, 1865, to rank from date. Benjamin Grierson, however, was appointed March 19, 1866, to rank from May 27, 1865, and Wager Swayne on May 1, 1866 (the last actual appointment), to rank from June 20, 1865. Both of the latter were junior to Smith by date of appointment but senior by date of rank.

(607) For some reason, *Appleton's Cyclopedia* and *The Union Army,* although both recording Smith's Mexican War service, fix the date of his birth as July 2, 1832, which would mean that he had been a commissioned officer prior to his fourteenth birthday.

The date within is from *Biographical Directory of the American Congress.*

(608) Swiggett, *The Rebel Raider,* 69.

(609) *Daily New Mexican* (Santa Fe), December 12, 1885, courtesy Mrs. J. K. Shishkin, Research Librarian, Museum of New Mexico Library, Santa Fe, to whom the author is also indebted for Smith's present place of burial.

(610) *Ibid.*

(611) He was tried by a general court-martial on five charges: "pillaging and marauding," "permitting the foregoing," "false mustering," "disobedience of orders," and "incompetency" but seems ultimately to have been dismissed "for presenting and collecting false and fraudulent accounts against the Government." (Special Orders, Vol. 2, 1863, Adjutant General's Office, National Archives.)

(612) His birthplace is sometimes given as Pennsylvania.

(613) Lewis, *Captain Sam Grant,* 407.

(614) For Smith's part in the court-martial of Porter, see Eisenschiml, *The Celebrated Case of Fitz John Porter, passim,* which is highly inimical to Smith. In the course of the 1879 hearing which exonerated Porter and recommended his restoration to the army, the Washington (D. C.), *Sentinel,* January 28, 1879 (cited in *ibid.*), commented that Smith was "a genius malignant. Tommy carries more genuine cussedness to the square inch than any man within the range of our acquaintance. . . ."

(615) The principal sources of information on Smith's ante- and postbellum careers are derived from an article written by his son-in-law for the *The Ojai* (Nordhoff, California), April 24, 1897, and in the "Proceedings" of the fiftieth anniversary of the Harvard class of 1841; both by courtesy of General Smith's grandson, L. A. Hopkins, Esq., of San Francisco.

(616) *Official Records,* XXI, 868. See also note 446 within.

(617) Smith's movement was designed as a cavalry screen for W. T. Sherman's advance on Meridian, which the latter felt would seriously cripple the activities of Confederate partisans in the area. Sherman moved into Meridian and destroyed everything within reach; Smith never reached Meridian, for N. B. Forrest whipped him from one position to another, finally sending him back to Memphis. (Lewis, *Sherman, Fighting Prophet,* 332-33; and Horn, *The Army of Tennessee,* 316.)

(618) "Ballyhooley, or Aghultie, a parish in the barony of Fermoy, county of Cork, and province of Munster, 4 miles (w. by n.) from Fermoy, on the road to Mallow. . . ." (Authority of Thomas Crosbie, Esq., Cork County, by courtesy of Mrs. S. H. Smith, La Jolla, California.)

(619) Green, *History of the M. W. Grand Lodge of Ancient, Free and Accepted Masons of Delaware,* 129-34.

(620) The American Irish Historical Society in New York is barely aware of his Irish birth, to say nothing of his accomplishments and antebellum career.

(621) *Official Records,* XXXII, Pt. 1, p. 52.

(622) Temple, *Notable Men of Tennessee,* 186-89. Spears was something of an elusive character and the author is indebted to a

number of individuals for data: Mrs. Kathryn P. Arnold, Chattanooga Public Library; W. W. Turner, Jasper, Tennessee; Jack H. Putnam and Leonard Hale, Pikeville, Tennessee; and Hon. Lawrence N. Spears, Chattanooga. Also see Wilson, *Under the Old Flag*, I, 282-83.

(623) *Official Records*, XXXIII, 639, 717-18.

(624) *Official Records*, XLI, Pt. 3, p. 498; unpublished records, Adjutant General's Office, National Archives.

(625) This command, whose colonel was Erastus B. Tyler, "was surprised while eating . . . breakfast . . . overpowered by superior numbers and scattered" at Cross Lanes, West Virginia, on August 27, 1861. The records do not show whether Captain Sprague was present. (*Official Records*, V, 118-19.)

(626) Sprague commanded the division for about two weeks in the latter part of October, 1864. (*Official Records*, XXXIX, Pt. 3, *passim*.)

(627) Sprague seems to have been on leave from January 29, 1865, to March 28, 1865. (*Official Records*, XLVII, Pt. 1, p. 49.)

(628) Stahel commanded the regiment and Louis Blenker the 1st Brigade of Dixon Miles's 5th Division, which was in reserve at Centreville. The extravagant claims made for the Germans in saving Washington are dismissed by *Battles and Leaders of the Civil War*, I, 194: "It [the division] had some skirmishing during the day and while covering the retreat of the army." But see Vasvary, *Lincoln's Hungarian Heroes*.

(629) Lewis, *Sherman, Fighting Prophet*, 406-407. Sherman felt that Stanley lacked "dash and energy."

(630) *The Union Army*, VIII, 254.

(631) *Official Records*, XXXVIII, Pt. 4, p. 217.

(632) *Official Records*, XXXIX, Pt. 1, p. 534, Starkweather's report, Pulaski, Tennessee, October 1, 1864 read: "My casualties have been large, particularly in captured men. . . ."

(633) *Official Records*, XLIII, Pt. 2, p. 725; Stanton to Sheridan, December 2, 1864: "Have you any objections [to Starkweather being assigned to duty with you]?" Sheridan to Stanton, same date: "I do not want General Starkweather. . . ."

(634) Gracie, *The Truth About Chickamauga*, 55.

(635) Reportedly, his confirmation by the Senate as brigadier general was also held up by articles in Steedman's newspaper which questioned the wisdom of immediate emancipation.

(636) It is generally stated (even by G. W. Cullum) that Steele commanded a brigade at Wilson's Creek; however, the returns show that he was in charge of four companies and that the 2nd Brigade of Nathaniel Lyon's army was directed by Lieutenant Colonel George Lippitt Andrews of the 1st Missouri Infantry, who is not to be confused with George Leonard Andrews, later a brigadier general and brevet major general of volunteers. (*Battles and Leaders of the Civil War*, I, 306.)

(637) General Steele was first buried in Lone Mountain Cemetery, San Francisco; his remains were moved to Woodlawn in 1912.

(638) *Official Records*, XXXVIII, Pt. 4, p. 157. He was not relieved from duty, however, until May 12. It is difficult to account for Stevenson's subsequent reappointment, his brevet promotion to

major general, and his appointment to the regular rank of colonel in 1866. The last was a highly prized plum which many prominent Civil War officers failed to secure when the army was expanded from twenty-nine regiments to fifty-nine in 1866. His prior service had been unexceptionable and he and McPherson seemingly did not get along. Apparently, he had one or more friends in high places.

(639) The city is inferential and the exact date is not ascertainable. On January 15, 1831, Stokes informed the Secretary of War by letter that "I was born in the State of Maryland, and now reside in the city of Baltimore. . . . My age is 15 last June. . . ." A genealogy of his second wife's family, coupled with the statement above, is authority for his birth in Hagerstown, although most published sources recite Baltimore. Stokes's obituary in the *New York Herald*, December 28, 1890, relates that "it was one of his peculiarities to conceal his age, even from his friends." It states, however, that he was born in Baltimore in 1814. Other sources, including census records, fix the year as 1816 and 1817, giving no month or day.

(640) See Lewis, *Captain Sam Grant*, 414-15.

(641) The Scandinavian version of his full baptismal name ·seems to have been Charles John Meuller Stohlbrand. He was carried on the army rolls as within.

(642) Sandburg, *Lincoln, The War Years*, III, 457.

(643) Charleston (South Carolina) *Sunday News*, February 4, 1894.

(644) See Catton, *Mr. Lincoln's Army*, 72-73, for an interesting outline of Stone's prior dealings with Governor John A. Andrew and Senator Charles Sumner of Massachusetts, which had apparently earned him the enmity of both.

(645) The arrest and imprisonment of Stone is without parallel in the annals of American military and/or civil jurisprudence. Despite the heavy demands on his time, President Lincoln cannot be wholly excused for abandoning Stone, a man whom he had trusted with his life. Even George B. McClellan could not save Stone; he was victim of a determination on the part of the Joint Committee on the Conduct of the War to avenge the death of one of their colleagues and to make it known that this was war to the knife, and a war to end slavery as well as to preserve the Union. For an account of what actually happened at Ball's Bluff as it related to Stone, cf., Richard B. Irwin, "Ball's Bluff and the Arrest of General Stone" in *Battles and Leaders of the Civil War*, II, 123-34, and Patch, *The Battle of Ball's Bluff*.

(646) This was an experiment inaugurated by Jefferson Davis, then Secretary of War. The cadets entering in 1854 were divided into two groups, those under eighteen being assigned to the five-year course. The plan was abandoned in 1861, when two classes were graduated: those who had entered in 1856 were graduated in May, and the cadets entering in 1857, in June.

(647) The quotation is from Russell (ed.), *The Memoirs of Colonel John S. Mosby*, 184. Latter-day romancers have tried to claim that Mosby's exploit was made possible by Antonia Ford, a young and pretty resident of Fairfax, who is said to have seen to it that Stoughton was plied with wine to such an extent that

Mosby found him in a welter of empty champagne bottles, after having been told by Antonia how and where to penetrate the Union defenses. Mosby categorically credits a deserter from the 5th New York Cavalry by the name of Ames with telling him where the gaps in the lines were and inferentially denied to Jeb Stuart that Antonia had anything to do with the surprise and capture of Stoughton. Stuart to Mosby, March 25, 1863 (*Official Records,* XXV, Pt. 2, p. 858), wherein Stuart asks him to send "whatever evidence you may be able to furnish of Miss Ford's innocence of the charge of having guided you in your exploit at Fairfax. . . ."

(648) Authority of *Harper's Weekly,* August 15, 1863, p. 515, col. 3, and pp. 525-26, which refers to Strong's "enfeebled condition."

(649) *Official Records,* LIII, 544.

(650) *Ibid.,* 560.

(651) *Official Records,* Series III, III, 1081-82, 1092.

(652) *Official Records,* XXIV, Pt. 3, pp. 171-72.

(653) Date of Stuart's death, authority of Detroit *Advertiser and Tribune,* September 12, 1868, courtesy Detroit Public Library. The *Biographical Directory of the American Congress* erroneously records his death on the twelfth.

(654) Letter to author from A. J. White Hutton, Chambersburg, February 1, 1957, who as a law student in Chambersburg remembered older men of the community speak of Colonel Stumbaugh.

(655) *The Union Army,* VIII, 260.

(656) Stumbaugh preferred to be called Colonel rather than General.

(657) He died suddenly while playing chess in his Topeka law office. (Letter to author from Kansas State Historical Society, March 7, 1957; the author is indebted to the society's secretary Nyle H. Miller for many courtesies.)

(658) Herman Haupt was the officer to whom this forthright declaration was made; he recorded it in his *Reminiscences of General Herman Haupt.*

(659) The four ships were the *Savannah, Vincennes, Constitution,* and *San Jacinto.* Sullivan was stationed at the Naval Academy when he resigned, but had never attended that institution, contrary to some published sources. (Letter to author from Elbert L. Huber, Chief, Navy and Military Service Branch, National Archives, Washington, May 17, 1962.)

(660) *Official Records,* XLVI, Pt. 2, pp. 553, 982. The reasons for his unpopularity are unclear. C. A. Dana wrote Edwin M. Stanton, June 5, 1863, that Sullivan had been relieved from duty at "the leased plantations" in Louisiana "for inertia."

(661) The author is indebted to the Oakland Public Library for data on Sullivan's postbellum career in California. His sister is said to have been the (second?) wife of Peter Hardeman Burnett, first governor of the state of California. (Oakland *Daily Evening Tribune,* October 21, 1890.)

(662) Lavender, *Bent's Fort,* 319-20.

(663) Catton, *Mr. Lincoln's Army,* 287-94.

(664) Swayne, by all accounts, was a gallant and accomplished officer whose contribution to the Federal cause as a regimental commander was in the highest degree creditable. However, it is

questionable wnether the rewards he received after the war were due to his own accomplishments or to his father's position and to the interest of his patron Oliver O. Howard.

(665) *Official Records,* XLVII, Pt. 2, p. 70.

(666) Sykes's nickname in the old army was "Tardy George."

(667) No particular reason for Taylor's resignation has been uncovered. He was shown in command of his brigade as late as December 31, 1862. (*Official Records,* XXI, 933.) Unpublished letters in the National Archives exhibit that his request to resign his commission was disapproved successively by Generals John C. Robinson, John F. Reynolds, and W. F. Smith—all attested to his merit. At length Adjutant General Lorenzo Thomas forwarded the resignation to the Secretary of War with the recommendation that it be accepted.

(668) Authority of Mrs. Maurice Moore, Lynchburg, Virginia, whose husband's mother was first cousin to General Terrill. (Letter to the author, February 13, 1954.)

(669) Cullum, *Biographical Register,* II, 533.

(670) H. G. Wright to Henry W. Halleck, September 2, 1862, gives the rather unusual circumstances attending Wright's endorsement of Terrill for advancement. (*Official Records,* XVI, Pt. 1, pp. 907-908.)

(671) Alexander McD. McCooks' report of Perryville. (*Ibid.,* 1040-41.)

(672) The author has been unable to unearth any record of Terrill's first burial, if any, and it may be that his remains were immediately conveyed to the Military Academy cemetery.

(673) The author has found no other instance of a volunteer officer of any grade being elevated to the grade of general officer in the Regular Army without holding one or more intermediate grades first.

(674) *Official Records,* Series II, VI, 841.

(675) *Official Records,* VII, 141.

(676) *The Union Army,* VIII, 17. Nebraska Territory furnished two regiments, a battalion, and two companies from an area embracing virtually everything between Kansas and Canada and Minnesota to the Continental Divide.

(677) *Official Records,* XLVIII, Pt. 1, p. 995.

(678) O'Connor, *Thomas, Rock of Chickamauga,* 60.

(679) There is no foundation in fact for the story that President Andrew Jackson handed Thomas his West Point warrant as a reward for heroic conduct in the Nat Turner uprising. This story is cited in Lewis, *Sherman, Fighting Prophet,* 57, upon the authority of a remark made by Sherman years after the event. The revolt occurred in 1831; Thomas was appointed to the Academy in 1836.

(680) Thomas' sisters later claimed that he would have dedicated himself to the Confederate cause save for the undue influence of his wife, a native of New York State. The latter categorically denied ever discussing the matter with him.

(681) *Appleton's Cyclopedia,* VI, 82.

(682) Authority of Mrs. James T. White, Cumberland, Maryland, a great-granddaughter of Thruston, letter to the author, November 12, 1957.

(683) Class rank was established beginning with the class of 1818. Thirty cadets graduated in 1814, one in 1813.

(684) See Note 590.

(685) *Official Records,* XLIII, Pt. 1, p. 723.

(686) Place of death, authority of Portland (Maine) *Eastern Argus,* May 1, 1895.

(687) *The Union Army,* VIII, 274.

(688) Comprising the present states of North and South Dakota.

(689) *Appleton's Cyclopedia,* VI, 127, and *The Union Army,* VIII, 274.

(690) Cf., the facts of Todd's life as set forth in *Biographical Directory of the American Congress,* 1924.

(691) *Journal of the Confederate States Congress,* Provisional Congress, proceedings of March 16, 1861, pp. 155-56. (Published as Senate Document No. 234, 58th Congress, 2nd Session [Washington, 1904].) The conclusion is more or less inescapable that one or more of his army comrades at some time or another caused Torbert to toy with the notion of "going South," also his native state Delaware was a slave state.

(692) The author has found no parallel to Torbert's later lack of promotion in the Regular service, in view of his high volunteer rank, brevet rank, and solid contributions to the Union cause. Numerous officers junior to him both in the regular and volunteer organizations became field-grade officers upon the expansion of the army in July, 1866.

(693) Freeman, *Lee's Lieutenants,* III, 597. One of Rosser's brigade commanders, Colonel T. T. Munford, declared that the fight was "the greatest disaster that ever befell our cavalry during the whole war." (*Ibid.*)

(694) Most sources, including the *Dictionary of American Biography,* record Totten's date of birth as August 23, 1788. The Washington (D. C.) *National Republican,* April 27, 1864, states that the silver plate upon his coffin reflects the date used herein. (Courtesy Yale University Library, October 21, 1957.) On the other hand, the inscription on his grave marker reads August 25, 1788. (Courtesy Mr. Al Johnson, Superintendent, Congressional Cemetery.)

(695) John Pope's report in *Official Records,* XII, Pt. 2, p. 48.

(696) Baird's report, *Official Records,* XXXVIII, Pt. 1, p. 755.

(697) *Official Records,* XXXIX, Pt. 2, p. 186 ff.

(698) Apparently greedy contractors who had been caught furnishing substandard arms brought sufficient political pressure on Andrew Jackson to cause him to deny Tyler's promotion to captain of ordnance.

(699) *Official Records,* V, 118-19. For other details of Tyler's career, cf., Ravenna (Ohio) *Republican Weekly,* February 4, 1891.

(700) *Official Records,* XXXVIII, Pt. 2, pp. 84-85.

(701) The return of May 31, 1863, for the Department of the Gulf exhibits Ullmann in command of the "Corps D'Afrique" of five regiments. A footnote, however, sets forth that only the officers of these regiments had been mustered and that the regiments themselves were not organized until August and September. (*Official Records,* XXVI, Pt. 1, p. 531.) Nevertheless, N. P. Banks's

official report (*ibid.*, 16) states: "General Ullmann's brigade, which had been raised during the campaign, also shared the labors of the siege. . ."

(702) *Official Records*, XXXI, Pt. 1, p. 101, states that "the bone has united . . . though the injured leg is 4 inches shorter than before." This is the only instance the author has found where amputation was not the immediate resort of the attendant surgeons.

(703) "He suffered from an incurable malady of the head and its passages, which ultimately became unbearable. . . ." Wilson, *Under the Old Flag*, II, 368.

(704) This inquiry was requested by Irvin McDowell himself.

(705) *Times* (London), July 27, 1886; *Boston Evening Transcript*, July 26, 1886; New York *Herald*, July 26, 1886. For certain facts the author is indebted to J. L. Van Alen, a great-great-grandson.

(706) Vandever was castigated during his tenure at Rome by the medical director of the Department of the Tennessee, who accused him of indifference in the procurement of supplies locally for the sick and wounded at the hospitals established there. "What are the suffering of sick men to a hackneyed and effete politician, when he finds himself unable to alleviate them without incurring the displeasure of ladies (?) who have remained in pleasant quarters while their husbands, sons, etc., are in the rebel army? It were as unreasonable to expect the Ethiopian to change his skin as for a man like this to be influenced by the instincts of a soldier. . . ." (*Official Records*, XXXVIII, Pt. 3, p. 56.) This statement was seemingly not taken seriously in more exalted circles.

(707) See *Official Records*, XI, Pt. 3, *passim*, for an interesting interchange of telegrams and letters between Van Vliet, Flag-Officer L. M. Goldsborough, commanding the Naval Station at Fortress Monroe, George B. McClellan, Edwin M. Stanton, and Secretary of the Navy Gideon Welles. Van Vliet seems to have stepped on the navy's toes by wiring a request for cooperation to Goldsborough, which the latter was pleased to construe as an order from a subordinate in another branch of the service. The ensuing tempest in a teapot may have caused Van Vliet to request relief and may also have been the reason for his non-confirmation as a brigadier general by the Thirty-Seventh Congress—the Senate at this time was dominated by men inimical to McClellan.

(708) There is a curious contradiction here between two of the most authoritative sources on the Civil War, one being to some extent a condensation, with additions, of the other. *Official Records*, XI, *passim*, record no mention of General Van Wyck; however, *Battles and Leaders of the Civil War* exhibits that during the battles of the Seven Days he was in command of his regiment in Naglee's brigade, J. J. Peck's division, Keyes's IV Corps, although no loss is reported in the command.

(709) *Official Records*, XLVII, Pt. 2, p. 121.

(710) *Official Records*, XXXIX, Pt. 2, p. 343. On January 17, 1865, Howard wrote Sherman, "I don't want Sweeny or Veatch. They

might be mustered out, with a view to the interest of the service, and in order to promote efficient, true, and hard-working men." (*Ibid.,* XLVII, Pt. 2, p. 70.)

(711) Viele's middle and last names are spelled variously by his descendants. One of his sons added an acute accent to the last *e* in Viele and another son adopted the pen name of Francis Vielé-Griffin; Griffin was his mother's maiden surname (General Viele was divorced from her in 1872). His middle name is also rendered as Ludovicus, Ludovickus, and Lodovickus. (Cf., *Dictionary of American Biography, Appleton's Cyclopedia,* and F. B. Heitman, *Historical Register.*) *Register of Graduates and Former Cadets* reduces his middle name to a common denominator by rendering it as Louis.

(712) H. W. Benham to David Hunter, April 16, 1862, in *Official Records,* VI, 140.

(713) Heitman's *Historical Register,* presumably reflecting army reports, records that he died July 7 of wounds received July 3. The historian of the 20th Maine states that the order promoting Vincent to brigadier general was read on July 10 to his old troops, who were ignorant of his death three days before. (Pullen, *The Twentieth Maine,* 147.) The order announcing his death is dated July 12. (*Official Records,* XXVII, Pt. 1, p. 620.)

(714) One of Vinton's uncles, Colonel D. H. Vinton (West Point, 1822) of the Quartermaster's Department, was brevetted brigadier and major general, U. S. Army, in 1865.

(715) During the Maryland campaign the 43rd New York is shown in command of its major. (*Battles and Leaders of the Civil War,* II, 599.)

(716) Vogdes was held originally as a hostage, along with a number of other Federal officers, for an equal number of captured Confederate privateersmen, who had been tried and condemned to be hung as pirates. The threat of retaliation in kind brought Washington to its senses, but endless bickering and red tape prevented Vogdes release until August 15, 1862. See *Official Records,* Series II, III and IV, *passim.*

(717) The War Department records list him as Adolph von Steinwehr, but index him variously under Steinwehr, Adolph von and Von Steinwehr, Adolph. Other authorities refer to him both as Steinwehr and Von Steinwehr, sometimes on the same page. Since both *Memorandum Relative to the General Officer* and Heitman have him listed under *V,* the author has followed suit, although both the *Official Records* and *Appleton's Cyclopedia* list him under *S.*

(718) *Official Records,* XXXII, Pt. 3, pp. 365-66.

(719) The brigade to which he had been assigned was led by a colonel during the Atlanta campaign.

(720) Buffalo *Express,* February 28, 1877, p. 2, col. 5.

(721) See, Paul E. Steiner, M.D., in *Military Medicine,* CXVIII, No. 5 (May, 1956), 493-95, citing the letters of a wounded Confederate surgeon who chanced to lie next to Wadsworth while the latter was dying.

(722) Courtesy of Mrs. Marie C. Preston, Geneseo, New York, in letter to author, September 11, 1957.

(723) Wagner's life is not to be found in any work of general reference. The author is indebted to Miss Louise Wood, Reference Librarian, Indiana Division, Indiana State Library, Indianapolis, for information from the *Indiana Magazine of History* (March, 1926), 46-47, for details of his career. However, this article is highly laudatory and noncritical—as well as inaccurate—in regard to his military career.

(724) *Official Records*, XLIV, 67. At twenty-six, Walcutt was one of the youngest full-rank general officers in the army.

(725) See Powell (ed.), *Officers of the Army and Navy (Volunteer)*, 262, who quotes from various official reports and dispatches.

(726) Agassiz (ed.), *Meade's Headquarters 1863-1865,* p. 106. Assistant Secretary of War Charles A. Dana was more blunt: "General Hobart Ward is under arrest for running away in the Wilderness battle. . . ." (Dana to Edwin M. Stanton, May 9, 1864, in *Official Records*, XXXVI, Pt. 1, p. 65.) Ward was not actually relieved until the twelfth, but Dana seems to have known of the intention to place him in arrest and reported it as a *fait accompli*. He was arrested on June 12 and ordered to Fort Monroe, but was dismissed from the service a month later without standing trial on court-martial.

(727) The author is compelled to note with what he trusts is pardonable pride that General Warner was his grandfather's brother.

(728) *Official Records*, XLIII, Pt. 2, p. 225.

(729) Controversies have raged for a century over the reasons for, and the manner of, Warren's relief from command of the V Corps at Five Forks. To summarize the debate: Sheridan would have relieved *any* corps commander of the Army of the Potomac placed under him; *no one* would have moved fast enough to suit him on that particular afternoon.

(730) Israel represented a Maine district, Elihu Benjamin (who added an *e* to his patronymic), an Illinois district, and Cadwallader, was one of Wisconsin's three representatives—all served in the Thirty-Fourth Congress (1855-57).

(731) There is considerable discrepancy in various sources in regard to the date of Watkins' birth, as well as to the place and date of his death. The data within is reconstructed from *The Union Regiments of Kentucky,* 73-74, and the New Orleans *Daily Picayune,* March 31, 1868. Other information was derived from Watkins' Pension File in the National Archives, Washington, D. C.

(732) See sketch of Rousseau within.

(733) *Official Records*, XIX, Pt. 1, p. 324.

(734) General Webster's great-niece, Miss Elizabeth Webster of Tryon, North Carolina, contributed information for an article on his career to the July 27, 1961, edition of *The Lake Forester* (Lake Forest, Illinois), which differs in minor respects from his sketch in *Dictionary of American Biography.*

(735) Place and date of Weed's birth, authority of Pension File, National Archives.

(736) Cf., sketches of Vincent and G. K. Warren, within.

(737) Colonel Ulric Dahlgren, son of the Union admiral, led a detachment of Kilpatrick's forces which went astray and came to grief. Dahlgren was killed: papers were found—or alleged to have

been found upon his body—which ordered the destruction of Richmond and the killing of Confederate civilian authorities. These were denounced in the South as barbaric and in the North as fraudulent and counterfeit. Proponents of both points of view are still debating this issue, with the preponderance of evidence pointing to the culpability of Dahlgren. (See Jones, *Eight Hours Before Richmond*.)

(738) Columbia, on the Susquehanna River, was the terminus of the first segment of the Pennsylvania Railroad running from Philadelphia. Freight was transferred at this point to canalboats which carried the merchandise to Hollidaysburg, and thence to Pittsburgh. The author is greatly indebted to Mrs. Gardiner Criswell, Librarian, Columbia Public Library, for information on General Welsh, some of which was abstracted from *Biographical Annals of Lancaster County, Pennsylvania*.

(739) Warner, *Generals in Gray*, 140.

(740) In July, 1864, West was on leave in the East while Jubal Early's raid on Washington was in progress. Accordingly, he wired Henry W. Halleck in Washington asking if there was anything he could do to help. The latter responded with the following: "We have five times as many generals here as we want, but are greatly in need of privates. Any one volunteering in that capacity will be thankfully received." (*Official Records*, XXXVII, Pt. 2, p. 196.)

(741) *Biographical Directory of the American Congress*, p. 1994.

(742) See the sketch within on Canby for details of this incident.

(743) Bigelow, *The Campaign of Chancellorsville*, 416.

(744) Assistant Secretary of War Charles A. Dana to Secretary of War Stanton, November 2, 1863: "I have to report Brigadier General Whitaker as drunk and disorderly in public. . . ." (*Official Records*, XXXI, Pt. 2, p. 55.)

(745) *Official Records*, XIX, Pt. 1, p. 798.

(746) White's five-line obituary appeared in the Chicago *Tribune* on May 13.

(747) Willcox was one of the senior brigadiers in service by date of commission, ranking John G. Parke by some four months. However, Willcox was never advanced beyond that grade except by brevet at the end of the war, despite his long record in division and (temporary) corps command, dating back to August, 1862. Parke, on the other hand, was commissioned major general on August 20, 1862, to rank from July 18, although much of his service in the war was as a staff officer.

(748) When the first Southern Pacific train reached Maley, Arizona, from the west in 1880, General Willcox, according to legend, was aboard and was received with acclamation; as a consequence the town was renamed Wilcox [*sic!*]. The error in spelling (suggestive of Major General Cadmus M. Wilcox of the Confederacy, who spelled his name with one *l*) was not rectified until 1889, when "Wilcox" became "Willcox." The original name of the community stemmed from one Mahley, through whose ranch the survey was run. Accordingly, the misspelling honors were about even. (Barnes, *Arizona Place Names*.)

(749) Williams' death certificate states that he was born in Kingston,

New York; however, his obituary in the Pittsburgh *Post*, June 2, 1891, gives his birthplace as within.

(750) All but one company of this regiment were recruited in Phila-delphia; the exception was Williams' Company, which was raised in Pittsburgh.

(751) *Official Records*, XXV, Pt. 2, p. 26.

(752) Joseph M. O'Donnell, Chief, Archives and History Division, U. S. Military Academy, to the author, June 18, 1962.

(753) New York *Daily Tribune*, December 2, 1897, which erroneously states that "he died . . . yesterday."

(754) Williams early life is taken from a most unflattering sketch by Captain Addison A. Stuart of the 17th Iowa, in *Iowa Colonels and Regiments*; wherein it is stated that "while in command of his regiment, he [Williams] was tyrannical, and, by a majority of both the officers and men, sincerely hated." (*Ibid.*, 96.)

(755) Boston *Journal*, March 26, 1866, courtesy Boston Public Library.

(756) See *Official Records*, XV, 26-29, for an account and drawing of this operation.

(757) Williams' antebellum career is derived from a printed pamphlet entitled, "Funeral Ceremony of the Late Brigadier General Thomas Williams," courtesy Burton Historical Collection, De-troit Public Library.

(758) Much of Williamson's sketch is taken from an article by Major General G. M. Dodge in *Annals of Iowa*, VI (October, 1903), published by the Historical Department of Iowa (now the Iowa Department of History and Archives, Des Moines, to which the author is indebted for a copy).

(759) General Willich did *not* serve "in all the movements and battles of the . . . Atlanta campaign and the march to the sea and through the Carolinas . . . ," as set forth in *Appleton's Cyclopedia*.

(760) *Battles and Leaders of the Civil War*, II, 218, 314.

(761) *Official Records*, XIX, Pt. 1, p. 307.

(762) *Official Records*, XXXVI, Pt. 2, p. 367.

(763) *Ibid.*, 16. The conclusion is more or less inescapable, although nothing concrete appears in the records, that Wistar's handling of his brigade on the foggy morning of May 16 left something to be desired. In this action Robert Ransom's division of P. G. T. Beauregard's forces overran the Federal division of Godfrey Weitzel, capturing General Charles A. Heckman, five stands of colors, and some four hundred other prisoners. Wis-tar's brigade was on Heckman's left. The operation as a whole was designed by Beauregard to isolate Benjamin F. Butler from his base at Bermuda Hundred but failed because of lack of con-cert between other subordinate commanders, notably W. H. C. Whiting. (See, *Lee's Lieutenants*, III, 483-95.) Strangely enough, in his own official report of the affair (*Official Records*, XXXVI, Pt. 2, p. 153), Weitzel quotes from Wistar's report, but the latter cannot be found.

(764) To understand Wood's rapid series of promotions, it is necessary to recognize that in August, 1861, the designations of the vari-ous mounted regiments were changed as follows: 1st and 2nd Dragoons became 1st and 2nd Cavalry; Regiment of Mounted

Riflemen became 3rd Cavalry; and 1st and 2nd Cavalry became 4th and 5th Cavalry. Those who resigned and joined the Confederacy were Colonel Fauntleroy, 1st Dragoons; Lieutenant Colonel G. B. Crittenden, Mounted Rifles; Colonel R. E. Lee and Lieutenant Colonel W. J. Hardee, 1st Cavalry (Old); and Colonel A. S. Johnston and Majors Early Van Dorn and E. K. Smith, 2nd Cavalry (Old). Wood's old regiment was the 1st Cavalry; he subsequently became colonel of the new 2nd Cavalry (old 2nd Dragoons).

(765) Controversy over this incident has raged unceasingly since 1863. O'Connor in his *Thomas; Rock of Chickamauga,* 40-41, represents Wood as virtually smacking his lips as he tucks W. S. Rosecrans' unfortunate order into his dispatch case, meantime remarking to "witnesses" that he "wouldn't think of questioning an order from General Rosecrans in writing." Unfortunately, citations are lacking. However, Rosecrans was at odds with his superiors in Washington: he and U. S. Grant were unfriendly and he was a devout Catholic in a Protestant army and administration. Wood, on the other hand was connected by marriage to the Lincolns and was a "loyal" Kentuckian.

(766) The author is greatly indebted to General Woodbury's grandson, Mr. William N. Woodbury of Birmingham, Alabama, for much valuable information, including a typescript copy of a memoir written by the General's widow in 1891, which recounts the days of April, 1861, in Wilmington and her departure therefrom. General Woodbury's father-in-law, Thomas Childs, brevet brigadier general, U. S. Army, the ninety-seventh graduate of West Point, and a native of Massachusetts, had married into a Virginia family. He died in 1853. His son (Mrs. Woodbury's brother, Frederick) an 1855 graduate of West Point, resigned his commission in March, 1861, and was a lieutenant colonel of artillery and ordnance in the Confederate Army during the Civil War. The family ties and affections were much in evidence when Mrs. Woodbury penned her recollections, for her brother is referred to as "Col. Childs," according to his Confederate rank.

(767) See, Catton, *The Coming Fury,* 176-82, for a detailed description of the firing on Fort Sumter which occurred on January 9, 1861.

(768) The rejection of Wright's original nomination apparently was due to the fact that he was appointed a major general in order to command the Department of the Ohio. When he was superseded by Ambrose E. Burnside in March, the necessity for the promotion disappeared. This is the only clue the author has been able to unearth. (See, *Official Records,* XXIII, Pt. 2, *passim.*)

(769) Zook's place and date of birth, authority of Frederick, *The Story of a Regiment.* There is also a sketch of Zook in Powell's *Officers of the Army and Navy (Volunteer),* 264, which is inaccurate in regard to his Civil War career but gives some details of his early life.

BIBLIOGRAPHY

THE PRINCIPAL CRITERION for inclusion of a name in the foregoing pages is the War Department publication of 1906, entitled *Memorandum Relative to the General Officers in the Armies of the United States During the Civil War, 1861-1865.* The work was issued by the Military Secretary's office, a bureau headed by General Frederick C. Ainsworth, who combined the duties of the Adjutant General's office with those of the newly created Record and Pension office. One of Ainsworth's principal subordinates was General Marcus J. Wright, formerly of the Confederate Army, the compiler of the memorandum and of several other invaluable source references to Union and Confederate officers.

General Wright was the official agent, for many years, of the War Department for the collection of Confederate records and as such made a monumental contribution to the *The War of the Rebellion: A Compilation of the Official Records of the Union and Confederate Armies* (70 volumes bound in 128 parts and a two-part atlas; Washington, 1880-1901). This compendium is, of course, a cornerstone upon which any phase of Civil War research must be based, and through its thousands of pages the military careers of the generals who wore the blue can, in most instances, be traced.

The next two most important sources consulted for definition were: F. B. Heitman, *Historical Register of the United States Army from its Organization . . . 1789-1903* (2 vols.; Washington, 1903), and George W. Cullum, *Biographical Register of the Officers and Graduates of the U. S. Military Academy* (3 vols.; Boston and New York, 1891), supplemented at ten-year intervals until the present day.

Several other prime sources of a biographical nature consulted were: *The Union Army* (8 vols.; Madison Wisconsin: Federal Publishing Company, 1908), which bears the imposing subtitle, "A History of Military Affairs in the Loyal States 1861-1865—Records of the Regiments in the Union Army—Cyclopedia of Battles—Memoirs of Commanders and Soldiers." The author has seen no other compendium as inclusive and authoritative as this; nevertheless, much of the work was farmed out and many of the biographical sketches of general officers, to which Volume VIII is devoted, draw heavily on such previously published works as *Appleton's Cyclopedia of American Biography* (6 vols.; New York, 1898), which contains many inaccuracies. Nevertheless, like *Dictionary of American Biography* (Centenary Edition; 11 vols.; New York, 1946), *Appleton's Cyclopedia* provided a convenient springboard for research in original sources.

Another rather obscure reference work has proved helpful, namely: *Official Army Register of the Volunteer Force of the United States Army for the Years 1861, 1862, 1863, 1864, 1865* (8 vols.; Washington: Adjutant General's Office, 1865). Any man who ever served as a volunteer officer, regularly mustered into United States service, or awaiting muster, at any grade, can be quickly located in this work.

Other published sources, each valuable in its own way, but consulted to·a lesser degree, follow:

Adams, Charles Francis. *Charles Francis Adams, 1835-1915: An Autobiography.* Boston and New York, 1916.

Adams, George W. *Doctors in Blue.* New York, 1952.

Agassiz, George R. (ed.). *Meade's Headquarters 1863-1865—Letters of Colonel Theodore Lyman, etc.* Boston, 1922.

Alexander, A. W. *Grant as a Soldier.* St. Louis, 1887.

Allen, William. *The Army of Northern Virginia in 1862.* Boston, 1892.

Anderson, C. C. *Fighting by Southern Federals.* New York, 1912.

Annals of the War, Written by Leading Participants North and South. Philadelphia, 1879.

Baker, Lafayette C. *The Secret Service in the Late War.* Chicago, 1874.

Barnes, Will C. *Arizona Place Names.* Revised and enlarged by Byrd J. Granger. Tucson, 1960.

Basler, Roy P. (ed.). *The Collected Works of Abraham Lincoln.* 8 vols. New Brunswick, New Jersey, 1953-55.

Bateman, Newton and Selby, Paul (eds.). *Historical Encyclopedia of Illinois and History of Jo Daviess County.* Chicago, 1904.

Battles and Leaders of the Civil War . . . Being for the Most Part Contributions by Union and Confederate Officers. Based upon the "Century War Series," edited by Robert U. Johnson and Clarence C. Buel. 4 vols. New York, 1887-88.

Beatie, R. H., Jr. *Road to Manassas,* New York, 1961.

Beatty, John, *Memoirs of a Volunteer (1861-1863),* ed. Harvey S. Ford. New York, 1946.

Beers, J. H. *Genealogical and Biographical Record of New London County, Connecticut.* n. p., 1905.

Benedict, G. G. *Vermont in the Civil War.* 2 vols. Burlington, 1886.

Bigelow, John, Jr. *The Campaign of Chancellorsville.* New Haven, Connecticut, 1910.

Biographical Annals of Lancaster County, Pennsylvania. Chicago, 1903.

Biographical Directory of the American Congress, 1774-1949. Washington, 1950.

Bowers, Claude G. *The Tragic Era.* Boston, 1929.

Bradford, Gamaliel. *The Army of Northern Virginia in 1862.* Boston, 1892.

Brown, Francis. *Raymond of the Times.* New York, 1951.

Bruce, Robert V. *Lincoln and the Tools of War.* New York and Indianapolis, 1956.

Campaigns of the Civil War. 16 vols. New York, 1881-85.

Catton, Bruce. *A Stillness at Appomattox.* Garden City, New York, 1953.

Catton, Bruce. *Glory Road.* Garden City, New York, 1952.

Catton, Bruce. *Grant Moves South.* Boston, 1950.

Catton, Bruce. *Mr. Lincoln's Army.* Garden City, New York, 1951.

Catton, Bruce. *Terrible Swift Sword.* Garden City, New York, 1963.

Catton, Bruce. *The Coming Fury.* Garden City, New York, 1961.

Cavanagh, Michael. *Memoirs of General Thomas Francis Meagher, etc.* Worcester, Massachusetts, 1892.

Chamberlain, J. L. *The Passing of the Armies.* New York, 1915.

Chicago: Pictorial and Biographical. Chicago, 1912.

Clark, Orton S. *The 116th Regiment of New York Volunteers.* Buffalo, 1868.

Cleaves, Freeman. *Meade of Gettysburg.* Norman, Oklahoma, 1960.

Cockrell, Monroe F. (ed.). *The Lost Account of the Battle of Corinth.* Jackson, Tennessee, 1955.

Collier, Henry M. *A History of Old Kinderhook.* n. p., 1914.

Collins, Richard H. (comp.). *History of Kentucky.* n. p., 1874.

Commager, Henry S. (ed.). *The Blue and The Gray.* 2 vols. New York, 1950.

Commemorative Biographical Record of Prominent and Representative Men of Indianapolis and Vicinity. Chicago, 1908.

Connelley, W. E. *Quantrill and the Border Wars.* New York, 1956.

Coppee, Henry. *Life and Services of General U. S. Grant.* Chicago, 1868.

Cox, J. D. *Military Reminiscences of the Civil War.* 2 vols. New York, 1900.

Crawford, S. W. *The Genesis of the Civil War.* New York, 1887.

Curtis, Newton M. *From Bull Run to Chancellorsville.* New York, 1906.

Cushing, Thomas, and Sheppard, C. E., *History of the Counties of Gloucester, Salem and Cumberland.* Philadelphia, 1883.

Daily [?]. *Greater Terre Haute and Vigo County.* Chicago, 1908.

Darnell, Ermina Jett. *Forks of Elkhorn Church.* Louisville, Kentucky, 1946.

Dearing, Mary R. *Veterans in Politics.* Baton Rouge, Louisiana, 1952.

De Leon, T. C. *Belles Beaux and Brains of the 60's.* New York, 1909.

Donald, David (ed.). *Divided We Fought.* New York, 1952.

Dorris, J. T. *Pardon and Amnesty Under Lincoln and Johnson.* Chapel Hill, North Carolina, 1953.

Doubleday, Abner. *Reminiscences of Forts Sumter and Moultrie in 1860-61.* New York, 1876.

Duke, Basil W. *Morgan's Cavalry.* New York, 1906.

Dunning, W. A. *Essays on the Civil War and Reconstruction.* New York, 1931.

Dyer, John P. *Fightin' Joe Wheeler.* Baton Rouge, Louisiana, 1941.

Eisenschiml, Otto. *The Celebrated Case of Fitz John Porter.* New York, 1950.

Eliot, Ellsworth, Jr. *Yale in the Civil War.* New Haven, Connecticut, 1932.

Encyclopaedia Britannica. 23 vols. and Atlas. Chicago and London, 1943.

Evans, Clement Anselm (ed.). *Confederate Military History: A Library of Confederate States History.* 12 vols. Atlanta, 1899.

Fiebeger, G. J. *Campaigns of the American Civil War.* West Point, New York, 1910.

Fisher, R. N. *Biographical Sketches of El Dorado Citizens.* El Dorado, n. d.

Fitch, John. *Annals of the Army of the Cumberland, etc.* Philadelphia, 1864.

Foster, John Y. *New Jersey and the Rebellion.* Newark, 1868.

Frederick, Gilbert. *The Story of a Regiment . . . 57th New York State Volunteer Infantry . . . 1861-1865.* Chicago, 1895.

Freeman, D. S. *Lee's Lieutenants.* 3 vols. New York, 1943-44.

Fry, James B. *Military Miscellanies.* New York, 1889.

Fuller, J. F. C. *Grant and Lee.* London, 1933.

Ganoe, W. A. *The History of the United States Army.* New York, 1924.

Gosnell, H. Allen. *Guns on the Western Waters.* Baton Rouge, Louisiana, 1949.

Gracie, Archibald. *The Truth About Chickamauga.* Boston, 1911.

Graham, W. A. *The Custer Myth.* Harrisburg, Pennsylvania, 1953.

Grant, Ulysses Simpson. *Personal Memoirs of U. S. Grant.* 2 vols. New York, 1885.

Green, Charles E. *History of M. W. Grand Lodge of Ancient, Free and Accepted Masons of Delaware.* Wilmington, 1956.

Hamersly, T. H. S. *Complete Regular Army Register of the United States: For One Hundred Years (1779-1879).* Washington, 1880.

Haskell, Frank A. *The Battle of Gettysburg.* Madison, Wisconsin, 1910.

Haskell, John C. "Memoirs." Unpublished MS., author's personal collection.

Hassler, Warren W., Jr. *General George B. McClellan.* Baton Rouge, Louisiana, 1957.

Haupt, Herman. *Reminiscences of Herman Haupt.* Milwaukee, Wisconsin, 1901.

Hay, Thomas R. *Hood's Tennessee Campaign.* New York, 1929.

Hempstead, Fay. *History of Arkansas.* St. Louis and New York, 1890.

Heyman, Max L., Jr. *Prudent Soldier, E. R. S. Canby.* Glendale, California, 1959.

Heyward, Du Bose, and Sass, Herbert. *Fort Sumter 1861-1865.* New York, 1938.

Historical Encyclopedia of Illinois and History of St. Clair County. Chicago, 1907.

History of Chicago, 1857-71. Chicago, 1885.

History of Wayne County, Indiana. 2 vols. Chicago, 1884.

Hoehling, A. A. *Last Train from Atlanta.* New York, 1958.

Horn, Stanley F. *The Army of Tennessee.* New York, 1941.

Horn, Stanley F. *The Decisive Battle of Nashville.* Baton Rouge, Louisiana, 1956.

Howard, O. O. *Autobiography of O. O. Howard.* New York, 1908.

Hunt, Aurora. *James H. Carleton.* Glendale, California, 1959.

Hunt, Aurora. *The Army of the Pacific.* Glendale, California, 1951.

Iowa Colonels and Regiments. Des Moines, n. d.

An Interesting Talk with General W. H. Powell. . . . Chicago, 1901.

James, Marquis. *They Had Their Hour.* Indianapolis, Indiana, 1934.

Johnson, Ludwell H. *The Red River Campaign.* Baltimore, Maryland, 1958.

Johnston, R. M. *Bull Run: Its Strategy and Tactics.* Boston, 1913.

Jones, Virgil Carrington. *Eight Hours Before Richmond.* New York, 1957.

Journal of the Confederate States Congress. Senate Document No. 234, 58th Congress, 2nd Session. 7 vols. Washington, D. C., 1904.

Keifer, J. Warren. *Slavery and Four Years of War.* 2 vols. New York, 1900.

Keleher, W. A. *Turmoil in New Mexico.* Santa Fe, 1952.

Keleher, W. A. *Violence in Lincoln County.* Albuquerque, New Mexico, 1957.

Kerby, Robert Lee. *The Confederate Invasion of New Mexico and Arizona.* Los Angeles, 1958.

Kincaid, Robert L. *The Wilderness Road.* New York, 1947.

Lamers, William M. *The Edge of Glory.* New York, 1961.

Lavender, David. *Bent's Fort.* Garden City, New York, 1954.

Leech, Margaret. *Reveille in Washington.* New York, 1941.

Lewis, Lloyd. *Captain Sam Grant.* Boston, 1950.

Lewis, Lloyd. *Sherman, Fighting Prophet.* New York, 1932.

Livermore, Thomas L. *Numbers and Losses in the Civil War in America: 1861-65.* Bloomington, Indiana, 1957.

Logan, John A. *The Great Conspiracy.* New York, 1886.

Lomax, Elizabeth L. *Leaves from an Old Washington Diary 1854-1863.* New York, 1943.

Long, E. B. (ed.). *Personal Memoirs of U. S. Grant.* Cleveland, Ohio, 1952.

Lonn, Ella. *Foreigners in the Union Army and Navy.* Baton Rouge, Louisiana, 1951.

Lord, Francis A. *They Fought for the Union.* Harrisburg, Pennsylvania, 1960.

Lossing, Benson J. *A History of the Civil War.* New York, 1912.

Macartney, C. E. *Mr. Lincoln's Admirals.* New York, 1956.

Maurice, Sir Frederick. *Statesmen and Soldiers of the Civil War.* Boston, 1926.

Maxwell, W. Q. *Lincoln's Fifth Wheel.* New York, 1956.

Meek, Basil. *Twentieth Century History of Sandusky County, Ohio.* . . . Chicago, 1909.

Memorial Record of Northeastern Indiana. Chicago, 1896.

Memorandum of Field Officers of Volunteers, U. S. Army, 1861-1865. The author's copy of this compilation lacks the title page; it was the personal copy of General Marcus J. Wright, former C.S.A., who was without a doubt the compiler; it was unquestionably a War Department publication.

Michigan Biographies. 2 vols. Lansing, 1924.

Miers, Earl S., and Brown, Richard A. (eds.). *Gettysburg.* New Brunswick, New Jersey, 1948.

Military Order of the Loyal Legion of the United States: "War Papers," "Personal Recollections of the Rebellion," "Sketches of War History," "Military Essays and Recollections," etc. Various state commanderies, various volumes, various places and dates of publication.

Papers of the Military Historical Society of Massachusetts. Various vols. Boston, various dates.

Miller, F. T. (ed.). *Photographic History of the Civil War.* 10 vols. New York, 1911.

Mills, Anson. *My Story.* (Privately printed.) n.p., n.d.

Mogelever, Jacob. *Death to Traitors*. Garden City, New York, 1960.

Monaghan, Jay. *Civil War on the Western Border*. Boston, 1955.

Monaghan, Jay. *Custer*. Boston, 1959.

Moore, Frank (ed.). *The Rebellion Record*. 12 vols. New York, 1861-71.

Morgan, James M. *Recollections of a Rebel Reefer*. Boston, 1917.

Munden, Kenneth W., and Beers, Henry P. *Guide to Federal Archives Relating to the Civil War*. Washington, 1962.

National Cyclopedia of American Biography. 37 vols. New York, 1892-1951.

Nevins, Allan. *Frémont, the West's Greatest Adventurer*. 2 vols. New York, 1928.

Nevins, Allan. *The War for the Union*. 2 vols. New York, 1959-60.

Nichols, Edward J. *Toward Gettysburg: A Biography of General John F. Reynolds*. University Park, Pennsylvania, 1958.

Nichols, Roy F. *The Disruption of American Democracy*. New York, 1958.

Nicolay, Helen. *Lincoln's Secretary*. New York, 1949.

Norton, David. *Sketches of the Town of Old Town*. n. p., 1881.

Norton, Oliver W. *The Attack and Defense of Little Round Top*. New York, 1913.

O'Connor, Richard. *Thomas: Rock of Chickamauga*. New York, 1948.

An Old Army Officer (Lieutenant Colonel O. H. Hein, U. S. Army). *Memories of Long Ago*. New York, 1925.

Palmer, John M. *Personal Recollections of John M. Palmer*. Cincinnati, Ohio, 1901.

Paris, Comte de. *History of the Civil War in America*. 4 vols. Philadelphia, 1875.

Patch, J. D. *The Battle of Ball's Bluff*. Leesburg, Virginia, 1958.

Pinchon, Edgcumb. *Dan Sickles*. Garden City, New York, 1945.

Porter, Horace. *Campaigning with Grant*. New York, 1897.

Post, Marie C. *The Life and Memoirs of Comte Regis de Trobriand*. New York, 1910.

Powell, William H. (ed.). *Officers of the Army and Navy (Volunteer) Who Served in the Civil War*. Philadelphia, 1893.

Powers, [?]. *History of the Eighty-fifth Regiment Pennsylvania Volunteer Infantry*. New York, 1915.

Pratt, Fletcher. *Eleven Generals*. New York, 1949.

Pratt, Fletcher. *Stanton—Lincoln's Secretary of War*. New York, 1953.

Pullen, John J. *The Twentieth Maine*. Philadelphia, Pennsylvania, 1957.

Putnam, George H. *A Prisoner of War in Virginia 1864-1865*. New York, 1912.

Rand-McNally. *Road Atlas—United States, Canada, Mexico*. 38th ed. Chicago.

Register of the Commissioned and Warrant Officers of the Navy of the United States, Including Officers of the Marine Corps, and Others, for the Year 1856. Washington, D. C., 1856.

Register of the Graduates and Former Cadets, U. S. Military Academy West Point, New York, 1948.

Roberts, Oliver Ayer. *History of . . . the Ancient and Honorable Artillery Company of Massachusetts, 1637-1688*. Boston, 1898.

Russell, C. W. (ed.). *The Memoirs of Colonel John S. Mosby*. Boston, 1917.

Sandburg, Carl. *Abraham Lincoln, The War Years.* 4 vols. New York, 1939.

Schaff, Morris. *The Spirit of Old West Point.* Boston, 1907.

Schofield, John M. *Forty-Six Years in the Army.* New York, 1897.

Schurz, Carl. *The Reminiscences of Carl Schurz.* 3 vols. Garden City, New York, 1909.

Shannon, F. A. *The Organization and Administration of the Union Army 1861-1865.* 2 vols. Cleveland, Ohio, 1928.

Sheridan, Philip H. *Personal Memoirs of Philip H. Sheridan.* 2 vols. New York, 1888.

Sherman, John. *Recollections of Forty Years.* 2 vols. New York, 1895.

Sherman, W. T. *Memoirs of W. T. Sherman.* 2 vols. New York, 1875.

Small, Abner. *The Road to Richmond.* Berkeley, California, 1957.

Southern Historical Society Papers. 49 vols. Richmond, 1876-1943.

Speed, Thomas. *The Union Regiments of Kentucky.* Louisville, 1897.

Steele, M. F. *American Campaigns.* 2 vols. Harrisburg, Pennsylvania, 1949.

Swanberg, W. A. *First Blood.* New York, 1957.

Swanberg, W. A. *Sickles the Incredible.* New York, 1956.

Swiggett, Howard. *The Rebel Raider.* New York, 1934.

Swinton, William. *Campaigns of the Army of the Potomac.* New York, 1882.

Taylor, Benjamin F. *Mission Ridge and Lookout Mountain.* New York, 1872.

Temple, O. P. *Notable Men of Tennessee.* New York, 1912.

Thayer, W. R. *Life and Letters of John Hay.* 2 vols. Boston, 1915.

Thomas, Benjamin P. (ed.). *Three Years with Grant.* New York, 1955.

Thompson, R. M., and Wainwright, Richard (eds.). *Confidential Correspondence of Gustavus Vasa Fox.* 2 vols. New York, 1928.

Townsend, W. H. *Lincoln and the Blue Grass.* Lexington, Kentucky, 1955.

Trobriand, Regis de. *Four Years with the Army of the Potomac.* Boston, 1889.

Tucker, Glenn. *Hancock the Superb.* New York, 1960.

The Union Regiments of Kentucky. Louisville, 1897.

U. S. Army Register. Washington, 1860-1866.

Vasvary, Edmund. *Lincoln's Hungarian Heroes.* Washington, 1939.

Waite, Otis F. R. *Vermont in the 'Great Rebellion.* Claremont, New Hampshire, 1869.

Ward, Willis C. *Orchard Lake and Its Island.* n.p., n.d.

Warner, Ezra J. *Generals in Gray.* Baton Rouge, Louisiana, 1959.

Weber, Thomas. *The Northern Railroads in the Civil War.* New York, 1952.

Weisberger, Bernard A. *Reporters for the Union.* Boston, 1953.

Welles, Gideon. *Diary of Gideon Welles.* 3 vols. Boston, 1911.

Werlich, Robert. *"Beast" Butler.* Washington, 1962.

Whipple, Charles H. *Genealogy of the Whipple-Wright, Wager, Ward-Pell, McLean-Burnet Families.* n.p., 1917.

Who's Who in New York. New York, 1906.

Wiley, Bell I. *Life of Billy Yank.* New York, 1952.

Williams, Kenneth P. *Lincoln Finds a General.* 5 vols. New York, 1949-1959.

Williams, T. Harry. *Lincoln and His Generals.* New York, 1952.
Wills, Charles W. *Army Life of an Illinois Soldier.* Washington, D. C., 1906.
Wilson, J. H. *The Life of John A. Rawlins.* . . . New York, 1916.
Wilson, James Harrison. *Under the Old Flag.* 2 vols. New York, 1912.
Wright, M. J. *Tennessee in the War 1861-1865.* New York, 1908.

Periodicals

Annual Association of Graduates, U. S. Military Academy, various issues.
Annals of Iowa, various issues.
Chronicles of Oklahoma, various issues.
Civil War History, various issues.
Harper's Weekly, various issues.
Harvard Graduates' Magazine, December, 1912.
Indiana History Bulletin, December, 1925.
Journal of the Illinois State Historical Society, various issues.
Kansas Historical Quarterly, various issues.
Military Medicine, May, 1956.
Montana, various issues.
Purple and Gold (Ann Arbor, Michigan), Winter 1959-60 issues.
Tennessee Historical Quarterly, various issues.
West Virginia History, various issues.
The Westerners (New York Posse Brand Book), Vol. LV, No. IV.